The Handbook of Managing and Marketing Tourism Experiences

The Handbook of Managing and Marketing Tourism Experiences

Edited by

Marios Sotiriadis
University of South Africa, Pretoria, South Africa

Dogan Gursoy
Washington State University, Pullman, WA, USA

United Kingdom – North America – Japan
India – Malaysia – China

Emerald Group Publishing Limited
Howard House, Wagon Lane, Bingley BD16 1WA, UK

First edition 2016

Copyright © 2016 Emerald Group Publishing Limited

Reprints and permissions service
Contact: permissions@emeraldinsight.com

British Library Cataloguing in Publication Data
A catalogue record for this book is available from the British Library

ISBN: 978-1-78635-290-3

Printed and bound by CPI Group (UK) Ltd, Croydon, CR0 4YY

ISOQAR certified
Management System,
awarded to Emerald
for adherence to
Environmental
standard
ISO 14001:2004.

Certificate Number 1985
ISO 14001

INVESTOR IN PEOPLE

Contents

List of Contributors   ix

Introduction
Marios Sotiriadis and Dogan Gursoy   xi

Part I   Planning: Design and Creating Tourism Experiences

CHAPTER 1   Experience-Based Service Design
             Özlem Güzel   3

CHAPTER 2   Experience-Centric Approach and Innovation
             Anita Zátori   21

CHAPTER 3   Crucial Role and Contribution of Human
             Resources in the Context of Tourism
             Experiences: Need for Experiential
             Intelligence and Skills
             Marios Sotiriadis and Stelios Varvaressos   45

CHAPTER 4   Tourism Destination: Design of Experiences
             Eyup Karayilan and Gurel Cetin   65

CHAPTER 5   Social Media and the Co-Creation of Tourism
             Experiences
             Marianna Sigala   85

CHAPTER 6   Experiential Tourism: Creating and
             Marketing Tourism Attraction Experiences
             Rachel Dodds and Lee Jolliffe   113

Part II   Managing: Organizing and Delivering Tourism Experiences

CHAPTER 7   Cultural and Experiential Tourism
Hilary du Cros   133

CHAPTER 8   Dragon Boat Intangible Cultural Heritage: Management Challenges of a Community and Élite Sport Event as a Tourism Experience
Fleur Fallon   155

CHAPTER 9   Collaborating to Provide Attractive Hotel Guests' Experiences
Marios Sotiriadis and Christos Sarmaniotis   175

CHAPTER 10   Managing Sport Tourism Experiences: Blueprinting Service Encounters
Chris A. Vassiliadis and Anestis Fotiadis   195

CHAPTER 11   Authenticity, Commodification, and McDonaldization of Tourism Experiences in the Context of Cultural Tourism
Medet Yolal   217

CHAPTER 12   Managing Experiences within the Field of Creative Tourism: Best Practices and Guidelines
Caroline Couret   235

CHAPTER 13   Greening as Part of Ecotourism to Contribute to Tourists' Experiences: A Destination Planning Approach
Elricke Botha and Willy Hannes Engelbrecht   261

CHAPTER 14   Managing Rural Tourist Experiences: Lessons from Cyprus
Anna Farmaki   281

CHAPTER 15   Service Innovations and Experience Creation in Spas, Wellness and Medical Tourism
Melanie Kay Smith, Sonia Ferrari and László Puczkó   299

Part III   Marketing: Communicating and Promoting Tourism Experiences

CHAPTER 16   The Role of Online Social Media on the Experience and Communication of Gay Events in a Tourist Destination: A Case Study of a Small-Scale Film Festival in Nice
S. Christofle, C. Papetti and M. Ferry   323

CHAPTER 17   Marketing Experiences for Visitor Attractions: The Contribution of Theming
Elricke Botha   343

CHAPTER 18   Marketing Culinary Tourism Experiences
Lee Jolliffe   363

CHAPTER 19   Managing and Marketing Tourism Experiences: Extending the Travel Risk Perception Literature to Address Affective Risk Perceptions
Ashley Schroeder, Lori Pennington-Gray, Maximiliano Korstanje and Geoffrey Skoll   379

CHAPTER 20   Promotion Tools Used in the Marketing of Sport Tourism Experiences in a Mature Tourism Destination
Crystal C. Lewis and Cristina H. Jönsson   397

CHAPTER 21   The Role of Information and Communication Technologies (ICTs) in Marketing Tourism Experiences
Kyung-Hyan Yoo and Ulrike Gretzel   409

Part IV   Monitoring and Evaluating Tourism Experiences

CHAPTER 22   Memorable Tourism Experiences: Conceptual Foundations and Managerial Implications for Program Design, Delivery, and Performance Measurement
Jong-Hyeong Kim   431

CHAPTER 23   Proposing an Experiential Value Model
within the Context of Business Tourism
Magdalena Petronella (Nellie) Swart   451

CHAPTER 24   Consumer Travel Online Reviews and
Recommendations: Suggesting Strategies
to Address Challenges Faced within the
Digital Context
Marios Sotiriadis and Ciná van Zyl   469

CHAPTER 25   Assessing Tourism Experiences:
The Case of Heritage Attractions
Gaunette Sinclair-Maragh   487

Conclusions: Issues and Challenges for Managing and
Marketing Tourism Experiences
Dogan Gursoy and Marios Sotiriadis   507

About the Authors   529

Index   541

List of Contributors

Elricke Botha	University of South Africa, Pretoria, South Africa
Gurel Cetin	Istanbul University, Istanbul, Turkey
S. Christofle	University of Nice Sophia Antipolis, Nice, France
Caroline Couret	Creative Tourism Network®, Barcelona, Spain
Rachel Dodds	Ryerson University, Toronto, Canada
Hilary du Cros	University of New Brunswick, Fredericton, Canada
Willy Hannes Engelbrecht	Independent Institute of Education, Gauteng, South Africa
Fleur Fallon	Formerly Sun Yat-sen University, Zhuhai, China
Anna Farmaki	Cyprus University of Technology, Limassol, Cyprus
Sonia Ferrari	University of Calabria, Rende, Italy
M. Ferry	Institut Paul Bocuse, Ecully, France
Anestis Fotiadis	I-Shou University, Kaohsiung, Taiwan
Ulrike Gretzel	University of Queensland, St Lucia, Australia
Özlem Güzel	Akdeniz University, Antalya, Turkey
Lee Jolliffe	University of New Brunswick, New Brunswick, Canada
Cristina H. Jönsson	The University of the West Indies, St Michael, Barbados
Eyup Karayilan	Istanbul University, Istanbul, Turkey
Jong-Hyeong Kim	Sun Yat-sen University, Guangdong, China

Maximiliano Korstanje	Palermo University Argentina, Buenos Aires, Argentina
Crystal C. Lewis	The University of the West Indies, St Michael, Barbados
C. Papetti	University of Nice Sophia Antipolis, Nice, France
Lori Pennington-Gray	University of Florida, Gainesville, FL, USA
László Puczkó	Budapest Metropolitan University of Applied Sciences, Budapest, Hungary
Christos Sarmaniotis	Alexander Technological Educational Institute of Thessaloniki, Thessaloniki, Greece
Ashley Schroeder	University of Florida, Gainesville, FL, USA
Marianna Sigala	University of South Australia, Adelaide, Australia
Gaunette Sinclair-Maragh	University of Technology, Jamaica, Kingston, Jamaica
Geoffrey Skoll	Buffalo State University, Buffalo, NY, USA
Melanie Kay Smith	Budapest Metropolitan University of Applied Sciences, Budapest, Hungary
Marios Sotiriadis	University of South Africa, Pretoria, South Africa
Magdalena Petronella (Nellie) Swart	University of South Africa, Pretoria, South Africa
Ciná van Zyl	University of South Africa, Pretoria, South Africa
Stelios Varvaressos	Technological Educational Institute (TEI) of Athens, Athens, Greece
Chris A. Vassiliadis	University of Macedonia, Thessaloniki, Greece
Medet Yolal	Anadolu University, Eskisehir, Turkey
Kyung-Hyan Yoo	William Paterson University of New Jersey, Wayne, NJ, USA
Anita Zátori	Corvinus University of Budapest, Budapest, Hungary

Introduction

Tourists desire a series of services that allow multiple options and experience opportunities. For tourists, the product is the total experience, covering the entire amalgam of all aspects and components of the experience encounter, including attitudes and expectations. Tourists generally perceive and evaluate their visit as an experience, even though the various services are offered by different operators. In fact, their visit consists of a structured series of services and providers/producers, which operate separately. From the supply side, the tourism offering is definitely a series of experiences achieved through a combination of a diverse array of products and services (Middleton, Fyall, Morgan, & Ranchhod, 2009). Hence, offering these experiences requires the involvement, partnering, and collaboration of a series of businesses (Gursoy, Saayman, & Sotiriadis, 2015).

The tourism experience is, by definition, "what people experience as tourists" (Sharpley & Stone, 2011, p. 1). Tourism destinations and providers of tourism services do nothing else than providing experience opportunities to people during their trips. What exactly is an experience? Literature suggests many different meanings and interpretations. According to a straightforward description, an experience is "the fact or state of having been affected by or gained knowledge through a direct observation or participation" (Merriam-Webster, 1993). Apparently, the customer experience is derived from the pursuit of fantasies, feelings, and fun. Experience refers to customers' wonderful memories associated with a place/location (destination); it is the core value of tourism consumption. In the broader social context, experience combines the actions of individual customers with the situations under which consumption will occur (Schmitt, 1999).

According to Sundbo and Darmer, "… experiences occur whenever a company intentionally uses services as the stage and goods as props to engage the individual" (2008, p. 11). Therefore, an experience occurs whenever companies intentionally construct it to engage customers. Every tourism company offers a customer experience. The more aware a business is of what type of experience is desired by consumers and by offering the type of experiences desired by consumers, the more likely they are to be successful.

Experience Economy: Anatomy of an Experience

Pine and Gilmore (1998) set out the vision for a new economic era, the experience economy, in which consumers are in search for extraordinary and memorable experiences. In the experience economy, during the last decades, the attention is shifted away from product or service delivery to the customer's experience as the value-added element (Mossberg, 2007; Pine & Gilmore, 1998; Schmitt, 1999; Schmitt, 2003). In an attempt to better analyze and contextualize the concept, researchers proposed various approaches regarding what creates experiences (see, e.g., Boswijk, Thijssen, & Peelen, 2007; Mossberg, 2007). However, Pine and Gilmore (1999) are less concerned with specific elements of what creates an experience. They instead suggest four main dimensions/realms of experiences along two axes: the customer's level of participation and the customer's connection with the environment or surroundings. The same authors suggest that an experience begins as an event where a tourist experiences (activity) an attraction or business (resources) within a particular context or situation. This event generates a reaction and that reaction results in a memory upon which the tourist reflects and creates new meaning. Ultimately the tourist, through this meaning-making process, both increases his or her understanding of the world and of the self as well.

While there are many ways to define an experience, Pine and Gilmore (1999) suggest the following equation depicting the "anatomy of an experience." Experience can be regarded as the entirety of the process consisting of the following formula (where the arrow means "causes"):

$$(\text{Activity} + \text{Situation} + \text{Resource}) \rightarrow \text{Event} \rightarrow \text{Reaction} \rightarrow \text{Memory} = \text{Experience}$$

It is believed that the experience formation takes place in consumers' mind, and the outcome of experience consumption depends on how the consumers, based on a specific situation or state of mind, react to the staged encounters (Mossberg, 2007; Pine & Gilmore, 1999; Schmitt, 2003). Obviously, the managerial functions of planning, designing, organizing, and marketing influence greatly the event or the type of an experience consumers are likely to have.

Tourism Experiences

Tourists travel for a variety of reasons: to escape, explore, understand, and participate. But at the core of the experience lies the providers of tourism services and the destination – the businesses and the place that deliver/provide something to the tourist to keep forever and share with others (Middleton et al., 2009; Morrison, 2013; Sharpley & Stone, 2011). Every tourist experiences a trip, holidays, or an attraction, but quality of their experiences depend on the activities and providers they select. Service is an essential component of delivery of most form of tourism activities. Services include but not limited to those functions that a tourist might or might not be able to perform for him or herself but in all cases choose someone else to perform it for them. Services take place at locations where the activity is offered (such as the travel, the accommodation, the food, the transportation, the communication, and the provision of souvenirs). Therefore, tourism activities require services provided by business; these set of services and activities form the tourism experiences. Further, it is generally accepted that tourism experiences have multidimensional facets. Walls, Okumus, Wang, and Kwun (2011) analyzed the theoretical underpinnings of customer experience by examining the definitions of experience and the contextual nature of customer experiences. Their study suggests that the perception of customer experience has numerous foundational origins that have complicated its growth as a viable and valued concept, and proposes a framework to better understand this construct in a tourism and hospitality context.

Providing tourists with memorable experiences is important for success in a highly competitive tourism marketplace (Kim, 2014). In order to gain a competitive advantage, it is crucial for organizations and companies to offer and deliver experiences that are demanded and valued by the market. There are numerous issues and challenges to be addressed in managing tourism experiences by tourism destinations and businesses ranging from the experience design to the management of experience creation and delivery that meets the customer's expectations (Lin & Liang, 2011). Literature has increasingly recognized the importance of managing the customer's experience (see, e.g., Berry, Carbone, & Haeckel, 2002; Morgan, Lugosi, & Ritchie, 2010; Schmitt, 2003). The customer experience has emerged as the single most important aspect in achieving success for companies across all industries. A successful customer experience management requires a strategy that focuses on the operations and processes of a business around the needs of the individual customer (Schmitt, 2003).

Managing and Marketing Tourism Experiences

In order to provide valuable and memorable experiences, tourism businesses and destinations have to manage and market efficiently and effectively the provision of tourism services and delivering experiences. From a managerial standpoint, the landmark work by Pine and Gilmore (1998, 1999) has generated widespread interest into a new management paradigm which emphasizes the transition from service delivery to experience creation and co-creation.

The motivation to design and stage valuable experiences stem from the fact that an experience is subjectively felt by an individual who is engaged with an event on an emotional, physical, spiritual, and/or intellectual level. As already mentioned, Pine and Gilmore (1999) defined four realms/dimensions of experiences, namely entertainment, educational, esthetic, and escapist. These dimensions are the components of the experience economy framework explored in various contexts, as presented below. The same authors provided five key points for which they called experience-design principles: theme the experience, harmonize impressions with positive cues, eliminate negative cues, mix in memorabilia, and engage all five senses.

Within the marketing realm, Holbrook and Hirschman (1982) suggested an experiential view of consumption, arguing that satisfaction is one component of experiences in addition to the hedonic, symbolic, and aesthetic nature of experiential consumption. Otto and Richie (1995), based on this experiential view, examined satisfaction of tourism experiences and asserted that subjective, emotional, and highly personal responses to various aspects of the service encounter are likely to result in varying levels of overall satisfaction. Further, Jennings and Nickerson (2006) have provided an assessment of and insights into the satisfactory quality experiences; however, there is no current consensus as to the definition of what constitutes "quality." Nevertheless, the most prevalent relationship is the connection of experience to service quality and to customer satisfaction (Ekinci, Riley, & Chen, 2001). This interrelationship and connection has been demonstrated by studies in various tourism contexts. It is believed that a valuable and memorable tourism experience will lead to customer satisfaction and post-consumption behavioral intentions (Oh, Fiore, & Jeoung, 2007).

Experience Economy Framework: Empirical Studies within Tourism Context and Settings

Literature suggests that the pertinent constructs of the experience economy model can be used to explain the experiential nature of tourism in various settings (see, for instance, Quadri-Felitti & Fiore, 2012). During the last decade, there has been an enthusiastic movement in the management and marketing literature toward the experience economy and its particular relevance to the tourism industry (Mehmetoglu & Engen, 2011; Titz, 2007). The experience economy framework briefly presented above has been empirically examined in various tourism contexts. Let us briefly present the main studies on applications of this framework in tourism contexts.

The first study was carried out by Oh et al. (2007) within the context of bed and breakfast accommodations. Authors proposed a measurement model that includes four realms of experience (i.e., entertainment, education, esthetics, and escapism) and four nomological consequences/antecedents (i.e., arousal, memory, overall quality, and satisfaction). The study performed by

Hosany and Witham (2010) investigated the relationships among cruisers' experiences, satisfaction, and intention to recommend. Mehmetoglu and Engen (2011) used the same framework to empirically examine the applicability of the four experiential dimensions within two different tourism contexts: an event and a built visitor attraction in Norway, both visited by domestic and inbound tourists. The study by Quadri-Felitti and Fiore (2013) evaluated the wine tourists' experiences in the Lake Erie wine region (USA). This study used an adapted version of the scale of the experience economy's dimensions to examine the impacts of four dimensions of experience economy on destination loyalty. Lastly, Correia Loureiro (2014) empirically explored the effect of the experience economy on place attachment and behavioral intentions through emotions and memory within the context of rural tourism, individuals experiencing rural holidays in the South of Portugal.

What are the main conclusions that could be drawn from the above studies? Three are, in our view, the main conclusions, namely (i) the experience framework (Pine and Gilmore's model) has been proved to be reliable and valid for measuring customers' experience within various tourism contexts; (ii) the relative importance/influence of four dimensions in estimating the experiential outcomes tend to vary from one context to the other; the four dimensions were found to operate differently in each tourism setting. All studies found that the correlation between the experience dimensions and the outcomes (memory, arousal, and overall perceived quality and satisfaction) was strong. However, the four dimensions differ in terms of their relative importance in explaining the outcome variables; and (iii) findings contradict Pine and Gilmore's assertion that simultaneous incorporation of the four dimensions is necessary.

The theoretical framework of experience economy, suggested by Pine and Gilmore challenged us to think about consumption experience in ways that resonated well with travel, tourism, and hospitality. However, they provided little in setting an agenda for the best practices or research beyond their basic concept. This is evidenced by the lack of development of the literature on the topic.

Additionally, the developments in the field of information and communication technology (ICTs) have revolutionized the business environment. The ICT revolution considerably influences consumer attitudes and behaviors and has a huge impact on tourists, tourism destinations, and providers of tourism services (Law, Buhalis, & Cobanoglu, 2014; Morrison, 2013). One of the main challenges in the digital environment and globalized travel and tourism markets is the rise of networking platforms or social media (SM) that allow tourists to interact and share their views and experiences with potentially unrestricted virtual communities (Sigala, Christou, & Gretzel, 2012; Xiang & Tussyadiah, 2014). SM platforms permit tourists to digitize and share online knowledge and experiences. All these technological developments offer benefits for both tourists and destinations, provide opportunities and raise challenges as well (Sigala et al., 2012). Indeed, SM have a considerable influence and impact, as part of tourism management and marketing strategy, on all aspects of the tourism industry. The reason for this is simultaneously simple and serious: they play a significant role in many aspects of tourism, especially in information search and decision-making behaviors, tourism promotion and in focusing on the best practices for interacting with consumers (Law et al., 2014; Sotiriadis & van Zyl, 2013; Xiang & Tussyadiah, 2014). Literature suggests that SM are increasingly relevant as part of tourism practices affecting destinations and businesses, as they are changing the ways in which information about travel and tourism experiences are disseminated (see, for instance, Munar & Jacobsen, 2014). The changes in tourists' behavior have a critical impact on the approaches and tools that tourism destinations and businesses have to adopt and use in managing and marketing their services and offerings in the digital environment. As argued by Sigala et al. (2012), SM are challenging existing customer services, marketing activities, and promotional processes in the tourism field. Apparently, the Internet and Web 2.0 provide tourism businesses and destinations with tools and applications to design, create and co-create, manage, market, and evaluate experiences for tourist consumers. Two crucial points in this field are to have the appropriate approach and to make effective use (Sotiriadis & van Zyl, 2015).

From the above discussion, it is clear that planning, design, management, and marketing of experiences for tourism markets constitute a focal challenge for tourism destinations and providers in a highly competitive marketplace. All businesses and organizations involved in have to address challenges and issues of providing high-quality experiences to tourists. This volume aims at bridging the gap in contemporary literature by carefully examining management and marketing issues of tourism experiences. Within this context, this volume (i) adopts an approach of strategic and operational management and marketing, and (ii) takes a tourism business and destination perspective to consider and analyze the main issues and aspects related to the three stages/phases of offering experiences to tourists: before, during and after the experience encounter.

This volume aims to explore and analyze the main issues and challenges in the field of tourist experiences from a strategic management and marketing perspective, and suggest the appropriate approaches in planning, managing, and marketing experiences for tourists. The specific objectives are: (i) to analyze the main issues and challenges related to tourism experience management and marketing; (ii) to present and discuss adequate analytical frameworks and tools; (iii) to explore the adoption and implementation of approaches to managing and marketing experiences in various tourism contexts and industries; and (iv) to discuss and analyze case studies illustrating approaches adopted, methods implemented, and best practices in addressing related issues.

In order to consider and analyze the various issues and aspects and to achieve its aims and objectives, this volume is structured into four parts, as follows. Part I "Planning: Design and Creating Tourism Experiences" deals with the planning tourism experiences and aims at considering and analyzing main issues and aspects of designing and creating experiences in tourism and encompasses six chapters. The first chapter, "Experience-based service design," by Özlem Güzel, presents a service design path built around various elements such as sensations, emotions, human relations, innovations, and values. It argues that experience-based service design contains different components, and that this service design should be established within three-steps, namely explore, design, and positioning. This process is illustrated using a case study on Singapore Airlines.

Chapter 2, entitled "Experience-Centric Approach and Innovation," is authored by Anita Zátori. It discusses the experience-centric strategy from the perspective of innovation management, its contribution to designing and managing valuable tourism experiences, especially in context of guided tours. It highlights the role of experience design and market intelligence in experience-centric service processes. The next chapter, "Crucial Role and Contribution of Human Resources in the Context of Tourism Experiences: Need for Experiential Intelligence and Skills," by Marios Sotiriadis and Stelios Varvaressos, discusses the issue of human resources within the context of tourism experiences. Specifically, it analyses and highlights the importance of a strategic approach to human resources management and suggests suitable tools and strategies. Micro-cases and examples are used to illustrate efficient human resources management tools and practices.

Chapter 4 entitled "Tourism Destination: Design of Experiences," by Eyup Karayilan and Gurel Cetin, proposes a conceptual model for designing tourism experiences at destination level and analyses the implications for main stakeholders (DMOs, host community, and tourism industry) in creating experiences for tourists. A case study highlights the determining role of destination features and that of stakeholders in involving tourists in experience production. Chapter 5, "Social media and the co-creation of tourism experiences," authored by Marianna Sigala, investigates the role and the impact of social media in influencing and shaping tourism experiences. This chapter adopts a Service Dominant Logic and co-creation approach and concepts for examining how the social media can influence interactions and participation that represent two major sources of tourism experiences. Author provides several arguments showing how social media enabled interactions and participation can facilitate, foster, and expand the experience co-creation process by altering: when, how, why, what, by whom, and how tourism experiences are co-created.

The last chapter of this part "Experiential tourism: Creating and marketing tourism attraction experiences," by Rachel Dodds and Lee Jolliffe, explores the current trend toward both creative and experiential tourism in cities in terms of development and marketing of local attractions. Creative tourism in cities is profiled through a literature review and further investigated by means of a case study at a local attraction in Toronto, Canada. The choice of a site was one of a creative city and the repurposing of a formerly industrial site for visitation. The study of Evergreens Brickworks demonstrates the use of marketing techniques to identify markets and match visitors with experiences.

Part II is devoted to management issues. It is entitled "Managing: Organizing and Delivering Tourism Experiences" and aims at approaching and analyzing issues of managing tourism experiences within various contexts, industries, and settings. The part features nine chapters, as follows. Chapter 7 "Cultural and Experiential Tourism," by Hilary du Cros, examines how sensitivity to event design and the creative process for an arts event also can have an impact on its ongoing management and tourism experience, by applying a new assessment tool, sustainable creative advantage (SCA), to gauge its performance. A case study approach is used to assess SCA for the Sculpture by Sea, Bondi, Sydney 2015, in order to discuss how its management enables satisfying arts leisure experiences. It is believed that the event could still be considered a fresh and inspiring experience for tourists. However, crowding on weekends can affect the experience for all participants. Tactile tours are a unique feature of the event and could be promoted more to tourists.

The next chapter "Dragon Boat Intangible Cultural Heritage: Management Challenges of a Community and Élite Sport Event as a Tourism Experience," authored by Fleur Fallon, presents three trends emerging from a review of the literature, namely: concern with balancing authenticity and profit-chasing; the phenomenal fast growth of the sport and the challenge to develop and maintain international control and governance; and seeking evidence of health and wellbeing benefits of Dragon Boat racing for breast cancer survivors. The study traces the growth of Dragon Boat racing from humble beginnings in 1976 as part of a local tourism strategy by the Hong Kong Tourist Association (HKTA) to position Hong Kong as more distinctive than a destination for shopping or with British colonial history appeal. The event is now a recognized world sport requiring a global strategy of co-operative alliances and is close to becoming an official sport in the Olympic Games. Author contends that emergent strategy and symbolic authenticity of intangible cultural heritage are key concerns for integrating special events as a central tourism experience.

It is believed that collaboration between tourism operations makes a significant contribution in providing special guest experiences and that a collaborative platform wisely designed creates a series of business benefits. Chapter 9, entitled "Collaborating to Provide Attractive Hotel Guests' Experiences," by Marios Sotiriadis and Christos Sarmaniotis, analyses the contribution of collaboration between businesses in providing valuable experiences in hotel settings. A case study from Italy is used to illustrate how hotel operations are collaborating to provide tourism experience opportunities. This collaboration offers a way of enriching and deepening guests' experiences, based on endogenous resources, and meeting the tourists' requirements.

Chris A. Vassiliadis and Anestis Fotiadis are the authors of next chapter "Managing Sport Tourism Experiences: Blueprinting Service Encounters." This chapter presents and analyses how the methodology of service blueprinting may contribute to managing and offering high quality experiences to sport tourists. It uses a combination of theoretical tools to develop a finalized services blueprint map for sport events. It is argued that observation, diaries, service blueprints, comment management, and FMEA (Failure Mode and Effects Analysis) are a range of corporate research approaches and management tools that can offer new insights into the theory and praxis of service management applications and can improve the sport tourism experiences.

The authenticity of tourism experiences and the commodification of tourism offering are two issues that attracted the interest of academic research. Chapter 11, entitled "Authenticity, Commodification, and McDonaldization of Tourism Experiences in the Context of Cultural Tourism" authored by Medet Yolal, discusses these dimensions of tourism experiences using a case study of a well-established destination (Cappadocia, Turkey). Author contends that destinations rely not only on authenticity of their attractiveness but also strive to attract tourists by tailoring experiences that will meet high-order needs of the tourists. However, these destinations are under threat by commodification and McDonaldization due to excessive use of the resources as a result of mass tourism.

The emergence of the creative and experiential tourism in general is only the visible part of the paradigm shift that is affecting the tourism industry, involving new challenges and opportunities. A contribution from a practitioner is provided in Chapter 12 "Managing Experiences within the Field of Creative Tourism: Best Practices and Guidelines." Caroline Couret shares her practical experience in creative tourism management and proposes some guidelines for DMOs interested in designing activities and plans in this field. Most of the analyses, examples, and observations are based on management of the *Creative Tourism Network*® and the approaches adopted by its members in managing their creative tourism offerings over the world. This chapter concludes with a series of applicable guidelines and suggestions for managers to cater to this niche market.

The growth of the ecotourism industry led to an increased emphasis on sustainable practices and called for greener practices to be incorporated in managing ecotourism destinations and operations. Chapter 13, entitled "Greening as Part of Ecotourism to Contribute to Tourists' Experiences: A Destination Planning Approach," by E. Botha and W. H. Engelbrecht, provides a brief overview of the green principles associated with developing ecotourism destinations. Green ecotourism destination planning is explained within the context of the tourism experiences to highlight aspects necessary for sustainable ecotourism destination development. Waterwheel, located in the Limpopo province of South Africa, is faced with this green development challenge and serves as a case study of planning and managing ecotourism experiences.

Anna Farmaki is the author of next chapter "Managing Rural Tourist Experiences: Lessons from Cyprus." This chapter assesses the management of the rural tourist experiences in Cyprus by implementing an exploratory research approach. It examines rural tourists' experiences in relation to travel motives and activities performed in rural areas in Cyprus, and explores overall satisfaction with the rural tourist experience with regard to several physical, social, and symbolic attributes derived from the literature review. Author elicits recommendations that can improve the tourist experience in rural areas. A refined segmentation strategy is proposed as well as the development of synergistic, innovative linkages among rural tourism stakeholders and across segments in the industry, with thematic clusters representing a favorable and suitable strategy.

Chapter 15 "Service Innovations and Experience Creation in Spas, Wellness and Medical Tourism," by Melanie Kay Smith, Sonia Ferrari, and László Puczkó, analyses the relationship between service innovation and experience creation within the context of spas, wellness, and medical tourism. This study provides an overview of service innovation theory and models, and then applies them to the spa, wellness, and medical tourism industries. Authors present a case study on Pärnu hospital in Estonia, where innovative practices are being implemented to improve the patients' experience. The main contribution of the empirical study is to identify the most important elements in the experiences of spa and wellness guests and tourists. Some aspects of innovation (such as design and technology) are not seen as important elements as expected; however, evidence-based treatments, medical services, and natural and local resources are valuable components.

The next part, Part III "Marketing: Communicating and promoting Tourism experiences," deals with marketing issues and approaches, and aims at considering and analyzing the functions and tools of communicating and promoting tourism experiences within various contexts and/or industries. This part includes six chapters as follows. Chapter 16, entitled "The Role of Online Social Media on the Experience and Communication of Gay

Events in a Tourist Destination: A Case Study of a Small-Scale Film Festival in Nice," by S. Christofle, C. Papetti, and M. Ferry, analyses the role of social media in experience sharing and communication of a gay film festival in one of the most popular world tourist destinations. This study implemented an exploratory research (qualitative study and netnographic analysis) for a single gay film festival (ZeFestival) to acquire insights on the adoption and uses of social media by both organizers (as communication tools) and festival goers (for experience sharing). The chapter is completed by formulating some recommendations for the adequate uses of these Web 2.0 tools at various stages — before, during, and after — of the event.

Chapter 17 "Marketing Experiences for Visitor Attractions: The Contribution of Theming," by E. Botha looks at similarities between the experience economy and Disneyization, with specific focus on theming as a means of enhancing tourism experience. Sophisticated tourists have brought with them the need to better understand their behavior and place more emphasis on experiences. The Addo Elephant National Park, South Africa, is presented as a case study that uses interpretation as a tool for theming. Several issues and guidelines related to theming are presented to highlight aspects which visitor attraction managers and marketers need to consider when seeking to use theming to improve or create a visitor experience. Author contends that the theme should be planned meticulously as it refers to several aspects not only in the experience itself but also in the experience cycle. It is therefore a quite complex tool to use that should not be taken lightly in order to benefit fully from the possible advantages.

The following chapter, "Marketing Culinary Tourism Experiences," authored by Lee Jolliffe, identifies issues in the development and marketing of culinary tourism experiences with the goal of determining the value of collaborative forms of product development and marketing. Author performs a literature review examining approaches to marketing of culinary experiences and identifies a gap in the study of collaborative approaches such as networking, partnering, and alliances. A case study investigates these themes. Through the analysis of an in-depth case study of an experiential culinary tourism event in a small city in Eastern Canada (a Restaurant Week), it is determined that informal collaboration in the form of partnership is essential to building and marketing collaborative culinary tourism offerings and experiences. This investigation has value for practitioners implementing collaborative forms in this field.

A different perspective and discipline approach to the thematic of tourism experiences is presented in Chapter 19 "Managing and Marketing Tourism Experiences: Extending the Travel Risk Perception Literature to Address Affective Risk Perceptions," by Ashley Schroeder, Lori Pennington-Gray, Maximiliano Korstanje, and Geoffrey Skoll. This chapter critically discusses the current risk perception literature in the tourism field and offers a solution through a more conceptual and operational definition of risk perceptions. Specifically, the inclusion of affective risk perceptions is added to the literature via the risk-as-feelings hypothesis. Authors contend that extension of the current literature enhances research moving forward. Hence, this chapter proposes a theoretical and conceptual model as a framework to address risk perception studies in tourism and travel. This model frames an operationalization of risk perception variables by providing clear measurement scales to be tested.

Many destinations are implementing sport tourism offerings to enhance their attractiveness and potential to satisfy tourists' desires for new experiences. This has led to a highly competitive sport tourism market and as a result destinations implement various marketing techniques and promotional tools. Chapter 20 "Promotion Tools Used in the Marketing of Sport Tourism Experiences in a Mature Tourism Destination," by Crystal C. Lewis and Cristina H. Jönsson, reports on a research conducted to acquire a better understanding of promotional tools to effectively and efficiently market sport tourism experiences. Findings indicated that promotional tools implemented in Barbados come along with problems of poor and insufficient sporting facilities. Furthermore, low collaboration between tourism providers and sporting entities hamper the success of Barbados as a sport tourism destination. It is argued that, while promotional tools are essential in attracting tourists, other elements must also be taken into consider to ensure that sport tourists will have adequate offerings and positive experiences. Ultimately this would lead to a successful sport tourism destination.

The last chapter regarding marketing of tourism experiences is entitled "The Role of Information Communication Technologies (ICTs) in Marketing Tourism Experiences," constitutes a contribution by Kyung-Hyan Yoo and Ulrike Gretzel. This chapter discusses the role of ICTs and the emerging trends and issues in marketing tourism experiences. Previous conceptual frameworks are reviewed and key issues and trends are identified as central for ICT-based tourism marketing. Authors suggest a conceptual model that outlines a technology-empowered marketing approach for co-created tourism experiences and identified key trends in marketing tourism experiences. Furthermore, case studies are presented to illustrate how the marketing issues could be translated into practical tourism marketing strategies, highlighting the integrated and strategic role of various tools ICTs. The chapter is completed with practical implications for ICT-based marketing of tourism experiences.

Last part (Part IV) "Monitoring and Evaluating Tourism Experiences" considers issues related to the stage of post experience encounter. It aims to present and analyze approaches and tools to monitor and evaluate the performance of tourism destinations and businesses in the field of tourism experiences. This part features four chapters as follows. Chapter 22 "Memorable Tourism Experiences: Conceptual Foundations and Managerial Implications for Program Design, Delivery and Performance Measurement," by Jong-Hyeong Kim, sought to overcome the current theoretical lack of understanding of the concept of memorable tourism experiences (MTEs) and to provide a conceptual framework for guiding destination managers who seek to design and deliver memorable experiences appropriate to their particular destination. This study investigated tourism experiential factors that enable and facilitate MTEs. The literature review and the content analysis and synthesis identified seven conceptual and theoretical components of MTEs, namely hedonism, refreshment, novelty, local culture, meaningfulness, knowledge, and adverse feelings. It then demonstrates the managerial importance of these theoretical components to the design of applicable destination programs and discusses the implications for destination managers of this understanding for designing, delivering, and evaluating programs.

Magdalena Petronella (Nellie) Swart is the author of next chapter, entitled "Proposing an Experiential Value Model within the Context of Business Tourism Experiences." This chapter argues that experiential value, satisfaction, and post consumption behavior may play an important role in acquiring information and knowledge creation on how business tourism organizations can use a structured model and to enhance service experiences. Author then suggests a theoretical framework for the development of a multi-item Business Tourist Experience Value Model, based on the Behavioral Intentions Model of Fishbein and Ajzen (1975). This model consists of an integration and re-assessment of different elements from a range of empirical studies. It is estimated that this theoretical model offers new practices into the measurement of experiential value, satisfaction, and post consumption behavior in a business tourism context. In other terms, business tourism managers can use these dimensions as guidelines on how to create valuable experiences for customers and achieve better performance.

Chapter 24 "Consumer Travel Online Reviews and Recommendations: Suggesting Strategies to Address Challenges Faced within the Digital Context," by Marios Sotiriadis and Ciná van Zyl, performs a synthesis of the academic research regarding the changes of tourist consumer behavior brought about by social media, and suggests a set of strategies for tourism businesses to address resulting challenges. Extensive literature reviews have been performed on the motivating factors and the effects of online reviews. This chapter focuses on the impact of online reviews on tourism businesses and outlines a series of adequate strategies formulated for business practitioners. Authors contend that this study provides practical recommendations/suggestions for tourism businesses in addressing the challenges and opportunities raised within the digital context.

The last chapter, entitled "Assessing Tourism Experiences: The Case of Heritage Attractions," by Gaunette Sinclair-Maragh, reports on an empirical investigation regarding tourism experiences in heritage attractions in Jamaica. It analyses the five principles of experience economy within the context of heritage attractions. This study aims to find out whether heritage attractions are using the principles of experience economy to provide a fulfilling experience to visitors. The principles of the experience economy are having consistent theme, using positive cues, eliminating negative cues, offering memorabilia, and engaging the five senses. This study provides insights on the implementation of experience economy principles in managing heritage attractions. Consequently, the same approach contributes to evaluate the performance of experience's outcomes.

The volume is completed by providing management and marketing implications and recommendations for tourism business and destinations to enable them to successfully create, manage, and market tourism experiences, as well as to effectively evaluate their performance in this field. Overall, this book provides conceptual and practical evidence for the critical importance of adopting and implementing management and marketing approaches and tools to address the challenges and seize the opportunities in the field of tourism experiences.

We would like to thank our colleagues and the researchers in the field of tourism and hospitality who have contributed to the *Handbook of Managing and Marketing Tourism Experiences*; you have given us reasons to initiate a project like this one. You are a true inspiration and source of this Handbook's birth, hoping that you would find the source useful. We as editors extent our sincere thanks to the Emerald Publishing and their highly skilled staff members for making this project a reality.

We hope that this book will generate a significant interest and discussion on design, delivery, and monitoring of tourism experience and provide a foundation for a much greater research contribution from both scholars and business practitioners. We strongly believe that this volume will be very useful for academics, researchers, and undergraduate and postgraduate tourism students. It will also be of interest to practitioners and entrepreneurs.

We hope you will enjoy reading this book.
Marios Sotiriadis
Dogan Gursoy
Editors

References

Berry, L. L., Carbone, L. P., & Haeckel, S. H. (2002). Managing the total customer experience. *MIT Sloan Management Review*, 43(3), 85–89.

Boswijk, A., Thijssen, T., & Peelen, E. (2007). *The experience economy: A new perspective*. Amsterdam: Pearson Education.

Correia Loureiro, S. M. (2014). The role of the rural tourism experience economy in place attachment and behavioral intentions. *International Journal of Hospitality Management*, 40(1), 1–9.

Ekinci, Y., Riley, M., & Chen, J. (2001). A review of comparisons used in service quality and customer satisfaction studies: Emerging issues for hospitality and tourism research. *Tourism Analysis*, 5(2–4), 197–202.

Fishbein, M., & Ajzen, I. (1975). *Belief, attitude, intention, and behavior: An introduction to theory and research*. Reading, MA: Addison-Wesley.

Gursoy, D., Saayman, M., & Sotiriadis, M. (2015). Introduction. In D. Gursoy, M. Saayman, & M. Sotiriadis (Eds.), *Collaboration in tourism businesses and destinations: A handbook* (pp. xv–xxvi). Bingley, UK: Emerald Group Publishing Limited.

Holbrook, M., & Hirschman, E. (1982). The experiential aspects of consumption: Consumer fantasies, feelings, and fun. *Journal of Consumer Research*, 9(2), 132–140.

Hosany, S., & Witham, M. (2010). Dimensions of cruisers' experiences, satisfaction, and intention to recommend. *Journal of Travel Research, 49*(3), 351–364.

Jennings, G., & Nickerson, N. (2006). *Quality tourism experiences.* Oxford: Butterworth-Heinemann.

Kim, J.-H. (2014). The antecedents of memorable tourism experiences: The development of a scale to measure the destination attributes associated with memorable experiences. *Tourism Management, 44*(1), 34–45.

Law, R., Buhalis, D., & Cobanoglu, C. (2014). Progress on information and communication technologies in hospitality and tourism. *International Journal of Contemporary Hospitality Management, 26*(5), 727–750.

Lin, J.-S. C., & Liang, H.-Y. (2011). The influence of service environments on customer emotion and service outcomes. *Managing Service Quality, 21*(4), 350–372.

Mehmetoglu, M., & Engen, M. (2011). Pine and Gilmore's concept of experience economy and its dimensions: An empirical examination in tourism. *Journal of Quality Assurance in Hospitality & Tourism, 12*(4), 237–255.

Merriam-Webster. (1993). *Merriam-Webster's collegiate dictionary* (10th ed.). Springfield, MA: Merriam-Webster Inc.

Middleton, V., Fyall, A., Morgan, M., & Ranchhod, A. (2009). *Marketing in travel and tourism* (4th ed.). Oxford: Butterworth-Heinemann.

Morgan, M., Lugosi, P., & Ritchie, J. R. B. (Eds.). (2010). *The tourism and leisure experience; consumer and managerial perspectives.* Clevedon: Channel View Publications.

Morrison, A. M. (2013). *Marketing and managing tourism destinations.* Oxon, UK: Routledge.

Mossberg, L. (2007). A marketing approach to the tourist experience. *Scandinavian Journal of Hospitality and Tourism, 7*(1), 59–74.

Munar, A. M., & Jacobsen, J. K. S. (2014). Motivations for sharing tourism experiences through social media. *Tourism Management, 43*, 46–54.

Oh, H., Fiore, A. M., & Jeoung, M. (2007). Measuring experience economy concepts: Tourism applications. *Journal of Travel Research, 46*(1), 119–132.

Otto, J., & Richie, J. (1995). Exploring the quality of the service experience; a theoretical and empirical analysis. *Advances in Services Marketing and Management, 4*, 37–61.

Pine, J. B., & Gilmore, J. H. (1998). Welcome to the experience economy. *Harvard Business Review, 76*(4), 97–105.

Pine, J. B., & Gilmore, J. H. (1999). *The experience economy: Work is theatre and every business a stage.* Boston, MA: Harvard Business School Press.

Quadri-Felitti, D., & Fiore, A. M. (2012). Experience economy constructs as a framework for understanding wine tourism. *Journal of Vacation Marketing, 18*(1), 3–15.

Quadri-Felitti, D., & Fiore, A. M. (2013). Destination loyalty: Effects of wine tourists' experiences, memories, and satisfaction on intentions. *Tourism and Hospitality Research, 13*(1), 47–62.

Schmitt, B. H. (1999). Experiential marketing. *Journal of Marketing Management, 15*(1), 53–67.

Schmitt, B. H. (2003). *Customer experience management: A revolutionary approach to connecting with your customers.* New York, NY: Wiley.

Sharpley, R., & Stone, P. R. (2011). Introduction: Thinking about the tourist experience. In R. Sharpley & P. R. Stone (Eds.), *Tourism experience; contemporary perspectives* (pp. 1–8). Oxon, UK: Routledge.

Sigala, M., Christou, E., & Gretzel, U. (Eds.). (2012). *Social media in travel, tourism and hospitality: Theory, practice and cases.* London: Ashgate.

Sotiriadis, M., & van Zyl, C. (2013). Electronic world-of-mouth and online reviews in tourism services: the use of twitter by tourists. *Electronic Commerce Research Journal, 13*(1), 103–124.

Sotiriadis, M., & van Zyl, C. (2015). Tourism services, micro-blogging and customer feedback: A tourism provider perspective. In J. N. Burkhalter & N. Wood (Eds.), *Maximizing commerce and marketing strategies through microblogging* (pp. 157–176). Philadelphia, PA: IGI Global.

Sundbo, J., & Darmer, P. (Eds.). (2008). *Creating experiences in the experience economy.* Cheltenham, UK: Edward Elgar.

Titz, K. (2007). Experiential consumption: Affect – Emotions – Hedonism. In A. Pizam & H. Oh (Eds.), *Handbook of hospitality marketing management* (pp. 324–352). Oxford, UK: Butterworth-Heinemann.

Walls, A. R., Okumus, F., Wang, Y. (R)., & Kwun, D. J.-W. (2011). An epistemological view of consumer experiences. *International Journal of Hospitality Management, 30*(1), 10–21.

Xiang, Z., & Tussyadiah, I. (Eds.). (2014). *Information and communication technologies in tourism 2014.* New York, NY: Springer.

Part I
Planning: Design and Creating Tourism Experiences

Aim: to consider and analyze related issues and aspects in various fields/contexts

1

Experience-Based Service Design

Özlem Güzel

ABSTRACT

Purpose – In the tourism sector, the differentiation is difficult in the commoditized market. The main challenge for businesses is to design the experiences which would create awareness and difference. With this foresight, this chapter aims to show an experience-based service design path built around various elements such as sensations, emotions, human relations, innovations, and values.

Methodology/approach – This chapter is based on extensive literature review, including books, journals, articles, conference papers, and search reports. Furthermore, the Singapore Airlines web page was used as an important source of information to examine the instructional path built suggested in the literature review.

Findings – As it has been determined by the general review, experience-based service design contains different components, and with these evaluations the experience-based service design was established in this chapter within three steps: explore, design, and positioning. Furthermore, on the case study of Singapore Airlines, the tracks of these three steps have been investigated. Especially, explore and design dimensions have been identified to be used mainly during the experience design.

Practical implications – From the highlights of the literature review, an instructional path for experience-based service design and implementation process is highlighted in three parts and this instructional path would guide business managers/experience engineers.

Originality/value – As the experience-based service design has been increasingly receiving the attention of the business' managers in the tourism sector, an overview examination of experience design, and being instructional guide will direct them to implicate the dimensions in practice.

Keywords: Experience marketing; experience design; service design; Singapore airlines

Introduction

Customers having many choices, but being less satisfied is the paradox of the 21st century (Prahalad & Ramaswamy, 2004). In this context, a new approach referred to as Customer Experience Management (CEM) has emerged as a new perspective for far-sighted businesses to use their capabilities and resources effectively in creating value and experience. This new approach has become a strategic competitive marketing tool for creating value as the traditional marketing has been losing its effectiveness in the 21st century (Gentile, Spiller, & Noci, 2007; Lasalle & Britton, 2003; Pine & Gilmore, 1999; Prahalad & Ramaswamy, 2004; Schmitt, 1999; Shaw, 2005; Smith & Wheeler, 2002). Shaw and Ivens (2002) refer the existence of the seven-point philosophy during customer experience design (CED). According to them, customer experience; must be a long-term competitive advantage source; must respond the customers' rational and emotional expectations consistently; should focus on stimulating the selected emotions; should be created with inspiring leadership; needs strong organization/motivated staff; must take the consumers in the center of experience implementations; should transform into the design of the brand.

If the industry is such an industry like tourism, experiences consist of the main core of the brand as it is one of the main sectors that recreative, unforgettable and attractive experiences could be created by evoking the emotions and feelings (Oh, Fiore, & Jeoung, 2007; Otto & Ritchie, 1996; Slatten, Mehmetoğlu, Svensson, & Svaeri, 2009; Williams, 2006). Schmitt (2013) states that the CEM framework is made up of five basic steps: analyzing the experiential world of the customer, building the experiential platform, designing the brand experience, structuring the customer interface and engaging in continuous innovation. Considering this framework within the literature review, it has been revealed the experience-based service design has many phases and dimensions. This chapter is going to provide a practical instructional path in three steps, including "explore, design and positioning" (EDP). Explore dimension contains exploring the business' self-sufficiency and understanding of the customer world as these are recognized as the beginning of the experiential journey. Design dimension refers to the preparation of the experience stage and involves experience value promise, actors, innovation and creativity, theme, and atmosphere. The positioning dimension contains the customer interface and placing into the customer's mind concluded with memorability. After a general review, a case study will be evaluated to follow the clues of experience design through these three dimensions.

Explore

The experience design process is defined as both science and art. In the scientific dimension, the customer expectations, needs, and priorities are discovered, the customer experience is mapped and the critical points are identified by focusing on the customer's senses (Smith & Wheeler, 2002). This dimension is named in this chapter as the explore dimension containing tips for the business about themselves and their customers to start their tourism experience design journey.

EXPLORING THE BUSINESS' SELF-SUFFICIENCY

CEM is created by exceeding the customers' physical/emotional expectations by designing inward (Shaw, 2005). Carbone and Haeckel (1994) see the acquisition of service experience design skills as the first phase of the experience-based design. The business managers should analyze on where they stand on the experience circle before the pre-design phase. In this context, Shaw (2005) has created a basic model to understand on which stage the business stands in the CEM circle. According to the model, there are four orientation areas including "inexperienced, operational, illuminated and natural." Inexperienced organizations focus on the products and these organizations are insensitive to customer needs. Their approach shapes on the philosophy; "take it or leave it" or/and "what do you expect from a product at this price."

On the next stage, operational organizations are those who realize the importance of the customer. However, these organizations, focusing on just the physical aspects of the customer experience (e.g., Quick response to the telephone), tend to ignore the other aspects of the experience (Cetin & Walls, 2016). In the third area, the organizations see the customer experience as important as the customers and transfer this foresight to all employees. These organizations are aware of the fact that emotions are a major component of customer experience and they implement new processes in order to evoke emotions. In the final stages, the natural organizations seeing the customer experience as the genes of business. They are aware of the critical role of emotions and feelings. Business leaders and all employees build the experience by using the theater as an experience stage together after identifying critical points (Shaw, 2005).

In order to reach the level of natural organizations, business should create a new wall for creating the experience containing effective values. Prahalad and Ramaswamy (2004) propose four activities to build up this wall; establishing a deep dialogue with the customers, improving customer interaction, taking advantage of new technological developments, and enabling the exchange of information.

UNDERSTANDING THE CUSTOMERS EXPECTATIONS

The customers' world must be understood by looking from the holistic perspective from different aspects in order to create the experience context before the designing (Thusy & Morris, 2004). Understanding what the target customers expect from the business and which values they look for have to be the critical steps of the experience design. The difficulty of obtaining the accurate understanding of how users feel about the products is the main challenge during the experience design (Kashimura, Kumagai, & Furuya, 2013). Moreover, Zaltman and Zaltman (2008) state that many businesses are facing with the problem named 'lack the depth' during the analysis of customers world. This lack of depth results because of the absence of thinking based on imagination, not having the benefit from the insights brought by different disciplines and not discussing the ideas coming from consumers. In order to eliminate the lack of depth from the perspective of creative paradigm and to establish the CED with effective values, customers should be included in the value creation and experience design process as being the continuously collaborative partners (Michelli, 2007; Prahalad & Ramaswamy, 2004; Schmitt, 2003; Smith & Wheeler, 2002; Tsai, 2005).

Kotler, Kartajaya, and Setiawan (2010) called this method as 'strengthen the customer' which let the customers have the opportunity to design their own experience by including into the business' mission. The analysis of the customers' lifestyles and their socio-cultural environment in which they live is an important step in understanding the customer world. In addition, for creating the personalized and unique experiences, flexible research methods should be used, particularly focusing on different interests and needs. In order to get realistic results, real stimulants should be used and the natural experiential environment should be observed during the research. Moreover, experience engineers should benefit from the customers' imagination world. Kashimura et al. (2013) offer collecting user complaints, making observations and conducting interviews in order to specify the user requirements and user's characteristics as they identify this step as human-centered design.

After the scientific process of the experience design has been completed the artistic dimension emerges containing the creativity and value creation as Smith and Wheeler (2002) refer. This next dimension is named in this chapter as the design.

Design

The design process being analogous to theatrical show contains creating experience value, actors (human resources), innovation and creativity, experience theme and experience atmosphere (scene).

EXPERIENCE VALUE PROMISE

Experiential value promise (EVP), constituting the basis of experience has to change the customers' lives and provide distinctive benefits (Knapp, 2008). Manschot and Visser (2011) define the value as the activity of assigning importance to a thing or an experience and they add that after experiencing a service through sensory perception, people produce an overall picture or feeling about how valuable an experience is. Similarly, Schmitt (2003, 1999) who define the experience as the changing the sensory, emotional, cognitive, behavioral and relational values with the functional value, describes the EVP as presented image.

EVP resides in the experience of consumption, including the symbolic and non-utilitarian aspects of use, such as fantasies, feelings and fun (Arnould & Thompson, 2005). So, it manifests itself in the form of emotions, testimonials, attitudes and users' behaviors (Manschot & Visser, 2011). So, Kotler et al. (2010) state that businesses have to focus on the mind (mission: satisfy/ values: be better), heart (mission: realize the desire/value: differentiate) and soul (mission: create love-compassion/value: make a difference) in the value-based matrix model. As the experiences create personal meaning for people, the EVP should be unique and personalized (Pine & Gilmore, 1999; Prahalad & Ramaswamy, 2004; Scott, Laws, & Boksberger, 2010). To achieve this, experience value should be established on five steps modules; sense, feel, think, act and relate (Schmitt, 2003).

CREATING ACTORS FOR EXPERIENCE SHOW

Experiences are the interactions, emerging as a result of the interactions with customers and employees (Lasalle & Britton, 2003; Pine & Gilmore, 1999; Prahalad & Ramaswamy, 2004; Shaw, 2005). So, after analyzing the customer expectations and creating the brand promise, the businesses should have an experientially focused business culture and employees (actors) to meet the expectations (Kotler et al., 2010; Schmitt, 2003; Shaw, 2005; Thusy & Morris, 2004). Carbone and Haeckel (1994) define the employees as the humanic clues. According to them, humanics determine the interpersonal relationship and customers' feelings, but humanics would be more effective when they are integrated with mechanics (atmospheric clues). While Smith and Wheeler (2002) define the internal resources as the intellectual capital/power which will fulfill the value promise, they offer four suggestions to the managers to build up the intellectual capital; (1) employ qualified staff, (2) train them in accordance with the brand value, (3) adopt their behaviors through the critical experience points, and (4) treat them like customers and reward their correct behavior (Smith & Wheeler, 2002). Also, experience being built deliberately for individuals, it requires the employment of the internal resources whose imagination have progressed in a holistic way (Pine & Gilmore, 1999; Thusy & Morris, 2004). Moreover, visionary leadership, strategic forecasting, entrepreneurial/innovative/collaborative environment, creativity, imagination development projects/training, social changes, different abilities/expertises and different idea-generating techniques should be used (Kotler et al., 2010; Martins & Terblanche, 2003; Papatya, 2006; Schmitt, 2003).

CONTINUOUS INNOVATION AND CREATIVITY

Experience design is a journey and this service delivery process consists of numerous touchpoints having the potential of continuous innovation and implementation within the new technological changes for the development/reproduction of the experiential value (Prahalad & Ramaswamy, 2004; Voss & Zomerdijk, 2007). Schmitt (2003) refers that the innovation adds value to the customer experience and improve the customers' lives by offering new solutions, so intrinsic prerequisite is needed during the production development stage. But the transition process through collaborative innovation, the experience is very difficult for many businesses focusing on the product and service as the experiential innovation require imagination and creativity. As the creativity is the production of the new/useful/valuable ideas (Martins & Terblanche, 2003), Kashimura et al. (2013) offer visualization methods focusing on flexible thinking for developing ideas from various perspectives such as workshops (for developing/visualizing creative ideas), experience table technique (presents the user's behaviors and experiences in chronological order), stage prototyping (the use of actual-scale mock-up with dummy equipment to provide a realistic environment), created experience case scenarios and business origami technique (visualize/finalize the scenario).

EXPERIENCE THEME

Businesses and destinations could create unforgettable experiences by drifting the people through the entertainment by real or imagined themes/stories (Carbone, 2004; Mossberg, 2007; Pine & Gilmore, 1999; Schmitt, 1999; Toffler, 1970). The theme is the basis of the experiences (Pine & Gilmore, 1999). Healey (2008) states that customers' buying behavior could be driven by storytelling and creating emotions as they are the critical drivers. Therefore, Toffler (1970) calls the artists as 'experience engineers' who will create the theme. An effective experience theme must be unique and compel the competitors (Mclellan, 2000); have to be focused on being a platform which adds value to the brand's style/appearance and contents (Schmitt, 2003) particularly for the brands that will enter into a new market with new products. John, Simons, and Bouwman (2009) show the emotional theme as the critical point for a successful experience. Pine and Gilmore (2005) refer five steps in creating the experience theme; building the theme, blending the experience with positive signs, eliminating the negative signs, associating with memorability and appealing to all five senses. Moreover, in order to create a fascinating and attractive theme, it should include elements that can completely change the reality; many attractions/ places should be created in an experience area (Pine & Gilmore, 1999).

EXPERIENCE ATMOSPHERE

The experiences created by real, imagined or virtual events are designed around many stimuli appealing to mind, sense and heart (Schmitt, 1999) as customers are being affected by the results of the interactions with these environmental stimulants (Robinette & Brand, 2001; Schmitt, 1999; Shaw, 2005). In this context, businesses should use their service area as the stage; their decor, products, and accessories as stage elements (Pine & Gilmore, 1999). Environmental scheme and image designed by business could be defined as the critical points that affect customer's service quality perception and these critical points affect the customer's emotional stimulation degree, resulting in approach or avoidance behaviors (Baker, Levy, & Grewal, 1992; Bowie & Buttle, 2009; Mehrabian & Russell, 1974; Zeithaml & Bitner, 2003). Thus, the consumer experience should be produced and marketed with the psychological foresight for transforming services into memorable experiences. As the physical performance of the business contains different elements, senses become information-gathering tools for people.

For example, the Starbucks transforming the daily coffee experience into the special Starbucks experience creates an authentic and unique experience different from competitors with the important contents attached to the service design such as interesting menu boards, floor boards, window front seats, coffee bags, table cloths etc. (Michelli, 2007). Massara and Pelloso (2006) propose a scale of the store environment, including the concept of the macro-, meso-, and micro-environment.

The macro-environment contains the exterior variable such as location, exterior signs, gardens and lawns, surrounding stores etc. The meso-environment contains the variables related with the structure of the interior such as employee uniforms, floor, carpets, lobby, decorations etc. The micro-environment includes elements which have close connections with the customers such as music, temperature, scents, colors, lights etc. Carbone and Haeckel (1994) define the sight, smell, taste, sound and texture as mechanics and they refer that by engineering customer experiences through the design and integration of mechanics, feelings and sub-experiences could be managed.

Pine and Gilmore (2005) also emphasize that experience occurs through the senses. At this point, the sensory marketing strengthens the impact of the brand on creating customer loyalty within the experience-based design approach (Molitor, 2007). Sensory experiences sending messages to all five senses create the feelings constituted by the emotional responses (Molitor, 2007). Further, the businesses' activating the multi-sensory bases leads; creating unforgettable memories and moments, strengthening the level of emotional connection between the customers and brand, effecting of the customers product quality/brand value/cost perceptions, creating dramatic effects on customers, finding buyers with higher prices and improving the trust through the brand (Lindstrom, 2007; Molitor, 2007; Shaw, 2005).

The sight which is frequently focused by the researchers as being the most powerful sensory stimuli activates the impressions; makes physical evidence meaningful; creates brand awareness; affects the customers' attention, interest, dynamism, emotion and entertainment level; highlights the aesthetic appearance; creates mental images; affects the customer satisfaction indirectly; leads the customers to buy or to eliminate the product (Creusen & Schoormans, 2005; Heide & Grønhaug, 2006; Hulten, Broweus, & Dijk, 2009; Lindstrom, 2007; Valenti & Riviere, 2008).

The auditory stimuli which is the easiest/cheapest/strongest factor that can be used to manage the service area has influence in creating a good service atmosphere; uncovering the emotions, feelings and excitement; increasing product consumption; making the product's functions understandable; increasing the entertainment level; evoking/creating the memories and emotions; increasing the amount of expenditure and the time spent in the service area (Hulten et al., 2009; Lindstrom, 2007; Mehrabian & Russell, 1974; Milliman, 1986; North & Hargreaves, 1996; Shaw, 2005; Turley & Chebat, 2002; Valenti & Riviere, 2008; Yalch & Spangenberg, 1990).

The scent stimuli mediate the formation of the 75% of human emotions; affects the customer moods/behaviors; revives the memories; destroys the bad perceptions/negative effects; creates a pleasing atmosphere; makes the customers spent more time in the service area (Bowie & Buttle, 2009; Hulten et al., 2009; Lindstrom, 2007; Shaw, 2005; Slatten, Krog, & Connolley, 2011). The sense of taste establishes a strong brand platform; strengthens the customer experience (Hulten et al., 2009; Valenti & Riviere, 2008) and tactile clues make any products more realistic and sensible (Lindstrom, 2007).

Being a practice of designing experience containing experience value promise, creating actors, innovation, creativity, theme and atmosphere, the experience design needs a holistic approach. This holistic approach is crucial to engage the consumers. Once the issue of design has been considered and established, the next stage is to approach the positioning of experience.

Experience Positioning

After the explore and design dimensions, the main issue in experiential marketing is to structure the customer interface and place into the customer's mind which is going result in memorability.

CUSTOMER INTERFACE

According to the experience model, the 'brand experience, customer interface and innovations' are the key drivers of customer equity, as the brand experience affects the process of gaining customers; the customer interface affects the memorability, and the innovation affects the additional sales (Schmitt, 2003). The customer interface affecting the memorability represents the exchange of information between businesses and customers. At this point Smith and Wheeler (2002) state that the businesses have to create accessibility when and where the customers want various intermediaries by exploring the new entry points. Pine and Gilmore (1999) offer personal and easily-remembered methods for interface and Volo (2010) offers a double-sided experience interface. In experience marketing approach active communication is being held in the service area, on the street, during the check-in time and even on online visits. Lo (2011) states that positive relational messages could be interpreted in 'care, important and trust' dimensions by using small details in the service scape that could evoke pleasant emotions such as welcome fruit, fresh flowers in hotel rooms, pleasant dream message card, accessory container, easy connection to the internet. Therefore, he states design is not only experienced functionally, aesthetically, and symbolically, but also interpreted relationally.

PLACING INTO THE CUSTOMERS MIND AND MEMORABILITY

Experiences are identified as the mental imprints (Aho, 2001) and occur between the sensations, perceptions (interpreting the emotions and feelings) and memory (Augustin, 2009; Bowie & Buttle, 2009; Lindstrom, 2007; Volo, 2010). Within this circle, people attribute values to the experiences consisting in their memory for a long time (Lasalle & Britton, 2003; Pine & Gilmore, 1999). Healey (2008) relates the brand experience with what is memorable. So, experience engineers should look forward to finding the way to take place in the customer's mind by the effects of *"cannot be found anywhere else"* and make the experiences memorable by fascinating and bewildering.

Physical environmental factors, sensory messages, connecting to the senses, emotional stimulation, myths, legends, personal relevance, novelty, surprises, learning, engagement and theme are seen as the tool for capturing the mind of the customers and memorability (Augustin, 2009; Bowie & Buttle, 2009; Carbone & Haeckel, 1994; Michelli, 2007; Otto & Ritchie, 1996; Pine & Gilmore, 1999; Shaw, 2005).

Massara and Pelloso (2006) introducing the concept of the macro-, meso-, and micro-environment state that the memorable experiences start from meso-environment elements to the micro-environment elements and customer's judgments occur in the mind. Therefore, the sensory experience has to focus within the meso- and the micro-environment to make the experience memorable and evoke the positive emotions. Smith and Wheeler (2002) state that in order to create a strong experience, a strong finish with unexpected surprises is very important and the experience presentations should be divided into parts to make the experiences more rememberable.

The experience-based service design has been examined in three dimensions (explore, design, positioning) as they are represented in this chapter and these dimensions' clues are going to be highlighted in the case study on Singapore Airlines.

CASE STUDY: SINGAPORE AIRLINES CUSTOMER EXPERIENCE DESIGN

"Service excellence has always been a key pillar of Singapore Airlines' brand promise, enabling us to retain our position as the world's most awarded airline for many years," said Senior Vice President of Products & Services, Tan Pee Teck on Singapore Airlines (SIA) website. From this statement, it is understood that SIA acknowledges the importance of CED as they focus on delivering an extraordinary flight experience. On SIA's web sites as their commitment, it is said that making every customer 'feel at home' when they fly with SIA has always been the cornerstone of their service philosophy.

The customers' preference is the foremost consideration in the creation process for new products. Singapore Airlines has signed a major contract with Accenture for the development of a new IT system to enable the airline to deliver an enhanced travel experience that focuses on meeting more of its customers' travel needs. The new CEM system, helping the staff to understand different touchpoints quickly, will be an important element to help their staff on the ground and in the air to take customer service to the next level. Training for all Frontline staff has commenced under the CEM program, with a focus on soft skills to create extraordinary moments in delighting customers. Innovation and customer service initiatives have propelled the growth of Singapore Airlines in the airline industry and creating the memorable travel experience such as full-size space-bed, free headsets, noise canceling headphones, connectivity, handset, alert service, global in-flight e-mail system, the internet, and phone check-in for all classes.

The Singapore Airlines Suites present individual cabin features sliding doors and window blinds, offering customers freedom and privacy. While the leather and wood materials, created in soothing natural hues, enhance the sense of serenity. For the first time ever in air travel, SIA offers a sleeping experience on a distinctively designed and standalone bed in personal space. The epitome of Asian grace and hospitality, the Singapore Girl has been synonymous with Singapore Airlines since her creation in 1972, an enduring symbol of SIA's impeccable service standards and quality customer care.

It is the first commercial figure to get its own wax statue in the world famous Madame Tussaud's Wax Museum in London. The flight staffs uniforms have been designed by Parisian couturier Pierre Balmain as compatible with the interior decors and the signature uniform in batik material reflects the Airlines' Asian heritage. As Lindstrom (2007) states SIA introduced Stefan Floridian Waters aroma which is blended into the hot towels before taking off and generally permeated the entire fleet of planes have become a unique and distinct trademark of Singapore Airlines, as the most of the passengers flying with SIA know this patent aroma.

At SIA, they provide a fine dining experience that will leave customers with indelible fond memories. SIA's gourmet menu spans a wide range of delectable treats thoughtfully created by an International Culinary Panel, exclusively designed tableware complemented with beverages carefully selected from around the world with elegantly in crystal ware. Moreover, Book the Cook service that enables customers to pre-order and have their gourmet main course specially prepared for them. SIA offers special assistance for children traveling by themselves. Throughout the journey customers' children from 5 to 18 years of age are always under someone's care if they are alone.

The Krisworld entertainment system for all classes at SIA introduces in-flight entertainment experience with touch screen handset. Singapore Airlines is the first airline offering 3D games in the fantastic interactive games selection. A wide variety of multiplayer games allows customers to challenge friends or fellow passengers in head-to-head battles. Moreover, with interactive application customers can learn a new language, keep up-to-date the current news and browse the highlights of the destination. With in-flight connectivity, it's simple to stay in touch with the internet.

Furthermore, a personal in-seat telephone allows customers to make their calls to virtually anywhere in the world via a global satellite network even at 35,000 feet. From comedy to the classics, customers can watch what they want and they could find more regional offerings from Europe, Australia, China, Japan, Korea and the subcontinent as well. The KrisWorld presents different radio channel, television programs, a selection of brand new single, new audio albums and hits from 1960 to 2014 taking the customer in memory lane down the past of classic icons.

As it is seen from the case study of SIA, experience-based service design is the genesis of the brand and the theoretical path of the experience-based service design mentioned in this chapter has been applied in a practical way. The customers' preference is the foremost consideration in the creation process for the new experience as they discover the touchpoints from the CEM system in "explore dimension." As the SIA's brand experience relies on technology, innovation, quality and excellent service design, the contents of the design dimension have been revealed mainly in the case study. Innovative initiatives, patent aroma, entertainment tools and the uniforms of the Singapore Girls support the memorable flight experience in positioning dimension. The data was compiled from SIA's website.

Conclusion

As the experiences being a set of emotions, creating meaning and relating to the moment, focusing on the experience-based service design is the way to push the customers in a dream world and make them loyal partners. With this foresight, an instructional path for experience-based design implementation process is highlighted in three parts in the chapter including EDP starting from examining the understanding the customer world and continuing with building up the experience scene and focusing on the configuration of the customer interface. The explore dimension is the starting point of the experiential journey. With the right output through the business and the customer, business managers can build up their philosophy making the individuals feel valuable and special.

Genuine customer experience could only be actualized and delivered on the core competency of design dimension. The most striking stage of tourism experience design is to determine the theme and the story of the experiences as the themes are the visual invitations of value promise. With the theme personalized meanings are created in customer's mind. The atmosphere is the physical evidence of the experiences highlighting the theme. The creation of the atmosphere, highlighting to customers' imaginations is the core activity of the experience design process as being the reflections of the dream world. At this stage, considering the relationship between the psychology and the consumption and discovering the ways appealing to multi-sense of the customers. The more an experience engages the senses, the more memorable the experiences will be.

As Schmitt (1999) being the founder of strategic experience module states that business managers should not ignore the neurobiological and psychological factors in experience design. In this context during the external and internal physical environment design, it is necessary to discover how the customers want to feel and how their emotions would be evoked as the experience marketing approach directs to the emotional, psychological, intellectual and spiritual scopes of the rational-emotional decision makers. Innovations based on the customer insights and technology should be included in all stages of experience design in order to think in an innovative way and move toward personalized customer focused service by initiatives.

The important thing is to target to the hearts, minds and souls of customers via customer interactions in order to make a place in the customers' memory, to recall them and to make them share their positive experiences with others as it has been stated in positioning dimension in the chapter. For offering the customers with the magic of experience, business should communicate with the customer at unlimited places in unexpected times with surprising methods.

To sum up, as the every single change in the economy causes the economic offerings going one step over, the experiences named as innovations reveal the curiosity through individualization/ privatization and satisfying the internal emotions. So, customers not only get entertained in the imaginary world designed around many factors such as sight, sound, taste, smell, color, human relations, activities and symbolic values but also see themselves as a part of this imaginary world built by *"dream engineering."* The experience-based service design could be examined in three dimensions (explore, design, positioning) practically as they are represented in this chapter and would be an instructional guide to implicate.

References

Aho, S. K. (2001). Towards general theory of touristic experiences: Modelling experience process in tourism. *Tourism Review*, 56(3/4), 33–37.

Arnould, E. J., & Thompson, C. J. (2005). Consumer Culture Theory (CCT): Twenty years of research. *Journal of Consumer Research*, 31(4), 868–882.

Augustin, S. (2009). *Place advantage: Applied psychology for interior architecture*. Hoboken, NJ: Wiley.

Baker, J., Levy, M., & Grewal, D. (1992). An experimental approach to making retail store environmental decisions. *Journal of Retailing*, 68(4), 445–460.

Bowie, D., & Buttle, F. (2009). *Hospitality marketing an introduction*. New York, NY: Elsevier Ltd. Publication.

Carbone, L. P. (2004). *Clued in*. Upper Saddle River, NJ: FT Prentice Hall.

Carbone, L. P., & Haeckel, S. H. (1994). Engineering customer experience. *Marketing Management*, 3(3), 8–19.

Cetin, G., & Walls, A. (2016). Understanding the customer experiences from the perspective of guests and hotel managers: Empirical findings from luxury hotels in Istanbul, Turkey. *Journal of Hospitality Marketing & Management*, 25(4), 395–424.

Creusen, M. E. H., & Schoormans, J. P. L. (2005). The different roles of product appearance in consumer choice. *Journal of Product Innovation Management*, 22(1), 63–81.

Gentile, C., Spiller, N., & Noci, G. (2007). How to sustain the customer experience: An overview of experience components that co-create value with the customer. *European Management Journal*, 25(5), 395–410.

Healey, M. (2008). *What is branding?* Geneva: RotoVision.

Heide, M., & Grønhaug, K. (2006). Atmosphere: Conceptual is- sues and implications for hospitality management. *Scandinavian Journal of Hospitality and Tourism*, 6(4), 271–286.

Hulten, B., Broweus, N., & Dijk, M. V. (2009). *Sensory marketing*. New York, NY: Palgrave Macmillan Publication.

John, R. A., Simons, L. P. A., & Bouwman, H. (2009). *Designing and testing service experiences (mobile, web, public displays) for airport transit*. 22nd Bled e-Conference eEnablement: Facilitating an open, effective and representative e-society. Slovenia. Retrieved from http://aisel.aisnet.org/bled2009/3. Accessed on June 14–17.

Kashimura, K., Kumagai, K., & Furuya, J. (2013). Experience design: Theory and practice. *Hitachi Review*, 62(6), 293–301.

Knapp, D. E. (2008). *The brand promise*. New York, NY: The McGraw-Hill Companies, Inc.

Kotler, P., Kartajaya, H., & Setiawan, I. (2010). *From products to customers to the human spirit; marketing 3.0*. Hoboken, NJ: Wiley.

Lasalle, D., & Britton, T. A. (2003). *Priceless: Turning ordinary products into extraordinary experiences*. Brighton, MA: Harvard Business School Press.

Lindstrom, M. (2007). *Duyular ve marka; 5 duyuyla güçlü markalar yaratmak*. İstanbul: Optimist Yayōnlarō.

Lo, K. P. Y. (2011). Designing service evidence for positive relational messages. *International Journal of Design*, 5(2), 5–13.

Manschot, M., & Visser, F. S. (2011). Experience-value: A framework for determining values in service design approaches. *4th world conference on design research*. Retrieved from http://studiolab.ide.tudelft.nl/studiolab/mmanschot/files/2011/12/IASDR-442-Manschot.pdf

Martins, E. C., & Terblanche, F. (2003). Building organizational culture that stimulates creativity and innovation. *European Journal of Innovation Management*, 6(1), 64–74.

Massara, F., & Pelloso, G. (2006). Investigating the consumer-environment ōnteraction through ōmage modeling technologies. *The International Review of Retail, Distribution and Consumer*, 16(5), 519–531.

Mclellan, H. (2000). Experience design. *Cyberpsychology & Behavior*, 3(1), 59–69.

Mehrabian, A., & Russell, J. A. (1974). *An approach to environmental psychology*. Cambridge: MIT Press.

Michelli, J. A. (2007). *Starbucks deneyimi, sōradanlōğō sōradōşōlōğa dönüştürmenin 5 ilkesi*. Optimist Yayōncōlōk, İstanbul.

Milliman, R. (1986). The influence of background music on the behavior of restaurant patrons. *The Journal of Consumer Research, 13*(2), 286–289.

Molitor, N. (2007). The sensory potential. *The Hub, November/December,* 34–36.

Mossberg, L. (2007). A marketing approach to the tourist experience. *Scandinavian Journal of Hospitality and Tourism, 7*(1), 59–74.

North, A. C., & Hargreaves, D. J. (1996). The effects of music on responses to a dining area. *Journal of Environmental Psychology, 16,* 55–64.

Oh, H., Fiore, A. M., & Jeoung, M. (2007). Measuring experience economy concepts: Tourism applications. *Journal of Travel Research, 46,* 119–132.

Otto, J. E., & Ritchie, J. R. (1996). The service experience in tourism. *Tourism Management, 17*(3), 165–174.

Papatya, N. (2006). İşletmelerde sōradōşō rekabet için yenilikçi pazarlama yaklaşōmō. *Pazarlama Dünyasō Dergisi, 20*(4), 42–46.

Pine, B. J., & Gilmore, J. H. (2005). *Pine & Gilmore's field guide for the experience economy.* Aurora, OH: Strategic Horizons LLP.

Pine, B. J., & Gilmore, J. H. (1999). *Experience economy: Work is theatre and every business is a stage.* Brighton, MA: Harvard Business School Press.

Prahalad, C. K., & Ramaswamy, V. (2004). *The future of competition; co-creating unique value with customers.* Brighton, MA: Harvard Business School Press.

Robinette, S., & Brand, C. (2001). *Emotion marketing.* New York, NY: The McGraw-Hill Companies, Inc.

Schmitt, B. (1999). *Experiential marketing: How to get customers to sense, fell, think, act, relate to your company and brands.* New York, NY: The Free Press.

Schmitt, B. (2003). *Customer experience management.* Hoboken, NJ: Wiley.

Schmitt, B. (2013). *Competitive advantage through the customer experience.* The EX Group. Retrieved from http://www.exgroup.com/thought_leadership/articles/competitive_advantage_cem.pdf. Accessed on August 29, 2015.

Scott, N., Laws, E., & Boksberger, P. (2010). *The marketing of hospitality and leisure experiences.* Abingdon: Routledge Publication.

Shaw, C. (2005). *Revolutionize your customer experience.* New York, NY: Palgrave Macmillan Publishers.

Shaw, C., & Ivens, J. (2002). *Building great customer experiences.* New York, NY: Palgrave MacMilanede.

SIA. (n.d.). Retrieved from http://www.singaporeair.com/en_UK/flying-with-us/. Accessed on July 13, 2015.

Slatten, T., Krog, C., & Connolley, S. (2011). Make it memorable: Customer experiences in winter amusement parks. *International Journal of Culture, Tourism and Hospitality Research, 5*(1), 80–91.

Slatten, T., Mehmetoğlu, M., Svensson, G., & Svaeri, S. (2009). Atmospheric experiences that emotionally touch customers a case study from a winter park. *Managing Service Quality, 19*(6), 721–746.

Smith, S., & Wheeler, J. (2002). *Managing the customer experience.* Essex: Prentice Hall Financial Times.

Thusy, A., & Morris, L. (2004). *From CRM to customer experience: A new realm for innovation*. Paris: Business Digest.

Toffler, A. (1970). *Future shock*. New York, NY: Pan American Copyright.

Tsai, S. P. (2005). Integrated marketing as management of holistic consumer experience. *Business Horizons, 48,* 431−441.

Turley, L., & Chebat, J. C. (2002). Linking retail strategy, atmospheric design and shopping behavior. *Journal of Marketing Management, 18*(1−2), 124−144.

Valenti, C., & Riviere, J. (2008). *The concept of sensory marketing*. Retrieved from http://www.diva-portal.org/smash/get/diva2:238806/FULLTEXT01.pdf

Volo, S. (2010). Conceptualizing experience: A tourist based approach. *Journal of Hospitality Marketing and Management, 18*(2−3), 111−126.

Voss, C., & Zomerdijk, L. (2007). Innovation in experiential services-an empirical view. In DTI (Ed.), *Innovation in services*. London: London Business School.

Williams, A. (2006). Tourism and hospitality marketing: Fantasy, feeling and fun. *International Journal of Contemporary Hospitality Management, 18*(6), 482−495.

Yalch, R., & Spangenberg, E. (1990). Effects of store music on shopping behavior. *The Journal of Consumer Marketing, 7,* 55−63.

Zaltman, G., & Zaltman, L. (2008). *Pazarlama metaforlarō, pazarlamanōn yeni çağōnda tüketicinin zihnini anlamak*. İstanbul: Marka Yayōnlarō.

Zeithaml, V., & Bitner, M. J. (2003). *Services marketing*. New York, NY: McGraw-Hill.

http://www.singaporeair.com/en_UK/flying-with-us/. Accessed on July 13, 2015.

2 Experience-Centric Approach and Innovation

Anita Zátori

ABSTRACT

Purpose – The aim of this chapter is to discuss the experience-centric strategy from the aspect of innovation management, its contribution to designing and managing valuable tourism experiences, especially in context of guided tours.

Methodology/approach – The study reviews literature on experience-centric approaches and innovation, it discusses the concepts of experience-centric innovation and experience innovation, particularly the role of experience design and market intelligence in experience-centric service processes. It analyzes empirical data from interviews with eleven tour providers.

Findings – Creating novel experiences through product innovation was found as the most common type of innovation on frames of guided tours. The group size was identified as an influential feature of the experience design, and imitation has proved to be a major threat. The role of knowledge management and dynamics of knowledge were explored, too, and tour guides were identified as experiential knowledge collectors and/or creators; thus their role in knowledge management is crucial alongside the market intelligence. In contract with theoretical proposition, costumer-driven innovation is not seen by tour providers as a crucial issue in creating memorable experiences.

Research limitations — The chapter studied only traditional guided tours where the customer meets the service provider, and the data was collected only in Budapest.

Originality/value — The chapter emphasized the role of market intelligence and experience design in the process of experience-centric service provision for a successful innovation — in frames of a theoretical model. The empirical results identified some main issues and obstacles in implementation of the experience-centric approach and innovative tools and processes in context of guided tours.

Keywords: Experience design; knowledge management; user-driven innovation; guided tours

Introduction

The tourism industry is in metamorphosis — it has been undergoing rapid and radical change for the past two and a half decades (Hall & Williams, 2008; Poon, 1993). New technology, more experienced consumers, and entirely different business models — such as the ones of sharing economy — are only some of the challenges facing the industry. The demand side has changed. Today's consumers have a different attitude toward consumption than previous generations. In general, they are not only better educated and wealthier, but also have access to more information than ever before. Tourists are looking for unique value, tailored experiences, special interest focus, experiences in a lifestyle destination setting, living culture, creative spaces and creative spectacles (Gross & Brown, 2006).

Nowadays, tourists look for experience rather than destination-driven products; thus it is important to create a rewarding tourism experience through innovation and service design (Weiermair, 2004). New tourism products offering a specific or a complex experience will become the main motives for travel decisions. Experiences offered or associated with the destination tend to determine the value of destinations, some DMOs are increasingly using this in positioning their destinations on the market (e.g., Incredible India campaign).

A part of the tourism sector tries to keep up with the newest demand trends, they design and create experience-centric products and processes to earn or maintain competitiveness. Experience-centric strategy is an evolving concept applied by an increasing number of DMOs, hotels, tour companies, and other tourism service providers.

It is argued that innovation is an under-represented subset of the experience context research (Hjalager, 2010), even if experience firms are very innovative, their innovation rate is significantly above other sectors' (Sundbo, Sørensen, & Fuglsang, 2013). The study aims to introduce and discuss the experience-centric strategy as an innovative approach, moreover, to analyze the role of innovation in designing experience offers and providing experiences.

A company applying experience-centric strategy is keen to generate the WOW-effect, because the surprise factor is one of the key value propositions for today's consumer. Therefore, experience-centric strategy can lead to competitive advantage, however, the intention to create the experience of surprise again and again, it requires continuous creativity and development which would not be possible without the implication of an innovative approach. The role of innovation in experience economy is inescapable in designing and creating effective and memorable tourism experiences.

Innovation is a relevant subject in research, due to its positive effect on economic performance, although Hjalager (2010) suggested that the consolidation of innovation phenomenon in tourism requires further theoretical and empirical studies. The chapter does not intent to focus on innovation as a phenomenon in itself; however, it discusses its role in the context of the experience-centric management and marketing approach, especially within the frame of guided tours. Guided tours have received little attention in academic literature (Wong & McKercher, 2012), even though they have an important role in destination experience creation.

Theory

THE EXPERIENCE-CENTRIC APPROACH AND CONCEPTS

The experience-centric approach is not uniform. The consumer experience concept emerged in the eighties (Holbrook & Hirschman, 1982), tourism management theory recognized this concept only when Pine and Gilmore (1999) came up with the concept of experience economy and introduced the experience-centric view to a wider audience. The concept of staged experience is one of the concepts of the experience-centric approach. Later Prahalad and Ramaswamy (2004) have called for a different strategic approach which allows customers to co-create their own experiences in search of personal meaning. The concept of value and experience co-creation shifted the debates from narrow notions of staging or production to broader concepts of experience creation, involving a wider range of agencies and processes (Sundbo, 1997). It is considered as another concept of the experience-centric approach. Although the concepts argue for different strategies, they still share a common ground, the main value proposition, which is the customer experience.

The experience-centric approach considers costumer experience as the locus of the value creation process, which aims to create memorable and unique experiences. Based on the similarities the different experience-centric concepts share, a conceptual frame for the experience-centric approach was identified (Zátori, 2014):

- Experience-centric approach aims for management of experiences, not products.
- Treats experience as content, formable, and developable, and not only as a part of a product, nor simply as a context.
- Believes that on the consumer side, traveling is increasingly about experiences, fulfilment, and rejuvenation.
- Enhances active participation and involvement of the consumer.
- Assigns a high importance to interaction with the consumer.
- Results in a knowledge-intensive process, which is not possible if the organization's main focus is on service provision.
- Consumers' anticipated experiences and points of interest are investigated.
- The anticipated experiences and points of interest are utilized in product, method, and experience environment development and innovation.
- New experience themes are in the center of innovation. A company should aim for an innovative approach in service design and management, to ensure novelty and surprise.
- Demonstrates itself through investments and marketing activity, too.
- Its strategy builds on intangible resources and utilization of goodwill, rather than on material resources.

- Believes that the creation of myths and stories ensures a steady foundation for successful experiences. Narrative should overcome facts and script.
- It encourages active participation of local community in creating tourism experience in the context of a destination.

The experience-centric approach in tourism equals to emphasizing the central role of the tourist and the consumer experience, which is evident based on its strategy, organization culture, innovation, product development, collaborations, marketing activity, and service provision.

INNOVATION, EXPERIENCE-CENTRIC INNOVATION, AND EXPERIENCE INNOVATION

Innovation refers to the process of bringing any new, problem solving idea into use; it is the generation, acceptance, and implementation of new ideas, processes, products, or services (Hall & Williams, 2008). Decelle (2004) classified innovation types based on their character: (1) technological and non-technological innovations, (2) according to the nature of the innovation: product or process innovation, organizational or market innovation, or "ad hoc" innovation, (3) according to the level of innovation and intensity of discontinuity: radical, incremental, or architectural innovation. Hjalager (2010) differentiates five categories in which innovation can take place: product innovation, processes innovation, managerial innovations (an internal shifts within an organization), marketing innovations, and institutional innovations.

Based on Schumpeter (1997), companies can introduce innovation in five areas: generation of new or improved products, introduction of new production processes, development of new sales markets, development of new supply markets, and reorganization and/or restructuring of the company. This definition clearly distinguishes innovation from minor changes in the product design or delivery, for example, adding service components or product differentiation.

Tourism as a service holds some unique features, such as low degree of technology culture compared to industrial models, thus to understand innovation, emphasis on non-technological forms of innovation play a major role, such as professional know-how, brands and service, and experience design. (Hjalager, 2010). The approach toward innovation in tourism is different than in other service industries. Tourism products are "experience goods par excellence, validated ex post facto by consumers, who commit their experience to memory and build upon it" (Decelle, 2004, p. 3), the consumption of tourism products involves the active participation of the customer (prosumer). In fact, tourism is a marketplace of experiences, and tourists provide the mental frames where the tourist experience happens (Volo, 2009).

By applying the experience-centric approach and accepting the fact that tourism is an experience economy, the definition of Schumpeter should be refined and the act of innovation in tourism defined as:

- generation of new complex tourist experiences,
- designing new experience themes and experience environments,
- introduction of new co-creative processes of experience enhancement,
- identifying and targeting new consumer segments based on their experience preferences,
- development of new supply markets with a focus on experience-based lifestyle attributes and tourist preferences,
- reorganization and introduction of new business models/ organizational structures/knowledge generating and sharing processes with the aim to enhance experiential value of the tourism product (i.e. experience offer).

EXPERIENCE-CENTRIC INNOVATION VS. EXPERIENCE INNOVATION

Experience-centric innovation is an innovation with the goal of enhancing customer experience. The focus of innovation in experience-centric strategy is both on context (experience environment – for example, physical evidence, vehicles, and processes – for example, co-creation methods) and content (interaction, themes, sensorial inputs). Although the latter one, the content, has a focal position and the context is in a subsidiary role in enhancing the creation of a novel and memorable experience.

Contradicting Stamboulis and Skayannis (2003) the chapter argues that tangible assets also play an important role in the development of outstanding experiences, as the development of some brand new experiences are costly – for example, virtual reality, simulations, purchasing a new technology – and require a bigger investment. However, we agree that the experience-centric strategy assigns a bigger importance to intangible assets (creativity, knowledge creation, know-how). It represents a strategy which can be used even by micro size companies, like one-two-man service providers, successfully. Sørensen and Jensen (2015) found that experience-centric innovation can raise the value of the tourist experience and the productivity of the company without incurring any significant cost.

Experience innovation is a form of experience-centric innovation. Experience innovation means creating an experience offer which provides a brand new consumer experience. Experience innovation is challenging, because from a psychological perspective, the nature of experience is subjective, thus a novel experience offer can be different for individuals based on their preferences, interpretations and past experiences. Although, there are some tourism products, such as those based on new technologies (e.g., oculus, augmented reality) or with a new designs e.g., segway, floating bus – which assure new experiences. Experience innovations are new tourism products entering the market successfully if they are introduced as experience products and if they provide an experience offer which has not been available previously (e.g., alternative tours, as explained later).

THE ROLE OF EXPERIENCE DESIGN AND MARKET INTELLIGENCE IN EXPERIENCE-CENTRIC VALUE CREATION

In order to be consumed, experience has to be produced (Pine & Gilmore, 1999; Stamboulis & Skayannis, 2003). However, a service provider cannot "produce" the experience, it emerges from the interaction between the experience offer (the provider & product) and the tourists (see Zatori, 2016). To be present at the "experience market" is possible through the production of experience offers. Successful experience offers provide a meaningful and memorable experience for the customer. To be able to design such a experience offer, information about their potential customers' anticipated experiences is needed.

Figure 1 aims to illustrate a process of experience-centric value creation, where customer experience is at the center of value creation. Market intelligence and experience design are the two cornerstones of the experience-centric value creation. Experience design refers to the marketing communication activity and to the on-site experience (co)creation. Marketing intelligence is highly important because effective experience design presupposes the accumulation of detailed information about the market segment's values, attitudes, behavioral patterns, and other preferences. Understanding the different values of customers is vital knowledge in experience design and innovation (Prebensen, 2014). Marketing intelligence's

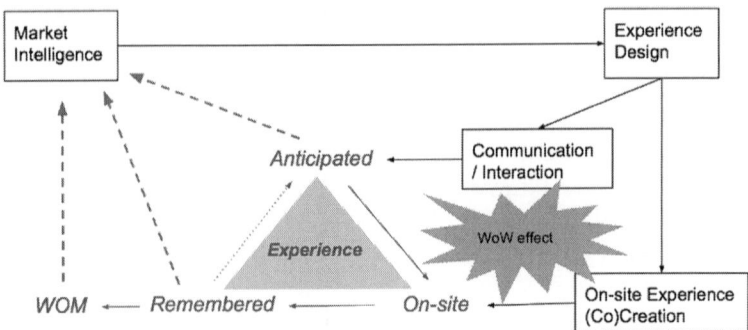

Figure 1.   The Role of Experience Design and Market Intelligence in Experience-Centric Value Creation.

role is to collect information about the anticipated, on-site, and remembered (memorable) experiences of consumers, and also the WOM (word of mouth) – in Figure 1 this process is indicated with dashed arrows. An experience-centric firm (and its frontline employees) are collecting information about the consumers' profile, needs, fantasies, experiential purposes, and behavior, during the service encounter, i.e. in the phase of (co)creating the on-site experience. Meanwhile it aims to develop knowledge, which then can be later utilized to enhance the experiential value of the provided service (Sørensen & Jensen, 2015).

Experience design should be able to utilize the information collected by market intelligence. The company's marketing communication activity (which is preferable a two-way communication) aims to create a dialogue by the engagement of the potential customer (Prahalad & Ramaswamy, 2004) which influences and forms the customer's expectations, moreover, it should arouse excitement to a level where the surprise factor, the so-called "WOW-effect," can be created during the consumption process. As the model acknowledges the process view of customer experience (Aho, 2001), anticipated experiences are viewed as the first phase of consumer experiences having a crucial influence on the formation of the on-site experience. Thus experience design does not focus on service provision only, but marketing communication is also viewed as its component. The design of attractive anticipated experiences might create high levels of consumer involvement which leads to a high level of active participation during the on-site service provision. For instance, the Art Institute of Chicago advertised its temporary

Van Gogh exhibition on Airbnb with a room installation looking exactly like the well-known paintings of the Van Gogh's room, and this led to a worldwide online awareness and involvement.

While designing on-site experiences, company-customer interaction (Pine & Gilmore, 1999; Prahalad & Ramaswamy, 2004), experience environment (Bitner, 1992; Prahalad & Ramaswamy, 2004), and customization (Prahalad & Ramaswamy, 2004; Prebensen & Foss, 2011) are issues to consider, as research on guided tours discussed it (Zátori, 2015). The result of the on-site experience design always depends on the customer, and her level of attitude, participation and experience involvement, because experience is co-created by the customer and the service provider (Binkhorst & Dekker, 2009; Prebensen & Foss, 2011). The customer and her experience are unique, subjective and a continuously changing phenomenon – which is illustrated with (blue) triangle in the model. The customer and the experience is not separated in the model, as the experience has a subjective character.

If the customer experience is meaningful and/or memorable enough, it will be remembered and even promoted by the customer in the form of online or offline (e.g., verbal) WOM. Remembered experiences also influence the next anticipated experiences of the customer – in the case of a repeated consumption/visit. The WOW-effect can be reached if the experience design of communication and on-site experience (co)creation is consistent, and leaves some room for unexpected events or experience elements. In case the firm does not target only the onetime consumer, it should repeatedly innovate and develop some novelties as surprise elements or surprising events. This requires an innovative and creative approach.

An experience-centric approach can be considered as a managerial innovation, because it reconstructs the process of value creation. Customer experience stands in the center. Market intelligence and experience design, with a strong focus on knowledge management, are of highlighted importance in the process, meanwhile, they also represent the core areas where innovations and product developments are initiated and designed. An experience-centric approach also means an innovation-focused strategy.

This is in line with Stamboulis and Skayannis (2003), according to whom, the process of experience design, compared to the standard production of the conventional tourist product, is new and innovative, and they describe it as a highly tacit, knowledge-creating process.

Knowledge is a prerequisite for tourism innovation (Hjalager, 2002), and customers are an important knowledge source for innovation (Foss, Laursen, & Pedersen, 2011). Sørensen and Jensen (2015) point out how the knowledge created in experience-centric service encounter can immediately lead to improved guest experiences. They also argue that on-site interactions, experience-centric service encounters and the so-called "experience encounters" situated in integrated experience environment are dynamic and personalized services requiring both employee's flexibility and experiential intelligence, while co-creating emotional consumer values.

The experience-centric approach suits the consumer-driven type of innovation (Hjalager & Nordin, 2011), which implies that the involvement of selected consumers in the process of experience design. User-driven innovation inspired by or being the result of needs, ideas and opinions derived from potential and/or an existing users, is a process reliant upon systematic activities that search for, acknowledge, tap, and understand the users' explicit, as well as implicit knowledge and ideas (Innotour, 2016).

THE CONTEXT: GUIDED TOURS

The destinations (DMOs) can use the experience-centric strategy for product, process and managerial innovation, too. According to Stamboulis and Skayannis (2003) to create a destination experience, a "myth" has to be developed, which is an organized, designed experience and an accompanying narrative in which the tourist will express the wish to live. This myth becomes a reason for the choice of destination. During the destination visit, tourists expect to be a part of the myth. The motivation for visiting a destination usually does not derive from its physical qualities, but from a strong spiritual and emotional image, the destination experience assumed by the tourist. The destination experience preference also affects the choice of the sightseeing tour.

Ooi (2005) sees the tours as destination experience mediators, but guided tours does not only have the ability to mediate the destination myth, they are also enhancers and creators of the destination experience. They are creators, because they fill up the destination experience offer with content through their sightseeing tour products, and during their interpretative work, they co-create the value and experience with the tour participants. Certainly, it is not only guided tours that fill up the destination experience offer with content, but other entities (e.g., DMO, cultural institutions) and environmental and cultural factors (e.g., architecture, atmosphere, lifestyle, landscape) provide experiences, too.

Tour guiding is more than a service provision; it is a process creating tourist experience even without the experience-centric strategy, however, when applying the strategy, the goal becomes creating unique and memorable experiences of emotional involvement, uplifted mood and discovery (Zátori, 2015), and the experiential value of the tourist experience is enhanced.

TOUR EXPERIENCE DESIGN

While designing a tour experience, tour guiding, tour content and schedule, experience environment (such as vehicles, technology, issues of comfort) and issues relating customization should be considered by the service provider. During a guided tour, tourists would rather expect to feel emotions than acquire knowledge, thus the transmission of knowledge during the tour should happen in an experience-focused and entertaining way (Zátori, 2013). It was also found that tour guides have the biggest influence on tourist experience, bigger than other elements of service provision – for example, experience environment, methods and level of customization (Zátori, 2015).

In the context of guided tours, a tour provider applying the staged experience concept aims to stage and perform the experience on a high level, and that is how it tries to engage the customer in the experience, however, this does not necessary provide a high degree of freedom for the customer, because it does not allow customization.

Tour providers using methods of experience co-creation approach aims to engage the customer by offering a large number of interaction points, and forms possibilities for experience co-creation and customization. By enabling customization, it creates an optimal degree of freedom for the tourist's experience involvement. Meanwhile, the consumer can decide to what extent and how they wish to be involved in the experience creation. This requires a higher degree activity and participation from the tourist.

Methodology

Qualitative, in-depth interview was applied as the method of primary data collection. During the interview, sightseeing tour providers – management and tour guides – were asked about their management strategy, innovation, product development, tour design considerations, marketing activity and methods and tools used during service provision. The sampling frame was created by listing and typology of all tour organizers of Budapest. Only guided sightseeing tour providers focusing on the city break segment of leisure tourism, that travel mostly individually, were included in the sample.

Random sampling was used: stratified sampling followed by systematic sampling. One managerial and two tour guide interviews were conducted with each tour provider included in the sample. In total, 11 interviews were realized with tour providers and 22 with tour guides. The data was collected in Budapest, during the high season (summer) of 2013. The interviews were carried out with a semi-structured method. The in-depth interview with the management took 60–100 minutes, while interviews with the tour guides took 15–35 minutes. The interviews were recorded.

The tour types were identified and named based on the main characteristics of the tours. The examined tour types are represented relatively equally in the sample. The sampling frame was evolved on the basis of the following tour types: small-group tours (three tour providers), big-group tours (three tour providers), and alternative tours (four tour providers).

This method meets the recent methodology trends of innovation research in tourism. Hjalager (2010) pointed out that currently, innovation studies in tourism rely on explorative and qualitative cases where the phenomenon is investigated and explained from a number of angles and where rigid definitions are less prevalent.

Small-group tour providers specialize in smaller size group tours, they usually organize walking tours, cycling tours and tours on segways for tourists visiting Budapest. Some tours are guaranteed (it is realized even with two participants), but others are held only if a minimal number of participants is reached. Participants of the tours are individuals forming random groups, but pre-arranged small-group tours are also common. Small-group tour providers of the sample are Budabike, Discover Budapest, Free Budapest Tours. Cityrama primarily provides small-group tours, but most of the tours are organized by bus, so they also share similarities with the second group of the sample (big-group tours).

Big-group tours are mostly bus tours. These tours, serving the needs of leisure and individual tourists, are mostly guaranteed tours, while the group is mostly formed randomly. The sample of big-group tours includes: RiverRide, a tour provider offering special, a "floating bus" bus-boat tours; Program Centrum and Eurama provide hop-on hop-off type (HoHo) sightseeing tours.

Alternative tour providers typically organize special themed tours for which a particular type of demand has formed, and it became popular among Budapestians. From a psychological perspective, all the experiences gained in an unusual environment – meaning a novelty for the individual can be considered a tourist experience. Local sightseeing tours provide novelty for the participants for two reasons – they are guided in less well-known parts of the city, and they uncover rare information and hidden stories. These tours shed light on unknown aspects of various locations and spaces which, up until that point, were hidden from the individual. The alternative tour providers are "alternative," because they apply different methods and tools than the traditional tour providers. Imagine Budapest, Unique Hungary, BUPAP, and Hosszulepes participated in the research as alternative tour providers.

The chapter raises a pair of research questions: to what extent do tour providers imply the experience-centric approach and its concepts; and what aspects and features of innovation demonstrate themselves while implying experience-centric approach. As it was already pointed out earlier, innovation and an innovative mindset is an important issue in experience-centric approach.

Findings and Discussion

The results showed that small-group tour providers and alternative tour providers are characterized by the experience-centric approach to the biggest extent. Regarding the management and operations of small-group tour providers, the concept of experience co-creation is prevalent, while in the case of alternative tour providers, the concept of staged experience creation and experience co-creation are both applied. The management perspective of both types are experience-centric, however, some fields and management aspects are still seeking development in this direction.

Big-group and bus type tour providers are characterized by the use of the experience-centric approach to a lower degree. The hindering facilities of acquiring experience-centric approach are arising from the specific features of the tour type (size of the group, the means of the transport causing passivity). However, they try to manage these hindering facilities with the aim to provide a better experience. In the case of hop-on hop-off type tour providers, the concept of experience co-creation offers untapped opportunities and suitable methods of development.

CREATING NOVEL EXPERIENCES THROUGH PRODUCT INNOVATION

Alternative tours

The latent demand identified by some service providers is locals wanting to discover their cities. Generally accepted fact is that locals are not primary customer segments of sightseeing tours. Sightseeing tours are typically developed for tourists visiting a destination or touring around multiply destinations.

Although it has changed lately: alternative tours became a demand trend, which is in continuous rise. These tours are typically organized in cities, and their market is rather complex. In Budapest, they can be seen as product innovations which met a latent demand among locals. According to an alternative tour provider (Unique Budapest), first it was for foreigners they targeted, then it turned out that locals were more interested. The supply market of alternative tours has grown, but demand has been growing along with it, thus tour variability became larger.

The experience offer: passion for the city, eager to learn more about the city, history, and their people from the past. Participants can learn personal stories from the past. to see those places where it happened − (authenticity). These kind of tours largely enhance authentic experiences − not only because of objective and subjective authenticity, but the intimacy of provided information (e.g., love stories, personal letters and pictures of people from the past) creates the impression of knowing something which others do not. An additional advantage is that it is a program to attend with others or alone.

In the case of alternative tours, learning is the main experience, but emotional and community experience also play important roles. Imagine Budapest supposes that for locals, a tour is a more memorable experience because what is shown to them is totally new or they have only known it from a different aspect – which means that the experience factor of the tour is higher because of the surprise and amusement.

Alternative tours brought new consumers to the guided tour market: locals. Sightseeing tours entered the leisure market for locals. But then, once the new product type became well-known for its uniqueness, DMCs, hotels (etc.) started to include them in their offerings for their clients and guests, and tourist demand for the product has increased, too, although the local segment still dominates. Why are these tours perceived as product innovations? Because they satisfy an emerging, a few years ago only latent consumer demand, the tour type introduced an entirely new experience, and built up a market based on this experience offer. Other reasons are that it brought a new segment to the sightseeing tour market, and that it is merely different in concept and methods than standard tours. This experience innovation is based both on non-technological product and process innovation.

Free-guided tours

Free-guided tours are a new concept of sightseeing tours which has been introduced lately, in the past decade across Europe, especially in city tourism. The concept of sharing economy has recently been a booming business model. However, free-guided tours were introduced to the tourism market even before the concept of sharing economy became widespread and Airbnb or Uber appeared. The business model of these tours is that one can participate in the tour free of cost, however, the unwritten (or written) tour ethic says to pay a tip at the end of the tour. The amount of the tip is flexible. Free-guided tours pay a big attention to the entertaining factor of the tour, and less to the educational one. The authenticity and quality control of provided information is not always under control of the management, in some cases, these tours are not even led by local guides, but "global nomads." Free-guided tours do not put an upper limit to group size, and heavily rely on social media sites – for example, recommendations on Trip Advisor. The concept of free-guided tours can be defined as a product and process innovation in itself, however, the concept to Budapest was introduced based on international know-how. However, it is doubtful if this tour type can be described as an experience-centric innovation, as the added value regards rather the business model, not the customer experience.

Product innovation in case of other tour types

Surprisingly, many tour providers of the analyzed segment use product innovation. Many of these are **technological product innovations**, such as the *RiverRide*'s floating bus or the *segway tour* of *Budapest Segway Tours*. RiverRide supposes that beside the "splashing" experience due to the special technological solution, experience deriving from the sightseeing is just additional, and what truly attracts tourists to choose this tour provider is the unique technology. In the case of segway tours, the novel, unusual tour experience is assured by the segway. Some tour participants try it for the first time, some have the preference to participate in a segway tour in every destination they visit. These tour types are using it as a unique selling proposition until a competition using the same technology does not enter the market, which can threaten their competitive advantage.

Sightseeing tours which include special experience elements are targeting to engage all five senses. **Gastronomic tours** have been a subject of a rising demand globally, just as other creative tours. The tours of *Discover Budapest* provide a complex experience promise, several experience factors are usually mixed – gastronomy, walking, shopping, break at a host location etc. This tour type does not need high technological investments, which makes it more threatened by imitators.

Themed tours are the primary examples of the staged experience concept. In every destination, the themes are different, matching the local "sense of place," culture and myths. For example, the *Ghost Tour* is a thematic sightseeing tour, too, it is a street theater show with an outstanding performance starring a guide dressed up as a ghost; however, it can be considered as a product innovation only locally, in Budapest. Some other themes are more original and place specific – for example, Dicta-tour (by Cityrama), which is about the socialist regime of 30–50 years ago.

DOES SIZE MATTER?

It was found that the group size of the tour influenced the practical implication of the experience-centric approach. Certainly smaller tour groups have a bigger potential to realize an experience-centric service due to the smaller number of tour participants. During the service provision, the small-group tour providers are measurably more consumer- and experience-focused, including the quality of interaction, as well as the involvement and activity of the tour participants. Small size groups are showed to be highly interactive, whereas interaction was not only realized through dialogues, but also with the aid of questions and tasks. Small-group tour providers pay outstanding attention to experience involvement beyond interactivity. As a tool of quality assurance, tour providers try to assure the personalized atmosphere of the tour by limiting the group size (number of participants).

Weiermair (2004) found that most tourism firms recognize the importance of product development, although rarely does this involve entirely new products or entirely new markets, rather a process of individualizing mass market (products) by product differentiation, product line extension by branding policies or by changing the cost (price) — quality-ratio of the product. This is not the case of guided tours — as analyzed in the previous part. Many of the guided tour providers introduced a new product or innovation to the destination market. A possible reason is that they interviewed mainly medium and large size tourism companies, and also tourism firms of different profiles, such as hotels, while tour providers are micro and small size companies offering intangible tourism products; thus they are more flexible to innovate.

IMITATION AS A THREAT

The findings show that tour providers try to assure the uniqueness of the tours with new ideas in terms of supplementary services and product packages (Program Centrum, Eurama), innovative product development (Cityrama, RiverRide, Discover Budapest), and cooperation in partnerships (Hosszulepes, Bupap, Cityrama). The small-group and alternative tour providers are trying to create a unique value by their experience offer, although most of them indicated a perceived danger of imitation by the competitors or newcomers. All of the tour providers included in the sample have unique product offers or at least additional products which distinguish them on the market.

In tourism and hospitality, innovations based on external knowledge readily accessed by competitors might be quickly and easily imitated (Souto, 2015). If innovation is driven by codified knowledge, the latter tends to circulate freely (Decelle, 2004). Although tour methods and tools do not count as readily accessed external solutions to adopt, the findings show that imitation is a serious hindering factor of keeping the newly introduced innovation a unique product, as tour providers can easily access each other's tours and collect information about them. In tourism, product innovation is visible and can be immediately imitated. This type of new knowledge is a public good, thus it results only in a sub-optimal level of production of innovations (Decelle, 2004). Innovators cannot keep the property rights associated with their innovations for themselves. To overcome these barriers, new knowledge and regulation of intellectual property rights, imitation, and diffusion patterns are required (Hjalager, 2010).

For those implying the experience-centric approach, it is important not to imitate innovative effects made elsewhere, but to build on a firm's or destination's own strength and core competencies, because it will be further strengthened and developed through knowledge management.

THE ROLE OF KNOWLEDGE MANAGEMENT AND DYNAMICS OF KNOWLEDGE

The experience-centric strategy is in fact a knowledge-intensive process that is neglected if the focus lies on service provision (Stamboulis & Skayannis, 2003). Knowledge must be created and utilized in the phase of experience design with respect to the formulating theme, content, schedule, and the technology choice. Customer's anticipated interests and preferences should be considered. However, knowledge is to be utilized and collected also in the phase of service provision and experience co-creation. Utilized, because customization is an important factor in the context of tourism industry, and more specifically in the case of guided tours, thus modification of the schedule might be the right decision to make in certain situations (e.g., based on customer's needs). Collected, because of further product development or innovation. The previously obtained knowledge – concerning the possible main interests of the consumers and the future experiences assumed by the consumers (Ooi, 2005; Wirtz, Kruger, Scollon, & Diener, 2003) – has to be put into use during the phase of production (including the creation of experience themes and the application of certain methods and techniques). Competencies concerning information and service provision, the intelligence of the company plays a key role, and the interaction with the consumer has to be highlighted among other business processes. Innovations of the experience-centric approach have to be centered on creating new experience themes.

Experiential knowledge from the tour is collected by guides. In micro and small size, non-hierarchical organizations (alternative and most of the small-group tour providers), direct, bottom-up knowledge sharing is emphasized, while in moderately hierarchical organizations (big-group tour providers and Discover Budapest), the process is centralized by a top-down initial, which does not have a positive effect on knowledge-intensive business processes – such as guided tours. In context of hotel industry, Sørensen and Jensen (2015) as a best practice found that information about guests derived from an experience-centric service encounter was noted in the hotel reservation system, so that this information could be transferred to other employees dealing with the guests, and to the management.

A distinction has to be made between codified knowledge: formal, recognized, taught, explicit (technical, theoretical, managerial) and tacit knowledge: spontaneously mobilizable learning and know-how (Decelle, 2004). In the context of guided tours, the latter has a more important role, it is one of the crucial indicators of guiding performance. According to Cooper (2006) capturing the tacit knowledge that resides in the tourism industry is one of the major challenges and to date has not been formally addressed by researchers. Hoarau and Kline (2014) explains how sharing of tacit and explicit knowledge between stakeholders in co-creational practices affects innovation processes in tourism.

In the case of the majority of tourism enterprises, there is an absence of R&D activity or market intelligence. Apart from a tourism firm's capacity to produce new knowledge derived from its activity, as in learning by doing, it is also important to consider the firm's capacity to acquire and absorb existing innovations, and to internalize knowledge that is codified and convert it into tacit know-how – into routines (Decelle, 2004).

CONSUMER-DRIVEN INNOVATION

Direct interaction should enhance the service provider's ability to create themes and interact with customers, as well as, its innovative capability regarding effectiveness and efficiency. The consumers' role in innovation processes is a current topic (Von Hippel, 2005) that deserves attention throughout the service sector, and which is highly applicable in tourism where consumer–producer interaction is closer than in many other types of enterprises (Hjalager, 2010).

Relationships with customers have always played a central role in tourism, such as the practice of listening to and learning from the customers when delivering a service. However, the involvement of customers as informants often seems to be coincidental and unsystematic, because numerous tourism companies and organizations do not employ distinctive and methodically organized approaches to tap ideas and inspiration from their customers (Hjalager & Nordin, 2011).

User-driven innovation is an approach for pro-active tourism service providers and destinations. Its synonym is costumer-driven innovation, and it is considered to fit well with the concept of experience-centric strategy. Responses from tourists are an optimal source of information that can lead not only to product or process developments, but to greater innovation as well. In the field of digital technology, there are plenty of cases where customers serve as the extended innovation staff.

However, the findings point out some shortcomings. Namely that customers do not always know what they really want, or what could be interesting for them. Thus most of the tour providers are skeptical about the individual suggestions from customers, even if they include this question in their questionnaire which aims to collect feedback from participants after the tour (all alternative tour providers imply this). The development of new themes is rather resource or market driven. For example, a new tour will be developed around a good presenter with an exciting topic, or actual events justify a certain topic (e.g., migration crisis in Budapest – a tour about Islam by Bupap).

Alternative tour providers invent the theme through own research or through an outside reference. They claim to never receive any theme ideas from the participants of the tour, which means that they do not find user-driven innovation in the context of product innovation as a useful method. However, the participants have the opportunity to add their own experience and knowledge to the tour, which presupposes a sort of co-created experience. This additional information can be useful for the content of the tour, as the guide can build that piece of information into the upcoming tour.

Instead of consumer-driven innovation, the development of the theme is usually realized through brainstorming among the members of the organizing team: "*It is important to offer an interesting theme, ... in which people are interested enough, which they will come for, which can be explored in a determined area and can be filled with interesting stories*" (Unique Budapest).

The findings show that despite the fact that customers actively participate in the experience co-creation and product development, costumer-driven innovation in new product development is not implied by the tour providers.

EXPERIENCE-CENTRIC INNOVATION FOR COMPETITIVE ADVANTAGE?

Although some tours are said to be complex from the aspect of experience promises, their feasibility and rentable nature were highlighted during the interview. Discover Budapest is referring to this fact as the main obstacle of the experience-centric perspective.

The tours of alternative tour providers (especially Imagine Budapest) used to be more thematic and staged (costumes, built in surprise elements and acts), but recently, after a few tours, they decided to eliminate these elements because of organizational circumstances and costs.

It is argued that innovation leads to higher market shares, a higher efficiency and easier realization of aims regarding turnover or profit (Hübner, 2002). Despite this fact, it is clear that experience-centric development is contradictory to cost effective strategy in short term; however, the long-term results might be better, as the experience-centric innovation might assure a sustainable competitive edge due to recommendations and/or returning customers.

It should also be considered that innovations might be less demanded in the first phase of introduction, in the so-called incubation phase, but as the supply and demand rises, and the take-off phase starts, the market becomes more structured, differentiation and branding strategies develop (just as it happened in case of alternative tour providers, discussed earlier). If the innovation cannot get through the incubation phase, it means that it is not successful, thus if not implemented and realized, it cannot even be regarded as an innovation. The conceptualization of innovations says that only new ideas, new approaches and inventions implemented and appropriated by users or customers can be viewed as innovations (Weiermair, 2004).

Conclusion

The chapter's aim was to discuss the experience-centric strategy from the perspective of innovation management, its contribution to designing and managing valuable tourism experiences, especially in the context of guided tours.

The theoretical contribution of the study lies in the fact that innovation has not been well explored yet neither in the frame of the experience-centric approach nor in the context of guided tours.

With the involvement of customers in the tourism experience creating process, tourism is becoming an information and relationship business (Weiermair & Peters, 2002), thus customer involvement is especially useful to map the preferences and anticipated experiences, and also to develop and run a market intelligence activity and effective knowledge management, which might be followed by enabling customer driven innovation.

One of the limitations of the study is that it analyzed only traditional guided tours where the customer meets the service provider. Mobile-based guiding applications were not included in the study, despite the fact that they realize or represent an important technology-based innovation activity, such as the implication of digital virtual reality – for example, augmented reality – into tour designs.

Data was collected only from tour providers based in Budapest, which represents another limitation of the study; thus the findings are mainly location-specific, further research in other locations would be needed to broaden the geographical boundaries of the findings and test them.

The availability of new technologies led to the development of new skills, new materials, new services, and new forms of organization. This is especially true for the last two decades. The technological development created new and changing consumer needs, but traditional guided tours are still dominant on the market. It can be questioned whether mobile-based or other digital guides are the real competitors of guided tours and guide books.

References

Aho, S. E. (2001). Towards a general theory of touristic experiences: Modelling experience process in tourism. *Tourism Review*, 56(3–4), 33–37.

Binkhorst, E., & Dekker, T. D. (2009). Agenda for co-creation tourism experience research. *Journal of Hospitality Marketing & Management*, 18(2–3), 311–327.

Bitner, M. J. (1992). Servicescapes: The impact of physical surroundings on customers and employees. *Journal of Marketing*, 56(April), 57–71.

Cooper, C. (2006). Knowledge management and tourism. *Annals of Tourism Research*, 33, 47–64.

Decelle, X. (2004). A conceptual and dynamic approach to innovation in tourism. *OECD conference on innovation and growth in tourism*. Swiss State Secretariat for Economic Affairs (SECO), Lugano, Switzerland, September 18–19, 2003. Retrieved from http://www.oecd.org/cfe/tourism/34267921.pdf. Accessed on February 20, 2016.

Foss, N. J., Laursen, K., & Pedersen, T. (2011). Linking customer interaction and innovation: The mediating role of new organizational practices. *Organization Science*, 22, 980–999.

Gross, M. J., & Brown, G. (2006). Tourism experiences in a lifestyle destination setting: The roles of involvement and place attachment. *Journal of Business Research*, 59, 696–700.

Hall, C. M., & Williams, A. M. (2008). *Tourism and innovation*. London: Routledge.

Hjalager, A. M. (2002). Repairing innovation defectiveness in tourism. *Tourism Management*, 23, 465–474.

Hjalager, A.-M. (2010). A review of the innovation research in tourism. *Tourism Management*, 31(1), 1–12.

Hjalager, A. M., & Nordin, S. (2011). User-driven Innovation in tourism – A review of methodologies. *Journal of Quality Assurance in Hospitality & Tourism*, 12(4), 289–315.

Hoarau, H., & Kline, C. (2014). Science and industry: Sharing knowledge for innovation. *Annals of Tourism Research*, 46, 44–61.

Holbrook, M. B., & Hirschman, E. C. (1982). The experiential aspects of consumption: Consumer fantasies, feelings, and fun. *Journal of Consumer Research*, 9(September), 132–140.

Hübner, H. (2002). *Integratives Innovationsmanagement. Nachhaltigkeit als Herausforderung für ganzheitliche Erneuerungsprozesse*. Berlin: Erich Schmidt.

Innotour. (2016). Retrieved from http://www.innotour.com/innovation-tools/user-driven-methods/. Accessed on February 12.

Ooi, C. (2005). Theory of tourism experiences: The management of attention. In T. O'Dell & P. Billing (Eds.), *Experiencescapes: Tourism, culture, and economy* (pp. 11–33). Copenhagen: Copenhagen Business School Press.

Pine, B. J., & Gilmore, J. H. (1999). *The experience economy: Work is theatre & every business a stage*. Boston, MA: Harvard Business School Press.

Poon, A. (1993). *Tourism, technology and competitive strategies*. Wallingford, CT: CAB.

Prahalad, C. K., & Ramaswamy, V. (2004). *The future of competition: Co-creating unique value with customers*. Boston, MA: Harvard Business School Press.

Prebensen, N. K. (2014). Facilitating for enhanced experience value. In G. A. Alsos, D. Eide, & E. L. Madsen (Eds.), *Handbook of research on innovation in tourism industries* (pp. 154–180). Cheltenham: Edward Elgar.

Prebensen, N. K., & Foss, L. (2011). Coping and co-creating in tourist experiences. *International Journal of Tourism Research*, 13(1), 54–67.

Schumpeter, J. (1997). *Theorie der wirtschaftlichen Entwicklung. Eine Untersuchung über Unternehmergewinn, Kapital, Kredit, Zins und Konjunkturzyklus* (9th ed.). Berlin: Duncker and Humblot.

Sørensen, F., & Jensen, J. F. (2015). Value creation and knowledge development in tourism experience encounters. *Tourism Management*, 46, 336–346.

Souto, J. E. (2015). Business model innovation and business concept innovation as the context of incremental innovation and radical innovation. *Tourism Management*, 51, 142–155.

Stamboulis, Y., & Skayannis, P. (2003). Innovation strategies and technology for experienced-based tourism. *Tourism Management, 24*(1), 35–43.

Sundbo, J. (1997). Innovation in the experience economy: A taxonomy of innovation organisations. *The Service Industries Journal, 29*(3–4), 431–455.

Sundbo, J., Sørensen, F., & Fuglsang, L. (2013). Innovation in the experience sector. In J. Sundbo & F. Sorensen (Eds.), *Handbook on the experience economy* (pp. 228–247). Cheltenham: Edward Elgar.

Volo, S. (2009). Conceptualizing experience: A tourist based approach. *Journal of Hospitality Marketing & Management, 18*(2), 111–126.

Von Hippel, E. (2005). *Democratizing innovation.* Cambridge, MA: MIT Press.

Weiermair, K. (2004). Product improvement or innovation: What is the key to success in tourism? *Conference on innovation and growth in tourism.* Swiss State Secretariat for Economic Affairs (SECO), Lugano, Switzerland, September 18–19, 2003. Retrieved from http://www.oecd.org/cfe/tourism/34267947.pdf. Accessed on February 20, 2016.

Weiermair, K., & Peters, M. (2002). Innovation and innovation behaviour in hospitality and tourism: Problems and prospects, "Tourism in Asia: Development, Marketing and Sustainability," *Fifth Biennial Conference, Conference proceedings*, Hong Kong (pp. 600–612).

Wirtz, D., Kruger, J., Scollon, C. N., & Diener, E. (2003). What to do on spring break? The role of predicted, on-line, and remembered experience in future choice. *Psychological Science, 14*, 520–524.

Wong, C., & McKercher, B. (2012). Day tour itineraries: Searching for the balance between commercial needs and experiential desires. *Tourism Management, 33*, 1360–1372.

Zátori, A. (2013). The impact of experience management perspective and tour guiding methods on tourist experience, In: D. Koerts, P. Smith, & O. Mitas (Eds.) *Conference proceedings, 3rd International research forum on guided tours*, The Netherlands, April 4–6 (235 p). NHTV University of Applied Science, Breda. NRIT Media (pp. 134–148).

Zátori, A. (2014). Az élménymenedzsment koncepcionális alapjai. [The conceptual base of experience management]. *Vezetéstudomány [Budapest Management Review], 45*(9), 57–66.

Zátori, A. (2015). *Tourist experience co-creation and management.* Saarbrucken: Lambert Academic Publishing.

Zatori, A. (2016). Exploring the value co-creation process on guided tours (the 'AIM-model') and the experience-centric management approach. *International Journal of Culture, Tourism, and Hospitality Research* (Accepted).

3

Crucial Role and Contribution of Human Resources in the Context of Tourism Experiences: Need for Experiential Intelligence and Skills

Marios Sotiriadis and Stelios Varvaressos

ABSTRACT

Purpose – In this chapter we aim to consider human resources (HR) within the context of tourism experiences. Specifically, our intention is to analyze and highlight the importance of a strategic approach to human resources management (HRM) and suggest suitable tools and strategies.

Methodology/approach – Extensive literature reviews were conducted on issues and aspects of HRM. Micro-cases and examples are used to illustrate efficient HRM tools and practices.

Findings – (i) HR have a significant contribution to make in overcoming the challenge of creating and managing experiences to meet customer expectations and achieve tourism business aims. (ii) The strategic management approach to HR is indispensable because consumption experience has shifted from the servicescape to the experiencescape environment. (iii) This evolution implies that tourism staff need to develop a new skills set.

Research limitations/implications – This study is explorative in nature, based on a literature review. Thus, more research-based knowledge and more empirical studies are needed to fully validate the chapter's suggestions.

Practical implications – Strategic HRM is a requirement for tourism businesses that aim to provide valuable tourism experiences. There is a need for experiential intelligence and a bundle of skills to fulfill the customized requirements and personal aspirations of contemporary tourists. The related strategies are also discussed.

Originality/value – The study offers insights into aspects of HRM in the context of tourism experiences and highlights the necessity of developing an extended bundle of skills.

Keywords: Human resources; tourism experience; experiencescape; experiential intelligence and skills; strategies

Introduction

Consumer experiences lie at the heart of the tourism industry. This industry is increasingly based on the consumption experience, and so providers and consumers interact more closely during all stages of their relationship (Shaw, Bailey, & Williams, 2011). The crucial role human resources (HR) play in providing high-quality experiences is well documented in the literature (Baum, 2006a; Cetin, Akova, & Kaya, 2014). The critical role of the customer-contact staff in the experience/service encounter has been extensively documented, as this directly affects the customer's perception of experience quality; tourists' perceptions are central to all tourism management activities (Solnet, 2008). It is for this reason that HR are considered to be one of the most valuable assets of tourism businesses in delivering memorable experiences and in achieving value creation for both tourists and businesses (Baum, 2005).

The critical role of human resources management (HRM) has been analyzed from various standpoints and perspectives, and so it is not our aim in this chapter to analyze all research agendas and concerns relating to this specific topic. However, a perspective that merits attention here is Service-Dominant Logic (S-D Logic). The concepts and ideas of this research stream provide a framework for examining provider–customer processes involved in co-creating the tourism experience. S-D Logic provides a conceptual framework for understanding how the consumer is becoming central to the development and marketing of tourism experiences through a process of co-creation with the provider (Cetin et al., 2014; Shaw et al., 2011). The co-creation process is just one critical dimension of S-D Logic, with other key elements being engaging more effectively with employees and understanding them as operant resources. If companies use their employees as operant resources they will be able to develop more innovative knowledge and skills, and in that way increase their competitive advantage (Lusch, Vargo, & O'Brien, 2007; Yang, 2008).

In this chapter we argue that HR are one of the key components and determining factors in providing valuable experiences within the tourism context. The main aim of the chapter is, therefore, to consider and highlight the contribution of strategic management of HR. This approach is indispensable for developing the new skills set required by staff of tourism businesses to meet the challenge of over-demanding tourists. The specific objectives of the chapter are (i) to briefly present the challenges and issues of HR within the tourism context; (ii) to view the field of HRM as a strategic function of tourism businesses; (iii) to discuss the shift from servicescape to experiencescape within the context of tourism, as well as the related evolution from emotional to experiential intelligence required of HR working for tourism businesses; and (iv) to outline the skills set required to provide tourists with a memorable experience and the supporting HR strategies. These issues are illustrated by a series of micro-cases.

Human Resources in the Tourism Field: The Importance of HRM Practices

The importance of employees for tourism companies has been well documented. Managers have the responsibility of "managing staff attitudes and behaviours for the mutual benefit of both parties: tourism companies and their employees" (Kusluvan, 2003, p. i). The literature indicates that there are two main challenges in designing and managing tourism experiences, namely (i) the relative intangibility of tourism services and (ii) the significant dependence on interpersonal interactions (Baum, 2005).

The perceived value derived by a tourist from an experience must be the driving force for all managerial decisions (Baum, 2006a; Solnet, 2008). The design and delivery of valuable tourism experiences requires the integration of all the organizational functions, such as operations, HR, marketing, and finance. Within this context, the organizational focus is on consideration of HR as strategic resources. General management and HRM in particular should be focused on how to create value for tourists and, in so doing, enhance the value of the company (Ford & Heaton, 2001).

The issue of strategic HRM will be discussed in more detail in the next section. But before that, the working environment and management style in tourism businesses merit brief consideration. This context has the potential to significantly affect the quality of experiences. Working conditions in tourism include work stress, casual work, tendency to low wages except where skills shortages act to counter this, tensions of low-pay work, unsociable hours and family unfriendly shift patterns, and monotonous and very hard work (Baum, 2006a). These conditions result in high levels of employee turnover, which is not conducive to providing consistently high levels of experience quality. Furthermore, these conditions do not help to foster a working environment that is customer focused and supports organizational citizenship, motivation and empowerment (Kusluvan, 2003; Solnet, 2008).

Therefore, management of tourism experiences implies a considerable focus on HR. Within this context, two issues require attention, namely the service/experience encounter and the role of customer-contact employees. A service encounter can be defined as the interaction between a tourist and a tourism company through its customer-contact employees. The outcomes of service encounters thus depend on the skills, knowledge, behavior, and performance of these employees. If successful, effective encounters can lead to many favorable outcomes, including satisfaction and positive word-of-mouth recommendation. Interactions with these employees are the experiences that tourists remember best, and employees who lack the skills and expertise to meet expectations can cause tourists to retain unpleasant memories of an experience (Sheng-Hshiung & Yi-Chun, 2004).

Customer-contact, or frontline, employees are a tourism company's primary interface with customers and, as such, are often perceived by the customer as part of the experience. Customers tend to measure service by the performance of the company's staff. A significant proportion of tourism experiences are delivered by people (tourism employees, managers, owners). Employees who deliver the service obviously have a direct influence on tourists' perception of their experience (Baum, 2006a).

A number of management strategies have been suggested to help tourism businesses manage service/experience encounters. These include (i) ingrained service culture that embeds the importance of customers into the organization's fabric; (ii) effective recruitment/HRM, ensuring that the right people are employed and that individual development continues throughout the term of employment; (iii) organizational culture which shapes the employees' responses to guests and also management's responses to their HR. The ability to adapt and respond properly is determined largely by the role HR play in the organization's culture (Kemp & Dwyer, 2001). A strong organizational culture increases behavioral consistency and enhances efficiency and effectiveness; (iv) the commitment of employees to the organization and its cultural strategy. Employees of an organization develop common perceptions which, in turn, affect their attitudes and behavior. The strength of that effect, however, depends on the strength of the organization's culture (Dwyer, Teal, & Kemp, 1999); (v) motivation: managers need to motivate employees continuously and provide them with ongoing feedback. It is vital that managers should support and acknowledge employees (Chiang & Jang, 2008).

From the summary above it may be concluded that HRM practices, such as recruitment and promotion policies, employee development, a reward system, employee communication, creation of organizational service orientation, training and staff empowerment, can make significant contributions to employees' engagement, skills, attitudes and behavior, and business performance (Ruzic, 2015; Wood, 1999). Most important, from the standpoint of our analysis, is that HRM practices contribute directly to the provision of high-value experiences.

MICRO-CASE 1: THE RITZ-CARLTON "GOLD STANDARDS"

The Ritz-Carlton Hotel Company is a management company that develops and operates luxury hotels throughout the world. The company operates 89 hotels in 29 countries and has 35,000 employees (Ritz-Carlton, 2015). Key product and service requirements of the customer have been translated into the Ritz-Carlton "Gold Standards," which include a credo, motto, three steps of service, service values, the 6th diamond and the employee promise (see below). These "Gold Standards" encompass the values and philosophy by which the company operates. Each employee is expected to understand and adhere to these efficiency standards. The responsibility for ensuring high-quality guest services rests primarily with employees.

> **The Ritz-Carlton credo:** "The Ritz-Carlton is a place where the genuine care and comfort of our guests is our highest mission. We pledge to provide the best service and facilities for our guests who will always enjoy a warm, relaxed yet refined ambience. The Ritz-Carlton experience enlivens the senses, instils well-being, and fulfils even the unexpressed wishes and needs of our guests."

> **The Ritz-Carlton motto:** "We are Ladies and Gentlemen serving Ladies and Gentlemen." This motto exemplifies the anticipatory service provided by all employees.

> **Three steps of service:** (i) A warm and sincere greeting. (ii) Anticipation and fulfilment of each guest's needs. (iii) Fond farewell. Give guests a warm good-bye.

> **Service values:** "I am proud to be Ritz-Carlton." This statement implies the following for employees: "I build

strong relationships and create Ritz-Carlton guests for life." "I am always responsive to the expressed and unexpressed wishes and needs of our guests." "I am empowered to create unique, memorable and personal experiences for our guests." "I understand my role in achieving the Key Success Factors, embracing Community Footprints and creating The Ritz-Carlton Mystique." "I continuously seek opportunities to innovate and improve The Ritz-Carlton experience." "I own and immediately resolve guest problems." "I create a work environment of teamwork and lateral service so that the needs of our guests and each other are met." "I have the opportunity to continuously learn and grow." "I am involved in the planning of the work that affects me." "I am proud of my professional appearance, language and behaviour." "I protect the privacy and security of our guests, my fellow employees and the company's confidential information and assets." "I am responsible for uncompromising levels of cleanliness and creating a safe and accident-free environment."

The 6th diamond: "Mystique, Emotional Engagement, and Functional."

The employee promise: "At The Ritz-Carlton, our Ladies and Gentlemen are the most important resource in our service commitment to our guests." "By applying the principles of trust, honesty, respect, integrity and commitment, we nurture and maximize talent to the benefit of each individual and the company." "The Ritz-Carlton fosters a work environment where diversity is valued, quality of life is enhanced, individual aspirations are fulfilled, and The Ritz-Carlton Mystique is strengthened." (Ritz-Carlton, 2015)

This example illustrates the importance of customer-contact employees and the appropriate work environment in creating a strong commitment to high-quality experiences. Given the importance of HR in the effective provision of tourism experiences, it is logical to consider the appropriate focus of HRM in greater detail. The following section suggests that the task should be seen as a strategic one, central to the success of any tourism company (Baum, 2006a).

Strategic Approach to Human Resources Management

HRM should adopt a strategic focus, thus allowing tourism companies to turn their staff into an important resource for competitive advantage (Wright & McMahan, 1992). A strategic approach implies above all a consideration of HRM over the long term as an asset/investment and revenue-generating resource. Tourism companies are constantly seeking ways to obtain a competitive advantage over competitors. There are many means available to try to achieve competitive advantage, including HR, innovation, quality, price, and location. A strategic approach aimed at creating a competitive advantage involves focusing on the creation of particular strengths inside the company. According to the resource-based view, competitive advantage can be achieved by capabilities that are internal to a company, including expertise, systems, and knowledge (Voola, Carlson, & West, 2004). This theory suggests that the key asset in attaining a competitive advantage is a company's HR.

A strategic view places great importance on people as a means to gain competitive advantage, particularly in tourism businesses with a high frequency of employee–customer interaction (Kusluvan, Kusluvan, Ilhan, & Buyruk, 2010). Wright and McMahan (1992, p. 298) define strategic human resources management (SHRM) as "the pattern of planned human resource deployments and activities intended to enable the firm to achieve its goals," and suggest that its application implies four components: (i) A focus on a firm's **human resources** as the primary resource to be strategically leveraged as a source of competitive advantage; (ii) The concept of **activities** highlights HR programs, policies and practices as the means to gain competitive advantage; (iii) Both **pattern and plan** describe the goal and the process of strategy, namely a consistent alignment or design which could also be described as "fit": vertical fit with the firm's strategy and horizontal fit with all HR activities aligned; and (iv) All planned HR activities are purposeful and focused on **goal achievement**. An SHRM approach is, therefore, largely about integrating the HR function into the strategic planning and operations of a company, particularly in the experiencescape where customers and employees interact frequently.

Scholars have argued that there is continued evidence for ongoing organizational delayering or lean management within tourism companies (Baum, 2015; Solnet, Kralj, & Baum, 2015). This is driven by cost pressure and the need to reduce the management levels within many companies. However, alongside this trend has been recognition of the value of an engaged staff, empowered to take decisions at the frontline without reference to the supervisory and managerial hierarchy. This process has extended organizationally into the execution of the HRM function (Gollan, Kalfa, & Xu, 2015), elaborated, in the context of tourism, by Solnet et al. (2015), who argue that the operational manager has a new role the execution of which has clear strategic implications. In this regard, Baum (2015) suggests that tourism companies facing future uncertainty urgently need organizational agility and flexibility. This implies that workforce fluidity (the capacity of a company to keep its HR aligned with business needs) is a requirement for companies operating in a dynamic environment. It is therefore believed that tourism industry managers should place greater emphasis on the HR function in their company and build up the appropriate organizational structure and culture in order to enhance tourist experiences and business performance.

MICRO-CASE 2: REFINED SERVICE AND EXQUISITE HOSPITALITY

This example illustrates the inculcation of a customer-focused attitude toward service that makes a hotel company a world-class leader. The Ritz-Carlton Hotel Company has set the bar for creating memorable customer experiences. Michelli (2008) explores every level of leadership within this company and suggests key principles that leaders at any company can apply to provide extraordinary customer experience. These include understanding the ever-evolving needs of customers, empowering employees by treating them with the utmost respect, and anticipating customers' unexpressed needs and concerns. Michelli further describes the innovative methods employed by Ritz-Carlton to create peerless guest experiences and explains how it constantly hones and improves them. Finally, he offers practical advice and leadership tools to help create and embed superior customer-service principles, processes, and practices.

One of the main implications of SHRM is that companies should focus on developing the skills required by their staff to provide experiences of high quality. The next section deals with this issue.

From Servicescape to Experiencescape and from Emotional to Experiential Intelligence: Skills Set for Providing Tourism Experiences

In the context of service experience, staff require a series of skills. These skills were initially based on what scholars termed "emotional labour" or "emotional intelligence" (Seymour, 2000) — employees are required to manage their emotions for the benefit of both customers and the company. To be most effective, tourism service employees must (i) be emotionally intelligent and understand which emotions are appropriate in different circumstances involving customers; (ii) be capable in terms of both tasks and interactions, because of the presence of customers (they must produce and engage simultaneously); (iii) adopt suitable attitudes and behaviors (more critical than technical skills); (iv) operate in an environment in which there are no formal mechanisms for employee control (a service culture must be in evidence to deal with unexpected circumstances); and (v) be "part-time marketers," in that they are expected to fully understand their company's offerings (Baum, 2006a; Solnet, 2008).

Furthermore, the literature reveals that skills in tourism are considered to include a wide-ranging "bundle of attributes" extending beyond the technical aspects of service delivery. These include "generic skills" (communication, problem-solving, information technology, and languages) within hospitality/tourism work (Baum, 2006a), as well as both emotional (Seymour, 2000) and esthetic (Warhurst, Nickson, Witz, & Cullen, 2000; Nickson, Warhurst, & Witz, 2003) dimensions as features within the bundling of tourism skills. Baum (2006b) suggests that skills bundling in services industries such as hospitality cannot be viewed solely in terms of the technical attributes of work, and thus emotional and esthetic dimensions have been added to the services skills bundle. The added dimension of "experience skills" within the "experience economy" suggested by Pine and

Gilmore (2013) constitutes a further component of this bundle (see 3.3).

Below we turn our attention to the shift from service to experience encounters and from emotional to experiential intelligence. This evolution involves an extended skills set.

EMOTIONAL LABOR AND INTELLIGENCE

Emotional demands are constantly made on tourism employees, who are required to be tolerant, amiable, positive and pleasant at all times. The ability to cope with such demands deserves recognition as a real skill (Baum, 2006b). Emotional demands were recognized as an additional dimension of generic skills by Seymour (2000), who considered the contribution of what she called "emotional labour" to service work, and concluded that this kind of work demands significant emotional elements in addition to overt technical skills.

In skills terms, effective emotional labor demands emotional intelligence (EI), defined by Goleman (1998) as "the capacity for recognizing our own feelings and those of others, for motivating ourselves, and for managing emotions well in ourselves and in our relationships" (p. 317). In practice, EI constitutes a measure of the degree to which individuals vary in their ability to perceive, understand and regulate their own emotions and those of others, and in their ability to integrate these with their own thoughts and actions. EI implies high levels of self-awareness and interpersonal skills.

To the requirements of EI in tourism can be added the skills demands of what Warhurst et al. (2000) describe as "aesthetic labour," that is, the skills required to present oneself, sound and behave in a manner that is compatible with the requirements of the job and with the expectations of customers. Esthetic labor is about appearance and the ability of customer-contact staff to understand and engage culturally with their customers on terms dictated by the latter. This requirement presupposes a certain level of prior education and cultural exposure as well as a commitment to remain up to date in these areas.

Baum (2006b) argues that the notion of EI does not fully encapsulate the breadth of working context in an experience economy. The nature of work has changed from its predominantly technical basis to include a range of sophisticated generic skills covering areas such as communications, languages and information technology as well as emotional and esthetic labor inputs. Tourism companies should therefore recruit employees who are able to fulfill the emotional and esthetic labor requirements of the work and who, as a result, are able to meet customers' experiential requirements. The main reason is that there has been a shift from service encounter to experience encounter.

EXPERIENCE ENCOUNTER

The experience economy is one in which consumers seek an integrated bundling of products and services in a way that generates responses across a range of their intellectual, emotional and esthetic senses. Baum (2005) states that tourism experiences generally rely on a number of encounters between tourists and tourism employees. The experience represents the essential motivation for customers to engage in the consumption of tourism services (Cetin et al., 2014).

Experience creation requires engagement from the customer, as well as functional and emotional involvement. This emotional involvement in experience creation relies on encounters between customers and companies who co-create experiences through two-way interactions (Boswijk, Thijssen, & Peelen, 2007). Because experiences are inherently personal, a company must ensure that tourists can co-create unique experiences with customer-contact employees (Ek, Larsen, Hornskov, & Mansfeldt, 2008). However, this requires that the encounter becomes an integrated part of the experience. In other words, experience encounters should be integrated with and activate the experiential attributes of the environment surrounding the encounter. An evolution from tourism service encounters to experience encounters leads to a different type of flexible and customized interaction between tourists and customer-contact employees. The study by Sørensen and Jensen (2015) suggests six distinctive characteristics of experience encounters in tourism, namely: dynamic, personalized, co-creation of emotional values, employee flexibility is key, experiential intelligence, and situated in integrated tourism experience environment.

Tourism service encounters offer functional value to tourists. Tourism experience encounters, on the other hand, contribute to developing knowledge about tourists' experiential purposes and latent desires and, consequently, enhance the experiential value of the tourism experience.

MICRO-CASE 3: TOURISM EXPERIENCE ENCOUNTERS IN A HOTEL

A very recent study argues that changing encounters between tourists and employees from service encounters to experience encounters, whose main function is experience creation, would raise the value of the encounters for tourists and increase the knowledge-creating potential in tourism. Sørensen and Jensen (2015) argue that traditional tourism service encounters limit knowledge creation and the development of knowledge about tourists' needs; tourism experience encounters, by contrast, support knowledge, and value creation. Their study suggests that if tourism service encounters are transformed into experience encounters by being integrated into the consumption environment to which they are related, this will create added experiential value for tourists and increase the creation of knowledge about consumers. An innovation field experiment in a retro design hotel in Copenhagen, Denmark has illustrated the potential of experience encounters to create knowledge and value. Analysis of the experiment revealed the benefits of experience encounters.

EXPERIENTIAL INTELLIGENCE AND SKILLS IN THE CONTEXT OF TOURISM

The shift from service to experience encounter, as briefly presented above, requires new skills of tourism staff. The experience economy is not solely about the experiences demanded by consumers. It is, equally, about the type of cultural and industry-specific experiences that employees bring into the workplace. Bryman (2004) considers the nature of work and experience delivery in the new consumption environment and identifies features of the required skills. The skills expected of employees go beyond their traditional technical core to include generic, emotional, and esthetic dimensions. This complex skills model is increasingly being recognized as a requirement for effective work in the services sector throughout the world.

As already mentioned, Baum (2006b) has explored the role of experiential factors in developing appropriate skills for hospitality industry employees, and proposed the concept of experiential intelligence (ExI) as a factor in the effective delivery of experience within the hospitality industry. The concept of ExI is representative of experiential and culturally based skills required in what Baum terms "skills bundle into an experience economy context." ExI is a kind of social capability that allows tourism employees to empathize and interact with their customers and identify with their expectations and requirements both experientially and emotionally (Baum, 2006b; Sørensen & Jensen, 2015).

Companies need to hire employees who are knowledgeable and experienced in the environment within which they will be operating. Direct engagement as a consumer is probably the most effective source of the requisite experiences that will equip employees with this type of intelligence. ExI represents the capability set that enables employees to empathize and identify with the expectations and requirements of their customers, based on a shared cultural and experience profile. In other words, employees must be able to place themselves both experientially and emotionally "in their customers' shoes." Substantially, ExI is a relative concept that is underpinned by the context of the interaction between guest and tourism employee.

The above-mentioned aspects make new demands on tourism employees who participate in co-creating experiences in experience encounters with tourists. Therefore, tourism companies need to implement strategies aiming at enhancing their HR in developing this skill set.

HR STRATEGIES FOR DEVELOPING EXPERIENTIAL SKILLS

Employees' ExI and flexibility are central in customized experience encounters which are integrated with the experience environment. Experiential skills go hand in hand with empowerment and organizational citizenship behavior. Ability and the willingness to accept empowered responsibility and to adopt organizational citizenship behavior in the tourism experience context depend on levels of understanding of tourists' needs implicit in higher levels of ExI (Baum, 2006b). It is believed that customer-contact staff must be engaged, involved, empowered and satisfied, and that they must be equipped with adequate tools. That is the reason why internal investment in developing HR is crucial in providing consistent, quality customer experience.

The main strategies in developing the experiential skills of HR in tourism include:

Emotional engagement and involvement: Employees' emotional engagement is central in providing valued experiences. Involvement of customer-contact employees means among other things giving them a voice to make suggestions.

Encouragement and motivation: employees should be encouraged to use their personal knowledge to assist tourists in co-creating their customized experiences. Managers should encourage employees involved in job or job-related decisions. It is vital that managers support and acknowledge employees (Chiang & Jang, 2008).

Guidance or guiding principles as a mobilizing force for companies: they help to form employee behavior and to channel employee actions and decisions in desired directions, and they are a tool for better preparing staff to respond to customer requirements (Harris, 2007).

Empowerment and flexibility: In practical terms empowerment means giving employees the responsibility for solving guests' problems. It is supported when employees are given flexibility to adjust services to particular customers' requirements, and this sustains creativity and knowledge development (Michelli, 2008). Employees must be open to the flexible creation of customized experience encounters.

Work engagement and job satisfaction: Engaged and satisfied employees are able to maintain high performance and provide enhanced quality of experience (Kusluvan, 2003; Kusluvan et al., 2010; Slatten & Mehmetoglu, 2010). The job satisfaction and engagement of customer-contact employees increase with the employee involvement and empowerment that is required in experience encounters (Zopiatis, Constanti, & Theocharous, 2014). In order to deliver quality experience and to satisfy customers these employees must be satisfied themselves.

Tourism involvement: encompasses an individual's long-term attitudes toward tourism activities. The study by Yeh (2013) confirmed the contributions of tourism involvement to work engagement and job satisfaction in the hotel industry. The findings of the study revealed that tourism involvement is positively related to work engagement, while both tourism involvement and work engagement are positively related to job satisfaction. Tourism business managers should therefore encourage customer-contact employees to become more involved in tourism and, consequently, develop their experiential skills (Yeh, 2013).

Continuous effective training and development is a good way to develop ExI. Employee training and setting more time aside for interactions with customers are very useful means to better employees' understanding of their guests, help employees to identify guests' needs and latent desires, and help employees go beyond functional service delivery to co-create emotional value with the guests (Baum, 2006b; Sørensen & Jensen, 2015). Simultaneously, it is the responsibility of the tourism business to create the appropriate organizational climate and working environment (Kusluvan et al., 2010). Therefore, tourism managers should make all the necessary support systems available to their staff to help them assume their new roles as "developers of individualised experiences" (Sørensen & Jensen, 2015).

The following case involving a strategic management approach illustrates some of the above-mentioned aspects.

MICRO-CASE 4: TOTAL QUALITY MANAGEMENT

Total quality management (TQM) is a strategic management approach and tool aimed at ensuring that organizational resources are dedicated to two key aims: (i) the satisfaction of all stakeholders involved in a business operation and (ii) the continuous improvement of quality services. It is an external recognition system for service excellence, certified by an independent organization. The seven categories on which companies are evaluated are leadership, information analysis, strategic quality planning, HR development and management, quality assurance, quality operating results, and customer satisfaction.

TQM is an integrated system of techniques and training based on the following five principles. (i) Commit to quality. Making quality a number one priority requires a supportive organizational culture. The first step toward TQM must involve active support and direction from senior management. (ii) Assess organizational culture. A select panel of managers and employees should examine the organization, with a focus on its culture, and assess the fit between that culture and TQM principles. This assessment would help management build on strengths, identify weaknesses, and set priorities. (iii) Focus on customer satisfaction. Customers are concerned about quality, and in fact define it for the organization. Companies that have successfully implemented TQM know what their customers really want, and consistently meet and exceed customer expectations. (iv) Empower employees. Although TQM is led from the top, the real work occurs bottom-up. Empowering employees requires training them to use their authority effectively, and redesigning some jobs to facilitate a team approach and modify practices. (v) Assess and measure quality efforts. Information gathering and analysis techniques should help identify causes of work-process problems and ways to solve them. TQM is based largely on rational thinking and problem-solving.

As can be seen, TQM is mainly about setting up and monitoring a program for continuous improvement of quality. The main strategy for ensuring steady quality improvement is empowering employees. The underlying principle is recognition of the role that employees play in the successful implementation of TQM. Furthermore, a focus on customer satisfaction must be built into the management processes and supported through an integrated system of information analysis, total employee participation, training, and the continuous effort to improve the quality of experience (Sotiriadis, 2011).

Conclusion

Currently the tourism industry is characterized by fierce competition and a more sophisticated and demanding consumer. Responses to these issues may determine the difference between success and failure. One of the main resources that is critical in overcoming such challenges is HR and their management.

In this chapter we have considered HR within the context of tourism experiences, and analyzed their crucial role. We argued that HR make a significant contribution to the design and management of tourism experiences to meet customer expectations and achieve tourism company aims, and suggested that the key lies in the strategic consideration of HR management. This approach is necessary because of the shift of consumption encounters between tourists and customer-contact employees from servicescape to experiencescape. This evolution implies that employees of tourism businesses require a new skills set.

Overall, in this chapter we offered insights into HR management practices and activities, and outlined the new skills set required for the effective delivery of tourism experiences. Within the new consumption environment, experiential intelligence and a new bundle of skills are required to satisfy the customized needs and meet the personal aspirations of contemporary tourists. The bundle of skills expected to be necessary in an experience economy context includes generic, emotional and esthetic dimensions, as well as experiential and culturally based skills.

Moreover, we also suggested suitable tools and a series of strategies for enhancing the experiential intelligence and developing the experiential skills of tourism employees. A number of micro-cases illustrated some aspects and strategies currently employed by tourism companies. This chapter could therefore be considered a contribution to a better understanding of the nature of the complex skills bundle required within the tourism industry in the era of the experience economy. In this regard, the strategies and tools suggested by SHRM are very suitable.

References

Baum, T. (2005). Making or breaking the tourist experience: The role of human resource management. In C. Ryan (Ed.), *The tourist experience* (pp. 94–111). London: Thomson.

Baum, T. (2006a). *Human resource management in tourism, hospitality and leisure: An international perspective*. London: Thomson.

Baum, T. (2006b). Reflections on the nature of skills in the experience economy: Challenging traditional skills models in hospitality. *Journal of Hospitality and Tourism Management, 13*(2), 124–135.

Baum, T. (2015). Human resources in tourism: Still waiting for change? A 2015 reprise. *Tourism Management, 50*(2), 204–212.

Boswijk, A., Thijssen, T., & Peelen, E. (2007). *The experience economy: A new perspective*. Amsterdam: Pearson Education.

Bryman, A. (2004). *The disneyization of society*. London: Sage.

Cetin, G., Akova, O., & Kaya, F. (2014). Components of experiential value: Case of hospitality industry. *Procedia – Social and Behavioral Sciences, 150*, 1040–1049.

Chiang, C.-F., & Jang, S. C. (2008). An expectancy theory model for hotel employee motivation. *International Journal of Hospitality Management, 27*, 313–322.

Dwyer, L., Teal, G., & Kemp, S. (1999). Organisational culture and strategic management in a resort hotel. *Asia Pacific Journal of Tourism Management, 3*(1), 27–36.

Ek, R., Larsen, J., Hornskov, S., & Mansfeldt, O. (2008). A dynamic framework of tourist experiences: Space-time and performances in the experience economy. *Scandinavian Journal of Hospitality and Tourism, 8*(2), 122–140.

Ford, R. C., & Heaton, C. P. (2001). Lessons from hospitality that can serve anyone. *Organizational Dynamics, 30*(1), 30–47.

Goleman, D. (1998). *Working with emotional intelligence*. New York, NY: Bantam.

Gollan, P., Kalfa, S., & Xu, Y. (2015). Strategic HRM and devolving HR to the line: Cochlear during the shift to lean manufacturing. *Asia Pacific Journal of Human Resource Management, 53*(2), 144–162.

Harris, P. (2007). We the people: The importance of employees in the process of building customer experience. *Journal of Brand Management, 15*(2), 102–114.

Kemp, S., & Dwyer, L. (2001). An examination of organisational culture – The Regent Hotel, Sydney. *Hospitality Management, 20*, 77–93.

Kusluvan, S. (2003). Employee attitudes and behaviors and their roles for tourism and hospitality. In S. Kusluvan (Ed.), *Managing employee attitudes and behaviors in the tourism and hospitality industry* (pp. 25–50). New York, NY: Nova Science.

Kusluvan, S., Kusluvan, Z., Ilhan, I., & Buyruk, L. (2010). The human dimension: A review of human resource management issues in the tourism and hospitality industry. *Cornell Hospitality Quarterly, 51*(2), 171–214.

Lusch, R. F., Vargo, S. L., & O'Brien, M. (2007). Competing through service: Insights from service-dominant logic. *Journal of Retailing, 83*(1), 5–18.

Michelli, J. (2008). *The new gold standard: 5 leadership principles for creating a legendary customer experience courtesy of the Ritz-Carlton Hotel Company.* New York, NY: McGraw-Hill Professional.

Nickson, D., Warhurst, C., & Witz, A. (2003). The labour of aesthetics and the aesthetics of organization. *Organization, 10*(1), 33–54.

Pine, B., & Gilmore, J. (2013). The experience economy: Past, present and future. In J. Sundbo & F. Sørensen (Eds.), *Handbook on the experience economy* (pp. 21–44). Cheltenham: Edward Elgar.

Ritz-Carlton. (2015). *Company website.* Retrieved from http://www.ritzcarlton.com/en/Corporate/. Accessed on October 20.

Ruzic, M. D. (2015). Direct and indirect contribution of HRM practice to hotel company performance. *International Journal of Hospitality Management, 49*(1), 56–65.

Seymour, D. (2000). Emotional labour: A comparison between fast food and traditional service work. *International Journal of Hospitality Management, 19*(2), 159–171.

Shaw, G., Bailey, A., & Williams, A. (2011). Aspects of service-dominant logic and its implications for tourism management: Examples from the hotel industry. *Tourism Management, 32*, 207–214.

Sheng-Hshiung, T., & Yi-Chun, L. (2004). Promoting service quality in tourist hotels: The role of HRM practices and service behaviour. *Tourism Management, 25*, 471–481.

Slatten, T., & Mehmetoglu, M. (2010). Antecedents and effects of engaged frontline employees: A study from the hospitality industry. *Managing Service Quality, 21*(1), 88–107.

Solnet, D. (2008). Supporting the contemporary tourism product: Service management. In C. Cooper & C. M. Hall (Eds.), *Contemporary tourism: An international approach* (pp. 307–343). Oxford: Elsevier.

Solnet, D., Kralj, A., & Baum, T. (2015). 360 degrees of pressure: The changing role of the HR professional in the hospitality industry. *Journal of Hospitality and Tourism Research, 39*(2), 271–292.

Sørensen, F., & Jensen, J. F. (2015). Value creation and knowledge development in tourism experience encounters. *Tourism Management, 46*, 336–346.

Sotiriadis, M. (2011). *Service quality in the hotel industry: Issues and challenges.* Saarbrucken, Germany: Lambert Academic.

Voola, R., Carlson, J., & West, M. (2004). Emotional intelligence and competitive advantage: Examining the relationship from a resource-based view. *Strategic Change*, *13*(2), 83–93.

Warhurst, C., Nickson, D., Witz, A., & Cullen, A. M. (2000). Aesthetic labour in interactive service work: Some case study evidence from the 'New Glasgow'. *Service Industries Journal*, *20*(3), 1–18.

Wood, S. (1999). Human resource management and performance. *International Journal of Management Review*, *1*(4), 367–413.

Wright, P., & McMahan, G. (1992). Theoretical perspectives for strategic human resource management. *Journal of Management*, *18*(2), 295–320.

Yang, J.-T. (2008). Individual attitudes and organizational knowledge sharing. *Tourism Management*, *29*(2), 345–353.

Yeh, C. M. (2013). Tourism involvement, work engagement and job satisfaction among frontline hotel employees. *Annals of Tourism Research*, *42*, 214–239.

Zopiatis, A., Constanti, P., & Theocharous, A. L. (2014). Job involvement, commitment, satisfaction and turnover: Evidence from hotel employees in Cyprus. *Tourism Management*, *41*(1), 129–140.

4 Tourism Destination: Design of Experiences

Eyup Karayilan and Gurel Cetin

ABSTRACT

Purpose – The aim of this chapter is to offer a conceptual model for tourist experiences in the destination and suggest implications for different stakeholders in creating experiences for tourists.

Methodology/approach – This conceptual paper explores tourist experiences based on previous literature and through a brief case. A holistic destination experience model is also suggested including the role of DMOs, host community and industry which are considered under the overall experiencescape.

Findings – Literature review and analysis of case study suggest that the destination experience can be framed based on the roles of different actors in a destination. Characteristic of the destination and stakeholders do play important roles in involving tourists in experience production.

Practical implications – Findings might provide insights to DMOs and other stakeholders in the destination concerning their roles in creating a holistic positive destination experience for tourists which is crucial for differentiation. Future research might also concentrate on different elements of destination experience and interrelationships of different stakeholders.

Originality/value – Although there are numerous papers on experiences from individual services (e.g., hotels, airlines, restaurants) in the destination, literature on overall stake-holder and creation of holistic destination experience has been overlooked. This chapter offers a theoretical model that would assist policy-makers to design experiences in the desti-nation by looking at the roles of different stakeholders and to improve the competitiveness of the destination.

Keywords: Destination experience; tourist experience; stakeholders

Introduction

Traditional tourist behavior concepts are no more sufficient in explaining changing tourist needs and motivations (Mossberg, 2007). From mid-80s the tourism product has been diversified toward more experiential and informative typologies. The com-mon characteristics of these travel types (e.g., adventure tourism, cultural tourism) are that they are more enriching, engaging, adventuresome and informative than traditional mass tourism (Zeppel & Hall, 1992). Packaged mass tourism products are increasingly supplemented by alternative tourism destinations (Butler, 1989) and many established trendy and superior quality sunlust destinations of the past are suffering today. Hence experi-ential offerings are becoming main determinants of destinations' long-term success (Pine & Gilmore, 1999; Ritzer, 2007).

Destinations are the core of the tourism product. The desire to visit them is the main motivation of most trips (Swarbrooke & Horner, 2007). Therefore destinations can be considered as the pull factor for tourists and might include factors like attractions, facilities, infrastructure, transportation, and hospitality (Mill & Morrison, 1985). Tourist destinations can also be framed as amalgam of services and activities (e.g., lodging, attractions) that create an overall experience of the area visited. The experi-ences created by destinations can be so powerful that travelers might create an emotional attachment to destinations (Hidalgo & Hernandez, 2001) and become loyal visitors. Therefore the value of destination lies in the quality and quantity of the experiences it offers (MacCannell, 1989).

Destinations can be considered as defined geographical areas with a political or legislative framework and understood as a unique space by its visitors (Barnes, Mattsson, & Sorensen, 2014). According to Framke (2002) destinations has several geographical levels and can be seen as an amalgam of attractions, services, facilities, infrastructure, landscapes, culture, hospitality, and events which requires coordination among different actors. From experience viewpoint destinations can be defined as places that facilitate the conditions of tourism experience (Sorensen, 2004). Hence tourist destinations in this study have been conceptualized as spatial brands that reflect a fusion of services, products and environment that form a total tourist experience in a geographic location. Therefore, rather than experiences with individual service providers this study focuses on the holistic experience produced in the destinations.

The aim of this chapter is to explore the destination experiences based on previous literature and through a brief case. A holistic tourist experience framework will also be suggested including the role of tourist, destination, and other stakeholders. Answers to four questions are sought:

- What is the destination experience?
- What are the various components of tourist experiences in destinations?
- How can tourist experiences be produced in the destinations? What are the roles of different stakeholders?
- How can tourist experiences be integrated into destination marketing?

LITERATURE REVIEW

Although there is an increasing interest in literature on customer experiences, the definition, conceptualization, components and measurement of tourist experiences are still ambiguous (Larsen, 2007). Measuring the overall experience in destinations is more complex than measuring it for individual service experiences because it extends a period of time and involves a synergistic interaction and consumption of integrated products and services simultaneously (Burns & Holden, 1995). The design of the hotel, interactions with locals, night life, landmarks, nature even the public Wi-Fi at the airport can be a part of the overall destination experience. Therefore on the total level there are many components that the traveler interacts and a holistic understanding of what creates the destination experience is important for all actors involved. Touristic products and their individual components should be coherent experiential whole (Sternberg, 1997). Thus to create a holistic positive experience destinations should go beyond traditional ways of packaging different products together and a new form of thinking is needed that would integrate actors, tourists, themes, stories, and communication in a unique way.

Moreover tourist experiences are subjective and depend very much on personal interpretations and perceptions. Different tourists from various cultural backgrounds and personal characteristics might interpret their experience differently in the same destination. Even for the same people, their moods at a particular moment might affect their perceptions. Destinations also differ in their characteristics and attractions. A beach holiday might include more passive elements of experience such as relaxation, esthetics and entertainment themes however a cultural tour might require more active involvement and education. Hence destination experiences are both subjective and context specific. Thus both pull and push factors should be considered when trying to analyze experiences in destinations.

Pine and Gilmore (1999) offered four realms of customer experiences as entertainment, educational, esthetic, and escapist experiences. The entertainment realm is related to events that make customer smile, this is the most basic experience (e.g., watching animation). Educational experiences are concerned with consumers' need to learn and understand (e.g., visiting museums). Esthetic experiences are related to customers' tendency to appreciate beauty and harmony (e.g., scenery). Escapist dimension of experiences refers to people's desire for a change and try new and different (e.g., adventure tour). Although these four realms have not been used in a destination setting, they have the potential to explain the destination experience as well.

Various other studies have acknowledged social interactions with locals, servicescape, public services, knowledge enhancement, feeling comfortable, and welcome, having challenges and active participation as important items that can be considered under the destination experience of travelers (Hood, 2004). Involvement also emerges as an antecedent of experiences and can be defined as the identification and interest of the tourist in the destination characterized by enjoyment and self-achievement (Selin & Howard, 1988). According to Jansson (2002), tourism experience involves a hedonistic aspect and a distinctive bodily and/or spiritual involvement. Authenticity, novelty, exoticism, meanings, and change were also used to describe tourist experiences (MacCannell, 1989; Mossberg, 2007).

Hosany and Gilbert (2010) found that love (e.g., passion, warm hearted), joy (e.g., cheerfulness, pleasure), positive surprise (e.g., amazement, astonishment) are emotions that can relate to experiences in the destinations. Barnes et al. (2014) also tried to define destination experiences using sensory (visual, aural, olfactory, gustatory and tactile; e.g., smell of the food), affective (feelings, emotions; e.g., feeling welcome), behavioral (physical actions; e.g., walk in the forest) and intellectual (knowledge enhancement; e.g., museums) factors. Kim, Ritchie, and McCormick (2010) also offered several dimensions of tourist experience. These are involvement, hedonism, happiness, pleasure, relaxation, stimulation, refreshment, social interaction, spontaneity, meaningfulness, knowledge, challenge, sense of separation, timelessness, adventure, personal relevance, novelty, escaping pressure, and intellectual cultivation.

Kim et al. (2010) argue that a memorable destination experience scale should include seven themes: hedonism, refreshment, local culture, meaningfulness, knowledge, involvement, and novelty. They also claim one of the distinguishing factors of an experience is its memorability. Larsen (2007) acknowledges the importance of memorability and defines tourist experience as a strong personal travel related event that is memorized. Thus destination experience is the multidimensional takeaway impression or outcome formed by different elements and it is a very difficult task to determine which are the key components Although destination experiences lacks a shared definition there are recurrent characteristics mentioned in the literature that can be used to offer a general framework and relationships.

Experiences a destination offers can also be used as a tool for differentiation and are able to create the necessary engagement between destinations and their visitors. Destinations should therefore focus on the specific customer segments that they think they can create better experiences for, try to understand them rather than simply focusing on the standards of general services. Las Vegas is a good case to support this claim. "What happens in Vegas stays in Vegas" evokes the *escape* rather than *education* which would be more appropriate message for a cultural city like Istanbul.

APPROACH AND CONTRIBUTION

A stream of research has already explored experiences in different settings in the destination such as attractions (Beeho & Prentice,

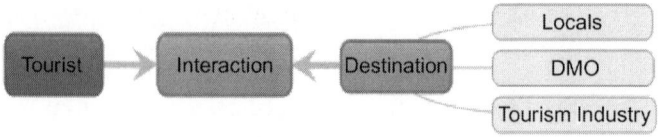

Figure 1.   The Process of Designing Destination Experience.

1997), adventure activities (Arnould & Price, 1993), lodging, and food (Cetin & Walls, 2016; Quan & Wang, 2004). However the overall tourist experience in the destination has been neglected. This chapter sets out to look at experiences from a broader destination planning perspective including the role of different stakeholders.

While doing so it aims to suggest a destination experience model as depicted in Figure 1 that would provide managerial implications particularly for DMOs. Identifying the experiential components of the vacation would also lead to better design of marketing strategies for destinations.

THE ROLE OF STAKEHOLDERS IN DESIGN OF TOURIST EXPERIENCE

Tourists' journey starts at home and includes a chain of events, activities and perceptions. A traveler usually faces with a plenty of challenges during the travel from information search to departure from the destination. Once in the destination they also interact with various actors depending on their motivations and activities they attend. Travelers in way co-create their own experiences by interacting with different elements and participating to different activities in the destination. There are numerous factors that have the possibility to affect the experience of tourists during this actual travel process.

Mossberg (2007) argues about three types of products that a tourist can experience in the destination. First typology refers to mass produced goods (e.g., souvenirs), the second group includes live products that requires tourists involvement and interaction (e.g., transportation, meals, accommodation) and the final group of products are basically value creating products that support another core product (e.g., atmospherics, arts, crafts, fashion, music, concerts, performing arts, films, architecture, design). She also refers to sensescapes (e.g., soundscapes, smellscapes, tastescapes, touchscapes) even mindscapes where tourists can dream, role play and experience new things while in the destination.

It should also be kept in mind that experience and motivations are the perceptual concepts that can naturally vary from one person to another. Moreover, as it is partially mentioned in the above argument, factors affecting the experience of visitors are not merely limited with stakeholders' behaviors and roles (Quan & Wang, 2004), tourists themselves are considered important players. Yet stakeholders are one of the main groups that affect the experience of tourists. It might also be argued that determining the role of stakeholders is a challenging task and a broad subject. However, some of these actors play a significant role in creation of tourists' destination experience such as the host community.

On the other hand, the roles of public and private sectors representatives are also essential. In this sense, roles of public sector and governmental bodies (e.g., DMOs, local governments, consulates, ministries, etc.) in creating a memorable tourist experience involves creating the facilitating environment, providing infrastructures and similar functions rather than merely trying to attract tourists to a destination (Beaumont & Dredge, 2010; Liang & Wang, 2010).

For instance, some governmental bodies such as Tourism Ministries which act as regulative institutions in most developing countries (Tosun, 2001), can directly apply or contribute to the destination marketing strategies. Yet application of these strategies are predominantly in the responsibility of private sector representatives (e.g., hotels, travel agencies, restaurants, recreation businesses) and depend on their performances (Dredge, 2001; Okumus, Okumus, & McKercher, 2007). Hence tourism businesses are also one of the main stakeholder groups that have a role in delineating the experience of visitors (Oh, Fiore, & Jeoung, 2007). For this reason, the contribution of tourism businesses on destination experience of visitors are also examined (Bordelon & Ortiz, 2015).

Host community

The role of the hosts in creating tourist experience can be examined based on their participation type, involvement purpose, and level of interaction with local tourism (Murphy, 2013; Smith, 2012). Firstly, locals' engagement with tourism industry for economic reasons might affect tourist experience. Considering novelty, authenticity, and experiencing different cultures as an important tourism motivation interacting with the hosts not only in public but also commercial stages would facilitate a better experience.

Because hosts usually have strong ties with local natural, social and cultural environment, their involvement in tourism industry may also minimize over-commercialization and negative side effects of tourism (Cetin, 2014; Tosun, 2001). Possible conflicts with tourism industry and tourists might also be prevented if locals are involved and an economic benefit is offered (McIntosh & Zahra, 2007; Zhang, Inbakaran, & Jackson, 2006). Participation of locals is a sine qua non for authenticity and the interaction with tourists which is crucial for a proper tourist experience. In this sense, the relationship between host communities' utilitarian and voluntary participation and tourists' experience can be better examined with some examples.

As a physical need all tourists eat at the destination and local food can become an important part of destination experience. There is an increasing interest among travelers for traditional and local foods. In this sense, a local restaurant serving authentic food by locals in a traditional setting can create a memorable experience (Quan & Wang, 2004). On the one hand, a local vendor selling handmade traditional products that have a local story can add to the experience of visitors (Isaac, 2008). By the same token, interaction with locals employed in these businesses can create positive experiences (Larsen, 2005).

In addition to the staff serving in the industry, other members of the local community can contribute to the tourist experience. Traditional hospitality, making tourists feel safe and welcome, being helpful, social and generous are important host features that facilitate a positive tourist experience. Besides the social interaction local culture, heritage, life style, traditions, and beliefs can influence the tourist experience (Salazar, 2005). Murphy (2013) defending participatory tourism also state that host community is a part of tourism product in a tourism destination. It is even possible to say that host communities can become a pull factor for some tourism destinations, particularly for communities that have unique socio-cultural structure and lifestyles (e.g., Samis in Scandinavia). In other cases the local way of doing things adds to the experience as in the case of a local man wearing Kilt in Scotland (Yeoman, Durie, McMahon-Beattie, & Palmer, 2005).

In a similar way, cultural festivals and events are also other common platforms for host-guest interaction. For instance, Rio de Janeiro's Carnival is one of the most famous example of event tourism. Many tourists take trips to Brazil to see Samba Dance and experience the local culture (Nurse, 2004). Camel races and oil wrestles in Turkey (Caliskan, 2010) and bullfight festivals in Spain (Tkac, 2014) can be considered as other examples. These festivals and events that are able to attract millions of tourists because of the experiences they offer.

However, it should also be mentioned that an event should not necessarily be a local authentic one to leave an impression on tourists. Hosts and guests can also interact during international organizations. For instance, host community and guests can intensively interact in Olympic Games (Ritchie, Shipway, & Cleeve, 2009). The common feature of these events is that they create the facilitating environment for interactions to occur between locals and travelers. Thus tourism activities and touristic spaces should be well-planned for a better and intensified interaction. Hence the destination management organizations and related government bodies have an important role designing the expriencescape at a destination.

DMOs

Public sector is recognized as one of the key tourism stakeholders (Hjalager, 2010). However, as it is discussed above the impact of governmental bodies on destination experience of visitors have some structural differences than other stakeholders. It is common knowledge that governmental bodies and public services offered by them have indirect effects on experience of visitors. For instance, some of the governmental bodies in a destination can directly fund or contribute to destination marketing but the implications of these strategies are predominantly under the responsibility of other tourism stakeholders (e.g., DMO, CVB) (Dredge, 2001; Okumus et al., 2007). Buhalis (2000) also criticize DMOs to be too concentrated on the needs of the stakeholders than the experiences of consumers.

There are also some basic services that should be supplied in a destination such as accessibility, cleanliness, landscaping, safety, and related infrastructure that also fall under the responsibility of governmental bodies. Without these basic services a positive experience is not possible. The super-structure in the case of tourism related services (e.g., lodging, F&B, attractions) should also be coordinated and facilitated through incentives.

Sheehan, Ritchie, and Hudson, (2007, cited in Elbe et al., 2009, p. 285) conclude from field research that DMOs should coordinate among stakeholders and act as an interface between buyers and sellers of the destination. DMOs should also audit activities of tourism industry in order to enhance the quality of services such as controlling the food safety and hygiene in restaurants and perform marketing communications concerning the destination (d'Angella & Go, 2009; Kim, Yuan, Goh, & Antun, 2009). That is to say the responsibilities of DMOs are not just providing infrastructure and super-structure but also coordinate the efforts related to the tourist experiencescapes and involve tourists as active participants for creation of their own experiences in the destination.

In this sense, DMOs can make numerous contributions to experience of tourists in the context of marketing and promotion. For example, DMOs can render the destination more attractive by promoting common touristic resources, cultural and historical landmarks. For instance, Eifel and Pisa towers are some famous landmarks in Europe. Large number of people visits France and Italy to see those unique landmarks which are extensively promoted by official mediums (Mazumdar, 2011). By the same token, Fairy Chimneys and cave houses landmarks that reflect the Goreme region in Turkey (Tucker, 2001). Additionally, landmarks can also be human made such as Petronas Towers in Malaysia (Vale, 1999) or Palm Jumeirah in Dubai (Bagaeen, 2007) which two are recently built manmade attractions used in official destination promotion.

In a similar vein, theme parks became main attractions in Orlando (Milman, 2001). However, landmarks and other attractions should not necessarily be manmade, historical or cultural. Indeed, natural attractions (e.g., wildlife, biodiversity, fauna, geography, etc.) can also be considered as touristic attractions. In this sense, kangaroos, for example, are associated with Australia and a large number of tourists travel there to see this rare fauna (Higginbottom, Northrope, Croft, Hill, & Fredline, 2004). Hence, protection, coordination and promotion of these values are another responsibility of DMOs. It should also be stated that most of aforementioned landmarks are also used in public-private sector collaborative promotion. Therefore private sector representatives (i.e., hotels, travel agencies) can also make contribution to the destination marketing.

Tourism industry

The performance and contribution of tourism industry (e.g., hotels, restaurants, tour companies) in creating positive experiences for tourists cannot be over stated. However their role in tourist experience of tourists should not be considered separate than DMOs activities since governmental bodies directly influence the business climate in a region. The collaboration between DMOs and tourism businesses is essential (e.g., infrastructure, investments, promotion) and linked in creating positive experiences to visitors. However, some activities and roles in experience creation fall solely under the responsibility of tourism industry.

Firstly, hotels in the destination are important to cover basic needs of tourists (e.g., shelter, food, etc.). However modern hotels are more concentrated on differentiating their services based on additional experiential services (e.g., atmospherics, spas, entertainment, etc.) besides their conventional functions such as offering a clean and comfortable bed (Aggett, 2007). In the context of hotels, vernacular architectures, usage of new technologies, CRM tools, guest relations, product bundling, and various other services should be taken into account for a proper guest satisfaction and experience.

In this sense, different researches indicate that small boutique hotels are becoming more popular and the destinations. It is also stated that there is an increasing trend that leads tourists to boutique hotels which have themed architectures. Importance of tangibles, atmospherics, physical environment, and servicescape are discussed as important elements of tourist experience (Cetin & Walls, 2016). For instance many entrepreneurs intended to invest in shophouse hotels in Singapore and similar plans seem to have emerged elsewhere internationally (Chang & Teo, 2009). This should not be surprising since the vernacular architectures stimulate nostalgic feelings and reflect heritage of a city. Perhaps, this type of lodging facilities have the possibly to become more popular in the form of architourism in the future.

Another major actor in tourism industry are the restaurants. Restaurants are becoming more estheticized (Arva & Deli-Gray, 2011) to create a positive experience for their guests. Corroborating with this Yang (2009), states that people do not only go to Häagen-Dazs to eat ice cream, they see ice cream as one of the ingredient of a romantic and childlike experience. Starbucks is also a popular example offering a distinctive customer experience to its customer using ambient physical clues (Michelli, 2013).

The tourists are more and more willing to leave their comfort zone, looking for local authentic restaurants rather than international chain restaurants which are also available anywhere in the world (Sengel et al., 2015). After all tourist travel for experiences that are not available in their regular environment. Offering a standard international menu does not create the desired experience any more, it only satisfies hunger. However eating at an authentic local restaurant also increases the opportunity to interact with locals and experience the local culture. This might also be the main reason why ethnic restaurants became so popular.

Consumers are looking for different and authentic. Tourists also seek ethnic and local restaurants to enrich their travel experiences. Confirming the importance of local restaurants in experience Sukalakamala and Boyce (2007) found that style of the uniform, traditional greeting, traditional music, interior and exterior design, interactions with locals and other distinctive features can be part of the authentic experience gathered from ethnic restaurants. Creation of experiences is discussed in a case study below.

CASE STUDY

Any activity that tourist attends in a destination have the potential to create an experience (e.g., visiting attractions, transportation, lodging, food, interactions with locals, etc.). However, it is better to examine an overall tourism destination to capture a holistic tourist experience. A case study can better contribute to understanding of destination experience discussed above.

There are many attractive tourism destinations that offer different experiences to their visitors and Istanbul can be considered among these experience intensive destinations for various reasons. First of all, Istanbul is one of the most visited tourism destination by volume considering other megapoles (Cetin, 2014). There is a continuous increase in international tourist flow to Istanbul as can be seen from Figure 2. Almost 13 million tourists visited Istanbul in 2015. In total, Istanbul has 72 public and private museums, 4 historic bazaars and more than 100 modern shopping malls. She was also crowned as the European Capital of Culture in 2010 and European Capital of Sport in 2012 (ICVB, 2014).

Secondly, Istanbul is a unique transcontinental city located between three continents. Besides its geographical location, Istanbul offers a rich cultural heritage since it has served as capital of two major empires (Kizilirmak & Cetin, 2015). It is possible to attend to various alternative type of tourism activities in Istanbul and each of them offer different experiences to visitors. However, cultural attractions and similar motifs

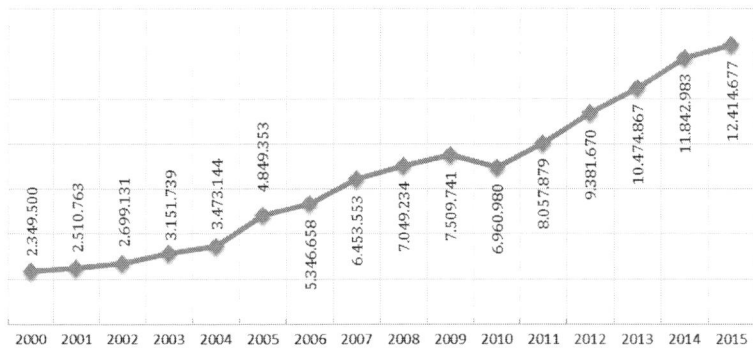

Figure 2. The Number of Tourists Visited Istanbul (2000—2015). *Source*: Provincial Directorate of Culture and Tourism (2015).

overwhelm on the characteristic of the destination. Perhaps, for this reason, it is selected as European Capital of Culture in the year of 2010 (Gunay, 2010). In the context of heritage tourism, Topkapõ Palace is one of landmarks attracting millions of visitors each year. The palace hosted the Ottoman dynasty for centuries and there are numerous cultural resources remained from Ottoman Empire such as Spoonmaker's diamond in treasury, military equipment and unique religious motifs and relics. Next to Topkapi the church of Holy wisdom Hagia Sophia stands overlooking to the Hipodrome from the Roman period. "Mevlevi Sema Ceremony" which is listed in UNESCOs Masterpieces of the Oral and Intangible Heritage of Humanity can also be experienced in Galata.

Ecumenical Patriarchate of Constantinople is another important sanctuary which hold a special place for Orthodox Christians (Svetlanamihić & Supić, 2014). Istanbul also offers Suleymaniye Mosque with its great calligraphies (Özsayiner, 2008) same like Blue Mosque which represent one of the great examples of tile art all over the world (Lu, Wang, Hua, Wang, & Li, 2011). These historical mosques, churches and synagogues offer a unique spiritual experience (Cifci, Kaya, & Akova, 2015) for tourists from different religions (Hackworth, 2005).

Besides its cultural attractions Istanbul has natural resources such as the Bosphorus, the waterway that separates Asia from Europe, beaches, forests, and islands that surround the city. The infusion of different cultures in the city also made food in Istanbul unique offering a wide variety of dishes, cooking styles and ingredients. Shopping in Istanbul is also both available in

traditional forms such as in Grand Bazaar offering authentic products as well as in modern shopping districts offering international brands and fashion products. The night life in Istanbul is
also well developed famous night clubs and entertainment districts are other resources for tourism experience in the city. Local
people are also considered social, friendly and value foreigners as
guests rather than strangers hence the term "Turkish hospitality"
which is also considered an important component of tourist
experience in the city (Cetin & Bilgihan, 2016).

Another hygiene factor for Istanbul to become an international destination is that it offers different qualities of accommodation facilities from word class luxury hotels to a number
of smaller hostels. Another facilitating factor for the city is its
accessibility, Istanbul can be reached from 199 countries with
direct flights, which makes it a convenient destination, easily
accessible. The city currently hosts around 13 million international tourists and 50% these tourists visiting the city are from
33 different countries. This international profile and other tourists visiting the city can also add up to tourist experience.

Marketing activities of DMO and CVB of Istanbul is also
concentrated to involve stakeholders and promote unique cultural elements in the destination. The DMO is also actively using
social media, produce virals (e.g., Turkish Tea), invite bloggers to
the destination and provide unique information about the city in
electronic media (e.g., howtoistanbul.com). They also coordinate
efforts with the industry by financing international fairs, events,
festivals and support joint promotional campaigns (e.g., Turkey
Home with Turkish Airlines).

Conclusion

As Arnould and Price (1993) put it the peak experience is something unique, unexpected and has a surprise dimension into it.
Quan and Wang (2004) argues a positive experience is only possible if the peak experience is accompanied by supporting experiences. The total experience quality in a destination therefore
depends both on peak and supporting experiences. This chapter
explores the creation of both peak and supporting destination
experiences based on different roles of stakeholders including
local people, DMO and tourism industry. Some implications are
mentioned below.

Firstly, participation of local community to tourism activities is crucial to offer a proper destination experience. From the industrial perspective, related governmental bodies can provide technical and financial support to local investors since locally owned businesses suffer from imperfect competition conditions particularly in the developing world (Tosun, 2000). Thus locals should be encouraged to invest in tourism, training and financial incentives should also be made available to hosts. DMOs also play a crucial role in creating the facilitating environment for desired experiences to emerge. By coordinating different public and private actors, promoting the destination, investing on infrastructure and lobbying with decision makers DMOs hold an important position. Secondly, DMOs can also encourage and promote cultural events, festivals, arts and other organizations that would improve tourist experience. Tourism industry's collaborative efforts and their awareness in creating tourist experiences should also be improved. The level of service supplied by the industry acts as a supporting experiential factor for travelers.

Both DMOs and individual service suppliers must understand the holistic experiential attributes the destination offers. Destinations should focus on developing new programs that people can experience and learn new things unique to the destination. Activities that involve challenge and make tourists explore their talents, skills and capabilities, increasing the level of social interaction both with the locals working in tourism services (e.g., hotels) as well as locals without any relation to tourism (e.g., in public transportation) would enhance experiences. Individuals who experience local culture is more likely to have a positive experience out of it; promoting local food, local architecture, farmers markets, and other activities that increase interaction with locals would also improve tourist experiences. These can also be used in destination marketing. For example local food is rarely utilized as a part of destination promotion. Using local clues is much more effective than using the images of beaches or international facilities that can be found pretty much in every destination in the World.

This study has some limitations. The conceptual framework offered above although supported with various literature, needs empirical validation. Future studies that explore tourist experiences in destinations would identify the specific roles of each stakeholders by looking at lived experiences of tourists at destinations. One might also look into impact of different personal characteristic of tourists in order to identify what type of experiences are sought by different tourist segments.

References

Aggett, M. (2007). What has influenced growth in the UK's boutique hotel sector? *International Journal of Contemporary Hospitality Management, 19*(2), 169–177.

Arnould, E., & Price, L. (1993). River magic: Extraordinary experience and the extended service encounter. *Journal of Consumer Research, 20*, 24–45.

Arva, L., & Deli-Gray, Z. (2011). New types of tourism and tourism marketing in the post-industrial world. *Applied Studies in Agribusiness and Commerce, 5*, 33–37.

Bagaeen, S. (2007). Brand Dubai: The instant city; or the instantly recognizable city. *International Planning Studies, 12*(2), 173–197.

Barnes, S. J., Mattsson, J., & Sorensen, F. (2014). Destination brand experience and visitor behavior: Testing a scale in the tourism context. *Annals of Tourism Research, 48*, 121–139.

Beaumont, N., & Dredge, D. (2010). Local tourism governance: A comparison of three network approaches. *Journal of Sustainable Tourism, 18*(1), 7–28.

Beeho, A. J., & Prentice, R. C. (1997). Conceptualizing the experiences of heritage tourists: a case study of Lanark world heritage village. *Tourism Management, 18*(2), 75–87.

Bordelon, B. M., & Ortiz, M. (2015). An exploratory study of the Destination Management Company (DMC): Building a profile.

Buhalis, D. (2000). Marketing the competitive destination of the future. *Tourism management, 21*(1), 97–116.

Burns, P. M., & Holden, A. (1995). *Tourism: A new perspective.* Upper Saddle River, NJ: Prentice Hall.

Butler, R. W. (1989). Alternative tourism: Pious hope or Trojan Horse? *World Tourism and Leisure, Winter*, 9–17.

Caliskan, V. (2010). Examining cultural tourism attractions for foreign visitors: The case of Camel Wrestling in Selçuk (Ephesus). *Turizam – International Scientific Journal, 14*(1), 22–40.

Cetin, G. (2014). Sustaining tourism development through city tax: The case of Istanbul. *E-Review of Tourism Research, 11*(1), 26–41.

Cetin, G., & Bilgihan, A. (2016). Components of cultural tourists' experiences in destinations. *Current Issues in Tourism, 19*(2), 137–154.

Cetin, G., & Walls, A. (2016). Understanding the customer experiences from the perspective of guests and hotel managers: Empirical findings from luxury hotels in Istanbul, Turkey. *Journal of Hospitality Marketing & Management, 25*(4), 395–424.

Chang, T. C., & Teo, P. (2009). The shophouse hotel: Vernacular heritage in a creative city. *Urban Studies, 46*(2), 341–367.

Cifci, I., Kaya, F., & Akova, O. (2015). Travel motivations and satisfaction levels of excursionists visiting: A case study of Haji Bektash Veli Museum. *Journal of Tourismology, 1*(1), 31–41.

d'Angella, F., & Go, F. M. (2009). Tale of two cities' collaborative tourism marketing: Towards a theory of destination stakeholder assessment. *Tourism Management, 30*(3), 429–440.

Dredge, D. (2001). Local government tourism planning and policy-making in New South Wales: Institutional development and historical legacies. *Current Issues in Tourism*, 4(2-4), 355—380.

Framke, W. (2002). The destination as a concept: A discussion of the business-related perspective versus the socio-cultural approach in tourism theory. *Scandinavian Journal of Hospitality and Tourism*, 2(2), 92—108.

Gunay, Z. (2010). Conservation versus regeneration?: Case of European capital of culture 2010 Istanbul. *European Planning Studies*, 18(8), 1173—1186.

Hackworth, N. (2005). *A hedonist's guide to Istanbul*. London: Hg2.

Hidalgo, M. C., & Hernandez, B. (2001). Place attachment: Conceptual and empirical questions. *Journal of Environmental Psychology*, 21(3), 273—281.

Higginbottom, K., Northrope, C. L., Croft, D. B., Hill, B., & Fredline, E. (2004). The role of kangaroos in Australian tourism. *Australian Mammalogy*, 26(1), 23—32.

Hjalager, A. M. (2010). A review of innovation research in tourism. *Tourism Management*, 31(1), 1—12.

Hood, M. G. (2004). Staying away: Why people choose. Reinventing the museum: Historical and contemporary perspectives on the paradigm shift, 150.

Hosany, S., & Gilbert, D. (2010). Measuring tourists' emotional experiences toward hedonic holiday destinations. *Journal of Travel Research*, 49(4), 513—526.

ICVB. (2014). Retrieved from http://icvb.org.tr/istanbul-by-numbers/#sthash. Gq29C8mY.dpbs. Accessed on February 7, 2016.

Isaac, R. K. (2008). Master of arts in pilgrimage and tourism. *Tourism and Hospitality Planning & Development*, 5(1), 73—76.

Jansson, A. (2002). Spatial phantasmagoria the mediatization of tourism experience. *European Journal of Communication*, 17(4), 429—443.

Kim, J. H., Ritchie, J. B., & McCormick, B. (2010). Development of a scale to measure memorable tourism experiences. *Journal of Travel Research*, 51(1), 12—25.

Kim, Y. H., Yuan, J., Goh, B. K., & Antun, J. M. (2009). Web marketing in food tourism: A content analysis of web sites in West Texas. *Journal of Culinary Science & Technology*, 7(1), 52—64.

Kizilirmak, I., & Cetin, G. (2015). A. P. D. G. The characteristics of Ahilik in grand bazaar and implications on tourist experience.

Larsen, J. (2005). Families seen sightseeing performativity of tourist photography. *Space and Culture*, 8(4), 416—434.

Larsen, S. (2007). Aspects of a psychology of the tourist experience. *Scandinavian Journal of Hospitality and Tourism*, 7(1), 7—18.

Liang, M. Z., & Wang, W. (2010). A study of government regulation of public tourism resources: Developing and protecting [J]. *Human Geography*, 6, 031.

Lu, W., Wang, J., Hua, X. S., Wang, S., & Li, S. (2011, November). Contextual image search. In *Proceedings of the 19th ACM international conference on Multimedia*. ACM (pp. 513—522).

MacCannell, D. (1989). Introduction. *Annals of Tourism Research*, 16(1), 1—6.

Mazumdar, R. (2011). Aviation, tourism and dreaming in 1960s Bombay cinema. *BioScope: South Asian Screen Studies*, 2(2), 129–155.

McIntosh, A. J., & Zahra, A. (2007). A cultural encounter through volunteer tourism: Towards the ideals of sustainable tourism? *Journal of Sustainable Tourism*, 15(5), 541–556.

Michelli, J. (2013). *Leading the Starbucks way: 5 principles for connecting with your customers, your products and your people*. New York, NY: McGraw Hill Professional.

Mill, R. C., & Morrison, A. M. (1985). The tourist system.

Milman, A. (2001). The future of the theme park and attraction industry: A management perspective. *Journal of Travel Research*, 40(2), 139–147.

Mossberg, L. (2007). A marketing approach to the tourist experience. *Scandinavian Journal of Hospitality and Tourism*, 7(1), 59–74.

Murphy, P. E. (2013). *Tourism: A community approach (RLE Tourism)*. Abingdon: Routledge.

Nurse, K. (2004). Trinidad carnival: Festival tourism and cultural industry. *Event Management*, 8(4), 223–230.

Oh, H., Fiore, A. M., & Jeoung, M. (2007). Measuring experience economy concepts: Tourism applications. *Journal of Travel Research*, 46(2), 119–132.

Okumus, B., Okumus, F., & McKercher, B. (2007). Incorporating local and international cuisines in the marketing of tourism destinations: The cases of Hong Kong and Turkey. *Tourism Management*, 28(1), 253–261.

Özsayiner, Z. C. (2008). Calligraphic inscriptions in the Sehzade, Süleymaniye and Selimiye Mosque. *Rocznik Orientalistyczny (Annual Of Oriental Studies)*, 61(2), 103–116.

Pine, J., & Gilmore, J. H. (1999). *The experience economy: Work is a theater and every business a stage*. Boston, MA: Harvard Business Press.

Provincial directorate of culture and tourism. (2015). Retrieved from http://www.istanbulkulturturizm.gov.tr/tr/turizm-istatistik/2015-y%C4%B1l%C4%B1-turizm-istatistikleri. Accessed on January 31, 2016.

Quan, S., & Wang, N. (2004). Towards a structural model of the tourist experience: An illustration from food experiences in tourism. *Tourism Management*, 25(3), 297–305.

Ritchie, B. W., Shipway, R., & Cleeve, B. (2009). Resident perceptions of mega-sporting events: A non-host city perspective of the 2012 London Olympic Games. *Journal of Sport & Tourism*, 14(2-3), 143–167.

Ritzer, G. (2007). Inhospitable hospitality. In *Hospitality: A social lens* (pp. 129–139). Oxford: Elsevier.

Salazar, N. B. (2005). Tourism and glocalization "local" tour guiding. *Annals of Tourism Research*, 32(3), 628–646.

Selin, S. W., & Howard, D. R. (1988). Ego involvement and leisure behavior: A conceptual specification. *Journal of leisure Research*, 20(3), 237–244.

Sengel, T., Karagoz, A., Cetin, G., Dincer, F. I., Ertugral, S. M., & Balõk, M. (2015). Tourists' approach to local food. *Procedia-Social and Behavioral Sciences*, 195, 429–437.

Sheehan, L., Ritchie, J. B., & Hudson, S. (2007). The destination promotion triad: Understanding asymmetric stakeholder interdependencies among the city, hotels, and DMO. *Journal of Travel Research*, 46(1), 64–74.

Smith, V. L. (Ed.). (2012). *Hosts and guests: The anthropology of tourism*. Philadelphia, PA: University of Pennsylvania Press.

Sorensen, F. (2004). *Tourism experience innovation networks*. Roskilde, DK: Center of Service Studies.

Sternberg, E. (1997). The iconography of the tourism experience. *Annals of Tourism Research*, 24(4), 951–969.

Sukalakamala, P., & Boyce, J. B. (2007). Customer perceptions for expectations and acceptance of an authentic dining experience in Thai restaurants. *Journal of Foodservice*, 18(2), 69–75.

Svetlanamihić, A. A., & Supić, D. (2014). Religious tourism and Serbian Orthodox Church. *Pilgrimage and Sacred Places in Southeast Europe: History, Religious Tourism and Contemporary Trends*, 14, 203.

Swarbrooke, J., & Horner, S. (2007). *Consumer behaviour in tourism*. Abingdon: Routledge.

Tkac, J. A. (2014). The role of Bullfighting and FC Barcelona in the Emancipation of Catalonia from Spain. *Revista de humanidades*, (23), 137–156.

Tosun, C. (2000). Limits to community participation in the tourism development process in developing countries. *Tourism Management*, 21(6), 613–633.

Tosun, C. (2001). Challenges of sustainable tourism development in the developing world: The case of Turkey. *Tourism Management*, 22(3), 289–303.

Tucker, H. (2001). Tourists and troglodytes: Negotiating for sustainability. *Annals of Tourism Research*, 28(4), 868–891.

Vale, L. J. (1999). Mediated monuments and national identity. *The Journal of Architecture*, 4(4), 391–408.

Yang, Y. S. (2009). *The resort hotel experience: Conceptualization, measurement, and relation to antecedents and consequences*. Doctoral dissertation. The Hong Kong Polytechnic University.

Yeoman, I., Durie, A., McMahon-Beattie, U., & Palmer, A. (2005). Capturing the essence of a brand from its history: The case of Scottish tourism marketing. *The Journal of Brand Management*, 13(2), 134–147.

Zeppel, H., & Hall, M. C. (1992). Arts and heritage tourism. In H. Zeppel, M. C. Hall, B. Weiler, & M. C. Hall (Eds.), *Special interesttourism* (pp. 47–69). London: Belhaven.

Zhang, J., Inbakaran, R. J., & Jackson, M. S. (2006). Understanding community attitudes towards tourism and host—Guest interaction in the urban—Rural border region. *Tourism Geographies*, 8(2), 182–204.

5 Social Media and the Co-Creation of Tourism Experiences

Marianna Sigala

ABSTRACT

Purpose – The chapter aims to investigate the role and the impact of social media in influencing and shaping (new) tourism experiences.

Methodology/approach – A service dominant logic and co-creation approach and concepts was adopted for examining how the social media can influence interactions and participation that represent two major sources of tourism experiences.

Findings – The chapter provides several arguments showing how social media-enabled interactions and participation can facilitate, foster, and expand the experience co-creation process by altering: when, how, why, what, by whom, and how tourism experiences are co-created.

Research limitations/implications – The chapter develops and argues a theoretical framework that needs to be further validated, refined, and expanded in various contexts.

Practical implications – The chapter provides several examples showing the practical implications on how tourists and tourism firms use the social media for enriching their interactions and participation in the co-creation of tourism experiences.

Social implication – The chapter also illustrates how the social interactions supported and fostered by the social media can be used for influencing, shaping and promoting specific tourism experiences (i.e., sustainable tourism behavior, socially responsible tourism development).

Originality/value – Past research on technology enhanced tourism experiences has adopted a phenomenological approach to explaining experience creation. The chapter expands this literature by advocating the individualized and the socially co-constructed nature of tourism experiences as well as by adopting an intersubjective approach for explaining how the social media enable an iterative process among the tourists' and their social context that in turn is responsible for the continuous formation of tourism experiences.

Keywords: Social media; experiences; tourism; co-creation; interactions; participation

Introduction

The social media have empowered tourists by changing: the way they access, share, distribute, discuss, and create information; with whom, how, and when they interact; and how and when they participate in business operations (Sigala, Christou, & Gretzel, 2012). In this vein, the social media transform the tourists from receivers of messages to experiences, from interpreters to creators of meaning, and from simply observers and consumers of tourism services to active actors. Active participation and interactions are sources of experiences, while they also increase the level of tourists' engagement into the experience and so, they make it more memorable (Campos, Mendes, Valle, & Scott, 2015). As the new tourists prefer to interact, learn, and apply knowledge rather than simply observe people and see places, a continuously increasing number of tourists and tourism suppliers are adopting the social media for enhancing the tourism experiences.

However, despite the increasing role of the Internet and the social media to transform tourism experience, the literature has been limited so far to provide a theoretical framework explaining how and why the social media can transform service encounters into experiential and valuable experiences. This is because most of the studies have primarily focused on simply describing the type of tourism experiences that single social media tools (e.g., blogs, social networks, and virtual words) can enable (Tussyadiah & Fesenmaier, 2009), and few recent studies (Neuhofer, Buhalis, & Ladkin, 2013, 2016) have also looked on the technology enabled experience co-creation possibilities in tourism. However, to better understand how to use the technologies for transforming tourism experiences, the focus should not be on the technology features and advances *per se*, but rather on how the technologies are impacting on the experience generation processes. As experiences are formed, shaped, and co-created through interactions and participation (Andrades & Dimanche, 2014), there is a need to understand how the social media influence the ways in which the various tourism actors interact and participate in tourism. Moreover, given the subjective and personal nature of tourism experiences, past studies have examined the impact of technology on tourism experiences from a single customer focused perspective. However, the latest marketing thinking recognizes that the individualized experiences are enabled but they also activate socially constructed experiences. The social media provide the tourists with a platform for creating and storing a memory of their past experiences as well as for sharing, promoting, and discussing their experiences. This stored memory of experiences and their discussions can in turn create fashions, modes and meanings that can ultimately influence the experience co-creation processes of individuals (what, how, and why people want to live specific experiences). In this vein, research investigating the influence of social media on tourism experiences should examine how the social media impact the formation of tourism experiences from both an individual customer centric and a wider service ecosystem perspective that recognizes the impact of the dialectical processes taking place among various actors and at various levels (i.e., individual, network, and market-economy level) on the formation of experiences.

In this vein, this chapter aims to investigate how and what tourism experiences the social media can enable and generate. To that end, the chapter focuses on examining how the interactions and participation supported by the social media can influence what we experience, how we experience it, and why we are experiencing it. As the social media empower customers and other stakeholders to co-create experiences and value, the chapter adopts a co-creation and service dominant logic (SDL) perspective and concepts for investigating the impact of social media on the tourism experience co-creation processes within a service eco-system. To that end, the chapter first explains the role of interactions and participation in forming experiences, and it then discusses how the features and the functionality of the social media can transform the former. The chapter also provides various examples showing how tourists and tourism firms use the social media for enhancing interactions and participation and enriching tourism experiences.

Interactions and Participation in Tourism Experiences: A Co-Creation and SDL Perspective

Experiences allow tourists to do things rather than just look at them and engage in activities that can help them to develop their identity, personal competencies and creative potential, as well as cherish meaningful personal narratives and stimulate intellectual growth. Thus, experiences arise from activities in which the tourists actively participate in various forms, i.e. cognitively/mentally, emotionally, physically, and/or spiritually (Campos et al., 2015). Active participation require tourists to use and share their skills and resources. Interactions of tourists with the tourism environment, its elements, other people and tourism information are also sources of experiences (Tussyadiah, Fesenmaier, & Yoo, 2008). Such interactions can also stimulate personal and/or collective identity (Kreziak & Frochot, 2011; Lugosi & Walls, 2013) which in turn gives a social and emotional dimension and meaning to experiences (e.g., desire to belong, communities).

In reviewing the literature, Campos et al. (2015) identified the major issues related to the generation of tourism experiences:

- experiences may engage individuals at different levels, for example, physically, emotionally, and/or intellectually
- experiences derive from interactions taking place not only between the firms and the customers, but also with objects, processes, the environment, and other individuals
- experiences are not generated only at the consumption stage (when the service is used), but across all the customer touch points during the whole customer lifecycle (i.e., before, during, and after consumption).

Hence, the customer experience is viewed as an evolution of the concept of relationship between the company and the customer, as it expands the experience generation process to include multiple interactions and at various customer touch points that the firm cannot even control (e.g., tourists to tourists interactions, customers' cognitive processes when interacting with tourism information) (Heinonen, Strandvik, & Voima, 2013). This also implies that tourism firms should try to create opportunities to integrate the tourists into all their value chain processes, as the greater the customer engagement and participation in various processes, the richer the customer experiences can become. This is in line with the co-creation and SDL perspectives advocating that value is not embedded in products/services, but rather it is co-created when people use the service/product, interact, and exchange resources with other actors, as well as participate in various value chain operations. In this vein, the customer experience is also defined (Gentile, Spiller, & Noci, 2007) as "*a set of interactions between a customer and a product, a company, or part of its organization, which provoke a reaction. This experience is strictly personal and implies the customer's involvement at different levels (rational, emotional, sensorial, physical and spiritual).*"

Experiences are also considered as subjective and highly personalized phenomena, and the phenomenology of experiences is usually analyzed in terms of their intensity, memorability, the meanings, and values (benefits) that the customers get (e.g., functional, emotional, cognitive, sensorial, social/relational experiences, and values) (Campos et al., 2015). The subjective nature of experience and value co-creation has also been at the core of the SDL foundational premises, but recent research (Edvardsson, Tronvoll, & Gruber, 2011) has started to shift from a purely phenomenological perspective towards an intersubjective orientation (rooted in social constructionism) for explaining experience co-creation. According to the latter, all knowledge is communal, contingent upon human practices, locally constructed in and out of interactions between individuals and their world, and developed and transmitted through socially mediated discourse. Within this perspective, the consumers' performance of socially constructed practices are deemed to frame consumer meaning and sense making of their situated brand experiences, which then become integrated in consumers' stock of social knowledge, thus impacting future brand experiences (Thompson, Locander, & Pollio, 1989).

In other words, experiences are enabled by and they actualize socially constructed experiences or else what we experience and how we interpret it is influenced, determined, and framed based on our social context, while what we experience creates meanings that in turn also shape, give, and maintain the form of our social context. This dialectical and reciprocal relation between individualized experiences and socially constructed experiences is enabled and fostered through the people's interactions that also expand beyond the firm-customer interactions (e.g., interactions with communities, family networks, institutions, and culture). This view recognizes that (a) lived experiences are not only personally defined and interpreted, but they are also framed by broader social conventions (e.g., cultural frames of reference, social norms), because such conventions both enable and constrain people's understanding and meaning of lived experiences and (b) experiences are formed and iteratively co-constructed in a dialectical fashion between socially constructed experiences, individualized, and collective experiences of others.

This intersubjective and social constructionism approach towards experience formation is compatible with the evolution of the SDL premises advocating that experiential value is co-created within a context (service ecosystem) that is: multilevel and socially defined (i.e., a shift from value-in-use to value-in-(social)-context). Thus, experiences are formed and evaluated within a three level context namely the micro, meso, and macro levels and a meta layer that allows for oscillation among the other three levels of context (Chandler & Lusch, 2014). The micro level represents individual evaluations of experiences, the meso level refers to relational norms and the macro level refers to collective meanings. Specifically, the meso level of context includes dynamic webs of actors, their relationships and their structural positions, who integrate and exchange resources to co-create value for themselves and for others (Vargo & Lusch, 2008). The macro level refers to the social norms or "institutions" that guide and/or motivate the actors' interaction and highlights that the social context of experience co-creation is not only composed by the variety of the actors' inter-connections and relationships.

In this vein, service ecosystems enable the formation of experiences at three levels: at a micro level, the believes, social values, perceptions and understandings of actors drive their behavior and evaluations of the experiential value creation processes and outcomes; at a meso level, networks enable access to resources through exchanges and interactions; and at a macro level, interaction within and among networks drives the (re)development of norms and meanings, which in turn are central for determining what resources are and how they can be integrated so, people can form their experiences and values. The impact of the micro level on experience formation is highlighted by the phenomenological nature of value, while studies measuring the impact of the composition, the links (weak or strong ties) and interactions among the actors of the service ecosystems highlight the impact of the meso level on experience creation (Chandler & Lusch, 2014). The macro level of service ecosystems suggests that as actors co-create value, they not only draw on, but they also contribute to the (re)formation of the social context through which value is derived. Indeed, it is generally agreed (Edvardsson et al., 2011; Kallio, 2015) that the interactions and integration of resources among actors contribute both to the co-creation of experiential value and to the "contextualization" or formation of the social context that frames these experiences. For example, Edvardsson et al. (2011) proposed the concept of "value in-*social*-context" as a means for studying how contexts are socially constructed through the enactment of practices and exchange of resources that lead not only to value creation but also to the formation and reformation of social structures.

Thus, from a co-creation and SDL perspective, the experience co-creation processes in a service ecosystem should consider not only "**who**" participates in resource exchange and value creation, but also (Ordanini & Parasuraman, 2012): the medium – "**what**" is exchanged for value; the meaning – "**why**" the exchange takes place; the usage – "**when**" value is realized; and the network – "**how**" interactions among actors are organized. The following sections use this framework of experience co-creation for discussing the impact of social media on tourism experience.

Social Media Features and Tourism Experiences

The proliferation of social media (e.g., blogs, wikis, forums, social networks, folksonomies) have transformed the way experiences and value are created, as social media are a principal engine fostering customer empowerment, engagement, and co-creation (Neuhofer, Buhalis, & Ladkin, 2012; Sigala et al., 2012). Indeed, by empowering tourists to interact; collaborate; generate; share; discuss; and co-construct information, experiences, and opinions, the social media support; and motivate tourists to connect, engage, and co-create their experiences with the firms and a plethora of actors on an unprecedented scale. Social media had turned the Internet into an immense space of empowered consumers, social interactions, and collaboration, whereby the tourists play a central role in both the co-creation and consumption of their experiences. In general, the social media possesses the following major features empowering the tourists to exchange resources and actively participate in the co-creation of their experiences and value:

- sharing: the social media enable tourists to share multimedia content (i.e., text, photos, videos) in a fast, efficient and international scale.
- (virtual) presence: the social media are accessible at any device, any place and any time, which creates a sense of always connectiveness with others and omnipresence; tourists never feel alone even if they travel alone; by sharing their experiences on social media, people get the sense that they are always (virtually) surrounded and observed by others (who might be known or unknown social media users, located in various geographical places and time zones), with whom they can also interact for exchanging opinions, experiences, and information resources. This feeling of the virtual social presence of others has significant effects on what tourists experience, why they wish to experience it and how they evaluate their experiences.
- Conversations: the social media enable the tourists to initiate and participate in dialogues for commenting and exchanging perspectives about experiences. Online dialogues and interactions can have a significant impact on the co-construction of content and meaning, which in turn influence the way tourists interpret, select, and evaluate their experiences
- Identity: tourists build and promote their identity by sharing content, interacting and networking with others. The construction of self-identity is also found to be one of the major motivators for using social media.
- Relationships: the tourists can use the social media for identifying, networking, and exchanging resources with others, which ultimately helps them build bonds and relations with them.
- Groups: the social media enable the tourists to create and participate in groups within which they can interact, collaborate, and co-create value. By participating in groups, the tourists

aggregate their power and resources in order to have a great influence in the economy and society (e.g., the Facebook group aiming to persuade tourists to boycott all-inclusive holidays in Greece and select independent holidays to support the locals, https://www.facebook.com/SupportGreeceBoycutAllInclusive/?fref=ts)

Social Media-Enabled Interactions and Tourism Experiences

Because of their features, the social media provide the tools to facilitate, enhance, and tourists' experiences in numerous ways by enabling interactions during all the stages of the tourists' journey:

- Before the trip, the tourists can search, access, and read travel information, reviews, experiences, as well as interact with others for: learning about destinations and their experience opportunities; planning their itineraries; and selecting tourism suppliers and services. By doing this, the tourists can reduces their risks in planning and purchasing something that does not meet their expectations, preferences, and interests as well as they can design fast and efficient personalized trip experiences.
- By viewing and sharing travel experiences and information on social media, the tourists gain a virtual experience and understanding of places, cultures, and destinations. In this vein, the social media enable a new type of tourism experience, which is usually referred to as immersive virtual, augmented reality or technology-mediated experience (Tussyadiah & Fesenmaier, 2009; Xiang & Gretzel, 2010)
- During their trip, the social media enable the tourists to stay connected and/or to connect with others (e.g., residents, friends, etc.) for sharing their experiences; obtaining travel resources and planning their trip on route; and enriching their tourism experience; and feel connected with their family/friends.
- After the trip, the social media provide the space whereby the tourists can reflect, revive, and create memories of their experiences by sharing their resources. By doing so, the tourists do not only enrich their own tourism experience, but they also create an online repository of travel resources that can be useful to others for planning and organizing their trips.

During the last decades, the increasing use of social media through mobile technologies enables the emergence of mobile and network sociality, as it pluralizes the time and social spaces whereby people can interact and keep social activities with others who are not even co-present. This, continuous and instant communication with others can enrich and trigger new tourism experiences through reflection, virtual presence, emotions, and new interpretations. For example, research shows that while traveling, people use access social networks through their smartphones for connecting with others for both functional and social reasons (i.e., doing work, checking e-mails, communication, entertaining, travel planning), which in turn impacts their emotions, place activities, and perceptions of experiences (Wang & Fesenmaier, 2013; Wang, Park, & Fesenmaier, 2012). In other words, accessing the social media through mobile technologies has a spillover effect whereby tourists carry out lifestyle habits and work while traveling, which however may in turn negatively inhibit their tourism experience (i.e., technology accessibility creates people an enhanced stressed to always stay connected with work and family/friends). Recently, Neuhofer (2016b) found that the omnipresence social connectivity enabled by mobile social media usage leads to value co-destruction and negatively influences the tourists' experience, because tourists perceive that the use of social media as: a barrier to escapism from everyday life and relaxation; an interference of "living" the experience; and a pressure and addiction (e.g., people's emotions and experiences are negatively influenced when they cannot access their social networks, interact with others, and check their messages).

Mobile research also confirms studies in human-computer interaction advocating that people can perceive technologies as social actors and develop social relations and perceptions with them. Travelers were found to assign three social roles to their smartphones (Tussyadiah, 2014a, 2014b): a companion, a personal assistant, and a personal guide/mentor. Hence, people anthropomorphize (i.e., attribute humanlike traits to non-human agents) and so, react/relate socially to smartphones in the same manner as they respond to other people. The tourists' perceptions of their mobile devices as "travel buddies" implies that technologies and social media can be viewed as a new actor influencing tourism experiences. Recent research in SDL recognizes that technology applications can have agency power and features and so, they can be regarded as co-creator actors.

In short, the social interaction affordances of the social media empower the tourists to enrich, enhance, and personalize their experiences by enabling them to augment their social capital. The social capital consists of three interrelated dimensions assisting tourists to interact and exchange resources for co-creating experiences:

• The structural capital representing the connection patterns among actors: the social media enable the tourists to find and interact with other experts, tourists, and virtual groups; networking ensures access to the necessary travel resources for co-creating tourism experiences
• The relational capital referring to the type and quality of an actor's personal relations; the closer the relation among social media users, the greater the commitment to exchange reliable and credible travel resources and collaborate/interact with others
• The cognitive capital referring to the degree to which an individual shares a common code and systems of meaning within a community. The share of travel experiences, opinions, reviews, and their discussions on social media create a permanent repository of travel resources that is accessible to others for future use. In addition, the scale and amount of these online public discussions can create but also promote travel fashions, lifestyles, and new meanings of tourism experiences. Hence, the cognitive capital identifies two major forces shaping and driving human behavior: mimicry and normative forces. The online promotion of travel experiences attracts the interest and travel desire of others, while due to peer pressures, tourists can be "forced" to select, live, and promote online tourism experiences that do not divert from the "peer group" behavior and/or from the online self-identity that they wish to construct and present online.

In other words, the concept of social capital enables us to understand the impact of social media on forming tourism experiences not only at an individual level, but also at a meso and macro level. At a meso level, the structural and relational capital show how the social media enable the tourists to find, create, and participate in networks in order to access and exchange resources for co-creating experiences in a service ecosystem. At a macro level, the cognitive capital explains how the social media support an intersubjective and social constructionism approach to tourism experiences, as the social media support the development of a dialectical process between individualized, collective/community and socially constructed travel experiences. For example, Payne, Storbacka, Frow, and Knox (2009) have shown how online customers' interactions and dialogues contribute to the co-construction and interpretation of brand meanings, experiences, and fashions.

Table 1 provides some examples showing how social media-enabled interactions developed at different ecosystem levels can influence the formation of tourism experiences. The examples recognize the continuous formation of tourism experiences in a dialectical fashion between socially constructed experiences, individualized and collective experiences. The social interaction affordances of the social media fortifies the intersubjective and phenomenological nature and generation processes of tourism experiences, and explain why the way tourists select, understand, and evaluate their experiences reflects both socially constructed and individualized meanings. This also means that experience formation is not always a deliberate process, but rather it emerges through the tourists' behavioral and mental processes when tourists' share, discuss, and interpret their experiences within their (online) social ecosystem. Consequently, research investigating tourism experiences should look beyond the line of visibility focused on visible customer-firm interactions, to the invisible mental life and social interactions of the tourists (as people having various and multiple social roles).

However, research investigating the meso and macro level impacts of social media-enabled interactions on the tourism experiences does not exist yet. Nevertheless, Magasic (2016) recently developed two new concepts (rooted in past tourism and namely, the "Selfie Gaze" and the "Social Media Pilgrimage") for explaining how the social media influence what and why we experience it.

Photographs have always been a mode of self-expression, and so, the phenomenon of taking and sharing a selfie on social media is currently receiving a high uptake as a mode of self-representation; online identity construction; communication; and appease of the crowd. Because of that, the tourists' journeys and experiences are lived in order to be photographed within the eyes and scrutiny of others. Past research has shown that people change their behavior when they are, or they believe that they are, under the scrutiny of others. Since the social media create a feeling of virtual social presence of others, the use of "selfie gaze" may drive and press tourists to seek out elements in the destination and in their experiences that they think that they will be

Table 1. Social Media Interactions Supporting the Formation of Tourism Experiences as an Iterative Co-construction Process between Individualized and Socially Constructed Experiences.

Level of interaction	How Interactions Take Place: Structure and Direction of Interactions among Actors and Objects in the Service Ecosystem	Description	Examples of Social Media Interactions
Macro level	We-in-content: collective social networked interaction with the online content	Tourists' collaborative interactions with online content for society use: how does our interactions can influence societal norms, values, lifestyles and fashions	Tourists aggregate their power and interactions for achieving a social goal (e.g., support sustainable traveling, volunteer tourism, environmental behavior while traveling, etc.): tourism crowdsourcing, crowdproduction and crowdfunding projects
Meso level	Me-to-we-in-content: individualized networked social interaction with online content	Tourists' individualized interactions with online travel content are networked for social use: how do we share online travel content for sharing, reflecting, and discussing our travel experiences?	Learn, network, follow, make friends, and interact with others through social media
	me&me&me&-with-content: individualized networked interact with online content	Tourists' individualized interactions with the online travel content are aggregated at a network (meso level): how does the overall interactions of others with the online content compare with my social values, experiences, and preferences?	Read all the comments, tags, likes, shares, etc. of online content

Table 1. (*Continued*)

Level of interaction	How Interactions Take Place: Structure and Direction of Interactions among Actors and Objects in the Service Ecosystem	Description	Examples of Social Media Interactions
Micro level	Me-with-the content: individualized interaction with online content	Tourists individually interact with online travel resources: how does the online content reflects and compares to my experiences, social values, and preferences?	Tagging, liking, disliking, favorite, follow, comment on online content (e.g., online photographs, videos, posts)
	Content-to-me: individualized passive reception of online content	Tourists consumes online travel content	Reading online reviews, looking at photos and videos

approved by the imagined online audience. This means that the social media travel era creates a selfie gaze paradigm whereby the tourists enact certain practices, live and share specific experiences, because their own self-representation may be viewed by their peers and a potentially unlimited audience. Hence, the "selfie gaze" impact of the social media on tourism experiences means that (Magasic, 2016) tourism experiences are lived with an audience in mind; selfies showing the ways and the feelings of tourists while experiencing their trips are carefully constructed to be consumed by others; self-esteem is built based on the fan base that the selfie can create; while the tourists' satisfaction does not derive from the experience itself, its performance and its appeal to the tourist, but it is rather determined by the number of the "likes," "shares," "followers," "friends," etc. generated by the sharing of the experience.

The concept of the "social media pilgrimage" recognizes the role of social media to enable and support a virtual, emotional, and imaginative mode of travel, preceding as well as running parallel to the physical journey (Magasic, 2016). This mediatized journey is enacted within the tourists' selfie gaze through that the tourists construct their self-presentation and their moments of the physical journey, which are in turn edited in ways that are conversant and compatible with the tourists' ideal self-image and the feedback received from the online audience. The feedback loop between the enactment of specific real experiences (for sharing them online and constructing self-identities) and the virtual mode of travel, implies that the social media play an integrative role between the mediatized and the actual physical tourism experience.

The selfie gaze and the social media pilgrimage recognize the affordances of the social media to transform the tourism experiences at a meso level (i.e., networks, audience, and peers) by influencing the way travel is experienced and the reasons why it is experienced. Indeed, based on a recent report (InterContinental Hotels Group, 2014): *"Younger generations no longer travel to 'discover' themselves, but to say something about themselves to their social peers. It may even be that these travellers now think about an experience in terms of how they will share it with others"* (p. 28). In other words, sharing travel experiences is a major reason for experiencing travel moments, which in turn highlights that the social media can function either as a mediator or as the core experience itself. However, the discussion of these two concepts has ignored the interplay and reciprocal influence between individualized and socially constructed tourism experiences. The mass social interactions afforded by the social media imply that one should also consider: the meso level impact of the others' individualized mediatized experiences on the individualized tourists' experiences and the macro level impact of the socially constructed experiences on creating trends, fashions, travel lifestyles, and cultures that in turn can constrain and enable the enactment and interpretation of individualized tourism experiences.

Social Media-Enabled Participation and Tourism Experiences

The social media have empowered tourists to become active co-designers, co-producers, and co-marketers of their personalized experiences (Sigala et al., 2012). Tourism firms are exploiting the social media tools for supporting the tourists' participation at any stage of the customer journey process and value creation system (Prahalad & Ramaswamy, 2004) (Table 2). Indeed, the use of social media have enabled new processes (e.g., crowdsourcing, co-production, co-creation, Neuhofer, 2016a) of how, when, and where consumers can play a role in the creation of their experiences. Co-creation means that both the firms and the tourists need to exchange and integrate their own resources for co-creating value (co-creation encounters). However, co-creation also takes place in the private spheres of the customer and the firm, which are usually invisible and out of the control of the other party (Heinonen et al., 2013). By providing their resources and participating in value operations as partial employees (prosumers), the tourists transform service encounters into meaningful and personalized experiences. However, the use of social media for developing experience co-creation opportunities creates value for both parties (Sigala, 2012):

- The tourists can design personalized and more meaningful experiences, get more satisfaction by controlling the quality and type of their experiences as well as from the experience co-creation process itself;
- The firms get value by: using customers as partial employees (operational efficiencies) and complementing/enriching processes traditionally performed only by the firm (employees) (e.g., market research is enriched with online customer data); and by designing customer touch points that enable customer

Table 2.   Social Media-Enabled Participation in Tourism Experiences: Co-Creation Opportunities and Processes.

Customer Sphere of Co-Creation Processes	Customer Learning and Interactions within the Customer Ecosystem			C2C Interactions, Participation and Interactions within Customer Communities, Crowdsourcing, Customer Collaborations
	Co-creation of tourism experience			
Customer journey	*Pre-trip*	*During the trip*	*After the trip*	
Co-creation: customer-firm encounters	↔	↔	↔	
Service value chain	*Service design and innovation*	*Service production and delivery*	*Marketing and after sales-support*	
Firm sphere of co-creation processes	Organizational design of experience co-creating opportunities			Integration of distribution channels, process re-engineering, employee-to-employee interactions, big data,
	Organizational learning, open innovation and dynamic capabilities			

participation, which is viewed and managed as both a customer learning and a customer experience — value enhancing opportunity (Sigala, 2017) in order to maximize customer engagement and attachment/loyalty to the firm.

Table 3 provides several examples showing how tourism firms have used the social media for designing and providing tourism co-creation opportunities that empower the tourists to participate as value co-creators into various operations. The highlighted value chain operations represent the processes whereby the customer and/or his/her customer-generated-content/resources are used for enriching and informationalizing the process. Customer participation in experience co-creation can be at any level of engagement: from very passive to very active such as

- Reading and viewing comments contributed by other customers for designing his/her own experience
- Commenting, sharing, discussing, and evaluating the comments — contributions of other customers
- Creating and contributing content and actions (e.g., creation of a blog, virtual community, creation, and upload of a video/photo)
- Using the firm's infrastructure not only for designing its own personalized experience but also for producing, selling, and promoting it (e.g., the application of Domino's pizza or Easycar car rental community that empower customers to become entrepreneurs and pizza/car rental providers by outsourcing operations such as production, delivery of pizzas, cleaning/insurance of cars, to the firms' infrastructure, and value chain system)
- Becoming the tourism entrepreneur him/her self (e.g., sharing economy whereby people become hoteliers/restaurateurs/travel guides selling and promoting their own services online, Sigala, 2014).

Conclusions

The chapter has shown that the social media do not only alter the nature of current experiences, but they also facilitate the transformation and continuous formation of experiences as well as the formation and creation of new types of tourism experiences, such as

Table 3. Co-Creation Opportunities of Tourism Experiences Supporting the Tourists' Participation into the Firm's Value Chain System Operations.

Service/Product Design	Production/Delivery/Operations	Marketing/Sales/Distribution, CRM	After Sales-Support
http://travel-brilliantly.marriott.com/your-ideas			
The travel brilliantly CE activity by Marriott is a crowdsourcing application enabling the customers to generate and share online ideas on how to innovate their travel and hotel experience. Ideas submitted by customers enable the firm to understand customers' expectations and needs, develop successful new services and inspire other customers to select the hotels and experiences			
	Meat & Seat program by KLM		
	When checking in, people can share their social profile (e.g., Google +, Facebook, Linkedin) with other checked-in passengers. The application allow travelers to see with whom else they are co-traveling and where this person is seating, so that they can select to seat next to a person with similar profile, interests and preferences. The application empower travelers to more actively participate in the "production" of their flight experience, take more control and responsibility of the quality of the flight experience that they can have, as well as promote to their social network friends their travel itineraries (e.g., online marketing).		
		theedit.sixsenses.com by **Six Senses Hotels Resorts Spas**	
		The hotel has developed a social media feed aggregator that aggregates user generated and brand content through the use of hashtags and key words in social platform posts from Facebook, Pinterest, YouTube, Twitter, and Instagram. The aggregated crowdsourced content is continuously published and updated daily on a dedicated micropage of the brands' website (theedit.sixsenses.com). The collection and publication of crowdsourced content can inspire and persuade website visitors to make an hotel booking, it reinforces and enhances brand image development, while by analyzing such content the company can better understands its customers, their needs, preferences, and uses of its resorts and spas, so that it can in turn feedback new product development processes.	

Table 3. (Continued)

Service/Product Design	Production/Delivery/Operations	Marketing/Sales/Distribution, CRM	After Sales-Support

The world's first Tweet Experience hotel. @SolWaveHouse Hotel, located in the beach of Magaluf (Mallorca) has created the first ever "Tweet Experience Hotel" in the world.

https://twitter.com/_solhouse

The hotel makes an innovative use of Twitter for supporting and fostering B2C and C2C co-creation and interactions in order to empower its guests to co-produce their hotel experiences. By using Twitter for sharing hotel experiences, socializing with other guests and liaising with hotel staff for customer support and concierge services, the guests are not only empowered to actively participate and co-create their hotel experience, but they also develop relationships with the brand, other guests, and the hotel brand community, while their generated content in Twitter can attract and inspire others to also book and stay at the hotel.

To co-create their Twitter experience, guests are offered free wifi Internet throughout the hotel resort and they are invited to share content and communicate with others through the hotel Twitter page by using related hashtags:

As soon as they book, guests join the #SocialWave community and they are invited to share their best moments
○ Guest service is available via Twitter @SOLWAVEHOUSE #HOUSESERVICE #HOUSESERVICE1. The "Tweet Concierge" is available from the moment that the guests make a reservation and after their departure
○ Guests can enjoy a very different and unique experience as well as receive exclusive assistance in the #TweetPartySuite rooms

The main engine of the whole experience is a virtual community called **#SocialWave**, only available from the hotel's wifi, to which clients can access from their mobile or electronic device, registering with their twitter accounts. Two Concierge on Twitter are devoted exclusively to meet guest requests via Twitter and generate conversation in this virtual community, acting as a link between all of them. Thus, guests can know and chat with each other, experience, flirt, compete in contests, share photos, etc. Every corner of the hotel is designed to engage in a new conversation. The hotel has also created the new **#PartySuites** spacious, equipped with all the details and up to 4 people. In these suites, users can enjoy with

Table 3. *(Continued)*

Service/Product Design	Production/Delivery/Operations	Marketing/Sales/Distribution, CRM	After Sales-Support

their friends treats like a bottle of champagne and special sports drinks on arrival, 20% discount on all bars and restaurants in Wave House, VIP hammocks and customizable mini bar, plus a free drink in the #TwitterPoolParty to be held every (Friday) at the hotel.

Guests feedback and content shared via Twitter can be later aggregated, analyzed, and interpreted for assisting the hotel with new product-service development processes.

The TripAdvisor business model heavily depends on the amount and quality of travel reviews uploaded by its users. To crowdsource content, foster/instil CE and motivate website users to upload content (travel reviews) and interact with the website (i.e., comment and rate others' reviews), Tripadvisor has gamified several of "operations/tasks" in which travelers have to get engaged. For example, travelers are motivated to upload travel reviews (play task), because they get "points" and badges. To ensure the upload of quality reviews, travelers' are also awarded with "helpful votes" and compliments by other users when their travel reviews are found useful. A scorecard also shows the (system and social) points gained by every website user when the user contributes content on the website either by uploading reviews and/or interacting (chatting) with other users. This funware does not only provides motivational affordances that induce the travelers to use the website tasks, but it also creates an engaging and gamefull user experience by generating experiential values and benefits to the users (such as, autonomy, achievement, competence and "competition"), that in turn lock users into a constant gamefull experience/flow whereby the users continuously strive to improve their travel profile, ego and self-esteem. Hence, the gamification of this CE application uses game mechanics that aim to trigger the travelers' motivation as well as create flow and gamefull experiences (psychological outcomes) that can in turn increase the travelers' engagement with the website tasks (i.e., support and foster CE and ensure the behavioral outcomes of CE).

Sharing economy online communities (accommodation airbnb.com, http://www.meetup.com citizen/residents groups and meetings/activities, uber. com for transportation, locals becoming travel guides, and selling travel services http://www.verylocaltrip.com/, https://www.triip.me/, https:// www.triip.me/rences, locals residents providing authentic meal experiences http://www.eatwith.com/, etc.)

Table 3.   (*Continued*)

Service/Product Design	Production/Delivery/Operations	Marketing/Sales/Distribution, CRM	After Sales-Support
		Customers become entrepreneurs and providers, producers, marketers, and distributors of their OWN tourism experiences. These type of tourism experiences are also supposed to be more authentic than the commercially available tourism experiences.	
	Customers are empowered to become tourism entrepreneurs by outsourcing part of the value chain operations to the firm		
	https://www.pizzamogul.com.au/#!/home		
	https://www.dominos.com.au/inside-dominos/pizza-mogul?gclid=Clidg_RwcsCFQoQvQodPf4NUA&gclsrc=aw.ds&dclid=CJmRnP_RwcsCFVCYvAodqtAAXg		
		Customers design and promote their own pizzas, use the infrastructure and value chain system of the firm for producing, selling, and delivering their own designed pizzas (outsource operations to the firm). Customers are rewarded for their co-creation efforts (pizza design, pizza's online promotion in social media) by obtaining a commission from Domino based on the sales' revenue generated by selling their pizzas.	
		https://carclub.easycar.com/?utm_source=broker_homepage&utm_medium=top_menu&_ga=1.155075068.518269460.1458351159	
		Customers use the infrastructure, value chain operations and online community of Easycar for: promoting and renting their own cars. Customers have to pay Easycar a fee and a commission for the services the firm provides them (e.g., insuring and cleaning the car, providing a platform for finding and evaluating the quality of potential customers to rent the car).	

Table 4.   The Role and Impact of Social Media in Co-creating Tourism Experience.

Dimensions of Experience Co-Creation Based on SDL and Co-creation	Social Media Influence
How experience value is formed	Social media enable tourists and actors to co-create experiences by connecting, networking, interacting, and exchanging travel resources (physical, cultural, political, social, economical)
	Tourism experiences are continuously formed in a dynamic, iterative, and emerging processes through actors interactions within the service ecosystem
Experiences are continually formed and not only deliberately co-created	The social media create a memory/repository of past experiences that creates fashions, modes, and meanings which in turn influence experience co-creation. In this vein, experience co-creation should go beyond the temporary (current) value chain system and it should include all the accumulated and past experiences of tourists that may influence the formation understanding, interpretation, and evaluation of future tourism experiences.
Where/when experience is co-created	Within and between the customer and the firm sphere (i.e., also outside of the control of the firm)
	During all the stages of the tourists' journey
	Along all the stages of the value creation chain
	Mobile and network sociality enabled by the ubiquitous access to social media expands experience co-creation at any place, any time, any device and with any actor (even if he/she is not co-present)
Who creates experiences	Social media themselves contribute to experience co-creation by being social actors (anthropomorphism effects)
A collective process but also individualized process	Customers, communities, firms, and various other connected actors

Table 4. (*Continued*)

Dimensions of Experience Co-Creation Based on SDL and Co-creation	Social Media Influence
Why experience is co-created	Social media influencing what and why we experience it by forming social values, norms, and institutions
	Social media are used for enriching and enhancing tourism experiences
	Social media use as the tourism experience itself
	Social media use for self-representation
What is co-created	A collective sense of tourism experiences, fashions, and travel trends
	An intersubjective but also individualized socially constructed tourism experience
	An authentic tourism experience co-created by the customers' themselves (e.g., sharing economy)

- Social media-assisted and facilitated tourism experiences (when tourists share travel resources for assisting others' travel planning processes)
- Social media-enriched and augmented tourism experiences (when online travel resources enable tourists to make experiences more personalized, meaningful, imaginative, and emotional)
- Social media-formed tourism experiences (when social media interactions among various actors at micro, meso, and macro level enable an iterative co-construction process of experience meaning, understanding, and evaluation)
- Social media-mediated tourism experiences (the virtual experience of a destination)
- Social media as the tourism experience itself (the use of the social media while traveling is the core and major purpose of having a tourism experience, that is, the social media become a tourism experience)
- Social media-empowered tourism experiences (when customers are empowered to participate and engage in the value co-creation processes of the firm, that is, the customer is embedded within the firm's value system)
- Social media-enabled tourism experiences (i.e., the use of social media for creating new types of tourism experiences, for example, when the customer uses the social media for becoming a tourism entrepreneur providing tourism experiences, for example, sharing economy, the customer uses the firm's infrastructure and value system for providing – marketing tourism experiences).

Social media-co-created tourism experiences are enabled and supported through interactions and participation that change the major dimensions of the co-creation generating processes. The chapters' arguments about the former are summarized in Table 4.

References

Andrades, L., & Dimanche, F. (2014). Co-creation of experience value: A tourist behavior approach. In N. Prebensen, J. Chen, & M. Uysal (Eds.), *Creating experience value in tourism* (pp. 95–112). London: CABI.

Campos, A. C., Mendes, J., Valle, P. O. D., & Scott, N. (2015). Co-creation of tourist experiences: A literature review. *Current Issues in Tourism, 15,* 1–32.

Chandler, J. D., & Lusch, R. F. (2014). Service systems: A broadened framework and research agenda on value propositions, engagement, and service experience. *Journal of Service Research, 32,* 26–38. doi:1094670514537709

Edvardsson, B., Tronvoll, B., & Gruber, T. (2011). Expanding understanding of service exchange and value co-creation. *Journal of the Academy of Marketing Science, 39*(2), 327–339.

Gentile, C., Spiller, N., & Noci, G. (2007). How to sustain the customer experience: An overview of experience components that co-create value with the customer. *European Management Journal, 66*(2), 395–410.

Heinonen, K., Strandvik, T., & Voima, P. (2013). Customer dominant value formation in service. *European Business Review, 25*(2), 104–123.

InterContinental Hotels Group. (2014). *We're all going on a smartphone vacation.* Retrieved from http://finance.yahoo.com/news/were-going-smartphone-vacation-200100591.html. Accessed on September 21, 15.

Kallio, K. (2015). Organizational learning in an innovation network – Enhancing the agency of public service organizations. *Journal of Service Theory and Practice, 25*(2), 140–161.

Kreziak, D., & Frochot, I. (2011). CO-CONSTRUCTION DE L'EXPÉRIENCE TOURISTIQUE Les stratégies des touristesen stations de sport d'hiver. *Décisions Marketing,* (64), 23.

Lugosi, P., & Walls, A. R. (2013). Researching destination experiences: Themes, perspectives and challenges. *Journal of DestinationMarketing and Management, 2*(2), 51–58.

Magasic, M. (2016). The 'Selfie Gaze' and 'Social Media Pilgrimage': Two frames for conceptualising the experience of social media using tourists. In A. Inversini & R. Schegg (Eds.), *Information and communication technologies in tourism 2016.* doi:10.1007/978-3-319-28231-2_13

Neuhofer, B. (2016). Value co-creation and co-destruction in connected tourist experiences. In *Information and communication technologies in tourism 2016* (pp. 779–792). Springer International Publishing.

Neuhofer, B. (2016a). Innovation through co-creation: Towards an understanding of technology-facilitated cocreation processes in tourism. In R. Egger, I. Gula, & D. Walch (Eds.), *Open tourism: Open innovation, crowdsourcing and collaborative consumption challenging the tourism industry* (pp. 17–33). Vienna, Austria: Springer Verlag.

Neuhofer, B. (2016b). Value co-creation and co-destruction in connected tourist experiences. In A. Inversini & R. Schegg (Eds.), *Information and communication technologies in tourism 2016.* Vienna, Austria: Springer Verlag.

Neuhofer, B., Buhalis, D., & Ladkin, A. (2012). Conceptualising technology enhanced destination experiences. *Journal of Destination Marketing & Management, 1*(1–2), 36–46.

Neuhofer, B., Buhalis, D., & Ladkin, A. (2013). A typology of technology-enhanced tourism experiences. *International Journal of Tourism Research.* doi:10.1002/jtr.1958

Ordanini, A., & Parasuraman, A. (2012). A conceptual framework for analyzing value-creating service ecosystems: An application to the recorded-music market. In S. L. Vargo & R. F. Lusch (Eds.), *Special Issue – Toward a better understanding of the role of value in markets and marketing* (Vol. 9, pp. 171–205). Review of Marketing Research. Bingley, UK: Emerald Group Publishing Limited.

Payne, A., Storbacka, K., Frow, P., & Knox, S. (2009). Co-creating brands: Diagnosing and designing the relationship experience. *Journal of Business Research, 62*(3), 379–389.

Prahalad, C. K., & Ramaswamy, V. (2004). Co-creation experiences: The next practice in value creation. *Journal of Interactive Marketing, 18*(3), 5–13.

Sigala, M. (2012). Social networks and customer involvement in New Service Development (NSD): The case of www.mystarbucksidea.com/. *International Journal of Contemporary Hospitality Management, 24*(7), 966–990.

Sigala, M. (2014). Collaborative commerce in tourism: Implications for research and industry. *Current Issues in Tourism, 14*, 1–10.

Sigala, M. (2017, in press). Social customer relationship management: Approaches, applications and implications in tourism and hospitality. *International Journal of Contemporary Hospitality Management*.

Sigala, M., Christou, E., & Gretzel, U. (2012). *Web 2.0 in travel, tourism and hospitality: Theory, practice and cases.* Farnham: Ashgate Publishers.

Thompson, C. J., Locander, W. B., & Pollio, H. R. (1989). Putting consumer experience back into consumer research: The philosophy and method of existential-phenomenology. *Journal of Consumer Research, 16*(2), 133–146.

Tussyadiah, I. P., Fesenmaier, D. R., & Yoo, Y. (2008). Designing interactions in tourism mediascape – Identification of patterns for Mobile 2.0 Platform. *Information and Communication Technologies in Tourism 2008*, 395–406.

Tussyadiah, I. P. (2014a). Social actor attribution to mobile phones: The case of tourists. *Information Technology & Tourism, 14*(1), 21–47.

Tussyadiah, I. P. (2014b). Toward a theoretical foundation for experience design in tourism. *Journal of Travel Research, 53*(5), 543–564.

Tussyadiah, I. P., & Fesenmaier, D. R. (2009). Mediating the tourist experiences: Access to places via shared videos. *Annals of Tourism Research, 36*(1), 24–40.

Vargo, S. L., & Lusch, R. F. (2008). Service-dominant logic: Continuing the evolution. *Journal of the Academy of Marketing Science, 36*(1), 1–10.

Wang, D., & Fesenmaier, D. R. (2013). *Transforming the travel experience: The use of smartphones for travel* (pp. 58–69). Heidelberg: Springer.

Wang, D., Park, S., & Fesenmaier, D. R. (2012). The role of smartphones in mediating the touristic experience. *Journal of Travel Research, 51*(4), 371–387.

Xiang, Z., & Gretzel, U. (2010). Role of social media in online travel information search. *Tourism Management, 31*(2), 179–188.

6

Experiential Tourism: Creating and Marketing Tourism Attraction Experiences

Rachel Dodds and Lee Jolliffe

ABSTRACT

Purpose – This chapter investigates the current trend toward both creative and experiential tourism in cities in terms of the development and marketing of local attractions.

Methodology/approach – Creative tourism in cities is profiled through a literature review and further investigated by means of a case study at a local attraction in Toronto, Canada. The choice of a site was one of a creative city and the re-purposing of a formerly industrial site for visitation.

Findings – The study of Evergreens Brickworks demonstrated the use of marketing techniques to identify markets and match visitors with experiences. The visitor segmentation method determined that pre-scheduled and bookable activities offered for locals need to be offered on a different basis for tourists, who may be one time visitors to the site. The product-market match process suggested areas in which products could be modified or indeed created.

Practical implications – This practical study offers lessons for other local visitor attractions and their managers desiring to identify market segments and match them with appropriate activities creating experiential tourism at the site level within the creative city context.

Originality/value – While many studies of the creative tourism concept and cities have been undertaken within the context of destinations this research offers a site-specific perspective as well as marketing perspective that will be of practical value to attraction managers.

Keywords: Creative tourism; tourism attraction; market segments; product-market match; Toronto

Introduction

This chapter investigates the current trend toward both creative and experiential tourism in cities. In particular, local attractions need tools to be able to create and market experiential tourism. The chapter thus explores the use of market segmentation and product-market match techniques to identify markets and match visitors with experiences at local attractions.

Through a literature review the chapter first considers the context for the development of "creative" tourist attractions and experiences, drawing on works on creative cities (Florida, 2014) and the creative class (Florida, 2005). Experiential tourism is part of creative tourism defined by Richards and Wilson (2007, p. 8) as tourism which offers visitors the opportunity to develop their creative potential through active participation.

In the context of the development and management of visitor attractions, it is essential that managers create and market effective visitor experiences (Swarbrooke & Page, 2012). In many cases, however, managers of smaller attraction often lack the marketing expertise to be able to adequately identify market segments and to create experiences for them (McKercher, du Cros, & McKercher, 2002). Therefore, managers are encouraged to diversify their products to meet the changing needs of tourists visiting attractions and the demand for more experiential products (Apostolakis, 2003). This chapter aims to fill that practical gap in the expertise of attractions managers, by providing an illustrative study that is a practical example of a market segmentation and product-market match from which lessons can be derived in general for other locally based visitor attractions. Exploring the concept of creative tourism within an urban regeneration context highlights the potential marketing of local attractions for tourism.

Literature Review

With a majority of the world's population now living in cities there is increased interest in the process of urbanization and the urban experience (Hall & Pfeiffer, 2013). While cities are considered social and economic hubs as well as generators of innovation and creativity, they also consume a disproportionate amount of nature resources (Irvine, 2012). Many urban green spaces are neglected in part due to suburbanization and deindustrialization and regeneration or re-purposing of buildings or areas is often seen as an answer. Unlike the process used in preservation and conservation where the building is maintained to the same physical conditions that it was previously, adaptive reuse or re-purposing of a building makes modifications and renovations to fit the new user's activities and needs (Horne, 2014). There are a number of causes for decline that include inner city-decline in areas where the industrial base is gone, replaced by the service sectors, often located elsewhere (Batty, 2012).

Arts and culture has been identified as part of the "creative economy" (Florida, 2005), and with regards to tourism, arts and culture may become part of regeneration projects or attractions in decline, thus employed to attract new visitors. As a consequence, there is a tendency for cities to adapt or copy regeneration ideas from other cities that can cause serial reproduction (Richards & Wilson, 2007). To address this dilemma of serial reproduction one of the most popular approaches is through the case by case nurturing of "creativity," "creative industries," and "creative communities."

Urban areas can incorporate cultural planning into their marketing campaigns and utilize the creative city model to rebuild decrepit areas (Grodach & Loukaitou-Sideris, 2007). As (Harvey, 1989, p. 9) explained, "the city has to appear as an innovative, exciting, creative and safe place to live or visit, to play and consume in," as festivals, spectacle and display, cultural events and the arts were increasingly appropriated as "symbols of [a] dynamic community."

Traditionally, municipal economic development efforts and strategies centered upon a variety of methods of encouraging businesses relocation to, as well as investment in a city (Grodach, 2012). Florida (2002), however, puts forth that creative people prefer authenticity, as a result making your city just like everyplace else is a sure way to kill its attractiveness. This new development approach is based on human creativity that is focused on supply-side intervention. Rather than focusing on ensuring shopping centers, sports stadiums and freeways, Florida (2002) indicates that cities can compete by developing creative urban environments. The approach in tourism for this sort of regeneration through creative tourism is defined as:

> tourism which offers visitors the opportunity to develop their creative potential through active participation in courses and learning experiences which are characteristic of the holiday destination where they are undertaken. (Richards & Raymond, 2000, p. 18)

According to the OECD, creative industries as they relate to tourism are:

> knowledge based creative activities that link producers, consumers and places by utilising technology, talent or skill to generate meaningful intangible cultural products, creative content and experiences. (OECD, 2014, p. 14)

In the shift from culture to creativity, spatial demands grows cultural institutions stimulate creative clusters and cities transform themselves into creative cities (Zukin, 1998). Cities that are most successful offer consumption and production, heritage and contemporary culture, as well as a cosmopolitanism that cannot easily be replicated or imported (Evans, 2007).

In the context of the "creative" movement many former industrial sites in cities have been regenerated for visitor use (Richards & Wilson, 2007). At these sites, new forms of tourism have been developed with an emphasis on both "authenticity," "creativity" and "experience" as tourism moves away from its former mass market and standardized approach (Richards, 2011). To achieve this approach, it is important for sites to be able to identify visitor markets in order to attract visitors who are interested in experiential tourism, in which they are co-creators (Tan, Luh, & Kung, 2014).

Four key factors influence the success of visitor attractions; the organization and its resources, the product, the market, and the management of the attraction (Swarbrooke & Page, 2012). In particular there is a need for the product to be matched with the attraction market and vice versa. What tools then are available to attractions to identify their markets and develop and deliver experiences for them?

Market segmentation plays a key role in the marketing strategy of almost all successful organizations (Lamb, Hair, & McDaniel, 2011, p. 97). This technique consists of first identifying group of people or organizations sharing one or more characteristics that cause them to have similar product needs and then dividing a market into meaningful, relatively similar, and identifiable segments or groups. Once market segments are identified existing product can be matched to identified visitor segment characteristics and from this comparison product innovations can be suggested. Understanding and implementing the principles of both market segmentation and a product/market match can be used by visitor attractions as guidelines to ensure they are meeting market needs and customer expectations (Boone & Kurtz, 2013).

Methodology

The study of an individual case is appropriate here as information is derived from multiple sources (market studies, documentation, participation observation) as well as being an appropriate method for considering marketing opportunities (Bonoma, 1985). Several types of sources and different data analysis procedures were incorporated as well as the use of primary and secondary data. The choice of a site in Toronto, Canada was one of a creative city and the re-purposing of a formerly industrial site for visitation. Toronto is seen as 7th among Canadian "creative cities" according to (Florida, 2012). There had however previous to this study been relatively little focus on re-purposing buildings or focusing on sustainable design and innovation to be a creative tourist attraction.

The first approach was examining data on tourism to Toronto and the Statistics Canada travel surveys. This includes reports on actual visitation to Toronto taken from Statistics Canada data that examines responses from a quantitative survey that asks respondents to report on whether they participated in several activities; this report focuses on "historic site," "nature park," "museum or art gallery" and "festival." Due to the structure of the surveys if the respondent has visited more than one destination on a trip it is not possible to know if the activities listed were participated in which destination. Therefore we can only say that visitors to Toronto participated in these activities at some point during their trip that may have included other destinations. This is more important for visitors who travel further who are more likely to include several destinations on one trip. However, it is still useful as it still illustrates an interest in these activities by different markets that visit Toronto (Ontario Ministry of Tourism, Cultue and Sport, 2011) and helps to identify key visitor preferences.

The second source is the Ontario portion of the Statistics Canada Motivations Survey (TAMS) that looks at behavior while on vacation to any destination (Ministry of Tourism, Governemnt of Ontario, 2007). This survey data was used to determine visitor segments based on activities and products sought. TAMS was conducted in 2006 and surveyed more than 31,000 Canadians and 60,000 Americans on "the recreational activities and travel habits ... (for) out-of-town, overnight travel behavior of one or more nights over the past two years providing detailed information on travelers' activities, travel motivators, places visited, type of accommodation used ... demographics and media consumption patterns." It asks people to report on their trip motivations and activities they participated in on vacations to all destinations in the last two years.

Third, best practice attractions worldwide were assessed for product offerings and types of tourism potential. Ten best practices were reviewed and visitor segments analyzed. The last stage of the research was to collect primary data. This was assembled through interviews conducted with management at the Evergreen Brickworks as well as neighboring sites to ascertain potential product development, sustainability efforts and current positioning and product offerings to potentially increase awareness and visitation to the site as a tourism attraction. Overall 15 interviews were conducted in the spring of 2011 and interviews lasted for approximately one hour.

Study

CONTEXT

The Evergreen Brickworks site in Toronto, Canada, was an old Brickwork and former quarry, located near the Don River in central Toronto, Canada. The Brickworks operated for nearly 100 years providing bricks for the construction of now well-known city landmarks such as Casa Loma, Massey Hall and the Ontario Legislature. Shaping the city's skyline, the factory at its peak produced over 43 million bricks per year (Irvine, 2012). "When the site closed, what was left was 42 acres of damaged ecosystem, 14 crumbling industrial heritage buildings and contaminated soil" (Irvine, 2012, p. 22).

The site was taken over by Evergreen and opened in 2010 as Canada's first large scale environmental community center and a venue for celebrating innovation in urban greening. The project involved renovating sixteen historic factory buildings through a process called adaptive re-use. Essentially this means that parts of the buildings are refurbished for use and parts are left for historical tours. The result was a sustainable community center with programs that celebrate the site's unique geological, industrial, and natural heritage (Evergreen Brickworks, n.d.). It is a unique site as it offers programs combining ecology, design, technology, and the arts in a hands-on, multi-sensory educational experience. The area includes walking and cycling routes, re-naturalized ponds, a farmers market, a children's area, arts, and craft programs. The site offers an opportunity to explore successfully adapted (and designated) industrial heritage buildings as a viable and sustainable enterprise. This is something that few formal industrial sites have been able to achieve and therefore there is opportunity to market the site as a tourism attraction.

The Brickworks can be viewed under the "creative" umbrella for two reasons. First, it is managed by Evergreen, whose mission to inspire green cities (Evergreen Brickworks, n.d.). Second, it is "creative" because of the site's transformation. The abandoned buildings of the Brickworks have been transformed into a cultural center with an environmental focus. Although the concept started as a community re-purposing approach for residents, it is now being examined in terms of "creative tourism." To the date of the study tourism had not yet really been established and few tourists had visited the site. A study aimed to determine key visitor profiles for the site in order to successfully target a client base that would be attracted to its offerings. Research identified key tourist markets to help understand the expectations and desires of ecological and environmental driven tourists in order to implement site and program enhancements at the attraction.

Market segmentation

The tourism product and services that the Brickworks offer broadly appeal to a number of North Americans while on vacation. Around 80% of Canadians and Americans participated in at least one of the activities available at the Brickworks while on vacation (TAMS, 2006). Five market segments for the Evergreen Brick Works were identified by using the data sources outlined in the methodology. They can be classified as Families, Foodies, Outdoor Activity Seekers, Nature and History Lovers and Sustainability Thought Leaders and Learners Segments and their specific activities (Table 1).

Almost 18 million Canadians participated in an activity available at the Brick Works while on vacation in the previous two years (or 84% of the adult traveling population). There were 12.9 million "foodies" (or 61.9% of the population), 11.4 million "nature history lovers" (55.6%), 7.3 million "families" (36.1%) and 6.1 million "outdoors" (31.2%) (Ministry of Tourism, Governemnt of Ontario, 2007).

In total 17 million Canadians participated in one of the above activities while on vacation to any destination in the previous two years, this is around 84% of all Canadian adults who traveled. In terms of where the largest source markets are, Toronto itself provides the largest number of people who do what the Brickworks does while on vacation, almost three million Torontonians met the criteria and account for 17% of all Canadians. Treating Toronto as a potential tourism market is obviously a wise idea. Offering Torontonians an alternative day out to other attractions that they may have visited several times before is a step that is no doubt being done already. One strategy that may not have been considered though is to encourage Torontonians to bring their visiting friends and relatives (VFR). A large number of Toronto's visitors are visiting friends or relatives, providing Toronto hosts with a new and alternative tourist attraction to entertain could produce traction in terms of increased visitor numbers for the Brickworks. Other Ontario cities as source markets do offer some potential, but there are also a large number of people from other parts of Ontario that could be considered potential visitors also. Montreal and the rest of Quebec, British Colombia, and Alberta also provide large population bases that participate in activities found at the Brickworks. When the size of each activity segment is compared we can see that foodies are the largest in number, closely followed by the nature and history lovers. Ottawa has a higher proportion of foodies (66%) and nature and history lovers (56%) than all

Table 1. Visitor Segments.

Families	Foodies	Outdoor Activity Seekers	Nature and History Lovers	Sustainability Thought Leadership and Learners
Ice-skating	Farmers' markets country fairs	Cycling – recreational cycling-same day	Hiking – same day excursion	Environmentally or socially conscious
Cycling – recreational cycling-same day	Food/drink festivals	Wilderness skills courses	Wildflowers/flora viewing	Seeking local, organic or fair trade products
Farmers' markets country fairs	Cooking/wine tasting courses	Hiking – same day excursion	Wildlife viewing – bird watching	Looking for hands-on learning experiences
Interpretive program at historic site or park	Restaurant dining-local ingredients/recipes	In-line/rollerblading	Interpretive program at historic site or park	Enjoy traveling and finding new experiences
Harvesting and/other farm operations			Well-known historic sites buildings	
In-line/rollerblading			Strolling around city fits buildings/architecture	

other Ontario source markets; however Kitchener is not far behind in either segment (65% and 55%). Looking at specific demographic information, there is little variation in age between the segments except for the "outdoors" group who are typically younger than the others. All four segments have higher average incomes than the total population, with the outdoors group earning the most overall.

Compared with the U.S. market the proportion of "foodies" and "nature and history lovers" is similar (63% and 50%), but the proportion of "families" and "outdoors" is much higher in Canada than in the United States (at 24% and 20%). In terms of where the largest source markets are, Toronto itself provides the largest number of people who do what the Brick Works does while on vacation, almost three million Torontonians met the criteria and account for 17% of all Canadians. Other large source markets in Canada include Montreal (2 million), other Quebec (1.9 million), British Colombia (2.5 million), and Alberta (1.9 million). In the United States, California, New York State, Texas, and Florida are the large source markets for Toronto tourism.

Product-market match

In order to attract tourism to a site, identifying product enhancements and program expansion opportunities is useful in order to determine what activities that these visitor segments may be interested in. This was done through a product-market match. For a product-market match, the current products and programs offered by the Evergreen Brickworks are matched with the five market segments identified (Table 2). Nearby attractions, background research, interviews, and a review of best practices were used to determine potential offerings that the Brickworks could consider. Overall the current programming efforts of Brickworks are well matched with potential visitor markets, however, few programs or activities are offered or made aware to visitors. Many programs are also pre-registered activities rather than daily or weekend tourism offerings.

According to Evans (2007) a destination must link producers, consumers and place to differentiate itself from others. Findings at the Evergreen Brickworks identify a number of unique selling points that fit within "creative tourism" and could be optimized to attract tourists. These include:

- Diverse offering of programs and activities for a variety of markets;

Table 2. Product-Market Match.

Visitor Profiles	Evergreen Offerings	Common Activities for Visitor Profile	Product Enhancement
Families	Community festivals/markets	Farmers markets/fairs/festivals	Kids tasting menu during events
	Gardens/workshops	Workshops/seminars	Brick making classes/children
	Summer camp/crafts programs	Family entertainment/movies	Nature-based scavenger hunts
	Child's play area/garden/programs	Restaurants/outdoor cafes/shopping	Outdoor café/ice cream/lemonade stand
	Self-guided tours	Interpretive programs/architecture/ historic sites	Guided tours in costume/character
	Cycling/hiking trails	Cycling/hiking	Geocaching
	Bird watching	Nature parks/beach/sunbathing/ swimming	Nature-based free weekend daycare
	Ice-skating/climbing wall	Ice-skating/rollerblading	Rollerblade rental
Foodies	Weekly Garden Market	Farmers markets/country fairs	
	Café Belong (Chef Brad Long)	Local food ingredients/dining/ outdoor cafes	Outdoor café/"taste local" festival
	Culinary events/courses (food, wine, pairings)	Food/drink festivals/Cooking/wine tasting courses/classes	Wine events
	Events (picnic in the park, earth day picnic, wild in the city)	Festivals/events	Local food events /meetings (i.e., Toronto Food Policy group)
	Gardening/stewardship	Experience architecture	
	Gardening stewardship workshops		

Table 2. (Continued)

Visitor Profiles	Evergreen Offerings	Common Activities for Visitor Profile	Product Enhancement
Outdoor seekers	Cycling/trails/skating workshops	Nature parks/birding/wildlife viewing/wilderness skills	Weekend outward bound survival skills courses
		Cycling/hiking/running/Climbing/canoeing/kayaking	Geocaching
	Café belong (chef brad long)	Local ingredients restaurants/outdoor cafes	Outdoor cafes
	Yoga	Yoga	
	Events environmentally themed	Viewing architecture/visiting historic sites	
Sustainability	Self-guided site tours/themes of green design, sustainability	Enjoy natural environmental experiences.	Self-guided sustainability trail/self-guided audio tours of LEED building
	Recycling days	Seek out opportunities to participate in authentic experiences	Provide guided/study tours for different interests (i.e., green building/architecture)
	Exhibits (better place Canada/sustainable transportation)	Seek out alternative/active transportation methods	Promote public transport (shuttle, bike parking, trail links, carpooling, etc.) Visitor guides/reduce their footprint
	Speakers series — Brickworks Forum on Leadership, Innovation and Sustainability		Site signage listing sustainability initiatives/Farm to table programs

- Unique natural and heritage attraction in an urban area;
- Leadership in environmental design techniques (LEED Platinum building);
- Multi-seasonal offerings;
- Nature experiences in an urban area (e.g., fall colors, bird viewing, hiking/cycling trails);
- Largest park based farmers market in Toronto;
- Many visitor activities are free.

These unique selling points of the Evergreen Brickworks were identified in part through the product-market match process informed from the stakeholder interviews and program review in the context of the visitor segmentation exercise.

Implications

The Evergreen Brickworks is well positioned to market and provide "creative" and experiences or "experiential tourism" to a consumer group who are seeking these experiences. The Brickworks has the tourism product and integrity in its sustainability initiatives to appeal to this high value market segment as the site offers a number of "experiences" rather than just products. This is in-line with the views of who note that creative tourism depends on the active involvement of tourists.

The local Toronto market provides a large population base of people who when they go on vacation enjoy the activities that the Brickworks has to offer. A marketing campaign targeted at locals and their VFR may be a useful strategy to ensure that locals become tourists within their own city. Toronto's current visitor market is varied, but the Brickworks has the potential to provide different tourists with a satisfying experience depending on their motivations and experience. The key is to market to different people with a message that will spark their interest and engage them. There are opportunities for partnering with marketing organizations and other attractions and service providers to package experiences together that will appeal to different visitor segments.

It is noted by (Evans, 2007) that new facilities alone do not create a creative city; therefore the Brickworks must work with other organizations and tourism organizations to profile the space alongside other attractions. Nor should they lose sight that their main market segment is the Toronto resident, rather than the tourist. The Brickworks is a charitable organization, and current and future marketing budgets are low, therefore paid advertising and promotion cannot be counted on to build brand awareness so the Brickworks' current experiences are what should be built to engage both residents and tourists. Experiential product and services are key in developing both "creative" and "experiential" tourism and packages and attractions which offer an authentic, unique experience is what will differentiate themselves from other similar attractions.

Although the Evergreen Brickworks is a unique attraction, there is a significant lack of awareness about the variety and scope of offerings that the site offers (many people have never heard of it). The site is not currently known to many tourism marketing bodies or tourism distribution companies and although there is potential for expansion into tourism markets, the largest source market is Toronto and VFR therefore optimizing this market should be a primary consideration.

Discussion

In this section we discuss and analyze the study results in the context of the objectives of the chapter and the literature review. The study of Evergreens Brickworks has demonstrated the use of market segmentation and product-market match techniques to identify markets and match visitors with experiences. These techniques are of particular import for attractions with a local audience that also wish to attract tourists. The visitor segmentation method can help managers to identify the fit between the profile of their attraction to local visitors and tourists, thereby identifying the motivations and interests of tourists that might differ and may lead to product innovation. For example, in the case of the Evergreen Brickworks pre-scheduled and bookable activities offered for locals would need to be offered on a different basis in order to be of interest to tourists, who may be one time visitors to the site. Likewise, the product-market match process can identify the suitability of current product offerings for both existing local audiences and visitors, suggesting areas in which products could be modified or indeed created. An example from the Evergreen Brickworks is the identification of the diversity of product elements including a restaurant, sustainability efforts (e.g., innovative energy uses, utilization of heritage and nature within interpretive tours), heritage building, and nature-based activities that can be matched with different visitor segments. The study of the Evergreen Brickworks also demonstrates how a site can employ experiential and creative tourism in an urban setting to differentiate themselves from other local visitor attraction offerings. This is a lesson that could be employed by other local attractions desiring to expand their visitor reach, by attracting tourists visiting their areas.

The study of the Evergreen Brickworks also demonstrated for other visitor attractions the importance of increasing awareness of their sites to potential audiences, and the identification of visitor segments is a tool that will help attractions to highlight partners it should align with in this process. The product-market match process can help sites such as the Evergreen Brickworks to profile their unique selling points (USPs) that can be optimized to engage, educate, and advocate, thereby increasing visitation and improving the visitor experience. For all attractions utilizing visitor segmentation and product match techniques strategies that follow should include marketing, partnership development, and product and site enhancements, thereby optimizing the future tourism potential of local attractions.

Conclusion

The contribution and value of this chapter in effectively managing and marketing high quality and memorable tourism experiences in the context of local tourism attractions has been to outline the use and value of market segmentation and market/product match techniques. This can be considered to be a key part of not only traditional marketing but also experiential marketing. The findings from the particular study pertaining to the use of creative tourism in marketing of an urban revitalization project, although specific to one Canadian site, can be applied to other destination sites worldwide and build upon those by Batty (2012) and (Malanga, 2004). Furthermore, as this study touches upon a particular attraction rather than the entire city therefore market research techniques and recommendations can be easier to replicate elsewhere.

References

Apostolakis, A. (2003). The convergence process in heritage tourism. *Annals of Tourism Research*, 30(4), 795–812.

Batty, M. (2012). Urban regeneration as self-organisation. *Architectural Design*, 82(1), 54.

Bonoma, T. V. (1985). Case research in marketing: Opportunities, problems, and a process. *Journal of Marketing Research*, 22, 199–208.

Boone, L., & Kurtz, D. (2013). *Contemporary marketing*. Boston, MA: Cengage Learning.

Evans, G. (2007). Creative spaces, tourism and the city. In G. Richards & J. Wilson (Eds.), *Tourism, creativity and development* (pp. 57–72). Routledge Creativity and Development. London: Routledge.

Evergreen Brickworks. (n.d.). *Evergreen brickworks*. Retrieved from www.evergreen.ca/

Florida, R. (2005). *Cities and the creative class*. Abingdon: Routledge.

Florida, R. (2014). *The rise of the creative class – revisited: Revised and expanded*. New York, NY: Basic Books.

Florida, R. L. (2002). *The rise of the creative class: And how it's transforming work, leisure, community and everyday life*. New York, NY: Basic Books.

Florida, R. L. (2012, July 12). Canada's most creative cities. *The Huffington Post*. Retrieved from http://www.huffingtonpost.ca/richard-florida/canadas-most-creative-cit_b_1608460.html

Grodach, C. (2012). Before and after the creative city: The politics of urban cultural policy in Austin, Texas. *Journal of Urban Affairs*, 34(1), 81–97.

Grodach, C., & Loukaitou-Sideris, A. (2007). Cultural development strategies and urban revitalization: A survey of US cities. *International Journal of Cultural Policy*, 13(4), 349–370.

Hall, P., & Pfeiffer, U. (2013). *Urban future 21: A global agenda for twenty-first century cities*. Abingdon: Routledge.

Harvey, D. (1989). From managerialism to entrepreneurialism: The transformation in urban governance in late capitalism. *Geografiska Annaler. Series B. Human Geography*, 3–17.

Horne, M. (2014). Temporary use of pop-up environment's potential for repurposing neglected buildings and spaces.

Irvine, S. (2012). Evergreen Brick works: An innovation and sustainability case study. *Technology Innovation Management Review*, 2(7), 21–25.

Lamb, C., Hair, J., & McDaniel, C. (2011). *Essentials of marketing*. Boston, MA: Cengage Learning.

Malanga, S. (2004). The curse of the creative class. *City Journal* (winter).

McKercher, B., du Cros, H., & McKercher, R. (2002). *Cultural tourism: The partnership between tourism and cultural heritage management*. Philadelphia, PA: Haworth Hospitality Press.

Ministry of Tourism, Governemnt of Ontario. (2007). *Travel activities and motivations of Canadian residents: An overview*. Toronto. Retrieved from http://www.mtc.gov.on.ca/en/research/travel_activities/TAMS%202006%20Overview%20Canadian%20Report.pdf

OECD. (2014). *Tourism and the creative economy*. (OECD Studies on Tourism). Paris: OECD Publishing.

Ontario Ministry of Tourism. (2006). *Travel activities and motivations survey (TAMS)*. Retrieved from www.tourism.gov.on.ca/english/research/travel_activities/index.html

Ontario Ministry of Tourism, Cultue and Sport. (2011). *Toronto visitor market report*. Toronto. Retrieved from http://www.seetorontonow.com/getattachment/7de27a85-eb45-44b3-af29-70dafc9875a1/Market-report-(full).pdf.aspx

Richards, G. (2011). Creativity and tourism: The state of the art. *Annals of Tourism Research, 38*(4), 1225–1253. Retrieved from http://doi.org/10.1016/j.annals.2011.07.008

Richards, G., & Raymond, C. (2000). Creative tourism. *ATLAS News*, 23, 16–20.

Richards, G., & Wilson, J. (2007). The creative turn in regeneration: Creative spaces, spectacles and tourism in cities. In *Tourism, culture and regeneration* (pp. 12–24). Wallingford, CT: CABI.

Swarbrooke, J., & Page, S. J. (2012). *Development and management of visitor attractions*. Abingdon: Routledge.

Tan, S.-K., Luh, D.-B., & Kung, S.-F. (2014). A taxonomy of creative tourists in creative tourism. *Tourism Management, 42*, 248–259.

Zukin, S. (1998). Urban lifestyles: Diversity and standardisation in spaces of consumption. *Urban Studies, 35*(5–6), 825–839.

Part II
Managing: Organizing and Delivering Tourism Experiences

Aim: to analyze issues of managing tourism experiences within various contexts

CHAPTER

7

Cultural and Experiential Tourism

Hilary du Cros

ABSTRACT

Purpose – This chapter looks at how sensitivity to event design and the creative process for an arts event also can have an impact on its ongoing management and tourist experience, by applying a new assessment tool, sustainable creative advantage (SCA), to gauge its performance.

Methodology/approach – A case study approach was used to assess SCA for the Sculpture by Sea, Bondi, Sydney 2015, in order to discuss how its management enables satisfying arts leisure experiences. Two key activities in the research were (1) in-depth interviews with organizers, full and volunteer staff, artists, gallery owners, and participants and (2) participant observation of touristic performances and other forms of engagement with the sculptures.

Findings – In its 19th edition, the event could still be considered a fresh and inspiring experience for tourists. However, crowding on weekends can affect the experience for all participants. Tactile tours are a unique feature of the event and could be promoted more to tourists, particularly the disabled.

Research limitations – Applying SCA needs careful timing, in order to collect information when interviewees are available and the event itself is running. Approaches should be made to organizers before, during, and after the event for information.

Practical implications – Event organizers could use SCA to understand more about controlling tourist experiences and how creative management and marketing of an event can have an impact on overall participant satisfaction.

Originality/value – Could also offer insights to academics studying glocality and events, the relationship of curatorial power to content/experience, or how such events can add to the study of leisurescapes in cultural tourism.

Keywords: Leisure; sustainable creative advantage; arts events; sculpture trails; tactile tours

Introduction

Cultural tourism provides numerous issues, challenges, and approaches for sustainable quality tourism experiences. An important principle to follow in order for these experiences to be repeatable is "The tourist experience must be controlled, which in turn controls the actions of the tourist" (du Cros & McKercher, 2014, p. 113). Tourism marketing and management therefore need to have a closer relationship than most people think for tourist experiences to be manageable and actually match tourist expectations when repeated. Consequently, integrating marketing aspects is vital to achieving sustainable cultural tourism.

Accordingly, there is a shortage of studies into arts events that look in detail at how the management and marketing of arts events can be enhanced, so that experiences can be kept fresh for repeat editions of an event, not allow a drain on the related arts ecology while attracting new and return visits of tourists. Communities and their arts ecologies that rely on such events and the experiences they generate would expect that academia might give them more of a priority. Hence, it is important that these events and experiences should receive more scrutiny by academics that consider sustainable cultural tourism one of their key research areas.

Arts events are special and not just another kind of special event, because of how they showcase the creative process for a particular art form(s). Repeatable arts events require more than the usual kind of performance assessment (e.g., SWOT analysis).

Knowing more about the nature and health of arts ecologies is important for understanding the enabling conditions for achieving sustainability in relation to arts events. Overall, there is a need for an arts event to maintain a Sustainable Creative Advantage (SCA), which is not as simple as a Sustainable Competitive Advantage (and completely different), in order to be considered to have characteristics of some or all of the above.

What is an SCA really? Building different kinds of capital for and beyond the community for a short answer, but a holistic concept such as SCA is more appropriate in this context than applying separate concepts of creative, cultural, social, or any other type of capital, particularly as most artists and arts academics do not warm to the word "capital" – it is too much associated with purely financial benefits in their minds. The term tries to encompass at least four kinds of capital under (social, cultural, human, and economic) under this umbrella term, as well as that creative spark that makes a really good arts event appeal to participants.

Arts events are a natural part of the "experience economy," as promoted by Pine and Gilmore (1999), as they showcase the cultural rhythms or creative synergies of a particular place. The definition of such experiential encounters is still being developed in the literature in relation to creative industries, events, and arts experiences in a tourism context (Kay & Polonsky, 2010). Quinn (2006) described arts festivals, in particular, as "socially significant cultural practices," which deserve consideration beyond their contributions to economic and tourism development "as a product to enliven a destination" (Quinn, 2006, p. 301). One danger identified in the study is that by running "a model tourism" event that highlights internationally known headliners local arts can be marginalized and alienated. A balance should be maintained when both local and international artists are invited to participate in an event.

This chapter will present Sculptures by the Sea (Bondi, Sydney) as a case study where the SCA assessment approach has been applied. The event has been studied over the last few years and the 2015 edition was examined in more detail in regard to it role in providing participants with a fresh and inspiring experience of Sydney's leisurescape. The goal was to see how the event can be sustained and improved over the long term and make some observation of its importance to local/global arts ecologies and the host community. So far SCA has only been applied to three events in Hong Kong by the author (du Cros & Jolliffe, 2014) and an opportunity exists to test it further with the

Sculptures event, which boasts some unique aspects, such as offering a guided tactile tour for disabled participants.

Literature Review

The previous work on arts events has occurred in a number of disparate disciplines, such as tourism, events management, arts management, anthropogy, cultural geography, and public policy. The chapter aims to outline a multidisciplinary approach to present the case study in a new light. The key areas where arts events need the most attention to create and maintain an SCA are glocal orientation and support, image, orientation and position, conceptual uniqueness, event experience, implementation, and management (du Cros & Jolliffe, 2014).

BUILDING GLOCALITY: ORIENTATION AND SUPPORT

What is meant by glocality in this context? The glocal concept comes from studies concerned with examining communities' relocalization of global trends in interaction with their local situation (Ganga, n.d.). It is used here, however, to denote a type of gloablized localism where an event that has proved to be highly successful in one location can be replicated elsewhere and which in doing so draws on both local and international arts ecologies.

Knowing more about the glocal orientation and support for an event is important for understanding the enabling conditions for achieving sustainability in relation to arts. Such conditions are also important for creating a sustainable advantage that is place-based and relies on available creative capital (creativity, creatives, creative processes, and cultural/arts ecologies) (Florida, 2002). The number and strength of arts community networks that might support the event and how the event could be considered a point of connection with these communities within an arts ecology (Stolarick & Florida, 2006). A successful event needs a critical mass of artists and art activities. Also, success only comes, if connections are strong and a healthy local/international balance is maintained (du Cros & Jolliffe, 2011; Mitchell & Fisher, 2010; Quinn, 2006).

MARKETING: BRAND, IMAGE, AND POSITION

Audience building for arts events often requires studies of audience impact and many arts organizations (particularly for the performing arts) conduct these regularly without specific reference to particular events (Preez & Bailey, 2010). Visual arts tend to rely on other indicators, such as through studies of social media responses or popularity competitions (Kay & Polonsky, 2010). Collecting more than basic demographic and psychographic information would assist the organizers in ensuring that the event is establishing its brand, image, and position in the eyes of its key market in the region, where the event maybe a new competitor (Shone & Parry, 2004).

Events with a public-spirited orientation, such as events with an intense local and educational purpose, would be seeking data about arts awareness and educational needs of the local community (Mitchell, 1992). Dividing this up into specific surveys for different participants may be too labor intensive for some organizations, while others drawing on voluntary and student assistance may prefer this approach. However, overly long surveys rarely get completed to the end, if they are not conducted face-to-face with some kind incentive offered (du Cros & Jolliffe, 2014).

CONCEPTUAL UNIQUENESS

Planning an arts event and re-inventing one have a certain amount in common in terms of ensuring conceptual uniqueness that will ensure for success and continuation as a repeatable cultural event. What is needed is a remarkable or dynamic element that can assist in marketing the event, so that it fits with its audience orientation and attracts the right partners, sponsors, participants or attendees. By audience orientation, it is meant whether it is principally held to attract a particular audience (e.g., art collectors or families looking for fun) or a mix. It also needs to be attractive to the artists or performers featured (du Cros & Jolliffe, 2014). The development of an event with conceptual uniqueness requires strongly supportive environment with visionary partners who can make things happen in that location. It is no accident that most event forms start in one place with this kind of social and institutional capital and then variants appear in other places with a similar supportive environment (du Cros & Jolliffe, forthcoming).

Finally, using or setting an event in an unusual context that catches the attention of audiences is another aspect of ensuring its conceptual uniqueness. This strategy requires some knowledge of the art form(s) or associated intellectual property. An event designer can explore new ways of constructing knowledge, new ideas, skills, and pathways that can be generated by the event.

Early examples of this strategy are Opera at the Pyramids, Giza, or Films at the Fort, Singapore, which are events that have reinvigorated these arts experiences by placing them outside in complementary locations.

EVENT EXPERIENCE

When the orientation of the event is identified in terms of who are likely to gain the key benefits from it (public sector, commercial sector, arts industry, artists/performers), a suitable approach is devised to evaluating event experience by participants. For instance, events planned to have a strong public/public sector orientation need to assess social impacts of and contributions to community cultural development in terms of providing enriching experiences. Goldbard (2006) has observed that there are at least six common goals in this case:

- Mutual and meaningful relationships are developed
- Opportunities are offered and taken to allow co-production of activities
- Participants notice a difference in their arts knowledge and skills, self-awareness, and personal growth as a result
- Satisfaction in the ability to communicate through arts media has grown
- Aims and expectations of participants have been advanced in terms of improving their potential
- Boosting of participant's confidence in partaking more fully in the arts.

Measuring many of these mostly intangible benefits is likely to require a data collection process that continues long after the event has been held. Developing a cyber community based on the event may be one way to track participants and their views. More traditional methods such as focus groups, in-depth interviews, and surveys can also have a role where there are the resources to conduct these activities.

Undertaking studies of event experience for any type of event should therefore occur before, during, and after in order to contribute to the continuous evaluation of the event. How an event is experienced could influence a participant or attendee's choice for years to come. Finally, information about event experiences can be used to suggest changes to just about any area associated with holding an event.

EVENT IMPLEMENTATION AND MANAGEMENT

Arts events that are larger in scale are also increasingly becoming subject to professional management regimes (Foley, McGillivary, & McPherson, 2009; Vogel, 2011). However, whether an event is professionally managed or not, there still needs to be an evaluation of how it has succeeded in being creative and sustainable, if it is to be ongoing. Four key areas for all arts events are likely to be:

1. Concept and content: appropriateness of conceptualization and selection process for artists/works/performers/activities/facilities/nature of participation by attendees
2. Timing: scheduling for timing of tasks associated with putting on the program/exhibition/ancillary activities/competition with similar events
3. Connectivity: quality of management of sponsors/partners/cross-cultural issues/media and communication/responsibility structures
4. Resourcing: that staff levels (both paid and volunteer), ability to source funding/handle sponsors, training needs, insurance, safety and security are all adequate and within budget.

The above aspects will require attention before, during, and after the event for the benefit of improving the event's ongoing experience for participants. Hence, repeatable arts and cultural events will need some kind evaluation, even if it is not SCA, to stay on track and continue to deliver exciting experiences. Whether they are professionally managed or not, it is important not to loose track of their glocal and audience orientations, market position, unique concept, key experiences offered, and effective implementation and management. Sculpture by the Sea, Australia, will be analyzed in relation to these criteria.

Methodology

The Australian example presented in this chapter deals largely with the Bondi edition (the first and original) of Sculpture by the Sea, held since 1997. The author has studied it at distance for several years then visited it over three days, during when the trail was staged as a public event from October 22 to November 9, 2015. Data was collected by in-depth interview with organizers, full and volunteer staff, artists, gallery owners, and participants.

Outputs for the event were analyzed such as catalogs, educational materials, and the commemorative publication (Sculpture by the Sea Inc., 2011). Participant observation was carried out of the trail and touristic performances and other forms of engagement. The organizers gave permission for the author to "shadow" some of the tactile tours offered and make observations.

Sculpture by the Sea

DEVELOPMENT OF A UNIQUE CONCEPT

That founder David Handley's background was not based in staging arts events makes the achievement and success of Sculpture by the Sea all the more significant. Instead, he was for many years a lawyer, then tried to break into film production. His unusual vision for this event was the culmination of 10 years of reflection about what he should do with his life. In 1993 he moved to Prague, where he was taken to an outdoor sculpture park that incorporated thirteenth century ruins, near the town of Klatovy in northern Bohemia. This was his first introduction to theatricality of sculpture and set him thinking about how to produce an experience that would convey this in a way other than through film (Handley, 2011).

The arts event's mission resulted from Handley's wish to create an iconic and free arts experience for Sydney linked to its natural heritage and landscape. Inspired by other outdoor large community arts events such as, "Opera in the Park" and "Symphony Under the Stars," he wanted it provide a sense of community that would result from partaking in enjoyable social and cultural activities that were not ticketed and not necessarily fringe. Handley observes that the kind of experience he was seeking for his event would be similar he hoped to one he felt while "playing amongst the ruins and sculptures one night with my Czech art school friends (where) I had my first experience of the power, if not majesty, of sculpture (Handley in Sculpture by the Sea, 2015a, p. 1)."

In 1996, after his return to Sydney, his friends, Marie-Volaine Poupart and Matt Kennedy, suggested he undertake the Bondi to Tamarama Coastal Walk (Handley, 2011). This walk is one of the first coastal walks established by local Sydney councils to encourage exercise and greater appreciation of the coastline's natural beauty (Waverley Public Library, 2009). His second breakthrough came on the walk, "all around me I saw natural plinth after natural plinth where sculptures of all descriptions could be installed" (Handley in Sculpture by the Sea, 2015a, p. 1).

Key protagonists in helping to stage the event successfully the first time were Waverley Council, Sydney Water, friends, artists, and academics. Of these, Anita Johnston at Waverley Council, which is responsible for managing the coastal walk granted permission (within 48 hours, probably a world record) for holding the event. Ron Robertson-Swann, a well-known Australian sculptor, advised Handley on matters relating to installing and siting sculpture along the coastal cliffs and beaches. Robertson-Swann's reputation and endorsement of the event helped attract other substantial artists to Sculpture by the Sea. From the beginning, organizers worked hard to present work of a high standard to the public, because they agreed that art "adored by the masses" need not be low quality (Handley, 2011; McDonald, 2011, p. 6; Sculpture by the Sea, 2015a).

GLOCAL ORIENTATION

The first event was held in 1997 featuring 64 works from artists mainly from southeastern Australia (Sculpture by the Sea Inc., 2011). Run from Handley's living room and staffed entirely by volunteers, the first exhibition started with a modest budget of AUD 11,000 of which AUD 8,000 was put toward awards for winning pieces (McDonald, 2011). Word-of-mouth through the artistic community elicited over 100 artist submissions for the first edition, while media interest, Council support and principal sponsor, Sydney Water (which sponsored the first Sculpture Prize and continues to support the event), also assisted with advertising costs (Sculpture by the Sea, 2015a).

The first exhibition had to be limited to daytime and therefore to one day only, because of a lack of a security budget. However, this had the benefit of allowing Waverley Council to see how the show would work, before authorizing a multi-day exhibition in 1998. Handley estimated that 25,000 people visited the 1997 exhibition (McDonald, 2011). For the 1998 event, the Sydney Organizing Committee for the Olympic Games (SOCOG) through the Artistic Director, Andrea Stretton, commissioned five Sculpture by the Sea exhibitions around Australia for the 1998 Sydney Olympic Cultural Olympiad.

The Olympiad edition was "one off" sponsorship boosted the event even more in the arts community, so that artists responded with over 260 sculptures being installed among five locations around Australia (Darwin, Noosa, Albany, Bondi, and the Tasman Peninsula) during the Olympiad. Handley estimated that the series of events attracted more than 200,000 visitors in total (Handley, 2011).

However, the organizers were not able to maintain each of these interstate exhibitions without the SOCOG funding, though Handley tried to keep Tasmania running with an exhibition included in the 2001 Tasmania wide arts fest "10 Days on the Island" on the Tasman Peninsula from Port Arthur Historic Convict Site to Eagle Hawk Neck. However, this proved to be unrepeatable, principally due to funding issues. In 2005, Sculpture by the Sea, Cottesloe, was launched instead and is held annually at Cottesloe Beach, Perth on Australia's Indian Ocean coast (Sculpture by the Sea, 2015a; Sculpture by the Sea Inc., 2011). It runs for 18 days, which is a few days longer than the Bondi edition.

With the advent of two trail events a year, Sculpture by the Sea now includes full time staff that often move between the two and boasts a broader funding base. It still does not attract any Federal/national funding though this could change with the political tides. The event now runs for two weeks in November in Bondi. In 2015, it was estimated that over 400,000 people visited the trail.[1] The Cottlesloe event in Western Australia earlier in March 2015 attracted 215,000 visitors.

More recently, some close link has formed with an overseas imitator that allows sculptures to move between the two. In June 2009 Sculpture by the Sea Aarhus – Denmark was launched, in association with the City of Aarhus and ARoS Aarhus Artmuseum, under the patronage of The Crown Prince and Crown Princess of Denmark. The royal couple visited the Bondi trail in 2000 and were inspired by it. The event is financially and legally independent of its Australian counterpart. It is put on by the city of Aarhus, Denmark, in collaboration with ARoS Aarhus Artmuseum. Nevertheless, the websites are linked and there is a flow of artists and artworks between them. It runs for four weeks and its first edition attracted over 500,000 people (McDonald, 2011; Sculpture by the Sea Aarhus, 2015).

Meanwhile, not many other places have established sculpture trails that also could be considered as impermanent and event-based as the trails at Bondi, Cottesloe, and Aarhus. Most have

---

[1]Interview with David Handley.

permanent sculptures, even if they refresh these works on a sporadic or regular basis. However, it was noticeable that when domestic tourists were interviewed during the Bondi edition most referred to sculpture trails established fairly recently in their hometowns and cities. Perhaps, Sculpture by the Sea's success has inspired a spate of civic sculpture trail building, at least in Australia.

Finally, Sculpture by the Sea should be seen as having developed a strong glocal orientation in order to be both popular and sustainable. It currently draws on both local and international arts ecologies. The event is juried and for 2015 had over 500 submissions from 19 countries. The proposals are reviewed by a curatorial panel, which changes from year to year and includes mostly leading authorities from public and private galleries. Once selected, the artists have six months to make their works and position them on the trail (Handley, 2015).

BRAND/CONCEPTUAL UNIQUENESS: FUSION OF SCULPTURE TRAIL, SALES PROMOTION, AND FESTIVAL

When Sculpture by Sea appeared on the art scene it could be argued that it is not just a new event but also a new arts event form. As discussed, it aims to provide free periodic outdoor access to high quality sculpture staged against a dynamic coastal setting. These are pieces that are judged for awards and available for purchase to collectors. The trail runs along the coast between two major Sydney beaches and through a series of parks where tents host a small sculptures exhibition, educational programs, and workshops, also free of charge (Sculpture by the Sea, 2015a).

Thus, it manages to be a fusion of commercial and community access for a mixed orientation, while being run as a trail, competition, art sales opportunity, and event. The temporal aspects noted by Morris and Cant (2007) with the Hebden Bridge Sculpture Trail are also evident here, but not as avidly as the role Sculpture by the Sea, Bondi, plays in Australian arts events calendar, where the major prize of AUD 60,000 is considered the sculpture equivalent of the country's prestigious Archibald Prize for portraiture by many artists.[2] Even the

---

[2]Interview with Peter Lundberg.

event's People's Choice Prize is considered of significance, and in 2015 was bestowed by Australia's prime minister, Malcolm Turnbull (Sculpture by the Sea, 2015b).

EVENT EXPERIENCE

Sculpture by the Sea has been an extremely popular event with a wide range of participants. Some sculptures invite interaction and some just offer a chance to think about what they are expressing (Plates 1 and 2). Public artist talks are aimed at both adults and children on the weekends and school children during the week. The children observed on the days the event was studied ranged between those who acted like the place was just another play-ground through to those who were fans of the event and came every year. One eight-year-old boy approached sculptor Peter Lundberg (during an interview) and recited the names of his winning sculptures and the years he had won prizes. Needless to say we were both stunned. Teens and young adults observed tended to be clearly art students and though some appeared to have just walked up from the beach according to their dress. No children or adults were observed looking bored and playing on their smart phones. Many local people (and even some from further away) brought their dogs, clearly seeing the event as either part of their

Plate 1.   Highly Interactive Sculpture.

Plate 2.   A Mix of Visitors Interacting with and Contemplating Sculptures.

daily routine or just another day out.[3] Hence, they contribute to the leisurescape of the event as viewed by tourists.

Adult and tourist experience can be more closely linked with photography and the general atmosphere of the event. 2015 winner of the sculpture photography prize, Rohan Hinton, observed that his work was successful due to his persistence to get the right moment:

> This year that meant heading out late at night, in the middle of a storm to capture *listen time passes* by Barbara Licha as it swayed under the storms wrath. There is something special about the night and early morning, when the world is quiet, and you can get closer to the sculptures. (Sculpture by the Sea, 2015b, p. 1)

Staff interviewed at the event stated that tourists seemed to take many more photos than locals. Tourists were more evident during the week and locals massed to the event on weekends. The experience differed depending on time of day, light, weather, and amount of crowding on the cliff walk. When it was

---

[3]Cottlesloe Council has banned dogs at the event even though the organizers have never requested it. Staff I spoke to thought unsupervized children knocking the sculptures around was more of a problem.

extremely congested, it was harder to appreciate the art and take photos many interviewees opined.

TACTILE TOUR EXPERIENCE

Tactile (touch and other interaction) experiences are provided to disabled children and adults and to troubled youth through free tactile tours (by appointment) run by occupational arts specialist volunteers sourced from large public galleries. From the research conducted for the study, Sculpture by the Sea (Bondi and Cottesloe) appeared to be the only sculpture trail or outdoor event that has offered this kind of tour. It started in 2009 and was offered initially to blind participants to assist their engagement with the sculptures. It has been expanded over the last their years to include people with other kinds of disability and troubled youth. Sponsorship covers the cost of hiring the arts professionals, who would normally provide this type of tour at major public galleries. The tours are therefore free, but by appointment.

The tours are also open to disabled tourists, if they are aware that these tours exist. The tours were not specifically promoted to tourists at the time of writing. The guides provide a level of interpretation about the sculptures appropriate to the age group they are guiding. Supervised interaction is encouraged with the agreement of the artists, who sometimes appear to give added information. Weather was playing a dampening role on the day the tours were observed, however children and adults who were attending the trail/event for the first time were still keen (Plate 3). The troubled youth who had attended the event for the third time were showing evidence of diminished returns over time. Refreshing the program for returnees from this group is probably wise to allow for the optimum experience.

KEY ISSUES IN PLANNING, MANAGEMENT, AND OPERATION THAT AFFECT TOURISM EXPERIENCES

For the most part, Sculpture by the Sea (Bondi edition studied) is an extremely well run event/trail that has thrashed out the worst of its problems over the last 19 years of being run annually. It has dealt with various growing pains (Handley, 2011; McDonald, 2011), while retaining important partners and sponsors. The tourism experience, however, is not one aspect that the organizers and staff spend a great deal of time reflecting upon, so some missed opportunities and minor problems exist.

Plate 3. Tactile Tour Operating in Challenging Weather.

The greatest missed opportunity is more recognition of how special the event/trail is in offering tactile tours. It may be that both Bondi and Cottesloe editions could become part of the traveling calendar for domestic disabled tourists, who have an interest in art or new experiences. Otherwise, the only other issue for enhancing tourist experiences is the lack of apps or directional signage in any language.

ASSESSING EVENT EXPERIENCE

Not much formal evaluation of the event or visitor experience has been tried by the Australian organizers for Sculpture by the Sea. However, the Danish version in Aarhus conducted a study in 2013 and posted a report on the event on the Internet. The interesting thing about this report is that, as well as the usual facts and figures, it also describes how artistic goals were being met by the event. Criteria for such goals are likely to be more subjective in nature than those for its economic impact or visitor satisfaction, while who is qualified to undertake their assessment is an interesting question.

The report states "artistic goals were also met, especially due to all the site-specific artworks that made this year's exhibition even more unique (Sculptures by the Sea Aarhus, 2013, p. 1)." It is highly likely that where arts events sometimes differ

from other special events is that appraisal of their relative quality of esthetic experience and artistic value is always going to
have to use arts criticism traditions as a framework that may
not be readily accessible or understandable to outsiders to the
arts world. However, that is not to say that such events ignore
the opinions of the public who are not arts professionals, but
who still gain pleasure from the esthetic arrangement of the
sculptures in the coastal landscape. The organizers of this event
state that they used a local market research company to undertake a visitor satisfaction survey and analysis, which is made
public in their exhibition report later in the year (Sculptures by
the Sea Aarhus, 2013).

For the first time this year, the organizers of Sculpture by
the Sea had asked staff to take clicker readings for visitor numbers. Estimates were based previously on eyeballing the crowds
passing along the path. The final estimate of just over 400,000
for the Bondi edition is consequently lower than previous years.
Tourists observed tended to be not that different to those visiting the Bondi Beach as a tourist attraction, except that there
were more arty and European types during the week. Bus tours
tended to be of elderly Australian tourists. No other bus tour
groups were observed taking the trail as maybe these do not
leave the beach or are advised by guides that the trail/event is
not worth visiting. The organizers and staff seemed satisfied
with this situation and lack of directional signage, though it
does work against independent tourists visiting, who would
benefit from the experience.

An assessment of Sculpture by Sea, Bondi, 2015 indicates
that it will need some minor tweaks and adjustments to maintain
its SCA, but otherwise will remain a success for many years more
if the SCA criteria continue to be met (Table 1).

Conclusion

Sculpture by the Sea (Bondi edition studied) could therefore still
be considered a fresh and inspiring experience for tourists on the
first time round, as it was for the author. However, a few cracks
are evident when talking to participants who have attended more
than once or from observing how crowding on weekends can be
allowed to affect the experience for participants. The lack of
apps or directional signage for independent tourists needs to also
be addressed, if it is retain its innovative image.

Table 1. Assessment of SCA for Sculpture by the Sea, Bondi, 2015.

SCA Criteria	Key Issues for SCA Criteria	Sculpture by the Sea
Glocal orientation/ support	What support is there for holding the event? How is the event playing a role in cultural/ arts ecologies (local/non-local) or in community cultural development (if relevant)?	Support from Waverley Council, Sydney Water, other sponsors, friends, artists, and academics. Commercial partners do drop out occasionally, but new ones join in, for example, Q Hotel.
		Event has become part of the arts scene and increasingly involves international as well as local artists. Its Facebook site actively promotes relevant activities conducted by its partners all year round, particularly participating local artists, galleries, and its imitator Aarhus in Denmark.
Brand image, orientation, and position	Is there any evidence the way the marketing that has shaped and presented the event has been effective in attracting participants/partners/sponsors/ media attention/goodwill from all sectors?	Event has been held since 1997 and has time to build up a following. Press kits are produced every year prior to both Bondi and Cottesloe events with associated early promotions. Gallery owners interviewed in 2015 opined that the brand is still very strong.
		The event still attracts positive publicity due to its proximity to Bondi Beach and due to greater interest in local visual arts since involvement of Australia's new prime minister over the last two years.
Conceptual uniqueness	Is the event standing out from others in some way that is positive and creative?	There is no other event with the same mix of activities, as well as overseas and local art artists, supported by a dynamic and enjoyable outdoor leisure experience, which is all for free.
Experience	What are the positive and negative elements of participants and others experience of the event before/during/afterwards?	Before: Some online resources are available prior to the event, but not always a huge amount of detail.
		During: The experience of being able to wander to or from Bondi Beach along the trail while appreciating the scenery and the sculpture is positive if the weather is good and it is not too crowded. Negative aspects include: rain, bottlenecks along paths and queuing

Table 1. (*Continued*)

SCA Criteria	Key Issues for SCA Criteria	Sculpture by the Sea
		to view small sculpture exhibition on weekends. Needs some apps and/or directional signage for independent tourists. Observation of the tactile tours revealed some minor problems sustaining interest amongst repeat participants. After: Not much use of Facebook page or website for this or other surveys evident, unlike the 2013 Aarhus study.
Implementation and management	What minor changes were made during implementation?	The Olympiad edition suggested other locations for the event. However, only Cottesloe in Western Australia has so far been successful for the organizers. More has been added more to the public education program and developed the first outdoor tactile tours for disabled participants.
	How effective were managers in ensuring the requirements of the four key areas of content, timing, connectivity and resources were fulfilled?	Content: It is a juried event that encourages high quality sculpture to be presented from international and local artists for viewing, sale and to compete for prizes. Timing: The event's position in the artworld calendar works well. However, tourists are not always aware of its existence and not many plan accordingly, unless they are domestic repeat tourists or art tourists. Connectivity: Still quite strong as the event has resolved various issues over the years. There is more media exposure than in previous years to the benefit of the local artists and arts ecology. Resources: The event organizers have achieved a high level of professionalism in managing resources after 19 years of holding the event. There is a risk that if current key individual organizers, such as David Handley or sponsors such as Sydney Water were to pull out for some reason resources would suffer accordingly. On a positive note, there is now a possibility of federal funding with the prime minister's interest.

The question then becomes, can it continue to sustain its creative advantage over the long term? On the weight of current evidence, it appears that unless there is a major change in circumstances or resources, the event should be able to maintain its current form for quite a few more years to come. However, it may be risky to extend the model to other locations in Australia, as the failure in Tasmania has shown.

Overall, importance of glocal arts ecologies for support is a big part of this success and should not be underestimated. As long as there is a refreshing diversity of sculptors prepared to present their work at these two event/trails in Bondi and Cottesloe, there will be fresh art for participants to enjoy. Other stakeholders appear to want to continue to support the event and so do the local residents.

This study has been the first time the new SCA assessment tool had been applied outside of Hong Kong. Data for most of the questions/issues that it requires was freely available from most people approached, although a few were too busy during the event itself for a long interview, unsurprisingly. Applying the approach therefore needs careful timing, if a greater depth of information is needed. However, because the author had been studying the example over a number of years this was not too much of a problem. Applying the approach within a shorter time-scale (such as the event duration only) could yield difficulties.

The SCA evaluation approach will continue to be tested by the author (and hopefully event organizers and other academics). It is likely that the results of this application will be of interest to academics studying glocality and events, the relationship of curatorial power to content/experience or how such events add to the leisurescapes in tourism. Consequently, it should become more obvious that arts events need and deserve their own specific evaluation method to remain a focus of creativity over the long term.

Acknowledgments

The author would like to thank the following people for their time and support in this research: David Handley, Ioni Doherty, Kat Remy, Peter Lundberg, and Petra Pattinson.

References

du Cros, H., & Jolliffe, L. (2011). Bundling the arts for tourism to complement urban heritage experiences in Asia. *Journal of Heritage Tourism*, 6(3), 181–195.

du Cros, H., & Jolliffe, L. (2014). *The arts and events*. Abingdon: Routledge (Taylor and Francis).

du Cros, H., & McKercher, B. (2014). *Cultural tourism*. Abingdon: Routledge.

du Cros, H., & Jolliffe, L. (forthcoming). Sculpture trails. What makes them work or not? *Journal of Heritage Tourism*.

Florida, R. (2002). *The rise of the creative class: And how it's transforming work, leisure, community and everyday life*. New York, NY: Basic Books.

Foley, M., McGillivary, D., & McPherson, G. (2009). Policy, politics and sustainable events. In M. J. Stabler (Ed.), *Tourism and sustainability: Principles to practice* (pp. 13–21). New York, NY: CAB International.

Ganga, R. N. (n.d.). European cultural institutions as glocalisms. The cases of the Fundacao de Serralves and the Contemporary Art Centre (Porto): 329–342. Retrieved from http://ler.letras.up.pt/uploads/ficheiros/10364.pdf. Accessed on October 29, 2015.

Goldbard, A. (2006). *New creative community. The art of cultural development*. Oakland, CA: New Village Press.

Handley, D. (2011). From idea to reality. In Sculpture by the Sea Inc. (Ed.), *Sculpture by the sea. The first fifteen years* (pp. 10–14). Sydney: Sculpture by the Sea Inc.

Handley, D. (2015). Founding Directors Note. *Sculpture by the sea nineteenth annual exhibition official catalogue*. Sydney: Sculpture by the Sea Inc.

Kay, P., & Polonsky, M. (2010). Creative industries and experiences: Development, marketing and consumption. *Tourism, Culture and Communication*, 10(3), 181–186.

McDonald, J. (2011). Sculpture by the sea: A retrospective. In Sculpture by the Sea Inc. (Ed.), *Sculpture by the sea. The first fifteen years* (pp. 6–8). Sydney: Sculpture by the Sea Inc.

Mitchell, P., & Fisher, R. (2010). From passenger to driver: Creativity and culture in rural communities. *Tourism, Culture and Communication*, 10(3), 187–200.

Mitchell, W. J. T. (1992). *Art and the public sphere*. Chicago, IL: Chicago University Press.

Morris, N., & Cant, S. (2007). Engaging with place: Artists, site-specity and the Hebden bridge sculpture trail. *Social and Cultural Geography*, 7(6), 863–888.

Pine, J., & Gilmore, J. (1999). *The experience economy*. Boston, MA: Harvard Business School Press.

Preez, K., & Bailey, J. (2010). *Artistic reflection kit. A guide to assist arts organizations to reflect on artistic vibrancy and measure their artistic achievements*. Canberra: Australia Council for the Arts.

Quinn, B. (2006). Problematising 'festival tourism': Arts festivals and sustainable development in Ireland. *Journal of Sustainable Tourism, 14*(3), 288–306.

Sculpture by the Sea. (2015a). *History*. Retrieved from http://sculpturebythesea. com. Accessed on December 11.

Sculpture by the Sea. (2015b). *Prime minister presents allens peoples' choice award*. Retrieved from http://sculpturebythesea.com/prime-minister-presents-allens-peoples-choice-prize/. Accessed on November 9.

Sculpture by the Sea Aarhus. (2015). *About*. Retrieved from http://en.aros.dk/ visit-aros/the-collection/sculpture-by-the-sea/. Accessed on January 26, 2016.

Sculpture by the Sea Inc. (2011). *Sculpture by the sea. The first fifteen years*. Sydney: Sculpture by the Sea Inc.

Sculptures by the Sea Aarhus. (2013). *Sculpture by the sea Aarhus has ended*. Retrieved from http://www.sculpturebythesea.dk/en/Medier/Nyheder/2013/ 3-kvartal/SxS-2013-slut.aspx. Accessed on November 16, 2015.

Shone, A., & Parry, B. (2004). *Successful events management: A practical handbook*. London: Thomson.

Stolarick, K., & Florida, R. (2006). Creativity, connections and innovation: A study of linkages in the Montreal region. *Environment and Planning A, 38*, 1799–1817.

Vogel, H. L. (2011). *Entertainment industry economics. A guide for financial analysis* (8th ed.). New York, NY: Cambridge University Press.

Waverley Public Library. (2009). *History of Tamarama beach*. Unpublished report. Waverley Public Library.

8

Dragon Boat Intangible Cultural Heritage: Management Challenges of a Community and Élite Sport Event as a Tourism Experience

Fleur Fallon

ABSTRACT

Purpose – This study traces the growth of Dragon Boat racing from humble beginnings in 1976 as part of a local tourism strategy by the Hong Kong Tourist Association (HKTA) to position Hong Kong as more distinctive than a destination for shopping or with British colonial history appeal. Dragon Boat racing is now a recognized world sport requiring a global strategy of co-operative alliances and is close to becoming an official sport in the Olympic Games. Emergent strategy and symbolic authenticity of intangible cultural heritage are key concerns for integrating special events as a central tourism experience.

Methodology/approach – This chapter presents three trends emerging from a review of the literature: concern with balancing authenticity and profit-chasing; the phenomenal fast growth of the sport and the challenge to develop and maintain international control and governance; and seeking evidence of health and well-being benefits of Dragon Boat racing for breast cancer survivors.

Findings – Survivors and élite athletes represent a symbolic authenticity connected to ancient Chinese intangible cultural heritage. Chasing profits by including cultural heritage as part of a particular tourism strategy has strengthened and protected the legacy of that heritage in unexpected ways. There are lessons for those charged with designing quality events and tourism experiences linked with intangible culture.

Research limitations/implications – Based on literature review only, but sets a framework for research in several directions.

Originality/value – Demonstrates the blurring of boundaries between tourism, events and sports, and how managers must be adept to shift strategy according to changing unexpected dynamics of threats and opportunities, yet still can adhere to symbolic authenticity to maintain integrity of intangible cultural heritage as a tourism experience.

Keywords: Dragon Boat racing; cultural heritage events; emergent strategy; symbolic authenticity

Introduction

The Double Fifth (Duan Wu) Festival, which celebrates the summer solstice on the fifth day of the fifth month in the Chinese lunar calendar, and promotes health and well-being, is more widely known in the west as the Dragon Boat Festival. The rise in popularity of Dragon Boat racing as a serious team sport in just four decades deserves particular attention as a case study of how special aspects of so called intangible cultural heritage customs can take on a new life of their own and become separate special events, not just held on one day of the year. Is Dragon Boat racing a passing fad or is it here to stay? Why and how did it become so popular as a sporting event and as a key tourism experience for domestic and international visitors? Is there a loss of authenticity due to the rise of popularity outside of China? Does this matter? Through examining this particular phenomenon, we may derive some lessons for design and strategic management of cultural heritage festivals as major tourism experiences.

Whilst racing Dragon Boats as a cultural activity has been linked to the drowning of the famous poet Qu Yuan over 2,500 years ago, Dragon Boat Racing as a sporting activity was initiated by the Hong Kong Tourism Association (HKTA) in 1976, and has emerged as a worldwide competitive sport for élite men and women athletes. Not only that, it has wide appeal for organizations as a substantive vehicle to promote team spirit, as typically a Dragon Boat carries between 10 and 22 paddlers, seated in pairs, plus a drummer and helm (steerer). Paddlers must synchronize their movement in time to the drum beat for best results. Additionally it is a community leisure sport that has been promoted widely by breast cancer survivors and evokes connections with the ancient Chinese Duan Wu festival rituals that involve protection from evil spirits and ill-health, and promotes community spirit, prosperity and good health. Without the intervention of the HKTA, who saw Dragon Boat racing as a vehicle to promote distinctive ancient Chinese rituals as part of the destination image of Hong Kong in order to attract international tourists, and by implication, chasing profits, the ancient Festival and Dragon Boat racing may well have become lost to a modern audience. This tourism strategy was a serendipitous moment in the modern era of Dragon Boat racing (Sofield & Sivan, 2003[1994]). As a rising sport at the élite and community level, Dragon Boat racing creates a special niche tourism experience as competitors and their supporters travel internationally.

This chapter outlines three key themes: Chinese concern with authenticity and protection of their intangible cultural heritage; changing priority challenges in strategic management during the growth of the sport outside Hong Kong; and the increasing popularity of Dragon Boat racing for breast cancer survivors as a strategy for healthy active living. With this dynamic interplay, Dragon Boat racing as a case study suggests particular learnings for the design of tourism, leisure, and sporting event experiences. Key concepts of intangible cultural heritage, authenticity, and strategic management are briefly outlined, followed by an exploration of the three themes emerging from the literature.

The Theoretical and Cultural Context

China's Dragon Boat Festival was inscribed in the UNESCO representative List of Intangible Cultural Heritage of Humanity in 2009. Intangible cultural heritage includes "traditions or living expressions inherited from our ancestors and passed on to our descendants, such as oral traditions, performing arts, social practices, rituals, festive events, knowledge and practices concerning nature and the universe or the knowledge and skills to produce traditional crafts" (UNESCO, n.d.). The only other Chinese Festival to be listed is the Qiang New Year Festival, besides examples in performing arts and specialized skills.

The UNESCO list citation reads: "The Dragon Boat Festival, comprising ceremonies, dances, performances, games, and the preparation of food and beverages, is carried out in an atmosphere of harmony that strengthens social cohesion, and is regarded and transmitted by the community from generation to generation as part of its cultural identity." The Festival is held throughout China with local regional variants. It is considered culturally important as it "strengthens bonds within families and establishes a harmonious relationship between humanity and nature. It also encourages the expression of imagination and creativity, contributing to a vivid sense of cultural identity" (UNESCO, n.d.).

Under the leadership of Mao Zedong in mainland China, the Festival was isolated and limited in scale (Oakes, 1999). Dragon Boat racing was neglected until the 1980s when it became acknowledged as a sport in China. Scholars became more active in focusing their attention on intangible cultural heritage identification and protection, especially after UNESCO recognized the Korean Dano Festival at Gangneung as intangible cultural heritage in 2005 (Barmé, 2007). The origins of the Korean Festival can be traced back to China's Duan Wu Festival. The Festival in China was reinstated as an official calendar event with a public holiday since 2008. The date varies, according to the fifth day of the fifth month (double fifth) in the Chinese lunar calendar.

In Hong Kong, still under British rule until the handover to China in 1999, the Festival, mostly celebrated by fishing communities, had declined in popularity due to modernization and commercialization (Sofield & Sivan, 2003[1994]). The Hong Kong Festival adaptation of the ancient Chinese tradition, centered around honoring Tin Hau, the Goddess of the Sea, in order to seek protection of fishing communities and to ensure future prosperity. In the 1970s the HKTA saw an opportunity to use a

Chinese cultural heritage festival as a hook to lure in more international tourists and to position Hong Kong as more than a shopping destination. With increasing tourism competition, such a strategy seeks to inform locals and visitors about the particular cultural heritage and acts as a champion for its protection and strengthening.

Chinese academics debate issues relating to authenticity of the Festival experience in tension with profit-chasing in more recent times (see the next section). In reviewing the literature on "authenticity," Li and Wall (2014, p. 25) conclude that authenticity is not a set of rigid rules relating to a particular culture in a particular place. It is a "dynamic, fluid, negotiated and creative process, and it constantly changes in response to the context and individual perspectives." Lew (2011) clarifies that this may include existential authenticity, that is, it is dependent on the experience of the tourist or visitor.

Dragon Boat racing is a case of adaptive authenticity, whose symbolism of community harmony, good health, and prosperity still resonates in the staging of Dragon Boat Racing Festivals. We might even call it "symbolic authenticity." This theme of change and adaptive authenticity also relates to key concepts linked with strategic management and experience design.

Mintzberg's (1987) definition of strategy is a dynamic one, and includes strategy as a plan, as a ploy, as a pattern of behavior, as a position within the competitive environment, and as a perspective. Mintzberg suggests that the traditional way of thinking about strategy implementation focuses only on deliberate strategies. However, many organizations begin implementing strategies before they clearly articulate mission, goals, or objectives, that is, strategy implementation may precede formal strategy formulation.

Mintzberg (1992) calls strategies that unfold in this way "emergent" strategies. Apart from rapid technology changes in transport, communications and knowledge management, political, and economic changes also signify a need to review and adapt strategy in the changing dynamics. More recently Mintzberg (2010) mentions the importance of collective thinking, co-operatives and networks for doing business. The story of Dragon Boat racing is an exemplar of both emergent strategy and symbolic authenticity. Based on the successful experience of a local tourism strategy, a large-scale emergent strategy for international governance of a world sport has evolved. As a fast growing sport, Dragon Boat Racing is becoming a major leisure experience for locals and a growing tourism market segment, with participants and supporters also engaging as tourists.

Before exploring the consequences arising from that first step – the lucky moment – to hold an international Dragon Boat racing competition in Hong Kong in 1976, a review of the concerns of Chinese academic scholars is presented.

Concerns about Authenticity and Profit-Chasers

There was a surge of studies by Chinese that focused on their cultural roots, including dragon rituals, and a revival in Dragon Boat racing traditions, especially in the lead up to the Year of the Dragon in 1988 (Oakes, 1999).

In considering the Dragon Boat Festival as a featured tourism experience, Chinese authors are concerned with balancing authenticity in honoring tradition and profit-chasing. However as the narrative of the Festival changed from ancient folk tradition to government shaping around commemorating historical events, "authentic tradition" remains varied and not easily verifiable across China. Huang (2007) compares the Festival with the Korean Gangneung Dano Festival, inscribed in UNESCO's World Intangible Cultural Heritage list in 2005. While both Festivals have a similar ancient origin, the Korean Festival remains closer to the original meaning of the sacrificial ceremony. There are many more variations of experience in China due to the larger population and wide geographical spread.

The tracing of the development of the Festival is covered by several authors, for example, Zhang (2007), Li and Huang (2010) and Huang and Yang (2011). Li and Huang (2010) provide an overview of studies about the Festival. The customs of the Festival are recorded in many ancient texts, and can be traced back to more than 5,000 years ago. In more recent texts there is evident conflict about the Festival meaning and tension between folk tradition and official government promoted events. The folk tradition centers on exorcising evil spirits, but has been subsumed in its promotion as a political government sponsored event to commemorate Qu Yuan, a poet-statesman in the state of Chu. He was exiled on suspicion of corruption, and when he heard that the state of Qin had conquered Chu, he committed suicide in 278 BC by drowning in the Li Mo, a river located in today's Hunan province. The story continues that fishermen paddled out to rescue him, and threw rice to the fish so they would not eat Qu Yuan. *Zongzi*, the special food that commemorates this story, is a sticky rice dumpling, wrapped and tied in leaves then steamed. Today, the Festival not only aims to maintain links with traditional culture through promoting special activities, (such as Dragon Boat racing), souvenirs and food, such as *zongzi*, but also promotes healthy lifestyles and a happy, harmonious family and community. As well as concerns about the dualistic nature of the Festival, scholars have been concerned with the function of the Festival in relation to the economy, entertainment and hygiene, and regional variations of the Festival within mainland China.

Lou (2010) is concerned about the role of mass media in relation to the development of intangible cultural heritage festivals. Although it may be an efficient promotion tool, media reporting is short-term and may only focus on economic gain (or loss) to the detriment of reinforcement of local cultural knowledge. Heritage protection must be considered as a long- term process.

Local case studies suggest tensions about integrating intangible cultural heritage elements in the tourism experience mix. Liu (2014) concludes that the Zigui Dragon Boat Festival, Hunan, acknowledged as the home town of Qu Yuan, had limited creativity, few activities and lacked financial support to create a cohesive and memorable experience to attract tourists. However, Liu, Fu, Wu, and Li (2011) are concerned that too many activities, souvenirs and entertainment on offer at the Guangxi Rong'an Dragon Boat Festival dilute the cultural heritage and may lead to misunderstanding about the Festival traditions as well as cause conflict between tourists and local residents. Finding the right balance between tradition and modernity, authenticity and commercialization, while respecting the rights of local residents is a complex task for the design of experience for events as a tourism drawcard. This is a similar concern for Zhu and Dai (2013), with their study of the Canoe Festival, held by the Miao ethnic minority group of Shidong town and its significant impact on the local economy. The Miao had continued to hold Dragon Boat races, but for some Han river towns in south-eastern Guizhou, Dragon Boat racing did not resume until 1994 (Oakes, 1999, p. 134). Festivals were then officially sanctioned as a way to promote sporting events for local teams, as well as a way to reconnect links to the past.

Some authors still express a concern about the decline of popularity for the Dragon Boat Festival, linked with a decline in the sense of a "we feeling" that expresses the national identity and spiritual approval of a nation (Sun, 2009). Yang (2005) adds that the common every day possibility of racing Dragon Boats, or of eating *zongzi,* decline in the spiritual aspects relating to history and poetry education of the Festival, plus globalization and the spread of western festivals and lack of government attention have contributed to the decline of appeal in the Dragon Boat Festival. Globalization processes are also a concern of Zhang (2007) and recommendations for drawing attention to, and improving the Festival in China parallel those of Lou (2010) and Liu (2014).

This set of articles, mostly written in Chinese, are internally and locally focused. Whilst the form and meaning of the Dragon Boat Festival has changed over time such that narrow debates about authenticity are on shaky ground, the rise in popularity of Dragon Boat racing globally has been extraordinary. Nearly every day somewhere in the world, there is a Dragon Boat race. The globalization process is working well in reverse. Originating from Hong Kong, "profit-chasing," in the form of tourism development and diversification of experience offerings by highlighting ancient Chinese traditions, has strengthened knowledge, and appreciation, of those traditions. The following section reviews this growth, including steps taken to honor the origin of ancient Chinese traditions.

Globalization Flow from East to the World – New Threats and Opportunities

Since 1976, as highlighted by Sofield and Sivan (2003[1994]), the renaissance of the Chinese Dragon Boat Festival into an international sporting event, had already begun, thanks to the HKTA's efforts to embed more distinctive Chinese characteristics into its destination image. HKTA's lead was quickly followed by both the Penang and Singapore Tourist Boards who also saw the value of using the Dragon Boat tradition as a way of promoting their own tourist attractions. It also should be noted that the HKTA took great care to collaborate with the local fishermen's association in order to honor and respect tradition. With the influence of modernization, the popularity of the Hong Kong's Tuen Ng (Dragon Boat Festival) had declined. The boats used for this traditional Festival were only used for this purpose, and brought out of storage four days before the Festival for the ritual awakening performed by Taoist priests (Sofield & Sivan, 2003 [1994], p. 14). With the formation of National Dragon Boat Associations in Europe, led by the British in 1985 and on other Continents, then the European Dragon Boat Federation (EDBF) in 1990 and International Dragon Boat Federation (IDBF) in 1991, followed by the Asian Dragon Boat Federation (ADBF) in 1992, the modern sport of Dragon Boating was quickly established and expanded throughout the world, with the IDBF introducing formal rules and regulations, standard boat designs, coaching and officiating schemes for the Sport. With the growth of popularity of Dragon Boat racing as a competitive and community sport, boats are not resting for long. Teams often practise together for several months before a competition. With more than 200 official events on the IDBF calendar, this means that "authentic" traditions are adapted, yet the essence of the Festival – good health and community harmony – remains firmly embedded in the practice of the sport and in the objectives and aims of the IDBF.

Today Dragon Boating is a "vibrant, effective and independent paddle sport." More than 80 countries have membership of the IDBF, with estimates of nearly 50 million participants in China, more than 300,000 in Europe, well over 100,000 in North America and many more hundreds of thousands in Asia, Oceania, and Africa. Hong Kong alone claims that 250,000 people take part annually in races celebrating the Dragon Boat Festival (IDBF, 2014). Table 1 presents a summary of milestones in the extraordinary 5,000 year history of Dragon Boat racing.

Although growth has been phenomenal, there have been major obstacles along the way. In sports governance only one organization is normally recognized at national and international levels by government agencies and multi-sport organizations. In terms of water sports involving paddles, there are two organizations: the IDBF, which is the recognized federation for Dragon Boating and the International Canoeing Federation (ICF), the recognized federation for Canoeing. However the ICF also holds an annual Dragon Boat Championship for the small percentage of its Members that are involved in the Sport.

In 1981, three Dragon Boats were sent to Nottingham UK to participate in demonstration races at the World Canoe and Kayaking Championship meeting. No subsequent action was taken by British Canoe Union or ICF to incorporate Dragon Boat racing into their organization. The ICF had declared that Dragon Boat racing was not a discipline of canoeing.

Table 1.   Major Milestones in the History of Dragon
Boat Racing.

5000–7000 BC	Duan Wu Festival and dragon boat racing evidence on archeological artefacts.
340–278 BC	Qu Yuan, exiled statesman/poet, suicides by drowning in the Li Mo (Mo River) in Hunan. The legend states fishermen paddled out in an attempt to rescue him and threw rice dumplings to the fish, so that they wouldn't eat Qu Yuan.
1949–1970s	In the new People's Republic of China, led by Mao Zedong, the Duan Wu Festival was banned.
1957	Hong Kong Tourist Association (HKTA) established by Hong Kong government to develop the tourism industry – narrow focus on hotel, shopping, food, and some special events.
1970s	Declining interest in traditional ceremonies in HK due to modernization and profit-chasing.
1976	HKTA encouraged the local Fishermen's Society to revive the Dragon Boat races, and with Cathay Pacific sponsored a Japanese team to participate in the first international Dragon Boat racing competition, held one week after the traditional festival; 300 rowers were involved.
1978	Part of destination image strategy and new badging: The Hong Kong Dragon Boat Festival – International Races, held in Victoria Harbor.
1979	First international Dragon Boat racing event held in Penang, Malaysia.
1981	Commercial sponsorship began; raised HK$200,000; plus "Row for Charity"; raised HK$86,000; 50 local teams; 7 international crews.
	Dragon Boats demonstrated at the World Canoe and Kayaking Championship in Nottingham, the United Kingdom with a three boat race series over 500 meters. No action was taken by British Canoe Union or International Canoeing Federation (ICF) to incorporate DB racing in their organization.
1984	First national Dragon Boat racing event held in mainland China.
1985	First formal Club established in Great Britain and racing commenced with boats transported to Nottingham for the 1981 demonstration races.
1986	Hong Kong presented four boats to Vancouver Canada at Expo 1986; Milton Wong & Associates formed the Lotus Sports Club; staged Dragon Boat races at Expo.
	False Creek **Racing Canoe** Club also formed a Dragon Boat club and helped organize the first annual Dragon Boat races in Vancouver; Venice Rowing Club and Circolo Canottieri

Table 1.   (*Continued*)

	Tevere Remo held first national event in Italy; New Zealand Dragon Boat Association was formed.
1987–1989	British Dragon Boat Racing Association (BDA) formed as the first National Federation in Europe. BDA developed the first written specification for a Dragon Boat based on the Hong Kong design of wooden boat but made in fiber glass (GRP). GRP Boats sent to Italy, the Netherlands, Sweden, and Germany with support from the HKTA in London and ad hoc racing commenced in Europe, with the first International Races held in Belgium.
1990	European Dragon Boat Federation (EDBF) was formed. EDBF recognized the Malmo Festival Dragon Boat Races as the first International Dragon Boat Racing Festival held in Europe.
1991	24 June, HK Dragon Boat Association (HKDBA) was formed as the local governing body of the sport – includes the Joint Association of HK Fishermen, and leading HK Clubs;
	International Dragon Boat Federation (IDBF) established, with Headquarters in Hong Kong, and 12 founding members: HK, PR China, Australia, Indonesia, Italy, Malaysia, Norway, Philippines, Singapore, Taiwan, the United Kingdom, and the United States.
1992	HKDBA registration as an affiliated member of the Amateur Sports Federation & Olympic Committee of HK.
	Asia DB Federation (ADBF) was formed, with responsibility for Asia.
	1st European Dragon Boat Championships held in Hazwinkle, Belgium.
1993	HK–128 local teams; 32 from overseas from 14 countries, including men and women, and the charity race raised HK $1.2 million for the HK Community Chest. HKTA sponsored 10 overseas crews and linked another 10 with commercial sponsors.
1995	1st IDBF World Nations Championships held in Yu Yang, China.
1996	Vancouver hosted the first International Dragon Boat Racing Festival held in North America, which incorporated the 1st IDBF Club Crew World Championships. First participation by novice women's cancer survivor team Abreast in a Boat, supported by sports physician Dr Donald McKenzie.
2002	The IDBF acknowledged the development of BCS survivor crews, formally welcomed them into the Dragon Boat family and confirmed its commitment to promote breast cancer awareness by providing a platform for BCS crews to participate in the sport at IDBF events.

Table 1.   (*Continued*)

2005	Dragon Boating included in the World Games as an invitational Sport. Korean Gangneung Dano Festival, inscribed in UNESCO's World Intangible Cultural Heritage list; similar origin as Duan Wu Festival, in ancient China.
	BCS Commission established, BCS crews raced in the 2005 IDBF World Championships.
2005–2006	Olympic Council of Asia (OCA) recognized IDBF as the official world international federation organizing DB racing and the ADBF as the IDBF Continental Federation with responsibility for the Sport in OCA Games.
	1st BCS Championships held in Singapore in September 2006.
2007	IDBF accepted into Membership of the General Association of International Sports Federation (GAISF), now SportAccord, as the DB Sports world governing body. DB racing recognized as an independent sport. The IOC confirmed its acceptance of the GAISF's decisions.
2008	Court of Arbitration for Sport confirmed the status of IDBF as the only official recognized world organization for Dragon Boating.
	The Duan Wu Festival in mainland China was recognized by the granting of a national public holiday.
2010	Dragon Boating included in the Asian Games. The International Breast Cancer Paddlers' Commission was established as an IDBF Commission – 150 teams in membership worldwide. First IBCPC Participatory Festival held in Canada.
2011	Led by IDBF, Alliance of Independent recognized Members of Sport (AIMS) was founded in 2011 by the 23 non-IOC recognized members of SportAccord.
2015	IDBF: 85 nations and territories have membership. Another 19 Countries are known to the IDBF as having an interest in Dragon Boating. 50 are required for IOC Recognition, a process that the IDBF is currently undertaking. 75 are required for acceptance as an official Olympic Games sport, once IOC Recognition has been obtained.
	20 year anniversary of Abreast in a Boat.
2016	40 years since first international Dragon Boat competition was held in Hong Kong. Official recognition of the IDBF as an Olympic Federation is a goal to achieve by end of 2016.

Source: Derived from "a brief history of the IDBF"; Sofield and Sivan (2003).

With growing interest in Dragon Boat racing from crews attending the annual Hong Kong International Races, especially in Europe after the 1981 demonstration races in Nottingham and in North America after the 1986 Expo in Vancouver Canada, when Hong Kong donated four boats to Canada, the IDBF was formed in June 1991 with 12 founding members, and headquartered in Hong Kong.

IDBF has gone from strength to strength, and the aim is to become an IOC Recognized International Federation by the end of 2016, which is the first step in the process of applying to become an Olympic Sport in a future Olympic Games. This strategic goal, now very strong and likely to succeed, follows the founding in 2011 of the Alliance of Independent recognized Members of Sports (AIMS) with 23 members. AIMS was accepted by the IOC as a SportAccord partner in 2015 and the AIMS goal now is to become an IOC Recognized Organization in 2016. Three sports within this alliance – climbing and mountaineering; flying disc (ultimate frisbee) and American football – have achieved individual acceptance as IOC Recognized Federations.

The aim of AIMS is to strengthen each individual sport, combine expertise, share knowledge and maintain close cooperation with the International Olympic Committee (IOC), so that the individual sport will achieve official recognition from the IOC. (IDBF, 2012)

However in the late 1990s and early 2000s, ICF attempted to take over the governance of Dragon Boat racing by inviting clubs to join their "family." ICF accepted that IDBF was the world governing body in 2003 but since 2005 organizes some Dragon Boat competitions for its members. IDBF was recognized as the official world governing body for Dragon Boat racing in 1999 and was admitted to full membership of SportAccord in 2007. In the same year IDBF conducted an open survey of Dragon Boat participants, who overwhelmingly identified with IDBF as the governing body and supported the move toward becoming an Olympics recognized ISF (International Sports Federation). The Court of Arbitration for Sport confirmed the status of IDBF in 2008. All international competitions are held using IDBF standards for boats and paddles, as well as competition rules. For technical details on standard specifications of boats, paddles and competition rules, go to the IDBF website idbf.org. Subject to meeting 54 criteria, IDBF expects to achieve IOC Recognized status by the end of 2016 (IDBF letter to National Sports Authorities, October 1, 2014).

Embedded in each club's constitution and strategic plans is the specific objective:

"Ensure that the historical and cultural heritage of dragon boating is acknowledged and protected" … by incorporating Chinese Dragon Boating traditions as appropriate at all regional/state events, as well as involving the local Chinese communities in Club activities (Dragon Boat Tasmania, 2013). Such clear intentions should allay concerns by Chinese authors and others, such as McCartney and Osti (2007) that the primary cultural heritage of the Festival is weakened as the focus shifts to Dragon Boat racing as a spectator entertainment and participant sport experience. Dragon Boat racing remains symbolically authentic and tied to its cultural roots, as it embodies the spirit of good health, fitness, and community spirit.

As well as competition at élite athletic level, IDBF also has developed a Community and Corporation Festival program with an emphasis on health and fitness, team spirit, and having fun. Along with international world and club championships, IDBF has over 200 events listed on its annual calendar, so there is a broad responsibility at different levels – junior, men, and women; novice and experienced athletes; company and community groups, including a special group for breast cancer survivors.

There is limited research about the involvement of corporations' involvement in Dragon Boating, other than as corporate sponsors but Dragon Boating is included in the World Corporate Games and in many of the Corporate Games held around the world at National Level as well as being featured in the World Fire Fighters' Games.

According to Brooke (2015) participants in Singapore like Dragon Boating for its camaraderie and social connectivity, but the experience is outside of their workplace, that is, separate from any sense of company teambuilding efforts. However from the growth in the number of Dragon Boat Festivals around the world today, community group and corporate interest in this team sport is growing. The next section looks at a particular community group. Recent literature, especially emanating from Canada, indicates an unexpected link to traditions and rituals, especially in relation to health and well-being.

Symbolic Authenticity and New Alliances

Studies on breast cancer survivors and their involvement with Dragon Boats have emerged from Canada since 1998. It was serendipitous that in 1986, Hong Kong presented four boats to Vancouver Canada at Expo 1986. Milton Wong & Associates formed the Lotus Sports Club and staged Dragon Boat races at Expo. False Creek Racing Canoe Club also formed a Dragon Boat club and helped organize the first annual Dragon Boat races in Vancouver. It took another 10 years of growing popularity before the first participation by novice women's cancer survivor team Abreast in a Boat.

Oh et al. (2004), cited by Parry (2008), note that in Canada where more than 22,000 women are diagnosed with breast cancer each year, the mortality rate showed a decline since 1986, and the five year survival rate was about 76 percent. As the number of breast cancer survivors was increasing with earlier detection and treatment, some women had begun to challenge the notion that they should not participate in active sports. They were supported by sports physician Dr Donald McKenzie from the University of British Columbia.

McKenzie (1998) noted that women had been advised to avoid strenuous activity after breast cancer surgery in order to prevent the increased risk of lymphedema, a chronic, irreversible swelling of the arms. McKenzie thought that Dragon Boating was an ideal exercise for this group of women. As a non-weight bearing exercise but with strenuous upper body activity, it would send a highly visible positive message to everyone with breast cancer. With proper training, it was deemed to be safe and offered physical health benefits by improving muscle mass and musculoskeletal and cardiovascular systems. Twenty four women aged between 31 and 62 years volunteered to form the first test team in February 1996. The only common criteria was that they were breast cancer survivors, who had survived six months beyond their last treatment. As a team sport with 22–26 paddlers, plus a drummer and helm (steerer), Dragon Boating also builds up a sense of togetherness and harmony. As a prescriptive exercise for a particular group, the Abreast in a Boat project included three workouts a week in the months leading up to the Vancouver competition.

So successful was the concept that the Abreast in a Boat Society, under the auspices of IDBF, participates annually in the Vancouver event, and now holds its own events, with 150 teams worldwide participating in 2015. The Society aims to support women (and men) with breast cancer to believe that they can lead full, active lives despite their physical limitations. This means that for each competition, there is an influx of 3,000–5,000 Dragon Boat tourists, comprising competitors, supporters and spectators. Typically visitors stay for four to seven days with one to two days of competition.

Several qualitative and quantitative studies have been conducted to gather evidence about the health benefits for breast cancer survivors who participate in Dragon Boat racing. Parry (2007, 2008) collected evidence to understand the broader health implications from a survivor's perspective. Her findings suggest changes to a "sense of self, personal identity, and health and well-being" across the five dimensions of social, emotional, physical, spiritual, and mental dimensions of health. The symbolism of the Dragon Boat racing is immensely powerful and works to support the quality and length of survivorship (Parry, 2007; Shermak, 2008, p. 210).

Women gain solidarity and emotional support in the shared history and are able to move beyond societal expectations of "how they should live out their life post-cancer" (Wilkinson, 2001, cited in Shermak, 2008, p. 10). See also McDonough, Sabiston, and Ullrich-French (2011).The mounting evidence suggests that not only is Dragon Boating safe for breast cancer survivors, but it has achieved wide acceptance in just two decades (Harris, 2012). Exercise-induced stressors are seen as positive, with strong correlation with feelings of self-esteem and overall well-being (Hadd, Sabiston, McDonough, & Crocker, 2010). The women have created their own ritual experiences, including dressing in pink, releasing pink flowers in the water to remember those who died, and a special saying "we seldom place, but we always win" (McKenzie, 1998, p. 377).

Chinese can be proud of the modern interpretation springing from the experience well of their ancient traditions related to health, happiness and prosperity and the dragon's protective spirit.

Conclusion

The cultural legitimacy and authenticity debate may have some merit, but its focus is narrow and detracts from what has been happening in the last four decades in the growth of Dragon Boat racing as an international competitive and community sport. From the IDBF documentation, Dragon Boat racing is alive and well, and honors the original purpose of the Festival for promoting and supporting community, with a focus on health and well-being benefits. Each race also begins with some rituals, adapted from the original awakening the Dragon spirit, and with Dragon heads on the bow, plus the rhythmic beating of the drum, intrinsic linkages with the Chinese origin are clearly on display around the world. Dragon Boat racing, which might seem an unlikely sport for breast cancer survivors, has been rising in popularity with special interest community groups and corporations. As a spectator sport, it is also an exciting event, which attracts locals and tourists to the event, as well as the large number of participants and supporters.

In relation to strategic management, and governance of the sport, IDBF experienced a threat from the ICF, after they declined to recognize Dragon Boat racing as a discipline of canoeing. IDBF has headed off these threats through close collaboration with its extensive networks across five continents and was proactive in initiating an alliance with other independent sports with the specific aim to become a fully accredited Sport and recognized Federation of the International Olympic Committee. They are close to achieving this goal within two years. It is remarkable that Dragon Boat racing has come so far, so fast in just four decades in gaining international recognition.

The initial steps of the HKTA to incorporate Dragon Boat racing as a local strategy for tourism experience distinctiveness has rapidly evolved into a global strategy for developing a world sport. World sport, by implication, attracts special niche tourists comprising competitors, coaches, friends, and family supporters, plus other spectators. In this case, a special cultural event, élite and community sport combine to create a new tourism niche market, and one that tourism managers can capitalize on by ensuring that the distinctive intangible cultural heritage elements of waking the dragon, and putting it to sleep at the end, the decorative dragon heads on the boats and the drumming style remain quintessential ingredients of the total experience. While it has moved from a once-a-year calendar community event to an almost every day sporting event, the world governing body, the IDBF, has built in constitutional mechanisms to ensure continuing recognition and protection of its Chinese cultural heritage traditions within the modern experience.

This chapter does not include a long review of literature on authenticity of ethnic tourism or strategy, but builds on the comprehensive survey already undertaken by Li and Wall (2010) and Mintzberg's well-known paper on the meaning of strategy. A deeper study, with interviews with stakeholders – organizers and participants, statistical analysis and surveys would enrich this broad brushstroke case study. Several research pathways are suggested, such as global sport governance challenges, corporate engagement with Dragon Boat racing, comparison of the benefits of Dragon Boat racing with other sports, as well as developing greater accuracy in participant statistics and specific contribution to economic and community value as a special tourism experience. The value of this chapter lies in indicating evidence of the spectacular growth of Dragon Boat racing, along with the challenges of formalizing structure and governance of a world élite sport and a special community sport, that may be part of a larger Festival and tourism experience, without loss of integrity and respect for its ancient origins in rituals that are symbolically authentic.

Acknowledgments

I am indebted for the learning and support of Guo You You, a student in the School of Tourism Management, Sun Yat-sen University, Zhuhai China for reading and summarizing several Chinese language articles. Thank you to Mike MacKeddie-Haslam, Honorary Life President of the International Dragon Boating Federation (IDBF) for taking the time to correct and to add insider detail for a more comprehensive chapter.

References

Barmé, G. (2007). Duanwu: The Sino-Korean dragon boat races. *China Heritage Quarterly*, *11*. Retrieved from www.chinaheritagequarterly.org/features

Brooke, M. (2015). Fongzi, dragons and corporate culture: An analysis of corporate dragon-boat paddlers' motivations. *Asia Pacific Journal of Sport and Social Science*. doi:10.1080/21640599.2015.1060037

Dragon Boat Tasmania. (2013). *Strategic plan 2014–2018*. Retrieved from http://dragonboattas.com.au/wp-content/uploads/2013/06/Strategic-Plan-2014-2018-Dragon-Boat-Tasmania.pdf

Hadd, V., Sabiston, C., McDonough, M., & Crocker, P. (2010). Sources of stress for breast cancer survivors involved in Dragon Boating: Examining association with treatment characteristics and self-esteem. *Journal of Women's Health*, 19(7), 1345–1353. doi:10.1089/jwh.2009.1440

Harris, S. (2012). "We're all in the same boat": A review of the benefits of Dragon Boat racing for women living with breast cancer. *Evidence-Based Complementary and Alternative Medicine*. doi:10.1155/2012/167651

Huang, J. (2007). A comparison between the Chinese and the Republic of Korea Double-Fifth Day from the perspective of calendrical folk custom features. *Journal of Zhejiang University (Humanities and Social Sciences)*, 37(4), 94–99 (in Chinese).

Huang, T., & Yang, W. (2011). Historical inheritance and contemporary renaissance of Double Fifth Festival. *Journal of Wenzhou University (Social Sciences)*, 24(4), 37–46 (in Chinese).

IDBF. (2014). *International Dragon Boat Federation letter to National Sports Authorities*, October 1. Retrieved from www.idbf.org

Lew, A. (2011). Understanding experiential authenticity through the best tourism places. *Tourism Geographies*, 13(4), 570–575.

Li, H., & Huang, Z. (2010). A review and the expectation of the Dragon Boat Festival culture: Relating research on the achievements and defects of researches in Hunan. *Journal of Hunan Agricultural University (Social Sciences)*, 11(1), 73–77 (in Chinese).

Li, Y., & Wall, G. (2010). Authenticity in ethnic tourism: Domestic tourists' perspectives. *Current Issues in Tourism*, 12(3), 235–254.

Li, Y., & Wall, G. (2014). *Planning for ethnic tourism*. Farnham: Ashgate.

Liu, S. (2014). Research on the suitability for the tour exploitation of intangible cultural heritage: A case survey of the Quyuan Hometown in Zigui County. *Yunnan Geographic Environment Research*, 26(4), 65–70 (in Chinese).

Liu, W., Fu, J., Wu, X., & Li, Z. (2011). Influence of traditional festival and event development on social culture in minority areas: A case study of Rong'an Dragon Boat Festival. *Journal of Hebei Institute of Physical Education*, 25(2), 85–88 (in Chinese).

Lou, Y. (2010). Research on communication by mass media about intangible cultural heritage: With the Dragon Boat Festival as a case study. *Journal of Zhejiang University*, 1–39 (in Chinese).

McCartney, G., & Osti, L. (2007). From cultural events to sport events: A case study of cultural authenticity in the Dragon Boat Races. *Journal of Sport & Tourism*, 12(1), 25–40.

McDonough, M., Sabiston, C., & Ullrich-French, S. (2011). The development of social relationships, social support, and post-traumatic growth in a Dragon Boating team for breast cancer survivors. *Journal of Sport & Exercise Psychology*, 33, 627–648.

McKenzie, D. (1998). Abreast in a boat – A race against breast cancer. *Canadian Medical Association Journal JAMC*, 159(4), 376–378.

Mintzberg, H. (1987). The strategy concept I: Five P's of strategy. *California Management Review*, 30(1), 25–32.

Mintzberg, H. (1992). Five Ps for strategy. In H. Mintzberg & J. Quinn (Eds.), *The strategy process* (pp. 12–19). Englewood Cliffs, NJ: Prentice-Hall International Editions.

Mintzberg, H. (2010). Developing leaders? Developing countries? *Oxford Leadership Press*, 1(2), 1–10.

Oakes, T. (1999). Eating the food of our ancestors: Place, tradition, and tourism in a Chinese frontier river town. *Eucemene*, 6(2), 123–145.

Parry, D. (2007). "There is life after Breast Cancer": Nine vignettes exploring Dragon Boat racing for breast cancer survivors. *Leisure Sciences*, 29, 53–69. doi:10.1080/01490400600983420

Parry, D. (2008). The contribution of Dragon Boat racing to women's health and breast cancer survivorship. *Qualitative Health Research*, 18(2), 222–233. doi:10.1177/1049732307312304

Shermak, S. (2008). *Digging in, moving on: The experiences of breast cancer dragon boat paddlers*. Thesis submitted for Masters of Social Work, Faculty of Graduate Studies, University of British Columbia.

Sofield, T., & Sivan, A. (2003 [1994]). From cultural festival to international sport-the Hong Kong Dragon Boat races. *Journal of Sport Tourism*, 8(1), 9–20.

Sun, W. (2009). The development direction of the Dragon Boat Festival: The design of the Festival activities. *Journal of East China Normal University*, 1–52 (in Chinese).

UNESCO. (n.d.). *United Nations educational, scientific and cultural organisation*. Retrieved from http://en.unesco.org/

Yang, L. (2005). On the culture of Dragon Boat Festival and its tourism value. *Journal of Yibin University*, 4(4), 9–13 (in Chinese).

Zhang, X. (2007). Researching on industrialization of the Chinese traditional festivals in the context of globalization: Dragon Boat Festival as an example. *Journal of Lanzhou University*, 1–46 (in Chinese).

Zhu, N., & Dai, G. (2013). Research on business promotion of traditional festival sports of minorities in Guizhou Province: Take the case of Dragon Canoe Festival in Shidong Town, Taijiang Countÿ. *Journal of Liupansui Normal University*, 25(4), 84–88 (in Chinese).

9 Collaborating to Provide Attractive Hotel Guests' Experiences

Marios Sotiriadis and
Christos Sarmaniotis

ABSTRACT

Purpose – The aim of this chapter is twofold: (i) to explore the issue of experience within the context of the hotel industry and (ii) to analyze the contribution of collaboration between businesses in providing valuable experiences in hotel settings.

Methodology/approach – Extensive literature reviews have been done on dimensions and outcomes of tourist experiences and on collaboration/business venture's contribution in providing memorable experiences in the hotel industry. A case study is then used to illustrate how hotel operations are collaborating to provide tourism experience opportunities.

Findings – (i) Collaboration between hotel operations makes a significant contribution in providing special guest experiences; (ii) Investment in business ventures is a good investment because it constitutes a potential source of competitive advantage; (iii) A collaborative platform wisely designed creates a series of business benefits.

Research limitations/implications – This study is explorative in nature. Based on a single case study of a business network, the suggestions are indicative rather than conclusive.

Thus, more empirical studies and analyses are needed to fully validate the chapter's suggestions.

Practical implications – The collaborative approach is a requirement for hotel businesses in providing valuable tourism experiences and in overcoming the issues and challenges arising within the context of experiential tourism. This collaboration offers a way of enriching and deepening guests' experiences, based on endogenous resources and meeting the tourists' requirements.

Originality/value – Offers insights on tourism providers' collaborations in offering attractive experience opportunities to their customers.

Keywords: Hotel industry; guest experiences; collaboration; network; Otium in Italy; managerial benefits

Introduction

Academic research and business reports have documented and highlighted the main challenges that the tourism industry in general and hotel industry in particular, have to address (Deloitte, 2010; Fyall & Garrod, 2005; Middleton, Fyall, Morgan, & Ranchhod, 2009). The key issues and challenges are in the field of tourist consumer behavior. Consumers are changing faster than ever before in both attitude and behaviors, and the hotel industry – traditionally more focused on the physical product – is waking up to a consumer who is demanding consistent delivery of the service promise and, in some segments of the industry, the experiential dimension will define a successful business.

It is argued that the most successful hotel providers will be those that are most able to efficiently engage with consumers and clearly differentiate their offering from their competitors. Delivering their service experience consistently will be vital to success. In the mid-market and budget-end of the market, tourism providers must combine value with experience to entice demanding consumers. Within this market context, tourism providers that are able to understand and meet the needs of these new consumers will be the most competitive; the main challenge is to be capable of responding creatively to new consumers' behaviors and trends. Let us point out three main trends: (i) the baby boomers generation – aged from 45 to 64 – is a key segment and should be targeted with "experiential" life-enhancing products, designed to appeal to their "forever young" attitudes and desire for experiential travel; (ii) the emphasis has to be on customized offerings; and (iii) price, quality, service experience, and convenience will continue to drive consumer spending.

Furthermore, within this increasingly challenging business environment, there is a particular characteristic of the tourism industry: interdependence. The travel and tourism sector can be viewed as comprising five component segments/industries: accommodation/hotels; attractions; transport; travel organizers; and destination organizations (Middleton et al., 2009). The hotel industry is inextricably linked with the other industries in the wider tourism and leisure industry. There are strong relationships between the hotel industry and other industries such as airlines and travel trade, which make up the wider tourism experience (Gursoy, Saayman, & Sotiriadis, 2015). The providers of tourism services are all linked and depend upon one another, that is, there is interdependence between them.

Within this context collaboration is a necessity rather than a luxury (Sotiriadis, Gursoy, & Saayman, 2015). The aim of this chapter is twofold: (i) to explore the issue of experience within the context of hotel settings and (ii) to analyze the contribution of collaboration in providing valuable experiences within the hotel industry and how this collaboration could be carried out to achieve managerial and marketing benefits for the participants. First, the main characteristics of experiential tourism are outlined. A review of relevant literature on consumer experiences and on collaboration is then undertaken, focusing on experiential dimensions and outcomes and how a business venture could have a significant contribution. This issue and related aspects are illustrated by using examples as well as a case study of a network providing attractive experience opportunities.

Experiential Tourism: Tourists' Requirements and Providers' Appropriate Approach

Experiential tourism constitutes the precise expression of inspirations and requirements of savvy and experienced tourists of this century. The term "experiential" constitutes a buzzword in tourism where tourists are looking for unique offerings and activities. While there is consensus that a demand for unique experiences continues to increase, there is no single definition for experiential tourism (Smith, 2006).

TOURISTS' ASPIRATIONS AND REQUIREMENTS

The rise in demand for experiential tourism is attributable to growing discontentment with the commercialization and homogenization of tourism (mass tourism) as well as the stressful pace of everyday life. It is estimated that three main elements underlie consumers' requirements: cultural immersion, specialized offerings and learning experiences, and flexibility (Mossberg, 2007; Tan, Kung, & Luh, 2013; Wong & McKercher, 2012). (i) Cultural immersion: tourists are looking for experiences exposing them to culture and landscapes that are different from those they are used to at home. They want to encounter unique cultures and experiences, eat local food, taste local drinks, meet locals and experience the place more than they have in the past. (ii) Specialized offerings and learning experiences: tourists are increasingly demanding specialized experience opportunities including gastronomic tours, volunteering experiences, as well as local produce tastings. Apparently, experiential tourists perceive their trip as a way to develop their knowledge and understanding. (iii) Flexible/customized trips: There is a demand for ways of exploring natural and historical resources and attractions beyond typical itineraries. They also have a strong desire to visit remote areas and have the opportunity to have a unique experience. It is important to provide tourists with the opportunity for a personalized itinerary.

What should the tourism businesses be doing differently to address the challenge and meet experiential tourists' requirements?

DIFFERENT APPROACH FROM PROVIDERS OF TOURISM SERVICES

Experiential tourism is by nature unique, therefore tourism providers willing to tap into this niche market must realize that there is no recipe for success. The main idea of a real experiential offering is a spectacular, unforgettable experience (Mossberg, 2007). This will take different forms for different consumers – a one-size-fits-all approach is unlikely to function with experiential tourists. This means that tourism providers have to be more creative, flexible and collaborative than ever before.

Collaboration: Providers must be in open and constant communication with other providers and suppliers of tourism services (Gopalan & Narayan, 2010). Through close collaboration with the other parties involved, a tourism provider is able to offer a high degree of personalization. For instance, if a group of tourists has a specific interest in local cuisine and gastronomy, then the entire experience can be tailored to suit their interests to encompass the crucial elements: selection of appropriate destination and of right time period, allocation of a specialist guide, and design of suitable activities. Additionally, tourism providers should not simply use the trend of experiential tourism as a marketing trick, but rather embrace the values that underpin the philosophy. Experiential tourism is more than a trend and certainly is not new. Tourists are not merely holidaymakers; they are visitors and travelers who are caring and savvy, have a world view regarding the environment, and a curiosity about local culture. They are very keen to interact with local populations and learn from them.

Providers of experiential tourism services and activities have to offer authentic and life-changing experiences that cannot be contrived or manufactured. Experiential tourism should be transformative; experiences changing the way the tourists consider the world in general, as well as the way they perceive themselves. Providers need to understand and experience activities themselves so they know they will add value for their customers by adding new/innovative elements (Wong & McKercher, 2012). Additionally, from a marketing perspective, providers should make use of social media and online platforms in terms of reviews, storytelling, and feedback. Online platforms and interactive websites are great tools for communicating and interacting with experiential tourists, as these platforms are great for experience sharing and storytelling, which is a key aspect of experiential tourism.

Micro-case – Example 1: Junior Ranger Experience, South Africa

African Hotels and Adventures (AHA) has put together an experiential package for the younger tourists. At Gondwana Game Reserve on the Garden Route, Eastern Cape, South African children from six years old can participate in a junior ranger experience. The participants have, besides hotel facilities, the following services and activities available to them:

- They receive a fun ranger's backpack and safari booklet to fill in throughout their stay.

- During game drives with their ranger, children will be taught how to identify mammals, birds, fynbos species and even stars.
- They will gain a greater understanding of conservation and the precious ecosystems.
- They will have a test by their ranger on what they have learned and will receive a level 1 Junior Ranger Patch and completion certificate, as well as a picture with their ranger for their safari book (*Source*: www.ahagroup.co.za).

Micro-case – Example 2: Hotel and Winery, Metsovo, Greece

On the edge of the Pindos Mountains in Metsovo (NW Greece), the Katogi Averoff Hotel & Winery combines a 15-room boutique hotel with an acclaimed winery, surrounded by steep slopes, vineyards, and woodland. It offers a fascinating one-hour tour of the winery with an audio-visual presentation of the wine-making process, followed by a tasting. Hotel rooms are, like the wines, divided into reds and whites; the best have the added bonus of balconies and fireplaces. The restaurant offers an array of local specialties for breakfast and lunch (*Source*: www.katogi-hotel.gr).

Hotel Industry and Guests' Experiences

The hotel industry is a component/segment of the hospitality industry encompassing hotels, motels, guest houses/bed and breakfasts, farmhouses, apartments/villas/flats/cottages, condominiums/timeshare resorts, vacation villages, caravan/camping sites, and inns (Middleton et al., 2009, p. 11). For leisure and tourism purposes, the hotel industry is integrally related to the attractions of a destination as well as being part of the facilities, improving their appeal.

HOTELS' OFFERING AS A SERVICE EXPERIENCE

Hotel products of all types are perceived by customers as experiences. The experience is organized and orchestrated to meet the identified needs and benefits sought by customer segments. It is very much the experience that is being sold. Consumers are selecting hotels according to the experience and type of trip they seek; their decisions will be based on the perceived benefits of the hotel product (Brotherton, 2005; Gilmore & Pine, 2002). With regard to the product components in marketing terms, Kotler and Keller (2006) suggested that they must be considered on three levels – core, formal, and augmented (i) The core product is the essential service or benefit designed to satisfy the identified needs of target customer segments. (ii) The formal or tangible product is the specific offer for sale stating what a customer will receive for his money. It is marketing an interpretation that turns the core into a specific offer. (iii) The augmented product comprises all the forms of added value providers may choose to build into their formal product offers to make the experiences they provide more attractive than competitors' offers to their targeted segments.

Micro-case – Example 3: Small Luxury Hotels of the World

Small Luxury Hotels (SLH) is a hotel consortium in the upscale/luxury market segment. A means of consortium differentiation is SLH's development of special customer experiences via the development of an extensive range of personalized packages that guarantee that "little something extra." SLH has set out to deliver ultimate active, gastronomic, spa or cultural experiences to targeted customers. In addition, SLH now recognizes that its pursuit of excellence does not need to be at the expense of the environment or the community in which a hotel operates. Through its "Caring Luxury" initiative, SLH encourages its hotel members to adopt responsible environmental, economic and social practices, which at the same time provide enriching and rewarding experiences for hotel guests. By practising Caring Luxury, SLH properties help to maximize the positive effects of tourism, such as creating jobs and benefiting small businesses, enhancing guests' awareness of local culture and traditions, and identifying ways to conserve and protect local surroundings (*Source*: Small Luxury Hotels (www.slh.com) and Fyall & Garrod, 2005).

Micro-case – Example 4: Gourmet break: Hotel Kritsa, Mount Pelion, Greece

In Portaria, central Greece, on the slopes of Mount Pelion – known for its rural villages and fresh-water springs – this delightfully welcoming, old-fashioned hotel offers cookery classes, either in the hotel itself or on a nearby farm. Using local ingredients and age-old recipes, guests learn to prepare traditional Greek dishes such as hearty stews and syrupy desserts. The guest rooms are peaceful and comfortable, and the best ones have balconies overlooking the main square. The hotel restaurant has outdoor tables on a terrace lined with potted hydrangeas and shaded by plane trees, and serves delicious dishes blending creative and traditional Greek cuisine. Hotel Kritsa can also help arrange hiking and canyoning in the countryside (*Source*: www. hotel-kritsa.gr).

HOTEL GUESTS' EXPERIENCES: CHARACTERISTICS AND INFLUENCING DIMENSIONS

The main challenge in the tourism and hotel industries is to offer special and spectacular experiences (Gilmore & Pine, 2002). Literature suggests that (i) tourism experiences are complex and (ii) hotel managers have to better understand consumer's experiences and to manage their offerings into the targeted market (Alcántara-Alcover, Artacho-Ramírez, Martínez-Guillamón, & Campos-Soriano, 2013). It is worth pointing out once again that experience is about perception. The importance of consumer perception in hotel experiences is generally advocated by literature (Brotherton, 2005; Sánchez, Callarisa, Rodríguez, & Miliner, 2006). They are influenced by physical elements (such as buildings and provision of food and drink), sensual benefits (experienced through sight, sound, touch and smell, and conveyed by the quality of design), and psychological benefits experienced as mental states of wellbeing, status, lifestyle and satisfaction (Middleton et al., 2009). Consumers' experience is mainly based on their deep-rooted reactions, feelings and perceptions, and relies primarily on their values system (Teng, 2011). In other words, a hotel experience is complex, encompassing dynamic and interactive relationships among different components, that is, psychological state and connection, interpersonal interaction, sensation, satisfaction, and perceived value from physical environment factors.

Some scholars argue that the challenge of creating unforgettable consumer experiences is the proper identification of specific characteristics that influence experiences, and gaining a better understanding of how these characteristics affect consumers' perceived value. Walls (2013) conducted a study on the structure of consumer experience and its role in influencing hotel guests' perceived value. He suggested a model that identifies influencing dimensions of consumer experiences and investigates their composition and the relative outcome on consumers' perceived value in a hotel setting.

The experience constructs are mainly physical environment dimensions and the human interaction dimensions as perceived by consumers. (i) Perceived physical environment construct: to create the desired consumer experience, hotels need to focus on providing the right setting, which includes physical dimensions that engage and enhance these experiences (Yuan & Wu, 2008). Literature suggests that there are four main physical environmental dimensions, namely: design attractiveness, layout/ease of navigation, upkeep, and physiological/ambience (Berry, Carbone, & Haeckel, 2002; Bitner, 1992). (ii) Perceived human interaction construct: a hotel should focus not only on its service, but also on the entire consumer experience it offers, including both physical environmental dimensions and human interaction dimensions (Bitner, 1992; Choi & Chu, 2001; Yuan & Wu, 2008). It is believed that there are five main dimensions of the human interaction construct, namely: caring/attentiveness, professionalism, reliability/trustworthiness, responsiveness, and guest-to-guest relations (Zeithaml, 1988).

Therefore, customers will form their value perceptions regarding their consumption experiences based on available environmental cues. Walls (2013) suggested that customer experiences with hotels will lead to certain consequences that are reflected in their **perceived value**. The dimension "perceived value" has been defined as "a consumer's overall assessment of the utility of a product or service based on perceptions of what is received and what is given" (Zeithaml, 1988, p. 14). This definition often refers to the trade-off between quality and price, which is a value-for-money conceptualization. Literature suggests that consumer behavior could be divided into three broad components (Bitner, 1992; Sheth, Newman, & Gross, 1991): (i) the affective or emotive component, that is, the emotional or feeling states; (ii) the cognitive component, that is, the intellectual or mental states; and (iii) the physiological or motivational component, that is, the "striving" states related to the tendency to treat objects as positive or negative goals. Sheth et al. (1991) and Bitner (1992) argued that emotive and cognitive components fundamentally influence consumer behavior.

The perceived value and customer satisfaction are also influenced by other factors such as guests' personality factors, for example, extraversion, agreeableness and neuroticism (Jani & Han, 2014). Further, it is estimated that perceived value influences customer satisfaction and post consumption behavioral intentions, that is, word-of-mouth, recommendation and loyalty/repurchase intentions. In sum, the guest experience is determined and influenced by a series of internal and external factors as illustrated by Figure 1.

In other words, the customers' perceived value is affected by their experience, which is, in turn, determined by the physical environment and human interaction dimensions in a hotel setting. Walls (2013) indicated that both the physical environment and the human interactions have a significant and positive relationship with perceived value, and are very important in creating

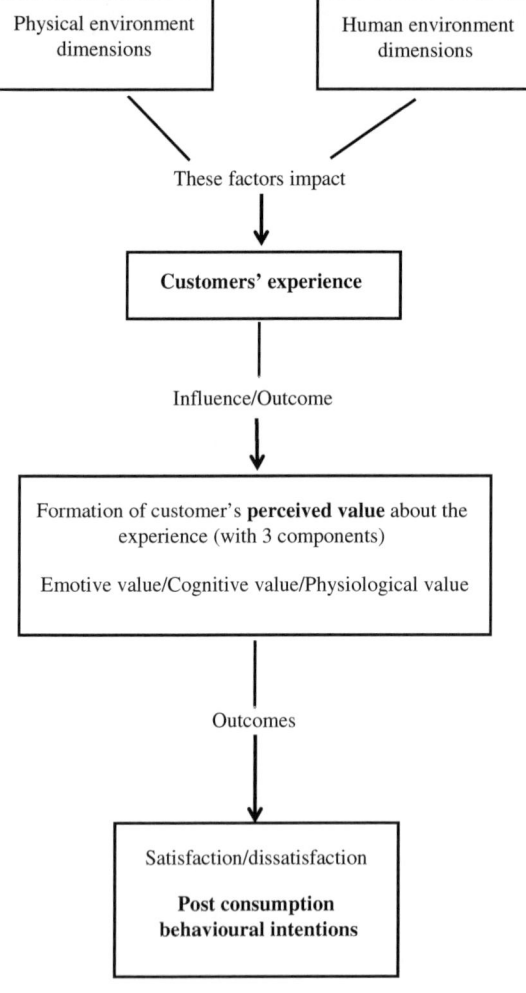

Figure 1.   Customer Experience: Dimensions, Influence on Perceived Value and Outcomes.

a positive hotel experience. Recognition of this emphasis can help managers emphasize how the physical environment and human interaction constructs impact perceived value (Oh, Fiore, & Jeoung, 2007).

It is worth pointing out that the tremendous growth of social media and consumer-generated content on the internet has inspired the development of the so-called "big data analytics," which are very useful in better understanding the relationship between hotel guest experience and satisfaction. The reviews posted by customers have become a valuable means by which hotel managers can better understand customer satisfaction and expectations (Xiang, Schwartz, Gerdes, & Uysal, 2015).

It is evident that the hotel guests' experiences are multidimensional and quite complex, and hotel operations must address the resulting challenges by adopting adequate approaches. This chapter argues that (i) collaboration and partnering could make a significant contribution in creating and managing hotel guests' experiences; and (ii) collaboration is a necessity rather than a luxury in a highly competitive hotel business environment.

Collaboration in Managing Hotel Guests' Experiences

Small and medium tourism enterprises (SMTEs) can provide adequate services and experiences to tourists who requesting tailored and customized experience opportunities. One effective way of doing so is collaboration. Collaborative forms in the business, such as alliances, networks and clusters, are seen as a framework providing SMTEs with managerial and marketing opportunities to operate locally and in a globalized and competitive business environment (Fyall & Garrod, 2005; Gursoy et al., 2015; Poon, 1993; Sotiriadis, Tyrogala, & Varvaressos, 2009). The issue of networks and clusters creation and how they can be used as an innovative process to support SMTEs' ventures has been examined by scholars (Novelli, Schmitz, & Spencer, 2006).

BUSINESS ALLIANCES: NETWORKS

One form of collaboration is networks that are described as "a specific type of relation linking a set of persons, objects or events" (Knoke & Kuklinski, 1983, p. 12). As globalization has involved increased pressure on SMTEs to be competitive, the concentration has to be on a local/regional level in order to achieve competitiveness through cooperation and collaboration (Gulati, 1998; Poon, 1993). Networking must be seen as a process that enables the partnering members to exploit their synergies and the complementarities between their outputs. Considering that through an alliance, a group of SMTEs can compete globally by cooperating locally; networks and clusters in tourism have experienced a dramatic growth. This collaborative framework has been extensively used in tourism industry, with niche markets gaining from networks building when their businesses are competing and collaborating at the same time, as they provide a series of business benefits for the providers involved (Novelli et al., 2006; Sotiriadis et al., 2009).

Networks provide organizations with access to knowledge, resources, markets and technologies (Inkpen & Tsang, 2005), and can operate as a strategic alliance if the companies involved enter into a voluntary arrangement of exchanging, sharing or co-developing products or services. Through this, new services and products are being developed, and a sustainable competitive advantage can be achieved by linking the network to the global marketplace.

Micro-case – Example 5: A business network in the hotel industry: Voluntary hotel chain

A voluntary chain is a very good example of a business network in the hotel industry. It constitutes a business partnership that involves independent hotels having common quality criteria. The main role of a voluntary hotel chain is to contribute to better management activities and to enhance the marketing communications and sales campaigns of hotel members. There are 37 voluntary hotel chains in France, for example, Hotels & Preference (H&P), Châteaux & Hôtels of Collection and PML Hotels. Let us briefly look at the example of H&P.

H&P is a French international hotel group composed of 150 mainly four- and five-star hotels. A hotel chain established in 2000, H&P today has more than 140 remarkable locations in 22 destinations worldwide, offering many activities such as golf, spas and gastronomy. The chain meets the expectations of customers enjoying luxury hotels as relaxing places with an intimate and friendly atmosphere. Each hotel meets high quality standards. H&P also has a hotel selection boasting spas and golf courses. The chain offers a "Preference Warranty" that includes: the lowest price/best rate guaranteed, customer service care, customers' verified reviews, and handpicked hotels.

To the potential members/partners, the chain H&P offers a contemporary hotel level of standing and impeccable service, accompanied in its development of upscale independent authentic hotels to continually improve members' image and positioning through marketing tools and online communications. In less than 14 years with nearly 10,000 rooms, H&P has become one of the top five independent luxury hotel chains. Its ambition is to significantly grow members' revenue across the fields of leisure, corporate and business by offering increased visibility thanks to eight international sales offices and a strong internet presence. By linking hotel property to H&P, a hotelier secures a significant place within the network of boutique and luxury hotels (Hotels & Preference, 2015).

MANAGEMENT AND MARKETING BENEFITS

The network is a collaborative form that has strong business objectives focusing on improving sales and profitability. This business alliance can generate a series of management and marketing benefits including (Bell, 2005; Novelli et al., 2006; Saxena, 2005; Sotiriadis et al., 2009): resource development and knowledge transfer between participants; exchange of valuable marketing information and technology; improved quality of service, improved business performance; encouraging different ways of coordination; improved organizational flexibility in addressing and meeting guests' requirements; innovation capacity; value chain establishment and enrichment; enhanced visibility; business referral and cross-marketing activities with other network members; the opportunity to enter other networks and clusters on a national and international level; building-up local businesses' critical mass; and enhancing improvement of local heritage and culture, and preservation of community values.

All the above benefits influence businesses' willingness to cooperate, create alliances, and actively work toward the long-term benefits derived from a collaborative use of resources. Services and products are combined in order to deliver the specific experience that tourists seek. These services can take various forms, one being routes and trails. The role of trails and routes as part of the tourism offering has been explored and their centrality to the tourist experience is well documented

(Sotiriadis et al., 2009; Timothy & Boyd, 2014). A route is often based on modern day conceptualization and designation of a circuit or course that links partnering tourism providers, as well as similar natural or cultural features into a thematic linear corridor. It is believed they have an important role in managing tourism resources/attractions and as facilitators of tourism experiences. This concept of route is used for management and marketing purposes, providing opportunities for experience, enjoyment, and satisfaction to a destination's visitors. Furthermore, the cross-organizational collaboration processes and activities in the tourism field are considerably enhanced by the knowledge management and ICTs frameworks and tools (Akoumianakis, 2014).

From the above synoptic discussion it is clear that the complex nature of experiences requires articulation in partnership and networks, allowing integrated product development and management (Denicolai, Cioccarelli, & Zucchella, 2010). It is therefore suggested that the collaboration and combination of forces and resources might be a recipe for success and performance improvement. Nevertheless, a number of key issues need to be considered and resolved in order to realize the above-mentioned potential benefits: (i) members should share consistent values and should be focused on the same targeted market segments; it is therefore imperative to select the appropriate partners; (ii) the arrangement also needs to be financially attractive to all participants, striking an equitable balance; (iii) choice of the appropriate collaboration structure (contractual form); and (iv) the services can be competitive, contributing towards making a hotel experience more attractive and unforgettable.

Case Study: Otium in Italy: Network to Provide Attractive Guests' Experiences

A very good example of collaboration between boutique hotel businesses and other tourism providers is presented in this case to illustrate how this kind of venture is implemented. This collaboration is in the form of a "grand tour" network. Independent boutique hotels are joining forces to offer an 18th-century experience, complete with vintage sports cars (Eames, 2015). This new "Grand Tour" is being offered by OTIUM, a nascent collaboration between independent owner-managed boutique hotels.

VENTURE'S PROFILE

The initial idea found its roots in the passion of three independent Italian hotel operators who realized the importance of discovering the true meaning of hospitality and uniqueness of the Italian culture. The aim of this venture, "Otium in Italy" – in the form of a business network – is to provide experience opportunities for a journey that "speaks to the senses and the soul, a place to be accepted for what we are, and discover who we want to be" (Otium in Italy, 2015). The idea is to connect through a unique journey, with stays at an exclusive collection of Italian properties, whose owners have been able to create unique places that ensure guests feel not only at home, but also part of the community and local culture. The network's aim is to create a group of linked properties that (i) tourists can conveniently book and travel between and (ii) offer history, character and the chance to meet and be personally looked after by the owners. To date, four properties have signed up but the objective is to have between eight and twelve in the network by the end of 2015.

NETWORK'S MARKETING CONCEPT: A LIFESTYLE "GRAND TOUR"

The network offers experiences based on the cultural background of the Italian "Grand Tour." Beginning in the late 16th century, the idea of the Grand Tour was a practice that introduced Englishmen, Germans, Scandinavians and Americans to the art and culture of Italy for the next 300 years. The Grand Tour not only provided a capstone to their liberal education, but also became a symbol of wealth and freedom. The Romans used the term "Otium" as synonymous with creativity, intellectual inquiry, and lightness of being (Otium in Italy, 2015). *Webster's Dictionary* defines it as "leisure with dignity."

The main concept is to provide experience opportunities while exploring Italy. The network offers an immersive itinerary that inspires the savvy traveler on a deeply personal level, creating emotion through the powerful medium of storytelling. Travelers can experiment with the idea of travel as experience and knowledge. The objective is to discover Italy through a sequence of landscapes, manners, cities and monuments. The network offers traveling experiences around culture, creativity, and enjoyment.

Here we look at some of the properties and services provided by this network.

BOUTIQUE HOTELS AND ACTIVITIES

The first boutique hotel is *Castello di Vicarello* in the Maremma region, Tuscany. This small castle was built by Knights Templar in the 11th century. The Castello is a fusion of design and gastronomy; its exterior is medieval but its interior is eclectic. Guests have access to the basics of Renaissance Italy, with Siena about 40 minutes away. The owners-operators themselves take visitors down into their vineyards for a tasting and show them how olive oil, salami and cheese are made. There are local craftsmen to visit, a spa, and two swimming pools. Additionally, guests can visit the nearby town of Pienza and a monastery where mass is sung in Latin.

Second hotel property is *Petrella Guidi*, in the hills of Montefeltro, west of San Marino in central Italy. This hotel is a small, castellated *borgo* (village) was first mentioned in 1225. For much of the 20th century this settlement was little more than an empty ruin, until it was stumbled upon in the 1970s by a group of artists and intellectuals. Among them was an Italian-Russian couple who combined three of the farm cottages and outlying buildings to construct this gem of a hotel, which has several levels. There is a *hammam* (Turkish warm baths), a private cinema, an indoor pool, and four suites, which can accommodate a maximum of eight guests. The owner-operator takes guests to the extraordinary nearby fortress town of San Leo, having a 12th century cathedral.

Third hotel operation is the San Lorenzo Mountain Lodge in South Tyrol in the foothills of the Alps — a German-speaking territory that became part of Italy after the First World War. The property was the former hunting lodge of a 16th century bishop. The landscape and the language change, the villages are better maintained and the churches turn Baroque. This lodge is a 500-year-old chalet of larch and pine. It is the simplest of network properties. The owner introduces guests to the world of mountainside golf and the task of chopping wood for the stove. He can arrange for a classic sports car to be delivered to the lodge for a drive in the mountains. In the evenings, guests can enjoy his wine cellar as well as his chef-produced meals.

As can be seen, "Otium in Italy" offers a unique experiential lifestyle journey through Italy. A series of unique experiences takes guests off the beaten track to experience Italian culture and heritage, all drawn together by a common thread of personal hospitality.

The basic concept is – in our view – sound, because there is a market for a modern day "Grand Tour"; the segment targeted being the mature baby boomers. The network is well-designed venture offering experience opportunities to lifestyle travelers. With flexibility and possible adjustments, it has the potential to provide customized experience and plan of activities meeting the aspirations of modern visitors. This business venture must be seen as a way to reinforce entrepreneurial cooperation and encourage further business development. It constitutes a venture combining the resources available to provide enriched and more attractive experience opportunities.

Conclusions and Management Implications

Hotel operators, along with the destination's visitor attractions – based mainly on intrinsic local natural, heritage and cultural resources – often share common strategic aims. That is the reason we are likely to see a more collaborative approach to achieving common benefits. Literature suggests that to be successful in the industry, hotel operations must provide a superior customer experience, and this must be done continuously and efficiently (Choi & Chu, 2001). In addition, hotels need to put more emphasis on improving the quality of their experience offering and in ensuring that the needs and expectations of their guests are being met.

From a managerial perspective, the customer experience has to be planned for, resources deployed, and personnel put in place to implement the plan. Value is a lived experience for the customer and is generally a trade-off between benefits and costs. In the hotel industry experience is delivered through a number of vehicles including partnerships, which provide more attractive guest experience opportunities. By entering into a business venture, hotels can also provide extra customer value and may gain a competitive advantage. Analyzing and understanding the guest experience as an emotionally and symbolically rich phenomenon, and anchoring it in a common, appealing, significant and distinctive route or theme (for instance, "Grand Tour"), may be a powerful way to combine the various elements and dimensions of the experience.

Based on the analysis, this chapter suggests that investment in business ventures and alliances is a good investment in the sense that it constitutes a potential source of sustainable competitive advantage. The main aim of a business network is, in our view, to generate business and market diversification. A collaborative platform wisely designed can offer a way of extending, enriching and deepening the hotel guests' experience, based on endogenous resources. The later and other distinctive elements might be used as a means of diversifying the experience and making it appealing to different individuals within the same market segment. The ultimate aim is to make the experience attractive, pleasant, interactive, diverse and meaningful.

References

Akoumianakis, D. (2014). Ambient affiliates in virtual cross-organizational tourism alliances; A case study of collaborative new product development. *Computers in Human Behavior, 30*, 773–786.

Alcántara-Alcover, E., Artacho-Ramírez, M. A., Martínez-Guillamón, N., & Campos-Soriano, N. (2013). Purpose of stay and willingness to stay as dimensions to identify and evaluate hotel experiences. *International Journal of Hospitality Management, 33*, 357–365.

Bell, G. G. (2005). Clusters, networks, and firm innovativeness. *Strategic Management Journal, 26*, 287–295.

Berry, L. L., Carbone, L. P., & Haeckel, S. H. (2002). Managing the total customer experience. *MIT Sloan Management Review, 43*(3), 85–89.

Bitner, M. J. (1992). Servicescapes: The impact of physical surroundings on customers and employees. *Journal of Marketing, 56*(2), 57–71.

Brotherton, B. (2005). The nature of hospitality: Customer perceptions and implications. *Tourism and Hospitality Planning and Development, 2*(3), 139–153.

Choi, T. Y., & Chu, R. (2001). Determinants of hotel guests' satisfaction and repeat patronage in the Hong Kong hotel industry. *Hospitality Management, 20*, 277–297.

Deloitte (2010). *Hospitality 2015: Game changers or spectators?* London: Deloitte LLP.

Denicolai, S., Cioccarelli, G., & Zucchella, A. (2010). Resource-based local development and networked core-competencies for tourism excellence. *Tourism Management, 31*(2), 260–266.

Eames, A. (2015). Grand tour with a modern spin, in "Life & Arts", *Financial Times (FT Weekend)*, March 21, p. 8.

Fyall, A., & Garrod, B. (2005). *Tourism marketing: A collaborative approach.* Clevedon: Channel View Publications.

Gilmore, J. H., & Pine, J. (2002). Differentiating hospitality operations via experiences: Why selling services is not enough. *Cornell Hotel and Restaurant Administration Quarterly, 43*(3), 87−96.

Gopalan, R., & Narayan, B. (2010). Improving customer experience in tourism: A framework for stakeholder collaboration. *Socio-Economic Planning Sciences, 44*(2), 100−112.

Gulati, R. (1998). Alliances and networks. *Strategic Management Journal, 19,* 293−317.

Gursoy, D., Saayman, M., & Sotiriadis, M. (2015). Introduction. In D. Gursoy, M. Saayman, & M. Sotiriadis (Eds.), *Collaboration in tourism businesses and destinations: A handbook* (pp. xv−xxvi). Bingley, UK: Emerald Group Publishing Limited.

Hotels & Preference. (2015). *Official website.* Retrieved from http://www.hotelspreference.com/fr/. Accessed on October 23.

Inkpen, A. C., & Tsang, E. W. K. (2005). Social capital, networks, and knowledge transfer. *Academy of Management Review, 30*(1), 146−165.

Jani, D., & Han, H. (2014). Personality, satisfaction, image, ambience, and loyalty: Testing their relationships in the hotel industry. *International Journal of Hospitality Management, 37*(1), 11−20.

Knoke, D., & Kuklinski, J. (1983). *Network analysis.* Los Angeles, CA: Sage.

Kotler, P., & Keller, K. L. (2006). *Marketing management* (12th ed.). Upper Saddle River, NJ: Prentice-Hall.

Middleton, V. T. C., Fyall, A., Morgan, M., & Ranchhod, A. (2009). *Marketing in travel and tourism* (4th ed.). Oxford: Elsevier.

Mossberg, L. (2007). A marketing approach to the tourist experience. *Scandinavian Journal of Hospitality and Tourism, 7*(1), 59−74.

Novelli, M., Schmitz, B., & Spencer, T. (2006). Networks, clusters and innovation in tourism: A UK experience. *Tourism Management, 27,* 1141−1152.

Oh, H., Fiore, A. M., & Jeoung, M. (2007). Measuring experience economy concepts: Tourism applications. *Journal of Travel Research, 46*(1), 119−132.

Otium in Italy. (2015). *Official website.* Retrieved from http://www.otiuminitaly.it/. Accessed on July 27.

Poon, A. (1993). *Tourism, technology and competitive strategies.* Wallingford, CT: CABI.

Sánchez, J., Callarisa, L., Rodríguez, R. M., & Miliner, M. A. (2006). Perceived value of the purchase of a tourism product. *Tourism Management, 27,* 394−409.

Saxena, G. (2005). Relationships, networks and the learning regions: Case evidence from the Peak District National Park. *Tourism Management, 26,* 277−289.

Sheth, J. N., Newman, B. I., & Gross, B. L. (1991). Why we buy what we buy: A theory of consumption values. *Journal of Business Research, 22*(2), 159−170.

Smith, W. I. (2006). Experiential tourism around the world and at home: Definition and standards. *International Journal of Services and Standards, 2*(1), 1−14.

Sotiriadis, M., Gursoy, D., & Saayman, M. (2015). Conclusions: Issues and challenges for collaborative forms in tourism businesses and destinations.

In D. Gursoy, M. Saayman, & M. Sotiriadis (Eds.), *Collaboration in tourism businesses and destinations: A handbook* (pp. 321−330). Bingley, UK: Emerald Group Publishing Limited.

Sotiriadis, M., Tyrogala, E., & Varvaressos, S. (2009). Contribution of networking and clustering in rural tourism business. *TOURISMOS: An International, Multi-Disciplinary Journal*, 4(4), 35−56.

Tan, S.-K., Kung, S.-F., & Luh, D.-B. (2013). A model of 'creative experience' in creative tourism. *Annals of Tourism Research*, 41(1), 153−174.

Teng, C.-C. (2011). Commercial hospitality in restaurants and tourist accommodation: Perspectives from international consumer experience in Scotland. *International Journal of Hospitality Management*, 30, 866−874.

Timothy, D. J., & Boyd, S. W. (2014). *Tourism and trails: Cultural, ecological and management issues*. Bristol: Channel View Publications.

Walls, A. R. (2013). A cross-sectional examination of hotel consumer experience and relative effects on consumer values. *International Journal of Hospitality Management*, 32(1), 179−192.

Wong, C. U. I., & McKercher, B. (2012). Day tour itineraries: Searching for the balance between commercial needs and experiential desires. *Tourism Management*, 33(6), 1360−1372.

Xiang, Z., Schwartz, Z., Gerdes, J. H., Jr., & Uysal, M. (2015). What can big data and text analytics tell us about hotel guest experience and satisfaction? *International Journal of Hospitality Management*, 44, 120−130.

Yuan, Y.-H. E., & Wu, C. K. (2008). Relationships among experiential marketing, experiential value, and customer satisfaction. *Journal of Hospitality & Tourism Research*, 32(3), 387−410.

Zeithaml, V. A. (1988). Consumer perceptions of price, quality, and value: A means-end model and synthesis of evidence. *The Journal of Marketing*, 52(3), 2−22.

10 Managing Sport Tourism Experiences: Blueprinting Service Encounters

Chris A. Vassiliadis and
Anestis Fotiadis

ABSTRACT

Purpose – This chapter aims to present and analyze how the methodology/approach of service blueprinting may contribute to managing and offering high quality experiences to sport tourists.

Methodology/approach – In this study we use a combination of theoretical tools to develop a finalized services blueprint map for sport events. The method consists of a literature review and a presentation of empirical findings. First, using a case study, we present the process through which a small-scale sport event blueprint map was constructed. Secondly, based on a meeting with the management staff and the use of diaries, we analyze the comments of tourists in the sport event area. Thirdly, we compare and describe the main contact points between the front-line staff and sport event tourists in a service blueprint. Finally we apply the six dimensional construct domain analysis of service experiences and combine this information in a table format for the Failure, Effect, and Action analysis.

Findings – This study shows that observation, diaries, service blueprints, comment management, and FMEA (Failure Mode and Effects Analysis) are a range of corporate research approaches and management tools that can offer new insights into the theory and praxis of service management applications and can improve the experiences of sports tourists.

Research limitations/implications – This study is related to sport rural events. Researchers have to check with the same method to study the results also in other sport events.

Practical implications – The analysis of Small-Scale Sport Event Services Blueprinting can be combined with other useful managerial tools, like the Failure Mode and Effects Analysis to better manage the contact points, the "moments of truth" of tourist experiences in the sport event service system. In addition, the SMF case study shows that it is useful to point out the problematic areas in the service system using combined methods and managerial tools with the aim of enhancing and contributing to better manage sport tourism event experiences.

Originality/value – It presents the new idea of combining theoretical constructs and measurement tools in order to blueprint, analyze, and create service customer experiences.

Keywords: Sport tourism; experiences; services blueprinting; failure mode and effects analysis

Introduction

According to Gibson (1998, p. 49) Sport Tourism can be defined as "leisure-based travel that takes individuals temporarily outside of their home communities to participate in physical activities, to watch physical activities, or to venerate attractions associated with physical activities." Participation in sport and tourism events can create unique leisure experiences for the participants (Perić, 2010; Ritchie & Adair, 2004). More and more small-scale events have been established over the last few years in an attempt to boost the economies of depressed countries and rural towns (Gibson, Kaplanidou, & Kang, 2012). Many other researchers have shown that sport events can affect a destination both socially and economically (Snelgrove & Wood, 2010). These destinations create sport events that will encourage the participation of non-professional or professional sport-tourists, promote local services, and encourage the consumption of local products and support involvement in local activities. As Higham (1999) mentioned, small-scale sports events usually function and operate within existing infrastructures, require minimal investment of public funds, and can generate a reliable and regular flow of visitors. Furthermore, these kind of events seem to minimize the effects of seasonality. Gibson, Willming, and Holdnak (2003) assert that these events are suitable for small or medium sized communities since they can provide proportionately more economic benefits than if they were conducted in larger cities.

For the service provider, customer participation can lead to the avoidance and minimization of their non-customer-oriented mistakes in the service delivery process but can also lead, through the continuing blueprinting service improvement system, to a higher quality output that sustains their customer markets on a long-term basis. Literature about small sport events and blueprinting services does not sufficiently highlight the basic processes that can be a script of small-scale sport event visitor behavior and their basic outdoor activities. This chapter aims to present and analyze how the methodology/approach of service blueprint may contribute to managing and offering high quality experiences to sport tourists.

Service Quality: Managing Perceptions

Many enterprises try to formulate and implement Strategic Marketing Planning with the aim of competing in the Service Industry Environment. The market competitiveness of a service enterprise can be built over the years if enterprises clearly focus on customer purchasing behavior. Service Quality is a key factor in designing service products because it is mostly related to non-tangible aspects of the services that affect the Satisfaction level and Loyalty behavior of customers (Chang & Chen, 1998; Cronin & Taylor, 1992; Gammie, 1992; Gummesson, 1998; Hallowell, 1996; Lasser, Manolis, & Winsor, 2000; Leonard & Sasser, 1982; Newman, 2001; Seth, Deshmukh, & Vrat, 2005; Sureshchander, Rajendran, & Anatharaman, 2002). Service systems, like sport events activities, should be efficient at delivering services at a high level (Berry, Parasuraman, Zeithaml, & Adsit,

1994; Hung, Huang, & Chen, 2003). In addition, based on Teece's notification, this kind of service model approach, like other business models, must be "honed to meet particular customer needs" (Teece, 2010, p. 192); If this is the managerial point the Service quality analysis can help to make the business models more customer-oriented (Andronikidis, Bellou, & Vassiliadis, 2008; Teece, 2010). Service quality analysis is based on the evaluation of two basic perceived aspects of service quality, namely the functional (Demand oriented service analysis, like customer evaluations of service attributes, consumer experiences per contact point, customer attitudes) and technical quality (Supply-oriented service analysis like technical systems, staff and skills, technology being used, etc.) aspects (Grönroos, 1984, 1991). Functional service quality is based on customer evaluations, these evaluations are the result of the comparison between the level of service quality expected and the level of service quality finally experienced from the delivery system of the service provider (Grönroos, 1991). Studies have pointed out that there are important direct relationships between, Perceived service quality (PSQ), Perceived customer value (PCV), Willingness to buy (WB), and Customer Perceptions (CP). More specifically, based on those studies, PSQ has a direct effect on PCV, Functional Service Quality as a part of the PSQ construct positively affects Technical service quality and Customer WB (Oh, 1999; Seth et al., 2005; Sweeney, Soutar, & Johnson, 1997). The Analysis of the Functional or Perceived Service Quality is based on attributes, which are important for customer service. The research work of Parasuraman, Zeithaml, and Berry (1985) is widely known to the research community and services business practice. Their first exploratory research analysis study, based on the results of 12 focus group studies, revealed a bundle of ten "potentially overlapping quality dimensions," namely the initial SERVQUAL item pool of 10 dimensions with 97 items for evaluation. Those ten dimensions were tangibles, reliability, responsiveness, communication, credibility, security, competence, courtesy, understanding and knowing the customer, and access (Parasuraman et al., 1985). In their following work the researchers used the Factor Analysis approach and Reliability Analysis to handle the problems of dimension purification and the refining of their related items. Following this approach they proposed a global measurement model of service quality analyses using five distinct service quality measurement dimensions, namely tangibles, reliability, responsibility, assurance, and empathy (Parasuraman,

Zeithaml, & Berry, 1988). This approach and many other research approaches are based on the idea that a service must be well defined by the service provider because service managers need to know how customers perceive the service quality of their service (Fotiadis & Vassiliadis, 2013) for service planning improvement purposes. These dimensions are very helpful for evaluating and improving the service quality delivery process and the perceived functionally focused service quality process. In this manner those quality dimensions can be an index for blueprinting, evaluating, developing understanding of managerial implications and developing long-term improvement in service products.

Service Encounters and Servicescapes: Blueprinting

Service encounters are "periods of time during which them a consumer directly interacts with a service" (Shostack, 1985, p. 243). They are the "service from the customer's point of view" (Bitner, 1990, p. 69). Solomon, Surprenant, Czepiel, and Gutman (1985) noted that it is important to create compatible service scripts with the scope to have a more realistic and clear vision about the whole service processes between the service providers and the customers. Blueprinting service encounters can be a useful tool for enforcing the empirical work that has been done and must be continued for the examination and consideration of the non-core attributes of service offerings, such as physical evidence of the supply and demand exchange environment, "Servicescapes," or the physical surroundings in which a service process takes place and where the service provider and the customer interact (Bitner, 1992; Rosenbaum, 2005; Zeithaml & Bitner, 2003). As shown in the different studies mentioned above, the Service Quality variable has a significant effect on customer satisfaction, loyalty and behavior. Service Quality includes Servicescapes that can be defined as a facility's exterior, for example, landscape design, weather conditions, outdoor emotional effects (smelling, hearing, etc.), signs, and interior characteristics, for example, ambiance, interior design, look and type of other customers and staff, interior design. Servicescapes can be organized in an open space or outdoor physical environment (i.e., outdoor sport tourism activities) or they can be a synthesis of exterior and interior spaces (i.e., Summer resorts; Hotel and recreation villages). Blueprinting can help the service managers to avoid omissions and mistakes like "flawed identification of customer needs," "errors in creating quality standards," "errors in designing the service" and errors because of the implementation of "inadequate business administration models" (Cetină, 2009). Service encounters and blueprinting can describe the pitfalls of the service delivery process (Brown & Bitner, 2007). Service blueprinting is a managerial approach used to clarify and enforce the practical aspects of service process design, analysis and improvement (Bitner, Ostrom, & Morgan, 2008). As a process oriented approach it consists of points of customer contact, physical evidence and related services provided to the customers. Services are analytically presented as onstage/visible contact employee actions, backstage/invisible contact employee actions and support processes that are important in supporting the customer-oriented service offer (Bitner et al., 2008; Kingman-Brundage, George, & Bowen, 1995; Shostack, 1992). Those levels of analyses are important for creating the everyday management praxis, which services blueprint maps. In the next case we implement this approach in order to build the final blueprint map for the Sfendami Mountain Festival (SMF) small-scale sport event. Customer contact-point service improvement based on service blueprints can create value for the active customers. A service provider can also enjoy some benefits from contact-point service improvement strategies, that is, through co-production, co-creation, synergies, or "co-value creation"; because he requires less managerial effort for the coordination of the service processes (Gummesson, 1994; Johnston & Clark, 2001; Vargo & Lusch, 2008). For the service provider this participation can lead to the avoidance and minimization of his non-customer-oriented mistakes in the service delivery process but also can lead, through the continuing blueprinting service improvement system, to higher quality output that sustains their customer markets on a long-term basis (Edvardsson, 1997).

Tourist Experience and Satisfaction

Literature suggests that quality measurement procedures must emphasize the quality of service experience that can explain the high portion of variance in satisfaction level evaluations (Chen & Chen, 2010; Kao, Huang, & Wu, 2008; Oliver, 1993). It is important to recognize the extraordinary experience that can be offered by extended leisure and tourism pursuits (Otto & Ritchie, 1996).

Managers can evaluate tourist experiences using e-technology like smartphones apps, web pages and e-mail lists, and e-mail communication (Jin, Lee, & Lee, 2015). The challenge in "Serviscapes" like the local small-scale tourism sport events, will in the future lie in the processes that can reform the tourist's experience of service, encounter, delivery, and environmental features. There is also a need to measure and understand the tourist's feelings. Otto & Ritchie, in their research work (1996), point out six dimensions that can contribute to the measurement and management of the affective components of the service experience, for example, the tourist feelings, namely the Hedonic (Excitement, Enjoyment, and Memorability), Interactive (Meeting people, Being part of the process, Having choice), Novelty (Escape, Doing something new), Comfort (Physical comfort, Relaxation), Safety (Personal safety, Security of belongings), and Stimulation (Educational and Informative, Challenging).

The Case of SMF, 2013: The Analysis of Sport Event Tourism Experiences in Practice

This study presents and analyzes the SMF, a small-scale tourism sport event. To achieve this we used the services blueprinting method and an FMEA (Failure Mode and Effects Analysis). The study tries to identify the service process and the related contact points of a real small-scale sport event case study based on the classical service blueprint theoretical construct. Second, the study tries to determine which actions improve the satisfaction levels of customers and which events can be improved by the service manager so as to avoid the high customer dissatisfaction levels that can affect the service quality strategy of an event provider. SMF is a two-day event organized every year during April at Sfendami, Pieria. The organizer is SFENDAMOS, a local non-profit company based in Sfendami in the region of Pieria, Northern Greece. In 2013 the event was being held for the 7th year. The aim of the event is to offer athletes, runners, mountain bikers, children, parents, and spectators, with a love of athletics and nature, as well as an experience of the area. The Hill of Prophet Elias where the festival will take place includes a campsite and immediate access to the race routes and tracks, as well as more events and new activities (Figure 2). The hill is 2.5 km from Sfendami. There are WC facilities and showers with hot water for the athletes and campers. There are eating and drinking facilities for all. The organizer offers the visitors a user friendly informative website in two languages (SMF, 2013).

Methodology

After a meeting with the management staff of SFENDAMOS, the authors built a list with basic contact points that are visible and which follows the activities that the visitors usually complete during their SMF participation. This information was critical for the

Ad/web site (be informed and participate with online registration, pay the participation fees)

↓

Small train station area (park the car in the village and continue with the local train)

↓

Outdoor parking area (arrival at the train parking area or at the car parking area near the sport event arena)

↓

Secretary & front office services (check in, check or pay the registration fees, take information and the athlete's handbag with visitor and athlete's instructions, competition routes and rules, the athlete's competition number, sport and sponsored accessories)

↓

Starting gate point in the sport arena (Exploring the area of the competition. Tour of the starting point and of the related services and facilities near the starting Gate; warming up)

↓

Management office and related activities (Giving attention to the competition rules and the running route)

↓

Starting and finishing: finish line in the sport arena (Running competition: Run, finish and take a handmade SMF medal)

↓

Management office and related activities (during the finish give the responsible staff some information about you and the running competition you have finished, be informed about the status of the competition and the total time of athlete's integrated running route)

↓

Secretary & front office services (check your final running time, take information about the other actions that you have to follow after ending the running route)

↓

WC douche & bathroom area (meet physical needs, body care and hygiene)

↓

Media, V.I.P. & medal ceremony event on the central outdoor stage (participate in awards, video creation and photo taking, stroll through the exhibition area)

↓

Pasta party & music event area (participate to the pasta party and the music event)

↓

Outdoor parking area (return to car or to the train station and depart)

Figure 1.   Flow Chart of the SMF Sport Event.

design of the physical evidence and customer actions in the service blueprinting approach (Figures 1–3). After the meeting 13 basic visible service provider and customer contact points, as well as the related activities that the small-scale sport tourists follow, were identified. Teamwork was very useful in preparing the final SMF blueprint map (Bitner et al., 2008). We present the five levels of the blueprint analysis, namely the Physical evidence, the Customer actions, the Onstage/visible Contact Employee actions, the Backstage/invisible employee actions and the Support processes of the SMF (2013) small tourism sport scale event in Figure 3. Moreover in our study we also use the services blueprinting method incorporating it with a Failure Mode and Effects Analysis (FMEA) (Seyring, Dornberger, Suveltza, & Byrnes, 2009). The FMEA process consists of three basic steps, namely the "Identification of processes and problematic areas," "Analysis with emphasis on the potential consequences" and finally "Action steps with the aim of identifying strategies" to avoid failures and problematic service processes per contact point

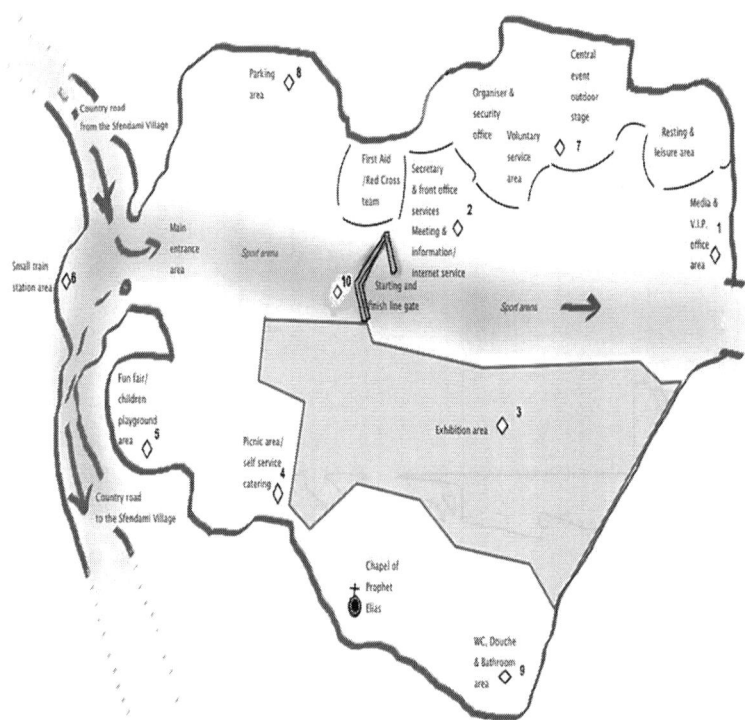

Figure 2.   The Area Map of the SMF Starting and Finishing Point.

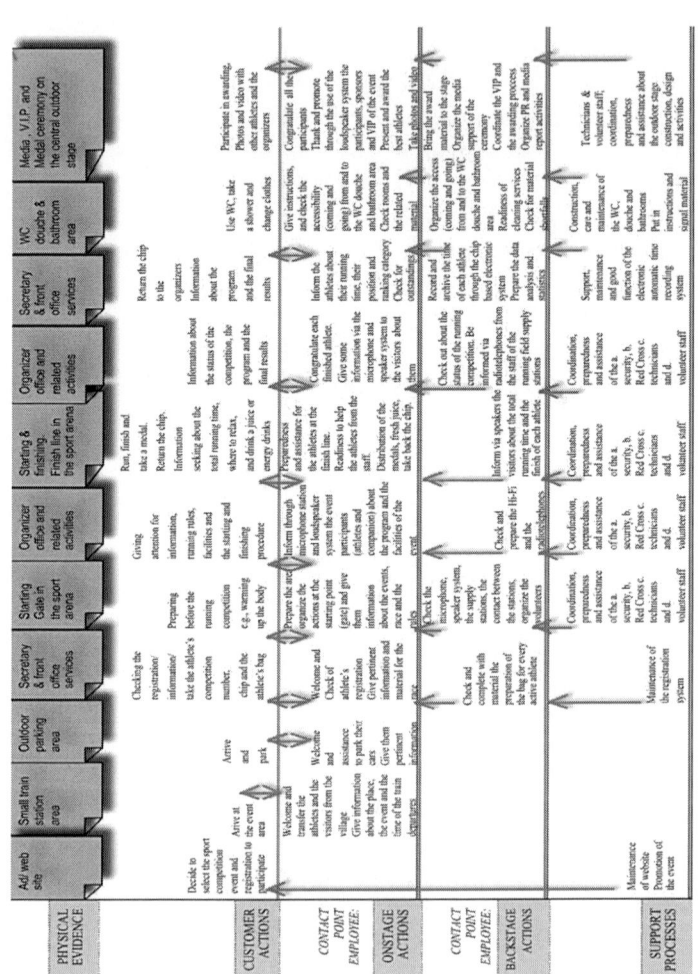

Figure 3.   Service Blueprint of a Visit to the SMF Small-Scale Sport Event.

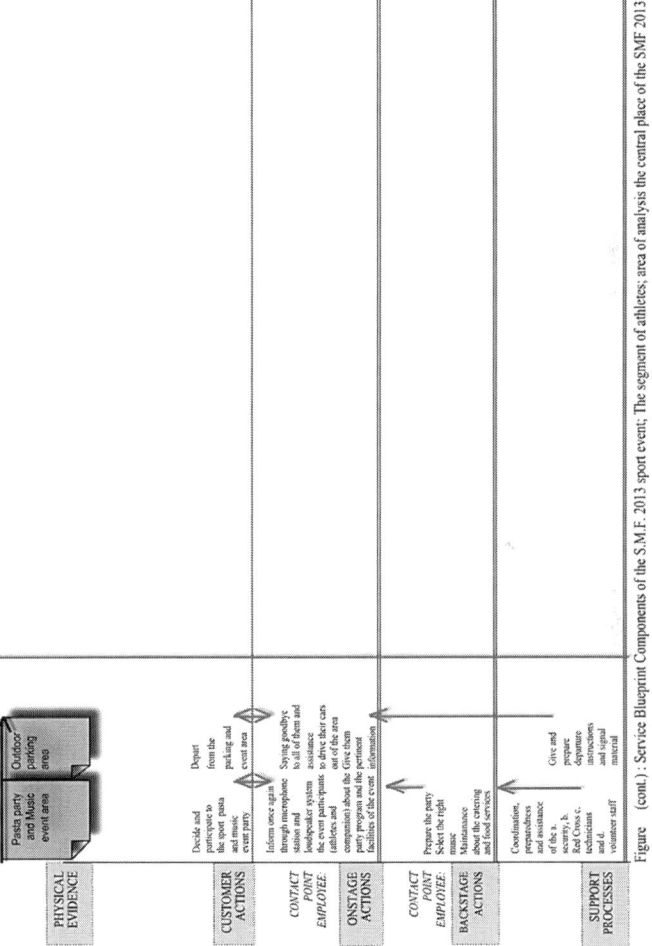

Figure 3.   (*Continued*)

Figure   (cont.) : Service Blueprint Components of the S.M.F. 2013 sport event; The segment of athletes; area of analysis the central place of the SMF 2013 basic sport event; Day of the running competition: 20 April 2013.

between customers and employees. The analysis is based on the evaluation of ten contact – point events (or else "moments of truth" for creating the tourist experience), (see also table 1 Service encounters: Positive and Negative Comments). For the "analysis of the potential consequences" we used Otto and Ritchie's (1996) six dimensional construct domain of service experience theory. The structure of this chapter ends with a proposal about the next steps that could be taken. In this last section the emphasis is on service strategy application and proposals to avoid future service blueprint failures that are related to specific contact points in the small-scale sport service system.

Diary Design

Diaries are useful tools for observation and tourist research participation (observation and tourist's comment selection) in a natural environment like the sport event area (Marino, Minichiello, & Browne, 2004). We finalized the diary style and format after checking the structural and design specifications for the specific sport event. In our diaries during the SMF (2013) event we developed descriptions and analyses for each time block, for the current situation and for the activities of the tourists in the sport event area. In addition, through observation and interviews, we identified the tourists' comments per contact-point. We used 26 field workers for the two-day period (April 20–21, 2013), with the aim of selecting, through observation and interviews, important comments that can help the management to evaluate their service in the natural environment of the SMF (2013) sport event arena. Each researcher noted by observation and comment selection important episodes and events per contact-point area. For each observation the procedure included notes about the researcher, the day of selection, the contact-point and the time frame of each observation of the research study. Additionally, in the main body of the diary the procedure included a semi-structured questionnaire with an open-ended format for indicating the customer comments per time block (from 8.00 until 20.00 with the use of six 2-hour time zones).

After the service process simulation, the description of the SMF services processes in a flow chart and in the Blueprint map (Figures 1–3) began. The main aim of the study approach was to process and analyze the Positive and Negative tourist comments per contact-point. As we have mentioned above those comments are the "experience moments" that the researchers selected per contact point based on their research diaries during the SMF event (Figure 4). In the service blueprint map we used the services taxonomy process of the five basic levels, namely Physical evidence, Customer actions, Onstage/visible Contact Employee actions, Backstage/invisible employee actions and Support processes (Bitner et al., 2008). The analysis of customer comments about service provision is a crucial point for this study because it helps failure point identification, related service design, and helps improve managerial decisions. In this part of our analysis we built a table to give a short account of the basic events that can have a positive and negative effect on the satisfaction level of the tourists. As mentioned above in the literature section, the tourists' satisfaction status is related with the tourists' experience and the related service contact points. After the selection of the events (based on the above comments) and their categorization per contact-point we developed the table mentioned above with the aim of having a synopsis of those critical moments. As we can see from table 1, 81.6% (31/38 events) of the diary events can negatively affect the satisfaction level of the tourists.

Using a combination of the above mentioned diary data pool and a table format for negative and positive aspects that affect the satisfaction status of the tourists; we are in a good position to identify negative events/experiences. In our study those are the: two (Secretary and Front Office services: Meeting and information/internet service), four (Catering area), five (Fun fair; Children Playground Area), six (Small Train Station Area), and nine (WC, Douche & Bathroom area) (Figure 4). Failures are identified in all the basic 10 contact points but we have identified only negative events/experiences in those five above. Next it is important to go forward with the identification of the potential consequences of each failure. To avoid a non-visitor-friendly atmosphere (i.e., Servicescape or Physical Environment) that can affect the satisfaction level and the whole experience of the visitors and of course their related loyalty and word of mouth, it is critical to invest in the improvement of the quality of Servicescape elements that can affect the tourists' experience (Laws, 1998).

Next we present the negative event(s) per contact-point, the characteristics that are related to the affective or emotional part of the service experience, and finally the potential consequences using Otto and Ritchie's (1996) six dimensional construct domain of service experience theory. Recognizing those basic relations we have built a table to give a synopsis of the Failure(s),

	Account of experience by "contact point"	Effect on satisfaction
	#1# VIP; Media & VIP Office Area	
1	The VIP visitors are very satisfied from the music event that took place during the intro to the sport competition and they express their positive feelings to the organizers	+
2	Some visitors select the VIP office area to find a place to rest and relax but the staff and the responsible volunteers suggest another place where they can relax.	–
	#2# Secretary and Front Office services: Meeting and information / internet service	
3	Failures that are related with the registration data process	–
4	Failures with the athlete's sport bag. In some cases the basic elements aren't included in the athlete's bag.	–
5	Visitors seek basic headache medication i.e., Aspirin, Depon, but the Secretary cannot serve them because they do not offer basic medications there	–
6	Visitors make negative comments about the free places in the camping area and the noisy and crowded situation in that area	–
	#3# Trade Show Area or Exhibition Area	
7	Visitors visit the trade show area in the morning of the sport competition day, but many exhibitors are not ready with their show rooms and show places	–
8	Visitors seek to mostly buy the SMF T-shirts. They find the T-shirts in the trade show area of the SMF event	+
	### Catering area	
9	Not enough tables and chairs (more benches and seats) near the food kiosk	–
10	Only meat and drinks without fruit and vegetable food and beverages	–
	#5# Fun fair; Children Playground Area	
11	There were problems with the availability of playground area staff. Early in the morning there was no one from the staff responsible for the area to care for the first guests in the playground area	–
12	There were not enough children's seats	–
	#6# Small Train Station Area	
13	Several complaints were expressed about the lack of frequency of the small trains	–
14	Complaints were expressed about the road dust kicked up by vehicles	–
15	Complaints were expressed about the behavior of private car drivers in the small train area	–
	#7# Red Cross Service; First Aid	
16	Immediate response of the Red Cross to four incidents (blood pressure, muscle cramps, beating creams, painkillers)	+
	#7b# Central Event Outdoor Stage; Resting and Leisure Area	
17	The staff do not immediately deal with the cleanliness of the central event outdoor stage area (people leave coffee packages in the area and water plastic bottles, workers had left nails in the grass)	–
18	Guests could not leave their luggage for safekeeping	–
19	Photographers during the event complain to each other about unprofessional behavior and work sharing	–
20	The awards and photo taking with athletes are pleasant moments for the visitors and the staff (all the people in the area enjoy this moment)	+
21	In the morning the music was too loud and the speakers were too noisy	–
	#8# The Parking Area	
22	Several parking problems. Many visitors cannot park and left the parking area (Cars are stuck in the mud)	+
23	It's not easy to find free parking places in the afternoon	–
24	The staff give instructions and direct the vehicles to and from the site	+
25	The staff does not help to release the vehicles that are stuck in the mud	+
	#9# WC, Douche & Bathroom area	
26	In the morning problems occurred in the toilets (paper, soap and an inadequate number of toilets for many users)	–
27	Accessibility is not easy (there were puddles and mud)	–
28	There were problems with cleanliness and hygiene in the female toilets, especially after 14.00.	–
29	Negative comments from the visitors about problems in the WC and Bathroom area, like small basins, no mirror(s), WC door (not closed well), non-existence of bench and seats and there was not enough light in the room	–
	#10# Starting & Finish Line Sport Competition Gate Area	
30	There are complaints expressed by visitors about WC, Douche signs and the related orientation signs for visitors in the area	–
31	Before the main sport race event they organize a race starting music event with the Brass and Fanfare Band of Kastoria	+
32	On the arrival of the first athletes the organizer and the staff give them medals and they are happy to have finished the race route	+
33	Problems with time recording	–
34	There are too many people who prevent the arrival of athletes at the finishing point	–
35	The noise in the finish point area makes it difficult to clarify the finishing time of the numbered athletes	–
36	Some athletes have indicated that there was a problem with the marking route tapes that were used to show the running route to athletes	–
37	Until 12.30 am several cars belonging to the sponsors and organizers remain in the or near the racing place, despite the announcements and appeals of the Secretariat	–
38	On arrival, some athletes thank the organizing body and the staff presents the athlete to the public and discuss his impressions of participating in the race	+

Figure 4.   SMF Research Study: Service Encounters and Positive/Negative Experiences and Episodes. *Note:* The number of the contact point is the service point in the area map (see the related area map before). Here, we only present the researcher diary comments that had negative or positive comments about the basis contact points.

Experience, Consequence(s)/Effects, and Management Actions (Figure 5).

Conclusions

Tourism sport event managers, can be encouraged, through the use of blueprints, to check all of the internal support systems and technological aspects of an event, as well as the employee-customer interactions that are required to create a distinctive customer experience. This chapter shows that observation, diaries, service blueprints, comment management and FMEA (Failure Mode and Effects Analysis) can act as a range of corporate research elements and management tools that give new insight into the theory and the praxis of tourism small-scale sport event customer and experience focused management applications. The case study shows that that synthesis of different tools can offer an alternative approach for services blueprinting improvement-planning procedures that arise from a diary based selection of comments. These comments reflect the problematic areas (failures) in different contact points of a service blueprint system. The management of the contact points in this blueprint system can be coordinated more easily, if we know those problematic areas that negatively affect the whole tourist experience. As the literature review shows, those dimensions develop the experience construct and can be qualitatively and quantitatively analyzed to give in depth information about the important aspects of, and the context of, the tourist experience. Given that these dimensions are important aspects in planning and organizing the customer quality improvement strategy of the event (see 3rd column of Figure 5), the management can build a long-term data pool about the failures and effects with the aim of avoiding similar circumstances and situations that may occur in the future and can affect satisfaction, word of mouth, the tourist experience and tourist loyalty, and hence the sustainability of the small-scale sport event (see "actions" in 5th column of the Figure 5). At the same time the positive comments can be the stable and diachronically sustainable competitive advantages of the SMF event product (see positive factors that affect the tourist satisfaction in Figure 4). The above analysis focuses mainly on how the methodology/approach of service blueprint may contribute to managing and offering high quality experiences to sport tourists. The analysis of Services Blueprinting can be combined with other useful

Contact point	Failure code	Related tourist experience construct domain	Potential consequence(s)/Effects	Actions
1	2	*Comfort*; they seek relaxation and physical comfort, *Interactive*; they want to be part of the process and to have a choice.	Conflicts that came out of misunderstandings e.g., psychological factors (comfort and interactive aspects) that can negatively affect the tourists experience of the friendly atmosphere that the event managers promote and promise in their advertising	Staff and volunteers inform the tourists about free sitting places in the area and relaxation opportunities using a notice that is printed in an instruction leaflet. Signposted places are made to inform the tourists during their entry into the area.
2	3–6	*Interactive*; they want to be part of the process and to having a choice, it is important for them to feel part of the event and the related Servicescape atmosphere. Also important is the *Hedonic* tourist experience dimension. Excitement, enjoyment and memorability are important aspects of their participation *Comfort* (e.g., emphasis on Relaxation & Physical Comfort to avoid noisy times and places) and the *Safety* (e.g., Health and Personal body safety) can be particularly useful information for them at this contact point.	Failures during the registration process of the athletes, gaps in the support needed, elements missing from athletes bags, problems with visitor health (medical services) and problems with visitors' peace of mind (a very noisy and crowded area to sleep and relax in the morning) can make tourists angry, and cause misunderstandings. Angry tourists can affect the mood of other visitors. When staff that cannot find instant solution(s), it gives a bad impression of the organizer's ability to meet the requirements of visitors. This situation(s) can also negatively affect the perceptions of the other visitors in the area.	Staff (secretary & front office personnel) must be trained and prepared. Failures in the e-registration process must be avoided and there should be effective control of the data recorded. If technical problems occur then they can use the conventional way of registering and recording. They can verbally inform the visitors about medical support and alternative places to relax so as to avoid noisy places (e.g., hours, places, lodgings). It's crucial that the staff in this contact point build a friendly atmosphere with politeness and prompt customer service. Signposted places and printed material e.g., for medical support and body & mind relaxation can enforce this effort.
3	7	*Hedonic*; they want to do something new and different they want to buy a T-shirt with the SMF logo, they want to taste the local products, *Interactive*; They want to meet local people and sport experts and have the choice to be in contact with them and the products and services of the trade show, *Stimulation*; they want to be educated and informed about the new sports technology, services and products.	Service accessibility, the need to have a choice during all the hours of the sport event festival and of course also in the morning hours. They must have the opportunity to visit the area of the trade show with the aim of avoiding noisy hours and crowded trade show areas.	Sponsors, sport experts, professional and local exhibitors must be on time and be prepared to show and to inform the visitors about their offers. The SMF management body must sign an agreement with them with the aim of respecting the necessary exposure regulation.
4	9,10	*Hedonic*; They want to enjoy the beverages and the food in a physical surrounding, *Interactive*; They want to meet their friends and other people on a common table, they want to have choice to select alternative food and beverages, *Comfort*; They want to have a nice place with a potential for physical comfort and relaxation and enjoy their food communally.	Shortages of alternative dining choices (i.e., healthy diet food and beverages) can affect the whole tourist experience of the organizers' promises to service the different and specific needs of the tourist event groups. Unsatisfied tourists in the catering area can share those comments with other common need driven tourists.	Define food and beverages and equipment criteria that are related to the needs of athletes and the other event visitors. Use those criteria to select the most suitable partner for the SMF catering area.
5	11,12	*Hedonic*; Parents and children seek enjoyment and excitement during the sport competition. They like to be in a place where children can play and have memorable times near the natural environment. *Interactive*; Parents want a place to meet and play with their children. They want to socialize with their children and find friends and meet other people in the playground area, *Comfort*; They like to find a comfortable playground for the children in the sports area. *Novelty*; They like to play outdoors and escape from the buildings and the playrooms in a city. *Stimulation*; Educational and informative playing activities are appropriate. *Security*; Parents want to feel secure about their children during their playing activities in the playground area.	Parents may not be satisfied with the service offered in the playground area if there is no adequate trained staff to undertake the, entertainment, recreation and childcare. Parents often want to feel secure that their children are safe, and can find facilities and friends to play with and experience socializing and educational & informational opportunities from meeting people. Unsatisfied parents and children form a negative perception about the services and facilities of the organizer. Negative Word of Mouth and weak intention to revisit the place with children is a possible scenario if they are unsatisfied from this contact – point.	Find the appropriate volunteers and staff. Motivate them and provide the suitable equipment for Children' playground area. Check and frequently approve the playing and playground activity plan and playground physical area (staff, opening hours, material and equipment).

Figure 5. Failure(s), Experience, Consequence(s)/Effects, and Actions for the SMF Study. *Note:* Where failure code(s) are the related code numbers of the failures in Figure 4.

6	13–15	*Hedonic*: Passengers seek enjoyment and excitement during the small train trip. They like to enjoy the landscape and remember memorable situations during the trip. *Interactive*: People like to take part in a small train trip, to meet and find friends and other people. *Comfort*: They like to have a comfortable and relaxing trip from and to the event area. *Novelty*: They like do something new; to make a trip with the small train. *Security*: Passengers want to feel safe during their trip	Passengers shouldn't feel upset with their transport services but should enjoy with pleasure the landscape and the route safely. So, when they arrive at the point of the event they will have the proper mood to participate actively and enthusiastically.	It's important to organize the departure and arrival timetables with the aim of developing a frequency plan of arrivals and departures that meets passenger's needs (i.e., avoid delays when place occupancy is achieved. Organize train departures at least every 35 minutes from and to the arrival and departure station points)
7	17–19, 21	*Hedonic*: Tourists seek enjoyment and excitement. They like to photograph themselves and to remember memorable situations. *Comfort*: They like to have a comfortable and relaxing stay near the central event outdoor stage of the event area. Music must be also clear and in the limits of the normal decibel volume *Security*: Tourists want to feel safe about their luggage. It is important to secure their belongings and their health and body from different risks (risk of injury).	Tourists' injuries affects the health and mood of visitors who were injured and those who accompany them. The event tourists feel uncomfortable with the loud music volume and unclear sounds, near the central event outdoor stage area	There is a risk of injury because the platform area; the outdoor stage isn't properly cleaned (there are nails on the floor). Cleaning service should clean the area before the start of the event. The technical staff should check the microphone and public loudspeaker system in the event outdoor stage area before starting the event.
8	22–23, 25	*Interactive*: The parking place is one of the first contact-points in the blueprinting process. It is important to meet the drivers and tourists in a friendly atmosphere before they enter the main sport event arena. Information on where to park and options for alternative parking spaces would be useful for them. *Comfort*: Most of the tourists change their clothes near their cars. The existence of changing rooms near the parking area is important. *Security*: Drivers and tourists want to feel safe about their cars and their belongings.	A lack of help and support from the non-welcoming staff in the Parking area can cause inconvenience and tensions between the drivers and staff and among drivers themselves.	Near the parking area there should be the appropriate equipment and staff support for the drivers (e.g., security service for their cars, sign system and staff to give information and help the car drivers and their cars that are stuck in the mud. The management staff has to seek for alternative parking places and combine the small train transportation opportunities with parking station points.
9	26–30	*Comfort*: Physical comfort and relaxation are important aspects for the tourists and they are also related to the contact-point WC, douche and bathroom area. *Safety*: Cleanness of the surrounding area and in the WC, douche and bathroom area are related to hygiene and the physical health of groups of tourists (Men, Women, and Children's physical needs).	Failures in the sign system, in offering facilities such as distinct spaces for women, men and children, information shortcomings, a lack of equipment in the area (benches, waiting chairs and cupboards); also a small number of alternatives on care and hygiene room facilities and problems in continued support of the WC, douche and bathroom cleanliness can together cause dissatisfaction with the quality of service that the organizer promotes through his web sites and his advertising material.	The spaces and the facilities in this area should cover the special needs of different groups of visitors (e.g., disabled people, men, women and children). They should be equipped and have the appropriate facilities before the starting day of the event. The cleaning service staff must check often e.g., every 15 minutes the situation in the area as well it must support the tourists by providing information and materials to the guests.
10	33–37	*Hedonic*: Athletes and their companions seek enjoyment and excitement about the sport competition. They like to be in a place where they have memorable experiences. *Interactive*: Athletes and their companions want to enjoy a suitable place to meet and race with other athletes. They want to socialize so want to find other people at the starting and finish line sport competition gate area. *Comfort*: They like to have relaxing facilities before and after the race. *Novelty*: They like to run in nature and escape the urban environment. *Stimulation*: Educational and informative services are very important for the athletes and their companions, like e.g., information about the position of each athlete in the race and running arena. *Security*: Athletes want to feel safe in the sport arena.	At this festival area the athletes are trying, to come into contact with others athletes but also to start to enjoy the running route. They leave their families and attendants to love their stay in the event area. The persons accompanying athletes are still waiting in the central event area and they like to be informed about the position of the athletes. They visit the other contact –points in the area for different reasons e.g. to buy local food products or a SMF t-shirt from kiosks in the exhibition area. After the arrival of the athletes at the finishing point the athletes seek food and beverages but also information about their total running time and the athletes' place categorization. If all of the above actions aren't organized e.g., like problems in time recording and correct athlete's time information services, but also problems in the running arena and the easy access from the starting and to the finishing point, this can cause situations that bring confusion and annoyance to the athletes. This situation can lead them to making negative comments about the organization of the event and the low value for money of their participation.	The organizing committee has to check the route and the recording system before the running event occurs. The TQM system can secure that the athletes can enjoy a memorable and exciting race without technical problems. The SMF broadcaster may indicate that athletes can relax and visit relaxation services e.g., maybe with the product service offerings of the related SMF sponsors. The Red Cross service is important for the athletes to feel safe so the presentation of this service from the broadcaster to the visitors, is very important.

Figure 5. (*Continued*)

managerial tools, like the Failure Mode and Effects Analysis to better manage the contact points, the "moments of truth" of tourist experiences in the sport event service system. In addition, the SMF case study shows that it is useful to point out the problematic areas in the service system using combined methods and managerial tools with the aim of enhancing and contributing to better managed sport tourism event experiences.

References

Andronikidis, A., Bellou, V., & Vassiliadis, C. A. (2008). Perceived service quality and patronage behavior in the auto-repair industry. *International Journal of Services, Economics and Management*, 1, 196−207.

Berry, L. L., Parasuraman, A., Zeithaml, V. A., & Adsit, D. (1994). Improving service quality in America: Lessons learned; executive commentary. *Academy of Management Executive*, 8, 32−52.

Bitner, M. (1990). Evaluating service encounters: The effects of physical surroundings and employee responses. *Journal of Marketing*, 54, 69−82.

Bitner, M. J. (1992). Servicescape: The impact of the physical environment surrounds customers and employees. *Journal of Marketing*, 56, 57−71.

Bitner, M. J., Ostrom, A., & Morgan, F. (2008). Service blueprinting: A practical technique for service innovation. *California Management Review*, 50, 66−94.

Brown, S. W., & Bitner, M. J. (2007). Mandating a service revolution for marketing. In R. F. Lush & S. L. Vargo (Eds.), *The service-dominant logic of marketing: Dialog, debate and directions* (pp. 393−405). Armonk, NY: M.E. Sharp.

Cetină, I. (2009). *Marketingul serviciilor. Fundamente and domenii de aplicare*. București: Uranus.

Chang, T. Z., & Chen, S. J. (1998). Market orientation, service quality and business profitability: A conceptual model and empirical evidence. *Journal of Service Marketing*, 12, 246−264.

Chen, C. F., & Chen, F. S. (2010). Experience quality, perceived value, satisfaction and behavioral intentions for heritage tourists. *Tourism Management*, 31(1), 29−35.

Cronin, J. J., & Taylor, S. A. (1992). Measuring service quality: A re-examination and extension. *Journal of Marketing*, 6(7), 55−68.

Edvardsson, B. (1997). Quality in new service development: Key concepts and a frame of reference. *International Journal of Production Economics*, 52, 31−46.

Fotiadis, A., & Vassiliadis, C. (2013). The effects of a transfer to new premises on patients' perceptions of service quality in a General Hospital in Greece. *Total Quality Management & Business Excellence*, 24, 1022−1034.

Gammie, A. (1992). Stop at nothing in the search for quality. *Human Resource*, 5(Spring), 35−38.

Gibson, H., Kaplanidou, K., & Kang, S. J. (2012). Small-scale event sport tourism: A case study in sustainable tourism. *Sport Management Review*, *15*, 160–170.

Gibson, H. J. (1998). Sport tourism: A critical analysis of research. *Sport Management Review*, *1*, 45–76.

Gibson, H. J., Willming, C., & Holdnak, A. (2003). Small-scale event sport tourism: Fans as tourists. *Tourism Management*, *24*, 181–190.

Grönroos, C. (1984). A service quality model and its marketing implications. European Journal of Marketing, *18*, 36–44.

Grönroos, C. (1991). The marketing strategy continuum: Towards a marketing concept for the 1990s. *Management Decision*, *29*, 7–13.

Gummesson, E. (1994). Making relationship marketing operational. *International Journal of Service Industry Management*, *5*, 5–20.

Gummesson, E. (1998). Productivity, quality and relationship marketing in service operations. *International Journal of Contemporary Hospitality Management*, *10*, 4–15.

Hallowell, R. (1996). The relationships of customer satisfaction, customer loyalty and profitability: An empirical study. *International Journal of Service Industry Management*, *7*, 27–42.

Higham, J. E. S. (1999). Sport as an avenue of tourism development: An analysis of the positive and negative impacts of sport tourism. *Current Issues in Tourism*, *2*(1), 82–90.

Hung, Y. H., Huang, M. L., & Chen, K. S. (2003). Service quality evaluation by service quality performance matrix. *Total quality Management & Business Excellence*, *14*(1), 79–89.

Jin, N. P., Lee, S., & Lee, H. (2015). The effect of experience quality on perceived value, satisfaction, image and behavioral intention of water park patrons: New versus repeat visitors. *International Journal of Tourism Research*, *17*, 82–95.

Johnston, R., & Clark, G. (2001). *Service operations management*. Harlow: Prentice-Hall.

Kao, Y. F., Huang, L. S., & Wu, C. H. (2008). Effects of theatrical elements on experiential quality and loyalty intentions for theme parks. *Asia Pacific Journal of Tourism Research*, *13*, 163–174.

Kingman-Brundage, J., George, W. R., & Bowen, D. E. (1995). Service logic: Achieving service system integration. *International Journal of Service Industry Management*, *6*, 20–39.

Lasser, W. M., Manolis, C., & Winsor, R. D. (2000). Service quality perspectives and satisfaction in private banking. *Journal of Service Marketing*, *14*, 244–271.

Laws, E. (1998). Conceptualizing visitor satisfaction management in heritage settings: An exploratory blueprinting analysis of Leeds Castle, Kent. *Tourism Management*, *19*, 545–554.

Leonard, F. S., & Sasser, W. E. (1982). The incline of quality. *Harvard Business Review*, *60*, 163–171.

Marino, R., Minichiello, V., & Browne, J. (2004). Reporting on events using diaries. In V. Minichiello, G. Sullivan, K. Greenwood, & R. Axford (Eds.),

Handbook of research methods for nursing and health science (2nd ed., pp. 393–410). Upper Saddle River, NJ: Pearson/Prentice Hall.

Newman, K. (2001). Interrogating SERVQUAL: A critical assessment of service quality measurement in a high street retail bank. *International Journal of Bank Marketing, 19*, 126–139.

Oh, H. (1999). Service quality, customer satisfaction and customer value: a holistic perspective. *International Journal of Hospitality Management, 18*, 67–82.

Oliver, R. L. (1993). Cognitive, affective and attribute bases of the satisfaction response. *Journal of Consumer Research, 20*, 1–13.

Otto, J. E., & Ritchie, J. R. (1996). The service experience in tourism. *Tourism Management, 17*, 165–174.

Parasuraman, A., Zeithaml, V. A., & Berry, L. L. (1985). A conceptual model of service quality and its implications for future research. *Journal of Marketing, 49*, 41–50.

Parasuraman, A., Zeithaml, V. A., & Berry, L. L. (1988). SERVQUAL: A multiple item scale for measuring customer perceptions of service quality. *Journal of Retailing, 64*, 12–40.

Perić, M. (2010). Sports tourism and system of experiences. *Tourism and Hospitality Management, 16*, 197–206.

Ritchie, B. W., & Adair, D. (2004). *Sport tourism: Interrelationships, impacts and issues*. Clevedon: Channel View Publications.

Rosenbaum, M. S. (2005). The symbolic servicescape: Your kind is welcomed here. *Journal of Consumer Behaviour, 4*, 257–267.

Seth, N., Deshmukh, S. G., & Vrat, P. (2005). Service quality models: A review, International. *Journal of Quality & Reliability Management, 22*, 913–949.

Seyring, M., Dornberger, U., Suveltza, A., & Byrnes, T. (2009). *Service blueprinting; Handbook*. Germany, Leipzig: International SEPT Program. May.

Shostack, G. L. (1992). Understanding services through blueprinting. In T. A. Swartz, D. E. Bowen, & S. W. Brown (Eds.), *Advances in marketing and management: Research and practice*. Greenwich, CT: JAI Press.

Shostack, L. (1985). Planning the service encounter. In J. Czepiel, M. Solomon, & C. Surprenant (Eds.), *The service encounter* (pp. 243–254). Lexington, MA: Lexington Books.

SMF. (2013). *Sfendami mountain festival*. Retrieved from http://www.sfendami.com/. Accessed on June 25, 2015.

Snelgrove, R., & Wood, L. (2010). Attracting and leveraging visitors at a charity cycling event. *Journal of Sport and Tourism, 15*, 269–285.

Solomon, R. M., Surprenant, C., Czepiel, J. A., & Gutman, E. G. (1985). A role theory perspective on dyadic interactions: The service encounter. *Journal of Marketing, 49*(Winter), 99–111.

Sureshchander, G. S., Rajendran, C., & Anatharaman, R. N. (2002). The relationship between management's perception of total quality service and customer perceptions of service quality. *Total Quality Management, 13*(1), 69–88.

Sweeney, J. C., Soutar, G. N., & Johnson, L. W. (1997). Retail service quality and perceived value. *Journal of Consumer Services, 4*, 39–48.

Teece, D. J. (2010). Business models, business strategy and innovation. *Long Range Planning, 43*, 172–194.

Vargo, S. L., & Lusch, R. F. (2008). Service-dominant logic: Continuing the evolution. *Journal of the Academy of Marketing Science, 36*, 1–10.

Zeithaml, V. A., & Bitner, M. J. (2003). *Service marketing: Integrating customer focus across the firm.* New York, NY: McGraw-Hill Higher Education.

11 Authenticity, Commodification, and Mcdonaldization of Tourism Experiences in the Context of Cultural Tourism

Medet Yolal

ABSTRACT

Purpose – The purpose of the chapter is to discuss the tourist experiences by tracing various perspectives and dimensions of authenticity, commodification, and McDonaldization.

Methodology/approach – The main debates on the authenticity of the tourism experiences and the commodification of the tourism product is examined. Further a relevant literature on the McDonaldization thesis is provided focusing on experiential dimensions of the tourism consumption.

Findings – Destinations rely not only on the object authenticity of their attractiveness but also strive to attract tourists by tailoring experiences that will meet high-order needs of the tourists. However, these destinations are under threat by commodification and McDonaldization due to excessive use of the resources as a result of mass tourism.

Practical implications – Destination managers and planners should focus on the experiences without compromising on authenticity, uniqueness, and genuineness of their destinations while refraining over-commercialization and McDonaldization of their offerings.

Originality/value – This chapter discusses the authenticity, commodification, and McDonaldization issues on the basis of a case study of a well-established destination.

Keywords: Authenticity; commodification; McDonaldization; experiences; cultural tourism; Cappadocia in Turkey

Introduction

The world we inhibit is no longer authentic-that it has become fake, plastic, a kitschy imitation (Gable & Handler, 1996). This is also reflected in the development of mass tourism which resulted in consumerism as the aftermath of the massive and often irreversible consumption of tourism resources (Singh, 2012). This materialistic consumption of tourism can be a destructive force both for tourists and destinations (Singh, 2012). The net result of mass tourism, therefore, has been the establishment of destinations for particular market segments which are very often remarkably similar-identikit destinations. Although it has been argued that escaping from the pressures of one's mundane environment in search for more authentic experiences is a primary driver in tourist motivation (Cohen, 2010), people rely on the optimum means that have been previously discovered and institutionalized in a variety of settings. Thus the search for maximum efficiency in increasingly numerous and diverse social and consumption settings is marked as McDonaldization, characterized by efficiency, predictability, calculability, and replacement of human with nonhuman technology in every aspect of the society (Ritzer, 1983).

Tourism is criticized to result in commoditization of areas in life of a community as a result of tourism development at the destination. Cohen (1988) notes that local culture generally serves as the principal example of such commoditization. In this vein,

Hughes (1995) underlines the fact that various economic, information, and population flows have profoundly influenced the ways in which cultures have become represented. However, a modernist anxiety goes hand in hand with desire to find the authenticity again whatever it costs. Therefore, those modern seekers who desire to overcome the opposition between their authenticity-seeking self and society have to look elsewhere for authentic life (Cohen, 1988).

Although authenticity, commodification, and McDonaldization of tourism industry is well scrutinized, there is still gap on the theoretical and empirical background of these concepts and their implications. Therefore, this chapter provides an overview of the tourist experience by tracing various perspectives and dimension of authenticity, commodification, and McDonaldization focusing on tourism experiences in the context of cultural tourism. After offering a review of the literature, the chapter presents a case study on the authenticity, commodification, and McDonaldization of a popular destination. The chapter ends with a discussion of maintaining and sustaining authentic cultural tourist experiences without endangering the development of tourism industry.

Authenticity in Cultural Tourism

The concept of authenticity was introduced into tourism by MacCannell (1973), and became the key concept in an emergent sociological paradigm for the study of tourism (Cohen, 1988, 2007, 2012; Hughes, 1995; Reisinger & Steiner, 2006; Wang, 1999). According to Thrilling, authenticity was first applied to museums where experts wanted to determine "whether objects of art are what they appear to be or claimed to be" (1972, p. 93). In a broader sense, MacCannel explains that it is the modernization of the society which determines the search for authenticity in every aspect of life. According to him, modern man has been condemned to look elsewhere, everywhere to see if he can catch a glimpse of it reflected in the simplicity, poverty, chastity or purity of others. In the establishment of modern society, the individual act of sightseeing is probably less important than the ceremonial ratification of authentic attractions as objects of ultimate value, a ratification at once caused and measurable to a certain degree by the time and distance the tourists travel to reach it (1973, p. 14). In this regard, Wang (2000, p. 215) argues that tourism is a form of "authenticity seeking" and of searching for meanings, not only in the sense of seeking authentic objects, but also in the sense of a quest for existential authenticity, by escaping from mainstream institutions and relaxing the rules of self-constraint associated with these institutions.

Tourism enables people to move from the constraints and inauthenticity of daily routines while offering a liminal place where societal constraints are suspended (Wang, 2000). Moreover, tourism involves both the supply and consumption of the commodity or of authentic experiences in which tourists can fulfill and actualize themselves. Further, tourism is also a part of generation, staging, and consumption of experiences through the manipulation of place and presentation of culture (Vutler & Carmichael, 2010). However, Mowforth and Munt (2008) warns that authenticity should be understood within a broader sense, since it is not just about the "real" other available all over the world, rather it is about the ability to witness and consume "real" lives too. Further, Wang (2000) suggests that the issue of authenticity may be less important in a number of kinds of tourism such as green tourism, holiday on the beach, hobby tourism, visiting friends and relatives, since what tourists seek are their own authentic selves.

Brown (1996) has classified authenticity into two: quest for authentic other and quest for authentic self. Further, Wang (1999, p. 49) has rendered the systematic account of authenticity: objective, constructive, and existential (subjective) authenticity. Objective authenticity refers to the authenticity of the original that the authenticity of the tourist experience depends on the toured object being perceived as authentic. In that sense, Culer (1981) notes that toured objects or toured others are experienced as authentic not because they are originals or reality but because they are perceived as the signs of authenticity. Reisinger and Steiner (2006) explains this as the genuineness of artefacts and events.

Constructive authenticity is the result of social construction where things appear to be authentic not because they are so but because they are constructed as such in terms of social viewpoints, beliefs, perspectives, or powers (Wang, 2000). Wang also suggests that tourists search for a symbolic authenticity as a result of social construction. Therefore, an object, a place or an experience meaningful for someone may be an absolute fake for another (Moore, 2002). However, Olsen (2012, p. 264) notes that power relations in social and cultural processes may be a significant factor in shaping the authenticity of the experience since people deem more "true to themselves" in some social context than in others.

Existential authenticity comprises personal or intersubjective feelings that are activated by the liminal process of tourist behaviors. Reisinger and Steiner (2006) suggest that existential authenticity has wider power in explaining tourist experiences as it can account for phenomena that are difficult to objectify such as nature experiences and interactions between tourists. In such liminal experiences, people feel that they are themselves much more authentic and more freely self-expressed than they are in everyday life (Wang, 2000).

Cohen (2010) argues that existential authenticity is commercially transformed into packaged experiences of holidays. Tourism is one way of accessing existential authenticity since it resists the logic and ethic of everyday reality and offers an intensified and concentrated experience of an alternative being-in-the-world (Wang, 2000, p. 65). However, McClinchey and Carmichael (2010) warn that tourists may grow tired of the staged performances and cultural representations, which is termed as "staged authenticity," where sense of place is apparently blurred. Therefore, cultural performances are shortened, parts/types of the performance are highlighted, staged, and performance is westernized to suit tourists' tastes and preferences (Hashimoto, 2002).

Hall (2012, p. 65) suggests that authenticity is born from everyday experiences and connections which are often serendipitous, not from things "out there." More recently, Pearce (2012) proposed the mundane subjective authenticity, which recognizes that everyday activities such as noting cultural and location differences and similarities as well as standing in line, watching a movie, dinking in a bar are real and genuine travel experiences with a different kind of authenticity value. Moreover, Cohen (1979, p. 192) believes that the existential tourist is one who lives in two worlds, the "world of the everyday," which is "devoid meaning and where he lives in exile, and the world of the trip, where he is his real self." Therefore, Brown (2013) suggests that not all tourists will experience tourism as a catalyst for existential authenticity. In this vein, "tourist moment" (Cary, 2004) or "existential moment" (Steiner & Reisinger, 2006) has the potential to create existential experiences while people are traveling. In this sense, Cohen (2005) argues that unexpected occurrence of natural events such as huge tsunami waves can be the most authentic moment which the vacationers can encounter during their visit.

Post-modernism as an articulation of facts with all its uncertainties, complexity and paradoxes has also been employed in the study of tourists and their search for authenticity. So-called "post tourists" are aware that the tourist experience is largely commodified, and that the search of authenticity is somewhat unavailing (Smith, 2009, p. 199). According to Cohen (1995, p. 16) two reasons can be identified: First, if the cultural sanction of the modern tourist has been the "quest for authenticity," then that of the postmodern tourist is a "playful search for enjoyment" or an "aesthetic enjoyment of surfaces" (1995, p. 21). Secondly, the postmodern tourist becomes more sensitive to the impact of tourism upon fragile host communities or tourist sites. Staged authenticity thus helps to protect a fragile toured culture and community from disturbance by acting as a substitute for the original and keeping tourists away from it (1995, p. 17). Imaginative, jarringly discordant innovations, bordering on the fantastic, may replace the longing for the wholeness of the pro-modern other, as the principal socially accepted manifestations of a novel kind of authenticity (Cohen, 2012, p. 261). Therefore, the future of tourism, according to Douglass and Raento (2004, p. 7) may well be restaged by the extraordinary success of such an "emblem of post-modernism" which thrives at being the embodiment of all that is opposed to authenticity.

CULTURAL TOURISM AND AUTHENTICITY

There has been a marked growth of interest in mass and minority (non-western) cultures, heritage, religious traditions, ethnicity, and environment and ecology. Cultural tourists are interested in the more experiential aspects of culture. In an international context, the way of life of a people can be a primary motivation as the authentic or intimate contact with people whose ethnic or cultural background is different from their own (Smith, 2009, p. 188). This increasing interest in others' culture has given rise to commodification of culture as bundles of experiences.

The authenticity of displayed culture is another debated area (Hashimoto, 2002). Pearce (1988) suggests that provided tourists placed a low value on authenticity they could still enjoy a cultural experience that was staged. Not all tourists would be upset and dissatisfied because of a perception that they had been manipulated to some extent. Although tourists claim to seek the "authentic" or "genuine" culture of the host communities, how far they can really accept and appreciate the "authentic" is always questionable (Hitchcock, King, & Parnwell, 1993). Hashimoto (2002, p. 221) argues that tourists often search for authenticity but their expectations do not go beyond the confirmation of their stereotypical images. When their images and ideas do not match the authentic cultural exhibitions, tourists tend to reduce dissonance by rejecting the authentic cultural exhibitions.

However, Pearce (1988) suggests that although tourists placed a low value on authenticity they could still enjoy a cultural experience that is staged. On the other hand, Sofield (2003) comments that not all tourists would be upset and dissatisfied because of a perception that they had been manipulated to some extent. Moreover, they do not want to spend all day watching the rituals which they may not understand, or they have such a busy travel itinerary that they cannot stay very long at any one site (Hashimoto, 2002, p. 221). Consequently, shopping and the purchase of tourism memorabilia is thought to be an enhancement and as integral part of the tourism experience (Ferdinand & Williams, 2010). These items can also be highly symbolic, fulfilling personal needs and desires for social status and provide opportunities for tourists to preserve their memories of finding the authentic during their visits.

EXPERIENCES IN THE FORM OF AUTHENTICITY SEARCH

Pine and Gilmore (1999) suggest that the human progress is divided into four stage: first, in the agrarian era, commodities were extracted from the earth, then during the industrial era, people manufactured goods. The industrial economy then gave way to the third economic era, the service economy, where services were delivered. Finally, the experience economy evolved, where the main economic offering is the staging of experiences. According to them, the newly identified offering of experience occurs whenever a company intentionally uses services as the stage and goods as props to engage an individual (1999, p. 11). Further, they suggest that commodities are fungible, goods are tangible, services are intangible, and experiences are memorable. In tourism, this can be justified by the fact that tourists migrate from mass consumption toward more authentic products and personal experiences for new meanings and self-actualization (Cooper & Hall, 2008). Similarly, Vutler and Carmichael (2010, p. 4) advocate that the tourism industries are also part of generation, staging, and consumption of experiences through the manipulation of place and presentation of culture. In order to respond to the changing needs of the tourists, that Poon (1993) defined as "new tourist," the tourism industry has developed experience-based products.

In the new experience economy, the quest for authenticity seeks out new experiences. Wang (2000) suggests that even when toured objects are totally inauthentic, authenticity-seeking is still possible because tourists can seek an alternative, namely existential authenticity, which is activated by their activities. As Mowforth and Munt (2008) suggest tourism can no longer rest upon cultural preservation and discovery of highland tribes and deep forest tribes, rather it has migrated to the quest for danger and risk. Therefore, people look for experiences that will educate, entertain, develop, and rejuvenate themselves either in their home environment or on holiday. This can be explained by "escape from" and "escape to" places or experiences that will help individuals set free from daily routine and associated tempos.

According to Pine and Gilmore (2007), there is no such thing as an authentic or inauthentic experience, as experiences happen inside us and are our internal reaction to the events unfolding around us. In line with this, MacCannell (1973) suggests that an authentic experience involves not merely connecting a marker to a sight, but a participation in a collective ritual, in connecting one's own marker to a sight already marked. For Smith (2009), this is a welcome development for non-traditional destinations, as they can now provide tourists with an alternative product and a broader range of activities.

Micro-Case/Example 1: Russian-US Crew, Space Tourist Return to Earth

Millionaire scientist and entrepreneur Gregory Olsen, one of the earliest space tourists, traveled to space with a Russian cosmonaut and an American astronaut in their Soyuz capsule. Olsen stayed in the orbit on the International Space Station for just over a week, paying a reported 20 million USD. Olsen waved and gave a big thumbs up, said: "I feel great. I can't wait to walk around, have real food and take a shower" (*Source*: *Turkish Daily News*, October 12, 2005).

Commodification of Cultural Tourism

Many societies in the process of tourism development were becoming increasingly commoditized through tourism should not have come as a surprise to scholars who have learned that there probably was no society, ever, in which some commoditization was not evident (Nash, 2007, p. 251). A prospective receiving society will not only be called upon to open its borders and its homes to foreign visitors, but to engage in a special kind of business, which involves the commoditization of culture, patrimony, traditions, social identity, certain population groups, and finally, to turn life itself into a tourist product (Lanfant, 2007, p. 134). Wang (2000, p. 188) suggests that commodification should be considered in two senses: first, tourism is commoditized and consumed as the end product of hedonic experiences and enjoyment as a result of cultural orientation toward marketing and consumption of the goods, services and experiences. Second, the consumption of tourism appears as symbolic consumption, which is related to the culture of status differentiation and market segmentation, in which the choice of products not only reflects the social position of individuals but also their tastes, social values, and lifestyle. This is explained by Mowforth and Munt (2008, p. 63) by the spread and intervention of capitalism into Third World where tourism had the effect of turning Third World places, landscapes and people into commodities. Consequently, touristic exploitation of societies results in fantastic exhibition of signs of identity and expectedly things are converted into touristic products (Lanfant, 2007). Therefore, culture is packaged, priced, and sold-like other consumer products.

Cohen (1988) suggests that MacCannell's views on authenticity assumed that the commoditization of an experience is destructive to the authenticity of the experience for both locals and tourists. In this regard, Greenwood (1989) notes that culture as a component of the tourism package is turned into an explicit and paid performance, and as a result empties the meanings by which people organize their lives. For example, in an account of tourism development in Bali, Picard (1996) summarizes the commodification of the culture and concludes that Balinese culture became reified and externalized in locals' own eyes, turning it to an object that could be detached from themselves in order to be displayed and marketed for others. However, Weaver and Lawton (2006) note that the commodification of culture may not necessarily be harmful. It is when the inherent quality and meaning of cultural artefacts and performances become less important than the goal of earning revenue from their reproduction or sale. In this vein, Cohen (2012) argues that craft products will remain authentic, even if produced for the tourist market, as long as they are not marked as "authentic" or "original." The falsification would be in the marking, not in the product itself (2012, p. 254).

According to Wang (2000), commoditization is universaliza- tion in which all single items are commoditized and offered to fit all tastes and preferences. Further, it is standardization, in which the quality of the same kind of commodities must remain similar and consistent. Moreover, commoditization is quantification in order to control costs and maximize profits (Wang, 2000). Through commodification, even the experiences are packaged as a saleable commodity which results in pseudo-events. In such, religious, pageantry and public celebrations, festivals, and events, culture itself and all its components and the relations are commo- dified and delivered to tourist markets as a packaged product, mostly far away from their original meanings. In order to qualify as a commodity that consumers will buy and consume, the pro- duct of tourism requires that uncertainty, risk, inconsistency, and contingency be reduced (Wang, 2000) which results in McDonaldization of the tourism businesses.

McDonaldization of the Tourist Experiences

In his classical work Ritzer (1983) underlines the significance of rationalization throughout America and other societies. According to him, in almost every sector of the society "more and more emphasis is placed on efficiency, predictability, calcul- ability, replacement of human by nonhuman technology, and control over uncertainty" (1983, p. 107). This process is termed by Ritzer as the "McDonaldization," borrowing from the popu- lar fast-food chain McDonald's being a pioneering exemplar of these trends. Over the years, the McDonaldization thesis has been used to interpret broad trends and tendencies across the tourism industry (Weaver, 2005). In this vein, Disney World represents a privatized, sanitized, aestheticzed, idealized world in which people can take refuge from the harsh realities of the out- side world. Craik (1997) suggests that these theme parks are much more appealing than many themed heritage attractions or museums because they can offer the visitor a more exciting, entertaining, and integrated experience. It is a world of fantasy and escapism, combining dreamscapes with simulations of real places, a curious blend of fiction and reality.

Disneyification of the experiences is a nightmare scenario according to Ashworth (2012, p. 279) in which pasts are condensed into easily consumed, bite-sized pieces lacking any authenticity. It is possible for the individual to leave his everyday world in search of authentic experience only to find himself surrounded once again by spurious elements such as would occur, for example, in a trip to Disney World (MacCannell, 1973, p. 152). Entire touristic communities and regions are now built up from spurious elements. However, Wang (2000) suggests that authenticity is an emerging process in which inauthentic experiences may become authentic by the time. Something in the beginning may be inauthentic or artificial can subsequently become "emergent authenticity" as time goes by as in the case of Disneyland (Cohen, 1988).

The original system of attractions is now overlaid with malls that entertain, amusement parks, virtual environments, indoor plastic rain forests, replicas of the pyramids, the Eiffel Tower and entire communities built by Disney and Dreamworks (MacCannell, 2007). Smith (2009, p. 31) argues that many tourist attractions constitute a kind of "tourist bubble" suspended in time and space, isolated from any real context, and providing the tourist with an idealized environment and experience. This mostly occur in "front" regions where hosts and guests meet. The back, by contrast, is the place not penetrated by the outsiders, where the residents relax and do "their own thing" away from prying eyes, where their behavior is "natural," and where they perform activities for reasons unassociated with and unaffected by an outside audience (Sofield, 2003, p. 270).

Cruise companies, all-inclusive resorts, and commercial tour operators have also tried to standardize their products in order to ensure consistency, predictability, and certainty, so that they supply the experiences precisely anticipated by their customers. For example, a package tour offers a visitor quick, accessible, and "soft" adventures in a pre-determined schedule. Similarly, all-inclusive resorts allow operators to serve large numbers of guests quickly, efficiently and in a way that leads to satisfaction (Crick & Campbell, 2007) which makes them an ideal fit with McDonaldization.

In criticizing the McDonaldization and large-scale commercial recreation, Zegre, Needham, Kruger, and Rosenberg (2012) note that this process threatens not only the vitality of the experience but also the sustainability of communities and resources. However, Weaver (2005) argues that McDonaldization and customization should not be viewed as mutually exclusive processes. According to Weaver the ascendancy of McDonaldization is far from absolute, due to the existence of niche markets and customization practices that are post-Fordist in nature.

Case Study: Cappadocia in Turkey: Authenticity, Experiences, and Commodification

Cappadocia is a historical region in Central Anatolia, Turkey, which owes its uniqueness and authenticity to tall columns topped with rocks as a result of erosion by wind and water forming present-day *fairy chimneys*. The name is believed to be Persian meaning "the land of beautiful horses." Even in earlier ages, people of this region realized that these soft rocks could be easily carved out to form houses, churches, and monasteries. Cappadocia was the home of the Jewish pilgrims, and it was also among the five Roman provinces in Anatolia addressed by Peter in his first letter (Wilson, 2010). Dwellings, castles, and even entire underground cities like Kaymakli and Derinkuyu were used as shelters and hiding places by early Christians who decorated these places with many examples of Byzantine art from the post-iconoclastic period. Cappadocia is currently an important tourist destination thanks to its fabulous landscape, exceptional natural wonders, and a unique historical and cultural heritage. Therefore, the genuineness and uniqueness of Cappadocia reflect the object authenticity of the region as defined by Reisinger and Steiner (2006).

Apart from natural and cultural attractions, Cappadocia offers distinctive experiences to its visitors. Hiking and sightseeing offer individuals a sense of being among these volcanic formations. Further, balloon ride over the landscape moves people to a magic land. "When we arrived at the site, it was like magic. We saw balloons scattered everywhere! The whole thing was beginning to feel very real by now and despite the cold, everyone's faces just lit up as if the cold air did not bother us at all" writes a commentator in Tripadviser. This comment is also a clear example for mundane authenticity. It can be argued that feeling cold during the balloon ride which takes places around 5:30 a.m. simply turns into a different kind of authenticity value as Pearce (2012) suggested. Furthermore, balloon ride itself enables a different type of experience by providing spectacular views and it is undeniable that this kind of experience is totally different from the routine. Therefore the experience could also be interpreted as a liminal experience which cuts the ties with mundane "earth-related life" and paves the way for "a distinct experience up in the air." This type of experience is another proof that consumption of breathtaking experiences through the manipulation of place should not always have to be destructive for the place itself.

Activities such as horse riding in the land of beautiful horses, pottery making which has its roots in Hittite period, tasting the wine that has a history goes back 7.000 years, do not only include aspects that play crucial role in presentation of the local culture but also offer unique and memorable experiences for the visitors as proposed by Pine and Gilmore (1999). However, development of tourism as a viable economic activity in the region, outmigration of the local people to other places, and immigration of people from other parts of the country have induced the community to change and lose its authentic culture (Tosun, 1998). Further, Tosun notes that emergence of large-scale accommodation establishments, souvenir shops, and bars has threatened the historical, cultural, and natural attractions. The development of mass tourism in an irresponsible manner has not only damaged the object authenticity of the region but also altered the social structure and locals' attitudes toward tourism and the tourists. Local cultural values have been used as a commodity and marketing tool. Many authentic cultural values have been over-commercialized by using them at the wrong place, wrong time, and with the wrong standards by mostly untrained performers (Tosun, 1998). In a recent paper Tosun (2000) reports his witness of a circumcision feast that has been presented as a tourist product. He writes "to be paraded in front of so many foreign people with different language and color should not be allowed and it becomes an additional stress factor for those boys kept waiting for the sake of tourists and money" (2000, p. 297). Consequently, over-commercialization and threats against the authenticity in the region has created a bundle of complicated problems that should be handled by the managers and local authorities in Cappadocia.

McDonaldization is evaluated in the same vein with mass tourism. Therefore, it becomes possible to find some reflections of the basic elements of McDonaldization in the region. From this point of view, "efficiency" is grasped as providing the things that tourists demand without any inefficiency (Kaelber, 2006,

p. 54). But those attempts for meeting the tourists' demands may also precipitate some undesirable results, especially when individuals choose a plan contrasting to the rest of region. This is also apparent in Cappadocia. The cave life of Cappadocia attracts the tourists. They can sleep in a cave, drink in a cave-bar and boutique hotels underline the availability of cave rooms and the fairy chimneys in their advertisements. The caves are up trending in value, and locals have begun to consider them as a valuable product. On the other hand, many of the cave houses are being stored in a very distinct way from the traditional ones (Tucker & Emge, 2010). In sum, locals try to offer every service in the same manner which tourists find it attractive. While this can lead a preservation of those caves, it also turns into a serious problem when those forms do not match with the general landscape.

Conclusions

Theories on authenticity, commodification, and McDonaldization point to each of these concepts as critical in understanding dimensions of tourist experiences. Hosting individuals traveling to specific destinations who are trying to satisfy their high-order needs such as authenticity seeking, prestige, and learning requires managers and planners to endeavor to maintain the authenticity of their destination, culture, and events. Indeed the case study has demonstrated that destinations rely on not only the object authenticity of their attractiveness but also strive to create experiences that would differentiate themselves from their competitors. As suggested by Pine and Gilmore (1999), a competitive edge will be gained by providers who are able to satisfy a consumer's search for personal achievement and transformation. Therefore, it is crucial for the political and developmental agendas to preserve their authenticity rather than develop places, cultures, and communities. Although the authenticity of the tourist experience is of importance, it is more crucial to ensure that local communities feel comfortable with their role as performers and entertainers (Smith, 2009). This includes the degree to which they are prepared to allow the commodification of their culture for touristic purposes.

This chapter has argued for greater attention to be paid to the role of authentic experiences in attracting and satisfying individuals. However, as suggested by Cohen (2007, p. 81), contemporary tourism may appear to be moving into the "post-authentic" age but authenticity is lurking beneath the surfaces of post-modern attractions, though in an inverted, and in the eyes of some, perverted guise. Therefore, ultimate goal for destination managers and planners to focus on the experiences without compromising on authenticity, uniqueness, and genuineness of the attraction while refraining over-commercialization and McDonaldization of the destination.

References

Ashworth, G. (2012). Do tourists destroy the heritage they have come to experience. In T. V. Singh (Ed.), *Critical debates in tourism* (pp. 278–286). Bristol: Channel View Publications.

Brown, D. (1996). Genuine fakes. In T. Selwyn (Ed.), *The tourist image: Myths and myth making in tourism* (pp.33–47). Chichester: Wiley.

Brown, L. (2013). Tourism: A catalyst for existential authenticity. *Annals of Tourism Research, 40*, 176–190.

Cary, S. H. (2004). The tourist moment. *Annals of Tourism Research, 31*(1), 61–77.

Cohen, E. (1979). A phenomenology of tourist experience. *Sociology, 13*, 179–201.

Cohen, E. (1988). Authenticity and commoditization in tourism. *Annals of Tourism Research, 15*, 371–386.

Cohen, E. (1995). Contemporary tourism-trends and challenges: Sustainable authenticity or contrived post-modernity? In R. Butler & D. Pearce (Eds.), *Change in tourism: People, places, progresses* (pp. 12–29). London: Routledge.

Cohen, E. (2005). Tourism and disaster: The tsunami waves in Southern Thailand. In W. Alejziak & R. Winiarski (Eds.), *Tourism in scientific research* (pp. 81–114). Krakow: Academy of Physical Education and Rzeszow, University of Information Technology and Management.

Cohen, E. (2007). Authenticity in tourism studies: Aprés la Lutte. *Tourism Recreation Research, 32*(2), 75–82.

Cohen, E. (2012). 'Authenticity' in tourism studies: Aprés la Lutte. In T. V. Singh (Ed.), *Critical debates in tourism* (pp. 250–261). Bristol: Channel View Publications.

Cohen, S. (2010). Searching for escape, authenticity and identity: Experiences of 'lifestyle travellers'. In M. Morgan, P. Lugosi, & J. R. B. Ritchie (Eds.), *The tourism and leisure experience* (pp. 27–42). Bristol: Channel View Publications.

Cooper, C., & Hall, C. M. (2008). *Contemporary tourism-an international approach*. Oxford: Butterworth-Heinemann.

Craik, J. (1997). The culture of tourism. In C. Rojek & J. Urry (Eds.), *Touring cultures: transformation of travel and theory* (pp. 113–136). London: Routledge.

Crick, A. P., & Campbell, A. (2007). McDonaldization, mass customization and customization: An analysis of Jamaica's all-inclusive hotel sector. *IDEAZ, 6*, 22–41.

Culer, J. (1981). Semiotics of tourism. *American Journal of Semiotics*, 1(1–2), 127–140.

Douglass, W. A., & Raento, P. (2004). The tradition of invention: Conceiving Las Vegas. *Annals of Tourism Researcl1*, 31(1), 7–23.

Ferdinand, N., & Williams, N. L. (2010). Tourism memorabilia and the tourism experience. In M. Morgan, P. Lugosi, & J. R. B. Ritchie (Eds.), *The tourism and leisure experience* (pp. 202–217). Bristol: Channel View Publications.

Gable, E., & Handler, E. (1996). After authenticity at an American heritage site. *American Anthropologist*, 98(3), 568–578.

Greenwood, D. (1989). Culture by the Pound: An anthropological perspective on tourism as cultural commoditization. In V. Smith (Ed.), *Hosts and guests: The anthropology of tourism* (pp. 171–185). Philadelphia, PA: University of Pennsylvania Press.

Hall, C. M. (2012). Consumerism, tourism and voluntary simplicity: We all have to consume, but do we really have to travel so much to be happy. In T. V. Singh (Ed.), *Critical debates in tourism* (pp. 61–68). Bristol: Channel View Publications.

Hashimoto, A. (2002). Tourism and sociocultural development issues. In R. Sharpley & D. J. Telfer (Eds.), *Tourism development: Concepts and issues* (pp. 202–230). Clevedon: Channel View Publications.

Hitchcock, M., King, V., & Parnwell, M. (1993). Tourism in South-East Asia: Introduction. In M. Hitchcock, V. King, & M. Parnwell (Eds.), *Tourism in South-East Asia* (pp. 1–31). London: Routledge.

Hughes, G. (1995). Authenticity in tourism. *Annals of Tourism Research*, 22(4), 781–803.

Kaelber, L. (2006). Paradigms of travel: From medieval pilgrimage to the postmodern virtual tour. In D. J. Timothy & D. H. Olsen (Eds.), *Tourism, religion and spiritual journeys* (pp. 49–63). London: Routledge.

Lanfant, M.-F. (2007). Constructing a research project: From past definite to future perfect. In D. Nash (Ed.), *The study of tourism: Anthropological and sociological beginnings* (pp. 122–136). Oxford: Elsevier.

McClinchey, K., & Carmichael, B. (2010). The role and meaning of place in cultural festival visitor experiences. In M. Morgan, P. Lugosi, & J. R. B. Ritchie (Eds.), *The tourism and leisure experience* (pp. 59–72). Bristol: Channel View Publications.

Moore, K. (2002). The discursive tourist. In G. M. S. Dann (Ed.), *The tourist as a metaphor of the social world* (pp. 41–60). Wallingford, CT: CABI.

Mowforth, M., & Munt, I. (2008). *Tourism and sustainability: Development, globalization and new tourism in the third world*. Oxon: Routledge.

Nash, D. (2007). The emergence of a new field of study. In D. Nash (Ed.), *The study of tourism: Anthropological and sociological beginnings* (pp. 223–253). Oxford: Elsevier.

Olsen, K. (2012). Staged authenticity: A Grande Idée? In T. V. Singh (Ed.), *Critical debates in tourism* (pp. 261–265). Bristol: Channel View Publications.

Pearce, P. L. (1988). *The Ulysses factor: Evaluating visitors in tourist settings*. New York, NY: Springer Verlag.

Pearce, P. L. (2012). Authenticity matters: Meanings and further studies in tourism. In T. V. Singh (Ed.), *Critical debates in tourism* (pp. 265−276). Bristol: Channel View Publications.

Picard, M. (1996). *Bali. Cultural tourism and touristic culture*. Singapore: Archipelago Press.

Pine, B., & Gilmore, J. (1999). *The experience economy: Work is theater and every business a stage*. Boston: Harvard Business School Press.

Pine, B., & Gilmore, J. (2007). *Authenticity*. Boston, MA: Harvard Business School.

Poon, A. (1993). *Tourism, technology and competitive strategies*. Wallingford, CT: CABI.

Reisinger, Y., & Steiner, C. (2006). Reconceptualizing object authenticity. *Annals of Tourism Research, 33*(1), 65−86.

Ritzer, G. (1983). The "McDonaldization" of society. *Journal of American Culture, 6*(1), 100−107.

Singh, T. V. (2012). Introduction. In T. V. Singh (Ed.), *Critical debates in tourism* (pp. 1−26). Bristol: Channel View Publications.

Smith, M. K. (2009). *Issues in cultural tourism studies*. Oxon: Routledge.

Sofield, T. H. B. (2003). *Empowerment for sustainable tourism development*. Oxford: Elsevier Science Ltd.

Steiner, C., & Reisinger, Y. (2006). Understanding existential authenticity. *Annals of Tourism Research, 33*(2), 299−318.

Thrilling, L. (1972). *Sincerity and authenticity*. Oxford: Oxford University Press.

Tosun, C. (1998). Roots of unsustainable tourism development at the local level: The case of Urgup in Turkey. *Tourism Management, 19*(6), 595−610.

Tosun, C. (2000). Challenges of sustainable tourism development in the developing world: The case of Turkey. *Tourism Management, 22*, 289−303.

Tucker, H., & Emge, A. (2010). Managing a world heritage site: The case of Cappadocia. *Anatolia, 21*(1), 41−54.

Vutler, S. Q., & Carmichael, B. A. (2010). The dimensions of the tourist experience. In M. Morgan, P. Lugosi, & J. R. B. Ritchie (Eds.), *The tourism and leisure experience* (pp. 3−26). Bristol: Channel View Publications.

Wang, N. (1999). Rethinking authenticity in tourism experience. *Annals of Tourism Research, 26*(2), 349−370.

Wang, N. (2000). *Tourism and modernity*. Oxford: Pergamon.

Weaver, A. (2005). The McDonaldization thesis and cruise tourism. *Annals of Tourism Research, 32*(2), 346−366.

Weaver, D., & Lawton, L. (2006). *Tourism management* (3rd ed.). Milton: Wiley.

Wilson, M. (2010). *Biblical Turkey: A guide to the Jewish and Christian sites of Asia Minor*. Istanbul: Ege Yayinlari.

Zegre, S. J., Needham, M. D., Kruger, L. E., & Rosenberg, R. S. (2012). McDonaldization and commercial outdoor recreation and tourism in Alaska. *Managing Leisure, 17*(4), 333−348.

12

Managing Experiences within the Field of Creative Tourism: Best Practices and Guidelines

Caroline Couret

ABSTRACT

Purpose – This chapter aims to share practical experiences in creative tourism management, in order to propose some basic guidelines for DMOs and DMCs interested in designing activities that cater to this new demand. Specifically, our intention is to analyze and highlight the basic criteria that most weighs to fit such a singular demand.

Methodology/approach – As practitioners, most of the examples, observations, and analyses are based on our daily management of the *Creative Tourism Network®* (CTN) and the solutions found by our members in the development of their creative tourism programs all over the world. These observations rely also on surveys and literature references.

Findings – (i) The emergence of the experiential tourism in general, and the creative one in particular, is only the visible part of the paradigm shift that is affecting the tourist industry, leading to the appearance of new opportunities and challenges. (ii) Amidst such a new and versatile context, it's important to analyze the factors that contribute to the experience achievement, in order to adapt them and guarantee the best practices. (iii) This enables to list down some guidelines and practical advises for managers to cater this new demand.

Research limitations/implications – This chapter is written simultaneously with the paradigm shift and thus limits the distance we can have on its evolution as well as on the study's completeness. It thus just pretends to provide a provisional balance of the current situation, contrasted with literature reviews.

Practical implications – The emergence of creative tourism implies a completely new form of management for both cultural and tourist fields that leads to the creation of specific skills and general guidelines to be adapted for different contexts.

Originality/value – The study, based on examples proposed by the CTN, offers a transversal overview of creative tourism, a sector that has not been deeply analyzed yet given its increasing growth. It is thus a novel approach, close to the practitioners' daily challenges.

Keywords: Creative tourism; tourist experience design; experience economy; communities' empowerment; disruption

Introduction

This chapter proposes reflections and practical tools for experiences the management has applied to the tourism field. Using creative tourism as a tourist paradigm for the experience economy, it aims to define the principles, best practices, and advices in order to help the stakeholders worldwide – whether private entrepreneurs or public DMOs – to launch their project or orientate their offer toward experiential tourism.

Since the appearance of the *Experience Economy concept* (Gilmore & Pine, 1998) and the origin of creative tourism (Richards & Raymond, 2000), there has been an increasing demand for a more participative, authentic, and creative tourist offer. Although this phenomenon has been arousing the interest of academics who are documenting this emergent sector through relevant literature, there still exists a gap between scientific and practical knowledge, and advices that are able to support the entrepreneurs worldwide to cater this new demand.

One of the reasons of this gap is the specificity of the experience itself, which hampers the researches by pretending to escape any standard product and model. Another reason is the adaptability and evolutive character of the creative tourism that hinders the elaboration of a general framework able to structure the best practices of the experience management. It is precisely this gap that we attempt to bridge in order to propose to the readers some common bases and practical tools to help them in their own project management.

The overview provided by the Creative Tourism Network®'s projects enables us to draw the main characteristics and challenges of this emergent sector. This study is thus oriented by academic sources but mainly powered by practical experiences in the field of creative tourism. This empirical approach relies on three sources: our own experiences as daily manager of CTN; a series of conversations with the operators and destinations that are already challenging for this new paradigm; and finally, the creative tourists' assessment – through the social media – of the activities that are proposed to them. The cases and examples have been selected from a wide array of projects and destinations worldwide in order to approach a certain objectivity as well as to cater with the most diverse readers' needs.

The Context of Creative Tourism: Opportunities and Challenges

CHANGES INTRODUCED BY THE EXPERIENCE ECONOMY AND THIS NEW SYSTEM OF VALUES

The first challenge that we had to face in writing this chapter was to delimit its scope. Indeed, although it looked relevant to consider creative tourism as a case of experiences and circular economies, it was required to include them in a very wider and complex frame, characterized by many interconnections, a rapidly growing evolution, and a disruptive impact upon the whole society.

The emergence of creative tourism is thus considered as a corollary of the experience economy. This means that a part of the factors that provoked such a paradigm shift is to be found in the same transfer of values from material products to intangible experiences and from a linear economy to a circular and multi-directional one. The changes came from the emergence of a new demand, empowered by the democratization of new technologies that turned the top-down model, which had shaped the tourist industry for decades, into a bottom-up approach, in which the tourists are now co-creators and prosumers of their own experiences.

This new demand, boosted by increasing environmental consciousness of the western society, puts the intangible values and personal development in front. *People no longer consume just what they need, but they buy goods and services which express their lifestyle and identity* (Richards, 2013). This is even more relevant in the tourism field, which is naturally conceived around emotions and a wide array of intangible insights.

In addition to this, *many people have increasingly pressured lives, which means that their creative activities are being squeezed into holidays as well. Holidays have therefore become more than just periods of rest and relaxation – they have become spaces for learning and self-development as well. The growth of "skilled consumption" is evident today* (Richards, 2013).

On the other side, the creative tourism concept meets the philosophy of the circular economy from the offer point of view as well. Indeed, for being considered as tourism in which the professionals have to be creative themselves in order to provide unique and innovative activities for the travelers, they have to "recycle" the existing insights and traditions to produce new stories and experiences, thereby creating new opportunities in this way. *After?* ... offering similar services worldwide and greeting the visitors with the same proposals (Bus City Tours, City Cards, etc.) since decades, this new context encourages them to distinguish their offers adding more participatory elements and creating unique experiences.

This new system of values is currently fostered by the millennials for whom the emphasis is no longer on the product but on the "atmosphere" and the (positive) effects of the experience in terms of skill development and connections with peers around the world.

They consider experiential and creative tourism as a good practice in circular economy that no longer relies on institutions – they don't trust – but on the loyalty of the society on its whole that seeks to create positive value and gives them a role in the optimization of resources and production of new meanings. A survey conducted by our team to a sample of 200 (millennial) guests in a hostel in Barcelona indicated that 58% were more interested in paying 40€ for a cooking class than 20€ for a visit to an historic monument (28%); none for both (10%), and n/a (4%). Millennials are also decisive agents for the expansion of sharing and collaborative consumption, that also strongly weighs on the development of experience economy in general and creative tourism in particular. This new model represents a double-edged element that, from the one hand, broadens and regenerates the tourism sector through new demands, but from the other hand, also imposes new rules – or absence of rules – for the new providers, in other words, new challenges.

ASSETS AND OPPORTUNITIES FOR CREATIVE TOURISM
Creative tourism as a lever for communities' empowerment

The tourist industry is probably one of the sectors in which this paradigm shift is most evident. Indeed, creative tourism brings new opportunities and challenges for the traditional/mainstream tourism. After decades of being formed with monographic activities, such as sun and beach, all-inclusive, city break, etc., it has to now face a long-tail market, characterized by a large number of niches requiring tailored experiences for extremely segmented groups.

In other words, the tourist offer that had been driving groups to the traditional hotspots ("What to see?") has to turn to participative activities involving small groups ("How to do?") in order to satisfy each traveler's exigence in its personal search of meanings and emotions ("Wow effect!").

Among these niches, creative tourism is certainly one that requires more attention and expertise as it can refer to a wide array of realms – craft, music, dance, gastronomy, photography, etc. – to design unique and meaningful experiences, and it caters to an already experienced audience. This means new opportunities for the local communities. Indeed, creative tourism, whose value is based on its entrepreneur's creativity, offers the local population the possibility to be involved in the tourism sector through the management of their own (micro)-project. It deals with an important asset for the tourism industry which is often criticized for its low-skilled and low-paying working places.

Artists, artisans, citizens, become the local culture these new travelers would want to meet. They no longer act as intermediaries between the tourists and the destination's heritage; they are the heritage. They generally propose educational activities that doesn't require infrastructure or investments: home cooking class, photographic routes, air painting holidays, traditional dance lessons, among an infinity. This is how the tourism sector is now counting on new actors like a Tuscan shoemaker, who teaches his art to the tourists, a Portuguese housewife who gives home cooking lessons, a Japanese farmer who shares his knowledge of bio culture, or an association that initiates the visitors to the French Provence or South Portugal's traditional dances. Although none of them has a professional vocation or training in tourism, they turn themselves into a growing number of travel purposes.

The women, who are particularly active within the artistic fields, are seizing those niches, to create their own microbusiness, which offer them more flexibility. The youths are also expected to be new ambassadors of destination, especially for millennial travelers. Through these educational programs, they not only add value to their culture and heritage, but they also improve their skills in a wide array of fields.

The CTN gathers an infinity of examples that can illustrate this phenomenon. The reason is that it precisely wants to guarantee the best practices for creative tourism by promoting activities that are authentic, and what a better way to do it than involving the base, that is to say the locals. All the members of the network offer a service of assessment and accompaniment to the local communities in order to empower them with these new professional activities, which also contributes to train them to perform new skills in terms of foreign language, ITCs, customer attention, management, etc.

Rethinking the role of the tourist organizations

Although IT platforms, boosted by the sharing economy, are trying to substitute intermediaries like tour operators or travel agencies, they just contribute to make them more essential as they have to find a balanced partnership between the local communities and the tourism companies in order to "package" and market the activity, while maintaining its authenticity and settle a sustainable system for the local communities. *"The creative tourism is a form of networked tourism, which depends on the ability of producers and consumers to relate each other and to generate value from their encounters"* (Richards & Marques, 2012).

Creative tourism thus represents new opportunities for the entrepreneurs, who can diversify their offer and cater this very

specific demand, just by collaborating with new content producers. This represents a great benefit for those who are tempted by
this new market as, on the one side, they have the possibility to
distinguish themselves with tailored activities, and on the other
side, they don't have to invest as they can commission the production of these tailored experiences to the local artists, artisans,
or cultural entities.

Among the other important assets that characterize creative
tourism, we can also mention its unseasonal demand, which
constitutes an incentive for many destinations that are traditionally polarized in one or two seasons in a year. It is, for
instance, the case of Ibiza Island, whose high season really
depends on the opening and closing period of the night clubs –
from May to September. For the rest of the year, proposals like
the creative tourism contribute to offer new purposes for the
tourists to go Ibiza for cooking course for singles, DJ workshop
for teenagers, painting retreat for seniors, among many other
activities.

By creating a new story to involve the tourists, DMOs and
DMCs demonstrate their ability to generate new business opportunities. Although a destination does not offer many different
versions by itself, creative tourism opens an infinity of possibilities to which the tour operators will have the responsibility to
make sense and make it attractive.

Obviously, this leads to new models of tourism management,
in which the companies no longer have to compete in terms of
standing and rates but have to reach the most demanding customers by proposing innovative and creative stays. The success key
of this new management will rely on their ability and flexibility
to partner with very different sectors. This is the reason why, in
order to be credible, profitable and above all sustainable for the
whole territory, the creative tourism management at the destination level, must go beyond the mere tourism sector and produce
value-added offers from cooperation between very different
actors in the territory, as well as from the collective intelligence
and entrepreneurship.

A holistic approach: The example of Saint-Jean-Port-Joli (Québec)

The creative tourists are very sensitive to the atmosphere, sense
of place, and its authenticity, and this holistic approach of destination management is essential to guarantee this loyalty with
these new visitors. Such an atmosphere cannot be produced
by mere digital transactions. In some cases, especially for

destinations that have to renew their clientele and "refresh" their image without investing in tangible, creative tourism appears as an opportunity.

This is the case of Saint-Jean-Port-Joli, a charming village situated in Quebec, along the Saint Laurent River. Its rich artistic heritage and the presence of many artists have been attracting domestic tourism for generations, in search of peaceful holidays. It's precisely to re-generate it by seducing a not-so-contemplative kind of visitors, that the Tourist Board, advised by Professor Habib Saïdi, Director of the Institute of Cultural Heritage (IPAC) of the University of Laval, launched the program "Saint-Jean-Port-Joli, Creative Village." All the ingredients to use creative tourism as a successful branding opportunity are present in this project.

1. The potential to attract creative tourists, thanks to its artistic vocation and the presence of artists and craftsmen who are still in activity, its harmonious and inspiring environment, its human size, the organization of cultural events and festivals.
2. The preliminary study and pilot project led by the IPAC with the participation of students of the University of Laval, in order to test, as millennials themselves, the activities that could appeal youth travelers.
3. The commitment of the tourism board.
4. The assignment of a coordinator with an artistic background exclusively devoted to the creative tourism program, who links the different sectors and create a story with the citizen.
5. A digital and informal campaign aimed to refresh the image of the village and to attract the youths.
6. The organization of as pilot creative stay for youth travelers, who deeply "shared" their experience on the social media.

This exemple shows how the creation of a new segment can, at the same time, impulse a virtuous circle acting positively on the heritage preservation, revitalization of the local economy, job creations, and branding. As a corollary effect, the fact of gathering inhabitants, artists and artisans in the same group of "creatives," contribute indoubtly to foster the social cohesion among the local communities and to enrich the friendly atmosphere of the destination. This is the objective of CTN, created in 2010 to highlight all these destinations that are engaged with this new form of tourism and are awarded as "Creative Friendly" for their respect for Best Practices.

NEW CHALLENGES

The essential awareness of changes

If the assets are numerous, there are also many challenges the professionals have to assume in order to cater the creative tourism demand. The first one is to be aware of the very fast paradigm shift that leads us to consider new tourists like travelers more interested in customized offerings than in mainstream ones and, for this reason, the model of management has to be adapted, from a former one, based on achieving short-term high economic profits, to a new one, integrating the concepts of training, inclusiveness, and sustainability. However, changes are slow and the reticence is sometimes fed by a generational conflict within the organizations, concerning a model that would not look as profitable as the traditional one, in terms of short-term benefits. Most of the big companies still consider niche tourism as a residual one, whose management is relegated to non-profit entities.

The same happens with a lot of traditional destinations that are still thought to be more efficient in terms of visibility, to concentrate their promotion in a unique icon instead of creating different segments. In both cases, the increasing demand for creative tourism will certainly be the only way to accelerate the change of mentality.

A mediator to guarantee the experience's eco-system

The second challenge for the tourist entrepreneurs and tourist boards is the willingness to attract these new travelers and to be aware that their expectations in terms of artistic knowledge and innovative offerings/experience require specific expertise. This means that they have to henceforth collaborate with professionals from many sectors. An error would be to consider it as a dilettante activity in margin of the tourism offer which would certainly maintain it in a permanent precariousness. Another one, would be to "package" the activity or experience without any sensibility.

This represents a barrier that is difficult to overcome in this field. Firstly, because the tourist entrepreneurs and the artists' ways of thinking are diametrically opposed to each other. They are always mutually distrusting. The tourist entrepreneurs consider that the industrial model cannot afford the artists' concept of work. According to tourist entrepreneurs the tourist industry model doesn't fit to the artists' working conception; similarly, according to the artists to collaborate with the (mass) tourism would be prejudicial for their creations. Mentalities are evolving, but it takes a while, that's why it looks more judicious to incorporate a new figure to act as an intermediary between both sectors. This "mediator," who is familiar to both sectors – the artistic and the tourist one – has to understand the tourist's demands and has to work hand-in-hand with the local community and the tour operators, to find a balance in designing an authentic, but marketable tourist experience.

Another challenge is to avoid multiplication, in the same area, of similar "creative experiences." This usually happens when a traditional activity, characteristic of a region, and is being declined and recycled as a tourist attraction. For instance, if in a same area different former ceramic factories propose similar basic workshops for the "visitors" (i.e., to say, for people who finds it by casuality) are invited to turn their own piece in a five minutes' time. The result is a standard offer, with a very low interactivity and consciousness of the place, that is abusively sold as an "experience." In this case, the moderator has to intervene by introducing meaning and creativity. The moderator thus assumes ethical responsibilities, as through the works he commissions to the locals; he has to ensure that the richness generated by the tourism sector returns improving the society.

As for example we could take the case of the *Barcelona Creative Tourism* platform, created by a non-profit cultural foundation with the aim to offer the tourists, customized and off-the-beaten path activities in the city. If part of the activities proposed in the platform, is directly organized by local entities (arts academies, dance and music school, cooking lessons, etc.), the foundation acts as a go-between, to design on-demand experiences commissioned by the tour operators eager to attract new profile of customers. Let us imagine a tour operator based in Madrid, who organizes a creative stay around Spain for U.S. tourists. He needs to contact artists currently working in Barcelona who would accept to hold workshops for tourists, which supposes the following:

1. To localize the artists, who normally used to work in discrete art studios unknown from the population.
2. To select them for their talent, relevance, but of course their ability to communicate and the capacity and access of their work space.
3. To convince them to take part in an activity that is far from their work conception.

4. To pact a fee that the artist will consider fair but not alienating.
5. To repeat the process for, as many artists as required, taking into account the distance between each place.
6. To be reactive in case one of them would cancel at the last minute.

So tour operators cannot realize different tasks or would not like to assume because they require very specific knowledge of the territory and wouldn't be profitable anyway.

Composing with the sharing economy

Another challenge which the tourism industry has to compete with is the sharing or collaborative economy imposed by the experience economy context and boosted by the development of new technologies. These new platforms and applications are very attractive to the new travelers, who value easy access to relevant information and apparent transparency, as well as interactivity with peers. Furthermore, they offer an integral experience that the established/mainstream industry still has difficulties to perceive and achieve. Indeed, what was considered as a customer experience within the traditional marketing model, was essentially focused on delivering services and offering assistance. It has now been considered as an integral unique experience that involves the tourist, from the phase of seduction to his viral recommendation of the experience or destination, passing through the realization of a meaningful activity that is full of "moments" and emotions.

Moreover, most of the new travelers are millennials and nomads or remote workers, which means that the new experience has to be as inclusive as well as in the sense of merging business and leisure.

This is just an example of how the creative tourism management has to set itself as a holistic one, involving different and complementary sectors, agents, as well as the tourists themselves, at all the levels of the experience.

In this way, the sharing economy grew rapidly until converting itself into a competitor of the tourist industry. Taking advantage of the democratization of the new technologies, the transfer of values related to the economic crisis, and being audacious enough to skirt the laws and bureaucracy, they also seized the opportunity of the emergence of the millennials, who feel completely identified to these new forms of living a travel experience before, during and after. They offer a permanent conversation with the communities. The tourist loves the stories with a human background, at the point that the "human experience" has turned into the core of all sorts of campaigns. We can mention Airbnb, with its campaign Mankind, that invites the traveler to explore the planet through a child's eyes, or BlaBlaCar, that pretends to humanize its communications with the initiative Members' stories, as well as a very long etcetera.

Once highlighted the general challenges the tourism industry has to overcome, the main difficulty for the practitioners and DMOs is to know how to reach this new target by offering attractive creative tourism experiences.

Creative Tourism Experience: An Analysis and Best Practices

The first step consists of (re-)delimiting a concept that has been evolving considerably since it appeared, given its adaptability to the local cultures and contexts. In some cases, the creative buzz supplanted the tourists' experience until reducing it as a trendy activity held in a "cool" atmosphere but with no participative or interactive features. According to Professor Greg Richards, although different places have their own definitions of creative tourism, there are commonalities among them, such as "active participation," "authentic experiences," "creative potential development," and "skills development" (Richards, 2011). We will rely on this definition by Professor Greg Richards to discuss point by point the criteria on which a creative tourist bases his valuation of a "creative experience."

PARTICIPATION

An active participation is essential for the tourist himself, as well as for creative tourism in general. From a tourist's point of view, participation is the key: an experience has to be lived.

That is why it is not a surprise if the creative tourism community has endorsed Confucius's words that perfectly illustrate the reason for creative tourism: *"Tell Me and I Will Forget; Show Me and I May Remember; Involve Me and I Will Understand."*

Although this may be the oldest reference to the creative tourism concept, there is a current revival through trends like "makers," "prosumers," who are looking for time in their daily life, to exert their creativity through after-work activities and DIY, holidays. They perceive creative tourism as a unique opportunity to develop new skills or new thoughts through meaningful vacations. It is believed that the participatory element remains the core of this tourism, as mentioned in the original definition. The growth of creative tourism has been identified as an extension of or a reaction to cultural tourism, in that creative consumers are looking for more interactive experiences which help them in their personal development and identity creation, rather than traditional cultural tourists (Richards, 2000; Richards & Raymond, 2000).

From the creative tourism sector in general, the participation means that, in addition to directly benefit from the activity itself, the creative tourists generate a system of "co-creation," in which companies work with the travelers to develop new experiences that link consumers and producers around a common interest, rather than traditional trade relationships. Whereas since decades, the tourist has been relegated to the role of a mere spectator and consumer who contributed to impoverish the tourism industries and destinations, that just copy/pasted ones with each other's.

Creative tourism depends heavily on tourist's active involvement, who are not just in a place and watching others, but instead interacting and co-creating the whole experience, actively learning about their surroundings, and applying this knowledge in order to develop their own skills (Richards & Wilson, 2006).

The process is more important than the result, as it reflects the transformation operated by the tourist, and it contributes, at a local level, to foster the cooperation between actors in the territories, which helps to revitalize local economic development. Furthermore, the tourists are more trustful if they are directly involved at all the levels of experience, including its design, production, and promotion. They are becoming autonomous "makers" of their own experiences, converting them into active stakeholders, as without their active participation, the creative experiences would not exist.

However, although participation is the core of the experience, creativity is the differentiator for this new generation of tourism.

CREATIVITY

The rise and democratization of the design among daily life products and spaces in the early 2000, tended to assimilate creativity with "arty," "trendy," "fashion." It is an amalgam against which the CTN has to fight all the time. Indeed, many destinations are to be concerned by the fact that most of their offer is based on traditions and intangible heritage, which is not what they consider "creative" in the sense on "new" or innovative as, for instance, the creative industries could be.

The question that most of the destinations that join the network ask us, is precisely, *"what do you mean by creativity?"* Of course, this issue could justify a single article but we will keep it focused on our current intent to draw the "recipe" for companies and DMOs willing to attract creative tourists. The question is hence, "how is the creativity expected by the creative tourists?"

Beyond the infinity of cases what we find in CTN, we share the following definition that considers creativity as *"the ability to create, to innovate, to generate new ideas or concepts, or new associations between existing elements, ideas and concepts."* This means that creativity in creative tourism refers to the concept of work-in-process and can be viewed as *informal learning systems that give the tourists the opportunity to develop their creativity in different contexts. These experiences are mostly related to everyday life, and the 'creativity-base' of creative tourism includes traditional crafts handicrafts-making, gastronomy, perfume-making, porcelain painting and dancing* (Richards & Wilson, 2006).

The creativity is thus shared by tourists as well as by suppliers, who invite them to experience the local traditions in a creative way. This is how all the destinations that have launched a creative tourism program give a second life to their intangible heritage. Although this heritage is usually dispraised by the locals themselves, the DMOs and local operators demonstrate their creativity to convert old-fashioned activities into attractive and unforgettable experiences.

We could give the example of the Tourist Board of the Brazilian City of Porto Alegre that wants to introduce the tourists to the Gaucha culture through a selection of workshops including dance, music, cooking, crafts, sewing, etc. The tourists participate in the tasting of each discipline and live an immersion into the local culture. This new form − that substitutes the typical craft demonstrations or folk performances − make the tourists feel themselves as protagonists of the local culture and the heir of the traditions. It's interesting to observe how they brilliantly recycle existing tourist resources like folklore, crafts and gastronomy – in order to create new experiences, able to seduce a wide array of tourist sub-segments, within this new generation of travelers (singles, seniors, premium, hipsters, eco-trendy, etc.).

Once again, the village of Saint-Jean-Port-Joli, in Quebec offers the perfect example of destination branding through creative tourism. As already mentioned, its visitors' profile were traditionally the local and multi-generational tourists, who spent their summertime in this relaxing place. Many artists live there but have no relationships with the tourists unless there is scarcity of sales. This is when the tourist board introduced creativity. First of all, in the name, the board added "Village Créatif" (Creative Village) to the name Saint-Jean-Port-Joli. They also contracted a cultural manager to act as a coordinator of artists, and artisans were equally considered as "the creatives." This attempt has been very successful and its positive effects are visible on the social cohesion of the village and, as a consequence, on the friendly atmosphere. The contents have also been refreshed as all the "creatives" shaped their abilities as interactive activities especially focused on the millennials target. They achieved their goal by proposing creative workshops on traditional activities like wood sculpture, wool weaving, luthery, etc. These activities, scheduled along a week, generated positive feedback that has been extensively reflected through the social media, thanks to their inclination to be technologically proactive. They converted themselves into prescriptors who are able to convince their fellows as well as help the destination to renew on its whole.

Another case is the one of the village of Biot, in the French Provence, that has a rich artistic tradition – the most outstanding artists lived there, Picasso, Matisse, Fernand Léger, among others – and still attracts creators from all over the world who are settling there. In order to turn this contemplative village into an active artistic hub, the Tourist Board involved the local artists and artisans in the creation of a platform that aimed to promote participative activities for tourists. *Biot Creative Tourism* thus offers a wide array of creative workshops adapted to different targets. One of the most successful is the team building organized for companies that "send" their employees to participate in a creative week at Biot where, through a program of glass blowing lesson, jewellery workshop, or photographic route, they develop their human, personal, and creative abilities. This contributes to associate the village of Biot to a new powerful brand, to diversify the artists' sources of income and to attract off-season tourists, just by introducing creativity in the traditional one.

Creativity is also to know how to tell new stories and to involve locals and tourists as the main characters. Storytelling converts traditional proposals into trendy ones.

In order to acquire better knowledge about the concept of "creativity" perceived by the creative tourists, we conducted a survey involving a sample of hundred 18–35-year-old participants of a craft workshop in Barcelona, between September and December 2015. The first question served to confirm that they had at least one creative tourism experience. The second one was to give a ranking to what is the meaning of creativity in a creative tourism experience. The ranking gave the following results: "creativity as a process" on the top (54%), followed by "inspiring atmosphere" (24%), "novelty" in third position (16%), and in the last position "trendy" (6%). No doubt that the idea the creative tourists have of "creativity" is at the opposite of the concept ordinary consumers would have. This copes with the idea that creativity for these tourists is not in a final product but a process that stimulates the desire to experiment and produce new meanings. It's favored by an inspiring environment, more than by a trendy one (that is supposed to be more formatted), and feels conceptually closer to novelty than to this latter.

Authenticity is, therefore, an important component of the creative tourism experience, to be taken into account by the practitioners and DMOs.

AUTHENTICITY

Another criterion that weighs in the creative tourists' appreciation toward the experience they have is its authenticity. But what is authenticity? According to Maisel (2009) many tourists desire to have experiences that are small, intimate, and on a human scale. Professor of Marketing, Barbara E. Kahn positions authenticity at the fourth level of the following evolutional approach:

1. Product orientation: Companies just manufacture goods and offer them.
2. Market orientation: consideration on customer needs and segmentation.

3. Customer experience: Adding to the other two factors some recognition of the importance of providing an emotionally positive experience to customers.
4. Authenticity: Products and service emerge from real soul of brand.

For Richards (2011) it lies in everyday life. In other words, tourists wish to participate in acts of everyday creativity which are closer to their real lives. But are their real lives what the tourists consider as "authentic?" In 2006, the United Nations Educational, Scientific and Cultural Organization's Creative Cities Network defined creative tourism as "travel directed toward an engaged and authentic experience, with participative learning in the arts, heritage, or special character of a place, and it provides a connection with those who reside in this place and create this living culture" (UNESCO, 2006). In order to develop creative tourism, industry practitioners must identify the activities which are closely linked to their region (Richards, 2005).

In Taiwan, the term "Creative Life Industry (CLI)" is used to describe the idea of creative tourism and is seen as part of the cultural and creative industries (Lin & Wu, 2010). Different from other cultural/creative industries, CLI focuses on everyday activities and aims to attract tourists rather than seeing creativity in purely artistic terms.

So, what makes an experience more authentic? What do the tourists previously know about the authenticity of cultural and creative experience that will be proposed? First of all, they will be more trustful if the channel through which he/she has been informed of the experience is – or at least looks – authentic. That's why, experiential marketing is betting on peer-to-peer communication. The tourists no longer trust the vertical promotional message, coming from the firms. They are in change, very demanding of their fellow travelers' reviews and advices. In 2014, a study led by the European Union showed that 64% of the Spanish travelers chose a destination by following their friends'/family's recommendations.

In addition to the channels, the content itself has to be authentic. If we take the example of food – which is probably the most universal need/activity – we observe that authentic local cuisine is considered as very important, including the youths. According to a *Topdeck*'s 2015 Global Youth Travel Survey, a popular provider of group travel for tourists aged 18–30, of the group surveyed (31,000 people from 134 different countries), experiencing a new culture (86%) and eating local foods (69%) were listed as common determining factors for motivating people aged 18–24 to travel – ahead of partying (44%) and shopping (28%). More specifically, 98% of younger generations ranked "eating local cuisine" as something that was very important (more than 5 out of 10) when they traveled.

If we focus for instance on the cooking classes for tourists that are emerging in the main urban destinations, we observe that, although they are sold as "experiences" to the tourists, and recognized as such by most of them, they are built on the same model and thereby their authenticity can be questioned. We examined a couple of such cooking schools in cities like Barcelona, Roma and Paris. They propose the same contents, are held in similar impersonal kitchens and propose what is considered as the local culinary speciality in the tourists' imaginary, but not necessarily in the locals' daily plates.

The same tourist products, the same stories are repeated everyday in each place that leads inevitably to a certain lack of authenticity. But this is compensated by the opportunity for them to realize a "routine" in a quite "exotic" context, which makes them feel as locals.

Does that mean that it is a tourist fake? Of course it is not part of the autochtons' habits. First of all, for what it concerns the schedule. Very few locals in Barcelona, Roma, or Paris would spend half a day to learn how to cook a supposedly typical meal, and then, in case they would, they'd probably disagree on what they consider as "typical", between a recipe that has been officially established as a culinary icon of the country or the food eaten by the locals in their daily life. Furthermore, locals used to have a dispraise for these "institutionalized specialties" as they associate them to mass tourism and the emergence of "tourist menu."

Hence, can we consider such cooking classes as true creative tourism experiences? The answer is yes, in the sense they foster the tourists' active participation and their inmesion in local culture, and they are associated to the creativity through the novelty.

But above all, the experience exists from the moment the tourists have a fully consciousness of it, and this is precisely what this kind of activities offer them: the possibility to keep linked to their reality as tourists – by sharing it with groups of peers – and an incursion in the local's life.

So, independently the experiences can be more or less authentic; another important criterion to take into account when designing a creative tourism experience is the awareness of the experience by the tourist.

AWARENESS OF THE EXPERIENCE

Awareness is, by nature, a completely intimate feeling, which is very difficult to perceive and integrate from outside. Nevertheless, it is possible to rely on factors that provoke it. Indeed, the experience, which doesn't generate "material" items, has other functions, such as a "change" or "transformation" of the inner-self. The awareness of these changes is the key for the experience success. *By the way, a once-and-done experience make people happier than the acquisition of a physical object. This is because a material thing, as being permanent, makes it easier to adapt to, and one of the enemies of happiness is pre-cisely the adaptation. Furthermore, our experiences are a bigger part of ourselves than our material goods anyway, we are the sum total of our experiences"* (Gilovich, Kumar, & Jampol, 2015).

Indeed, experiences are also paradoxically as intimate as they are a potential connector between individuals. *"Outer interactions" and "inner reflections" construct the model of tourists' creative experience. "Consciousness/awareness" is a prerequisite for "creative experience," differentiating it from other types of experiences* (Tan, Kung, & Luh, 2015).

This awareness has to be reflected in the time dimension – pre-experience, in-experience, and post-experience – as well as in the spatial one (the sense of place). Both dimensions contribute to create memory that will convert into nostalgic, for the past and anticipatory, and for future experiences. The creative tourism managers take care of the details that will propitiate this nostalgic state, not only during the experience but also before and after. The experiential marketing is the most powerful way to spread these authentic contents through viral support.

Regarding pre-disposition, a good example is the one of Creative Tourism Namur (Belgium). As proposed by the Tourist Board of Namur, every creative experience is personified by its tutor. This predisposes the creative tourist who feels like a special guest by "personally knowing" an autochthon, prior to his stay.

This awareness is easy to canalize during and after the experience as the social media play an important role to crystal-lize the moment. Even a personal sensation is thus shared and cultivated by the community, until being exploited by the suppliers themselves. Social media like Instagram for instance, offer many possibilities to form virtual communities that will foster and spread the experience memory. The examples of campaigns that use this nostalgic element are infinite. All the communication campaigns do it in such a way.

HOLISTIC APPROACH

After all, this leads to have a holistic approach for the creative tourism experience design, which represents a big shift for the traditional tourist industry. All the tourists' practitioners agree that they have to achieve the following steps: "to attract/to convert (into sales)/to win the loyalty of customers. Most of them pretend to do it through the use of big data, which bring them essential information regarding each tourist's behavior, needs, and expectations, but if it represents, nowadays, an interesting source of information, they have to be managed carefully in the case of creative tourism in order to be integrated to a "story."

But the creative tourists are precisely, "creative," which means that they are versatile and do not conform with a single model. They need to permanently experiment new things, which makes relegates the use of Big Data to a second level. This implies a tailored attention required to produce a customized experience.

The holistic approach means as well the integration of storytelling as a part of the experience and not just a communication tool. This will make it understandable, believable, and attractive. The tourist has to feel himself as a protagonist of the story. In this case, any information provided by "big data" could help to avoid the possible interferences — in terms of cultural references and consumption habits — that would break the "charm" of the experience.

This injection of meaning makes the difference between a creative tourism experience and a mere participative — and yet artistic-activity. That's why the activities proposed in all-inclusive resorts, for instance, can be assimilated to entertainment but does not represent creative tourism experiences, in the sense they don't provide a human and holistic experience able to transform the individual.

In addition to all the factors that we have just mentioned, what weighs in a traveler's satisfaction is the creative activity realized by the tourist during his stay, and this forms the core of the tourists' experience valuation. One of the most efficient tools to measure it at this moment, is the digital platforms through which the travelers share their reviews, with specific details that can be documented in a wide array of consumers' profiles.

Guidelines: Some Practical Recommendations

As the very subjective and evolutive character of the creative tourism sector makes difficult the elaboration of exhaustive guidelines, we will essentially focus on the main principles to be followed by the practitioners eager to design this kind of ephemeral tourist experiences. These principles or guidelines are based on our daily experience as coordinators of the CTN, and of course, on the *Best Practices* of this emergent tourist trend, that are part of our missions.

(1) First of all, to **involve** the tourists in the process of construction of the "creative experience." Indeed, by knowing how the creative process has been constructed, tourists can maximize their creative experience. In the same philosophy as with the circular economy, the creative tourist has to feel himself as an important piece of cooperation between actors in the territories who can contribute to revitalize the local economic development. *Creative tourism depends heavily on tourist's active involvement, who are not just in a place and watching others, but instead interacting and co-creating the whole experience, actively learning about their surroundings and applying this knowledge in order to develop their own skills* (Richards & Wilson, 2006). This means that creative tourists are a group of active stakeholders, as without their active participation, the creative experiences would not exist.

(2) But at the same time, this involvement is really depended on the capacity of the experience **to immerse the tourist**. It should, for that, to have an – at least apparent – "accidental harmony," that reassures the tourist and immerses him into the experience. This is a very delicate step because, if a certain amount of "naturality" can facilitate their immersion – by demonstrating them that it is not the perfection but the reality – the minimum failure can jeopardize the whole experience. This failure can both be related to imperfection but also to the overly perfection, which could be considered as fake.

These advices are related, for instance, to the authenticity of the venue where the activity is held. In the case of workshops with artists, the success is mostly guaranteed if the tourists have the surprise effect to penetrate into the artist's personal and creative "universe." That's why the art studio has to be minimally adapted to the safety standards but has to keep its fortuity and bohemian atmosphere. The creative tourists are searching for activities with "controlled risk" – above all if they are holidaying with their family – but in a home environment that makes them feel privileged to share the artists' intimacy.

The challenge for artists and operators is precisely to find the balance in order to "package" them as a marketable tourist offer, while maintaining their authenticity and settling a sustainable system for the local communities in general. The training and accompaniment of these new suppliers to "shape" the activities and adapt them to different targets – within the creative tourism sector – is essential.

(3) Launching a creative tourism project requires to be very professional and rigorous in the **selection** of the artists or locals who will intervene in the learning process as an "outer interaction." This is an error that many operators make when they "design an experience" and they try to achieve profitability by contracting low-paid tutors or instructors, who lack specific knowledge. It is thus the responsibility of the (Creative) tourism sector to involve, train, and professionalize the local communities. This role should be assumed by a "mediator" who is familiar with both sectors (the artistic and the tourist one).

(4) The **role of moderator** is completely new for the private companies and DMOs, that have been essentially focused on the promotion of existing offers. Henceforth, they all have to deal with a new kind of partners – the creatives – whose philosophy can be at the opposite end of the tourism trade priorities. In this sense, there is a lack of human resources in the tourist sector; it's important for the entrepreneurs and DMOs to contract professionals from the cultural management, for instance, to bridge the gap between the tourist industry and the creative suppliers.

(5) For what concerns the experience itself, in addition to the authenticity, the practitioners have to guarantee a **high-level of expertize in each specific realm.** *Creative tourists have*

intellectual *needs and limited time, so that they want to make the most of their stay to 'gain knowledge' and 'self-improvement' through participating in creative experiences* (Siow-Kian Tan/Shiann-Far Kung/Ding-Bang Luh). The tutors/instructors must be "knowledge-rich" and must show their "professionalism" when they are teaching. Artists are thus expected to share their knowledge in a professional frame but without losing their identity and spontaneity. They also have to adapt themselves to the rules and features of the tourist activity, in terms of duration, time optimization, language, and didactic skills.

(6) **Beneficial to the community**: Another important factor to be taken into account in a mid-term vision is the fact that the **creative tourism sector must generate wealth that must be returned improving the society**. This especially refers to the communities' empowerment, through trainings, as well as economical vitalization and job creation. This means that each actor – whether private or public – has to develop responsible and sustainable actions, as well as invest in project monitoring, professional assessments, etc. This makes particularly relevant the role of mediators. On the contrary, digital platforms created through sharing economy neither offer the same guarantee nor does it provide any value-added offer, as they just propose a conglomeration of participative and generally peer-to-peer offers that might lack professional background and territorial development interest.

(7) Involvement: The tourists' involvement is the key elements at the marketing level as well. It is now recognized that consumers are using virtual communities and other online social sharing formats to share ideas and contact fellow consumers who are seen as more objective information sources, and the tourist industry is certainly one of the most representative. It is thus important to stop differentiating the tourist and the local. They are the same one and everybody is someone's tourist. It is then important to consider the experiential and viral marketing as the main one to reach the creative tourists in spite of their specificity. The institutional promotion no longer reaches the millennials nor the new travelers, who are much more sensible to storytelling, as far as it is really integrated to the experience. In other words, through storytelling, marketing is part of the experience. Peer-to-peer communication and influencer marketing are certainly the

fastest growing aspect of digital public relations. In addition to their short-term efficiency to attract tourists, they also contribute to permanently enhance *talkability* of a destination or tourist experience, especially the ones that are not among the world hotspots. One of the most successful cases in the previous months, was the one of the hotel Adare Manor (Ireland), that converts a supposed incident into a viral worldwide marketing campaign. The establishment created a buzz campaign around a "supposed" incident. The toy bunny rabbit that was left behind by its owner during a holiday at a five-star hotel and became internet hit after being pampered by staff, who documented its luxurious solo stay on social media. Of course, these channels represent as well relevant sources of information for providers to shape the most adapted offering to their potential customers. The travelers who participate in the "virtual communities" often share in-depth insight on themselves, their lifestyles, and any information very valuable for tourist marketers to cater this new demand.

(8) **The role of DMOs:** In the same way it is essential to involve the tourist in the design of their own experience, the Destination Management Organizations also have to go beyond the mere promotion of the existing tourist attraction, and to generate values through coordination of the local communities and stakeholders. This new role is key for the destinations to maintain their position within this new paradigm that is no longer based on competition, but on their differentiation through authenticity, local cohesion, and creativity. Therefore, DMOs not only have a leading role in promoting and marketing tourism destinations but, more importantly, steer destination development. It is believed that it is crucial for destinations to adopt a midterm vision and invest on human resources that are able to foster partnerships that beneficiate the local economy, create educational opportunities, and highlights the intangible heritage. As the towns of Loulé (Portugal) and Saint Jean Port Joli (Québec) did, the creative tourism can be used as a cohesion tool to generate synergies from small initiatives and entrepreneurs from other sectors.

Finally – although it has not been explicitly expressed in this chapter – the tourists have to be the most responsible, to discuss their experiences and to support the local businesses.

Conclusion

As already mentioned, this chapter cannot unfortunately claim to be an exhaustive handbook for practitioners and DMOs to develop and market creative tourism experiences. The reason is that this niche tourism activity is currently amidst of a paradigm shift of the economy in general — essentially due to the "uberization" of the economy — and more specifically of the tourism industry. This chapter attempted to define the main lines of these changes, at this stage, in order to offer the stakeholders some guidelines that will help them to advance in the good direction and above all to respect, at each step, the best practices of the creative tourism.

Changes are slow, but they offer this way a great opportunity to change the priorities and the ways to reach them. In this sense, we are living the perfect moment to satisfy the new values proposed by the new generations and to put them in practice in a new and responsible tourist offering.

References

Gilmore, J. H., & Pine, J. (1998). *The experience economy*. Brighton, MA: Harvard Business Press.

Gilovich, T., Kumar, A., & Jampol, L. (2015). Research dialogue a wonderful life: Experiential consumption and the pursuit of happiness. *Journal of Consumer Psychology, 25*, 152–165.

Kahn, B. E. (1998). Dynamic relationships with customers: High-variety strategies. *Journal of the Academy of Marketing Science, 26*, 54–61.

Richards, G. (2013, May). Interview by Belinda Saile. El Pais.

Richards, G. (2015). *Creativity and tourism: The state of the art*. Creative Tourism Trend Report, 1.

Richards, G., & Marques, L. (2012). Exploring creative tourism: Editors introduction. *Journal of Tourism Consumption and Practice, 4*(2), 1–11.

Richards, G., & Raymond, C. (2000). Creative tourism. *ATLAS News*, no. 23, pp. 16–20.

Richards, G., & Wilson, J. (2006). Developing creativity in tourist experiences: A solution to the serial reproduction of culture? *Tourism Management, 27*(6), 1209–1223.

Tan, S.-K., Kung, S.-F., & Luh, D.-B. (2015). A model of "creative experience" in creative tourism. *Annals of Tourism Research, 41*, 153–174.

13 Greening as Part of Ecotourism to Contribute to Tourists' Experiences: A Destination Planning Approach

Elricke Botha and Willy Hannes Engelbrecht

ABSTRACT

Purpose – The growth in the ecotourism industry has increased emphasis on sustainable practices. Despite the fact that ample research has been conducted on sustainable ecotourism practices, many ecotourism destinations fail to become sustainable. The growth of the ecotourism industry and the global population has called for greener practices to be incorporated in developing ecotourism destinations. Waterwheel, located in the Limpopo province of South Africa, is faced with this green development challenge and serves as a case study (located at the end of the chapter) for this chapter.

Methodology/approach – This chapter gives a brief overview of the green principles associated with developing ecotourism destinations. Green ecotourism destination planning is explained within the context of the tourists' experience to

highlight aspects necessary for sustainable ecotourism destination development.

Findings — Even though the green market is still in its
infancy, tourists are increasingly demanding green accommodation. A green, sustainable ecotourism destination can only
be developed if green principles are incorporated from the
input phase. The input phase (e.g., building materials and
infrastructure systems for water and energy) determines the
output phase (e.g., operational materials, activities, suppliers,
activities, and marketing) and, subsequently, the level of sustainability. It is therefore crucial to plan for these aspects
and the level to which the destination aims to adhere to these
aspects, as they are costly.

Originality/value — Even though research on the green economy is not a new phenomenon it has only recently trickled
down to ecotourism development. This explains the lack of
research currently experienced in the literature of ecotourism
and a gap that should be addressed urgently. Although this
chapter only briefly discusses green ecotourism development,
the aspects highlighted in the chapter provides other
researchers with research opportunities to pursue in an effort
to bridge the gap.

Keywords: Greening; ecolabeling; ecotourism;
sustainability; experience; Waterwheel

Introduction

Ecotourism is considered one of the fastest growing sectors in
tourism with annual growth estimated at 10−15% worldwide
(Ayob, Saman, Hussin, & Jusoff, 2009; Nwahia, Omonona,
Onyeabor, & Balogun, 2012; Shrivastava, 2014). Ecotourism
contributes an estimated 9% to the Gross Domestic Product
(UNWTO, 2015), however, this growth may put sustainability,
which ecotourism aspires to, in jeopardy.

Various definitions of ecotourism exist (Geldenhuys, 2009),
because there is little agreement as to what precisely ecotourism
entails (Mason, 2008). Ceballos (1987), the first author to define
ecotourism, defines it as traveling to relatively undisturbed or
uncontaminated natural areas for studying, admiring or enjoying
the scenery, wild plants, animals, and any existing cultural

manifestations. Regardless of the definition of ecotourism being used, Geldenhuys (2009) and Walker and Walker (2011) explain that an analysis of all the existing definitions indicate that ecotourism is nature-based, environmentally educating, and sustainably managed.

Sustainability gained predominance over the years (Frey & Gervers, 2016), resulting in the green economy (Bina, 2013). The term *green* has been exploited by various organizations, but in the tourism industry it refers to the intention of tourism destinations to be more efficient and effective in their management practices. It highlights the importance of ecotourism destinations implementing stronger environmental protection and conservation practices to minimize negative environmental impact (UNEP, 2013). With the positive change in tourist behavior and attitude toward environmentally friendly products and services (UNEP, 2013), ecotourism destinations have to ensure that they answer tourist demands.

This chapter will explain the importance of greening and planning for greening in a South African ecotourism destination.

Planning Green Ecotourism Destinations

Ecotourism destinations must become greener or more environmentally friendly to ensure sustainability (Cooper, 2012). This is, however, only possible if all stakeholders get involved (Powell & Ham, 2008) and focus on the implementation of green principles and practices. Typical stakeholders include the government (local, provincial, and national), suppliers, the local community, educational institutions and, most importantly, the tourists.

The government is the most prominent stakeholder in addressing environmental sustainability. It has significant influence on regulatory frameworks and access to information needed to address environmental sustainability. Since sustainability is a global issue, governments have to liaise with industry experts in technology, environment and manufacturing to find innovative ways of assisting and guiding ecotourism destinations in becoming more conscious of their environmental impact (Chan & Ho, 2006; Walker & Walker, 2011). It is in governments' best interest to drive the process of becoming greener as this will motivate and get the private sector on board with being environmentally friendly. Governments can provide financial support in particular, which will assist ecotourism destinations in implementing environmentally friendly practices and supplying regular updates on changes. Since green practices are a costly investment that private organizations cannot always afford, the tourism industry depends on this kind of support from government (Chan & Ho, 2006).

Financial constraints lead to ecotourism destinations only implementing some green principles, like low-flow shower heads, twin toilet flush systems, and towel reuse programs. These practices do not, however, constitute an efficient green destination; it merely minimizes environmental impact. Further costly aspects that affect ecotourism destinations include employee training, certification, and maintenance of specialized environmental friendly equipment (Chan & Ho, 2006).

Although certification is expensive, the government could subsidize ecotourism destinations that are certified as effective and efficient ecotourism destinations that implement environmental best practices (Chan & Ho, 2006). Walker and Walker (2011) explain that eco certification is open to all ecotourism organizations where ecotourism experts audit the destination against ecotourism criteria to determine their sustainability, efficiency, and effectiveness. Certification has significant benefits for ecotourism destinations, including updates on environmentally friendly practices, marketing awareness and benchmarking against similar destinations (Walker & Walker, 2011). Considering tourists' increased demand for more environmentally friendly practices (KamalulAriffin, Khalid, & Wahid, 2013), certification would assist ecotourism destinations in addressing the majority of tourists' demands.

Tourism destinations rely on a variety of suppliers to produce products and services for tourists (George, 2014). These products and services are often manufactured for both tourism and non-tourism sectors (Cooper, Fletcher, Fyall, Gilbert, & Wanhill, 2008). Ecotourism destinations that are fully aware of their tourists' demands will be able to determine the additional suppliers needed to be fully functional and operational in terms of green principles (Cooper, 2012). It is important that ecotourism destinations source manufacturers that can supply products and services that are certified as environmentally friendly to support sustainability practices (Rishi, 2014). By using suppliers from the local community, the ecotourism destination will further illustrate its degree of participation in ecotourism principles (see ecotourism pillars later in this chapter). Local suppliers could provide organic vegetables, locally produced organic tea or even environmentally friendly cleaning products.

Local communities are an extremely important stakeholder in ecotourism destinations as providers of cultural artefacts or cultural education to tourists (see ecotourism pillars later in this chapter). As they should form part of the ecotourism destination's practices, they too should promote environmentally sustainable lifestyles. The ecotourism destination should, as far as possible, support local community upliftment programs and educate the community about the importance of being environmentally conscious and preserving natural resources (UNEP, 2013). Local communities have significant influence on the ecotourism destination if there are benefits involved for them and receiving their approval on the implementation of environmental practices would be an added bonus.

At a more indirect level, educational institutions are also considered stakeholders in the ecotourism sector. Educational institutions can assist ecotourism destinations in improving current or assisting with new development practices through various ecotourism research projects (Suki & Suki, 2015). These research projects can assist the ecotourism destination in addressing the tourists' needs.

In general, the tourism industry's success and sustainability depends on tourists. Tourists are, therefore, an important stakeholder to consider when planning green ecotourism destinations (Walker & Walker, 2011). Current trends indicate that tourists opt for destinations that are environmentally friendly (George, 2014), allow them to participate in creating the value they seek (Middleton, Fyall, Morgan, & Ranchhod, 2009) and that are greener. Ecotourism destinations must adapt to these demands and ensure a memorable experience. Keeping this in mind, consider Geldenhuys's (2009) ecotourism pillars and Pine and Gilmore's (1999) experience economy.

Geldenhuys (2009) explains that there are four ecotourism pillars: (i) conservation and promotion of the natural and cultural environment; (ii) sustainable management of the environment; (iii) participation of the local community, which contributes to the fourth pillar; and (iv) tourist satisfaction. These four pillars must be incorporated at every ecotourism destination to truly reflect ecotourism. The experience with these pillars must, however, be memorable to ensure satisfied tourists. It is against this background that Pine and Gilmore's (1999) experience economy will be considered.

Pine and Gilmore (1999) explain that there are four realms of a customer's (or tourist's) experience: (i) entertainment, (ii) education, (iii) escape; and (iv) esthetics. According to Pine and Gilmore (1999) experiences that are compelling are those that include all four of these realms. What ecotourism destinations have to consider is how they contribute toward all four of these realms in order to create a memorable experience.

Starting with the *escapist* experience, Vespestad and Mehmetoglu (2010) explain that tourists can actively participate in river rafting, kayaking or mountain climbing and therefore immerse themselves in activities associated with ecotourism. *Escape* can also be referred to as a motive. Ecotourists consider *escape* the most important motive to visit ecotourism destinations (Chan & Baum, 2007; Kruger, Saayman, & Hermann, 2014). They seek the tranquillity of nature to escape their demanding routines. Nature does, however, also contribute to the *esthetics experience*. Vespestad and Mehmetoglu (2010) refer to nature's aesthetic (i.e., *esthetics*) appeal that differentiates one experience from another and impacts the ecotourism destination's competitiveness.

Nature plays an additional role in ecotourism experiences. Ecotourism destinations are known for the *educational experiences* that they offer, where tourists can learn more about the natural and cultural environment (Kang & Gretzel, 2012; Walker & Walker, 2011). This educational role is usually fulfilled by means of interpretation. According to Ham and Weiler (2007) as well as Ballantyne, Packer, and Sutherland (2011) interpretation adds value and quality to the tourists' leisure experience. Ecotourism destinations therefore not only contribute toward the tourists' *education*, but can also contribute toward *entertainment* by means of delivering interpretation services. The various green aspects incorporated in the design of an ecotourism destination would provide ample opportunity for interpreting these aspects for both educational and entertainment purposes.

Ecotourism destinations have the ability to create and sustain tourist demand by implementing continuous informative marketing campaigns on the aforementioned aspects. They must, however, ensure that they continuously rejuvenate their ecotourism products and service offerings to ensure high levels of satisfaction and tourist loyalty (Akama Kieti, 2003; Engelbrecht, 2011).

Sustainable Management Tools and Approaches for an Ecolodge

With the growing concern for the depletion of natural resources in relation to the growth of the world's population (Marsiglio, 2015), more emphasis is being placed on sustainable development. For this reason, the impact of tourism destination development on natural resources is always a concern. In South Africa, one of the five strategic priority areas for action set out in the National Framework for Sustainable Development is sustaining ecosystems and using natural resources efficiently (DEA South Africa, 2016). Even though only a framework has been developed thus far, the intention is to prepare a detailed action plan and implementation phase (DEA South Africa, 2016). It is clearly an aspect that should be addressed at different levels in South African government.

Even though sustainability is at the core of ecotourism, ecotourism destinations fail to fully comply with this aspect. McLaren (2003) explains that sustainable tourism should include integrated planning that challenge the tourism industry at *every* level. These levels could include the different life cycle phases of developing a new destination. The next sections will address these life cycles.

GREEN DEVELOPMENT

The tourism and hospitality industry depends on high-energy consumers who demand luxury and comfort (Jauhari & Verma, 2014). A general rule associated with the impact of accommodation on the environment is that the more luxurious the accommodation, the more energy will be used and the larger the impact (UNEP & UNWTO, 2012). Accommodation establishments are built based on the demand for heating, cooling, lighting, cooking, and cleaning; these practices are not always in harmony with sustainability principles. Legrand, Sloan, Wagmann, and Rheindorf (2014) explain that the hospitality industry has made tremendous progress over the years in managing outputs (i.e., waste, energy consumption), but the differentiating factor today is the input stage (i.e., choice of materials construction methods). According to Jauhari and Verma (2014), the building sector accounts for 40% of the total energy required to build new buildings and has potentially significant energy and environmental impacts. It is against this background that the hospitality industry, especially those that strive for sustainability, such as ecolodges, should make crucial decisions at the input stage as it will affect the output stage (Legrand et al., 2014). A development's environmental impacts should be assessed with the life cycle assessment (LCA), explained by Sasidharan and Font (2001) as:

1. Life cycle inventory – identifying and quantifying energy consumption, raw materials, and waste discharge;
2. Environmental impact analysis – environmental impacts produced by inputs and outputs over the life of the destination;
3. Improvement analysis – use of information gathered in the previous steps to reduce the environmental impacts.

Various decisions must be made for green development at input level, but tourist needs must never be forgotten. Baker, Davis, and Weaver (2013) found that tourists' concern about the luxury of green hotels impacts their intention to stay at the hotel and perceptions about comfort and green initiatives as cost-cutting, affects their willingness to pay for the hotel accommodation. As early as input level, no compromise should be made on luxury or comfort; guests must be assured of quality.

In South Africa, the Tourism Grading Council of South Africa (TGCSA) is a "recognised and globally credible quality assurance body for tourism products in South Africa" (TGCSA, 2013). The TGCSA has a range of minimum requirements that different accommodation types (i.e., guesthouses, hotels, lodges, and bed and breakfasts) must adhere to. An associated star grading mounted on the establishment's wall indicates adherence to these requirements and serves as a sign of quality and good service. Currently, the TGCSA's minimum requirements do not make provision for greening aspects associated with each accommodation type. South Africa does, however, have other green certification initiatives such as Fair Trade in Tourism South Africa (2016), Green Leaf Environmental Standard (GLES, 2015) and Heritage Environmental Rating Programme (2016) which might be valuable options to consider for developing green buildings along with the TGCSA. Along with these possibilities, entrepreneurs can make use of online self-help tools to assist with informed decision-making in the input stages of development (more about this in the case study).

Green operations

Environmentally friendly and sustainable operations at ecotourism destinations are vital in minimizing the environmental impact of tourism on natural resources. Pratt, Rivera, and Bien (2012) indicate several challenges associated with green operations. These challenges include energy and greenhouse gas emissions, water consumption, waste management, loss of biological diversity, effective management of built and cultural heritage, and planning and governance. Each of these aspects will be briefly explored in the following.

Energy can be saved in innovative ways, including using censored LED energy-efficient light bulbs (Nandi, 2014), constructing buildings to face north (especially in South Africa) for an increase in natural light and heating, and isolation in buildings. Ecotourism destinations should consider purchasing energy-efficient equipment that can be used at the destination. Alternative forms of transportation and activities should be found if the current ones have a negative impact on the environment (Sharma, 2014; Walker & Walker, 2011).

It is equally important that destinations save water. It is crucial that ecotourism destinations aiming to be greener, find ways in which water can be recycled and used optimally (Pratt et al., 2012; UNEP, 2013). Tourist destinations are known for high water use. This perception can be changed if destinations find innovative ways of minimizing their water consumption.

The implementation of gray (recyclable) and black (non-recyclable, contaminated) water practices could assist tourism destinations in optimally managing their water consumption (Saayman, 2009). Such practices will assist destinations in determining the volume of water used and the percentage that can be recycled. Ecotourism destinations should determine the types of human waste that could contaminate the water and how this water can be recycled and used for other purposes at the destination (UNEP, 2013).

Hard waste refers to, amongst others, paper, glass, tins, plastic and kitchen waste (Saayman, 2009). Ecotourism destinations should ensure that there is a safe area where waste can be sorted and included in other national recycling initiatives. Climate change, exploitation of natural resources, introduction of alien species, pollution, the disturbance of wildlife and waste are all types of damage that a tourism destination can inflict on a region's biodiversity (Pratt et al., 2012).

Ecotourism destinations have to ensure that there are implementation, monitoring, and evaluation plans in place for all operational duties. These plans will increase destination efficiency. The destination should be managed and governed through the principles and practices of ecotourism and greening associations to ensure optimal conservation and sustainability.

CREATING DEMAND

A new product does not automatically have consumers; companies have to create demand. This also applies to tourism. Unlike products, tourism is a service and intangible. This may make it difficult to create a demand or market. Rishi (2014) explains that green or sustainable tourism marketing requires careful selection of the elements in the marketing mix. Some of these elements are discussed in previous sections and illustrate what one should consider when developing an ecotourism destination. Most important is that ecotourism destinations should abstain from greenwashing.

Greenwashing takes place when organizations market themselves as green, but have implemented little, if any greening principles and practices. These organizations have vague communication and marketing strategies and send out false impressions of the ecotourism destination to increase revenue without any efforts focused on conserving the natural environment (Nandi, 2014; Ringham, n.d.; Smith & Font, 2014). It is crucial that ecotourism destinations are certified (ecolabeling) to communicate credibility. Certification is, however, costly and time-consuming and some associations advise against it. Various green certifications exist and each has their own logo, which tourists do not always recognize (GHA, 2016).

With or without certification, ecotourism destinations that provide green products should communicate or market their green products and services effectively. Marketing material should portray the ecotourism destination as luxurious and comfortable and messages should refrain from green aspects for cost-cutting, but rather incorporate it for conservation purposes (Baker et al., 2013; Lee & Oh, 2014). This requires ecotourism destinations to choose their pricing strategies carefully to support the correct message.

Creating demand is challenging because there is not a substantial, evenly spread number of tourists who make sustainable choices (Rishi, 2014). This poses a challenge for ecotourism destinations that wish to attract the green market. Nevertheless, promotions can be used to position the ecotourism destination and motivate ecotourists to use green products and services (Rishi, 2014). Promotions and distribution channels should be carefully selected to create a more educated ecotourist in terms of sustainability, but also to eventually attract more, greener eco-tourists to the destination.

Waterwheel Green Ecolodge Near Tzaneen and Haenerstburg, South Africa

Waterwheel is registered as a charity trust (i.e., Galasiers) and is situated on the Onverwacht farm, just outside Haenertsburg toward Tzaneen in the Limpopo province of South Africa. The land on which it is situated was specifically bought to provide a free breakaway for volunteers or employees at various South African charities. Waterwheel is considering several funding sources to sustain its charity work, including a separate luxury ecolodge as the main source of funding.

As this ecolodge is still in the planning phase, several key decisions should be taken to ensure that it is feasible. It is beyond the scope of this chapter to explain the various business plan decisions that should be considered, but this section will address some of the aspects discussed earlier in this chapter. These aspects pertain to green development, green operations and creating demand for Waterwheel as a green ecodestination.

GREEN DEVELOPMENT

Environmental economics

As defined by the TGCSA, the proposed accommodation Waterwheel wishes to develop is classified as a lodge. A lodge is "a formal accommodation facility providing full or limited services located in natural surroundings beyond that of an immediate garden area, without any game" (TGCSA, 2014). As Waterwheel is aspiring to a luxury ecolodge, the TGCSA's four or five-star grading is recommended for development. However, several of the four and five-star grading aspects is in contradiction with greening principles, therefore alternative methods must be explored to fulfill these grading requirements. Some of the contradicting requirements include the amount of electricity plugs necessary (bedside lights, hair dryers, dress table/desk light and bar fridge), systems that use electricity (hot water and heating and cooling systems) and the installation of both a shower and bath in guest rooms. The Excellence in Design for Greater Efficiencies (EDGE) is a software application that assists construction planning and hypothetical cost savings by considering energy saving (reflective roof paint or roof insulation), water efficiency (low-flow shower heads or dual-flush toilets) and material efficiency (window frames or flooring) (EDGE, 2016).

GREEN OPERATIONS

Daily operations form part of the construction of the accommodation. Due to Waterwheel's location, trustees made an informed choice to erect a waterwheel on the property that generates electricity from the Letaba River (Plate 1). This was decided due to the immense capital investment necessary to lay and render

Plate 1.   Waterwheel to Generate Electricity. *Source*: Supplied by Authors

electrical services from the South African grid. This is also a calculating plan to work around the South African power outages experienced in 2008 and once again in 2014/2015 (Eskom, 2015). Generating one's own electricity is not only a solution to power outages; it is more environmentally friendly. The trustees of Waterwheel are concerned about the human impact on the environment and recognize that efforts should be made to conserve it for future generations. The trustees' philosophy also informed the environmentally friendly sewage system (Plate 2) that is designed and implemented on standard, with the necessary civil engineering certification in place. This sewage system flows through a range of processes that naturally purifies the sewage.

The trustees feel strongly about the impact of CO_2 emissions and planted a plantation of trees to counteract greenhouse gas emissions and supply extra O_2 to the environment. Waterwheel's current input activities are already on track to positively counter output activities.

Plate 2. Sewage System. *Source*: Supplied by Authors

A lot of green aspects were already considered and are to be incorporated further in the accommodation development, including waste management (by guests and during construction). Environmentally friendly product packaging, biodegradable amenities, and activities with a minimal environmental impact that are locally sourced should be considered.

The Haenertsburg and Tzaneen areas, between which Waterwheel is situated, have a variety of activities which makes additional activities at Waterwheel unnecessary and motivates participation in the community's activities. In this way the impact on the environment is minimized. As Waterwheel aims to be an ecotourism destination, some form of activity is required to add to the guests' experience; ecotourists are, after all, well-educated and expect information-rich experiences (Jurdana, 2009). Waterwheel's green aspects, such as the Letaba river, provide ample opportunity to educate tourists and ensure memorable experiences (see Chapter 17).

CREATING DEMAND

One of the most challenging aspects of a newly developed tourism business is creating product demand. A starting point for all developments is considering the potential target market. Waterwheel's obvious target market is green tourists, a market that, in South Africa, is currently quite small and on which data is scarce. Nevertheless, this market should not be forgotten and marketing campaigns or distribution channels should be put in place to attract these tourists as the market grows. Fortunately, the green market associates well with ecotourists who would also make use of the product and in some cases, these ecotourists are also green tourists. Ecotourists is a more viable market to focus efforts on and as the green market develops, the already developed distribution channels will attract green tourists.

It is extremely important to attract tourists through distribution channels. Considering Waterwheel's situation, there are three distribution channels (apart from the website that should be developed to market them directly) that must be considered. These channels can be approached indirectly (i.e., through other platforms) worldwide, nationally and regionally.

Worldwide Trip Advisor (2015) is the largest internationally known travel site that offers advice from millions of travelers to enable other travelers to plan and book their trips. This platform enables tourists to co-create potential tourists' experiences through their own experiences.

On a national level, Eco Atlas (2015a) is a South African website that enables tourists to search for ecotourism products. This site uses 20 ecolabels that inform tourists of associated tourism business' sustainable goals, allowing them to make informed travel decisions. Being part of the Eco Atlas website enables networking between relevant ecosuppliers, partners, and best practices through the Eco Atlas Forum. Further marketing avenues include Twitter, Facebook, a blog, and other relevant media (Eco Atlas, 2015b).

The Magoebaskloof Tourism (2015) site is a regional website of the Magoebaskloof and Haenertsburg area where Waterwheel is located. This site lists accommodation, activities, shopping and dining opportunities, and information about the area. It also provides contact information, but has no instant booking and availability options. It is, however, important to be part of this site to indicate that Waterwheel is part of the local community (one of the four pillars of ecotourism). Being part of the local community's tourism initiatives is important as Waterwheel should be making use of local services and products to gain support from the local community through business referrals.

Conclusion

Tourists across the globe are much more conscious of their impact on the natural environment and are continuously finding ways to be more environmentally friendly. They are willing to pay higher prices if it means that local labor conditions are fair, products, and services provided are organic, the negative impact on the environment is minimized, environmental sustainability is guaranteed, and more funds are used to increase the conservation of natural areas and decrease the footprint of tourists in significant natural tourism attractions (Han, Hsu, & Sheu, 2010; Suki & Suki, 2015). Ecotourism destinations have to ensure that they are continuously identifying factors that influence the experience of tourists at the destination and manage these factors accordingly to maintain optimum visitor experience which could lead to a competitive advantage in the sector (Engelbrecht, 2011, p. 86). This supports the notion that tourists' experience is based on the perception, expectations, and level of satisfaction whilst visiting the ecotourism destination (Boshoff, Landman,

Kerley, & Bradfield, 2007). Ecotourism destinations have to be proactive in ensuring tourists a memorable experience before, during and after their visits to an ecotourism destination. This could lead to a more conscious tourist and support of global sustainability.

References

Akama, J. S., & Kieti, D. M. (2003). Measuring tourist satisfaction with Kenya's wildlife safari: A case study of Tsavo West National Park. *Tourism Management*, 24(1), 73–81.

Ayob, M. Z., Saman, F. M., Hussin, Z. H., & Jusoff, K. (2009). Tourists' satisfaction on Kilim River Mangrove Forest Ecotourism Services. *International Journal of Business and Management*, 4(7), 76–84. doi:10.5539/ijbm.v4n7p76

Baker, M. A., Davis, E. A., & Weaver, P. A. (2013). Eco-friendly attitudes, barriers to participation, and differences in behavior at green hotels. *Cornell Hospitality Quarterly*, 55(1), 89–99. doi:10.1177/1938965513504483 cqx.sagepub.com.

Ballantyne, R., Packer, J., & Sutherland, L. A. (2011). Visitors' memories of wildlife tourism: Implications for the design of powerful interpretive experiences. *Tourism Management*, 32(4), 770–779. doi:10.1016/j.tourman.2010.06.012

Bina, O. (2013). The green economy and sustainable development: An uneasy balance? *Environment and Planning C: Government and Policy 2013*, 31, 1023–1047. doi:10.1068/c1310j

Boshoff, A. F., Landman, M., Kerley, G. I. H., & Bradfield, M. (2007). Profiles, views and observations of visitors to the Addo Elephant National Park, Eastern Cape, South Africa. *South African Journal of Wildlife Research*, 37(2), 189–196. doi:10.3957/0379-4369-37.2.189

Ceballos, L. H. (1987). The future of ecotourism. *Mexico Journal*, 1(987), 13–14.

Chan, J. K. L., & Baum, T. (2007). Motivation factors of ecotourists in ecolodge accommodation: The push and pull factors. *Asia Pacific Journal of Tourism Research*, 12(4), 349–364. doi:10.1080/10941660701761027

Chan, W. W., & Ho, K. (2006). Hotels' environmental management systems (ISO 14001): Creative financing strategy. *International Journal of Contemporary Hospitality Management*, 18(4), 302–316. doi:10.1108/09596110610665311

Cooper, C., Fletcher, J., Fyall, A., Gilbert, D., & Wanhill, S. (2008). *Tourism: principles and practices* (4th ed.). Harlow: Prentice Hall.

Cooper, C. (2012). *Essentials of tourism*. Harlow: Pearson.

Department of Environmental Affairs, South Africa. (2016). *National framework for sustainable development: Department of environmental affairs*. Retrieved from https://www/enviornment.gov.za/?q=content/documents/strategic_docs/national_framework_sustainable_development

Eco Atlas. (2015a). *About eco ATLAS.* Retrieved from http://ecoatlas.co.za/about

Eco Atlas. (2015b). *Get listed on eco Atlas.* Retrieved from http://ecoatlas.co.za/get-listed

Engelbrecht, W. H. (2011). *Critical success factors for managing the visitor experience at the Kruger National Park.* Potchefstroom: NWU. Dissertation – M.Com. Retrieved from http://dspace.nwu.ac.za/bitstream/handle/10394/6928/Engelbrech_W_H.pdf?sequence=2

Eskom. (2015). *Short history of electricity in South Africa.* Retrieved from http://eskomfail.co.za/short-history/

Excellence in Design for Greater Efficiencies (EDGE). (2016). *EDGE calculates operational savings and reduced carbon emissions for your building as measured against a base case.* Retrieved from http://www.ifc.org/wps/wcm/connect/Topics_Ext_Content/IFC_External_Corporate_Site/EDGE/How+it+works/

Fair Trade in Tourism. (2016). *Get certified.* Retrieved from http://www.fairtrade.travel/get-certified

Frey, A., & Gervers, S. (2016). Green economy and tourism. In H. Schwägermann, P. Mayer, & D. Xi (Eds.), *Handbook event market China* (pp. 139–151). Oldenbourg: De Gruyter.

Geldenhuys, S. (2009). Ecotourism criteria and context. In M. Saayman (Eds.), *Ecotourism: Getting back to basics* (pp. 1–29). Potchefstroom: Platinum Press.

George, R. (2014). *Marketing tourism in South Africa* (5th ed.). Cape Town: Oxford University Press.

Green Hotels Association (GHA). (2016). *Certification??* Retrieved from http://www.greenhotels.com/

Green Leaf Environmental Standard (GLES). (2015). *Green leaf eco standard.* Retrieved from http://www.greenleafecostandard.net/

Ham, S. H., & Weiler, B. (2007). Isolating the role of on-site interpretation in a satisfying experience. *Journal of Interpretation Research, 12*(2), 5–24. Retrieved from http://www.interpnet.com/NAI/interp/Resources/Publications/Journal_of_Interpretation_Research/Archive/nai/_publications/JIR_Archive.aspx?hkey=7f4c07ef-bdd9-4bae-9858-0b73facfbe19

Han, H., Hsu, L. T., & Sheu, C. (2010). Application of the theory of planned behaviour to green hotel choice: Testing the effect of environmental friendly activities. *Tourism Management, 31*(3), 325–334. doi:10.1016/j.tourman.2009.03.013

Jauhari, V., & Verma, T. (2014). Designing sustainable hotels: Technical and human aspects. In V. Jauhari (Eds.), *Managing sustainability and tourism industry: Paradigms and directions for the future* (pp.1–40). Oakville: Apple Academic Press.

Jurdana, D. S. (2009). Specific knowledge for managing ecotourism destinations. *Tourism Hospitality Management, 15*(2), 267–278.

KamalulAriffin, S. N., Khalid, S. N. A., & Wahid, N. A. (2013). The barriers to the adoption of environmental management practices in the hotel industry: A study of Malaysian hotels. *Business Strategy Series, 14*(4), 106–117. doi:10.1108/BSS-06-2012-0028

Kang, M., & Gretzel, U. (2012). Effects of podcast tours on tourist experiences in a national park. *Tourism Management*, *33*(2), 440–455. doi:10.1016/j. tourman.2011.05.005

Kruger, M., Saayman, M., & Hermann, U. (2014). First-time versus repeat visitors at the Kruger National Park. *Acta Commercii*, *14*(1), 1–9. doi:10.4102/ac.v14i1.220

Lee, S., & Oh, H. (2014). Effective communication strategies for hotel guests' green behaviour. *Cornell Hospitality Quarterly*, *55*(1), 52–63. doi:10.1177/ 1938965513504029

Legrand, W., Sloan, P., Wagmann, C., & Rheindorf, L. (2014). From output to input: The emissions to principles of sustainable hotel design. In V. Jauhari (Eds.), *Managing sustainability and tourism industry: Paradigms and directions for the future* (pp. 41–73). Oakville: Apple Academic Press.

Magoebaskloof Tourism. (2015). *Home*. Retrieved from www.magoebaskloof-tourism.co.za/index.php

Marsiglio, S. (2015). Economic growth and environment: Tourism as a trigger for green growth. *Tourism Economics*, *21*(1), 183–204. doi:10.5367/te.2014.0411

Mason, P. (2008). Managing the natural resources for tourism. In P. Mason (Eds.), *Tourism impacts, planning and management* (2nd ed., pp.151–164). Abingdon: Routledge.

McLaren, D. (2003). *Rethinking tourism & ecotravel* (2nd ed.). Bloomfield: Kurmarian Press Inc.

Middleton, V. T. C., Fyall, A., Morgan, M., & Ranchhod, A. (2009). *Marketing in travel and tourism* (4th ed.). Oxford: Butterworth-Heinemann.

Nandi, S. K. (2014). Efficient equipment: Sources for sustainability in the hotel industry. In V. Jauhari (Eds.), *Managing sustainability and tourism industry: Paradigms and directions for the future* (pp. 363–386). Oakville: Apple Academic Press.

Nwahia, O. C., Omonona, B. T., Onyeabor, E. N., & Balogun, O. S. (2012). An analysis of the effect of Obudu community participation in ecotourism on poverty. *Journal of Economics and Sustainable Development*, *3*(8), 25–36. Retrieved from http://www.iiste.org/Journals/index.php/JEDS/article/view/2304

Pine, B. J., & Gilmore, J. H. (1999). *The experience economy: Work is theatre & every business a stage*. Boston, MA: Harvard Business School Press.

Powell, R. B., & Ham, S. H. (2008). Can ecotourism interpretation really lead to pro-conservation knowledge, attitudes and behaviour? Evidence from the Galapagos Islands. *Journal of Sustainable Tourism*, *16*(4), 467–489. doi:10.1080/09669580802154223

Pratt, L., Rivera, L., & Bien, A. (2012). *UNWTO: Tourism in the green economy: background report*. Madrid: UNWTO. Retrieved from http://www.unep. org/greeneconomy/Portals/88/documents/ger/ger_final_dec_2011/Tourism%20in %20the%20green_economy%20unwto_unep.pdf

Ringham, S. (n.d.). *Greenwashing eco (?) tourism in New Zealand: What climate change?* Retrieved from https://scholar.google.co.za/scholar?q=greenwashing+ in+tourism&btnG=&hl=en&as_sdt=0%2C5&as_ylo=2012&as_yhi=2016

Rishi, M. (2014). Marketing sustainability in the hospitality and tourism industry. In V. Jauhari (Eds.), *Managing sustainability and tourism industry: Paradigms and directions for the future* (pp. 137–180). Oakville: Apple Academic Press.

Saayman, M. (2009). Managing parks as ecotourism attractions. In M. Saayman (Ed.), *Ecotourism: Getting back to basics* (pp. 345–383). Potchefstroom: North-West University, Leisure Publications.

Sasidharan, V., & Font, X. (2001). Pitfalls of ecolabelling. In X. Font & R. C. Buckley (Eds.), *Tourism ecolabelling: Certification and promotion of sustainable management* (pp. 105–119). Wallingford: CABI Publishing.

Sharma, S. (2014). Sustainable culinary practices. In V. Jauhari (Eds.), *Managing sustainability and tourism industry: Paradigms and directions for the future* (pp. 303–334). Oakville: Apple Academic Press.

Shrivastava, M. (2014). Responsible ecotourism – Todays need. *Indian Journal Applied & Pure Biology, 29*(1), 195–196. Retrieved from http://www.biology-journal.com/fulltext/v29i1/ijapb29-1-30.pdf

Smith, V. L., & Font, X. (2014). Volunteer tourism, greenwashing and under-standing responsible marketing using market signalling theory. *Journal of Sustainable Tourism, 22*(6), 942–963. doi:10.1080/09669582.2013.871021

Suki, N. M., & Suki, N. M. (2015). Consumers' environmental behaviour towards staying at a green hotel: Moderation of green hotel knowledge. *Management of Environmental Quality: An International Journal, 26*(1), 103–117. doi:10.1108/MEQ-02-2014-0023

The Heritage Environmental Management Company. (2016). *Heritage Environmental Rating Programme.* Retrieved from http://www.heritagesa.co.za/

Tourism Grading Council of South Africa (TGCSA). (2013). *About the TGCSA.* Retrieved from http://www.tourismgrading.co.za/about-the-tgcsa/

Tourism Grading Council of South Africa (TGCSA). (2014). *Tourism grading council of South Africa: Grading criteria and minimum requirements: Game lodge/nature lodge accommodation.* Retrieved from http://www.tourismgrading. co.za/get-graded/whats-in-it-for-me/grading-criteria-3/

Trip Advisor. (2015). *Fact sheet.* Retrieved from www.tripadviro.co.za/ PressCentre-c4-Fact_Sheet.html

United Nationals Environmental Programme (UNEP). (2013). *Green economy and trade – trends, challenges and opportunities.* Retrieved from http://www. unep.org/greeneconomy/GreenEconomyandTrade

United Nations Environment Programme (UNEP), & World Tourism Organization (UNWTO). (2012). *Tourism in the green economy: Background report.* UNWTO, Madrid. Retrieved from http://www.unep.org/greeneconomy/ Portals/88/documents/ger/ger_final_dec_2011/Tourism%20in%20the%20green_ economy%20unwto_unep.pdf

United Nations World Tourism Organisation (UNWTO). (2015). *Tourism high-lights.* Madrid, Spain: UNWTO. Retrieved from http://www.e-unwto.org/doi/ pdf/10.18111/9789284416899

Vespestad, M. K., & Mehmetoglu, M. (2010). The relationship between tourist nationality, cultural orientation and nature-based tourism experiences. *European Journal of Tourism Research, 32*(2), 87–104. Retrieved from http:// search.proquest.com/docview/763259157/fulltext?accountid=14648

Walker, J. R., & Walker, J. T. (2011). *Tourism: Concepts and practices.* Upper Saddle River, NJ: Pearson Education.

14 Managing Rural Tourist Experiences: Lessons from Cyprus

Anna Farmaki

ABSTRACT

Purpose – The purpose of this chapter is to evaluate the management of the rural tourist experience in Cyprus. In doing so, it specifically attempts to examine rural tourists' experiences in relation to travel motives and activities performed in rural areas in Cyprus, explore overall satisfaction with the rural tourist experience with regard to several physical, social, and symbolic attributes derived from the literature review and elicit recommendations that can improve the tourist experience in rural areas.

Methodology/approach – An exploratory research approach was utilized, whereby 70 open-ended casual interviews were conducted with domestic and international tourists visiting rural areas in Cyprus.

Findings – Main findings derived from this study include the realization that the rural tourism experience is fragmented and largely shaped by travel motives, regional characteristics, support services, and service provision.

Practical implications – A refined segmentation strategy is proposed as well as the development of synergistic, innovative linkages among rural tourism stakeholders and across sectors in the industry, with thematic clusters representing a favorable proposed strategy.

Originality/value – Although the study is centered on a single case, theoretical and practical implications may be derived with regard to the demand aspects of rural tourist experiences. In turn, such insights may be transferrable to other rural destination contexts.

Keywords: Rural tourism; tourist experience; travel motives; satisfaction; destination management; Cyprus

Introduction

Rural tourism is a favorable developmental strategy for several destinations due to the economic and social benefits it can yield, not only to rural regions but also to tourist destinations overall. On one hand, rural tourism is regarded as a catalyst for economic and social growth in remote communities. Indeed, rural tourism has become one of the most popular rural development strategies adopted by destinations especially following the decline of traditional agrarian industries. Arguments have been put forward that tourism offers a range of benefits to rural communities such as employment opportunities, re-population of rural areas, social development through public facilities and services improvement, the revitalization of local crafts, customs and traditional culture, the promotion of locally produced products, and the protection of nature and the environment (Binns & Noel, 2002; Bramwell, 2004; Cawley, 2007; Ribeiro & Marques, 2002; Sharpley, 2002). On the other hand, in destinations where tourism has been concentrated in coastal areas, rural tourism development has been extensively considered as a means of diversification of the tourism product. Promoted in island contexts as a counterpoint to mass tourism, rural tourism has emerged from a supplementary niche to a sector of its own (Barke, 2004; Cánoves, Villarino, Priestley, & Blanco, 2004; Tchetchik, Fleischer, & Finkelshtain, 2006).

Unsurprisingly, innumerable academic articles and books have been devoted to the study of rural tourism, employing numerous angles, and perspectives. While academic attention has concentrated initially on the potential benefits rural tourism may yield, in recent years a departure of academic focus is noted toward the practicalities of rural tourism development. Despite the enthusiasm surrounding the rhetoric on rural tourism, it has become clear that the reality is somewhat challenged, as destinations show inability in meeting expectations of rural tourists (Ribeiro & Marques, 2002). Several problems have been identified in extant literature, stemming primarily from the poor planning and implementation of rural tourism projects as well as poorly coordinated marketing efforts. For example, lack of collaboration (Waayers, Lee, & Newsome, 2012; Wilson, Fesenmaier, Fesenmaier, & Van Es, 2001), minimal economic contribution compared to the high developmental capital required (Sharpley, 2002), seasonal profits and employment opportunities (Wilson et al., 2001), lack of government support (Hall, 2004; Wang & Krakover, 2008), poor satisfaction levels among tourists, and lack of entrepreneurship (Kommpula, 2014; Ryan, Mottiar, & Quinn, 2012; Sharpley, 2002) have been identified as primary challenges to successful rural tourism development.

This important array of work performed on rural tourism lends two important insights. First, rural tourism is an increasingly valuable developmental strategy for destinations, and as such, it will continue to attract considerable scholarly attention. Secondly, rural tourism falls victim of not only the challenges facing the tourism industry but also the limitations related to rural regions, which impair the successful development of rural tourism. Inevitably, as the competitiveness of rural destinations remains questionable, the advancement of understanding of rural tourist experiences gains potency. A central theme of this chapter is the management of the rural tourist experience. Scholars unanimously agree that understanding of the type of tourists attracted to rural tourist regions, the underlying motives for traveling to rural areas and the dimensions influencing the rural tourist experience is pivotal in the planning, management and marketing of rural tourism. It is widely accepted that their examination will improve destination competitiveness, decision-making, tourism planning, destination management and marketing. For example, monitoring the tourist experience may lead to product, market and process improvements that can increase the willingness of revisiting the destination and tourist satisfaction.

Tourist experiences is a core theme in tourist discourse, however, within rural tourism studies the difficulties facing the successful performance of rural tourism business has led to the heightened need to consider the tourist experience sought in rural settings. Acknowledging that understanding of rural tourism demand aspects will contribute to destination competitiveness, this chapter examines the management of the rural tourist experience in the island of Cyprus. Using insights of empirical investigations performed on rural tourist motivations and satisfaction, this chapter attempts to evaluate the perceptions of tourists visiting selected rural villages in Cyprus with regard to a series of attributes pertaining to rural tourism. In turn, the chapter aims at informing practitioners and academicians on the planning and management aspects of rural tourism experiences through the provision of a several propositions, which may be transferrable to other destination contexts. The chapter begins with a review of the meaning and dimensions of the rural tourism experience, before presenting the study context and the methodology adopted. Following, discussion centers on the key themes pertaining to the management of rural tourism experiences in Cyprus. Lastly, recommendations are offered that can be transferred across similar destinations attempting to improve their rural tourism product and consequently the rural tourism experience.

The Rural Tourism Experience

The concept of rural tourism is an ambiguous one, which has been ill-defined over the years. The notion that it refers to tourism taking place in rural areas is far too simplistic and has long been abandoned. This departure in conceptualization has led to attempts to identify certain criteria that can be employed in the definition of rural tourism. Some parameters that seem to be universally accepted include small-scale development, locally controlled and nature-based tourism (Lane, 1994). However, these fail to consider the traditional aspects of the countryside and related activities. According to Pena, Jamilena, and Molina (2012) different terminology has been used to describe rural tourism activity (farm, green, adventure, and eco-tourism) in an attempt to incorporate the multi-faceted nature of rurality. An OECD report (1994) states that rurality can be understood upon three dimensions: (a) population density and size, (b) land use, and (c) traditional community identity. Hence, rural tourism conceptualization needs to include a range of characteristics that relate to the rural context in which a range of activities are performed. Therefore, subsequent attempts to define the term centered on "the range of activities and amenities provided by farmers and rural people to attract tourists to their areas" (Gannon, 1994, p. 5), whereas Bramwell and Lane's (1994) definition included the activities and interests in farms, nature, adventure, sports, health, education, arts and heritage taking place in countryside. Also, Pedford (1996) added rural customs and folklore, local and family traditions, values and beliefs to the definition of rural tourism. Despite these conceptualization attempts, the interpretation of what constitutes rural tourism seems to vary among countries and regions (Hall, 2010).

The vagueness surrounding the conceptualization of rural tourism stems, to a great extent, from the rural contextual setting in which tourism develops. For instance, there is a varying degree of rurality (Cloke, 1977) as some regions are more remote than others, with smaller populations, few employment opportunities and poor infrastructure. Murdoch and Marsden (1994) suggested that rurality should not be viewed only geographically but also in terms of developmental policy as some rural areas are preserved against development and others are encouraged, through subsidies to the local community, to exploit employment opportunities offered by tourism. Hall (2010) posited that many rural areas display urban characteristics and further suggested that the distinction between different types of rural regions is not clear as rural tourism activities may be offered in settings that are not predominantly rural or might be offered on a large-scale. In addition to contextual ambivalences, rural tourism conceptualization is further entangled by the large variety of activities affiliated to rural tourism which range from nature-based to adventure-oriented activities. Typical rural activities may include walking, climbing, canoeing, rafting, skiing, swimming, hunting, nature study, cycling, heritage observation, small-scale conventions, rural festivals, and relaxation (OECD, 1994). As a result, rural tourism has become synonymous to a polymorphous tourism product, highly associated with agro-tourism, eco-tourism, and alternative tourism (Roberts & Hall, 2001). The multi-faceted nature of rural tourism entails that a variety of motivations are associated with the rural tourism product, producing a wide range of tourist experiences.

According to Sharpley and Stone (2010) to consume tourism is to consume experiences. Therefore, an evaluation of destination and/or business performance needs to consider tourist

experiences. The need to evaluate tourist experiences is highlighted in recent years due to the noticeable change in tourist
needs and travel motives. By definition, the term "tourist
experience" is problematized by the different components it
encompasses such as tourist motivations, demand factors, typologies of tourists, tourist perceptions, and destination image. An
examination of tourist experiences centers on the measurement
of destination attributes, the interaction with which influences
tourist perceptions. Such elements may include facilities,
attractions, destination image, and service level. Alegre and
Garau (2010) argued that attributes can be classified into categories and distinguished between instrumental (i.e., accommodation facilities, restaurants, infrastructure, etc.) and expressive
attributes (i.e., activities, authenticity, hospitality of local community, etc.). Nonetheless, the same destination may produce
diverse tourist experiences for different tourists. This assumption is adopted in recent tourism studies, which view tourist
experiences as a relative rather than absolute truth (Uriely,
2005).

Particularly within rural tourism, the variation in activities
and pursuits leads to a challenging evaluation of rural tourist
experiences. Indeed, Page and Getz (1997) argued that tourists,
depending on the experience sought, will be attracted to rural
areas for different reasons including tranquillity, nature, scenery,
recreation, adventure and traditionality. Similarly, Kastenholz
(2000) agreed that not all rural tourists seek rurality to the same
extent whereas Farmaki's findings (2012) confirm that different
types of rural tourists exist as different motives drive tourists to
visit rural areas. Pena et al. (2012) argued that rural tourism has
its own characteristics that distinguish it from other tourism
forms. Evidently, an evaluation of rural tourism experiences
needs to consider natural, cultural, heritage, and accommodation
resources as well as services belonging to the rural environment.
As Kastenholz, Carneiro, Marques, and Lima (2012) concluded
the rural tourism experiences comprise of social, emotional, and
symbolic dimensions. Hence, an evaluation of the management
of rural tourism experiences needs to consider travel motives,
activities performed at the destination and satisfaction with a
variety of physical and social attributes. In evaluating rural tourist experiences in Cyprus, these dimensions were considered. In
the section below, an overview of rural tourism development in
Cyprus is provided together with an explanation of the data collection methods employed.

Methodology

STUDY CONTEXT

Rural tourism development in Cyprus is not recent. Before Cyprus gained independence in 1960, the majority of the island's tourists were attracted to the island's mountainous interior. However, Cyprus's tourism development efforts coincided with the mass coastal tourism explosion in the 1970s, leading to the island becoming a popular sea and sun destination in the Mediterranean. As tourist facilities were developed along the island's coastline, Cyprus' rural areas diminished in popularity. Nonetheless, the acknowledgment of the negative impacts of mass tourism in the 1990s, led to the realization that Cyprus had to redirect tourism development toward rural areas across the island. The rationale for this strategy was two-fold. First, by investing in rural tourism the island could diversify its main product offering and complement its "sea and sun" product. Second, through rural tourism development the principles of sustainable development could be achieved. The tourist authorities of Cyprus envisaged that through rural tourism the tourist season could be extended and the tourist experience would be improved, as rural tourism was widely regarded as a vehicle for promoting traditional culture, preserving nature and encouraging regional economic growth. Thus, the Cyprus Tourism Organisation (CTO) established the Laona project in 1989, with the aim to restore 26 buildings in five villages including accommodation units, tavernas and a visitor center (Sharpley & Sharpley, 1997). Also, the CTO initiated financial incentive schemes, where interest on loans undertaken by owners of traditional properties to restore and convert into tourism establishments, was partly subsidized. By 1998, approximately $4 million were invested by the private sector on restoration of 60 traditional buildings with the government spending about $500,000 in subsidies and by 1999 a total of 444 bed spaces were created (Cyprus Tourism Organisation [CTO], 1999).

Simultaneously, a multi-faceted promotion program to endorse what was labeled "agro-tourism" began including advertising, exhibitions at agricultural consumer shows, travel trade education trips and the production of an agro-tourism guide. In order to intensify promotional efforts, the CTO established the Cyprus Agrotourism in 1995, whereby marketing efforts concentrated on promoting traditional culture through educational programs for local communities and training courses centered on Cypriot traditional dance, music, and crafts (Sharpley, 2002). In the years that followed, similar organizations were established to facilitate promotion and support for "agro-tourism" such as the Cyprus Sustainable Tourism Initiative and the regional tourism companies, which were responsible for the development and promotion of tourism in peripheral areas of the island. The efforts to develop rural tourism in Cyprus appeared successful initially, as the supply of agro-tourism units almost doubled between 1999 and 2010. From 51 accommodation units in 1999 to just less than 100 in 2013, rural accommodation units were developed in villages across the four major regions of the island (Troodos, Pafos, Larnaka, and Limassol and Paralimni area).

However, the increase in the supply of accommodation units does not indicate success. Recorded tourist arrivals in rural accommodation units accounted for approximately 1% of total tourist arrivals to Cyprus (which amounted to 2.3 million in 2014), whereas occupancy rates in rural accommodation units in the same year accounted for only a fifth of their potential. The low occupancy rates of the rural accommodation units have also been highlighted by Sharpley (2002), who questioned the success of rural tourism development in Cyprus. With demand for rural tourism fluctuating according to the season and with the high prices offered deterring locals visiting rural areas, the need to evaluate rural tourist experiences is imperative.

RESEARCH OBJECTIVES

The evaluation of rural tourist experiences in Cyprus was driven by three primary objectives. Firstly, tourist experiences in relation to travel motives and activities performed to rural areas in Cyprus were explored. Secondly, the overall satisfaction of tourists visiting rural areas in Cyprus was examined with regard to several physical, social and symbolic attributes derived from the literature review. Thirdly, tourist perceptions over the rural tourism product of Cyprus was sought and associated recommendations.

Due to time and budgetary constraints, the research which employed a qualitative exploratory approach, focused on selected rural villages including Troodos, Platres, Foini, Lofou, Omodos, Kalavasos, Agros, Scarinou, Lefkara, and Liopetri. Overall, 70 short open-ended interviews were employed with tourists who visited the above-mentioned rural areas in Cyprus from November 2011 to March 2013. Out of the total sample, 50% Cypriot and 50% were foreigners. Table 1 illustrates the number of respondents according to country of residence.

Table 1.   Number of Interviewees by Country of Residence.

Cypriots	The United Kingdom	Germany	Russia	Scandinavia	France	Greece
35	8	7	7	6	4	3

Although the demographic profile of the respondents was not rigidly recorded, it was noted that 76% of the sample were of an older age group (from 55 to 74 years old) who had traveled with their spouse. The rest of the sample were of a younger age group, traveling with children. The respondents were selected upon convenience and approached in key areas including regional museums (such as the Troodos Nature Museum and Lefkara Wax museum), information centers, the village square, and restaurants/shops. After the interviewer explained to respondents the main purpose of the study, she obtained their verbal consent in participating to the research before asking a series of questions. The interviews were short so as not to distract visitors from other activities they were engaged in and were primarily casual conversations, in which the interviewer took notes. The conversations were not recorded, however, where appropriate the interviewer gained the consent of tour guides and travel agency employees accompanying the visitors in conducting the interviews. Following data collection, the interviews were transcribed using the notes of the interviewer and then analyzed thematically by reading the text numerous times and identifying thematic categories in relation to the objectives driving the study.

Findings

MOTIVATIONS AND ACTIVITIES

A variety of motives were identified in relation to visitation to the rural areas, with domestic tourists notably visiting rural villages for different reasons than foreigners. For instance, the majority of domestic visitors argued that they visited the villages for relaxation and as an escape of their busy daily life in the city. The brief interaction with the tranquil environment and nature was the main driver for visitation. In addition, spending time with their family and/ or spouse in a calm surrounding was identified as a key motive for visitation. Most Cypriots visiting rural areas were not identified as particularly active tourists, as the activities with which they mainly engaged were limited to dining and walking around the villages.

Nonetheless, a small number of locals were reported to have shown interest in more active hobbies including cycling and skiing during the winter. On the other hand, foreign tourists visiting the villages reported a greater variety of motives. For example, British, Germans, Scandinavians and French stated an inherent interest in nature, which drove their visitation to the villages and surrounding rural environment. Particularly, Scandinavian tourists reported cycling as a key activity which they performed throughout the duration of their visit whereas some British, Germans and French tourists identified trekking as a key activity. Interestingly, Russians and Greeks visiting the rural areas were mostly interested in the traditional cultural attractions of the areas such as byzantine churches, monasteries and thematic museums. Some Cypriots and Germans also stated that they visited byzantine churches during their time in the rural villages, however, this was not identified as the primary motive predisposing visitation.

Moreover, it was found that a significant percentage of the foreigners visiting the rural areas were not particularly interested in either the nature or the cultural aspect of the villages. In contrary, they were identified as organized mass tourists who stayed in coastal regions but visited the rural areas as part of a daily excursion. Some of these visitors did not know the names of the villages they visited, neither did they engage in any activities or interact with locals. Rather, they purchased a few souvenirs but were not interested in learning about the environment and/or traditional culture of the villages. Farmaki's (2012) work on rural tourist motivations in Troodos distinguished rural tourists by their purpose of travel, their interest in either culture, nature or adventure, and by their level of interaction with the activity and/or environment. Building on this seminal work, this study may conclude that rural tourists can be divided into categories depending on the way of travel to the rural areas (i.e., organized mass tourists vs. independent tourists), their primary motive for visiting (i.e., culture, nature, or other) and the degree of interest and participation they exhibit in terms of learning about the local culture and environment (i.e., passive tourists vs. active tourists). This categorization may prove helpful to tourism practitioners in terms of segmenting and targeting the rural tourism market.

SATISFACTION ACROSS SEVERAL ATTRIBUTES

Satisfaction with a series of attributes related to the rural areas also exhibited varying responses, although these were not found to be influenced by nationality. For a more informed categorization and understanding of key attributes, these were divided into physical (including characteristics such as accommodation, restaurants, infrastructure, accessibility, shopping facilities, etc.) and social/symbolic (including characteristics such as activities performed, authenticity, traditional character of village, hospitality of local community, service quality, etc.). In general, most tourists reported an overall satisfaction with the physical characteristics of the villages, stating that accessibility to the villages was good as is infrastructure. Additionally, those visitors staying in rural accommodation expressed high satisfaction with the facilities. Nonetheless, in relation to social/symbolic characteristics rural tourists expressed less satisfaction and negative perceptions, with a majority of Cypriots complaining about the expensiveness of restaurants and accommodation units. High prices were not identified as a problem by most foreigners. Rather, they indicated toward poor service quality, uncleanliness of the surrounding environment, and lack of activities and attractions as primary weaknesses of the Cyprus rural tourism product. For instance, tourists interested in cycling stated that although cycling routes exist, there are no attractions or facilities (such as equipment replacement shops) along the routes. The lack of attractions and facilities deteriorates the interest of cycling routes. Furthermore, independent tourists visiting thematic museums and wineries complained about these establishments being closed during weekdays. On the contrary, organized mass tourists who had visited such attractions had not expressed similar complaints.

The lack of activities was also reported by several Cypriots who argued that they would like a greater variety of primarily family-oriented activities to be offered. Additionally, both foreign tourists and locals stated that they would like more information regarding certain activities, attractions and events as they said they were unaware of their existence prior to the visit, arguing that information provision could have helped them plan their visit better. An important weakness identified by primarily foreign tourists was the poor service quality offered in restaurants, attractions and shops. Specifically, some respondents identified unskilled foreign staff as a key problem which diminishes the authenticity and traditionality degree of the experience. Respondents highlighted that if employees, whether local or foreign, are to be employed in rural establishments they need to know the language, basic geography and facts about the region in order to provide better service and information when needed. A few respondents

went a step further and stated that the authentic Cypriot experience they anticipated was ruined when an Asian employee was
showing visitors how local cheese was made.

Interestingly, satisfaction expressions appeared to differ
according to the region and type of tourist. For instance, villages
that are more touristic were not favored by locals who stated
they are too busy. Similarly, some foreigners claimed they had a
negative experience when visited popular villages that attract
hordes of organized mass tourists. On the other hand, some rural
regions that are less developed and more remotely located were
identified by tourists as providing a less interesting experience
due to the lack of activities and attractions on offer.

RECOMMENDATIONS

In general, most local respondents expressed an overall satisfaction with the rural tourism product of Cyprus contrary to foreign
tourists who had opposing opinions. On one hand, organized
mass tourists stated that they had the opportunity of seeing
another side of the island, albeit their little involvement in activities and attractions related to the rural nature and culture.
Therefore, for organized mass tourists a positive experience was
expressed. On the other hand, for foreign visitors traveling independently comparisons with previous experiences they had in
other destinations impaired their satisfaction. Several respondents
gave their recommendations over the potentiality of the improvement of their rural experience. These included improvements in
information provision, service, quality, variety of activities and
attractions offered, and cleanliness of surrounding environment.
The availability of activities and attractions seemed to be a central point mentioned by both locals and foreigners with respondents suggesting more kids or family-oriented activities, more
events and festivals related to traditional culture and more convenient opening hours for museums and stores including weekdays
and weekends. Interestingly, some foreign respondents commented on the need to preserve the rural character of the villages and
to avoid over-development. Nonetheless, the same tourists
acknowledged that their experience in the rural areas is largely
shaped by the availability of key facilities such as toilets and coffee shops, concluding that a balance is needed between modernization attempts and preservation of the traditional character of
Cyprus.

Discussion and Conclusions

Devesa, Laguna, and Palacios (2009) warned against treating rural tourist demand homogeneously as this may lead to negative tourist experiences. This study is an indication of the underlying assumption that the rural tourism experience is fragmented and largely influenced by tourist motives, expectations, prior experience, and regional characteristics. As Kastenholz and Lima (2011) stated the rural tourist space can be adjusted, with elements combined, in order to appeal to different market segments. The multiplicity of rural tourist segments is a key conclusion of this study. Rural tourists have been found to differ and the need to categorize them into distinctive segments with relation to their motives, degree of interest with specific aspects of rurality and level of involvement in activities is imminent. The study also reported varying opinions with regard to the rural tourism experience in Cyprus. Specifically, the lack of activities and attractions seems to be a focal point which the tourism authorities need to address if the experience of rural tourists is to be improved. Indeed, an over-dependence on accommodation provision has been reported in previous studies (Farmaki, 2014; Sharpley, 2002). However, accommodation makes up one element of several constituting the tourist experience. In order to prolong the length of stay of visitors in the rural regions and enrich the tourist experience, it is important that a variety of activities and attractions appealing to different groups of tourists are required. In addition, a better organization and coordination of development and marketing efforts is required among key stakeholders in providing an enjoyable experience to rural tourists. The availability of attractions and facilities is not adequate as the effectiveness of service delivery is pivotal in the tourist experience. Sharpley's (2002) research highlighted lack of business knowledge and expertise as key obstacles in the development of rural tourism in Cyprus. Thus, training rural tourism entrepreneurs and providing marketing support are essential tactics that regional tourism boards need to take into consideration.

Additionally, the rural tourist experience seems to be influenced by regional characteristics. Indeed, varying levels of rurality have been identified and thus segmenting regions in terms of development scale, rather than geography, is essential. For instance, infrastructural provisions can be made to rural areas that seek to develop further whereas rural regions aiming at preserving their secluded character may target a different type of rural tourist. Park and Yoon (2009) suggested that in regions with limited natural resources rural tourism development should focus on activities, whereas an option for local communities with distinctive natural environments but with low investment capability is targeting to rural tourists who seek less active holidays. The use of rural regions as a base for destinations' efforts to minimize the pressures of spatial tourism development and diversify their tourism products should address site-specific characteristics in addition to tourist needs.

As rural tourism development evolves through the lens of sustainability, it becomes apparent that the multi-faceted character of the rural tourism experience requires an integrated developmental effort. For instance, hard and soft networks can be developed, with the first being focused on shared business objectives such as co-production and co-marketing and the second deriving from member associations driven mostly by shared interests. Horizontal and vertical networks as well as formal and informal networks of cooperative nature may be established to make maximum use of rural resources and enhance the development of support services and promotion. For example, an online platform can be formed from an association of rural tourism entrepreneurs with the support of regional tourism boards which would provide information regarding the availability and type of activities and attractions in regions. In addition, clustering appears as a promising tactic that can enhance the competitiveness of rural regions. Thematic clusters could be formed and different combinations of rural resources, in relation to tourist needs and regional characteristics, can be made. Such thematic routes have been successfully developed in other destinations such as Italy and Spain, whereby cycling routes have been developed along thematic product such as gastronomy. Thematic clusters allow for the utilization of common infrastructure for innovative processes to be established and networking possibilities to be exploited.

Micro-case – Ktima Georgiadi, Scarinou

Ktima Georgiadi is a family agro-tourism business, located in the village of Scarinou. Starting as a donkey farm, the business expanded rapidly as demand from both domestic and international visitors grew. Currently, Ktima Georgiadi encompasses a donkey farm, accommodation rooms, a restaurant, an olive oil museum and shops while offers a wide range of activities such as cooking classes, picking oranges from the trees, riding donkeys, and making olive oil. Contrary to other agro-tourism businesses on the island which have struggled to maintain a clientele, Ktima Georgiadi represents an example of success. Much of the farm's success stems from the management tactics of the owner, Mr. Pieris Georgiades. Once an employee in the tourism industry himself, he has utilized his knowledge of the industry and network with foreign tour operators, which secure a steady flow of international visitors throughout the year. Additionally, Mr. Georgiades has collaborated with entrepreneurs from nearby villages, such as jewellery makers and winery owners, by allowing them to use a specified space in his farm to sell their products. In this way, Mr. Georgiadis enriches the tourist experience of the visitors in the farm. Recognizing the values of donkey milk, Mr. Georgiades has gone a step further and formed a partnership with the Cyprus University of Technology to transform donkey milk into power for exporting (*Source*: www.ktima-georgiadi. com).

Rural regions are by nature limited in their capabilities, hence, they should recognize their interdependencies. Although the rural space can provide opportunities for niche tourism

Table 2. Recommendations for Efficient Management of Rural Tourist Experience.

Recommended Actions

- Prioritize development according to regional rural resources
- Make training obligatory in order to improve service quality
- Encourage entrepreneurship through education and financial support
- Develop appropriate infrastructure
- Develop niche products such as culture, health, natural, adventure, etc. (thematic clusters)
- Build image for rural tourism through coordinated marketing
- Enhance e-promotion
- Segment rural tourists by level of interest and motive
- Offer incentives (i.e., tax credits) for development of restaurants and related tourist products (Incentivize vertical linkages)
- Improve local transportation between rural areas and thematic routes (i.e., wine routes)
- Encourage organization of collaborative events to support cluster formation
- Flatten structure of industry by promoting associations and cluster groups
- Incentivize horizontal linkages
- Provide incentives for external firms to act as co-operators or co-sponsors of rural tourism development

development, the use – or reuse – of the rural environment needs to be carefully conducted in order to prevent the loss of the traditional characteristics that make rural regions distinctive. Da Cunha and Da Cunha (2005) suggested that a region suitable for tourism development should have cultural, natural, and social characteristics that underline its identity, should be accessible, have support services and facilities and follow good marketing strategies. Nonetheless, not all rural regions have the same capabilities and resources to effectively develop, manage, and promote rural tourism. Innovative synergies are required between tourism sectors and across other sectors of the economy. Table 2 provides a set of propositions related to the management and marketing of rural tourist experience.

References

Alegre, J., & Garau, J. (2010). Tourist satisfaction and dissatisfaction. *Annals of Tourism Research*, 37(1), 52–73.

Barke, M. (2004). Rural tourism in Spain. *International Journal of Tourism Research*, 6(3), 137–149.

Binns, T., & Noel, E. (2002). Tourism as a local development strategy in South Africa. *The Geographical Journal*, 168, 235–247.

Bramwell, B. (2004). Mass tourism, diversification and sustainability in Southern Europe's coastal regions. In B. Bramwell (Ed.), *Coastal mass tourism: Diversification and sustainable development in Southern Europe* (pp. 1–31). Clevedon: Channel View Publications.

Bramwell, B., & Lane. (1994). *Rural tourism and sustainable rural development*. Clevedon: Channel View Publications.

Cánoves, G., Villarino, M., Priestley, G. K., & Blanco, A. (2004). Rural tourism in Spain: An analysis of recent evolution. *Geoforum*, 35(6), 755–769.

Cawley, M. (2007). Integrated rural tourism: Concepts and practice. *Annals of Tourism Research*, 35(6), 316–337.

Cloke, P. J. (1977). An index of rurality for England and Wales. *Regional Studies B*, 11, 31–46.

Cyprus Tourism Organisation. (1999). *Annual Report 1999*. Retrieved from www.visitcyprus.biz. Accessed on September 14, 2011.

Da Cunha, S. K., & Da Cunha, J. C. (2005). Tourism cluster competitiveness and sustainability: Proposal for a systemic model to measure the impact of tourism on local development. *Brazilian Administration Review*, 2(2), 47–62.

Devesa, M., Laguna, M., & Palacios, A. (2009). The role of motivation in visitor satisfaction: Empirical evidence in rural tourism. *Tourism Management*, 31, 547–552.

Farmaki, A. (2012). A comparison of the projected and perceived images of Cyprus. *Tourismos*, 7(2), 95–119.

Farmaki, A. (2014). Satisfaction with the rural tourism product of Cyprus. *International Journal of Tourism Policy*, 5(4), 249–268.

Gannon, A. (1994). Rural tourism as a factor in rural community economic development for economies in transition. *Journal of Sustainable Tourism*, 2(1 + 2), 51–60.

Hall, C. M. (2010). *Sustainable rural area tourism: Development and issues.* Conference paper. Retrieved from http://www.edsconference.com/content/docs/ papers/Hall,%20M.pdf. Accessed on November 31, 2012.

Hall, D. (2004). Rural tourism development in south-eastern Europe: transition and the search for sustainability. *International Journal of Tourism Research*, 6, 165–176.

Kastenholz, E. (2000). The market for rural tourism in north and central Portugal: A benefit segmentation approach. In D. Richards & G. Hall (Eds.), *Tourism and sustainable community development* (pp. 268–284). London: Routledge.

Kastenholz, E., Carneiro, M. J., Marques, C. P., & Lima, J. (2012). Understanding and managing the rural tourism experience – The case of a historical village in Portugal. *Tourism Management Perspectives*, 4, 207–224.

Kastenholz, E., & Lima, J. (2011). The integral rural tourism experience from the tourist's point of view: A qualitative analysis of its nature and meaning. *Tourism and Management Studies*, 7, 62–74.

Kommpula, R. (2014). The role of individual entrepreneurs in the development of competitiveness for a rural tourism destination: A case study. *Tourism Management*, 40, 361–371.

Lane, B. (1994). What is rural tourism? *Journal of Sustainable Tourism*, 2(1 + 2), 7–21.

Murdoch, J., & Marsden, T. K. (1994). *Reconstituting rurality: Class community and power in the development process.* London: University College of London Press.

OECD. (1994). *Tourism strategies and rural development, Report.* Retrieved from www.oecd.org/industry/tourism/27555218.pd. Accessed on November 3, 2012.

Page, J., & Getz, D. (1997). *The business of rural tourism.* London: Thomson Business Express.

Park, D. B., & Yoon, Y. S. (2009). Segmentation by motivation in rural tourism: A Korean case study. *Tourism Management*, 30(1), 99–108.

Pedford, J. (1996). Seeing is believing: The role of living history in marketing local heritage. In T. Brewer (Ed.), *The marketing of tradition* (pp. 13–20). Enfiled Lock: Hisarlink Press.

Pena, A. I. P., Jamilena, D. M. F., & Molina, M. A. R. (2012). Validation of cognitive image dimensions for rural tourist destinations: A contribution to the management of rural tourist destinations. *Journal of Vacation Marketing*, 18(24), 261–273.

Ribeiro, M., & Marques, C. (2002). Rural tourism and the development of less favoured areas – between rhetoric and practice. *International Journal of Tourism Research*, 4, 211–220.

Roberts, L., & Hall, D. (2001). *Rural tourism and recreation: Principles to practice*. Wallingford, CT: CABI Publishing.

Ryan, T., Mottiar, Z., & Quinn, B. (2012). The dynamic role of entrepreneurs in destination development. *Tourism Planning and Development*, 9(2), 119–131.

Sharpley, R. (2002). Rural tourism and the challenge of tourism diversification: The case of Cyprus. *Tourism Management*, 23(3), 233–244.

Sharpley, R., & Sharpley, J. (1997). *Rural tourism: An introduction*. Oxford: International Thomson Business Press.

Sharpley, R., & Stone, P. R. (Eds.). (2010). *Tourist experience: Contemporary perspectives*. Abingdon: Routledge.

Tchetchik, A., Fleischer, A., & Finkelshtain, I. (2006). *Rural tourism: Development, public intervention and lessons from the Israeli experience*. Discussion Paper No. 12.06. Retrieved from http://departments.agri.huji.ac.il/economics/en/publications/discussion_papers/2%20006/index.htm. Accessed on October 26, 2013.

Uriely, N. (2005). The tourist experience: Conceptual developments. *Annals of Tourism Research*, 32(1), 199–216.

Waayers, D., Lee, D., & Newsome, D. (2012). 'Exploring the nature of stakeholder collaboration: A case study of marine turtle tourism in the Ningaloo region', Western Australia. *Current Issues in Tourism*, 15(7), 673–692.

Wang, Y., & Krakover, S. (2008). Destination marketing: Competition, cooperation or competition? *International Journal of Contemporary Hospitality Management*, 20(2), 126–141.

Wilson, S., Fesenmaier, D., Fesenmaier, J., & Van Es, J. (2001). Factors for success in rural tourism development. *Journal of Travel Research*, 40, 132–138.

15 Service Innovations and Experience Creation in Spas, Wellness and Medical Tourism

Melanie Kay Smith, Sonia Ferrari and László Puczkó

ABSTRACT

Purpose – The main purpose of this chapter is to analyze the relationship between service innovation and experience creation in the context of spas, wellness and medical tourism. The objectives include providing an overview of service innovation theory and models and applying them to the spa, wellness and medical tourism sectors.

Methodology/approach – Primary research was undertaken with the purpose of identifying the most important elements in the experiences of spa and wellness guests and tourists. An online questionnaire was collected from 17 different types of spa and wellness facilities from 56 countries including all kinds of spa, wellness hotels, and retreats. Information given was based on three major demand segments: local customers, domestic tourists, and international tourists. A case study is also given of Pärnu hospital in Estonia, where innovative practices are being implemented to enhance the patient experience.

Findings – Findings suggested that some aspects of innovation (e.g., design and technology) are not as important as expected, but evidence-based treatments, medical services, and natural and local resources are.

Research limitations/implications – The research gives important insights into customer preferences and current and future trends; however, the research only focused on operator rather than consumer perspectives. This would require further research.

Practical implications – The research findings provide useful information to operators who are trying to create innovative, unique, and competitive customer services.

Originality/value – Existing service innovation models are applied to new sectors (spa, wellness and medical tourism) and new insights are given into how these sectors can increase innovation and enhance customer experiences.

Keywords: Service innovation; experience creation; spas; wellness; medical tourism

Introduction

Wernz, Thakur-Wernz, and Phusavat (2014) suggest that although innovation in the service industries has been an important element in industry, it was not systematically studied until the 1980s. Service innovations in the spa, wellness and medical tourism sectors are especially important because of the inseparable nature of the guest or patient experience. Close interactions with employees (e.g., doctors, therapists) are fundamental. Engen and Magnusson (2015) suggest that interaction represents a focal point for innovating activities and processes (e.g., interaction between client and supplier or hosts and guests). They emphasize the important role of front-line employees in service innovation coupled with the support of middle management. The spa, wellness and medical tourism sectors have become more and more competitive globally in recent years. Competitive advantage usually ensues from service innovation because of improvements in service novelty, quality, and customer satisfaction (Hertog, Van der Aa, & de Jong, 2010). Eisingerich, Rubera, and Seifert (2009) suggest that service innovation management and the relationships between organizations affect the operation of spa businesses and Grissemann, Pikkemaat, and Weger (2013) suggest that innovative hotels (many of which now have spas) are more successful than their non-innovative competitors. One of the most important reasons to innovate in all sectors is to improve the guest or tourist experience, and the spa, wellness and medical tourism sectors are no exception.

Experiences and Innovations in Services

Frequently, in today's experience economy (Pine & Gilmore, 1999) in which customers are always looking for new and memorable consumer experiences, leisure and tourism companies become more and more market-oriented, trying to offer unique and multi-sensory experiences to visitors (Berry, Carbone, & Haeckel, 2002). Health, wellness and medical tourism are services mainly based on highly subjective and intangible elements, with a complete involvement (not only physical and mental, but also emotional, social, or spiritual) of the customer during the consumption experience (Ferrari, Puczkó, & Smith, 2014). For this reason, but also because of the prolonged contact with the customer and the atmosphere, which affects perceptions, the servicescape plays an important role during the delivery process, contributing to create scenic atmospheres that immerse the consumer in experiences (Firat, Dholakia, & Venkatesh, 1995; Shostack, 1977).

Services have specific characteristics that distinguish them from goods. They are intangible and inseparable (meaning that there is no tangible good to buy and to bring home and that for many services the customer must be physically present during the delivery). They are also heterogeneous and variable (namely it is difficult to standardize performances and quality) (Lovelock, 1980; Normann, 2000; Parasuraman, Zeithaml, & Berry, 1985; Shostack, 1977). Services are processes, in which normally during the encounter the customer becomes a co-producer and therefore has a very important role together with front-line personnel. As a consequence of intangibility, it is difficult to describe and promote a service and for clients it is hard to form expectations and evaluate the received service, which creates a certain degree of uncertainty.

There are, however, different degrees of immateriality, depending on the importance of tangible elements (such as equipment and machinery). Intangibility increases the importance of the tangible elements available to the customer as indirect indicators of quality (Aubert-Gamet & Cova, 1998). The search for quality indicators (called by many scholars cues) during the purchasing process is, therefore, challenging and all the material elements, including physical environment, affect the formation of expectations and perceptions. The cues could be color, music and sounds, lighting, space and function, layout and design, artefacts and plants. All of these are especially important in the context of spas, for example. According to Bitner (1992), the physical environment has effects on individual (consumers and personnel) behavior, interactions, cognitive and emotional responses of customers, and level of overall customer satisfaction (Ferrari, 2015). They are an important component of the offer in wellness tourism (Correia Loureiro, Almeida, & Rita, 2013).

To program innovations strategically, managers have to identify the most important cues for their customers. The cues, consciously or unconsciously perceived by the consumer through the sensory system, are contained in all the service components that can be perceived or experienced by customers while in contact with the company. They transmit messages directly or indirectly and can, therefore, be considered as drivers of experience (Carbone, 2004). Cues are mostly found in the physical environment and in the behavior and attitude of the front-line personnel. There are two categories of cues related to consumption experiences: the signals relating to the functionality and reliability of the service offered and those that refer to the emotional experience of consumption (Berry et al., 2002).

A consequence of inseparability of services is perishability. In fact, as production and consumption are simultaneous, it is impossible to store services to make the supply more flexible and adapting it to irregular demand flows. For all of these reasons it appears impossible to speak of innovation in the service sector solely adapting the models used in manufacturing, even if this has been attempted since the 1980s when they began to study service innovation. In those early years, in fact, some researchers decided to study technical innovations in services by means of the same instruments created to understand the production processes of goods (Salter & Tether, 2006; Wernz et al., 2014). However, the first to underline the differences between services and goods production was Barras (1986), who observed that while in manufacturing the innovation pattern is normally focused first on products and later on processes, in services it is the contrary. In fact, in this second case, the earlier emphasis is on delivery processes (often using ICT to improve efficacy) and only subsequently the attention is switched to offered products (trying to improve them through learning and customization activities).

In addition, because of the high degree of heterogeneity in the service sector it is impossible to speak of a unique innovation pattern. Lovelock (1984) created a model that is based on the newness of the offer or of the delivery process. It describes the different categories of new services, distinguishing between radical innovations (new services, start-up businesses and major innovations) and incremental innovations (service line extensions, service improvements, and style changes). However, although the management of new service development (NSD) has become an important competitive element in many service industries (Fitzsimmons & Fitzsimmons, 2000; Johnson, Menor, Roth, & Chase, 2000; Menor, Tatikonda, & Sampon, 2002), it is still among the least studied subjects in service management literature.

Service Innovation in Spas, Wellness and Medical Tourism

Many of the generic models that have been developed for the services sectors can be applied and adapted to the spa, wellness and medical tourism sectors. Table 1 shows how new services can be classified in this field.

Kozak and Gürel (2015) make the point that service innovation improvements are often likely to be small but continuous rather than completely new and radical, especially in the service sector; for example, hospitality, because this approach costs less and is less risky. Service innovations are therefore frequently small and continuous changes to service delivery rather than the creation of totally new services (Hertog et al., 2010; Sundbo, 1997). For this reason, scholars say that in service sectors innovation is incremental more than radical and although more services are becoming standardized and high-tech, the changes will give birth to innovations that can create new markets (Berry, Shankar, Parish, Cadwallader, & Dotzel, 2006). As stated by Berry et al. (2006) innovations creating new markets differ from others in terms of two variables: the type of offered benefit and the degree of service "separability." As for the first aspect, the innovation can be related to the offer of a new core benefit or to

Table 1.   Classification of New Services: Wellness and Spa Examples.

Type of Innovation	Description	Wellness/Spa Examples
Radical innovations		
Major innovation	New services for markets as yet undefined; innovations usually driven by information and computer-based technologies	Introduction of wearable/ hearable technology to health, wellness
Start-up business	New services in a market that is already served by existing services	Creation and introduction of a spa brand for Evian
New services for the market presently served	New service offerings to existing customers of an organization (although the services may be available from other companies)	Healthy food/drink suggestion in a weekly alert to members
Incremental innovations		
Service line extensions	Augmentations of the existing service line such as adding new menu items, new routes, and new courses	Introduction of a spa journey for men (eforea by Hilton).
Service improvements	Changes in features of services that currently are being offered	Introduction of new (e.g., green skincare) brand to the spa menu
Style changes	Modest forms of visible changes that have an impact on customer perceptions, emotions, and attitudes, with style changes that do not change the service fundamentally, only its appearance	Changing the visual brand elements (e.g., SpaFinder)

Source: Adapted from Menor et al. (2002).

a new benefit in the delivery process. The second aspect is related to the degree of "separability," which depends on the need for the customer to be present during the service encounter or not. In fact, some services could be delivered remotely (i.e., online shopping, telemedicine), while for others, such as wellness and spa tourism services, it is impossible. Combining these two dimensions Menor et al. (2002) created a matrix (Figure 1) that managers can use to understand better how and where to invest in innovation to gain a durable competitive advantage. However,

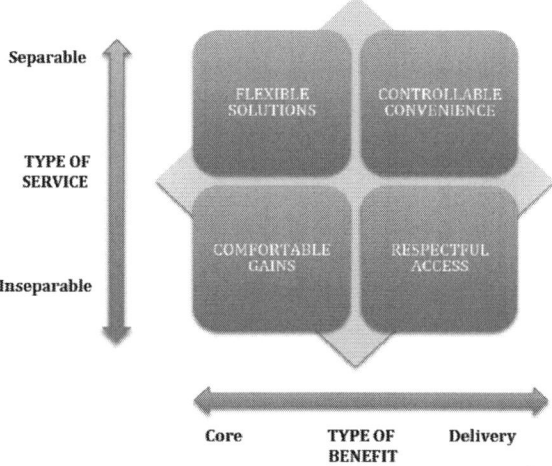

Figure 1. The Four Types of Market-Creating Service Innovations. *Source*: Adapted from Berry et al. (2006).

they have to take into consideration the fact that service innovations are more easily imitated, so they spread more rapidly and, for this reason, normally are less profitable (Boone, 2000).

In the matrix, the "Flexible Solutions" cell represents the case of high separability services and innovations in terms of a new core benefit. In this situation the service can be consumed in a different moment and place from that of production. In the case of the "Controllable Convenience" cell separability is also high, but the innovation is present in the delivery processes creating new markets and offering clients better ways to reach and use the service. Normally these innovations are based on new technologies or a creative design of the delivery process. The cell of "Comfortable Gains" comprises services in which consumption and production are simultaneous and the innovations are focused on a new core benefit. The aim is to provide new experiences to customers with higher quality standards in terms of comfort or emotions, to differentiate the offer. The last cell is that of "Respectful Access." It is related to inseparable services and innovations in terms of a new delivery benefit. In this case the firms know that the customer will be there during the production and consumption processes. These firms show respect for their customers' time and presence, offering easier access, a good layout and location, minimum waiting times, parking, good signage, and more competent, motivated, and empathic contact-personnel.

The spa and wellness industry is not exempt from market innovations that can enhance guest experiences (as well as creating market advantage for service providers). The authors of this chapter adapted the four market-creating service innovations to the wellness and spa industry. There are several good examples that represent the innovative nature of the industry.

In terms of Flexible Solutions the introduction of so-called "wearables" has changed how customers gain the benefits of using the service regardless of where they actually are (e.g., for tourists too). The wearables (as wareable.com, 2016 states) tap into the connected self — they are laden with smart sensors, and make use of a web connection, usually using Bluetooth to connect wirelessly to a smartphone. They use these sensors to connect to a person, and they help them to achieve goals such as staying fit, being active, losing weight, or being more organized This new technology is used primarily in the wellness and fitness world. These wearables collect, monitor, and analyze information and the users are free from the constraints of time and place.

In the domain of Controllable Convenience the wellness and medical world can benefit from several e-health solutions. E-health (according to WHO, 2016) is the transfer of health resources and healthcare by electronic means, for example, E-health portals like eHealth Ontario (2016). E-health from the customers' perspective has several areas such as the delivery of health information for health consumers (and health professionals). E-health can improve public health services in general and at personal level. E-health solutions can provide users with the freedom of having access to health, wellness-related information and recommendations anytime they look for them (including on holiday). Another example is a wellness center (e.g., in hotels) that are open 24/7. These provide guests with the flexibility that business guests especially appreciate.

The wellness and spa world has been creating more and more experiences that can be categorized as Comfortable Gains. Signature treatments or fusion services are essential elements of creating unique and competitive brand and customer experiences. The 2015 IWSTM data (as discussed in more depth in the latter part of this chapter) showed that every third wellness and spa facility has already created at least one signature treatment or service (TOHWS, 2015). Most of these treatments are tailor-made for the guest or co-created involving the guest actively in the delivery, thus enhancing the guest experience to the maximum. The data considered many cases from Asia, where wellness and spa providers created so-called "Myspa experiences" which are tailor-made, special massages and treatments which are delivered in the guests' own villas. Spa therapists are exploring how guests can take an active role in the service delivery, for example, providing alternatives for scents, music or oils to be used for a specific treatment. Guests can decide which of the various alternatives they prefer for the selected treatment.

The Respectful Access innovation category also contains examples from the wellness and spa world. The rather successful US company Massage Envy introduced a compelling value proposition to prospective clients. The massage salons were located in strip malls. Thus, the service moved to the location where the potential clients are already and with competitive pricing strategies (e.g., standard memberships) could make the benefits of regular massages available and accessible both to traditional as well as new segments. Another example was the Urban Massage company (London, the United Kingdom), which offered short massages to men, but not at salons or spas but where men tend to be, that is, in pubs!

Health, wellness and medical tourism enterprises generally offer highly inseparable services. In the last decades, companies in these sectors were looking for innovations creating new markets both in terms of new core and delivery benefits. In fact, these are mature and saturated markets often in the last stage of their life cycle. Traditional sauna visits in certain countries, such as Germany or Austria could be considered saturated services. The innovation here therefore was the incorporation of entertainment and shows to sauna visits (e.g., Wellness and Spa Resort Quellenhof in South Tirol). Now, the entertainment factor (e.g., Aufguss or sauna ceremonies) is an essential element to most sauna worlds in these countries. Sauna masters even compete at the European Sauna Master Championships, which are held in spa resorts. However, it is still necessary to try to develop even further and to look for new customers and markets through service and delivery innovations. Today, when studying these industries, it is possible to see that innovations had significant effects in both directions, moving towards an enlargement of the range of offered services, a quality improvement, a higher level of customer satisfaction through new ways of delivering existing services, the creation of new markets with innovative offers, and the attraction of new clients, also by means of technological innovations. The incorporation of local elements (e.g., natural assets, herbs, stones, etc.) to the wellness or spa provision is currently one common form of innovation. For example, adding ginseng to thermal waters is one of the ways thermal facilities in South Korea translate the innovation to their guests. In the South Korean culture and tradition ginseng has several favorable qualities which then being combined with thermal water creates a rather special and memorable guest experience.

Deesomlert and Sawmong (2013) undertook research on spas in Thailand. The findings revealed that market orientation factors, service orientation factors, organizational factors, and service innovation factors were factors influencing the business performance of spas for health in Thailand. They found that market orientation factors were the most important, followed by service orientation factors, organizational factors and service innovation factors, respectively. Regarding service innovation, the executives interviewed in their research mentioned giving superior customer benefit as the most important, followed by continuous operational innovation, customer experience management, investment in employee performance, and price competition/affordability. They stated that the findings were consistent with the research of Berry et al. (2006). They found that service innovation was a combination of technology innovation, business model innovation, organizational social innovation, and demand innovation in added value in the aspect of services and creating new service systems. In addition, their findings are also consistent with the findings of Eisingerich et al. (2009), who studied service innovation management and the relationship between the organizations affecting business performance.

Berry et al. (2006) suggest that medical services are a prime example of where service innovation is extremely important. The reasons they give are because service delivery staff are central to the customer experience; secondly, the customer has to be physically present; thirdly, there is usually no tangible product or brand name attached. The exception may be branded spa products (e.g., cosmetics) or famous hotel chains with spas. Healthcare is typically an inseparable service and Berry et al. (2006) give the example of transforming a hospital emergency room (ER) experience into a calmer and more comforting one by improving the waiting room, facilitating patient registration, using electronic information boards, etc. Wu (2013) suggests that hospitals need to take more inspiration from hotels enhancing not only the physical environment and design, but also the service quality. This can include hotel-like rooms and catering, welcoming lobbies, social, communal and green spaces, as well as concierge or guest services. He suggests that spas and wellness centers could also be located in hospitals to offer a variety of benefits to many user groups or organizations. This can optimize patient healing, as well as providing treatments for employees, for example. Wernz et al. (2014) quote the example of Bumrangrad International Hospital in Bangkok, Thailand as an example of a hospital that has adopted practices which are usually found only in hospitality and other service sectors. This includes the customer experience for non-medical services (e.g., food, shops, and accommodation). The case study below gives the example of Pärnu Hospital in Estonia, which is especially innovative and is also starting to attract medical tourists as well as local resident patients.

Case Study: Pärnu Hospital, Estonia

It was just recently (last century) when hospitals were terrifying places for the patients with blank gray walls and long empty hallways. Medical personnel were dressed in white and unknown activities were going on behind closed doors and operating rooms. The whole atmosphere was not welcoming and calming, instead it added stress to the worrying patient. Luckily, innovative visionaries started to see that hospitals can no longer proceed like that, things have to change.

The modern concept of a hospital is to make patients feel more like at home in a somewhat welcoming place which supports the healing process rather than making the condition even worse. Foundation Pärnu Hospital is one of the excellent examples from Estonia where creation of a welcoming atmosphere is a major part of the customer journey. How is this done? Firstly, the need for doing so has to be defined, recognized and accepted by the managing board and only then can it be carried out by employees in charge of PR and all the others. Actually, the main reason people are in healthcare is their willingness to help and provide good care for the ones in need.

Modern hospitals provide services that help the customers take care of themselves before they get sick and need to see

(continued)

a doctor. For this purpose, Pärnu Hospital has opened just recently a Rehabilitation and Well-Being Center, where one can enjoy the calming and soothing effect of water therapies and exercise their body with professional physiotherapists and trainers. They can calm their mind in a relaxation room while sitting in a massage chair and enjoy the positive effects of light therapy.

When talking about a hospital, concerts and educational exhibitions are not the first activities that come to mind, but this is exactly what is done in Pärnu Hospital. Customers come to the hospital usually with some health problem and while waiting for their appointment they have an amazing chance to enjoy a wide variety of arts exhibitions. We are collaborating with different embassies whose photo exhibitions are taking our customers on a journey to different countries, may it be China, Hungary, Sweden, the United States or Austria. In addition to that, we collaborate with local and international artists, whose work touches the hearts of many. Over the span of one year we have had more than twenty exhibitions in four different areas of the hospital.

Concerts, dance shows and different plays in the main entrance foyer and our conference room bring joy and musical experiences and help to forget about problems even for 30 minutes. Usually, there are more than thirty performances in a year. Last year, one of the most popular and fascinating concerts was a Tibetan yogi's mantra concert. On a regular day, there is always calming music playing in the background as part of the musical therapy.

The above mentioned cannot be carried out without people, who are the most important resource in healthcare. It is truly vital that most of the employees understand the main idea and the concept of a modern hospital where patients are more like customers with whom we collaboratively take care of their health and well-being.

(Case study by Errit Kuldkepp, Marketing Specialist, Pärnu Hospital, 2016)

Borg, Gratzer, and Ljungbo (2014) state that a consequence of increased competition in global medical tourism is the need to specialize in hospitals, clinics, and medical research institutes. Innovation is described as being different from invention, as it also includes seeing how new ideas come into use through actual implementation. This might involve interconnections between activities, organizations, research, development, production and marketing, as well as between producers and end users. Innovation in the medical sector can be a lengthy process because of safety and regulation, as well as funding for research or new technology. So-called "smart specialization" is advocated as an approach for increasing competitiveness in the international medical tourism arena. Midtkandal and Sörvik (2012) describe smart specialization as "a strategic approach to economic development through targeted support for research and innovation. It involves a process of developing a vision, identifying the place-based areas of greatest strategic potential, developing multi-stakeholder governance mechanisms, setting strategic priorities and using smart policies to maximize the knowledge-based development potential of a region" (p. 1).

RESEARCH DATA ON SPAS, WELLNESS AND MEDICAL TOURISM EXPERIENCES

As mentioned earlier in the chapter, data was collected in 2014 by the authors for the Tourism Observatory for Health Wellness and Spa (published in 2015) in order to identify the role tourism and tourists play at various spa and wellness facilities worldwide. Data was collected from 17 different types of spa and wellness facilities from 56 countries. (e.g., including all kinds of spa, wellness hotels, and retreats). An online questionnaire was distributed using an existing database of co-operating industry partner associations, chains, and individual operators. Information was collected from three major demand segments: local customers, domestic tourists, and international tourists. The whole data set is not presented here, but instead those parts that are most relevant to spa and wellness service innovation and tourist experiences. This data can give important insights into which types of innovation are the most important from different points of view, for example, that of clients and that of managers, and to understand if there is a gap and if so, what type? Such data is useful to inform operators of trends in customer preferences and can be essential to service innovation and experience creation in the future. In fact, in many cases, managers do not have a clear vision of their customers' expectations and levels of satisfaction referring to the various elements of offered services in terms of core benefits and delivering processes. For this reason, sometimes they invest in elements that are less important than others for the customers and less effective in terms of competitiveness. It could be an interesting starting point for future in-depth research on this subject.

One of the most interesting findings from this research concerns motivations of the tourists. Treatments remain the most important motivation for international guests. Location is also a relevant factor for international/foreign guests. Somewhat

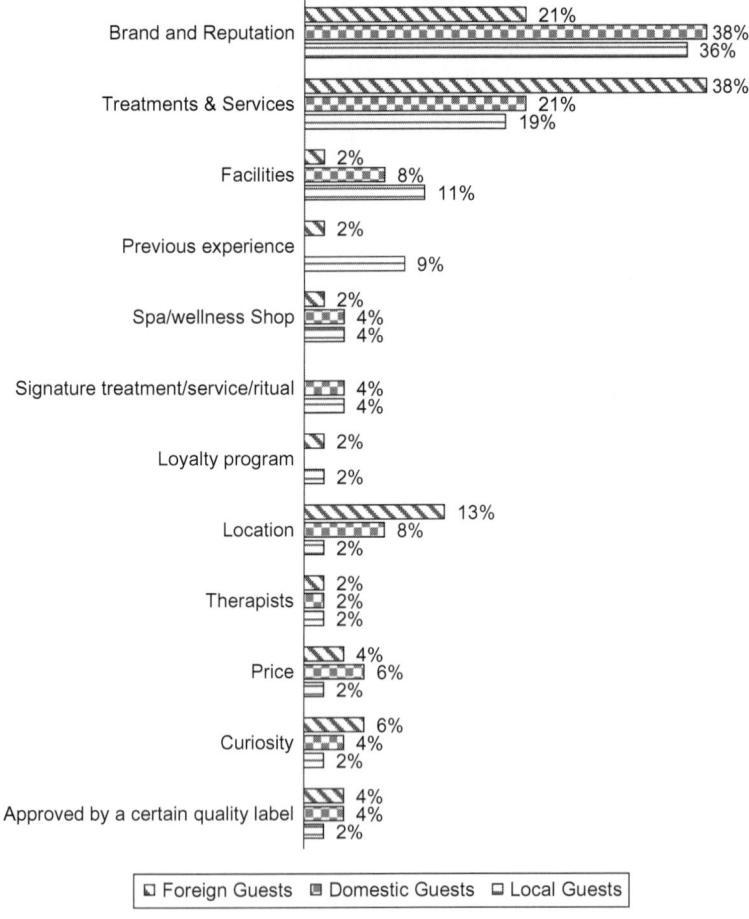

Figure 2. Motivations of Spa and Wellness Guests.

unexpectedly, technology, design, or fashion have no real impact on motivation and decision making. This is a very telling finding since many facilities keep investing large sums into technology/ equipment and/or design in the hope of attracting more guests (Figure 2).

There are relatively few differences between the three guest groups when popular services were asked about. Massages were the most popular services on offer in wellness and spa facilities. International guest data showed an interest in medical services at wellness and spa facilities. Lifestyle-oriented services are also popular (Figure 3).

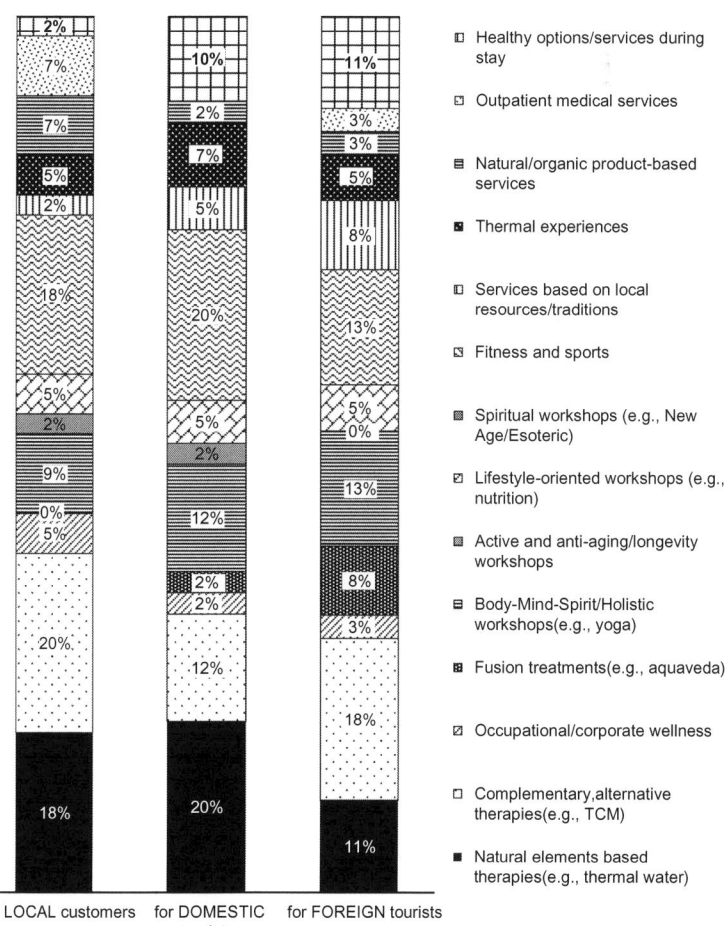

Figure 3. Most Popular Services in Spas and Wellness Centers.

In cases where spa and wellness services are not the core service, it is important to consider which guest services can be packaged with spa and wellness. Weddings/honeymoons, beach, or golf have traditionally been common complementary services, as well as skiing packages in winter. It can be seen from Figure 4 that several other services are also popular, such as cultural activities or adventure.

Signature treatments and services are essential elements of creating unique and competitive brands and customer experiences. More than a third of the respondents from spas and wellness facilities have already created at least one signature treatment or service (Figure 5).

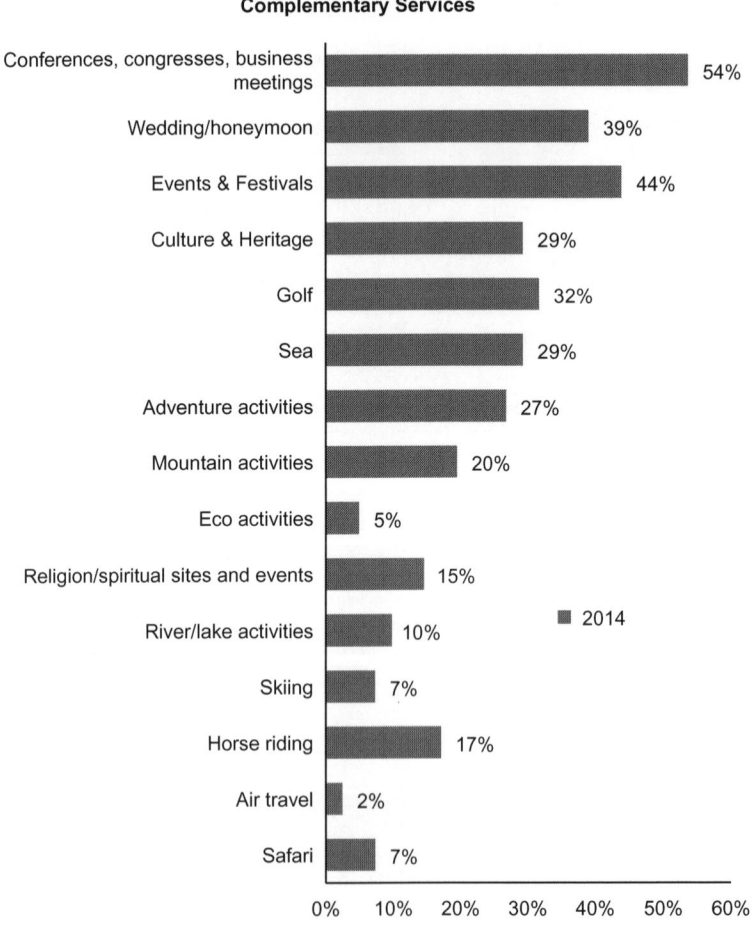

Figure 4. Complementary Products and Services.

Africa	Very diversified: rituals, massages, detox treatments based on local ingredients
The Americas	Mainly rituals, based on global brands, plus energizing massages, welcome packages Mud treatments Ayurvedic treatments
Asia	Mainly complex rituals (e.g. wraps, massages, scrubs, facials). My spa experiences (special massage, treatments in own villas), as well as energizing treatments based on local products and specialities. Luxury services, e.g., pearl powder
Australia/New Zealand	Mud and bath therapies based on local resources as well as underwater massages Indigenous Aboriginal massage techniques
Europe	Local resources in treatments: Amber, thermal water, mud, Nordic plants Holistic treatments: co-listening
Middle-East	Local traditions incorporated: Camomile, mint

Figure 5. Signature Treatments by Region.

There is a clear shift in the market to natural resources with proven impacts and evidence (Figure 6).

It can be seen from this data that there were a few surprises even for the operators of spas and wellness services, who might have imagined that some aspects of innovation (e.g., design and technology) would be more important for the creation of guest experiences. Although most facilities have developed signature treatments, they do not seem to be as popular with guests as operators imagined. Although massages are still the most popular service, guests may not be inclined to try out new types of signature massages, especially if they are significantly more expensive. On the other hand, operators may not have anticipated that evidence-based medical services and natural and local resources and therapies would become so popular, as well as lifestyle and holistic services. This information gives important insights into customer preferences and current and future trends, which is essential for operators trying to create innovative, unique, and competitive customer services.

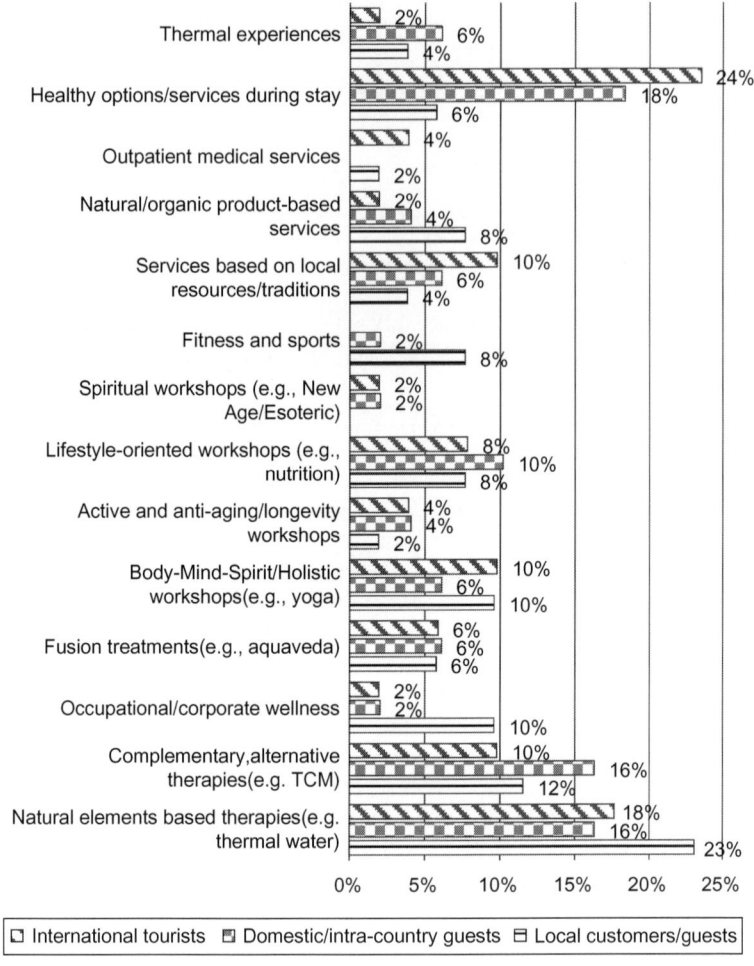

Figure 6.   Services Becoming Popular in Spas and Wellness Facilities.

Conclusion

The inseparable nature of the spa, wellness and medical tourism sectors means that it is especially important to consider service innovation in the creation of guest experiences. Treatments and therapies depend on close interaction with healthcare practitioners and therapists, and they are essential to the quality of the service delivery. More recent models of delivery include strong elements of co-creation with tailor-made packages and treatments. "Comfortable gains" mean that customers are more and more involved in their own experience creation. Although the research data suggested that technology might not be as important as operators imagined, "flexible solutions" (e.g., wearables) are becoming more and more sophisticated and can easily be used on holiday as well as at home. "Controllable convenience" also means that tourists are never far from specific medical advice, even when away from home. There are also significant efforts being made to make the medical experience more comfortable and less anxiety-inducing. The servicescape can be of considerable importance for spas, wellness and medical facilities, and even though the research data suggested that design may not be as important as operators thought, the atmosphere of spas and wellness facilities depends very much on highly subjective and intangible elements such as design, light, color, scent, and music. Although Deesomlert and Sawmong's (2013) research on spas suggested that service innovation factors are not as important as market orientation factors, service orientation factors or organizational factors, it can be seen from this chapter that service innovation nevertheless play an extremely significant role in the (co)creation of spas, wellness and medical tourist experiences.

References

Aubert-Gamet, V., & Cova, B. (1998). Servicescape: From modern non-places to postmodern common places. *Journal of Business Research*, 44, 37–45.

Barras, R. (1986). Towards a theory of innovation in services. *Research Policy*, 15(4), 161–173.

Berry, L. L., Carbone, L. P., & Haeckel, S. H. (2002). Managing customer experience. *MIT Sloan Management Review*, 43(3), 85–89.

Berry, L. L., Shankar, V., Parish, J. T., Cadwallader, S., & Dotzel, T. (2006). Creating new markets through service innovation. *MIT Sloan Management Review*, 47(2), 56–63.

Bitner, M. J. (1992). Servicescapes: The impact of physical surroundings on customers and employees. *Journal of Marketing*, 56(April), 57–71.

Boone, T. (2000). Exploring the link between product and process innovation in services. In J. A. Fitzsimmons & M. J. Fitzsimmons (Eds.), *Service development. Creating memorable experiences* (pp. 92–110). London: Sage.

Borg, E. A., Gratzer, K., & Ljungbo, K. (2014). Innovation and specialization strategies in medical tourism: Evidences from Europe. *4th annual international conference on business strategy and organizational behaviour*. GSTF, 47–50.

Carbone, L. P. (2004). *Clued in: How to keep customers coming back again and again.* Upper Saddle River, NJ: FT Prentice Hall.

Correia Loureiro, S. M., Almeida, M., & Rita, P. (2013). The effect of atmospheric cues and involvement on pleasure and relaxation: The spa hotel context. *International Journal of Hospitality Management, 35,* 35−43.

Deesomlert, S., & Sawmong, S. (2013). Factors influencing service innovation and business performance of spa for health in Thailand: Empirical study. *International Journal of Business, Marketing, and Decision Sciences, 6*(1), 136−156.

eHealth Ontario. (2016). Retrieved from https://www.ehealthontario.ca/portal/server.pt/community/home/3090. Accessed on February 14.

Eisingerich, A. B., Rubera, G., & Seifert, M. (2009). Managing service innovation and interorganizational relationships for firm performance to commit or diversify? *Journal of Service Research, 11,* 344−356.

Engen, M., & Magnusson, P. (2015). Exploring the role of frontline employees as innovators. *The Service Industries Journal, 35*(6), 303−324.

Ferrari, S. (2015). Experiential tourist products: The role of servicescape. In N. Ryan (Ed.), *Emerging innovative marketing strategies in the tourism industry* (pp. 211−230). Hershey, PA: IGI Global.

Ferrari, S., Puczkó, L., & Smith, M. (2014). Co-creating spa customer experience. In J. Kandampully (Ed.), *Customer experience management: Enhancing experience and value through service management* (pp. 187−203). Dubuque, IA: Kendall Hunt.

Firat, A. F., Dholakia, N., & Venkatesh, A. (1995). Marketing in a postmodern world. *European Journal of Marketing, 29*(1), 40−56.

Fitzsimmons, J. A., & Fitzsimmons, M. J. (Eds.). (2000). *Service development. Creating memorable experiences.* London: Sage.

Grissemann, U. S., Pikkemaat, B., & Weger, C. (2013). Antecedents of innovation activities in tourism: An empirical investigation of the alpine hospitality industry. *Tourism, 61*(1), 7−27.

Hertog, P. D., Van der Aa, W., & de Jong, M. W. (2010). Capabilities for managing service innovation: Towards a conceptual framework. *Journal of Service Management, 21*(4), 490−514.

Johnson, S. P., Menor, L. J., Roth, A. V., & Chase, R. B. (2000). A critical evaluation of the new service development process: Integrating service innovation and service design. In J. A. Fitzsimmons & M. J. Fitzsimmons (Eds.), *Service development. Creating memorable experiences* (pp. 1−32). London: Sage.

Kozak, M. A., & Gürel, D. A. (2015). Service design in hotels: A conceptual review. *Tourism Review, 63*(2), 225−240.

Lovelock, C. H. (1980). Towards a classification of services. In C. Lamb & P. Dunne (Eds.), *Theoretical developments in marketing* (pp. 72−76). Chicago, IL: American Marketing.

Lovelock, C. H. (1984). Developing and implementing new services. In W. R. George & C. E. Marshall (Eds.), *Developing new services* (pp. 44−64). Chicago, IL: American Marketing Association.

Menor, L. J., Tatikonda, M. V., & Sampon, S. E. (2002). New service development: Areas for exploitation and exploration. *Journal of Operations Marketing*, *20*, 135−157.

Midtkandal, I., & Sörvik, J. (2012). What is smart specialisation? *Nordregio News Issue 5*. Retrieved from http://www.nordregio.se/en/Metameny/Nordregio-News/2012/Smart-Specialisation/Context. Accessed on January 20, 2016.

Normann, R. (2000). *Service management: Strategy and leadership in service business* (3rd ed.). Chichester: Wiley.

Parasuraman, A., Zeithaml, V. A., & Berry, L. L. (1985). A conceptual model of service quality and its implications for future research. *Journal of Marketing*, *49*(4), 41−50.

Pine, B., & Gilmore, J. (1999). *The experience economy: Work is theatre & every business stage*. Boston, MA: Harvard Business School Press.

Salter, A., & Tether, B. S. (2006). *Innovation in services through the looking glass of innovation studies*. Background paper for Advanced Institute of Management (AIM) Research's Grand Challenge on Service Science.

Shostack, G. L. (1977). Breaking free from product marketing. *Journal of Marketing*, *41*(April), 73−80.

Sundbo, J. (1997). Management of innovation in services. *The Service Industries Journal*, *17*(3), 432−455.

TOHWS. (2015). International wellness & spa tourism monitor. TOHWS. Retrieved from https://drive.google.com/file/d/0Bzev74rN3_ysdUVHWlRHRzJn WDhPZjRrOERRR2ltaE1rNE1Z/view?pli=1. Accessed on February 14, 2016.

Wareable.com/. (2016). Retrieved from http://www.wareable.com/wearable-tech/what-is-wearable-tech-753. Accessed on February 14.

Wernz, C., Thakur-Wernz, P. T., & Phusavat, K. (2014). Service convergence and service integration in medical tourism. *Industrial Management & Data Systems*, *114*(7), 1094−1106.

WHO. (2016). *E-Health*. Retrieved from http://www.who.int/trade/glossary/story021/en/. Accessed February 14.

Wu, Z. (2013). The application of hospitality elements in hospitals. *Journal of Healthcare Management*, *58*(1), 47−62.

Part III
Marketing: Communicating and Promoting Tourism Experiences

Aim: to approach and analyze the marketing
function within the same or other contexts
and/or industries

16 The Role of Online Social Media on the Experience and Communication of Gay Events in a Tourist Destination: A Case Study of a Small-Scale Film Festival in Nice

S. Christofle, C. Papetti and M. Ferry

ABSTRACT

Purpose – To know the role of online social media (OSM) on the experience and communication of a gay film festival (ZeFestival) in a tourist destination: Nice, France

Methodology/approach – Literature review accompanied with a qualitative study and netnographic analysis.

Findings – Informs on the use of OSMs by both organizers and festival goers, with a much poorer involvement of stakeholders than was envisaged. Proposes avenues for finding the causes of this lack of communication and sharing of the online experience.

Research limitations/implications – An exploratory study of a single gay film festival. The research work should be extended to other gay cultural events in Nice and France as a whole.

Practical implications – Recommendations for online experience sharing and communication before, during, and after the event.

Originality/value – This theme has been hardly broached on an international scale and never in a French context.

Keywords: Cultural gay event; online communication; touristic destination; online experience

Introduction

The gay population's average income is 59% higher than that of heterosexuals.[1] Consequently, the marketing sector is increasingly interested in the gay community, even though the latter is a minority community that is difficult to target. To do so, some territories are developing policies aimed at this target, banking on accommodation, places to go out and events.

Lesbians, gays, bi, and trans (LGBT)[2] events and places to go out are "coming out into the open," as explained by Leobon (2006), and are nowadays intended for everyone, whether residents or tourists. Thus, numerous territories, and in particular a number of international tourist destinations, organize or sponsor gay events in order to provide the ferments of an experience, secure a welcoming image, and increase the positive effects as regards a "gay-friendly" image.

---

[1]2012 figures: 51,000€/year against 32000€/year http://www.atlantico.fr/decryptage/51-000-euros-salaire-moyen-gay-superieur-celui-hetero-timetosignoff-331114.html
[2]Lesbian, Gay, Bisexual, and Transgender.

Yet, despite the interest for a destination to promote such events, we observe that, although a number of studies have been devoted to gay tourism and its various forms and spatial diffusion (Jaurand & Leroy, 2011; Jaurand, 2010; Venske, 2015; Waitt & Markwell, 2006), the theme of gay event-organizing is either less developed or focused on sports (the Gay Games, Krane & Waldron, 2000) and festive events (gay prides, queer carnivals, Waitt & Markwell, 2006). Few studies are devoted to gay cultural events.

Furthermore, although reflections on the online experience of a destination are on the increase (Milano, 2010), such literature rarely takes into account the experience of an event via online media and its role on the event's real-life experience. The experience during an event is physical: encounter, emotion, even body (dancing, singing, sport …) but in recent years the online experience has been added. Moreover, gays are keen users of online social media (OSM): indeed, the virtual sphere is a space that enables a community with affinities to interact and discuss whilst benefitting from anonymity and the respect of private life with neither fear nor taboo; Cooper et al. (1999) talk about triple A for "Anonymous, Affordable and Accessible." The issue of the use of the internet and OSM by homosexuals has been studied mainly in regard to dating where the virtual character of exchanges helps to release inhibitions, to cybersex, double-dealing processes, and those of identity retranslation (Filluzeau, 2002). However, we consider that these studies can be applied to encounters in general terms and to encounters at events.

The issue that we intend to develop concerns the role of OSM on the promotion and real-life experience of gay cultural events and its possible repercussions on the image of the host territory. We chose to study the subject in Nice, which sets itself up as a gay-friendly town and a place of gay tourism, and we'll take a more specific interest into the gay and lesbian film festival, ZeFestival.

This theme leads us to raise a number of questions:

– Can a gay film festival foster an experience related to the internet and more particularly to OSMs? What would be the main objectives of such online communication: to inform, debate, share the experience?
– In Nice, a world famous tourist town, could there be a location effect? Would the town's demographic and functional characteristics influence the intensity and sharing of an

experience connected both with the homosexual community and culture? Conversely, does the real-life experience of the festival and its sharing on OSMs influence the perception of the destination's image?

Literature Review

GAY CULTURAL EVENTS AND GAY FILM FESTIVALS

An increasing number of research works is devoted to event-organizing (Christofle & Ferry, 2016; Getz & Page, 2016). Gay event-organizing is often analyzed through large-scale festive, playful, sports and tourist events, for example, the homosexual "bandas" at the Rio de Janeiro carnival (Gontijo, 2004). Nowadays, gay events are increasingly considered as contributing to turning a "stigmata" into a social and spatial resource, notably in the sector of tourism (Melián-González, Moreno-Gil, & Araña, 2011). Some authors are studying places with either a gay identity or appropriated by gays, in environments as different as Paris,[3] Montréal,[4] Santiago,[5] and Cape Town[6] ... (Astudillo Lizama, 2014; Giraud, 2013; Leroy, 2010; Venske, 2015). Taking part in a gay event, in developed and democratic countries, can also be part of both a group and individual experience for nonhomosexuals, sympathizers, or merely people attracted by the event's merry and playful aspect (Waitt & Markwell, 2006). There are also gay cultural events which are less "visible" because they are less exuberant and festive, but which are worth studying because they give an interesting outlook on the gay event experience. These are events referring to an asserted and assumed homosexual culture via, among others, gay film festivals which started in the years 1980.

The definition of a festival as given by Getz (2010) underlines human interactions as the core of the experience. Such experience is at the same time personal and social. Festival designers are particularly interested in the way human interactions influence participants and how to succeed in obtaining that such relational expectations be assuaged in order to give the event and Matheson (2005) speak of authentic experiences and of "emerging

---

[3]France.
[4]Canada.
[5]Chile.
[6]South Africa.

authenticity." This observation is shared by MacCannell (1973): in fact, festivals can be considered in terms of artistic characteristics with an increasingly omnipresent social component. Then the festival goer's experience is not to do with music, films or theater, but is above all social. Festivals appear to include the concept of *gregariousness* (Crompton & McKay, 1997) with a "known-group socialization" phenomenon, or socialization with an undifferentiated and *a priori* unknown public. Festival goers seem to first identify with the event itself: "festivals encapsulate identity, in terms of the nation state, a sense of place, and the personal and heterogeneous identities of a people" (Matheson, 2005). A festival can be seen as a particular and atypical social context in which different individuals understand, accept, and share common values. Therefore, festival goers would be eager to become actors of that social theater. They would negotiate among themselves a number of standards and values based either on customs or on tradition and expressed in a physical or conceptual manner (Bruner & Kirshenblatt-Gimblett, 1994).

This is an interesting point in so far as social media are based on such socialization: individuals meet over shared values and, free from constraints of time and space, develop communities of similar people sharing these values, and reasons to be together. Thus festivals are real destinations where people go to share common values and a collective objective whilst developing relations with similar individuals. Therefore, one can easily presume that OSM play an *a priori* not insignificant role in how a festival works. This is what we now intend to test out.

THE ROLE OF OSMs ON THE EXPERIENCE OF A GAY FILM FESTIVAL

Among the different typologies that have been proposed we have selected the one from Kaplan and Haenlein (2010) because it classifies social media according to their social presence/media richness and self-presentation/self-disclosure.

These criteria lead to a social media classification:

- Social networking sites (e.g., Facebook, LinkedIn)
- Blogs
- Content communities (YouTube, Flicker, Scribd, Slideshare, Delicious)
- Collaborative projects (Wikipedia, Wikitravel)
- Social worlds (Second Life)
- Virtual games (World of Warcraft).

Fotis, Buhalis, and Rossides (2012) added microblogs (i.e., Twitter), consumer reviews and rating websites (i.e., TripAdvisor, Epinions), and internet fora (i.e., ThornTree, Fodor's Travel Talk).

The reach of the media, accelerated by digital technology, enables people to live an experience from home, without leaving their everyday lives (Uriely, 2005). Urry (2001) thus argues: "The development of computer-assisted mediation tools has caused a compression of time and space, enabling people to experience tourist activities by using several modes of travel: physical, virtual or imaginary." Several authors then demonstrate that activities connected to social media are already part of the experience (Tussyadiah & Fesenmaier, 2009) and modify it.

OSMs, characterized by their rapidity, convenience, anonymity, and virtual nature, are digital tools which are particularly effective for developing social movements in the consumer sector (Neveu, 2010). They make it possible to spread information quickly and on a large scale several weeks ahead of the event and to develop the necessary relations to mobilize a sufficient number of people (Grappin-Schmitt, 2010; Neveu, 2010). A certain form of connectivity is necessary to find and coordinate individuals, and include among others a good use of OSMs (Neveu, 2010).

The diffusion and mediation tools constitute the very message? The aim is not to communicate something but to communicate with somebody, which is exactly the purpose of a festival as defined above. Thus, the aim on social media which is to virtually communicate with the "other," that "other" who shares common values, is the same as in a festival where communication with the other, the link with the other, are achieved in a real place and space. Music, art, and cinema are pretexts for a further quest which is to go toward the other, to meet that person who is different from self and shares a common objective. Social media also enable virtual communities to meet over a shared objective: enabling people to communicate, exchange views, and debate. So, we can easily suppose that social media contribute to that same quest for a common objective.

Furthermore, the social proximity achieved online continues in the physical world (Glassey & Pfister, 2004), because virtual communities create opportunities to meet: theme evenings etc. Even though they do not allow to totally free oneself from spatial and cultural constraints, they often work as catalysts for encounters. Thus we can conclude that OSMs are tools that develop in festival communication.

Our working hypotheses are as follows:

(1) One presumes that OSMs are much used at a gay festival held in a tourist town which is involved in the contemporary digital development. How intense is online communication in regard to this festival? What are its main objectives? What role does it play (or not) in the experience of the event?
(2) We can thus formulate a second hypothesis on the possible role of communication on the way the tourist destination, Nice, is perceived. Is there an influence of the online communication on the perception of the venue via the festival or does such perception remain essentially offline?

Methodology

FIELD OF THE STUDY

To answer these questions, we studied a small-scale film festival. At present, two gay film festivals are held in Nice every year: the In&Out festival and ZeFestival. The latter is organized by the Polychromes association, an association of volunteers whose objective goes far beyond event organizing. Indeed, Polychromes is a cultural association[7] created in 2006. This association intends to "promote all forms of culture by or for lesbians, gays, bi, and trans (LGBT) by opening to society as a whole and by doing so, spread the positive and assumed identity of homosexuality and gender issues."[8] In addition to the film festival, Polychromes organizes various activities focused on singing, theater, discovering the Alpes-Maritimes heritage, etc. In 2008, Polychromes launched in Nice the first LGBT film festival on the French Riviera, which in 2012 became ZEFESTIVAL and now screens its films in the whole region, from Nice to Marseille and Toulon. The festival takes place every year from end September to mid-October and includes previews, national releases, and previously never released films, with meetings/debates with national and international directors, actors, and lecturers (lgbt.zefestival. fr). The festival attracts a yearly average of 2,000–3,000 people

---

[7]200 members.
[8]http://www.polychromes.fr/index.php?option=com_content&view= article&id=2&Itemid=6. Consulted on January 13, 2016.

and is sponsored by community, cultural, and institutional[9] partners. Although the festival has recently been spreading in the
Provence-Alpes-Côte-d'Azur region, most events are held in Nice,
a Mecca of tourism, leisure, and events (Christofle, 2014). Nice is
the capital of a vast event and tourist continuum, the Côte
d'Azur, which welcomes an annual 11 million tourists spending
5 billion euros during their stay and accounting for 77 million
hotel nights in 2014 (CRT Riviera, 2016)[10] and which is our field
of study. Moreover, the town where the festival takes place is of
particular interest for the study of OSMs. Indeed, in February
2015, Nice has been listed in the World's Top 5 of *Smart Cities*
and in 2015 opened a "Smart City Innovation Center," a collaborative platform which is unique in France and brings together
researchers, universities, and companies. The Côte d'Azur's digital sector is developing in an environment which is favorable to
innovation and the use of digital networks. Actually, digital technology at the service of tourism is one of the town's priorities;
the "e-tourism and mobility" component is one of five key sectors of strategic activities to be developed.

METHODOLOGICAL APPROACH: QUALITATIVE STUDY AND NETNOGRAPHIC ANALYSIS

To our knowledge, no empirical study has been carried out on
the role of OSMs in the organization and real-life experience of a
gay community cultural event and its possible effects on the
perception of the destination's gay image. Moreover, the rare
existing studies have been carried out in the United States and we
have no data on the subject in a French context. We wish to
show how the festival participants and its organizers used OSMs
to inform or bring acquaintances, and how they perceived

---

[9]ARC-LGBT (Acteurs Réseau Culturel): Réseau Francophone des
Acteurs Culturels LGBT of which Polychromes is a founding member,
ATCA (Association des Transgenre de la Côte d'Azur) CFdT, F3C-côte
d'Azur, the LGBTI Alpes maritimes relay of the Amnesty International
association, the LGBTI Bouches du Rhône relay of the Amnesty
International association, Association héliotrope Nice, visual artist
Patrick Moya, the BELLADONNA 9Ch group, the Centre LGBT Côte
d'Azur, lle Muséa, Les méduses Nice, on one side and on the other:
Ville de Nice, Ville de Marseille, Conseil Départemental des Alpes-
Maritimes, lConseil Régional Provence–Alpes-Côte d'Azur.
[10]http://cms.cotedazur-tourisme.com/userfiles/file/ChiffresCles2014.pdf,
consulted on January 13, 2016.

whatever communication on the event already existed in OSMs. Also, we want to understand whether the OSMs perceived real-life experience has an impact on the perceived image of the tourist destination.

We chose to first carry out a qualitative study based on semi-directive individual interviews, a method which is particularly adapted to an exploratory study. Those interviewed during the event were living the experience at the same time as they were asked questions.

We interviewed 39 participants: 21 men, 16 women, a trans-sexual, and a person describing itself as "in-between." The average age is 49.[11] All live in the Nice area, except from a man from Paris and another from Monaco (Table 1).

We completed this qualitative survey with a netnographic analysis. The interest is that "netnography provides marketing researchers with a window into naturally occurring behaviors, such as search for information by, and communal word of mouth discussion between consumers," as stressed by Kozinets (2002). ZeFestival, carrier, and symbol of gay culture, seems altogether suited for this kind of study. Therefore, the approach is double; it consists in measuring the results of Google searches and the study of Facebook pages relative to the event (before/during and after the event) with the number of publications, interactions, and

Table 1.   Description of the Methodological Approach.

Sample	39 individuals; average age: 49 [20:77];
	Marital status: single: 20/in a heterosexual couple: 5/in a homosexual couple: 14
	Socio-professional categories: Executive: 12/Employee: 9/Retired: 6/Intermediate: 6/Self-employed, shopkeeper, company head: 3/Student: 2/Unemployed: 1
Themes of the interview	– Description of the population interviewed – Knowing the gay environment generally and in Nice, and perception of the Nice destination's gay-friendly character – Use and perception of OSMs in general and in the organization and real-life experience linked to the festival
Data processing	Recording and full re-transcription of all views expressed; Manual theme processing and working out how often the various themes appear.

---

[11]The youngest is 20 years old and the oldest 77.

sharing. These will be our only criteria because there are no other OSMs relating to the event.

Results/Findings and Discussion

RESULTS OF THE QUALITATIVE STUDY

Perception of the destination: Poor knowledge of labels

Only four participants are aware that Nice was the first town in France to obtain the "Gay comfort" label in 2011. Now, this label, awarded by the gay and lesbian travel international association, rewards the policy of the Nice Office du Tourisme et des Congrès (OTC) and people working in tourism (hotels, restaurants, transport, etc.) that adapt their hospitality and train their personnel to suit this clientele. Likewise, efforts made by Nice institutions get little media coverage: only eight of 39 people know the slogan "Nice, irisée naturellement (Nice, naturally iridescent)," launched by Nice OTC with a view to asserting the quality of its gay-friendly tourism offer.

Actually, what they know about gay events, places to go out and bars is mostly concentrated on a few names: Queernaval, the In&Out, and ZeFestival as regards festivals, the Pink Parade (name given to the Gay Pride in Nice) as regards events, the Six, Gossip Bar, Bar Bitch, Malabar Station, and Glam as regards gay places to go out and bars. In Nice, although there are a few events and places acknowledged as gay and festive, the town's homosexual geography seems to be very limited, which may explain the hesitation of those interviewed to consider that Nice is a destination which is really known and appreciated by gays.

Perception of the destination: Discrepancy between the perception and the reality of facts

We have to admit that those interviewed have a low perception of the destination's "gay-friendly" character: 30 out of 39 consider Nice as hardly or not much "gay friendly," far behind in the rating in comparison with Paris[12] (mentioned as a gay tourist destination by 15 of 39 people), San Francisco,[13] Sitges, and Barcelona[14]

---

[12]France.
[13]The United States.
[14]Spain.

(each mentioned by 10 people), Berlin,[15] New York,[16] and Ibiza[17] (each mentioned by seven people) and finally London[18] and the Canary Islands.[19] In terms of perceived image, the two words that most come into mind to the festival participants when Nice is mentioned are "sea" and "sun," far ahead of "gay." So, these people, who should be sensitive to the gay cause and to the initiatives developed by Nice (obtaining a label, targeted communication, etc.) have a very low perception of Nice as a "gay-friendly" town whereas the municipality directly contributes to financing ZeFestival!

To sum up, the presence of five positive elements detected by the interviewed – Good climate/Gay scene/Nightlife/Gay-friendly environment/Good beaches (the first five in the list of criteria defining the expectation of gay tourists in regard to a tourist destination according to Melián-González et al., 2011, p. 1032) – could give an inkling that Nice has the potential to become a gay tourist destination but those interviewed are hardly aware of the fact owing to their practical experience in situ. Therefore, we may presume that the use of OSMs could help to reinforce the festival experience.

The use of OSMs and the gay experience

Very interesting studies show that the internet enables individuals to manage an identity or behavior perceived as deviant or discreditable more easily owing to the fact that the cyberspace preserves anonymity. Furthermore, the high reactivity of websurfers to create virtual communities enables them to reinforce group identity and get rid of a feeling of personal, social, or geographical isolation. Therefore, social geography should not ignore the new territory formed by the content of services available through the internet network. Yet, our own results diverge with the results of these studies which tend to indicate that using OSMs for exchanging views and interacting on shared issues should be favored by that community. In fact, the overall use of OSMs by the gays interviewed in Nice is low: 19 spend less than two hours per day on OSMs (less than an hour for 10 of them).

---

[15]Germany.
[16]The United States.
[17]Spain.
[18]The United Kingdom.
[19]Spain.

Only 10 belong to an online gay community. However, a surprising result needs underlining: most of the interviewed think that gay people are keen users of OSMs whereas they are not personally. Therefore, the image they project on the members of their community differs from their own real-life situation.

Online social media and events

Numerous studies highlight the important role of OSMs on the development of a sense of belonging to a community, in particular in the case of actions with a political or community purpose. In the present case, two interesting variables stand out to explain why people take part in ZeFestival: "activism" and "because there are too few gay events." Therefore, we could legitimately suppose that, a fortiori, OSMs should play a preponderant role to rally people. Yet, under a third of the interviewed invited their friends via the OSM. Likewise, under a third of them post information or photos during the festival and contribute to the online communication; at the same time, over half of them wish that there be more advertising on the internet. In the end, they favor the word of mouth and direct communication.

RESULTS OF THE NETNOGRAPHIC STUDY

Contrary to our early expectations, the netnographic analysis reveals a low presence of the event on the internet. Indeed, apart from an automatic page generator referring to the festival's definition given by Wikipedia, not a single Facebook page is devoted to the event, and the automatically generated page has only 17 "Likes." There is no publication, the page is blank. In parallel, the page of the Polychromes association has only 866 followers. Table 2 presents the main results of the study of the association's Facebook page before, during, and after ZeFestival in Nice, Toulon, and Marseille. We note that there is not a single reference to the event after it ended. There is no desire to prolong the experience, and yet we know that OSMs play a role before, during and after an event, notably for giving visibility to the event's success and encourage people to take part in the next festival. The participants' feedback on the experience is not exploited.

This table highlights the low level of communication by the organizers. On the other hand, a publication generates 3.8 "Likes" on average, which is low. Also, it is interesting to note that during the event, a number of posts have had 0 "Likes" and comments.

Table 2.   Levels of Communication by ZeFestival Organizers.

Period	Towns	Number of Posts	Number of Likes	Number of Shares	Number of Comments
Before	Nice	14 (beginning to D-12)	66	2	3
During		21	68	18	0
After		0	0	0	0
Before	Toulon	2	6	0	0
During and after		0	0	0	0
Before	Marseille	9	36	1	0
During and after		0	0	0	0
	TOTAL	46	176	21	3

Examining Google's searches reveals over 39 million results with the event's name. This preliminary search works both in French and in English, because the key words are significant in both languages. Therefore, a problem of homonymy can be raised in terms of communication. So, a second search was launched, adding the towns where the event is held and the year. The search "ZeFestival Nice 2015" has generated the lowest number of pages referenced by Google – 848: Marseille gets 2,200 and Toulon 1,570. Therefore it appears that the Nice event is proportionally the least attended, which may seem paradoxical bearing in mind the organizing association's vivacity and dynamism. Moreover, it shows that ZeFestival has little online coverage whereas the same search launched for the In&Out[20] gay festival generates 13,200 results. Even if we add the results for Toulon and Marseille to those obtained for Nice, the total for ZeFestival is disappointing. The competitor seems to have a much better online communication.

DISCUSSION

The Facebook page and "posts" are hardly active and online communication has a purely informative role. The netnographic study

---

[20]Another gay film festival in Nice, resulting from the split between various members of the organizing association.

shows that ZeFestival's external communication pattern is essentially traditional – newspapers, mainly local (Nice Matin) and a few posts. We observe that the event is more publicized in Toulon and Marseille (number of Google searches); this means that the festival has a presence on line, which is in no way driven by the organizers, but instead by the community and participants.

The low intensity of the role of OSMs in the experience and communication of ZeFestival's organizers and goers teaches us a lot. At first sight, we are surprised, even disappointed by the fact that the role of OSMs is poorer than we envisaged in a tourist destination that claims to be "gay friendly" and a "smart city," with little interaction, the OSMs used mainly for information purposes by the organizers and the experience hardly commented and shared by participants via OSMs.

To sum up:

- Our research work has an innovative character because of the originality of the theme, which is hardly developed on a global scale and non-existent in France: the role of the online experience through a gay cultural event in a tourist destination.
- The results are often paradoxical, in view of the hypotheses that were formulated. In the light of the literature, the interest of Nice for new technologies, the focus on a gay population ... we expected that the role of the online experience during ZeFestival in Nice would be important, with intense and varied online interaction. Yet our results show that the members of the gay population that we interviewed, even those who use OSMs, attribute a much lower role than expected to this online communication.
- Is this due to the low use of OSMs by the organizers, as underlined by the netnographic analysis? To the relatively high average age[21] of the festival's organizers and participants, which is characteristic of Nice's demography with a higher number of seniors than in other French towns, bearing in mind that the very active use of OSMs is a generation phenomenon?
- Beyond the location and generation effect, could there be an explanation linked to the way the organizing structure

---

[21]Except for the association's president who is 30 years old.

works? The latter's aim is to enable its members to share face-to-face pleasant moments via meetings, outings, dances, etc. and to promote gay culture; ZeFestival has the same objective. The study shows that ZeFestival is indeed attended by the association's members and sympathizers who come to see films, of course, but also and above all to meet, exchange views and keep the local LGBT community alive. *In fine*, despite the present development of the digital experience, ZeFestival's participants and organizers remain in a pattern of face-to-face experience with communication and experience feedbacks that are interpersonal and internal to the community.

– *De facto*, owing to the low level of online communication and exchanges, the influence is limited and has little impact on the external perception of the experience linked to the festival and the Nice destination.

Contribution of the Approach

Our main suggestions to the organizers are of a managerial nature: to propose avenues to develop the communication on the festival via OSMs, in order to attract more people, build up a loyal audience and thus ensure that more external audiences will attend the next events. OSMs have significant advantages: they are free, quick, anonymous, and do away with time and space limits. However, communicating information is not enough, above all it has to be passed on to the right relays and transmitters. The best thing would be to rely on those people who participate directly (and without charge) to an online communication about the event; this would help to from a group and ensure a greater success of the festival by fostering a real online experience. To achieve this, we suggest that the organizers create an OSMs community for the festival with a dedicated Facebook page and including the "famous" 1% of those individuals who are at the origin of the information posted on OSMs. The 90-9-1 rule is used to describe the three types of OSM user profile (Lampe & Johnston, 2005). "User participation often more or less follows a 90-9-1 rule: 90% of users read or observe, but don't contribute. 9% of users contribute from time to time, but other priorities dominate their time. 1% of users participates a lot and account for most contributions: it seems as if they don't have lives because they often post just minutes after whatever event they just comment" (Li et al., 2011).

Regarding post-event communication, the organizers could build up a "collective intelligence" on socio-digital media (Litvin, Goldsmith, & Pan, 2008); for example, by encouraging experience feedback by e-festival goers. Well-structured customer relations through the social media may contribute to building loyalty and to an interesting return on investments. Indeed, perpetuating customer relations may lead customers to spontaneously become a company or a brand's e-ambassadors (Miranda & Papetti, 2014), to recruit future members for future festivals. "In addition to the in-situ experience, an online event life is now a complete process as far as pre and post-event are becoming more and more crucial to communicate on and about the event. People can select to attend or not through careful design of online communication and event managers can enhance customer's experiences by maximizing anticipation of an enjoyable experience (through communication)" (Getz & Carlsen, 2006).

Conclusion: Limitations and Future Directions

This exploratory study focuses on a single gay cultural event of a relatively small scale (2,000–3,000 attendees) organized by a militant association.

Therefore, the team in charge of the festival's organization and communication is small, which may partly explain the event's poor online promotion, due perhaps to the fact that the team underestimates the importance of OSMs for the event's promotion and development: nevertheless we should mention that most of the attendees regret the lack of online advertizing and communication about the festival, which drastically limits the role of OSMs in the festival experience ...

We should now carry on analyzing other gay events in Nice and elsewhere in France. Indeed, in view of the fact that the subject has yet been hardly developed, numerous questions remain unanswered and research must be carried out on other similar festivals in order to understand whether the behaviors described are specific to ZeFestival or whether the conclusions can be applicable generally ...

References

Astudillo Lizama, P. (2014). Existe-t-il un quartier gay à Santiago du Chili? Appropriation et distanciation d'un modèle urbain importé. *Annales de géographie*, 699(5), 128.

Bruner, E. M., & Kirshenblatt-Gimblett, B. (1994). Maasai on the lawn tourist realism in East Africa. *Cultural Anthropology*, 9(4), 435−470.

Christofle, S. (2014). « Côte d'azur et «évènementiel»: Leadership territorial et renouvellement de destinations? » dans S. Christofle (dir.). Tourisme, destinations et entreprises: Leadership territorial dans le luxe, l' «évènementiel » et les TIC, Mondes du Tourisme, hors-série, pp. 43−58.

Christofle, S., & Ferry, M. (2016, à paraître). Tourisme et évènementiel: modélisation et analyse d'un système interfacique, communication au colloque international, Rendez-vous Champlain: *Tourisme et événementiel.*

Cooper, A., Scherer, C. R., Boies, S. C., & Gordon, B. L. (1999). Sexuality on the internet: From sexual exploration to pathological expression. *Professional Psychology: Research and Practice*, 30, 154−164.

Crompton, J. L., & McKay, T. L. (1997). Motives of visitors attending festival events. *Annals of Tourism Research*, 24(2), 425−439.

CRT Riviera. (2016). Retrieved from http://cms.cotedazur-tourisme.com/user-files/file/ChiffresCles2014.pdf. Accessed on January 13, 2016.

Filluzeau, D. (2002). Des processus de socialisation homosexuels aux usages socio-sexuels d'internet: Des lieux réels aux lieux virtuels, cheminements identitaires et espaces de socialisation. Mémoire de DEA de sociologie à l'université de Nantes, sous la direction de Deniot J. et Léobon A, pp. 29−34.

Fotis, J., Buhalis, D., & Rossides, N. (2012). Social media use and impact during the holiday travel planning process. In M. Fuchs, F. Ricci, & L. Cantoni (Eds.), *Information and communication technologies in tourism 2012* (pp. 13−24). Vienna: Springer-Verlag.

Getz, D. (2010). *Events studies: Théory, research and policy for planned events* (2nd ed., p. 468). London: Elsevier.

Getz, D., & Carlsen, J. (2006). Quality management for events. In B. Prideaux, G. Moscardo, & E. Laws (Eds.), *Managing tourism and hospitality services: Theory and international applications* (pp. 145−155). Cambridge, MA: CABI Publishing.

Getz, D., & Page, S. J. (2016). Progress and prospects for event tourism research. *Tourism Management*, 52, 593−631.

Giraud, C. (2013). Le « Village Gai » de Montréal. Une aventure urbaine minoritaire. *Espaces et sociétés*, 154(3), 200.

Glassey, O., & Pfister, B. (2004). Liens numériques, lien social? Analyse des rapports entre innovations technologiques et dynamiques sociales, *Conférence Internationale "ICTs & Inequalities: the digital divides" "TIC & Inégalités: les fractures numériques"* Paris, Carré des Sciences 18−19 novembre.

Gontijo, F. (2004). « Quand Momus passe sous l'arc en ciel … La construction sociale des images identitaires homosexuelles dans le carnaval de Rio de Janeiro ». *Sociétés*, 2(84), 100.

Grappin-Schmitt, S. (2010). Flash mob. Repères, cahier de danse, 1(25), 10.

Jaurand, E. (2010). Construire des territoires d'un autre genre? Perspectives géographiques sur des territorialités marginales dans l'espace touristique. Tome III. Dossier d'habilitation à diriger des recherches. Université de Nice-Sophia Antipolis. UFR Espaces & Cultures. 160 p.

Jaurand, E., & Leroy, S. (2011). "Bienvenue aux gays du monde entier". Tourisme gay et mondialisation. Mondes du Tourisme, 299−309.

Kaplan, A., & Haenlein, M. (2010). Users of the world, unite! The challenges and opportunities of social media. Business Horizons, 53, 59−68.

Kozinets, R. V. (2002). The field behind the screen: Using netnography for marketing research in online communities. Journal of Marketing Research: February, 39(1), 61−72.

Krane, V., & Waldron, J. J. (2000). The gay games: Creating our sport culture. In K. Schaffer & S. Smith (Eds.), The Olympics at the millennium: Power, politics, and the Olympic games (pp. 147−164). New Brunswick, NJ: Rutgers University Press.

Lampe, C., & Johnston, E. (2005). Follow the (slash) dot: Effects of feedback on new members in an online community. International conference on supporting group work, ACM Press, Sanibel Island (pp. 11−20).

Leobon, A. (2006). "Vers une géographie des espaces de visibilité et de rencontre LGBT (lesbiennes, gais, bi et transsexuels), en France et au Québec" dans "territorialités, mobilités, conflits" Colloque ESO? collection Géographie sociale des PUR.

Leroy, S. (2010). Le Paris gay. Éléments pour une géographie de l'homosexualité. Annales de géographie, 646(6), 114.

Li, X., Zhang, X., Cui, P., Fu, Z., Yang, S., & Cui, B. (2011). The visualization of mass information in social network with a holistic view, Conférence EVA (Electronic Visualisation and the Arts), Londres.

Litvin, S. W., Goldsmith, R. E., & Pan, B. (2008). Electronic word-of-mouth in hospitality and tourism management. Tourism Management, 29, 458−468.

MacCannell, D. (1973). Staged authenticity: Arrangements of social space in tourist settings. American Journal of Sociology, 79(3), 589−603.

Matheson, C. M. (2005). Festivity and sociability: A study of a Celtic music festival. Tourism, Culture and Communication, 5(3), 149−163.

Melián-González, A., Moreno-Gil, S., & Araña, J. E. (2011). Gay tourism in a sun and beach destination. Tourism Management, 32, 1027−1037.

Milano, R. (2010). Cosa fare e cosa non fare nella Rete turistica. Il caso Italia.it. In G. Granieri & G. Perri (Eds.), Linguaggi digitali per il turismo (pp. 47−48). Milan: Apogeo.

Miranda, S., & Papetti, C. (2014). Les nouveaux paradigmes du tourisme mobiquitaire, Hors-série de la revue Mondes du tourisme, décembre.

Neveu, E. (2010). Médias et protestation collective, in E. Agrikoliansky et al. (coord.), Penser les mouvements sociaux, Paris, La Découverte « Recherches », 245−264.

Tussyadiah, I., & Fesenmaier, D. R. (2009). Mediating tourist experiences: Access to places via shared videos. Annals of Tourism Research, 36(1), 24−40.

Uriely, N. (2005). The tourist experience: Conceptual developments. *Annals of Tourism Research*, *32*, 199–216.

Urry, J. (2001). *Globalising the tourist gaze*. Retrieved from http://www.comp. lancs.ac.uk/sociology/papers/Urry-Globalising-the-Tourist-aze.pdf

Venske, E. (2015). Pink tourism in Cape Town: The development of the post-apartheid gay quarter. In A. Diekmann & M. K. Smith (Eds.), *Ethnic and minority cultures as tourist attractions* (p. 202–214). Bristol: Channel View Publications.

Waitt, G., & Markwell, K. (2006). *Gay tourism. Culture and context* (p. 334). New York, NY Haworth Hospitality Press.

17 Marketing Experiences for Visitor Attractions: The Contribution of Theming

Elricke Botha

ABSTRACT

Purpose – This chapter looks at similarities between the experience economy and Disneyization, with specific focus placed on theming as a means of enhancing the visitor's experience. Sophisticated tourists have brought with them the need for research to explain their behavior and place more emphasis on experiences. The Addo Elephant National Park, South Africa, is presented as a case study that uses interpretation as a tool for theming.

Methodology/approach – This chapter is approached from a marketing perspective on visitor attractions. Several issues and guidelines related to theming are presented to highlight several aspects which visitor attraction managers need to consider when seeking to use theming to enhance or create a visitor experience.

Findings – What was evident from the literature is that the theme is the most important aspect in all models (i.e., the experience economy, Disneyization, and interpretation). The theme should be planned meticulously as the theme refers to several aspects not only in the experience itself, but also in the experience cycle. It is therefore a quite complex tool to use that should not be taken lightly in order to benefit fully from the advantages it offers.

Originality/value – The value of this chapter lies in the fact that several models and their similarities were presented with an underpinning tool called theming. As not much research have been done on theming, the guidelines presented by all the models have been considered in a systematic manner that would assist visitor attraction managers in forming a better understanding of the use of the tool and issues related to it. With this said, there are several aspects highlighted in the chapter which necessitate more research in order to assist managers effectively in designing effective themes.

Keywords: Experience economy; Disneyization; theming; visitor attractions; interpretation; Addo Elephant National Park

Introduction

The rising number of sophisticated tourists who are far removed from the mass tourism offerings has led to the growing importance of tourism research to explain their behavior (Middleton, Fyall, Morgan, & Ranchhod, 2009, p. 15; Moutinho, Ballantyne, & Rate, 2011, p. 83). We find ourselves in the post-industrial economy where research is increasingly focused on new trends in tourist behavior by placing emphasis on the "experience" of tourists. The new tourists are seeking experiences that are meaningful to them and are prepared to participate in creating the value they seek (Middleton et al., 2009, p. 15). The tourism industry therefore finds itself at a stage where service needs to be re-packaged and presented as experiences (Hayes & MacLeod, 2007, p. 45), as the experience is seen as an element of connecting production and consumption (Anderson, 2007, p. 47).

As a result of this shift toward experiences, Pine and Gilmore (1999, p. 98) have coined the term "experience economy." They explain that experiences are a distinct economic offering from services, as services are different from goods. Although Pine and Gilmore (1999) indicate that this concept can be adopted in any industry, the tourism industry seems to be the forerunner in recognizing the importance of experiences. Disneyland, launched on July 17, 1955 by the Disney Corporation, is a well-known visitor attraction in the tourism industry and it has embraced the idea of experiences since the 1950s (Disney Corporation, 2015). Even more so, Disney's success with creating experiences has led to the term Disneyization (Bryman, 1999). Research is increasingly focusing on these two concepts to explain tourists' behavior, to test the validity of each concept and to attempt to create guidelines for managers and marketers. Even though these concepts are relatively novel in tourism research, they have lately come under some scrutiny. Morgan, Elbe, and de Esteban Curiel (2009, p. 205) explain that the emphasis of performance and the overuse of examples from Disney have led to ideas that the experience economy is superficial and product-centered rather than customer-centered. Nevertheless these concepts seem to have some merit as both revolve around theming.

The aim of this chapter is therefore to analyses the use of theming in a tourism context as a tool to enhance the visitor experience and hence to provide guidelines to assist visitor attraction managers and marketers.

Section 1: The Experience Economy and Disneyization

As tourists in the modern economy are more educated, mature, and demanding, the notions of mass tourism are far removed from these tourists. This necessitates tourism providers to be more consumer-centric (Morgan et al., 2009, p. 15; Moutinho et al., 2011, p. 83), hence the importance of tourist experiences as a means to create a closer link between the tourist and the tourist provider (Hayes & MacLeod, 2007, p. 46).

Amid the various theoretical frameworks explaining tourists' experiences, Pine and Gilmore's (1999) experience economy has become very popular (Quadri-Felitti & Fiore, 2012, pp. 5–6). The experience economy delineates four realms of customer experiences, which are referred to as the 4Es of experience. Experiences are categorized according to whether they require active or passive interaction (seen in the form of a horizontal line that halves a circle), and whether the experience results into absorbed or immersed tourist participation (vertical line that halves the circle). Even though detail on each realm is beyond the scope of this chapter, some attention will be given to the center of this model. The center of the circle/model (i.e., where the horizontal and vertical lines cross) is regarded as enriching experiences, which are the most compelling experiences (Pine & Gilmore, 1999, p. 43) since they encompass all the realms and therefore may be referred to as memorable experiences. As every service provider wants to aim for this center, Pine and Gilmore (1999) provide principles to assist service providers in creating these memorable experiences. These principles include aspects like providing a compelling and memorable theme to help tourists organize their impressions; using positive cues that affirm the nature of the experience; providing memorabilia as a physical reminder of the experience; and engaging all four senses to enhance the chosen theme (Pine & Gilmore, 1999, pp. 46–61). It is precisely these principles or guidelines which guide one to recognize their similarity to Disneyization.

Disneyization is defined as a "process by which the principles of the Disney theme park are coming to dominate more and more sectors of American society as well as the rest of the world" (Bryman, 1999, p. 26). Disneyization was developed by Bryman (1999) as a parallel to Ritzer's (1993) McDonaldization. McDonaldization refers to the principles of predictability, efficiency, calculability, and control, which dominate sectors more and more. Disneyization, however, draws attention to the principles demonstrated by Disney theme parks and is in many ways parallel to McDonaldization, except for the calculability dimension (Bryman, 1999, p. 26). The principles of Disneyization are indicated as theming, de-differentiation, merchandising, and emotional labor (Bryman, 1999, p. 29). These principles are also strikingly similar to the experience economy's principles for a memorable experience.

One should remember that Disneyization only refers to organizational principles. Hancock (2005, pp. 546, 547) explains that Disneyization has been devised with an introductory market in mind and only provides descriptions related to organizational principles. As such, not much have been said to elaborate on Disneyization as only a type of guideline. This chapter specifically focuses on theming based on this characteristic of an organizational principle and some similarities between Disneyization and the experience economy.

Section 2: Theming

The use of themes has gained increasing popularity. This is due to the fact that it leads to several managerial and marketing benefits for tourism businesses. Literature explains that the benefits of theming include that theming contains useful information for the process of planning and marketing meaningful and memorable experiences; creates an initial perception of quality, communicates value or acts as a value-adding factor; boosts attendance or repeat visits; provides a memorable experience; influences the place tourists are visiting and how they behave; is a means of effective word-of-mouth advertising; allows for coordination of retail merchandise; also allows for coordination of offerings that attract certain market segments; and creates a competitive advantage, especially if the theme is related to a location that is difficult to duplicate (Agapito, Valle, & Mendes, 2014, p. 226; Mossberg, 2007, p. 71; Wassler, Li, & Hung, 2015, p. 8; Wong & Cheung, 1999, p. 321). Clearly it is worthwhile to consider theming as an approach to create memorable experiences.

Services automatically turn into experiences when themes are used. Moreover, themes are a successful way of connecting various services and products (Gilmore & Pine, 2002, p. 92). Theming has not been defined precisely within the tourism literature, which might be the case because the concept is in part self-explanatory. Mossberg (2007, p. 69, 71), however, explains that the theme is the underlying concept for everything staged in a particular place; shows the total offering; and creates a meaningful experience by communicating the core values in an understandable and memorable way.

The "place" to which Mossberg (2007) refers in her definition can range to several tourism sectors. The most obvious places where themes are used are theme parks like Disney World and Universal Studios. Apart from these attractions, some holiday destinations revolve around a central theme like Las Vegas and Sun City in South Africa. Even the accommodation sector has moved to themed hotels with examples ranging from Las Vegas to Hello Kitty hotels in China (Wassler et al., 2015). Further to the obvious themes like Mexican or Italian restaurants, the food sector is also increasingly adopting themed restaurants like the Prison Restaurant in Tianjin, China, or the bathroom-themed Modern Toilet Restaurant in Kaohsiung, Taiwan.

Interestingly, Lorentzen (2009, pp. 834–835) explains that "place" also involves a branding component where providers try to create a wish of the consumer to "be there." Applying a theme to locations or objects therefore infuses a thought of attractiveness and creates something more interesting than they actually are (Poursani, 2013, p. 165). A theme helps to project an image (an intrinsic part of marketing) and quality of the place by means of the tangible facilities and props (Wong & Cheung, 1999, p. 322). It is therefore quite noticeable that themes have a specific role in attracting tourists to a specific destination or visitor attraction that amplifies the role of themes in the pre-experience stage.

It is essential to remember that consuming an experience should be viewed as a process that takes place in three stages, namely pre-experience, tourist experience, and post-experience (Tynan & McKechnie, 2009, p. 508). As illustrated above, themes assist the tourists in anticipating and preparing themselves for the experience. But anticipation and preparation are preceded by a decision-making process. Not to go into too much detail, but this decision-making process is quite important for tourism businesses, especially from a marketing perspective. Tourism businesses compete against one another to form part of the potential tourists' brand awareness set in order to stand a chance of becoming the preferred choice to visit (Decrop, 2010, p. 95). This process where tourists consider the destinations or attractions they may visit is referred to as choice sets in decision-making and is perhaps the most difficult part of marketing, since tourists are so diverse.

Gross and Pullman (2012, p. 46) argue that themes are usually determined by management in a top-down manner; they follow a type of product-centric approach. Binkhorst and Den Dekker (2009, p. 314) have a different opinion. They argue that the visitor should be the starting point as they "co-create" their experiences. It is therefore extremely important to research tourists' needs in order to not only create satisfactory visitor attractions, but also to market these attractions according to those specific needs. Even if Gross and Pullman (2012) are correct, very few studies have aimed to determine the effect of theming in the pre-experience stage. More research has been done on the effect of theming during the experience stage.

As explained earlier, a service automatically turns into an experience when a theme is used (Gilmore & Pine, 2002, p. 92), but theming is quite a complex phenomenon (Wassler et al., 2015,

p. 13). The complexity is evident when one considers the factors shown in Figure 1 and becomes even clearer when one looks at these factors in relation to the principles of the experience economy and Disneyization.

Pine and Gilmore (1999, p. 46) explain that the theme helps tourists to organize their impressions of the tourism business. However, the effectiveness of these impressions depends on the fact that the theme is applied consistently. Muñoz, Wood, and Solomon (2006, p. 224) state that the structure or place where the experience is provided should meet the physical design of the theme, with atmospheric elements to inspire authenticity and employees that conform to the theme.

From a marketing perspective, the physical environment includes aspects like ambient conditions (i.e., music and lighting), layout (including the functionality of facilities) and signs, symbols and artefacts that communicate a certain image of the tourism business (Mossberg, 2007, p. 65). It could be in the light of these physical environment criteria that Pine and Gilmore (1999, p. 59) suggest that tourism businesses should engage all five senses of tourists. The physical environment could also play a role in de-differentiation as applied in Disneyization. De-differentiation refers to a trend that entails that the different forms of consumption become interlocked with one another and increasingly difficult to distinguish (Bryman, 1999, p. 33). This is quite noticeable in theme parks and amusement parks, where the selling of food and various goods are done under one theme. Other sources refer to this factor as the servicescape. This specifically refers to designing and constructing an attractive setting for visitors

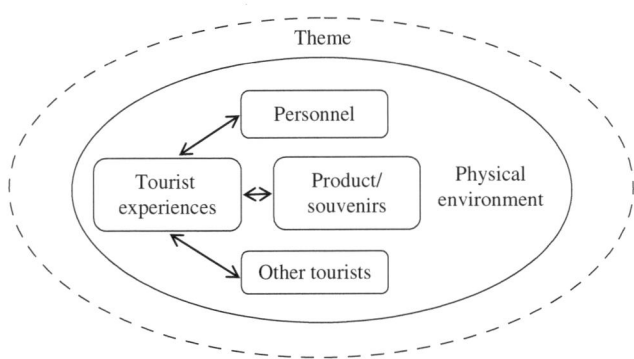

Figure 1. Factors Influencing the Tourist Experience. *Source*: Adapted from Mossberg (2007).

(Dong & Siu, 2013, p. 542), which has shown to impact pleasure-feeling emotions (Kim & Moon, 2009, p. 152). However, Mossberg (2007, p. 66) suggests that more research is necessary into this aspect to assist tourism businesses in designing stimulating tourism environments and hence in contributing toward their image.

Together with the physical environment, encounters with service personnel also have an impact on the tourist experience and the image of the tourism business. In fact, service personnel are such an essential component of the tourist experience that Disneyization principles include them as emotional labor (Bryman, 1999, p. 40). Disney employees use language in a distinctive way to give the impression that they are having fun and are not engaging in real-life work. Surprisingly, this requirement is mostly accepted by Disney's employees (Bryman, 1999, p. 41). This could be why Pine and Gilmore (1999, p. 52) suggest that tourism businesses should use positive cues in order for tourists to affirm their experiences. Bærenholdt and Jensen (2009, p. 362) explain that performative work (i.e., emotional labor) requires personnel to gain experience themselves in order to facilitate the experiences of visitors. This ensures that the encounters with visitors become more than superficial and rather a form of common social understanding between the visitor and personnel. Considering the intangibility of tourism service, to a degree, more research is necessary on service encounter characteristics in various tourism contexts (Mossberg, 2007, p. 67). Gross and Pullman (2012, p. 53) indicate that the implementation and context (i.e., simple interaction like Disney vs. complex interaction like a boutique hotel) in which theming is provided can create conflict and interpretation differences between managers and employees.

It is important for tourism managers to attract and entertain tourists, but the post-experience is equally important to complete the experience cycle. There are some aspects of themes that are specifically evident in the post-experience stage. Products and souvenirs, which are associated with both the experience economy and Disneyization, are one such aspect. The experience economy explains that souvenirs are an extension of the experience. Souvenirs or memorabilia serve as physical reminders of the experience tourists had on site (Pine & Gilmore, 1999, p. 57). They are a tangible reminder of the tourists' consumption which would otherwise have been an intangible experience (Mossberg, 2007, p. 68). Bryman (1999, p. 38) argues that more money can be made (by feature films) through merchandise. The author confirms that restaurants like Hard Rock Café use merchandise, such as t-shirts, as walking advertisements. It is therefore not surprising that Mossberg (2007, p. 69) suggests that further research is necessary to determine how souvenirs are linked to a theme, how they influence the experience and, even more, how they affect marketing.

Further to the above, Binkhorst and Den Dekker (2009, p. 315) note that tourists are rarely included as partners in the process of building experiences. Today it is customary that tourists share their experiences on social media platforms, applications and websites like Audiosnacks (i.e., podcasts) and TripAdvisor. In a sense tourists co-create the image of a tourism business and communicate expected experiences to other tourists via word-of-mouth marketing.

It is also important to mention the impact that the local community might have on tourists' experiences. The focus here is specifically on the encounters with experts in the local community who give tourists lessons about local gastronomy, art, pottery, painting, dancing, and the language (Binkhorst & Den Dekker, 2009, p. 318). During these activities tourists help in creating their own experiences and provide value far beyond the immediate experience. These experiences are cherished as memorable and are specifically important for positive word-of-mouth marketing. Communicating interesting information or teaching tourists specific skills are better known as interpretation.

Section 3: Interpretation as a Means of Theming

Interpretation is defined by Tilden (1977, p. 8), the father of interpretation, as "an educational activity which aims to reveal meanings and relationships through the use of original objects, by first-hand experience, and by illustrative media, rather than simply to communicate factual information." Although interpretation is mostly used in national parks to convey the park's preservation, conservation, and educational goals (Chen, Hwang, & Lee, 2006, p. 1167), interpretation has also been used in other tourism contexts such as museums, destinations with specific historical significance, zoos, botanical gardens and galleries. As the definition suggests, all these contexts use interpretation to communicate and educate the visitor about the specific context's significance, usually with some sort of explanatory information.

One should note here that interpretation is either a necessary component of the visitor experience or it is the experience itself (Kuo, 2002, p. 95; Moscardo, 1998, p. 5). In order to understand the aforementioned, the role of interpretation in the experience cycle should be considered.

For reasons of clarity the role of interpretation in the experience phase (see Figure 2) of the experience cycle will be considered first as it is the most noticeable. Interpretation as an experience echoes Stewart, Hayward, Devlin, and Kirby's (1998) primary and secondary interpretation classifications. These classifications respectively denote interpretation that is immediately identifiable as interpretation and auxiliary to the wider activity (Stewart et al., 1998, p. 260). Primary and in a sense also secondary interpretation, as the definition of interpretation suggests, are educational activities that can be done in person (e.g., by a tour guide) or non-personal (e.g., via audio comments or information boards at exhibits). Interpretation can be distinguished from other forms of factual informational transfer since the audience is non-captive and hence do not have to pay attention (Ham, 1992, p. 6). It is therefore designed according to specific guidelines to make sure that tourists stay captivated. In short, these guidelines

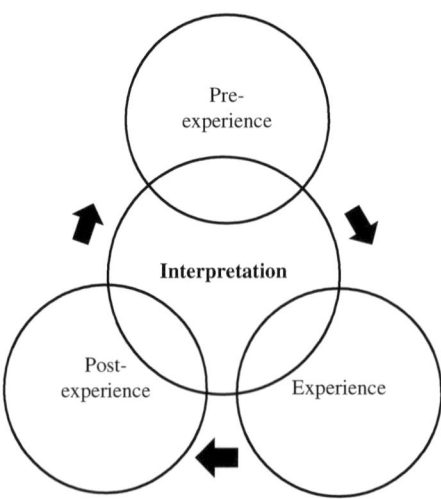

Figure 2.   The Role of Interpretation in the Experience Cycle. *Source*: Author's own compilation.

are known as the EROT model for the development of effective interpretation (Ham, 1992, pp. 8–28). Interpretation should be:

- *Enjoyable*: Interpretation should be developed in a conversational tone with exhibits that are game-like, participatory, and use different senses and lively colors. Presentations should also contain humor where possible, music or two-way communication to entice the visitor to participate.
- *Relevant*: Information should be linked to what the visitors know and rather use examples, analogies, and comparisons than technical terms. Further to this the interpretation should be personal, they should enable the visitor to use self-referencing and they should include categories where visitors can be labeled.
- *Organized*: Logical trains of thought should be used to organize ideas. Present information in five of fewer ideas.
- *Themed*: Interpretation should have the qualities of a story where the theme (e.g., the rhinoceros is endangered) rather than the topic (e.g., rhinoceros) should be presented in chronological order with a beginning and an end.

The theme in particular conveys the moral of the story and links tangible (e.g., geological formations) and intangible (e.g., what is represented by the tangible element – beliefs, values) elements to add power and relevance to tourists' experiences (Ham, Housego, & Weiler, 2005, p. 13). This leads to an enhanced visitor experience, which is one of the goals of interpretation along with protecting resources, protecting visitors form hazards and broadening the visitor's perspective on a place or idea (Ham, 1992, p. 4; Ham et al., 2005, p. 3; Kuo, 2002, p. 88; Lewis, 1980, p. 31; Ward & Wilkinson, 2006, p. 16).

More than the obvious educational aspect of interpretation (i.e., primary and secondary interpretation), there is also an obscure form or classification of interpretation which impacts the tourists' experience or, as Moscardo (1998) explains, a necessary component of the experience. This interpretation echoes Stewart et al.'s (1998) tertiary interpretation, for example informal conversations, with regard to interpretation services with staff and even visitor management techniques incorporated at the destination. These visitor management techniques can be further classified into physical (viewing platforms, fences restricting entrance, zoning), regulatory (reducing traffic congestion, ensuring visitor safety), and economic (park-and-ride schemes, increase fees for seasonal use, fines for littering) techniques that impact the visitors' educational experience (Kuo, 2002, p. 89). Tertiary interpretation therefore refers to the interpretation that impacts the tourists' experience but is not seen as the experience per se.

With reference to the experience cycle, tertiary interpretation's role is specifically clear in the pre- and post-experience phases. Tertiary interpretation is also known to be advertisements on TV or in magazines (which play a clear role in attracting visitors). It is furthermore seen as merchandising (Stewart et al., 1998), with memorabilia that play a role as a physical reminder of the experience visitors had. One should also note the impact of the educational experience on the post-experience. Both Powell and Ham (2008, p. 484) and Zeppel and Muloin (2008, p. 285) find that interpretation within a nature-based experience has an impact on tourists' philanthropic support for conservation. Even though research pertaining to marketing and interpretation is quite scarce, it is obvious that a satisfactory experience would lead to return visits, positive word-of-mouth and loyalty.

Regardless of the experience cycle phase, the theme used in interpretation obviously plays an important role. The theme combines all the factors illustrated in Figure 2 (physical environment, tourists' experience, other tourists and personnel). An interpretation example from South Africa that incorporates a theme in a visitor attraction is the Ulwazi Interpretation Centre situated in the Addo Elephant National Park.

Section 4: Case Study of the Ulwazi Interpretation Centre, Addo Elephant National Park

The Addo Elephant National Park is the third largest national park in South Africa and the only park to accommodate the big 7 (elephant, lion, buffalo, leopard, rhinoceros, southern right whale, and great white shark). It is situated in the far south of the country (SANParks, 2015a). Land was set aside for elephants in 1925 and proclaimed as the Addo Elephant National Park in 1931 (SANParks, 2015a). The Park was founded in an area where elephants were hunted in the past until they were on the verge of extinction. Not only has the Park succeeded in growing the number of elephants in the area from 16 to over 600, but owing to several conservation interventions the Park now also hosts several other animals (SANParks, 2015a). Although the Park is now concerned about conserving biodiversity, the elephants attract visitors to the Park (M. Taplin, personal communication, October 8, 2015). In fact, the legendary Hapoor, who was the Park's dominant elephant for 24 years and who had a deep hatred for humans, is the focal point of the Ulwazi Interpretive Centre in the Park (SANParks, 2015b) (Plate 1).

The illustrative panels in the Ulwazi Interpretive Centre explain the rich history of the Park and provide ample information to help guests understand the nature of the legendary "dominant elephant, Hapoor." A family tree of all the elephants in the Park is portrayed just below Hapoor to show guests the relevance of human and elephant generations. Further to this, the Centre provides fascinating information about the evolution of elephants (left of Hapoor; see Plate 2) and educational information about their special features (right of Hapoor; see Plate 3).

Elephants' ability to communicate over long distances is demonstrated with an interesting parabolic dish display which guests can use to experience this remarkable phenomenon. The

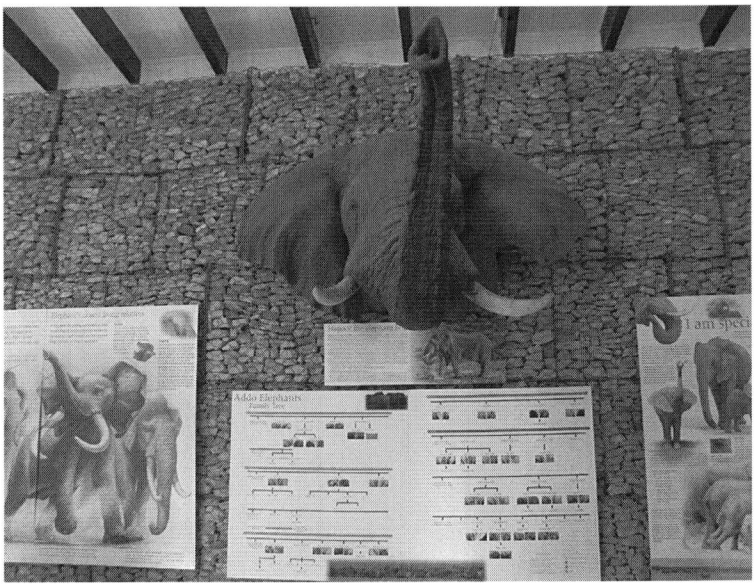

Plate 1. Hapoor. *Source*: Supplied by author.

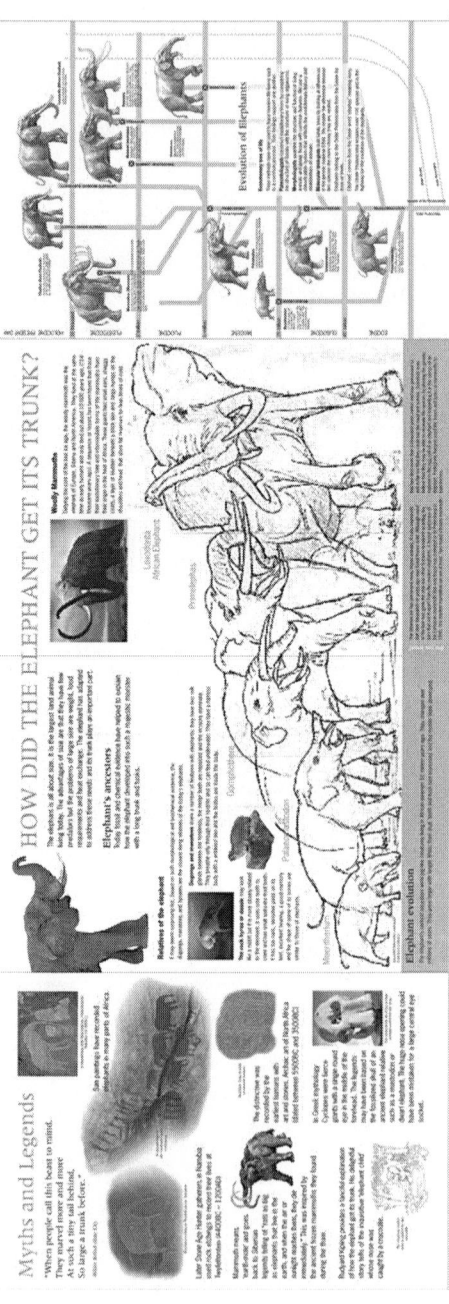

Plate 2.   Evolution of Elephants. *Source: SANParks (2015c).*

Plate 3. Elephants' Special Features. *Source*: SANParks (2015c).

Plate 4. Elephant Whisperer. *Source*: Supplied by author.

"elephant whisperer" is two parabolic dishes placed opposite each other to illustrate and explain how any sound, even a whispered voice, is reflected from one dish (similar to an elephant ear) to the other dish (Plates 4 and 5).

Plate 5.   Elephant Whisperer. *Source*: Supplied by author.

Plate 6.   Elliegym. *Source*: SANParks (2015c).

Even the elephant jungle gym (the Elliegym) that forms part of the illustrations just outside the center is developed as a life-size example of an average elephant where guests can compare their size to that of the elephant (Plate 6).

Even though a great deal of information in the center focus on elephants, the center also houses other educational displays that are relevant to the Park. These include displays with information about the geology of the Park, reptiles, nocturnal animals, islands, dinosaurs, marine animals, Bushmen, fauna and flora, the Xhosa culture in the area, rocky shores, fresh water and biomes (M. Taplin, personal communication, October 8, 2015).

The name of the center was chosen from suggestions of staff. It was Temba Mangcaka's suggestion to name the center Ulwazi, which means "knowledge" (M. Taplin, personal communication, October 8, 2015). The playful, yet interesting and informative displays clearly justify the center's name. The Ulwazi Interpretive Centre is a good example of the application of Ham's (1992) EROT guidelines: the current center is *enjoyed* by both young and old (M. Taplin, personal communication, October 8, 2015), displays are indeed *relevant*, they are *organized* in the center according to themes and there is an overarching *theme* (i.e., elephants) as well as subthemes. In an effort to organize the information even better the Park is planning to theme the information about the Park to tell one story and to link all the aspects of the Park so that the information flows from one board to the next. Moreover, the Park wants to increase the floor space of the center, create a booklet on the interpretive center that could be sold in the Park and at other outlets, and provide information on the environmental education center that forms part of the interpretive center (M. Taplin, personal communication, October 8, 2015).

Conclusion

The purpose of this chapter was to consider theming as a means of creating an experience. In order to do this several models were considered, with specific emphasis on comparing and finding similarities between the experience economy and Disneyization. Even though several similarities have been found, theming seems to be the overarching aspect that combines all the other similarities (such as the physical environment, staff, tourists, and souvenirs). This makes theming quite a complex tool to use, especially when one considers its role in the experience cycle. Theming therefore relates to a variety of managerial aspects at the attraction, while experiences are created but can also be taken further to the pre-experience in the form of marketing and post-experience where previous tourists co-create potential tourists' experiences. Although theme parks are the most obvious attractions that have used themes for quite some time, attractions that provide interpretation to tourists were presented as a case study that also uses theming. Even though interpretation has several guidelines for effective design, theming is regarded as the overarching aspect that either forms part of the experience (i.e., marketing or positive word-of-mouth) or it is the experience itself (i.e., exhibition with a theme to educate visitors). The Ulwazi Interpretive Centre in the Addo Elephant National Park of South Africa was presented as one such example. More research is necessary to determine the impact of theming on several aspects in order to provide comprehensive guidelines to attraction managers.

References

Agapito, D., Valle, P., & Mendes, J. (2014). The sensory dimension of tourist experiences: Capturing meaningful sensory-informed themes in Southwest Portugal. *Tourism Management*, *42*(June), 224–237. doi:10.1016/j.tourman.2013.11.011

Anderson, T. D. (2007). The tourist in the experience economy. *Scandinavian Journal of Hospitality and Tourism*, *7*(1), 46–58. doi:10.1080/15022250701224035

Bærenholdt, J. O., & Jensen, H. L. (2009). Performative work in tourism. *Scandinavian Journal of Hospitality and Tourism*, *9*(4), 349–365. doi:10.1080/15022250902978710

Binkhorst, E., & Den Dekker, T. (2009). Agenda for co-creation tourism experience research. *Journal of Hospitality Marketing & Management*, *18*(2–3), 311–327. doi:10.1080/19368620802594193

Bryman, A. (1999). The Disneyization of society. *The Editorial Board of the Sociological Review*, *47*(1), 25–46. doi:10.1111/1467-954X.00161

Chen, H. J., Hwang, S. N., & Lee, C. (2006). Visitors' characteristics of guided interpretation tours. *Journal of Business Research*, *59*(10), 1167–1181. doi:10.1016/j.jbusres.2006.09.006

Decrop, A. (2010). Destination choice sets: An inductive longitudinal approach. *Annals of Tourism Research*, *37*(1), 93–115. doi:10.1016/j.annals.2009.08.002

Disney Corporation. (2015). *Disney history*. Retrieved from https://thewaltdisneycompany.com/about-disney/disney-history/1950-01-01–1959-12-31

Dong, P., & Siu, N. Y. (2013). Servicescape elements, customer predispositions and service experience: The case of theme park visitors. *Tourism Management*, *36*(June), 541–551. doi:10.1016/j.tourman.2012.09.004

Gilmore, J., & Pine, J. (2002). Differentiating hospitality operations via experiences: Why selling services is not enough. *Cornell Hotel and Restaurant Administration Quarterly*, *43*(3), 87–96. doi:10.1016/S0010-8804(02)80022-2

Gross, M. A., & Pullman, M. (2012). Playing their roles: Experiential design concepts applied in complex services. *Journal of Management Inquiry*, *21*(1), 43–59. doi:10.1177/1056492610395928

Ham, S. (1992). *Environmental interpretation: A practical guide for people with big ideas and small budgets*. Golden, CO: North American Press.

Ham, S., Housego, A., & Weiler, B. (2005). *Tasmanian thematic interpretation planning manual*. Hobart: Tourism Tasmania. Retrieved from http://www.tourismtasmania.com.au/__data/assets/pdf_file/0014/16313/interpretation_manual.pdf

Hancock, P. (2005). Disneyfying Disneyization. *Ephemera Reviews: Theory & Politics in Organization, 5*(3), 545−550. Retrieved from https://www.researchgate.net/profile/Yiannis_Gabriel/publication/241453495_Production_and_Consumption_It%27s_All_Work/links/0c96052ecae4fa665b000000.pdf#page=104

Hayes, D., & MacLeod, N. (2007). Packaging places: Designing heritage trails using an experience economy perspective to maximize visitor engagement. *Journal of Vacation Marketing, 13*(1), 45−58. doi:10.1177/1356766706071205

Kim, W. G., & Moon, Y. J. (2009). Customers' cognitive, emotional, and actionable response to the servicescape: A test of the moderating effect of the restaurant type. *International Journal of Hospitality Management, 28*(1), 144−156. doi:10.1016/j.ijhm.2008.06.010

Kuo, I. (2002). The effectiveness of environmental interpretation at resource-sensitive tourism destinations. *International Journal of Tourism Research, 4*(2), 87−101. doi:10.1002/jtr.362

Lewis, W. J. (1980). *Interpreting for park visitors*. Philadelphia, PA: Eastern Acorn Press.

Lorentzen, A. (2009). Cities in the experience economy. *European Planning Studies, 17*(6), 829−845. doi:10.1080/09654310902793986

Middleton, V. T. C., Fyall, A., Morgan, M., & Ranchhod, A. (2009). *Marketing in travel and tourism* (4th ed.). Oxford: Butterworth-Heinemann.

Morgan, M., Elbe, J., & de Esteban Curiel, J. (2009). Has the experience economy arrived? The views of destination managers in three visitor-dependent areas. *International Journal of Tourism Research, 11*(2), 201−216. doi:10.1002/jtr.719

Moscardo, G. (1998). Interpretation and sustainable tourism: Functions, examples and principles. *Journal of Tourism Studies, 9*(1), 2−13. Retrieved from http://www.cabdirect.org/abstracts/19991804806.html

Mossberg, L. (2007). A marketing approach to the tourist experience. *Scandinavian Journal of Hospitality and Tourism, 7*(1), 59−74. doi:10.1080/15022250701231915

Moutinho, L., Ballantyne, R., & Rate, S. (2011). Consumer behaviour in tourism. In L. Moutinho (Ed.), *Strategic management in tourism* (2nd ed., pp. 83−126). Cambridge, MA: CABI.

Muñoz, C. L., Wood, N. T., & Solomon, M. R. (2006). Real or blarney? A cross-cultural investigation of the perceived authenticity of Irish pubs. *Journal of Consumer Behaviour, 5*(3), 222−234. doi:10.1002/cb.174

Pine, B. J., & Gilmore, J. H. (1999). *The experience economy: Work is theatre & every business a stage*. Boston, MA: Harvard Business School Press.

Poursani, E. T. (2013). Semiotics of the known and unknown. *Semiotics*, 163–174. doi:10.5840/cpsem201315

Powell, R. B., & Ham, S. H. (2008). Can ecotourism interpretation really lead to pro-conservation knowledge, attitudes and behaviour? Evidence form the

Galapagos Islands. *Journal of Sustainable Tourism*, *16*(4), 467–489. doi:10.1080/09669580802154223

Quadri-Felitti, D., & Fiore, A. M. (2012). Experience economy constructs as a framework for understanding wine tourism. *Journal of Vacation Marketing*, *18*(1), 3–15. doi:10.1177/1356766711432222

Ritzer, G. (1993). *The McDonaldization of society*. Thousand Oaks, CA: Pine Forge.

South African National Parks (SANParks). (2015a). *Addo Elephant National Park: Introduction*. Retrieved from http://www.sanparks.co.za/parks/addo/

South African National Parks (SANParks). (2015b). *Natural & cultural history: Hapoor*. Retrieved from http://www.sanparks.co.za/parks/addo/tourism/history.php

South African National Parks (SANParks). (2015c). Copyright 2011 SANParks. Reprinted with permission.

Stewart, E. J., Hayward, B. M., Devlin, P. J., & Kirby, V. G. (1998). The "place" of interpretation: A new approach to the evaluation of interpretation. *Tourism Management*, *19*(3), 257–266. doi:10.1016/S0261-5177(98)00015-6

Taplin, M. (2015). Addo Information.

Tilden, F. (1977). *Interpreting our heritage* (3rd ed.). Chapel Hill, NC: University of North Carolina Press.

Tynan, C., & McKechnie, S. (2009). Experience marketing: A review and assessment. *Journal of Marketing Management*, *25*(5–6), 501–517. doi:10.1362/026725709X461821

Ward, C. W., & Wilkinson, A. E. (2006). *Conducting meaningful interpretation: A field guide for success*. Golden, CO: Fulcrum Publishing.

Wassler, P., Li, X., & Hung, K. (2015). Hotel theming in China: A qualitative study of practitioners' views. *Journal of Travel & Tourism Marketing*, *11*(2), 1–18. doi:10.1080/10548408.2014.933727

Wong, K. K. F., & Cheung, P. W. Y. (1999). Strategic theming in theme park marketing. *Journal of Vacation Marketing*, *5*(4), 319–332. doi:10.1177/135676679900500402

Zeppel, H., & Muloin, S. (2008). Conservation benefits of interpretation on marine wildlife tours. *Human Dimensions of Wildlife: An International Journal*, *13*(4), 280–294. doi:10.1080/10871200802187105

18 Marketing Culinary Tourism Experiences

Lee Jolliffe

ABSTRACT

Purpose – This chapter identifies issues in the development and marketing of culinary tourism experiences with the goal of determining the value of collaborative forms of product development and marketing.

Methodology/approach – A literature review examines approaches to marketing of culinary experiences identifying a gap in the study of collaborative approaches such as networking, partnering, and alliances. A case study investigates these themes.

Findings – Through the analysis of an in-depth case study of an experiential culinary tourism event in a small city in Eastern Canada (a Restaurant Week) it is determined that informal collaboration in the form of partnership is essential to building and marketing collaborative culinary tourism products and experiences.

Practical implications – This investigation has value for academics studying culinary tourism development and for practitioners implementing collaborative forms of the development and marketing of such tourism offerings and experience.

Originality/value – In the context of culinary tourism, a case study illustrates the value of collaboration in developing and marketing experiential culinary products. Findings indicate informal collaborative partnerships are essential to building and marketing culinary tourism products and experiences, addressing a gap in the literature and providing value for practitioners.

Keywords: Culinary tourism; collaboration; restaurant week

Introduction

The market for culinary tourism is encouraged by a number of overall trends in tourism, including but not limited to: the drive for differentiation of destinations, interest in authentic and experiential activities, foodies and their lifestyle and interests. There is also a growing public interest in where food comes from leading consumers to want to connect with farmers, food producers and chefs to experience local food. In the push to develop new offerings, products and experience opportunities for this new emerging market, practitioners need tools and techniques for developing and bringing to market experiential culinary tourism offerings.

This chapter will document and analyze the marketing function in culinary tourism, particularly in the case of collaboratively developed tourism products that encourage participation of both stakeholders and consumers. As culinary tourism is an assembled or experiential tourism product in which tourists are co-creators, marketing is an essential function in the formation of the culinary tourism product. Since many culinary tourism products consist of different elements provided by a wide variety of partners (e.g., food-related tours, festivals, and events) yet bundled together as one product the topics of collaboration and partnership are significant to the creation and marketing of culinary tourism experiences.

The contribution of this chapter will be to look at the marketing of culinary tourism from the perspective of developing collaborative experiential tourism by assembling culinary elements, contributing to the development of new and practical perspectives related to the creation and marketing of culinary tourism. This will address an existing gap in both the academic and practical literature on culinary tourism. By taking as its focal point the experience of cultural tourism the chapter can delve into the methods and techniques for the design and development of the product, as well as through the examination of existing culinary tourism products provide new insights and perspectives on culinary tourism product marketing.

Following a literature review and problem statement a case study approach will be adopted. The case study methodology is particularly appropriate as the topic is broadly defined, covers contextual conditions and relies on multiple, not singular sources of information (Yin, 1994). Information for the case study will be gathered through interviews, participant observation and examination of existing documentation and reports on the culinary event profiled. Analysis of an in-depth case will allow for the extraction of both theoretical implications and practical insights into the co-creation of collaborative experiential culinary tourism products as well as the role of marketing in this process.

Literature Review

The academic examination of culinary tourism began with the book *Culinary Tourism* (Long, 1998) in which the author, using a folkloristic approach, curated a collection of works examining culinary tourism in public and commercial, private and domestic, constructed and emerging contexts. Issues and cases, development, management and markets for culinary were identified in another volume providing an overview rather than achieving depth on any aspect (Hall, Cambourne, Sharples, Macionis, & Mitchell, 2003). Subsequent research related to culinary tourism has focused on food as a tourism resource (Henderson, 2004), the attractiveness of food to tourism (Cohen & Avieli, 2004), the relationship of food to tourism (Henderson, 2009), and the role of food tourism in sustaining regional identity (Everett & Aitchison, 2008). Culinary tourism trends have been identified as reflecting the rise of the experience economy and reflecting new trends in product development (Richards, 2012). Several authors have recently focused on the niche market for foodies (Getz, Robinson, Andersson, & Vujicic, 2014). There has also been a practical handbook that provided an overview of many different areas of developing and managing culinary tourism experiences (Wolf, 2014).

Other works have examined market niches and branding of culinary tourism (Hall et al., 2003; Hashimoto & Telfer, 2006). One volume had a focus on the marketing of culinary tourism (Hall, 2013) with contributions on the role of government in marketing food tourism. The broader role of culinary tourism in regional development was examined (Boyne, Hall, & Williams, 2003). Market segments have been generally discussed and identified in the literature to date and recently authors have identified in detail the motivations of a particular segment, that of foodies (Robinson & Getz, 2012). The positioning of culinary tourism on a national and regional basis has been identified by several authors (Estevez, 2015; Hashimoto & Telfer, 2006) identifying the key role of partnerships in profiling culinary tourism to external markets.

The literature on collaboration in tourism businesses is relevant to examining the theme of partnering in culinary tourism (Gursoy, Saayman, & Sotiriadis, 2015). Collaboration can occur in the form of partnerships or strategic alliances that are relevant to the development of experiential tourism products found in culinary tourism. In particular in the development of experience-based products business networks, partnerships and alliances offer the opportunity for smaller tourism operators to cooperate together to develop and market experiences. Stakeholder involvement at a variety of levels is acknowledged as essential for the collaborative development of tourism experiences. In terms of culinary tourism stakeholders need to take advantage of co-operation, which has been identified as a primary growth strategy for such tourism (Estevez, 2015). Wolf (2014) also highlights the benefits of collaborative networks in developing culinary tourism products. Both collaboration and co-operation can be accomplished through networks, partnerships, or strategic alliances. Specific collaborations in culinary tourism may take different forms, orientated toward the launching of specific products or projects or as strategic marketing alliances (Estevez, 2015). Collaboration among stakeholders was identified as an important factor for the development of a regional approach to the marketing of culinary tourism in a particular region of Germany (Ottenbacher & Harrington, 2011).

Events are one type of experiential tourism product reflecting the trend toward collaboration within the move toward experiential tourism. A UNWTO report on food tourism has identified events as the most common form of marketing such as tourism (Richards, 2012). Wolf (2014) indicated that food events should strive to be self-funded after no more than three years. A specific strategic planning framework for culinary events and assets has been proposed by Sotiriadis (2015) as an integrated approach to the planning of culinary tourism activities. Others have examined the role of food festivals in nurturing among visitors a connection with a destination (Rand, Heath, & Alberts, 2003). Food-related festivals and events are recognized as the ideal location for visitors such as today's foodies to experience authentic local cuisines

(Robinson & Getz, 2012). Events featuring cuisine allow for the participation and collaboration of local stakeholders and the bundling of individual culinary experiences, such as tasting, demonstrations or dining into a culinary tourism product that can be featured as reflective of local cuisines (Hashimoto & Telfer, 2006). This reflects current trends toward authenticity and local experiences. Food then is more than just sustenance; it is for visitors a means of experiencing destinations.

Another method for creating culinary tourism experiences is to establish a culinary trail through partnership of various producers and food service providers. Such trails may have a regional culinary focus as in The Aaran Taste Trail (Boyne, Williams, & Hall, 2002) or on a particular food or beverage in a regional context as with the Waterloo-Wellington Ale Trail (Plummer, Telfer, & Hashimoto, 2006). The creation of such culinary trails or routes requires networking and partnering of both food producers and providers and co-operation with local destination-marketing agencies.

Many of the works cited above focus on food-related tourism development and destination markets. Sotiriadis (2015) found that in order for a destination to be successful in culinary tourism it is necessary to be strategic and develop linkages among stakeholders. Using the case of Canada (Hashimoto & Telfer, 2006) examined culinary branding as creating a place where the cuisines of the world come together noting that the various regions also have potential for being identified and marketed through cuisine. Telfer (2000) noted the importance of strategic alliances between food producers, restaurants, and chefs in terms of the development of culinary tourism in Canada's Niagara region. In the case of Argentina Estevez (2015) identified the importance of interaction between culinary tourism stakeholders, noting both formal collaboration in the form of alliances or partnerships and informal collaboration in the case of particular projects. Local food has also been shown in the case of South Africa to have an important role in destination-marketing, as a means of differentiating locales (Rand et al., 2003). Local food products and experiences that are conceived of as authentic can symbolize the place and culture of a destination (Sims, 2009). In Scotland food-related collaborative tourism initiatives have been recognized as important to regional development (Boyne et al., 2002).

However, more work is needed on relevant themes in terms of partnership and collaboration in culinary tourism (Estevez, 2015). Existing contemporary marketing theories and techniques

Table 1.   Collaborative Forms for Developing and Marketing
Culinary Tourism Experiences.

Forms	Characteristics	Examples from Literature
Networking	Informal Exploratory Establishing goals	Culinary tourism campaign in region of Germany (Ottenbacher & Harrington, 2011)
Partnerships	Informal/formal Common goals Important for small and medium enterprises	Waterloo-Wellington Ale Trail (Plummer et al., 2006)
Alliances	Formal Strategic goals Membership criteria	Isle of Aaran Taste Trail (Boyne et al., 2002)

that apply to this work such as networking, co-marketing and cross-promotion (Boone & Kurtz, 2013) as well as strategic alliances and partnerships (Lamb, Hair, & McDaniel, 2011) are relevant to this discussion. A theme worthy of further investigation is that of how aspects of cuisine are collaboratively grouped into offerings or experiential opportunities and what the role of marketing is in that process. Specific examples of collaboration in culinary tourism demonstrate the different levels and range of joint efforts that exist in terms of creating culinary tourism products and experiences (Table 1).

How then are culinary components grouped or assembled into experiential culinary tourism products? What is the role of marketing in terms of partnerships, strategic alliances and co-marketing in terms of developing forms of culinary-based tourism experiences? An in-depth case study is developed in this chapter as a means of investigating these themes. The theoretical basis for investigating this problem is found in the literature previously reviewed on collaborative forms, in terms of business networks, partnerships, and alliances from a marketing perspective.

Case Study

CONTEXT

Illustrating the issues and aspects of culinary tourism production and marketing identified in the literature review is the following in-depth case study of a culinary tourism product in the city of Saint John, New Brunswick, Canada. The choice of Saint John is both one of convenience and also suitable for investigation as cuisine has been adopted as part of the tourism brand for Canada and its regions (Hashimoto & Telfer, 2006). While identifying a Canadian cuisine has remained elusive there is agreement that the various regions of the country have distinctive cuisines (Jacobs, 2009). The Canadian Tourism Commission in their effort to create a culinary tourism brand also focused on the culinary distinctiveness of the various regions of the country as reflected by both immigration and physical geography that shaped distinctive cuisines (Deneault & Canadian Tourism Commission, 2002).

The city of Saint John demonstrates characteristics of the East Coast regional cuisine also noted by Hashimoto and Telfer (2006). This maritime city in Eastern Canada has a cuisine infused with local products that reflect its coastlines, rivers and forests, including seafood, duels, blueberries, and apples as well as colonial ties and traditional trade routes. East Coast cuisine has influences from the British, the Acadians, and the Loyalists (who came north from the United States in 1783) and Atlantic seafood has become a recognizable part of the appeal. Local products reflect the physical geography and climate of the region. Traditional local food products include seafood, blueberries, molasses, maple syrup, dulse, and apples.

For example, the global wild blueberry industry is confined to Northeastern North America, with the province producing 25% of Canadian output (12% globally) (New Brunswick Department of Agriculture, n.d.). A local company, Crosby's is the sole company in Canada responsible for importing, processing, and distributing molasses, a by-product of sugar production in a trade that links back to the Saint John Port's historic ties to the sugar producing islands of the Caribbean (Jolliffe, 2012). Much of the world's maple syrup is produced in Eastern North America and New Brunswick is the third largest producer after Quebec and Vermont. Maple syrup has become part of the culinary tourism product through festivals (such as the Maple Capital of Atlantic Canada Festival, in Saint Quentin, N.B.), sugar shack operations open to the public through the season and maple syrup sold as souvenirs in locations such as the historic Saint John City Market. Dulse is also a characteristic produce utilized in cuisine and sold as a souvenir. Blueberries, maple syrup, and dulse are all noted as native Canadian food plants (Jacobs, 2009).

The regional cuisine of New Brunswick can be experienced through food service outlets (restaurants, cafes) as well as by participating in one of a number of culinary tourism events held across the province. There are a number of small-scale food events and festivals, including The Fundy Food Festival, a charity event held annually in Saint John and specific community food festivals reflecting local foods such as Riverview's Maple Syrup Festival. Weekly farmers markets are also held across the province, connecting consumers with local food experiences. Several cities host restaurant weeks including Fredericton (Dine Around Freddy) and Saint John (Chop Chop) and the latter is featured in this case.

THE CONCEPT

The concept of the restaurant week originated in New York City in 1992, and has since been replicated in various forms around the world. The basic idea is that participating restaurants provide a special menu and price during a specific time period that is normally slow for these establishments, creating a demand for their product and developing a new customer base (Hochwarth, 2005). A study conducted in 2015 has shown that establishments participating in Restaurant Week had a 54% increase in first time diners and a 38% boost in total diners during a two-week event period (Restaurant Hospitality, 2015). At times restaurant weeks have also been employed to bring people back to restaurants after a crisis such as those organized in New York city after the 9/11 attacks in the city (Green, Bartholomew, & Murrmann, 2004).

THE EVENT

For a week, twice a year for a week in both fall (November) and winter (February) seasons, restaurants in the historic uptown of Saint John offer patrons a special menu at an attractive price for lunch or dinner during the Chop Chop Restaurant Week. The bi-annual week-long event, established in 2009 serves to create a buzz in the uptown, encouraging patrons to try new restaurants and to return to favorite ones. Contributing food establishments create special plated menu items at attractive prices, which encourage participation. In November 2015, 24 participating food establishments offered Chop Chop diners an appetizer plate for $8, a two-course lunch for $13, and a three-course dinner for $31.

Many of the individual restaurant menus for the week feature local ingredients, identified above as characteristic of the East

Table 2. Example of a Dinner Menu from a Restaurant Participating in Chop Chop.

Restaurant/Chef	Courses
Port City Royal/ Jakob Lutes	*First course* – Corn and leek broth with root vegetables and croutons
Chef and Owner	*Second course* – River John Blue Potato Puree with Lady Ashburn Pickles and choice of: Poached Boston Bluefish, Charred Onion, Creamed Leek -OR- Tourtiere
	Third course – Bread Pudding with Buttercup Squash, Pear and Brown Sugar Sauce

Coast regional food production and cuisine exhibited in the province of New Brunswick. Examples of menu offerings highlight the interpretation of the regional cuisine and the use of local products as well as the playfulness of the chefs in creating new interpretations of the regional cuisine (Table 2). For example, the entry from the chef/owner of Port City Royal indicates "Inspired by his love of New Brunswick, he is drawn to its complex culinary history and our place within it" (Uptown Saint John, 2015). From both an experiential tourism and marketing perspective this is important in terms of branding cuisine for tourism, providing both locals and visitors with opportunities to experience these distinctive culinary traditions. The creation of the special menus for the week also provides the restaurants and their chefs with a platform for strategic product innovation and customer feedback regarding new items. Demand for dining is therefore increased by reasonable price points for Chop Chop plates at both lunch and dinner.

PARTNERSHIP

The event is developed and administered by Uptown Saint John, the local business improvement association, funded by a levy paid by business property owners. It thus represents retailers including restaurants and other food service establishments in the historic uptown of Saint John. In terms of collaboration the Restaurant Week had developed organically as a networked event and form of promoting the Uptown, loosely organized by the association that co-ordinates promotion in the form now of a poster, web site, social media (Facebook and Twitter) and radio advertising. In the early years of the event established in 2009 participating restaurants paid small marketing fee, however as the event gained momentum the marketing costs were able to be absorbed into the budget of the association. Uptown Saint John now indicates that the chefs of the 24 participating restaurants, most of which are independently owned and in some cases owned by chefs, provide a strong level of support for the event, welcoming the opportunity to create new and innovative menu items and to attract a new clientele (Tissington and Hanson, Personal Interview, January 19, 2016).

After six years of operating the event, and at the suggestion of the participating chefs, the Chop Chop event was rebranded for Fall of 2015, with a new poster showing the group of chefs. A dedicated web site featuring stories about the individual chefs and their restaurants was also developed. It is interesting to note that the photograph of the group of chefs on the event poster was a serious one (Figure 1), whereas the photo of the group on the web site is more playful. Uptown Saint John has indicated that this rebranding of the event was an important refresh of an already popular event as it enhances visitor experience of the events by providing personal backgrounds of the chefs and their establishments on the web site (Tissington and Hanson, Personal Interview, January 19, 2016). Local radio interviews with the chefs were also organized immediately before the event week.

In terms of the characteristics of partnership reflected in the literature the Chop Chop event represents an informal arrangement (there is no written agreement and currently no marketing fee) of the restaurants occupying buildings that are part of the business improvement district. It also reflects the character of other partnerships in culinary tourism by having common goals (of promoting business in the Uptown area) and being important for small to medium enterprises. The event demonstrates the value of business-orientated partnerships (Lamb et al., 2011) in assembling and then marketing what is essentially an experiential product. Participating restaurants are for the most part independently owned and operated but are united through their membership in the business improvement association. The restaurant week offers these food service establishments who are essentially competitors a means of collaborating with each other in developing an audience for culinary experiences in Saint John. The event has played a role in developing a vibrant restaurant scene in the central business district of this historic city.

Figure 1.   Chop Chop Poster 2015. Source: With permission from Uptown Saint John.

In 2015 the event also had a partnership with The Lunch Connection, an organization that provides free hot lunch programs to deserving children and youth in Saint John. With $1 from every Chop Chop plate sold being given directly to this charity this was also a way for the event and Uptown Saint John to give back to the community. The group of chefs from participating restaurants participated with the association in presenting quite a large cheque to The Lunch Connection. The networked partnering reflected by this giving back to the community is possible because of the shared goals of both Uptown Saint John and the group of restaurant chefs working together to develop the culinary scene of the city.

MARKETING

The Chop Chop event is made known through traditional promotional techniques, such as a poster, a dedicated web page (Chop Chop, 2015), the web pages of participating restaurants and radio spots. In addition the event employs social media, for example, through a Facebook page and the use of Twitter. Targeted sponsored advertisements on Facebook are also employed to promote the event.

The event benefits from the networked efforts of Uptown Saint John, the business development association along with those of the participating restaurants who also market the event through their own websites and social media sites. The menus for each individual site are available not only on the Chop Chop restaurant week web page but also on the websites of individual establishments. Co-marketing partnerships such as this one offer fresh opportunity for promotion (Bucklin & Sengupta, 1993). The value of cross-promotion is also reflected in this case (Boone & Kurtz, 2013). These are particularly important approaches when marketing experiential culinary tourism, for the customers who are involved in the co-creation of the product need to be attracted to participate.

A key marketing partner and acknowledged sponsor for the Chop Chop Restaurant Week is Discover Saint John, the destination-marketing agency. As this agency is involved in destination-marketing the experiential culinary tourism products such as the restaurant week is an important part of the branding of the city. The event reflects a destination-orientated form of collaboration noted by Gursoy et al. (2015).

Other marketing partners include two local radio stations that Uptown Saint John often works with, a food wholesale that supplies some of the participating restaurants and a local brewery. The participation of sponsors from food-related sectors reflects the strong support that has been developed for the Chop Chop event since its establishment in 2009.

Discussion

The Chop Chop event profiled above demonstrates the grouping of culinary components into a product and the value of an informal partnership for the collaborative marketing of culinary tourism. By bundling together special culinary experiences an augmented product is created, that invents an opportunity for innovation and serves to reinforce and build upon the existing customer base. Embracing a variety of both traditional and new marketing techniques also enables the event to reach a broad customer base of both existing and new clientele. The refresh in the branding of the event accomplished in 2015 has also served to give promotional materials a new look and appeal, to continue to be relevant to the participating restaurants and to the participating customers while also appealing to new audiences.

For the restaurants this event also provides an opportunity to work collaboratively with each other, contributing to the development of the culinary scene in the city. For the organizer, Uptown Saint John, the event is a means to achieve their objectives as a business improvement association, promoting and highlighting the retail experience in the Uptown. This is important for the historic city center, for as with other cities in North America much of the retail had moved to shopping malls on the outskirts of the city, and the unique mix of small shops and restaurants in the Uptown is just beginning to emerge as a key influencer in making the central area of the city into a destination for locals and visitors. In this way the organization Uptown Saint John is employing strategic planning to achieve their results.

The Chop Chop event furthermore contributes to the efforts of Discover Saint John in marketing dining experiences in the uptown as part of the tourism product and reflects the collaborative efforts of tourism operators in the city to build tourism experiences. The restaurant weeks therefore support the destination in creating a competitive advantage through its experiential culinary offerings (Sotiriadis, 2015). In a way the restaurant week creates for a short time a culinary route and focused culinary experience in the compact and historic center of the city of Saint John. This is an attribute currently reflected in destination marking efforts but that could also be harnessed in a more formally constructed year round route for visitors to experience the regional cuisine through dining in the restaurants of this historic city.

Conclusion

This chapter has shown the benefits of the collaborative development and marketing of culinary tourism experiences through networks, partnerships, and alliances. It has identified through an in-depth case of a culinary tourism product that partnering between organizations and supporting networks made up of members is essential to both the development and the cooperative marketing of such experiences. In this way the chapter contributes toward furthering existing research on the effective marketing of high quality and memorable tourism experiences in the field of culinary tourism. Building on previous research on what is necessary for the branding of culinary tourism (Hashimoto & Telfer, 2006) and the benefits of taking a strategic approach to the marketing of such products (Sotiriadis, 2015) the chapter furthers our understanding of how to establish common goals to develop and market such tourism. It highlights the importance of collaborative forms of product development and innovation in marketing in terms of both networking and partnering that will be applicable for both academics and practitioners in the growing area of experiential culinary tourism. In the case of the restaurant week in the city of Saint John this work contributes to our understanding of how a strategic approach to developing culinary tourism experiences can benefit destination branding and marketing, a lesson that will be applicable to other cities wishing to identify themselves with regional cuisines.

References

Boone, L., & Kurtz, D. (2013). *Contemporary marketing*. Boston, MA: Cengage Learning.

Boyne, S., Hall, D., & Williams, F. (2003). Policy, support and promotion for food-related tourism initiatives: A marketing approach to regional development. *Journal of Travel & Tourism Marketing*, 14(3−4), 131−154.

Boyne, S., Williams, F., & Hall, D. (2002). On the trail of regional success: Tourism, food production and the Isle of Arran Taste Trail. In A.-M. Hjaljar & G. Richards (Eds.), *Tourism and Gastronomy* (pp. 91–114). London: Routledge.

Bucklin, L. P., & Sengupta, S. (1993). Organizing successful co-marketing alliances. *The Journal of Marketing, 57*(2), 32–46.

Chop Chop. (2015). Retrieved from http://uptownsj.com/chop-chop-2015.html. Accessed on January 10, 2015.

Cohen, E., & Avieli, N. (2004). Food in tourism: Attraction and impediment. *Annals of Tourism Research, 31*(4), 755–778.

Deneault, M., & Canadian Tourism Commission. (2002). *Acquiring a taste for cuisine tourism: A product development strategy.* Ottawa: Canadian Tourism Commission.

Estevez, L. (2015). Are partnerships necessary in culinary tourism? In D. Gursoy, M. Saayman, & M. D. Sotiriadis (Eds.), *Collaboration in tourism businesses and destinations: A handbook* (pp. 155–173). Bingley, UK: Emerald Group Publishing Limited.

Everett, S., & Aitchison, C. (2008). The role of food tourism in sustaining regional identity: A case study of Cornwall, South West England. *Journal of Sustainable Tourism, 16*(2), 150–167.

Getz, D., Robinson, R. N., Andersson, T. D., & Vujicic, S. (2014). *Foodies and food tourism.* Oxford: Goodfellow Publishers.

Green, C. G., Bartholomew, P., & Murrmann, S. (2004). New York restaurant industry: Strategic responses to September 11, 2001. *Journal of Travel & Tourism Marketing, 15*(2–3), 63–79.

Gursoy, D., Saayman, M., & Sotiriadis, M. D. (2015). *Collaboration in tourism businesses and destinations: A handbook.* Bingley, UK: Emerald Group Publishing Limited.

Hall, C. M. (2013). *Wine, food, and tourism marketing.* London: Routledge.

Hall, C. M., Cambourne, B., Sharples, L., Macionis, N., & Mitchell, R. (2003). *Food tourism around the world development, management and markets.* Oxford: Butterworth-Heinnemann.

Hashimoto, A., & Telfer, D. J. (2006). Selling Canadian culinary tourism: Branding the global and the regional product. *Tourism Geographies, 8*(1), 31–55.

Henderson, J. C. (2004). Food as a tourism resource: A view from Singapore. *Tourism Recreation Research, 29*(3), 69–74.

Henderson, J. C. (2009). Food tourism reviewed. *British Food Journal, 111*(4), 317–326.

Hochwarth, P. (2005). The genius of restaurant week. *Restaurant Hospitality, 89*(7), 62–68.

Jacobs, H. (2009). Structural elements in Canadian cuisine. *Cuizine: The Journal of Canadian Food Cultures.* [Cuizine: Revue Des Cultures Culinaires Au Canada.], *2*(1), 62–68. Retrieved from https://www.erudit.org/revue/cuizine/2009/v2/n1/039510ar.html?vue=resume. Accessed on January 10, 2016.

Jolliffe, L. (2012). *Sugar heritage and tourism in transition.* Bristol: Channel View Publications.

Lamb, C., Hair, J., & McDaniel, C. (2011). *Essentials of marketing*. Bingley: Cengage Learning.

Long, L. M. (1998). *Culinary tourism* (Vol. 55). Lexington, KY: University Press of Kentucky.

New Brunswick Department of Agriculture. (n.d.). *Industry overview: New Brunswick Wild Blueberries*. Retrieved from http://www2.gnb.ca/content/dam/gnb/Departments/10/pdf/Agriculture/WildBlueberries-BleuetsSauvages/A10e2010.pdf. Accessed on January 15, 2016.

Ottenbacher, M. C., & Harrington, R. J. (2011). A case study of a culinary tourism campaign in Germany: Implications for strategy making and successful implementation. *Journal of Hospitality & Tourism Research*, 3–28.

Plummer, R., Telfer, D., & Hashimoto, A. (2006). The rise and fall of the Waterloo-Wellington Ale Trail: A study of collaboration within the tourism industry. *Current Issues in Tourism*, 9(3), 191–205. doi:10.2167/cit/194.0

Rand, G. E. D., Heath, E., & Alberts, N. (2003). The role of local and regional food in destination marketing. *Journal of Travel & Tourism Marketing*, 14(3–4), 97–112.

Restaurant Hospitality. (2015). *Study: Restaurant week deals build business, boost bottom line*. January 24, 2015. Retrieved from http://restaurant-hospitality.com/consumer-trends/study-restaurant-week-deals-build-business-boost-bottom-line. Accessed on January 10, 2016.

Richards, G. (2012). *Food and the tourism experience, A Global Report on food tourism*. UNWTO: Madrid.

Robinson, R. N., & Getz, D. (2012). Getting involved: 'Foodies' and food tourism (p. 176). Presented at the CAUTHE 2012: The new golden age of tourism and hospitality; Book 2; Proceedings of the 22nd Annual Conference, La Trobe University.

Sims, R. (2009). Food, place and authenticity: Local food and the sustainable tourism experience. *Journal of Sustainable Tourism*, 17(3), 321–336.

Sotiriadis, M. D. (2015). Culinary tourism assets and events: Suggesting a strategic planning tool. *International Journal of Contemporary Hospitality Management*, 27(6), 1214–1232.

Telfer, D. J. (2000). Tastes of Niagara: Building strategic alliances between tourism and agriculture. *International Journal of Hospitality & Tourism Administration*, 1(1), 71–88.

Uptown Saint John. (2015). *Chop Chop*. Retrieved from http://uptownsj.com/chop-chop-2015.html. Accessed on January 20, 2016.

Wolf, E. (2014). *Have fork will travel: A practical handbook for food & drink tourism professionals*. Seattle, OR: World Food Travel Association.

Yin, R. (1994). *Case study research: Design and methods*. Beverly Hills, CA: Sage.

19 Managing and Marketing Tourism Experiences: Extending the Travel Risk Perception Literature to Address Affective Risk Perceptions

Ashley Schroeder, Lori Pennington-Gray, Maximiliano Korstanje and Geoffrey Skoll

ABSTRACT

Purpose – This chapter discusses the current risk perception literature in the tourism field. The chapter critiques the literature and offers a solution through a more conceptual and operational definition of risk perceptions. Specifically, the inclusion of affective risk perceptions will be added to the literature via the risk-as-feelings hypothesis. Extension of the current literature will enhance research moving forward.

Methodology/approach – The chapter will provide a literature review, propose a conceptual model, and operationalize the risk perception variables.

Findings – The outcome of this chapter is to provide a conceptual model as a framework to address risk perception studies in tourism and hospitality in the future. The model will provide clear measurement scales to be tested.

Originality/value – This chapter gives a much needed theoretical and conceptual foundation to the study of risk perceptions in the travel and tourism literature.

Keywords: Risk; fear; tourism; affective risk perceptions; risk as feelings

Introduction

Given the economic significance of tourism to most economies around the world, crises can have devastating impacts on the destination, tourism system, and economy (Tourism Crisis Management Initiative (TCMI), 2015; United Nations World Tourism Organization (UNWTO), 2011). In the past two decades, we have seen continued growth in these events, as there has been a documented increase in the quantity and severity of both nature-induced and human-induced crises across the globe in modern times (Drabek, 2009). This increasing prevalence of crises has highlighted the significant need to prioritize safety and security issues in the tourism industry (Pacific Asia Travel Association (PATA), 2011). In addition, increasing pressure is being put on destinations and tourism organizations to effectively manage their businesses and safeguard both their visitors and their images (TCMI, 2015).

While tourism academics have taken an organizational attribution approach to defining a crisis (e.g., Faulkner, 2001; Prideaux, Laws, & Faulkner, 2003; Scott & Laws, 2005), tourism practitioners have taken a different approach to defining a tourism crisis. Specifically, PATA (2003) defined a tourism crisis as "any situation that has the potential to affect long-term confidence in an organization or a product, or which may interfere with its ability to continue operating normally" (p. 2). Similarly, UNWTO (2005) defined a tourism crisis as "any unexpected event that affects traveler confidence in a destination and interferes with the ability to continue operating normally" (p. 11). Accordingly, practitioners have focused on determining when a situation becomes a crisis in terms of consumer confidence and business operations within the tourism system. Through the consumer confidence element, both PATA (2003) and UNWTO's (2005) definitions recognize that if tourists perceive a situation to be a crisis, it should be considered as a crisis and managed accordingly.

In practice, the monitoring of tourists' risk perceptions is increasing in attention in the current environment. At the same time, there is increasing criticism of the travel risk literature (Korstanje, 2009; Pennington-Gray & Schroeder, 2013). Criticisms have primarily focused on the conceptualization and operationalization of perceived risk. Accordingly, the purpose of this chapter is to move the travel risk literature forward by proposing a theory-based model for the study of travel risk so as to provide a strong theoretical foundation for destination risk management.

Literature Review

Over the past three decades, the tourism literature has examined the role of risk perceptions in an effort to gain a better understanding of the factors that influence travel decision-making in these uncertain times. However, major criticisms of the existing body of knowledge related to travel risk stem from a lack of conceptual clarity and a lack of theoretical underpinnings.

Overall, the conceptualization and measurement of travel risk perceptions have not been consistent with the theoretical frameworks of travel risk studies. For example, Sönmez and Graefe (1998a, 1998b) indicated that protection motivation theory was one of the theories that guided their research. However, the conceptualization of perceived risk according to the theory was not applied in their study. Rather, Sönmez and Graefe (1998a) defined risk perception level as "the amount and types of risk potential tourists associated with international tourism" (p. 128). Thus, even when travel risk studies have adopted a theoretical lens, the conceptualization of travel risk has lacked strong theoretical underpinnings.

The fields of health behavior (Maddux & Rogers, 1983; Rogers, 1975, 1983) and psychology (Loewenstein, Weber, Hsee, & Welch, 2001) consider risk perceptions to be multidimensional. For example, protection motivation theory, one of the most established health behavior theories, suggests that risk perceptions consist of an evaluation of the perceived vulnerability to and perceived severity of a risk (Floyd, Prentice-Dunn, & Rogers, 2000; Maddux & Rogers, 1983; Rogers, 1975, 1983). Several tourism studies have adopted the perceived vulnerability measure of risk perceptions (Floyd, Gibson, Pennington-Gray, & Thapa, 2004; Kozak, Crotts, & Law, 2007; Law, 2006; Pennington-Gray, Kaplanidou, & Schroeder, 2013; Pennington-Gray, Schroeder, & Kaplanidou, 2011; Schroeder & Pennington-Gray, 2014; Schroeder, Pennington-Gray, Donohoe, & Kiousis, 2013; Schroeder, Pennington-Gray, Kaplanidou, & Zhan, 2013), while few have measured perceived severity (Kozak et al., 2007; Law, 2006). Thus, while theory considers perceived risk to be multidimensional, travel risk studies have tended to consider risk perceptions to be unidimensional. Provided that protection motivation theory is often cited as the theoretical framework for travel risk studies, tourism scholars have generally had a problem with conceptualizing and measuring travel risk perceptions in accordance with the guiding theoretical framework of their studies.

Often times, the operationalization of travel risk has lacked any theoretical underpinnings. For example, simplistic measures such as a 1–5 scale of very safe-very risky (Sönmez & Graefe, 1998a) have been used. Also, the measurement of travel risk has been derived from either the travel risk literature or the destination image literature (Schroeder, Pennington-Gray, Kaplanidou, et al., 2013). Those who have turned to the destination image literature have suggested that travel risk is a component of destination image because risk factors are included in destination image studies (Qi, Gibson, & Zhang, 2009). However, destination image has often been operationalized through a series of either Likert-type scales or semantic differential scales (Echtner & Ritchie, 2003). Accordingly, measures of perceived risk based on the destination image literature have tended to lack theoretical underpinnings, which is also a shortcoming of the destination image literature.

In addition, while travel risk studies have considered risk perceptions to be either a factor which prevents travel or one which influences one's image of a destination (before travel), the field of health behavior focuses on the cognitive processes from which risk is perceived (Maddux & Rogers, 1983; Rogers, 1975, 1983). This research also occurs prior to engaging in the behavior; however, it uses a psychological paradigm to understand both cognitive and affective influences of risk (Loewenstein et al., 2001; Slovic & Peters, 2006). Therefore, adapting the conceptualization of risk perceptions from the health behavior and psychology literature can provide a deeper understanding of the processes that tourists go through when evaluating travel risk, rather than a simple measure of "what prevents you from traveling?" or "what is your image of the destination?"

Korstanje (2009) has also argued that the study of risk perceptions is contextually important to understand and that asking about risks prior to travel is merely an exploration of anxiety. He suggests that there is a lack of direct stimuli which is the critical element necessary to form risk perceptions. He argues that studies which are conducted prior to the trip (Lepp & Gibson, 2003) are not measuring perceived risk, although the authors claim they are.

Lyng (2008) argues the opposite to Korstanje (2009), and suggests that risk perceptions can be constructed and reconstructed through narratives. The argument here is that risk is more fluid in its interpretation and evaluation. This then challenges the notion that risk is not just a categorization (e.g., political, health, crime), but, rather, a distinction between cognitive perceptions of risk, uncertainty, and emotion (fear, anxiety, and excitement).

Furthermore, the existing body of knowledge related to travel risk has primarily focused on risk perceptions. However, there are a variety of other risk-related constructs studied in other academic disciplines. Thus, in order to consider additional risk-related constructs in the context of travel, there is a need for an interdisciplinary approach to the study of travel risk. By doing so, the travel risk literature must recognize that the study of risk is not new. The health behavior and psychology literature, for example, are more advanced and have a vast body of knowledge related to risky decision-making that should be integrated with the existing body of knowledge related to travel risk. For example, perceived efficacy is an important risk-related construct in the fields of health behavior (Floyd et al., 2000; Maddux & Rogers, 1983; Rogers, 1975, 1983) and psychology (Bandura, 1977, 1982, 1986, 1992) that is understudied in the travel risk literature. Therefore, future travel risk research must take an interdisciplinary approach by integrating knowledge from several different disciplines, including health behavior and psychology.

In summary, the main criticisms of the existing body of knowledge stem from a lack of conceptual clarity and a lack of theoretical underpinnings. Overall, the travel risk literature needs to reconceptualize and reoperationalize travel risk perceptions.

There is also a need to consider additional risk-related constructs which can be integrated with the existing travel risk literature to provide a deeper understanding of the role of risk in travel decision-making, such as affective risk perceptions, perceived severity, perceived vulnerability, and efficacy beliefs (in terms of response efficacy and self-efficacy). Thus, there is a need to create a testable model and operationalize the constructs proposed.

Extension of Risk Perceptions

Taking the major criticisms of the travel risk research into consideration, this chapter adopts a theoretical lens guided by protection motivation theory and the risk-as-feelings hypothesis.

PROTECTION MOTIVATION THEORY

Protection motivation theory (PMT) (Rogers, 1975, 1983) is considered to be one of the most prominent models in the field of health behavior (Weinstein, 1993). Albeit referenced in the tourism literature (Sönmez & Graefe, 1998a, 1998b), the theory has neither been operationalized effectively nor tested. PMT was originally developed as a theory of fear appeals (Rogers, 1975); however, the theory was later revised into a general attitudinal change model (Maddux & Rogers, 1983; Rogers, 1983). Particularly, by adding the self-efficacy construct, PMT became an attitudinal model which focused on the cognitive processes which mediate behavioral change (Maddux & Rogers, 1983; Rogers, 1983). As a general attitudinal change model, PMT offers a framework for understanding the reason for attitudinal and behavioral change in risky situations (Floyd et al., 2000). Prentice-Dunn and Rogers (1986) suggested that PMT is comprehensive enough to be applicable to any context involving risk.

A core assumption of PMT is that individuals go through two cognitive processes when deciding whether or not to engage in a behavior to protect oneself from a risk (Rogers, 1983). First, individuals go through a threat appraisal process in which they evaluate risk in terms of perceived severity and perceived vulnerability (Floyd et al., 2000). Perceived severity represents the perceived level of harm to an individual that is associated with the event (Rogers, 1975). Perceived vulnerability represents the perceived likelihood that a threatened event will occur (Rogers, 1975). Second, individuals go through a coping appraisal process in which they evaluate behaviors to cope with risk in terms of response efficacy and self-efficacy (Floyd et al., 2000). Response efficacy represents the perception of the effectiveness of a recommended behavior in protecting oneself from a risk (Floyd et al., 2000). Self-efficacy represents the perception that an individual is able to successfully perform a recommended behavior in an effort to protect oneself from a risk (Floyd et al., 2000).

The reason that PMT assumes that the threat appraisal process comes before the coping appraisal process is that an individual must perceive a risk before assessing whether they will engage in a behavior to reduce a risk or not (Floyd et al., 2000). The outcome of the two cognitive mediational processes is that the threat appraisal and the coping appraisal processes come together to stimulate, maintain, and guide engagement in risk reduction behaviors (Floyd et al., 2000). It is important to note that PMT does not assume that decision makers are rational (Floyd et al., 2000). Rather, cognitive and motivational biases are believed to have an effect on all PMT constructs and the two cognitive evaluation processes (Floyd et al., 2000).

RISK-AS-FEELINGS HYPOTHESIS

The risk-as-feelings hypothesis, a concept originating from the field of psychology, suggests that both affective and cognitive risk perceptions directly influence decision-making (Loewenstein et al., 2001). According to the risk-as-feeing hypothesis, individuals comprehend risks via two different methods – one relies on a cognitive approach, which is established on the basis of logic and reasoning, while the other depends on an affective approach, which involves people's emotions and affective responses (Loewenstein et al., 2001). Risk perceptions reflect the cognitive approach, since individuals normally analyze a risky situation through reasoning (perceived severity and perceived vulnerability) (Slovic & Peters, 2006). This applies equally to tourists, whose risk perceptions are situation- and destination-specific, and result from people's thorough assessment of the situation (Kozak et al., 2007).

Emotions or affective risk perceptions reflect the affective approach. As such, research has found that emotions such as anxiety, dread, fear, and worry directly influence reactions to risky situations (Loewenstein et al., 2001). Emotions associated with the affective consequences, in return, have an effect on cognitive evaluations (Loewenstein et al., 2001). Research has suggested that affective risk perceptions are represented by three major constructs: uncertainty, worry, and anxiety.

Interestingly, the risk-as-feelings hypothesis suggests that while cognitive risk perceptions and affective risk perceptions directly influence risky decision-making, there is also an interaction between these two types of risk perceptions. Therefore, the risk-as-feelings hypothesis acknowledges that cognitive risk perceptions and affective risk perceptions may be associated with one another (Loewenstein et al., 2001). Furthermore, scholars have also suggested that affective risk perceptions may be causally linked (Buhr & Dugas, 2009). Much of the ongoing research in psychology supports this causal string which starts with one's uncertainty, which influences worry, which influences anxiety (Buhr & Dugas, 2009).

Affective risk perceptions play a crucial role in the mitigation or inflation of risks. One of the authorities in the psychology of affection is Cass Sunstein. He argues that risks are often inflated due to bad decisions, which is a combination of two psychological mechanisms, the neglect of probability and the heuristic of risk. The theory says that risk assessment is previously determined by emotional disposition instead of rational evaluation — cognitive activity. Sometimes people delve into the worst possible situations due to failure to inquire properly about the real cause of danger. Here we also see that Sunstein (2003) suggests that affective risk perceptions are antecedents of cognitive risk perceptions.

Affective Risk Perceptions in the Travel Literature

Within the travel literature, Reisinger and Mavondo (2005) found that there is a high correlation between risk perceptions and the degree of anxiety a person may feel. They found that tolerance of uncertainty seems to play a vital role in threat perceptions. Aversion to risk is associated with intolerance of uncertainty. Moreover, the fear of traveling has been discussed by Korstanje (2011). In a study on Nomad tribes, he found that not only were Nomads unfamiliar with risks, but they also perceived the geography as a continuum not a "here" or "there." Nomads had a sense that ownership of property and sedentary lifestyles was confining. For this reason, they felt that to have "fear" of travel was something that settlers would exhibit rather than those who move from place to place. It was a sign of sedentary societies.

Yang and Nair (2014) also addressed concerns with the measurement of risk perceptions. Although they did not consider worry, anxiety, fear, and uncertainty as being dimensions of affective risk perceptions, their model did include these concepts. They suggest two paths to worry – one triggered by an event and the other triggered by an object. They suggest that uncertainty leads to worry if the stimuli is an event, while fear leads to anxiety which leads to worry when the stimuli is an object. In contrast, based on Buhr and Dugas (2009), it is contented that uncertainty leads to anxiety which leads to worry which represents affective risk perceptions. The affective risk perception is an antecedent to the cognitive risk perception (in terms of the perceived severity of and perceived vulnerability to a risk). We argue this needs to be tested in the context of travel.

DEVELOPING A THEORY-BASED CONCEPTUAL MODEL FOR THE STUDY OF TRAVEL RISK

Through the development of a theory-based proposed conceptual model, this chapter seeks to advance knowledge related to travel risk by integrating the existing body of knowledge related to risk in the fields of health behavior and psychology with the travel risk literature. Specifically, this chapter integrates PMT and the risk-as-feelings hypothesis with the existing body of knowledge related to travel risk in an effort to reconceptualize the risk-related constructs studied in the context of international travel based on theory.

The development of the proposed conceptual model focused on the relationships between the risk-related constructs as framed by PMT and the risk-as-feelings hypothesis. Notably, of the risk-related variables included in the proposed conceptual model, only perceived vulnerability has been studied extensively in the travel risk literature. Therefore, the proposed conceptual model considers the role of the understudied risk-related variables of perceived severity, affective risk perceptions, self-efficacy, response efficacy, and engagement in a risk reduction behavior. In addition, PMT's threat appraisal process was extended with the inclusion of affective risk perceptions, which were derived from the risk-as-feelings hypothesis. Further, in accordance with the core assumption of PMT, perceived risk and perceived efficacy were entered in a causal string in which individuals go

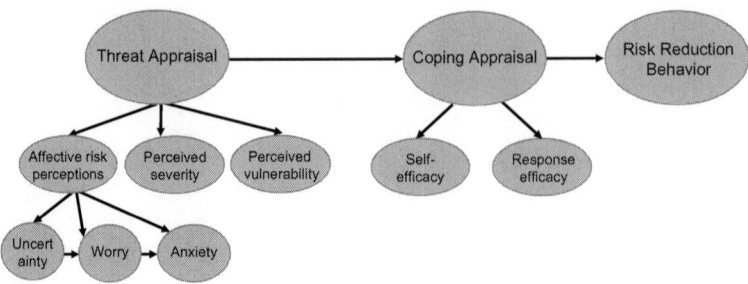

Figure 1. Conceptual Model to Understand the Role of Affective Risk Perceptions in Relation to Cognitive Risk Perceptions and Risk Reduction Behaviors.

through the threat appraisal process before the coping appraisal process (Floyd et al., 2000). The proposed conceptual model is presented in Figure 1.

Operationalizing Travel Risk

As previously noted, going from theory to operationalization has been a challenge for travel risk scholars. Current measures have mainly failed to capture the multidimensional nature of risk. A possible solution to this challenge is to look outside and turn to other fields that have extensively studied these constructs. Thus, the authors adopted measures of the risk-related constructs from the health behavior and psychology literature. The survey questions, items, and original source are provided in Table 1.

It should be noted that the measures were adapted to reflect the dynamic nature of tourism because in the health behavior literature, for example, studies have focused on topics such as AIDS prevention and breast cancer screenings. Further, tourism scholars should adapt the items to reflect the relevant risks of the destination of focus and the risk reduction behaviors should be specific to this type of risk.

Affective risk perceptions have been operationalized using three main scales: (1) Loewenstein's personal safety scale, (2) the Penn State Worry Questionnaire, and (3) Buhr & Dugas's Intolerance of Uncertainty. Loewenstein's personal safety scale consists of three semantic differential scales which are overviews of affective risk. The items include relaxed-anxious, fearless-fearful, and assured-worried. This is conceptualized as the

Table 1.   Operationalization of Risk-Related Constructs.

Variable	Survey Question and Items	Source
Affective risk perceptions	Using the rating scales below, please indicate how you feel when you think about your personal safety while visiting (destination) for leisure purposes.	Loewenstein et al. (2001)
	1. Relaxed-anxious 2. Fearless-fearful 3. Assured-worried	
	Worry (Penn State Worry Questionnaire) – a 5-question scale to measure worry levels after the introduction of an anxiety-provoking situation. Using the scale below, please indicate on a 7-point scale ranging from 1 = strongly disagree to 7 = strongly agree	Meyer et al. (1990)
	1. The majority of my thoughts are about risky situations related to my upcoming trip 2. I am not worried about encountering a risky situation on my upcoming trip 3. I am worried about the consequences of a risky situation on my upcoming trip 4. I am not worried about my trip 5. I find it easy to dismiss my worrisome thoughts	
	Uncertainty (Intolerance of Uncertainty), 27 items related to the idea that uncertainty is stressful and upsetting, uncertainty leads to the inability to act, events are negative and should be avoided. On a five point scale from 1 = "not at characteristic of me" to 5 = "entirely characteristic of me," please respond to the following:	Buhr and Dugas (2002)
	1. Uncertainty about travel makes me uneasy, anxious, and stressed 2. My mind can't be relaxed if I don't know what will happen tomorrow when I am on vacation	

Table 1. *(Continued)*

Variable	Survey Question and Items	Source
Perceived severity	Please indicate your level of agreement with the following statements, on a scale of 1–5 (where 1 = strongly disagree and 5 = strongly agree). 1. If I were a victim of (risk type) while visiting (destination), I would experience serious negative consequences 2. It would have a serious negative impact on me if I were a victim of (risk type) while visiting (destination) 3. If I were a victim of (risk type) while visiting (destination), it would be harmful to my well-being	Witte et al. (1998)
Perceived vulnerability	Please indicate your level of agreement with the following statements, on a scale of 1–5 (where 1 = strongly disagree and 5 = strongly agree). 1. It is likely that I will be a victim of (risk type) while visiting (destination) 2. I am at risk for being a victim of (risk type) while visiting (destination) 3. My chances of being a victim of (risk type) while visiting (destination) are high	Witte et al. (1998)
Self-efficacy	How confident are you in your ability to perform the following behaviors to ensure your personal safety while visiting (destination), on a scale of 1–5 (where 1 = very unconfident and 5 = very confident)?	Witte et al. (1998)
Response efficacy	Please indicate how effective you believe the following behaviors would be in ensuring your personal safety while visiting (destination), on a scale of 1-5 (where 1 = very ineffective and 5 = very effective).	Witte et al. (1998)
Intentions to engage in a recommended risk reduction behavior	Please indicate the likelihood that you would engage in the following behaviors to ensure your personal safety while visiting (destination), on a scale of 1–5 (where 1 = very unlikely and 5 = very likely).	

overview scale for affective risk perceptions. The Penn State Worry Questionnaire (Meyer, Miller, Metzger, & Borkovec, 1990) consists of five questions related to worry. The questions are responded to on a 7-point scale and represent such items as "The majority of my thoughts are about risky situations related to my upcoming trip." Finally, the uncertainty scale is a 27-item scale measured on a 5-point scale. This scale asks such questions as "my mind can't be relaxed if I don't know what will happen tomorrow when I am on vacation." None of these constructs have been tested in the travel literature. In addition, the causal relationships have not been tested.

The two main constructs which represent threat appraisal are perceived severity and perceived vulnerability. Perceived severity is represented by three questions on a 5-point scale (Witte, Cameron, Lapinski, & Nzyuko, 1998). The three items in the perceived severity scale are: (1) If I were a victim of (risk type) while visiting (destination), I would experience serious negative consequences; (2) It would have a serious negative impact on me if I were a victim of (risk type) while visiting (destination); (3) If I were a victim of (risk type) while visiting (destination), it would be harmful to my well-being. The second construct is perceived vulnerability. It is also measured on a 5-point scale and includes such statements as: (1) It is likely that I will be a victim of (risk type) while visiting (destination); (2) I am at risk for being a victim of (risk type) while visiting (destination); (3) My chances of being a victim of (risk type) while visiting (destination) are high.

The two main constructs which represent coping appraisal are self-efficacy and response efficacy. Self-efficacy is measured by one item which relates to one's confidence in their ability to perform a behavior to keep the tourist safe. The item is specific to the risk. For example, if the risk is related to terrorism, then the risk reduction behavior that tourists may engage in to ensure their personal safety might include registering with your embassy prior to travel. Response efficacy relates to the effectiveness of whether those behaviors can keep you safe. The combination of both self- and response efficacy represent one's ability to cope with the risk. This coping appraisal is an antecedent of engaging in the risk reduction behavior.

Risk reduction behaviors are risk-specific. This construct may consist of one or many behaviors to keep the tourist safe. Such behaviors may be represented as: buying travel insurance (health), not venturing off the resort property (crime), making copies of your passport (crime), keeping a low profile (crime), or having a plan to alert friends and family you are safe in the event of a disaster (natural and terrorism).

Conclusion

This chapter first provided an overview of major criticisms of the travel risk literature. In an effort to address these criticisms, this chapter proposes a conceptual model to understand the risk-related constructs of perceived risk (perceived vulnerability, perceived severity, affective risk perceptions), perceived efficacy (self-efficacy, response efficacy), and engagement in a recommended risk reduction behavior. Adopting a theory-based, interdisciplinary approach to the conceptualization and operationalization of risk-related constructs can provide a more holistic understanding of the role of risk in travel decision-making. In particular, a majority of the risk-related variables (i.e., perceived severity, affective risk perceptions, self-efficacy, response efficacy, and engagement in a recommended risk reduction behavior) have not been studied in the context of international travel. Therefore, testing of the proposed conceptual model can provide a better understanding of the dynamic processes between the risk-related constructs, as well as their role in the destination choice process.

The authors consider this chapter to be one of the first steps in the process of moving the travel risk literature forward. An obvious next step in the process is to test the proposed conceptual model. As previously noted, going from theory to operationalization has been a challenge for travel risk scholars. Current measures have mainly failed to capture the multidimensional nature of perceived risk. A possible solution to this challenge is to look outside and turn to other fields that have extensively studied these constructs. For example, tourism scholars can adopt the measures used in health behavior and psychology. However, it should be noted that the measures will need to be adapted to reflect the dynamic nature of tourism because in the health behavior literature, for example, studies have focused on risk associated with topics such as AIDS prevention and breast cancer screenings. Another next step in the process is to test the proposed conceptual model in a variety of settings (e.g., different destinations, different types of risk, different tourist origin markets). Such research is necessary to refine the proposed conceptual model.

References

Bandura, A. (1977). Self-efficacy: Toward a unifying theory of behavioral change. *Psychological Review*, *84*, 191–215.

Bandura, A. (1982). Self-efficacy mechanism in human agency. *American Psychologist*, *37*, 122–147.

Bandura, A. (1986). *Social foundations of thought and action: A social cognitive theory*. Englewood Cliffs, NJ: Prentice Hill.

Bandura, A. (1992). Exercise of personal agency through the self-efficacy mechanism. In R. Schwarzer (Ed.), *Self-efficacy: Thought control of action* (pp. 3–38). Washington, DC: Hemisphere.

Buhr, K., & Dugas, M. J. (2002). The intolerance of uncertainty scale: Psychometric properties of the English version. *Behaviour Research and Therapy*, *40*(8), 931–945.

Buhr, K., & Dugas, M. J. (2009). The role of fear of anxiety and intolerance of uncertainty in worry: An experimental manipulation. *Behaviour Research and Therapy*, *47*(3), 215–223.

Drabek, T. (2009). *The human side of disaster*. Boca Raton, FL: CRC Press.

Echtner, C. M., & Ritchie, J. R. B. (2003). The meaning and measurement of destination image. *The Journal of Tourism Studies*, *14*(1), 37–48.

Faulkner, B. (2001). Towards a framework for tourism disaster management. *Tourism Management*, *22*, 135–147.

Floyd, D. L., Prentice-Dunn, S., & Rogers, R. W. (2000). A meta-analysis of research on protection motivation theory. *Journal of Applied Social Psychology*, *30*(2), 407–429.

Floyd, M. F., Gibson, H., Pennington-Gray, L., & Thapa, B. (2004). The effect of risk perceptions on intentions to travel in the aftermath of September 11, 2001. *Journal of Travel & Tourism Marketing*, *15*(2–3), 19–38.

Korstanje, M. (2009). Re-visiting risk perception theory in the context of travel. *e-Review of Tourism Research*, *7*(4), 68–81.

Korstanje, M. E. (2011). The fear of traveling: A new perspective for tourism and hospitality. *Anatolia*, *22*(2), 222–233.

Kozak, M., Crotts, J. C., & Law, R. (2007). The impact of the perception of risk on international travellers. *International Journal of Tourism Research*, *9*(4), 233–242.

Law, R. (2006). The perceived impact of risks on travel decisions. *International Journal of Tourism Research*, *8*(4), 289–300.

Lepp, A., & Gibson, H. (2003). Tourist roles, perceived risk and international tourism. *Annals of Tourism Research*, *30*, 606–624.

Loewenstein, G. F., Weber, E. U., Hsee, C. K., & Welch, E. S. (2001). Risk as feelings. *Psychological Bulletin*, *127*, 267–286.

Lyng, S. (2008). Risk-taking in sport: Edgework and reflexive community. *Tribal Play: Subcultural Journeys through Sport*, *4*, 83–111.

Maddux, J. E., & Rogers, R. W. (1983). Protection motivation and self-efficacy: A revised theory of fear appeals and attitude change. *Journal of Experimental Social Psychology, 19,* 469–479.

Meyer, T. J., Miller, M. L., Metzger, R. L., & Borkovec, T. D. (1990). Development and validation of the Penn State worry questionnaire. *Behavior Research and Therapy, 28,* 487–495.

Pacific Asia Travel Association (PATA). (2003). *Crisis: It won't happen to us.* Bangkok: PATA.

Pacific Asia Travel Association [PATA]. (2011). *Bounce back: Tourism risk.*

Pennington-Gray, L., Kaplanidou, K., & Schroeder, A. (2013). Drivers of social media use among African Americans in the event of a crisis. *Natural Hazards, 66*(1), 77–95.

Pennington-Gray, L., & Schroeder, A. (2013). International tourist's perceptions of safety & security: The role of social media. *Matkailututkimus, 9*(1), 7–20.

Pennington-Gray, L., Schroeder, A., & Kaplanidou, K. (2011). Examining the influence of past travel experience, general web searching behaviors, and risk perceptions on future travel intentions. *International Journal of Safety and Security in Tourism/Hospitality, 1*(1), 64–89.

Prentice-Dunn, S., & Rogers, R. (1986). Protection motivation theory and preventive health: Beyond the health belief model. *Health Education Research, 1,* 153–161.

Prideaux, B., Laws, E., & Faulkner, B. (2003). Events in Indonesia: Exploring the limits to formal tourism trends forecasting methods in complex crisis situations. *Tourism Management, 24*(4), 475–487.

Qi, C. X., Gibson, H. J., & Zhang, J. J. (2009). Perceptions of risk and travel intentions: The case of China and the Beijing Olympic Games. *Journal of Sport & Tourism, 14*(1), 43–67.

Reisinger, Y., & Mavondo, F. (2005). Travel anxiety and intentions to travel internationally: Implications of travel risk perceptions. *Journal of Travel Research, 43,* 212–225.

Rogers, R. W. (1975). A protection motivation theory of fear appeals and attitude change. *The Journal of Psychology, 91*(1), 93–114.

Rogers, R. W. (1983). Cognitive and physiological processes in fear appeals and attitude change: A revised theory of protection motivation. In J. Cacioppo & R. Petty (Eds.), *Social psychophysiology.* New York, NY: Guilford Press.

Schroeder, A., & Pennington-Gray, L. (2014). Perceptions of crime at the Olympic Games: What role does media, travel advisories, and social media play? *Journal of Vacation Marketing, 20*(3), 225–237.

Schroeder, A., Pennington-Gray, L., Donohoe, H., & Kiousis, S. (2013). Using social media in times of crisis. *Journal of Travel & Tourism Marketing,* Special issue on Social Media, *30*(1–2), 126–143.

Schroeder, A., Pennington-Gray, L., Kaplanidou, K., & Zhan, F. (2013). Destination risk perceptions among U.S. residents for London as the host city of the 2012 Summer Olympic Games. *Tourism Management, 38*(October), 107–119.

Scott, N., & Laws, E. (2005). Tourism crises and disasters: Enhancing understanding of system effects. *Journal of Travel & Tourism Marketing, 19*(2–3), 149–158.

Slovic, P., & Peters, E. (2006). Risk perception and affect. *Current Directions in Psychological Science, 15*(6), 322–325.

Sönmez, S. F., & Graefe, A. R. (1998a). Influence of terrorism risk on foreign tourism decisions. *Annals of Tourism Research, 25*(1), 112–144.

Sönmez, S. F., & Graefe, A. R. (1998b). Determining future travel behavior from past travel experience and perceptions of risk and safety. *Journal of Travel Research, 37*(2), 171–177.

Sunstein, C. R. (2003). Terrorism and probability neglect. *Journal of Risk and Uncertainty, 26*, 121–136.

Tourism Crisis Management Initiative (TCMI). (2015). *Welcome.* Retrieved from http://tcmi.hhp.ufl.edu/

United Nations World Tourism Organization [UNWTO]. (2011). *Toolbox for crisis communications in tourism.* Madrid: UNWTO.

United Nations World Tourism Organization [UNWTO]. (2005). *Evolution of tourism in the tsunami-affected destinations.* Madrid: UNWTO.

Weinstein, N. D. (1993). Testing four competing theories of health-protective behavior. *Health Psychology, 12*(4), 324–333.

Witte, K., Cameron, K. A., Lapinski, M. K., & Nzyuko, S. (1998). A theoretically based evaluation of HIV/AIDS prevention campaigns along the trans-Africa highway in Kenya. *Journal of Health Communication, 3*, 345–363.

Yang, C. L., & Nair, V. (2014). Risk perception study in tourism: Are we really measuring perceived risk? *Procedia – Social and Behavioral Sciences, 144*(20), 322–327.

20

Promotion Tools Used in the Marketing of Sport Tourism Experiences in a Mature Tourism Destination

Crystal C. Lewis and
Cristina H. Jönsson

ABSTRACT

Purpose – It is observed that many destinations are implementing sport tourism offerings to enhance their ability to attract visitors through satisfying their desires of new experiences. This has led to a highly competitive sport tourism market and as a result destinations engage in various marketing techniques and promotional tools to gain an advantage. For that reason this research was undertaken to acquire a greater understanding of the importance of promotional tools to successfully and efficiently market sport tourism experiences.

Methodology/approach – The construct of this study comprises of two stages. The aim of the first stage is to evaluate the specific tools used to promote sport tourism and sport tourism experiences in Barbados by examining the responses of various sporting and tourism bodies. The second stage of this research was conducted to present and analyze how marketing/promotional tools could contribute to better market sport tourism experiences.

Findings – The research found that many of the promotional tools implemented in Barbados during their marketing process correspond with those used internationally. However, problems of poor and insufficient sporting facilities as well as little collaboration between tourism and sporting entities, hamper the success of Barbados as a sport tourism destination. This further minimized Barbados' ability to market favorable tourism experiences. This therefore shows that while promotional tools are essential in attracting tourists, other elements must also be taken into consideration to ensure sport tourists have positive experiences which would lead to a successful sport tourism destination.

Originality/value – Few studies in this area have been undertaken in the Caribbean. This study attempts to fill this gap by examining the implementation of sport tourism offerings to attract visitors to Barbados.

Keywords: Sport tourism; Caribbean; Barbados; promotional tools; tourism marketing

Introduction

Sport and tourism have been combined to create a recent phenomenon known as sport tourism. According to Weed and Bull (2004), "sports tourism is a social, economic and cultural phenomenon arising from the unique interaction of activity, people and place." On the other hand, marketing is one of the oldest concepts within the business industry. Marketing is "the all-embracing function that links the business with customer needs and wants in order to get the right product to the right place at the right time" (Riley, 2012).

Marketing and more specifically the promotional tools used for marketing are essential components for tourism destination marketing organizers (DMOs) as these tools can be used to create and sell an experience even before the visitor arrives on location. As such there is a high degree of importance placed on using these components to communicate and attract sports tourists to a tourism destination. For this reason, "promotional tools" was considered for this research, specifically focusing on the case of Barbados.

Over the years, tourists' travel motivations have evolved. Tourists are increasingly more experienced and demanding and seek a wide range of experiences (Peric, 2010). Visitors are also seeking more interactive holidays which are aligned with continued healthier lifestyle choices. This change has led to sports tourism becoming a multi-million dollar component to the wider tourism industry (Lashley, 2014 in Sporting Barbados, 2014).

Barbados, a tourism destination which has long been successful in attracting visitors with the sun, sea and sand experience, is now recognizing the importance of collaborative efforts between sports and tourism. For that reason, many recent tourism developments have been formed with a particular focus on sport. In doing this, Barbados' government has its goals set "to position Barbados as the number one sports tourism destination in the Caribbean, offering diverse and exciting opportunities for visitors, as well as the local communities, which result in direct economic and other benefits" (Caribbean360, 2013).

As of 2006, Barbados has hosted many sports clubs, teams, and groups in various sporting disciplines for 10 to 20 years (Elcock, 2005; Yearwood, 2006). In addition to this, Barbados has had a successful track record in hosting many local, regional, and international sporting events. Sport and tourism event organizers can use the successes of these past events hosted to market the experiences felt by sport tourists.

More specifically, Barbados has an annual sport tourism calendar of fixed events which include but is not limited to: the Sandy Lane Gold Cup, Run Barbados Festival, Mount Gay Round Barbados Race Series, and Sol Rally. These sporting events attracted several tourists to the destination and accounted for an estimated 1.1–1.5% of the total visitor arrivals between 2010 and 2014 (Ministry of Tourism, 2014). The one key factor for the continued success of these events in particular is the additional activities surrounding the sport; where cultural exhibitions such as song and dance add value to the event.

This value-added, in the form of an experience for current sport tourist can aid in repeat visitation as highlighted by Perner (2008) who state that a good experience may lead to continued use. Additionally, an experience can also act as a pull or motivating factor for new sport tourists. This is supported by

Marketing-Schools.org (2012) who state that this motivation at its most basic level is dictated by emotional experience.

The following sections will review sport tourism and tourism promotion literature, which is followed by the methodology and a discussion of the study results. A conclusion with implications for the study ends this chapter.

Review of Literature

Sport tourism has become a regularly applied strategy for many mature tourism destinations seeking to rejuvenate the tourism products and services being offered (Weed & Bull, 2004). The replication of this strategy across many destinations has led to a highly competitive industry. Therefore, the presence of effective marketing practices is of great importance in distinguishing destinations from each other through the creation of distinct images. To aid in a destination's marketing effort is the use of promotional tools. Destination Marketing Organizations (DMOs) have a variety of promotional tools at their disposal, that can be used individually or in combination with others. These tools are used not only to communicate a particular message to potential and current customers (The Chartered Institute of Marketing, 2009), but also to entice the tourists by marketing an experience.

The promotional tools covered in this research include advertising, personal selling, sales promotions, direct marketing, publicity and public relations, sponsorship and finally internet and e-Marketing which were identified by Esu and Ebitu (2010). Advertising, the most popular form of promotion is used to inform and create awareness about a product or a service to current and prospective customers. This particular promotional tool can be experienced through the use of tourist board brochures, consumer and trade magazines, television, radio, and newspaper (Honarvar, 2009 in Kashkuli, Moharramzadeh, & Ghalehgir, 2014).

Personal selling unlike advertising is more target group specific and focuses on customer needs. Examples of this type of tool can be seen at World Travel Market with various destination representatives, through the use of video conferencing and through interactive computer links. On the other hand, sales promotion is seen as a short-term inducement of value to arouse interest in new customers and create repeat sales in buying a good or service (Onditi, 2012). This can be seen when tour operators offer combination packages or two for one ticket sales.

Direct marketing is another promotional tool that focuses on targeting a specific group of persons and has the ability to build long-term relationships with customers. An example of direct marketing is the mailing of sporting catalogues to regular customers (Onditi, 2012).

Similarly to advertising, publicity and public relations are used to communicate with the general public and reach a wide audience. The difference between the two is that publicity pertains to communication in a newspaper such as news release and feature articles while public relation deals with the managerial process of publicity for example, press launches, and personality appearances.

One of the most recently added promotional tools is that of sponsorship which is described as a business agreement between two parties. The sponsor provides money, goods, services or experience and in exchange, the sponsored party offers rights and associations that the sponsor utilizes commercially (Lagae, 2005). This is often seen when major companies sponsor teams with sporting apparel and in exchange the athlete wears the clothing and aids in the marketing of the company.

Finally, the internet and e-Marketing has become popular promotional tools with the advances in technology. The internet permits two-way communication between organization and customer by using social media platforms, website and online forums while e-Marketing deals with the buying and selling of products and services via the internet. E-Marketing and tourism leads to online tourism which allows tourists to search for details on destinations, facilities, price and availabilities and get a look into the destinations they are considering. Additionally, according to MarketingFind Inc. (2015) consumers come together online and share their experiences with each other. This sharing of experiences can be noted on TripAdvisor and other internet platforms which can use the experiences of past visitors as pull factors to attract new consumers. Chiu and Ananzeh (2012) further adds, "Nowadays, the Internet is widely used because it is an inexpensive communication tool presented in multiple languages to provide the delegates with adequate information and could greatly affect consumers' perceived image through creating a virtual experience of a destination." While Reino and Hay (2014) state "Sites such as YouTube, Trip Advisory and Expedia also give users a forum to share and rate their experiences, and so anyone who comments about a destination/product, are now part of the marketing process."

Research has shown that many destinations around the world showcase their features in similar ways (Marketing-Schools.org, 2012) while using similar promotional tools. Marking-Schools.org (2012) further state that general marketing principles note that the more emotionally involved a consumer is with a product or brand, the more likely they are to purchase that product or brand. This emotional involvement comes from experiences. Supporting this is Mulec (2010) stating that the brand is not only a trademark (logo or icon), but an experience and image that signals a value system and positioning. It is a promise of an experience that the visitor can expect from the destination. Furthermore, branding is perhaps the most powerful marketing weapon available to contemporary destination marketers confronted by tourists who are increasingly seeking lifestyle fulfillment and experiences (Toolkit on Poverty Reduction through Tourism, 2012).

Empirical Study

The approach to understanding the implementation of sport tourism as a promotional tool to attract visitors to a tourist destination requires greater empirical attention, given the limited research in the area. As a result, the present study seeks to address this concern by examining promotional tools used in Barbados' tourism sector. Implementing sport tourism offerings to enhance a destination's ability to attract visitors has led to a highly competitive sport tourism market. This in turn has led to tourism destinations engaging in various marketing techniques and using promotional tools to gain an advantage.

METHODOLOGY
Research Approach and Sampling
To fulfill the requirements of this research a qualitative approach was adopted. Purposive sampling was used and the sample group comprised of stakeholders that represent various sporting associations, sport event organizers, and tourism representatives in Barbados. These stakeholders were specifically targeted for this research as they were most likely to have direct knowledge of the subject matter being researched and as such be able to provide the researcher with the information necessary to complete this study. The number of respondents was not predetermined as is

the norm with purposive sampling during which respondents are interviewed until "nothing new comes from the data – a point called saturation" (Patton & Cochran, 2002).

Data Collection Procedures

The data collected for this research was carried out using both primary and secondary data sources. The secondary data used in this research were governmental reports and publications, organization statistical reports, academic journal articles, reports prepared by universities and economists, website articles and newspaper articles. These data types were used as they provided a representation of past and on-going research conducted on a consistent basis from reliable sources. The qualitative method of in-depth interviews with informed respondents was chosen as it provided the opportunity to converse one on one with the respondent.

Research Instrument

The research instrument is an interview schedule comprised of four sections. The first section entitled "SECTION A – General Sports Tourism" is made up of three questions which focus generally on sport tourism and aims to capture the opinion of the respondents as it relates to sport tourism.

"SECTION B – Barbados' Sport Tourism," the second section, includes five questions which have a greater emphasis on the sport tourism sector in Barbados. The question pertained to the opinion of respondents to the prominence of sport tourism in Barbados, and the sport tourism experiences provided by both tourism and sporting bodies.

The third section entitled "SECTION C – Marketing Barbados' Sport Tourism and Experiences" is the main focus of the interview and is necessary to fulfill the objectives of the research. Comprising of six questions, this section focuses on the geographical locations targeted during sport tourism marketing and the promotional tools used in the process. It also captures the experiences of the sport tourists and how these experiences are in turn marketed by the tools to attract new sport tourists to the island.

"SECTION D – The Future of Barbados' Sport Tourism," the final section in the interview schedule focuses on the future of sport tourism in Barbados with regards to product expansion, enhancement, and improvement. These questions are important in determining the likelihood of further developments in the sport tourism industries as well as strategies employed by local organizations. Additionally, capturing the response of these questions would aid in enhancing sport tourists experiences. The knowledge from this section would assist in the development of the discussions section of this research.

The interview schedule is constructed with all open-ended questions. This particular format allows the rapport between interviewer and interviewee to be built, permitting a smooth flowing conversation. It also allows respondents to express themselves freely on the subject area while expanding on certain points and explaining specific comments made.

Data Analysis Procedures and Validity

A thematic analysis was used in order to analyze the information received from the interviews the researcher utilizes.

For several years, some qualitative researchers have deemed validity as not being applicable in qualitative research (Golafshani, 2003). Furthermore, Cho and Trent (2006) highlighted the fact that during these years, concerns with the issues of validity in qualitative research have grown. However, it is stated that in qualitative research, "the research is the instrument" for measuring validity. Additionally, validity in qualitative research involves determining the degree to which the researchers' claims about knowledge correspond to the reality being studied (Cho & Trent, 2006).

As such, in this study, validity of the data is proven from the point of selecting the sample. The persons selected to participate in this research were specifically chosen as they possess the knowledge needed to fulfill the objectives of this study. The procedures of audio recording, taking notes, and transcribing the recordings of the interviews allowed for accuracy in reporting what was said by the interviewee. These methods ensured that credibility of the research is upheld thereby proving the validity of the data. In addition, taking into consideration the ethical concerns posed above was another means of assuring validity of this research.

DISCUSSION OF RESULTS

From the results obtained, it is noted that several of the promotional tools identified by Kitchen and Pelsmacker (2004), Honarvar (2009), and Esu and Ebitu (2010) are implemented by both tourism and sporting entities in Barbados. These practices demonstrate an alignment of the promotional tools used to market sport tourism in Barbados with those used internationally.

It was further noted that these tools are used to communicate the attractions and entice visitors to the destination through the creation of unique and distinguishing destination images. Additionally, the promotional tools but more specifically, the internet and the social media platform which allowed tourist to share and discuss their experiences, were also used to aid in the marketing of a variety of elements experienced the sport tourist. However, it is important to note that while there is no single tool that can be implemented alone and reap success for the destination, all the promotional tools can be used to effectively and efficiently market the experiences of sport tourist. Fyall and Garrod (2005 in Mulec, 2010) reinforces this by saying, successful delivery of the wider tourism product is dependent on close working relationships, interdependencies and interactions with numerous other stakeholders, enabling the tourism organization to provide a seamless experience for its customers.

The results clearly show that Barbados is aligned with the standard and international practices of tourism marketing however Barbados has been unable to achieve competitive advantage over its competitors due to the lack of facilities and cooperation between the relevant bodies. Due to all that was identified, the researcher is in full support of Bidokhti and Nazari (2009 in Kashkuli et al., 2014) who stated that "balancing main policy-making, developing infrastructures, noticing tourism attractions, advertisement activities and regulating strategies are effective in tourism industry development" and by extension sports tourism.

Conclusion and Implications

This research set out to achieve four specific objectives which were designed to depict an overall picture of Barbados as a sport tourism destination and the specific promotional tools used during the marketing process. Along with an analysis to determine whether these promotional tools could contribute to enhanced marketing of sport tourism experiences. The objectives pertained to the current state of sport tourism in Barbados, the role that tourism bodies play in marketing Barbados as a sport tourism destination, the specific tools used to promote Barbados as a sport tourism destination as compared to established global practices and to acquire a greater understanding of the importance of promotional tools to successfully and efficiently market sport tourism experiences.

The results showed that Barbados is an ideal destination to develop sport tourism, due to its year-round tropical weather, as it allows for out-of-season competition and training opportunities for international sports teams. However, very little has been done by authorities to capitalize on this fast growing tourism niche. Additionally, it was found that many of the promotional tools implemented by both tourism and sporting bodies during their marketing process are aligned with practices used internationally. It was also noted that the promotional tools were used to market the experiences of sport tourism and also create images and emotional connections to the experiences the sport tourist may seek. However, it was also identified that issues such as inadequate sporting facilities and lack of collaboration between tourism and sporting entities greatly hampers the ability to portray or market satisfactory experiences and in turn affects the success of Barbados as a sport tourism destination.

References

Bidokhti, A., & Nazari, M. (2009). Marketing role in tourism industry development. *Management Perspective Magazine, 32*, 49−68.

Chiu, L. K., & Ananzeh, O. (2012). Evaluating the relationship between the role of promotional tools in MICE tourism and the formation of the touristic image of Jordan. *Academica Turistica, 5*(1), 59−73.

Cho, J., & Trent, A. (2006). Validity in qualitative research revisited. *Qualitative Research, 6*(3), 319−340.

Elcock, Y. (2005). Sport tourism in Narnados: The development of sport facilities and special events. *Journal of Sport & Tourism, 10*(2), 129−134.

Esu, B., & Ebitu, E. (2010). Promoting an emerging tourism destination. *Global Journal of Management and Business Research, 10*(1), 21−28.

Fyall, A., & Garrod, B. (2005). *Tourism marketing: A collaborative approach.* London: Channel View Publications.

Golafshani, N. (2003). Understanding reliability and validity in qualitative research. *The Qualitative Report, 8*(4), 597−607.

Honarvar, A. (2009). *Codifies Iran sport tourism marketing strategy.* PhD thesis, Tarbiat Modarres University, Tehran, Iran.

Kashkuli, F. E., Moharramzadeh, M., & Ghalehgir, S. (2014). The role of advertisement factors in development of sport tourism industry of Fars Province. *Physical Education of Students, 3*, 61−66.

Kitchen, P. J., & Pelsmacker, P. (2004). *Integrated marketing communications.* London: Routledge.

Lagae, W. (2005). *Sports sponsorship and marketing communications. A European perspective.* Harlow: Financial Times/Prentice Hall.

Lashley, S. (Eds.). (2014). Foreword. In Hiles (Ed.), *Sporting Barbados 2014* (10th ed.). Bridgetown: Hiltop Publications Ltd.

MarketingFind Inc. (2015). *Web marketing promotional tools and techniques.* Retrieved from http://www.marketingfind.com/articles/web_marketing_promotional_tools_and_techniques.html

Marketing Tourism. Marketing-Schools.org. (2012). Retrieved from http://www.marketing-schools.org/consumer-psychology/marketing-tourism.html

Mulec, I. (2010). Promotion as a tool in sustaining the destination marketing activities. *Turizam, 14*(1), 13–21.

Onditi, A. (2012). An evaluation of promotional elements influencing sales of an organization: A case study of sales of agricultural and non-agricultural products among women groups, Homa-Bay District, Kenya. *International Journal of Business & Social Sciences, 3*(5), 296–313. Retrieved from http://ijbssnet.com/journals/Vol_3_No_5_March_2012/33.pdf

Patton, M. Q., & Cochran, M. (2002). *A guide to using qualitative research methodology.* Retrieved from http://fieldresearch.msf.org/msf/bitstream/10144/84230/1/Qualitative%20research%20methodology.pdf

Peric, M. (2010). Sport tourism and system of experiences. *Tourism and Hospitality Management, 16*(2), 197–206.

Perner, L. (2008). *Promotion: Integrated marketing communication.* Retrieved from http://www.consumerpsychologist.com/intro_Promotion.html

Reino, S., & Hay, B. (2014). *The use of YouTube as a tourism marketing tool.* Retrieved from http://eresearch.qmu.ac.uk/2315/1/2315.PDF

Riley, J. (2012). *What is marketing?* Retrieved from http://www.tutor2u.net/business/marketing/what_is_marketing.asp

Strategy for Sports tourism on the cards in Barbados. Caribbean 360. (2013, July). Retrieved from http://www.caribbean360.com/sports/strategy-for-sports-tourism-on-the-cards-in-barbados

The Chartered Institute of Marketing. (2009). *How to achieve an effective promotional mix.* Berkshire: Membership Services. Retrieved from http://www.cim.co.uk/files/promotionalmix.pdf

The International Labour Office. (2012). *Toolkit on poverty reduction through tourism. Promotion and marketing in tourism.* Retrieved from http://www.ilo.org/wcmsp5/groups/public/—ed_dialogue/—sector/documents/instructionalmaterial/wcms_218329.pdf

Weed, M., & Bull, C. (2004). Sport tourism as a diversification strategy in Malta. In Weed & Bull (Eds.), *Sport tourism: Participants, policy and providers* (pp. 153–163). Oxford: Elsevier Butterworth-Heinemann.

Yearwood, G. (2006). Sports tourism events: A measure of the benefits of stakeholders in Barbados. In Jayawardena (Ed.), *Caribbean tourism: More than sun, sand & sea* (pp. 294–314). Bridgetown: Ian Randle Publishers.

21 The Role of Information and Communication Technologies (ICTs) in Marketing Tourism Experiences

Kyung-Hyan Yoo and Ulrike Gretzel

ABSTRACT

Purpose – To analyze and discuss the role of ICTs and the emerging trends and issues in marketing tourism experiences.

Methodology/approach – Previous conceptual frameworks are reviewed and key issues and trends are identified as central for ICT-based tourism marketing. Case studies are presented to illustrate how the marketing issues could be translated into practical tourism marketing strategies.

Findings – (1) Based on the literature, a conceptual model that outlines a technology-empowered marketing approach for co-created tourism experiences is presented. (2) The identified key trends in marketing tourism experiences include the changing overall role of marketers, a growth in mobile marketing opportunities, the emergence of smart destinations and their varied implications for marketing. (3) The case studies show the integrated and strategic role of social media platforms, hashtags, photography, location-based geofilters, augmented reality and videography in marketing tourism experiences.

Originality/value – This chapter conceptually outlines the technology-empowered tourism marketing approach and the role of marketers and various other players in tourism experience co-creation. The case studies provide practical implications for ICT-based tourism marketing.

Keywords: Information and Communication Technology (ICT); tourism experience; tourism marketing; conceptual paper

Introduction

Experience has been identified as an important concept in tourism studies (Uriely, 2005). A great deal of previous studies has been dedicated to advancing our understanding of tourism experiences from psychological, anthropological and sociological perspectives (e.g., Cohen, 1979; Csikszentmihalyi & LeFevre, 1989; Jennings et al., 2009; MacCannell, 1973). However, recent advances in information and communication technologies (ICTs) have revolutionized the way travelers plan, consume, create, perceive and share their experiences (Buhalis, 2003; Stamboulis & Skayannis, 2003; Wang, Park, & Fesenmaier, 2012) and this requires new ways of conceptualizing what tourism experiences involve. Experiences that are increasingly mediated by ICTs also require new marketing and management approaches. As a consequence, tourism and hospitality businesses are faced with both opportunities and challenges (Gretzel, Fesenmaier, Formica, & O'Leary, 2006; Law, Buhalis, & Cobanoglu, 2014).

Given the significant impacts of ICTs on tourism businesses, some researchers have discussed the role and impacts of ICTs in tourist experience design/management and tourism marketing. However, most research emphasizes the consumer perspective. Gretzel and Jamal (2009) foresaw the emergence of a new "Creative Class" of tourists who uses technologies to create, mediate and reconstruct their experiences. McCarthy and Wright (2004) also noted that the technology serves either as a mediator or the core experience itself for tourist experiences. Neuhofer, Buhalis, and Ladkin (2014) argued that tourism companies and tourists can co-create a "technology-empowered experience" when they use interactive, immersive and persuasive technology. Wang and her colleagues (2012) specifically look at the impact of smart phones on tourism experiences. Marketing and management perspectives on the topic are not as prominently available. Yoo and Gretzel (2010) discussed the changing marketing functions as a result of increasing use of Web. 2.0 technologies. Tussyadiah (2014a) outlines consequences of increased technology mediation for tourism experience design. In addition, the recent book by Benckendorff, Sheldon, and Fesenmaier (2014) provides an overview of the impacts of ICTs applications in all sectors of the tourism industry. While these studies have provided insights regarding the role of ICTs in tourism, and specifically their impact on the tourist experience, there is still a lack of literature that examines the role of ICTs in tourism marketing.

There is a dearth of knowledge in particular in relation to how marketers can effectively communicate, convincingly deliver and best stage these technology-mediated tourism experiences. Pine and Gilmore (2011) predicted that the next competitive battleground for companies lies in staging compelling and memorable experiences. In tourism marketing, creating a meaningful and memorable experience has long been a core value for marketers and various ICTs have been used to support and enhance tourism experiences (Neuhofer et al., 2014). With the rapid advances of social and mobile technologies and also increasing integration of ICTs in the tourism industry, it is ever more important to understand how ICTs can be effectively used for marketing tourism experiences.

Pine and Gilmore (2011) also proposed a new economic value, namely "Transformation," which companies create on top of experiences. They explained that transformations are "effectual outcomes that guide customers to change some dimension of self" (Gilmore & Pine, 2007, p. 47), which goes beyond creating a memorable experience. The emphasis is on authenticity, relevance and meaning. Many recent tourism studies have also argued that tourist experiences are not simply staged by companies but co-created with the tourists (Binkhorst & Den Dekker, 2009; Prebensen & Foss, 2011) and ICTs play an integral role in the co-creation process (Neuhofer et al., 2014). This new business paradigm raises many questions for tourism marketers. What is the role of marketers and how can tourism marketers effectively manage the co-creation process? How can tourism marketers maintain quality when the experiences are created with tourists? What are the effects of tourists' involvement on their experiences and do they involve transformations? This chapter seeks to discuss and analyze these issues. For this purpose, relevant previous findings and conceptual frameworks are reviewed, key issues and trends are identified and overall implications for ICT-based tourism marketing are drawn. Further, case studies are presented to illustrate how the discussed marketing issues could be translated into practical tourism marketing strategies. This chapter closes with a summary and an agenda for future research.

Literature Review

ICTS AND THE TOURISM EXPERIENCE

Tourism is a highly information-intensive industry (Shanker, 2008). The advances of ICTs have transformed the industry structure and practices in designing and delivering tourism experience as well as tourist experience consumption. Existing literature confirms the significant role of ICTs in the tourism experience (e.g., Gretzel, Fesenmaier, & O'Leary, 2006; Neuhofer et al., 2014).

Several studies discussed the opportunities that ICTs open for tourism organizations to support and enhance tourist experiences. Stamboulis and Skayannis (2003) claimed that the customization and flexibilization supported by ICTs lead to a new experience-based tourism that distinguishes experience as a separate and valuable commodity. Buhalis and O'Connor (2005) argued that ICTs enable tourism organizations to dynamically differentiate and specialize their products which allow travelers to personalize their tourism experiences. In a recent study, Buhalis and Amaranggana (2015) noted the importance of analyzing Big Data to build smart tourism destinations that could enhance tourism experiences through offering more personalized products/services.

A great deal of studies has discussed how ICTs have fundamentally changed tourist experiences. Gretzel et al. (2006) argued that ICT tools, in particular the smartphone, play critical roles in shaping the tourist experience across all stages of a trip, including the extensive dreaming/planning phase before and recollection phase after. Indeed, Wang, Xiang, and Fesenmaier (2014) found that the use of smart phones for travel transforms tourist experiences. The findings of Kim and Tussyadiah (2013) show that the more tourists are engaged in social media communication during their trip, the more social support they get, which contributes positively to their tourism experience. A study by Lo and McKercher (2015) suggests that digital photography and social media redefine tourist gazes and thus tourism experiences. Their findings illustrate how tourists use social media and photographs to create, manage and manipulate their ideal identity and experience. Dinhopl and Gretzel (2016) conceptualized how videography mediates tourist experience and argued that the videography-mediated experiences differ from the experience mediated by photography because of the more seamless integration of video technology into tourism experiences. Kang and Gretzel (2012) found that podcast tours at a national park increase perceived social presence and mindfulness, which in turn enhance tourist experiences. Tussyadiah (2014b) suggested that people's interaction with personal wearable technology augment their physical surroundings and, as a result, enhance their experiences.

The trends of experience co-creation and collaborative consumption with the advances in ICTs are discussed in several recent studies. Neuhofer et al. (2014) noted that two most significant advances in the area of experience are the increasing level of co-creation and integration of ICTs. They conceptualize an "experience hierarchy" that depicts the relationship between the level of technology integration and the type of tourist experience. The hierarchy proposes four levels of experience in terms of technology and respective increase in co-creation. The levels include conventional experience (1), technology-assisted experience (2), technology-enhanced experience (3) and technology-empowered experience (4) (see Figure 1). The phenomenon of the sharing economy and collaborative consumption are emerging issues in tourism that further illustrate how the increasing influence of ICTs facilitates the creation and sustenance of online peer-to-peer communities like Airbnb and Uber (Sigala, 2014; Tussyadiah & Pesonen, 2015) and how tourists increasingly communicate and co-create their experiences with local residents and other tourists through such ICTs.

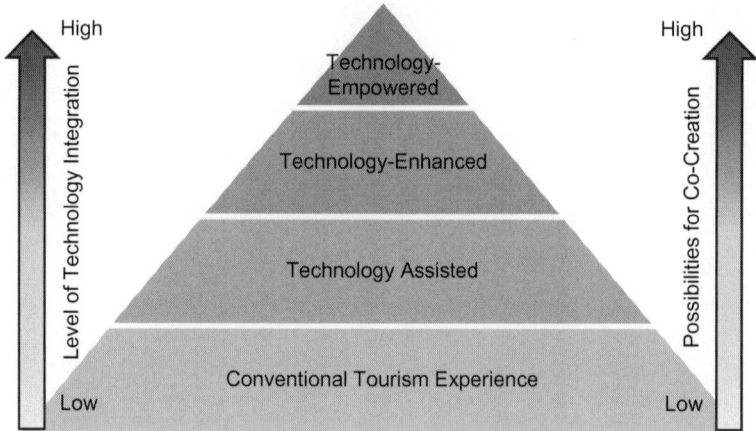

Figure 1. Experience Hierarchy. *Source*: Adapted from Neuhofer et al. (2014)

These trends show that ICTs are increasingly key to positive tourism experiences and therefore should be taking on an integral role in the marketing of such tourism experiences.

ICTS IN TOURISM MARKETING

Given the growing applications of ICTs across all tourism sectors, many researchers have examined the development, the role and impacts of ICTs in tourism marketing. The dominant topic investigated was the effectiveness of different online marketing strategies including websites, social media, and search engines (Law et al., 2014) and a number of recent studies examined the role of social and mobile technologies in tourism marketing (e.g., Wang et al., 2014).

Researchers have long identified the website as a key marketing channel for tourism destinations (Gretzel, Yuan, & Fesenmaier, 2000). With ever more sophisticated Web-based tools available, tourism websites themselves have the potential to deliver engaging experiences. Website design has therefore become an integral element of tourism marketing. Luna-Nevarez and Hyman (2012) analyzed the websites for the 235 top global destinations in terms of six design characteristics and suggested the destination marketing organizations (DMOs) should rely on design elements that promote positive perceptions. The findings of Kim and Fesenmaier (2008) also indicate that the website design factors, in particular usability and inspiration-related factors, form the users' first impression, which affects the persuasiveness of destination websites. Lee, Gretzel, and Law (2010) suggest that vivid and sensory descriptions on destination websites are a way for marketers to make their websites more persuasive. Lee and Gretzel (2012) also investigated how other website features influence travelers' destination selection. Their findings show that pictures included on the destination website induce mental imagery, which significantly influences the website visitors' attitude and expectations toward the destination.

Some studies discussed the importance of search engine marketing in tourism. O'Connor (2009) analyzed a randomly selected sample of 90 hotel properties worldwide and found that most hotels are performing well in their search engine optimization; however, they did not strategically use the paid search advertising which resulted in their favorable organic search positions being compromised by third party sites' paid ads. Pan, Xiang, Law, and Fesenmaier (2011) presented a dynamic model of search engine marketing and noted the important role of search engine marketing in designing and implementing strategic online destination marketing. Search engines are critical for tourists in their search for tourism experiences and therefore require careful attention from tourism marketers in their efforts to promote tourism experiences online.

Over the past few years, a growing number of studies have reported the significant role and impacts of social media and user-generated contents in tourism marketing. Gretzel and Yoo (2013) claimed that tourism marketing has fundamentally changed with the advance and popularity of social media. They noted that social media marketing functions span across all elements of marketing including the classic 4Ps (product, price, promotion, and place) of marketing, customer relations and research (Yoo & Gretzel, 2010). The social media focused book edited by Sigala, Christou, and Gretzel (2012) provides various Web 2.0 enabled tourism marketing applications and practices including DMOs' social media marketing, meeting planners' social media use as well as discussions of the impacts of social media on hotels' price strategies. Hays, Page, and Buhalis (2013) identified social media as a good marketing tool for DMOs to reach a global audience with limited resources. Some studies also discussed the emerging marketing tactics for specific social media platforms such as Facebook (Kwok & Yu, 2013) and Twitter (Hay, 2010; Sevin,

2013). These academic publications illustrate the increasing penetration of social media in tourism marketing and emphasize the need to better understand how social media can be effectively used to market tourism experiences.

Recent studies have also underlined the value of other innovative ICTs including mobile technologies (Wang et al., 2014), virtual reality (Guttentag, 2010; Jung, Chung, & Leue, 2015), and wearable technologies (Tussyadiah, 2014b). Because of mobile technologies, many travelers today make their decisions on the move which opens up new opportunities to connect and engage travelers (Wang et al., 2014). The experiential nature of virtual reality enables the provision of rich data to prospective travelers who seek destination information (Guttentag, 2010) and augmented reality technology is getting ever easier to access and use today with the growing availability and enhanced capabilities of mobile technologies (Jung et al., 2015; Yovcheva, Buhalis, & Gatzidis, 2012). Context-aware mobile technologies are especially important for tourism marketing, as they make sure messages are tailored to the needs of on-the-go travelers (Lamsfus, Wang, Alzua-Sorzabal, & Xiang, 2015). Overall, mobile ICTs provide marketers with new opportunities to shape experiences and push relevant information.

These studies indicate that the advances of information technologies have changed the role of marketers and require changes in their strategies to reach and engage target audiences. Smith (2012) insisted that tourism marketers today should provide travelers the most relevant and customized information. As he explained, travelers today have access to a great amount of information and need someone to help them find the right information. Marketers increasingly compete for this position as the most important information source as ICTs make it easier for tourists to tap into other sources of knowledge to inform their experiences.

Drawing from this literature, Figure 2 proposes a framework that recognizes the increasing interconnectivity and complexity of information exchanges and experience co-creation in the context of the technology-empowered experience. The model illustrates that the separate, disconnected and rigid one-way service creation, production/delivery and consumption of the traditional marketing approach differs significantly from the combined, interconnected, interactive and co-created approach empowered by a variety of technologies. The changing role of tourism

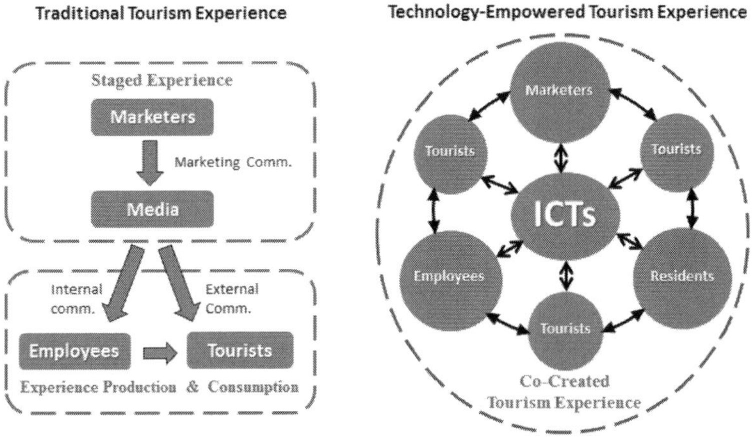

Traditional Tourism Experience   Technology-Empowered Tourism Experience

Figure 2. Role of Marketing in Traditional versus Technology-Empowered Tourism Experiences.

marketers as facilitators rather than "owners" of tourism experiences is obvious, as is the central position taken on by ICTs.

Key Trends in Marketing Tourism Experience

The review of previous studies shows that tourism marketing is undergoing significant changes that create new challenges as well as opportunities. This section discusses the key emerging trends and issues in marketing tourism experience identified in the literature.

Changing Role of Marketers: As indicated in Figure 2, the connected and technology-empowered travelers today do not need marketing content to learn about tourism products and services. Due to the growing information overload, they rather need credible sources that can provide quality information that is personalized. As the tourists' demand changes, new roles of marketers emerge. Marketers today are expected to be the "trusted experts" who can provide not only accurate but especially relevant information (Smith, 2012) as the rapid growth of information online creates challenges for end users to find the right information. The role as an "experience curator" is also emphasized. Growing numbers of tourists create, mediate and reconstruct their experience using various ICTs (Gretzel & Jamal, 2009) and they often need to connect and aggregate information. Marketers can serve as the experience curators for tourists by showing them the most relevant information and providing the technologies (e.g., mobile applications with suggested attractions and activities) to support experience creation. Another important role of marketers today is the "content creator" who creates stories. While the tourist experience traditionally only encapsulates the phase when tourism services are consumed at a destination (Sorensen & Jensen, 2015), the experience can be extended to pre- and post-stages by consuming and sharing travel stories. Many ICTs like websites, social media and mobile applications enable tourists to narrate their stories (Gretzel, Fesenmaier, Lee, & Tussyadiah, 2011) and make the stories sharable. Marketers need to emulate such consumer practices. Advantages of building narratives into tourism systems were already outlined by Gretzel and Fesenmaier in 2002. Miralbell, Alzua-Sorzabal, and Gerrikagoitia (2014) explain that a narrative structure of tourist information inspires empathy in readers toward the destination which influences their travel decisions. Tussyadiah, Park, and Fesenmaier (2011) argue that stories convey important knowledge about destinations and help tourists learn. Pulizzi (2012) suggests that storytelling is growing in importance for marketers and is key to attracting and retaining consumers. Tourism marketing therefore needs to increasingly take advantage of the storytelling capabilities of ICTs. In addition, marketers have become "entertainers" who provide visually appealing, entertaining and highly shareable contents via ICTs. Entertaining Facebook posts with photos receive more likes and comments (Kwok & Yu, 2013) and including props at the destination that can be integrated into tourists' videos may result in increased immersion during the experience (Dinhopl & Gretzel, 2016). Due to their shareability, such ICT empowered marketing contents can also be used by tourists to influence other consumers in a more natural way than would be possible for marketers directly. Tourism marketers can play a strategic role in shaping such conversations among consumers (Gretzel & Yoo, 2013). As such, they become custodians rather than pure managers of the reputation of the tourism brands they represent.

Mobile Marketing: Wang and Fesenmaier (2013) argue that the use of smart phones collapses the three-stage model of travel experience. The pre- and post- consumption stages are eliminated or shortened and the consumption stage is extended. This change suggests that increased numbers of tourists simultaneously plan, make decisions, consume and share their experiences during trips using their smart phones. Given the pervasive use of mobile technology, more and more tourism marketers involve mobile technologies in their marketing strategies. Several studies found that the use of mobile technologies during trips can create spontaneous deviations which result in a change of travelers' en-route activities (Kramer, Modsching, Hagen, & Gretzel, 2007; Wang & Fesenmaier, 2013; Wang et al., 2012). The mobile device capabilities enable marketers to access the up-to-date and situation specific information about the consumers' external context while they are on move (Haekkilae et al., 2009). This means tourism marketers can reach out to travelers with highly targeted and context-relevant messages at the right time and place. Recently, Buhalis and Foerste (2015) proposed "social context mobile marketing (SoCoMo)" as a new marketing framework that increases value for all stakeholders at the destination and thus encourages co-creation of tourism experiences. They defined SoCoMo as "an advanced systematic method of context marketing on smart mobile devices that integrates social media to empower co-creation of value" (p. 155). This marketing approach incorporates internal contextual data (e.g., preference, emotional status) collected from social media and the external contextual data (e.g., location, traffic) retrieved from mobile devices to craft a highly relevant marketing message. With the customized message, tourism marketers engage the travelers and promote a dynamic conversation for co-creating value and experience. Such a marketing approach opens up new opportunities for tourism marketers but also challenges them as this integrated approach often requires sophisticated big data-mining techniques, knowledge and skills of mobile technologies/applications as well as expertise in designing strategic integrated marketing communication.

Marketing within Smart Destinations: Gretzel, Sigala, Xiang, and Koo (2015) define smart tourism as "tourism supported by integrated efforts at a destination to collect and aggregate/harness data derived from physical infrastructure, social connections, government/organizational sources and human bodies/minds in combination with the use of advanced technologies to transform that data into on-site experiences and business value-propositions with a clear focus on efficiency, sustainability and experience enrichment" (p. 181). Buhalis and Amaranggana (2015) also

stress the need for collaboration among various destination stakeholders in order to realize marketing in the context of smart
tourism. The role of destination marketers at a smart destination
is therefore one of a marketing coordinator, data clearinghouse
and infrastructure provider. Smart destinations rely on a number
of "smart" technologies, most prominently sensors, beacons,
RFID (radio-frequency identification) and NFC (near-field communication) in combination with smart phones and mobile apps
to allow for integration between physical and virtual destination
layers. The City of Barcelona, for instance, offers bus shelters
with USB ports so tourists can charge their phones while waiting
and Amsterdam uses beacons to let tourist signage translate itself
into different languages when tourists approach it with their
mobile phones. Augmented reality technologies also play a critical part in delivering data that is harnessed through smart systems (e.g., weather sensors) to tourists in a way that enhances
rather than disrupts the experience. The key to marketing within
smart destinations is to understand tourism experiences in situ
and to develop technologies and provide information that can
enhance them. However, the ultimate smart tourism experiences
are those that are personalized, context-sensitive and monitored
in real-time (Gretzel et al., 2015). Such real-time, big data-driven
and pervasive marketing requirements challenge tourism marketers enormously as old approaches to content creation and marketing communication do not work in this case, specialized
technical knowledge is needed, and traditional marketing tools
are limited in their ability to support smart tourism marketing.

Best Practices/Case Studies

CURATING AND CO-CREATING VISITORS' EXPERIENCE: #VISITPHILLY PHOTO SPOTS

Visit Philadelphia, hosted by the Greater Philadelphia Tourism
Marketing Corporation, implemented an integrated marketing
campaign, *With Love, Philadelphia XOXO*, which includes various projects designed to engage visitors using social media. One
of the projects was *#Visitphilly Photo Spots* which provided visitors a number of photo spots where they could take photos with
special With Love-branded structures at Philadelphia's highly fre-
quented and iconic places. The project was promoted as a part of
the *With Love, Philadelphia XOXO campaign* through advertising, social media platforms and the joint marketing efforts with

partners. The promotion strategically used social media and employed a #visitphilly hashtag to encourage visitors to tag their photos with the hashtag and share them on social media. A specific webpage was created for the project at Visitphilly.com, the official visitor site for the Greater Philadelphia Area. The page included an interactive map that shows the photo spots for With Love-branded structures as well as other spots for Philadelphia photo opportunities such as the Rocky statue and the Philadelphia Museum of Art steps. The visitors could also find photo tips for individual spots and the "Read More" links to the pages provided descriptions of places, open hours, ticket information as well as nearby attractions, restaurants and accommodations information (see Plate 1 for a screen shot of the campaign webpage). This campaign is a best practice example that shows how marketers can stage an experience for visitors and what support ICTs can provide to help tourism marketers co-create experiences with tourists and encourage the visitors to share these experiences with a

XOXO Letters at the Independence Visitor Center

CREDIT: PHOTO BY J. FUSCO FOR VISIT PHILADELPHIA

The best place to begin a trip to the City of Brotherly Love, the Independence Visitor Center will also be home to a set of Visit Philly's XOXO Letters this summer.

Photo tip: The XOXO Letters are perfectly situated so your photo can have Independence Hall — the birthplace of both the Declaration of Independence and the U.S. Constitution — in the background.

VIEW ON MAP   READ MORE ▸

Plate 1.   Screen Shot of #Visitphilly Photo Spot Campaign Webpage for the Independence Visitor Center. *Photo Credit:* Photo by J. Fusco for VISIT PHILADELPHIA®

wide audience of others through ICTs. According to the annual report of Visit Philadelphia (2015), people have used its hashtag, #visitphilly, more than 100,000 times on Instagram and 86 percent of out-of-towners reported increased interest in visiting because of information they found on social media platforms.

SOCIAL CONTEXT MOBILE MARKETING: SNAPCHAT GEOFILTERS

Snapchat's location-based geofilters are in-app overlays for Snaps that can be accessed in certain locations (Snapchat.com, 2016). The application users can choose and add the filters to their photos to show their location and/or activity. Some hospitality brands have recently created sponsored geofilters to provide engaging and playful experiences to visitors and an effective way to promote brands via spreading messages through consumers' personal social networks. McDonalds created a set of geofilters including the filter featuring a cheeseburger and fries. W hotel also launched filters with different messages like "You wish you were here" and "Current situation." The brand-sponsored geofilters provide a new marketing opportunity for tourism and hospitality marketers. Tourism is highly related to spatiotemporal movement (Xia, Ciesielski, & Arrowsmith, 2005) and the information relevant to space and time can be more persuasive. Since the brand-sponsored geofilters are accessible when the visitors are at the locations and provide a fun opportunity to communicate one's location and experience to others, consumers feel comfortable to add the brand image and message to their photos and share with their contacts. The playfulness of this practice also encourages visitors to engage with a brand in an authentic way, therefore facilitating the experience co-creation process. While Facebook's sponsored posts or Twitter's promoted tweets are designed based on traditional push marketing approaches that interrupts the users to deliver their messages (Tran, 2015), Snapchat geofilters provide context-specific images in a way that allows for much better integration of marketing messages in the visitor experience.

ENHANCING VISITORS' EXPERIENCE WITH AUGMENTED REALITY: ROYAL ONTARIO MUSEUM

Augmented tourism experience is defined as "A complex construct which involves the emotions, feelings, knowledge and skills resulting from the perception, processing and interaction with virtual information that is merged with the real physical world surrounding the tourist" (Yovcheva, Buhalis, & Gatzidis, 2013, p. 27). The Royal Ontario Museum in Toronto hosted an exhibition in 2012 named "Ultimate Dinosaurs" that used Augmented Reality (AR) technologies to provide visitors with new experiences beyond what was physically possible in the museum. The museum provided iPads and the visitors could use augmented reality technology that allowed them to virtually flesh out dinosaur skeletons to see what the dinosaurs looked like with skin and how they would have moved and behaved (Rieland, 2012). They could also click on the on-screen hotspots on the mobile devices to learn more about specific dinosaurs and were able to take a keepsake photo with the augmented reality graphic dinosaur at the museum plaza. A mobile application was also developed for the exhibition that visitors could download on their phones (Royal Ontario Museum Website, 2016). This case shows how advanced ICTs, in particular augmented reality, enhance the museum visitors experience and create the marketing competitiveness of tourism products/services.

Conclusion

This chapter illustrated the many types of ICTs (web-based, social media, location-based, virtual and augmented reality, mobile and smart technologies) and their varied impacts on tourism experiences, tourist expectations and visitor needs. It painted a picture of a highly technology-based tourism experience that offers new interplays between marketers and tourists and lots of avenues for experience as well as marketing content co-creation. It offered a conceptual framework to show how ICTs have disrupted the exclusive rights of tourism marketers to tourism experience creation and promotion by facilitating new connections among tourists themselves, with marketers, with residents and with employees. It discussed not only emerging opportunities for marketers to take advantage of new ICTs but also urged tourism marketing to realize its increasing dependence on technology and its need to adjust strategies and tactics aimed at developing and selling compelling tourism experiences. It listed a number of trends that illustrate how tourism marketing is changing and presented examples of how tourism marketers have tried to use emerging ICTs for the marketing of tourism experiences.

The literature review acknowledged the many ways in which the phenomenon of ICTs in tourism and their impacts on tourism experiences have been studied and showed a strong emphasis on consumer perspectives. Understanding consumers and their ICT related perceptions and behaviors is essential for tourism marketers and more research is needed on how these change as new technologies enter the playing field. Indeed, consumer perspectives on smart tourism experiences are currently missing from the literature. There is also a growing need to continue research on dimensions and effects of technology-empowered experiences. That technology automatically leads to better experiences is a dangerous assumption and systematic research is needed to identify the circumstances under which ICTs indeed enhance and empower tourism experiences. Such knowledge can greatly inform tourism marketers' attempts to design competitive experience products.

The chapter further emphasized the changing role of marketing and the need of marketers to redefine themselves as trusted experts, curators, experience facilitators, reputation custodians and storytellers. The trends identified in the chapter raise important questions about the type of knowledge and skills these new tourism marketers need and to what extent tourism marketers have shifted their assumptions and implemented new practices. Research is needed to answer these questions. There is also a growing need for research that looks at marketing effectiveness in these new technological contexts. Performance measurement has not yet been defined and informed for many of the forms of tourism marketing discussed in the chapter, such as the use of augmented reality and beacons.

The main take-away of the chapter, from both a theoretical as well as practical perspective, is that ICTs continue to impact tourism experiences and disrupt tourism marketing practice in fundamental ways. This requires constant questioning of existing models and approaches. As outlined by Gretzel et al. (2000), it also requires a general attitude to change as the new normal and an appreciation of technology as a critical foundation for all tourism marketing-related activities. It further calls for innovation and creativity in thinking about how tourism experiences can be better supported and communicated with the help of the ever greater variety of ICTs available.

References

Benckendorff, P., Sheldon, P. J., & Fesenmaier, D. R. (2014). *Tourism information technology* (2nd ed.). London: CABI.

Binkhorst, E., & Den Dekker, T. (2009). Agenda for co-creation tourism experience research. *Journal of Hospitality Marketing & Management*, *18*(2–3), 311–327.

Buhalis, D. (2003). *eTourism: Information technology for strategic tourism management*. Amsterdam: Pearson Education.

Buhalis, D., & Amaranggana, A. (2015). Smart tourism destinations: Enhancing tourism experience through personalisation of services. In I. Tussyadiah & A. Inversini (Eds.), *Information and communication technologies in tourism 2015* (pp. 377–389). Heidelberg: Springer.

Buhalis, D., & Foerste, M. (2015). SoCoMo marketing for travel and tourism: Empowering co-creation of value. *Journal of Destination Marketing & Management*, *4*(3), 151–161.

Buhalis, D., & O'Connor, P. (2005). Information communication technology revolutionizing tourism. *Tourism Recreation Research*, *30*(3), 7–16.

Cohen, E. (1979). A phenomenology of tourist experiences. *Sociology*, *13*(2), 179–201.

Csikszentmihalyi, M., & LeFevre, J. (1989). Optimal experience in work and leisure. *Journal of Personality and Social Psychology*, *56*(5), 815.

Dinhopl, A., & Gretzel, U. (2016). Conceptualizing tourist videography. *Information Technology & Tourism*, *15*(4), 395–410.

Gilmore, J. H., & Pine, B. J. (2007). *Authenticity: What customers really want*. Boston, Massachusetts: Harvard Business School Press.

Gretzel, U., & Fesenmaier, D. R. (2002). Building narrative logic into tourism information systems. IEEE Intelligent Systems, November/December 2002, pp. 59–61.

Gretzel, U., Fesenmaier, D. R., Formica, S., & O'Leary, J. T. (2006). Searching for the future: Challenges faced by destination marketing organizations. *Journal of Travel Research*, *45*(2), 116–126.

Gretzel, U., Fesenmaier, D. R., Lee, Y.-J., & Tussyadiah, I. (2011). Narrating travel experiences: The role of new media. In R. Sharpley & P. Stone (Eds.), *Tourist experiences: Contemporary perspectives* (pp. 171–182). New York, NY: Routledge.

Gretzel, U., Fesenmaier, D. R., & O'Leary, J. T. (2006). The transformation of consumer behaviour. In D. Buhalis & C. Costa (Eds.), *Tourism business frontiers: Consumers, products and industry* (pp. 9–18). Oxford: Elsevier.

Gretzel, U., Sigala, M., Xiang, Z., & Koo, C. (2015). Smart tourism: Foundations and developments. *Electronic Markets*, *25*(3), 179–188.

Gretzel, U., & Yoo, K.-H. (2013). Premises and promises of social media marketing in tourism. In S. McCabe (Ed.), *The Routledge handbook of tourism marketing* (pp. 491–504). New York, NY: Routledge.

Gretzel, U., Yuan, Y., & Fesenmaier, D. R. (2000). Preparing for the new economy: Advertising strategies and change in destination marketing organizations. *Journal of Travel Research*, *39*(2), 146–156.

Guttentag, D. A. (2010). Virtual reality: Applications and implications for tourism. *Tourism Management*, *31*(5), 637–651.

Haekkilae, J., Schmidt, A., Maentyjaervi, J., Sahami, A., Akerman, P., & Dey, A. K. (2009). Context-aware mobile media and social networks. In *Proceedings* of the 11th conference on human-computer interaction with mobile devices and services, Munich, Germany.

Hay, B. (2010). Twitter Twitter—But who is listening? A review of the current and potential use of Twittering as a tourism marketing tool. Retrieved from http://eresearch.qmu.ac.uk/1500/. Accessed on February 2016.

Hays, S., Page, S. J., & Buhalis, D. (2013). Social media as a destination marketing tool: Its use by national tourism organisations. Current issues in Tourism, 16(3), 211—239.

Jennings, G., Lee, Y. S., Ayling, A., Lunny, B., Cater, C., & Ollenburg, C. (2009). Quality tourism experiences: Reviews, reflections, research agendas. Journal of Hospitality Marketing & Management, 18(2—3), 294—310.

Jung, T., Chung, N., & Leue, M. C. (2015). The determinants of recommendations to use augmented reality technologies: The case of a Korean theme park. Tourism Management, 49, 75—86.

Kang, M., & Gretzel, U. (2012). Effects of podcast tours on tourist experiences in a national park. Tourism Management, 33(2), 440—455.

Kim, H., & Fesenmaier, D. R. (2008). Persuasive design of destination web sites: An analysis of first impression. Journal of Travel Research, 47(1), 3—13.

Kim, J., & Tussyadiah, I. P. (2013). Social networking and social support in tourism experience: The moderating role of online self-presentation strategies. Journal of Travel & Tourism Marketing, 30(1—2), 78—92.

Kramer, R., Modsching, M., Hagen, K., & Gretzel, U. (2007). Behaviouralimpacts of mobile tour guides. In M. Sigala, L. Mich, & J. Murphy (Eds.), Information and communication technologies in tourism (pp. 109–118). Wien: SpringerWienNewYork.

Kwok, L., & Yu, B. (2013). Spreading social media messages on Facebook: An analysis of restaurant business-to-consumer communications. Cornell Hospitality Quarterly, 54(1), 84—94.

Lamsfus, C., Wang, D., Alzua-Sorzabal, A., & Xiang, Z. (2015). Going mobile defining context for on-the-go travelers. Journal of Travel Research, 54(6), 691—701.

Law, R., Buhalis, D., & Cobanoglu, C. (2014). Progress on information and communication technologies in hospitality and tourism. International Journal of Contemporary Hospitality Management, 26(5), 727—750.

Lee, W., & Gretzel, U. (2012). Designing persuasive destination websites: A mental imagery processing perspective. Tourism Management, 33(5), 1270—1280.

Lee, W., Gretzel, U., & Law, R. (2010). Quasi-trial experiences through sensory information on destination web sites. Journal of Travel Research, 49(3), 310—322.

Lo, I. S., & McKercher, B. (2015). Ideal image in process: Online tourist photography and impression management. Annals of Tourism Research, 52, 104—116.

Luna-Nevarez, C., & Hyman, M. R. (2012). Common practices in destination website design. Journal of Destination Marketing and Management, 1(1—2), 94—106.

MacCannell, D. (1973). Staged authenticity: Arrangements of social space in tourist settings. *American Journal of Sociology, 79*(3), 589–603.

McCarthy, J., & Wright, P. (2004). Technology as experience. *Interactions, 11*(5), 42–43.

Miralbell, O., Alzua-Sorzabal, A., & Gerrikagoitia, J. K. (2014). Content curation and narrative tourism marketing. In Z. Xiang & I. Tussyadiah (Eds.), *Information and communication technologies in tourism* (pp. 187–199). Switzerland: Springer International Publishing.

Neuhofer, B., Buhalis, D., & Ladkin, A. (2014). A typology of technology-enhanced tourism experiences. *International Journal of Tourism Research, 16,* 340–350.

O'Connor, P. (2009). Pay-per-click search engine advertising: Are hotel trademarks being abused? *Cornell Hospitality Quarterly, 50*(2), 232–244.

Pan, B., Xiang, Z., Law, R., & Fesenmaier, D. R. (2011). The dynamics of search engine marketing for tourist destinations. *Journal of Travel Research, 50*(4), 365–377.

Pine, B. J., & Gilmore, J. H. (2011). *The experience economy.* Boston, Massachusetts: Harvard Business School Press.

Prebensen, N. K., & Foss, L. (2011). Coping and co-creating in tourist experiences. *International Journal of Tourism Research, 13*(1), 54–67.

Pulizzi, J. (2012). The rise of storytelling as the new marketing. *Publishing Research Quarterly, 28*(2), 116–123.

Rieland, R. (2012). Augmented reality livens up museums. *Smithsonian.com.* Retrieved from http://www.smithsonianmag.com/innovation/augmented-reality-livens-up-museums-22323417/. Accessed on February 2016.

Royal Ontario Museum. (2016). Retrieved from https://www.rom.on.ca/en/exhibitions-galleries/exhibitions/past-exhibitions/ultimate-dinos/augmented-reality. Accessed on February 2016.

Sevin, E. (2013). Places going viral: Twitter usage patterns in destination marketing and place branding. *Journal of Place Management and Development, 6*(3), 227–239.

Shanker, D. (2008). ICT and tourism: Challenges and opportunities. In *Conference on Tourism in India – Challenges Ahead,* 15, p. 17.

Sigala, M. (2014). Collaborative commerce in tourism: Implications for research and industry. *Current Issues in Tourism,* 1–10. Retrieved from http://www.tandfonline.com/doi/full/10.1080/13683500.2014.982522

Sigala, M., Christou, E., & Gretzel, U. (Eds.). (2012). *Social media in travel, tourism and hospitality: Theory, practice and cases.* Burlington, VT: Ashgate Publishing.

Smith, A. (2012). Reaching your audience in the digital age: Key research trends to watch. Pew Internet Project Presentation. Retrieved from http://www.pewinternet.org/2012/09/06/reaching-your-audience-in-the-digital-age-key-research-trends-to-watch/. Accessed on January 2016.

Snapchat.com. (2016). Retrieved from https://www.snapchat.com/. Accessed on January 2016.

Sorensen, F., & Jensen, J. F. (2015). Value creation and knowledge development in tourism experience encounters. *Tourism Management, 46*, 336–346.

Stamboulis, Y., & Skayannis, P. (2003). Innovation strategies and technology for experience-based tourism. *Tourism Management, 24*(1), 35–43.

Tran, T. (2015). *Social millennial today: How brands can market to millennials on snapchat*. Retrieved from http://www.socialmediatoday.com/special-columns/taictran/2015-09-04/social-millennial-today-how-brands-can-market-millennials. Accessed on February 2016.

Tussyadiah, I. P. (2014a). Toward a theoretical foundation for experience design in tourism. *Journal of Travel Research, 53*(5), 543–564.

Tussyadiah, I. (2014b). Expectation of travel experiences with wearable computing devices. In Z. Xiang & I. Tussyadiah (Eds.), *Information and communication technologies in tourism* (pp. 539–552). Switzerland: Springer International Publishing.

Tussyadiah, I. P., Park, S., & Fesenmaier, D. R. (2011). Assessing the effectiveness of consumer narratives for destination marketing. *Journal of Hospitality & Tourism Research, 35*(1), 64–78.

Tussyadiah, I. P., & Pesonen, J. (2015). Impacts of peer-to-peer accommodation use on travel patterns. *Journal of Travel Research*, 1–19. doi:10.1177/0047287515608505

Uriely, N. (2005). The tourist experience: Conceptual developments. *Annals of Tourism Research, 32*(1), 199–216.

Visit Philadelphia (2015). *Visit Philadelphia 2015 annual report*. Retrieved from http://www.visitphilly.com/2015-visit-philadelphia-annual-report/. Accessed on January 2016.

Wang, D., Park, S., & Fesenmaier, D. R. (2012). The role of smartphones in mediating the touristic experience. *Journal of Travel Research, 51*(4), 371–387.

Wang, D., & Fesenmaier, D. R. (2013). Transforming the travel experience: The use of smartphones for travel. In L. Cantoni & Z. Xiang (Eds.), *Information and communication technologies in tourism 2013* (pp. 58–69). Berlin, Heidelberg: Springer-Verlag.

Wang, D., Xiang, Z., & Fesenmaier, D. R. (2014). Adapting to the mobile world: A model of smartphone use. *Annals of Tourism Research, 48*, 11–26.

Xia, J., Ciesielski, V., & Arrowsmith, C. (2005). Data mining of tourists spatio-temporal movement patterns: A case study on Phillip Island. In Y. Xie & D. Brown (Eds.), *Proceedings of the eighth international conference on geocomputation* (pp. 1–15). University of Michigan, August 2005.

Yoo, K.-H., & Gretzel, U. (2010). Web 2.0: New rules for tourism marketing. *41st Annual Proceedings of the travel and tourism research association conference*. San Antonio, TX, June 20–22, 2010. Travel and Tourism Research Association.

Yovcheva, Z., Buhalis, D., & Gatzidis, C. (2012). Overview of smartphone augmented reality applications for tourism. *e-Review of Tourism Research, 10*(2), 63–66.

Yovcheva, Z., Buhalis, D., & Gatzidis, C. (2013). Engineering augmented tourism experiences. In L. Cantoni & Z. Xiang (Eds.), *Information and communication technologies in tourism 2013* (pp. 24–35). Berlin: Springer-Verlag.

Part IV
Monitoring and Evaluating Tourism Experiences

Aim: to consider and analyze issues and aspects related to the stage of post experience encounter

22 Memorable Tourism Experiences: Conceptual Foundations and Managerial Implications for Program Design, Delivery, and Performance Measurement

Jong-Hyeong Kim

ABSTRACT

Purpose – This chapter sought to overcome the current theoretical lack of understanding of the memorable tourism experiences (MTEs) phenomena and provide a conceptual framework for guiding destination managers who seek to design and deliver memorable experiences appropriate to their particular destination.

Methodology/approach – This chapter employed literature-based research methods. More specifically, it sought to (1) summarize the understanding of MTEs gained from a review of others' work, and conduct a retrospective examination of my own empirical research on the topic; and (2) convey the insights I have formulated regarding the implications for destination managers of this understanding for designing, delivering, and evaluating programs, which may increase the probability a visitor will return home with truly memorable experiences.

Findings – The literature review and the content analysis and synthesis identified seven conceptual and theoretical components of MTEs, such as hedonism, refreshment, novelty, local culture, meaningfulness, knowledge, and adverse feelings.

Practical implications – The current study suggested what characteristics of tourism experiences lead to strong memorability and how to measure each component of MTEs. Thus, the findings provide important implications for destination managers to develop tourism programs that last long in visitors' memories.

Originality/value – Previous researchers suggested some practical strategies to prepare environments and design experiences. However, a comprehensive, theoretically sound understanding of the fundamental factors of MTEs was left out. This study investigated tourism experiential factors that enable and facilitate MTEs. It also tried to demonstrate the managerial importance of these theoretical components to the design of "on the ground" destination programs, which initially create excitement and anticipation among potential visitors (within the context of a highly competitive marketplace), to the point where a given destination is selected over a multitude of others and where it subsequently delivers the kind of high-quality "truly memorable" experiences that fully meet the inflated expectations initially "promised" by the destination brand.

Keywords: Tourism experience; memorable tourism experience; memory; performance measurement

Introduction

> Premed, 4.0 GPA, 44 MCATs, President, American
> Legion Math League ... We have 76 applicants this year,
> only one of whom will get the scholarship and most of
> whom have resumes just as impressive as yours ... The
> Robinson [scholarship] is going to go to someone who
> dazzles. Somebody who just jumps off the page. You
> need to really explain to us what makes you special.
> What life experience separates you from all the rest.
> (Luketic, 2008)

This quote from the movie *21* is of particular relevance to the
tourism industry. To become or remain competitive in the fiercely
competitive marketplace that characterizes international tourism,
destination managers must provide their visitors with truly memorable experiences (MEs). To provide support to industry managers, certain researchers have studied the factors that influence
and shape participants' perceptions of their visitation experience
(e.g., servicescape; Bitner, 1992). They have emphasized that spatial layouts and the functionality of the physical surroundings, as
well as related symbols and artifacts, should be systemically managed to provide quality experiences. However, such practices in
the tourism industry focus more on augmenting and beautifying
the superficial appearances of facilities and equipment (e.g.,
design and architecture) rather than developing unique, memorable content for the visitation experience.

Unfortunately, the effectiveness of these efforts does not
endure. Competitors can easily copy the attributes of most tourism products, and tourism is becoming increasingly more homo-
genized or "McDonaldized" (Ritzer, 1998). These uniformities
across destinations mean that managers face difficulty in providing tourists with the unique MEs they crave. Tourists may be
amazed by the scale and modern technology of on-site attractions
but feel hollow when recalling the travel experience. Hosany and
Witham (2010) noted that marketing approaches that merely
focus on functional product attributes and inherent quality are
inadequate for dazzling tourists' senses, and ultimately for providing unforgettable tourism experiences.

To address the importance and urgency of providing MEs,
researchers have recognized the need and discussed ways to deliver
MEs (Berry, Carbone, & Haeckel, 2002). Researchers have also
asserted that positive cues help businesses affirm the nature and

value of the experience and that sensory stimulants accompanying experiential immersion enhance the efficiency and memorability of the experience. Of particular note is Pine and Gilmore's treatise on the "Experience Economy" (Pine & Gilmore, 1998), which represents a pioneering initiative, from a "how-to" perspective, particularly regarding the use of "theater" in delivering primarily functional experiences as opposed to MEs. Specifically, Pine and Gilmore suggested the (a) development of a theme for an experience, (b) harmonization of impressions with positive cues, (c) elimination of negative cues, (d) interaction of memorabilia, and (e) engagement of all five senses. Berry et al. (2002) also emphasized the importance of the environment in which the experience is provided, and of engaging the five senses in designing customer experiences. While it is commendable that researchers have provided some practical strategies to prepare environments and to design experiences, one of the most important discussions (i.e., the underlying conceptual content of the programs) has been left out. Therefore, to support tourism managers in developing cost-effective programs that provide lasting memories, more progress must be made in investigating and understanding the experiential factors that enable and facilitate MEs.

Understanding the Essence of Memorable Tourism Experiences (MTEs)

In analyzing and integrating the key ideas gained from a review of the existing literature, I noted the following key questions: (a) What are the underlying theoretical components of an experience that lead to creating an experience that is truly memorable? and (b) Can relatively routine tourism experiences be successfully translated into MEs? If yes, how? In summary, the ultimate focus has been on identifying the components of the tourism experience that lead to memorability. More specifically, I analyzed and synthesized the contents of extant articles, papers, and books concerning this experience to identify the key components of the experience considered essential to creating MTEs. This process involved (a) reviewing the literature that specifically pertains to tourism experiences and (b) cross-referencing the memory literature with that tourism experience literature.

ANALYSIS AND SYNTHESIS: THE CONCEPTUAL/THEORETICAL COMPONENTS OF TOURISM EXPERIENCES IN GENERAL

Twelve experiential components that constitute tourism experiences in general were identified in the literature. Consistent with extant tourism experience research (Otto & Ritchie, 1996), these factors represent the underlying theoretical and conceptual components of the tourism experience. The components are given in Table 1.

Table 1. Conceptual Components of the Tourism Experience.

Component of the Tourism Experience	Definition of Component	References
Adverse feelings	Negative psychological feelings, such as anger, sadness, irritation, and frustration	Larsen and Jenssen (2004), Ryan (1991), Wirtz, Kruger, Scollon, and Diener (2003)
Hedonism	A feeling of pleasure, fun, and amusement that excites oneself	Dunman and Mattila (2005), Grappi and Montanari (2011), Mannell and Kleiber (1997), Otto and Ritchie (1996)
Local culture	An experience of host cultures by observing and/or encountering local people	Morgan and Xu (2009), Weiler and Yu (2008)
Refreshment	A psychological feeling of being refreshed	Hull and Michael (1995), Mak, Wong, and Chang (2009)
Knowledge	Information, facts, or experiences known by an individual	Blackshaw (2003), Otto and Ritchie (1996), Weiler and Yu (2008)
Meaningfulness	A sense of great value or significance	Jamal and Hollinshead (2001), Noy (2004), Wilson and Harris (2006)
Novelty	A psychological feeling of newness resulting from having new experiences	Dunman and Mattila (2005), Farber and Hall (2007), Weiler and Yu (2008)
Relaxation	A feeling of comfort and pleasure without involving physical activity	Chandralal and Valenzuela (2013), Mannell, Zuzanek, and Larson (1988)
Stimulation	Arousal of feelings that heighten and/or invigorate oneself	Arnould and Price (1993), Bolla, Dawson, and Harrington (1991), Obenour, Patterson, Pedersen, and Pearson (2006)

Table 1. (*Continued*)

Component of the Tourism Experience	Definition of Component	References
Social interaction	A feeling of connection and group identity with travel partners and/or local people	Ap and Wong (2001), Arnould and Price (1993), Obenour et al. (2006)
Happiness	A feeling of joy that springs from the heart	Bolla et al. (1991)
Challenge	An experience that demands physical and/or mental ability	Lee, Dattilo, and Howard (1994), Mannell and Iso-Ahola (1987)

CROSS REFERENCE ANALYSIS: IDENTIFYING THE CONCEPTUAL AND THEORETICAL COMPONENTS OF MTEs

To better understand the components of the tourism experience and the manner in which they affect individuals (and potentially lead to memorability), I examined the conceptual components of the tourism experience, an examination based on cross-referencing the literature on tourism with that on memory accordingly.

The literature review and the content analysis and synthesis identified a subset of seven conceptual and theoretical components of MTEs: (a) hedonism, (b) refreshment, (c) novelty, (d) local culture, (e) meaningfulness, (f) knowledge, and (g) adverse feelings. The following describes the nature of these seven factors and their roles in creating MTEs.

Hedonism

Tourism researchers have long recognized that tourism and leisure activities possess a predominantly hedonic component. Unlike other activities and products, people primarily seek enjoyment (hedonism/pleasure) while "consuming" tourism products (experiences). Consistent with the notion that the primary purpose of consuming leisure-related products is to pursue hedonic or pleasurable experiences, an emotional component is a significant aspect of tourism experiences. In one of the earliest empirical studies on this topic, Otto and Ritchie (1996) reported that tourism products and services are rich in attributes and are primarily consumed for hedonic purposes. This finding is consistent with a wide range of evidence, subsequently documented in the tourism literature. For example, Dunman and Mattila (2005) identified hedonism as a major determinant of the perceived value of cruise travel.

Refreshment

Next to hedonism, refreshment, or relaxation and renewal, is probably the most defining basic component of tourism activities. Turner and Ash (1975) contended that the temporary distance of tourists from their regular environment allows them to suspend the power of the norms and values of their daily lives and think about their own lives and societies from a different perspective. People satisfy their psychological need to escape from boredom and seek solitude, or relaxation, by engaging in travel experiences (Cohen, 1979). Turner and Bruner (1986) elaborated on Dilthey's distinction between "mere experience" and "an experience" from an anthropological perspective (p. 35). Mere experience is simply the passive endurance and acceptance of events. In contrast, "an experience" like a rock in a Zen sand garden stands out from the evenness of passing hours and years, and forms what Dilthey called a "structuring of experience." Moreover, in a study that identified factors enhancing the memorability of tourism experiences, Kim (2010) contended that the feeling of being refreshed positively influences people's memories of travel.

Novelty

In the tourism literature, novelty seeking has been consistently discussed as another important component of the subjective tourism experience as well as a popular motivation for an individual to travel (Dunman & Mattila, 2005; Farber & Hall, 2007). Travelers tend to choose a destination where the culture and lifestyles are different, to satisfy their need and desire to experience something new or "other, something" that cannot be found in their home countries (Pearce, 1987). Of particular significance in relation to the understanding of MTEs is the fact that the memory literature has reported a strong causal connection between novelty and human memory (Reder, Donavos, & Erickson, 2002). More specifically, memory researchers have contended that unusual, atypical, or distinctive events are better remembered than "typical" events. Tourism researchers who studied the components of MTEs found that individuals recall and remember novel tourism experiences better than other experiences (Kim & Ritchie, 2014).

Social Interaction and Local Culture

Unlike other customer product experiences, tourism experiences are co-created by involving people in experience-based situations (Ryan, 1998). In the tourism setting, customers often share the setting together with others and influence each other's tourism experiences. Furthermore, tourists increase their understanding of the local culture by interacting with residents in a destination. In the tourism literature, experiencing local culture has been discussed as an important motivational factor for traveling (Funk & Bruun, 2007; Sharpley & Sundaram, 2005). In MTE studies, Kim, Ritchie, and McCormick (2012) and Kim (2010) found that experiencing local culture makes travel more meaningful and memorable. Additionally, Morgan and Xu (2009) stated that interacting with the local culture and people allowed travelers to construct unique and memorable holiday experiences.

Knowledge

Tourism researchers have also reported that people wish to learn new things and develop new insights and skills because of their tourism experiences (Poria, Reichel, & Brian, 2006; Richards, 2002). Tourism motivation studies suggest that one of the push motivations that predispose individuals to travel is to satisfy the need to gain knowledge. For example, many people travel in response to the urge to acquire new knowledge and understanding of the destinations they visit (particularly areas such as history, culture, and food). While studying antecedents of MTEs, Chandralal and Valenzuela (2013) found that authentic local experiences that provide learning opportunities to visitors are memorable. For example, their study participants' strongly remembered local food and culinary experiences associated with how they are consumed and how unique and different they are.

Meaningfulness

Because meaning is essential to happiness and well-being (Baumeister & Vohs, 2002), people strive to find meaning in life (Frankl, 1985). Similarly, people search for meaningful experiences within their travel and tourism activities, such as seeking a sense of physical, emotional, or spiritual fulfillment through tourism, rather than pursuing mere escapism or a hollow search for authenticity (Callanan & Thomas, 2005; Digance, 2003;

Noy, 2004). Since travelers are more sophisticated today, they increasingly seek unique and meaningful travel experiences to satisfy their needs and desires (Robinson & Novelli, 2005). For example, some individuals consider a tourism experience an inner journey of personal growth and self-development, rather than the mere consumption of sights, faces, and places. Chandralal and Valenzuela (2013) supported this notion by finding that most of their study participants referred to their past tourism experiences as memorable, as they had gained personally significant outcomes, such as self-development, relationship development, and enhanced family well-being.

Adverse Feelings

The pursuit of pleasurable, positive feelings is the primary motivation for participating in tourism experiences. However, tourists can unexpectedly realize negative emotions or feelings during their tourism experiences. If these emotions are sufficiently intense, they can result in negative MEs. Severely adverse feelings are evoked by the occurrence of an accident or a highly negative service or tourism experience. Since the main tourism products are service-related and thus have an inconsistent nature (largely derived from the inevitability of human error), tourists can always develop adverse feelings (e.g., anger and frustration) during their tourism experiences. Not surprisingly, as complaint behavior studies have reported, such occurrences exert more significant influence on customer dissatisfaction than on satisfaction (Kim & Chen, 2010): "people remember these sorts of negative emotional events better than ordinary events that occurred equally long ago" (Christianson, 1992, p. 194).

Management Practice for the Design and Delivery of MTEs

In order to provide managers with guidance on how to best deliver MTE components and provide this guidance in a systematic, integrated manner, I now explore the implications of the understanding gained from the previous discussion, with a view to translating them into "service encounter, service delivery, and service environment specifics" (Otto & Ritchie, 1996, p. 173). Accordingly, I examine the different management practices (see

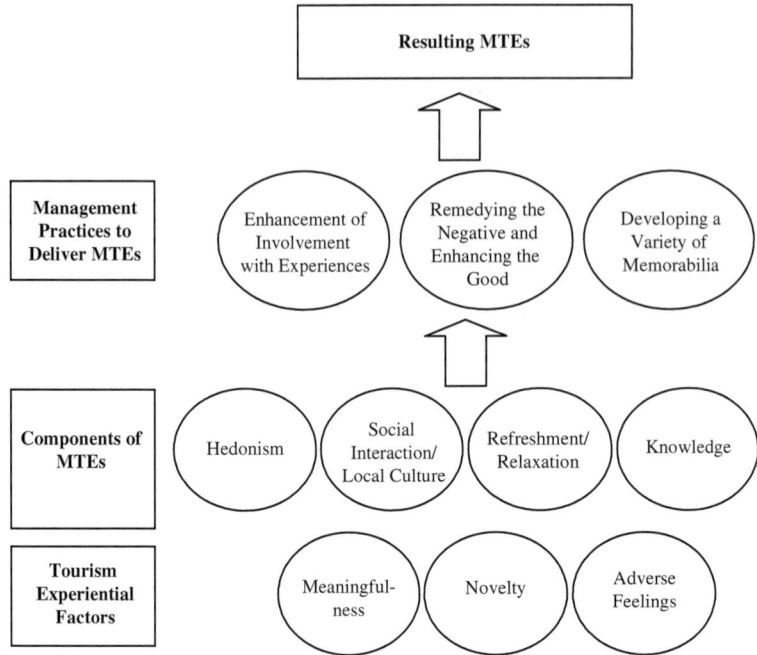

Figure 1.   A Conceptual Framework for the Design and Delivery of MTEs.

Figure 1) related to the design of various tourism programs and destination environments that collectively provide visitors with the underlying components of an MTE (as shown in Table 2).

In summary, responses to the challenge of translating theoretical understanding into practical guidance are given in the managerial framework in Figure 1. This framework has as its foundation the seven components of MTE that managers must seek to deliver (in varying degrees) during tourism experiences. In addition to these foundational components, I recommend to DMOs the three major kinds of management practices that as means to effectively translate the total set of conceptual components of an experience into real-world MTEs. Briefly, these three practices are (a) enhancement of involvement with experiences; (b) actions to remedy or offset negative or adverse effects from experiences, while taking steps to strengthen the good or positive effects arising from the experience; and (c) comprehensive programs of memorabilia that play the critical role of reinforcing the MEs within the individual's memory. These memorabilia may take many forms, from the mundane to the exceptional, from

Table 2.   Tourism Environments/Programs which Destination Managers May Design/Implement within Tourism Destinations to Deliver the Underlying Components of MTEs.

Component of Experience	Management Program/ Environment	Types of Tourism
Hedonism	Develop pleasurable and amusing programs as well as environmental cues	Adventure tourism, extreme tourism, sports tourism, event tourism
Social interaction/ local culture	Develop tour routes in which visitors can freely interact with locals	Agritourism, cultural tourism, rural tourism, backpacking
Refreshment	Develop programs in which visitors can experience a feeling of relaxation and recovery from their everyday life	Cruise tourism, spa tourism, nature-based tourism, sun and sand tourism, nautical tourism, water tourism, hunting tourism
Knowledge	Utilize interpreters as well as interpretive commentaries and signage in order to provide more detailed information about the destination areas	Heritage tourism, archaeological tourism, genealogy tourism
Meaningfulness	Develop programs in which visitors experience personal growth and self-development	Volunteer tourism, religious tourism, educational tourism
Novelty	Create novel atmospheres in the experience environment and expose visitors with unique features of service encounters	Space tourism, wildlife tourism, cyber-tourism

highly popular photographs and diverse physical souvenirs to the finding of a lifelong partner. The purpose of memorabilia is to help facilitate the MTE's recall.

In applying my managerial framework, I strongly urge destination managers to remember that tourists subjectively construct their own personal experiences by taking fragments from different programs and environments and reassembling them. Different kinds of tourism that seek to satisfy each underlying component of the MEs will have limitations. For example, the novelty of a particular experience is significantly constrained by an individual's total set of experiences. Therefore, generalizing how specific kinds of tourism programs or experience environments might satisfy the novelty component needs of the general population of visitors is difficult. Furthermore, since no destination marketer wants his or her visitors to develop negative memories about the destination program, the experiential component "adverse feeling" is not included in the conceptual framework as a component of MTEs a destination should seek to deliver. Consequently, this section discusses only the management and marketing practices (programs and environments) related to each positive component of MTEs. Additionally, when applying the framework, destination managers must remember that a given experience may not satisfy all of the underlying components of an ME and should ideally seek at all times to deliver visitation experiences that satisfy all components of MTEs. Realistically, however, a destination manager must recognize that any destination, in all likelihood, is capable of delivering only some subset of the components of MTEs. Accordingly, the destination manager must first identify the MTE components the destination is capable of delivering competitively and subsequently identify those segments of the travel market to which those components have particular appeal. I now identify and examine the programs and environments that destination managers might employ to deliver the components of an ME.

Enhancing Involvement

People remember a personally relevant and meaningful experience more than a non-relevant one. People's involvement with travel experiences significantly increases their memories of the experiences (Kim et al., 2012). Two phases of tourism experiences exist in which travelers develop involvement: planning and on-site. In the former, during which diverse preparations are necessary (e.g., arranging transportation and accommodations), people often visualize themselves actually involved in the activity. Various emotions (e.g., anxiety and exhilaration) and expectations of the experience can develop from these visualizations. Therefore, destination managers should develop comprehensive marketing strategies that build positive perceptions across all components of the destination experience and thus strengthen people's desire to visit. Emphasizing physical clues and employing metaphors and vivid images in advertising can be an effective method for encouraging people to develop interest in the destination and curiosity about the tourism programs.

In the on-site phase of tourism experiences, marketing managers can enhance tourists' involvement by designing programs in which tourists can actively participate. Briefly, when customers find themselves immersed in an activity, they are more likely to have an ME. Markwell (2004) also emphasized multisensory participation that allows visitors a feeling of "being there" and extends beyond the "gaze" associated with tourist experiences. Destination managers should develop tourism programs where tourists are co-producers of their experiences.

Remedying the Negatives and Enhancing the Positives

Due to the dynamic nature of tourism experiences, an unexpected event, such as an accident, illness, loss of valuables, or even contest win, can happen at any time. Because of these unanticipated events, feelings of surprise, anger, frustration, happiness, etc., are evoked. Depending on the characteristics of the experiences, they may be either positive or negative. Researchers studying human memory have suggested that these unexpected, emotionally laden, and consequential events lead to "flashbulb memory," which lasts longer than ordinary events (Talarico & Rubin, 2003). Thus, unexpected occurrences in people's tourism experiences are retained better in their memories. The Canadian Tourism Commission (2004) highlighted the importance of surprise as an integral part of memorable travel experiences. The intensity of positive surprises correlates significantly with positive word-of-mouth (Derbaix & Vanhamme, 2003) and influences overall satisfaction (Vanhamme, 2000).

Since negative events during travel can result in negative word-of-mouth advertising and/or loss of market share, destination managers should seek to resolve any service failure. Indeed, the service recovery literature suggests that a business can take advantage of a service failure because employing effective recovery strategies can produce a "service recovery paradox," or a situation in which the satisfaction levels of customers who received excellent recovery or compensation are higher than those of customers who experienced no service breakdowns in the first place (Heung & Lam, 2003; Kotler, Bowen, & Makens, 2003). Researchers studying service recovery have contended that customers expect fairness in the recovery process to make up for the losses that occurred during a service failure (McColl-Kennedy & Sparks, 2003). Thus, destination managers should ensure that recovery efforts provide benefits that customers believe make up for their losses equitably.

Discounts for future visits, replacement of service, employees' empathy, and explanations for the service failure can all be used to handle service failure situations.

Destination managers should develop events and/or situations that surprise their visitors in a positive way. Even a minor change in management practices can create positive MEs. Gilmore and Pine (2002) described examples of creating MEs by surprising customers. The examples include the MGM Grand Hotel & Casino in Las Vegas, which provides a unique morning call service. Guests wake up to recorded voices of celebrities who have performed in the hotel, creating fun MEs simply because the visitors never expected to hear celebrity voices. Such events result in feelings of delight, a mediator of MEs. In summary, destination managers should layer pleasantly surprising experiences on top of existing services.

Developing a Variety of Memorabilia

Tourists always collect memorabilia, such as souvenirs, to remind them of their tourism experiences and to show people back home what the experiences were like. Destination managers should develop diverse memorabilia that include not only objects belonging to current souvenir typologies but also more ordinary objects, such as nail clippers, that begin functioning as souvenirs later, after the tourist's return home. Objects acquired explicitly as souvenirs often lose their sentimental value over time, while practical articles brought home from a journey often acquire sentimental meaning in retrospect (Collins-Kreiner & Zins, 2011).

In addition to developing a diverse range of souvenirs, another way to promote the memorability of tourism experiences is designing a memory point at various sites in a destination area. The photographs taken at memory points reinforce visitors' memories of their tourism experiences after they return home, thus creating a recollection stage of multiphase experiences.

Measuring Managerial Performance in Achieving Experience Memorability

Because MTEs design and delivery have only recently received attention in the literature, understandably, there has been even less attention paid to measuring the effectiveness of the delivery of MTEs. However, the following measures will perhaps be viewed as a useful point of departure. I refer to a set of scales developed to assess the degree to which an individual perceived that he/she received satisfaction across each/any/all (6) positive components of MTEs. Briefly, this set of scales, which I have developed and tested, may provide a useful tool for enabling visitors to indicate the degree to which they experience a visit that

1. Was hedonistically memorable
2. Was refreshingly memorable
3. Was memorably different/unique
4. Was socially/culturally memorable
5. Taught something new/some memorable skill
6. Generated something especially meaningful – generated memorable involvement in something?
7. Generated a memorably bad experience?

Conclusion

Commenting on the importance of delivering MTEs, Ritchie and Crouch (2003) stated,

> The implication of the search for experiences is that each and every destination manager must attempt to view his or her destination not simply as a place to visit and a place to do things, but, more importantly, as the provider of visitor experiences – preferably enjoyable, memorable experiences – that will generate high levels of visitor satisfaction and the subsequent favorable word-of-mouth advertising that is essential to both competitiveness and sustainability. (p. 2)

However, current tourism marketing approaches focusing on functional product attributes and quality seem ineffective in delivering MEs. In particular, researchers should pay more explicit and careful attention to the central role of identifying tourism experiential factors that last longer in visitors' memories. Therefore, to facilitate a better understanding of how tourism programs can help people gain MEs, I explicitly integrated tourism literature with memory literature.

The framework for assisting destination managers in designing and delivering programs and environments that will enhance each destination's ability to deliver the components of MTEs is specifically tailored to the particular strengths and appeals of the destination in question. This conceptual assessment of the managerial practices best suited to delivering MTEs in any context represents a pioneering attempt to capture the experience's components that are potentially available at a particular destination and to match them with management practices that have the highest probability of delivering a visitation experience subjectively perceived as truly memorable by visitors when they are evaluating their destination experiences.

The review of the tourism and memory literature related to experiences and the subsequent content analysis and overall synthesis of my findings revealed that MTEs are composed of seven underlying conceptual components. Thus, tourism visitation experiences should be carefully designed to ensure they include the six positive components of a potential MTE – and, to the extent possible, avoid negative, or adverse, components, which can easily undo many months and years of careful planning.

To conclude, I formulated a conceptual framework (see Figure 1) identifying a range of management practices for assisting destination managers in strategic planning and program design within DMOs. The recommended managerial practices will greatly enhance the likelihood that visitors will experience a truly memorable destination visit. I suggested enhancing visitor involvement as co-producers of their experiences, remedying negative experiences and enhancing positive ones (e.g., dealing with stressful events and surprising visitors in positive ways), and diversifying memorabilia as ways to enhance the probability of delivering MTEs. The framework provides recommendations for designing and delivering tourism programs and "experiencescapes" that will provide visitors with the underlying components of MEs a destination can deliver.

Destination managers could also use the study results to develop rating or evaluation criteria. They may learn how their businesses rank against others across memorable experiential factors and management practices by asking visitors' questions about competitors. Since consumers have become more information oriented when deciding on destination areas, this competitive information could be transferred to advertising efforts and program development.

References

Ap, J., & Wong, K. K. F. (2001). Case study on tour guiding: Professionalism, issues, and problems. *Tourism Management, 22*, 551–563.

Arnould, E., & Price, L. (1993). River magic: Extraordinary experience and the extended service encounter. *Journal of Consumer Research, 20*, 24–45.

Baumeister, R. F., & Vohs, K. D. (2002). The pursuit of meaningfulness in life. *Handbook of positive psychology* (pp. 608–618). New York, NY: Oxford University Press.

Berry, L. L., Carbone, L. P., & Haeckel, S. H. (2002). Managing the total customer experience. *MIT Sloan Management Review, 43*(3), 85–89.

Bitner, M. J. (1992). Servicescapes: The impact of physical surroundings on customers and employees. *Journal of Marketing, 56*(2), 57–71.

Blackshaw, T. (2003). *Leisure life: Myth, modernity, and masculinity*. New York, NY: Routledge.

Bolla, P., Dawson, D., & Harrington, M. (1991). The leisure experience of women in Ontario. *Journal of Applied Recreation Research, 16*(4), 322–348.

Callanan, M., & Thomas, S. (2005). Volunteer tourism: Deconstructing volunteer activities within a dynamic environment. In M. Novelli (Ed.), *Niche tourism: Contemporary issues and trends* (pp. 183–200). New York, NY: Elsevier.

Canadian Tourism Commission. (2004). *Defining tomorrow's tourism product: Packaging experiences*. Research Report, 2004–2007, pp. 1–41.

Chandralal, L., & Valenzuela, F.-R. (2013). Exploring memorable tourism experiences: Antecedents and behavioural outcomes. *Journal of Economics, Business, and Management, 1*(2), 177–181.

Christianson, S. A. (1992). Do flashbulb memories differ from other types of emotional memories? In E. Winograd & U. Neisser (Eds.), *Affect and accuracy in recall: Studies of flashbulb memories* (pp. 191–211). New York, NY: Cambridge University Press.

Cohen, E. (1979). A phenomenology of tourist types. *Sociology, 13*, 179–201.

Collins-Kreiner, N., & Zins, Y. (2011). Tourists and souvenirs: Changes through time, space, and meaning. *Journal of Heritage Tourism, 6*(1), 17–27.

Derbaix, C., & Vanhamme, J. (2003). Inducing word-of-mouth by eliciting surprise – A pilot Investigation. *Journal of Economic Psychology, 24*(1), 99–116.

Digance, J. (2003). Pilgrimage at contested sites. *Annals of Tourism Research, 30*(1), 143–159.

Dunman, T., & Mattila, A. S. (2005). The role of affective factors on perceived cruise vacation Value. *Tourism Management, 26*, 311–323.

Farber, M. E., & Hall, T. E. (2007). Emotion and environment: Visitor' extraordinary experiences along the Dalton Highway in Alaska. *Journal of Leisure Research, 39*(2), 248–270.

Frankl, V. E. (1985). *Man's search for meaning*. New York, NY: Simon & Schuster.

Funk, D. C., & Bruun, T. J. (2007). The role of socio-psychological and culture-education motives in marketing international sport tourism: A cross-cultural perspective. *Tourism Management*, *28*(3), 806–819.

Gilmore, J. H., & Pine, J. B. (2002). Differentiating hospitality operations via experiences: Why selling services is not enough. *Cornell Hotel and Restaurant Administration Quarterly*, *43*, 87–96.

Grappi, S., & Montanari, F. (2011). The role of social identification and hedonism in affecting tourist re-patronizing behaviours: The case of an Italian festival. *Tourism Management*, *32*(5), 1128–1140.

Heung, V. C. S., & Lam, T. (2003). Guest complaint behavior towards hotel restaurant services. *International Journal of Contemporary Hospitality Management*, *15*(5), 283–289.

Hosany, S., & Witham, M. (2010). Dimensions of cruisers' experiences, satisfaction, and intention to recommend. *Journal of Travel Research*, *49*(3), 351–364.

Hull, R. B., & Michael, S. E. (1995). Nature-based recreation, mood change, and stress reduction. *Leisure Sciences*, *17*, 1–14.

Jamal, T., & Hollinshead, K. (2001). Tourism and the forbidden zone: The underserved power of qualitative inquiry. *Tourism Management*, *22*(1), 63–82.

Kim, J.-H. (2010). Determining the factors affecting the nature of memorable experience of travel experiences. *Journal of Travel & Tourism Marketing*, *27*(8), 780–796.

Kim, J.-H., & Chen, J. S. (2010). The effects of situational and personal characteristics on consumer complaint behavior in restaurant services. *Journal of Travel & Tourism Marketing*, *27*(1), 96–112.

Kim, J.-H., & Ritchie, J. R. B. (2014). Cross-cultural validation of a Memorable Tourism Experience Scale (MTES). *Journal of Travel Research*, *53*(3), 323–335.

Kim, J.-H., Ritchie, J. R. B., & McCormick, B. (2012). Development of a scale to measure memorable tourism experiences. *Journal of Travel Research*, *51*(1), 12–25.

Kotler, P., Bowen, J. T., & Makens, J. C. (2003). *Marketing for hospitality and tourism*. Upper Saddle River, NJ: Prentice-Hall.

Larsen, S., & Jenssen, D. (2004). The school trip: Travelling with, not to or from. *Scandinavian Journal of Tourism Research*, *4*, 43–57.

Lee, Y., Dattilo, J., & Howard, D. (1994). The complex and dynamic nature of leisure experience. *Journal of Leisure Research*, *26*, 195–211.

Luketic, R. (Director). (2008). *21* [Film]. Columbia Pictures, Los Angeles.

Mak, A. H., Wong, K. K., & Chang, R. C. (2009). Health or self-indulgence? The motivations and characteristics of Spa-Goers. *International Journal of Tourism Research*, *11*(2), 185–199.

Mannell, R., & Iso-Ahola, S. E. (1987). Psychological nature of leisure and tourism experience. *Annals of Tourism Research*, *14*, 314–331.

Mannell, R., & Kleiber, D. (1997). *A social psychology of leisure*. State College, PA: Venture.

Mannell, R., Zuzanek, J., & Larson, R. (1988). Leisure state and flow experiences: Testing perceived freedom and intrinsic motivation hypotheses. *Journal of Leisure Research*, *20*(4), 289–304.

Markwell, K. (2004). Constructing, presenting and interpreting nature: A case study of a nature-based tour to Borneo. *Annals of Leisure Research*, 7(1), 19–33.

McColl-Kennedy, J. R., & Sparks, B. A. (2003). Application of fairness theory to service failures and service recovery. *Journal of Service Research*, 5(3), 251–266.

Morgan, M., & Xu, F. (2009). Student travel experiences: Memories and dreams. *Journal of Hospitality Marketing & Management*, 18, 216–236.

Noy, C. (2004). This trip really changed me: Backpackers' narratives of self-change. *Annals of Tourism Research*, 31(1), 78–102.

Obenour, W., Patterson, M., Pedersen, P., & Pearson, L. (2006). Conceptualization of a meaning-based research approach for tourism service experiences. *Tourism Management*, 27, 34–41.

Otto, J. E., & Ritchie, J. R. B. (1996). The service experience in tourism. *Tourism Management*, 17(3), 165–174.

Pearce, D. G. (1987). *Tourism today: A geographical analysis*. Harlow: Longman.

Pine, J. B., & Gilmore, J. H. (1998). Welcome to the experience economy. *Harvard Business Review*, 76(4), 97–105.

Poria, Y., Reichel, A., & Brian, A. (2006). Heritage site management: Motivations and Expectations. *Annals of Tourism Research*, 33(1), 162–178.

Reder, L. M., Donavos, D. K., & Erickson, M. A. (2002). Perceptual match effects in direct tests of memory: The role of contextual fan. *Memory & Cognition*, 30(2), 312–323.

Richards, G. (2002). Tourism attraction systems: Exploring cultural behavior. *Annals of Tourism Research*, 29(4), 1048–1064.

Ritchie, J. R. B., & Crouch, G. (2003). *The competitive destination: A sustainable tourism perspective*. Wallingford: CABI.

Ritzer, G. (1998). *The Mcdonaldization thesis*. Sage, London.

Robinson, M., & Novelli, M. (2005). Niche tourism: An introduction. In M. Novelli (Ed.), *Niche tourism: Contemporary issues, trends and cases* (pp. 1–14). Oxford: Elsevier Butterworth-Heinemann.

Ryan, C. (1991). *Recreational tourism: A social science approach*. London: Routledge.

Ryan, C. (1998). Saltwater crocodiles as tourist attractions: A pilot study. *Journal of Sustainable Tourism*, 6(4), 314–327.

Sharpley, R., & Sundaram, P. (2005). Tourism: A sacred journey? The case of ashram tourism, India. *International Journal of Tourism Research*, 7(3), 161–171.

Talarico, J. M., & Rubin, D. C. (2003). Confidence, not consistency, characterizes flashbulb memories. *Psychological Science*, 14, 455–461.

Turner, L., & Ash, J. (1975). *The golden hordes: International tourism and the pleasure periphery*. London: Routledge.

Turner, V. W., & Bruner, E. M. (1986). *The anthropology of experience*. Urbana, IL: University of Illinois.

Vanhamme, J. (2000). The link between surprise and satisfaction: An exploratory research on how best to measure surprise. *Journal of Marketing Management, 16*(6), 565–582.

Weiler, B., & Yu, X. (2008). Case studies of the experience of Chinese visitors to three tourist attractions in Victoria, Australia. *Annals of Leisure Research, 11*(1–2), 225–241.

Wilson, E., & Harris, C. (2006). Meaningful travel: Women, independent travel and the search for self and meaning. *Tourism, 54*(2), 161–172.

Wirtz, D., Kruger, J., Scollon, C. N., & Diener, E. (2003). What to do on spring break? The role of predicted, on-line, and remembered experience in future choice. *Psychological Science, 14*, 520–524.

23 Proposing an Experiential Value Model within the Context of Business Tourism

Magdalena Petronella (Nellie) Swart

ABSTRACT

Purpose – The relevance of the use of business models in the measurement of tourist experience has been questioned. Therefore, the purpose of this chapter is to suggest a theoretical framework for the development of a multi-item Business Tourist Experience Value Model.

Methodology/approach – Against the Behavioural Intentions Model of Fishbein and Ajzen (1975), an alternative Business Tourist Experience Value theoretical model is suggested. This model consists of an integration and re-assessment of different elements from a range of empirical studies.

Findings – Experiential value, satisfaction, and post-consumption behavior may play an important role in acquiring information and knowledge creation on how business tourism organizations can use a Business Tourist Experience Value model to enhance service experiences.

Research limitations/implications – Due to the explorative nature of the Business Tourist Experience Value theoretical model, more empirical studies are needed to investigate, test and validate the model.

Practical implications – Results from the theoretical discussion support the inclusion of experiential value, satisfaction, and post-consumption behavior as part of the Business Tourist Experience Value model. Due to the magnitude of the relationships among these dimensions it is expected that the theoretical and practical implications may complement each other. Therefore business tourism managers can use these dimensions as guidelines on how to create valuable experiences for their tourists and perform better.

Originality/value – This theoretical model offers new practices into business tourism managers' measurement of experiential value, satisfaction, and post-consumption behavior in a business tourism context.

Keywords: Business tourist; experiences; experiential value; intention; post-consumption behavior; satisfaction

Introduction

Are business tourist experiences influenced by the modeling of experiential value, satisfaction, or post-consumption behavior? Do we need a new business model to deal with changes in business tourism experiences? We would like to avoid a new business model, as many scholars (Booms & Bitner, 1981; Parasuraman, Zeithaml, & Berry, 1988; Siu, Wan, & Dong, 2012; Swart, 2013) have proposed these kind of models, such as DINESERV, RENTQUAL, SERVQUAL, SERVPERF, Servicescape and the Service Quality Scorecard (SQSC) to name a few. Yet we do need to create something like it (Sørensen & Jensen, 2015). From these studies it is evident that no one-size-fits-all solution exists and most researchers will use some combination of proposed business models to formulate their own model.

Business tourism is one of the fastest growing sectors in the tourism industry, but little is known about the application of different business models in the measurement of experience value, satisfaction, and post-consumption behavior. A new, radical and profound idea for creating experiential value and satisfaction that stems from different schools of thought and the application of unconventional methodologies is required. Future studies should also focus its research scope on other forms of special interest tourism (SIT), such as business tourism, to compare the overall conclusions of these models (Peric & Wise, 2015; Swart, 2013). This will require an integration of different elements from business models and to examine the relationship between these different business models, variety of experiences, and performances. Therefore, this exploratory journey must begin with a straight-forward step to re-assess some of the fundamental literature related to experiential value, satisfaction, and business tourist post-consumption behavior.

Despite the voluminous body of research on service quality (Parasuraman et al., 1988) and experience (Sørensen & Jensen, 2015), it is poorly understood in a business tourism context. As a result, business tourism managers and organizations overlook one of the most potent tools of service experience, namely value (Swart, 2013), that they have at their disposal. Researchers have spent decades to explore the impacts, nature and sources of service quality systematically (Cronin & Taylor, 1992; Grönroos, 1984; Parasuraman et al., 1988; Siu et al., 2012). But it was Swart (2013) who assessed the Customer Value Perspective as a variable of a SQSC in a Business Tourism context. It is therefore argued that by increasing the value customers (or business tourists) get from their experiences, they are more likely to turn those value perceptions into positive experiences.

According to consumer and social psychologists, people who are confident of their beliefs have shown a greater possibility to buy, buy sooner, and spend more (Tormala & Rucker, 2015). A positive experience is the catalyst that turns attitudes into action, brings beliefs to life and instills them with meaning, business tourists must have certainty about their beliefs of the value experiences they can get when engaging with the service providers. It is important that when business tourists decide to buy a service, it "feels right" and they have a sense that they will have a valuable experience and feel satisfied. Researchers support the empirical testing of "experience value," however, the challenge remains that this is still subjective and depends on the beliefs and behaviors of the business tourist (Swart, 2013). It is against this background that the following literature framework is proposed in Figure 1.

The chapter is structured as follows. First, the concepts business tourist and business tourism are discussed to inform the literature framework and to provide context for the literature study. Second, experiential value and satisfaction are defined,

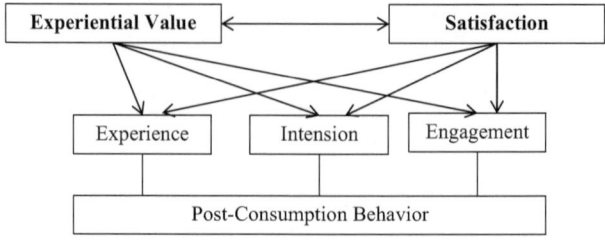

Figure 1. Theoretical Framework. *Sources*: Fishbein and Ajzen (1975), Lauring (2013), Peric and Wise (2015), Pine and Gilmore (1998, 2013), Sørensen and Jensen (2015), Swarbrooke and Horner (1999), Swart (2013).

and suggestions are made about how these factors may provide new opportunities for knowledge development and value creation in business tourism. Third, the relationships between experiential value and satisfaction are highlighted and suggestions are made on how these factors influence business tourist post-consumption behavior. Fourth, a new experiential value and satisfaction business tourism model to assess business tourist post-consumption behavior is proposed. Finally, the main conclusions of the chapter are summarized and discussed.

Business Tourism

In tourism, we differentiate between two main categories of tourists, namely business and leisure tourists (Rogers, 2003). These two categories function in an economic environment and are referred to as the "demand force," as tourists move through the tourism system (Davidson, 1994 as cited in Rogers, 2003, p. 22). The United Nations (UN) World Tourism Organisation (WTO, 1999, p. 139) associates leisure "… with people taking photos, buying souvenirs, having limited contact with residents and staying for short periods of time."

Although business tourism is considered to be a fairly young phenomenon in academic research, it is regarded as one of the oldest forms of tourism (Shone, 1998). Spa towns and the exchange of agricultural products among Roman-British communities in England and Ireland dates back more than 2000 years. Small-scale traders, such as artisans, are regarded as the earliest business tourists; as they traveled for hundreds of kilometers to trade their products (Swarbrooke & Horner, 2001). In the modern era, most of the business tourism research and application stem from adopting management and marketing theories. Today, the business tourism industry is regarded one of the fastest growing segments in the tourism industry (ITB Berlin Convention, 2008). Getz (1997) was one of the first authors to investigate the impact of events and their evolution over the past two decades.

In the 1990s, academia and industry referred to the acronym MICE (Meetings, Incentives, Conventions and Exhibitions/ Events) (South African Tourism, 2004, p. 15). In the early 2000s MICE was commonly known as business tourist or business events, depending on your geographical location. Davidson (1994 as cited in Swarbrooke & Horner, 2001, p. 3) was one of the first authors to define business tourism as "… people travelling for a purpose, which is related to their work," while Swarbrooke and Horner (2001, p. 3) included "… all the aspects of the experience of the business traveller." In addition Medlik (2003, p. 29) refers to business tourism as "trips and visits made by employees and others in the course of their work, including attending meetings, conferences and exhibitions." Business tourists stay away from their home for at least one night to conduct business and are regarded as "true" tourists by Rogers (2003, p. 20). In South Africa, Swart (2007, p. 41) states that "… business tourism includes elements of people who travel for work-related activities (i.e., meetings, conferences, and exhibitions) and who stay away from their home for at least one night," while South African Tourism (2008) refers to the attendance of a conference, event, exhibition, incentive trip, or a meeting, by a tourist, as business tourism. More recently, George (2011, p. 552) postulates that business tourism is "… the provision of facilities and services to the millions of delegates who annually attend meetings, congresses, exhibitions, business events, incentive travel and corporate hospitality."

The concept business tourist is more commonly used in Europe and the United Kingdom (Davidson, 1994 as cited in Rogers, 2003; Swarbrooke & Horner, 2001, p. 3), while in Australia reference is made to business events (Tourism Australia, 2005). Academia and industry leaders still argue about which concept must become the generally accepted term. However, it is view of the author that business tourism is a more suitable concept for the development of a business tourism experience value model, based on previous research done in this field (Swart, 2013). Therefore, for the purpose of this chapter and in the context of the literature review, reference will be made to business tourism or business tourists.

Campbell (2009) is of the opinion that one of the key purposes of business travel is to maintain a strong relationship with
customers. The average number of nights business tourists spend,
together with their average expenditure per trip are used to measure business tourists' contribution to the national economy.
Earlier we referred to the "demand force of tourism"; from a
business tourism perspective this may include *associations* (such
as the International Congress and Conference Association –
ICCA), *companies* (such as Show on Scan) or *individuals* (such
as a business man) who use the services offered by the tourism
industry (Ramsborg, 2006). Most of the tourism sub-sectors,
such as accommodation and transport operators, are regarded as
the suppliers of business tourism experiences (British Tourist
Authority, 2005; Scottish Executive News, 2004), who provide a
bundle of characteristics and experiences (Sørensen & Jensen,
2015). Over the past decade, business tourism has become more
complex because of the need to create more value for the business
tourist, as end-user (IMEX, 2005). The proposed business tourism experience value model will be investigated based on experiences offered by the tourism sub-sectors, as suppliers, to meet the
needs of the business tourists, as the demand force.

Experiential Value

According to Baum (2007), the service encounter is critical in the
end-user's experience of tourism, as production and consumption
are inseparable functions. Furthermore, service includes performing certain functions and solving people's problems. The moment
when tourism consumption meets tourism production is critical
to the economics of tourism experiences, as the tourist plays an
important role in the creation of value (Peric & Wise, 2015), the
rise in value and to enhance knowledge to stimulate more tourism (Sørensen & Jensen, 2015). In understanding the value
experience, one needs to understand that it stems from service
quality literature. In service quality the expectation and experience gap is known, and therefore value experience happens
during the "moment of truth" (Sørensen & Jensen, 2015).
Assurance, empathy, responsiveness, reliability and tangibility
(Parasuraman et al., 1988) are the factors affecting service experiences, but Lopez, Hart, and Rampersad (2007) argue that
different service quality dimensions may also exist, which require
further investigation. As the relationship between service quality

and experiential value has been highlighted, it is necessary to define service quality to have a well-rounded understanding of experiential value. Many scholars have tried to define service quality (Chou, Liu, Huang, Yih, & Han, 2011; Hume, 2008; Hutchinson, Lai, & Wang, 2009; Ismail, Haron, Ibrahim, & Isa, 2006), but Swart (2013, p. 38) was one of the first researchers to define service quality from a business tourism perspective, as "... a narrow or no discrepancy between expected services and perceived services, where perceived services are evaluated based on the technical (What?) and functional (How?) nature of a bundle of service dimensions in the service encountered at a business tourism destination."

From these discussions it is evident that experience value is an extension of how we understand service quality. Therefore experience value is regarded as a tool that can be applied at interpersonal, managerial and organizational level effectively. Customers evaluate a service before and after receiving it (Lehtinen & Lehtinen, 1982), but normally have prior beliefs about the service quality. This creates challenges for tourism managers as decisions about the value of a service are not made in isolation (Dabholkar, Shepherd, & Thorpe, 2000; Haelsig, Swoboda, Morschett, & Schramm-Klein, 2007; Iyengar, Ansari, & Gupta, 2007), but rather by a combination of different service encounters, such as experience, intention and engagement. Sørensen and Jensen (2015) argue that an integration of tourism service encounters with tourism experiences will create added experiential value and increase the creation of knowledge about these tourists.

Satisfaction

Customer satisfaction has become a dominant topic in the research field (Ismail et al., 2006), as it has the potential to influence a consumer's behavioral intention (Cronin, Brady, & Hult, 2000). Hume (2008, p. 353) defines satisfaction as "... the attitude resulting from the comparison of the expectations of performance and the perceived performance of the service experience." Investigations into satisfaction refer to the interrelationship among the psychological variables, from a psychology and applied behavioral science perspective, are popular approaches in business research. A strong relationship exists between customer satisfaction and employee behavior (Kong & Jogaratnam, 2007), therefore Swarbrooke and Horner (1999) postulate that tourist satisfaction is influenced by the effective human resource management of employees. If tourist satisfaction increases, the employee satisfaction increases, which may reduce the employee turnover, lower business expenses and increase revenue for the tourism organization (Sørensen & Jensen, 2015).

Successful tourism business management requires an understanding of consumer psychology and the psychological process of a tourist during the pre- and post-tourism experiences (Swarbrooke & Horner, 2001). Yet, Del Bosque and Martín (2008) highlight the relative unknown influences of psychological processes when they are integrated with tourist satisfaction. Based on the customer's ability to judge their consumption experiences, the cognitive-affective influence of satisfaction has been confirmed (Bigné, Andreu, & Gnoth, 2005). However, stronger evidence exists about the affective influence of satisfaction on the behavior of business tourists (Swart, 2013). Therefore satisfaction can be defined from a business tourism context as "… a cumulative perspective of a business tourist's general attitude or feeling, generated by cognitive and emotional aspects, toward a destination, based on an accumulated evaluation of the different components and features to which tourists are exposed during the pre-purchase, purchase, and post-purchase phases, resulting in fulfilment" (Swart, 2013, p. 106). Although much research has been conducted on customer satisfaction, the application in tourism and business tourism requires its own methodology for a holistic understanding of the concept (Brunner-Sperdin, Peters, & Strobl, 2012; Swart, 2013).

Dimensions for Experiential Value and Satisfaction

Three dimensions for testing experiential and satisfaction are proposed, namely experience, intention, and engagement. All three dimensions are discussed in the sections below, followed by a motivation for the inclusion of these dimensions in the measurement of experiential value and satisfaction.

EXPERIENCE

Extraordinary experiences have an influence on how societal discourses support individual exploration, self-actualization, and spontaneity (Lauring, 2013). Nearly four decades ago Wagner

(1977) argued that experience can free tourists from stressful routes. As in the case of services, experiences are developed before the departure to the destination (Bigné, Sánchez, & Sánchez, 2001). Sørensen and Jensen (2015) observed a change from service to an experience-based encounter, where the functional and experiential attributes are integrated with the employees to enhance the larger tourism experience and to co-create emotional value to tourists. Tourists also want to be in charge of creating their own valuable experiences. Four broad experience dimensions are known, namely esthetic, educational, entertainment, and escapist experiences (Pine & Gilmore, 1998). Peric and Wise (2015) applied these experience categories to sports tourism, but its application in a business tourism context is lacking. However, business tourists who travel for business tourism related activities can belong to the active realm of Pine and Gilmore's (1998) concept, as discussed below:

- **Esthetic experience (E1):** when business tourists are likely to minimize active participation as they have little effect on the event, for example when delegates attend an AIDS conference, they are just part of the audience and observe the discussions, without making an active contribution.
- **Educational experience (E2):** business tourists are likely to have a more active participation in the event, but their participation is still marginal rather than having a real impact, for example when a delegate attends an AIDS conference to learn more about the disease and to gain knowledge about how to support people living with HIV and AIDS.
- **Entertainment experience (E3):** business tourists who are passive participants in the event, as their connection with the event is more out of interest than making an impact. An example is when delegates travel to Durban, South Africa, to experience the destination more than attending the AIDS conference itself.
- **Escapist experience (E4):** this is a combination of the knowledge a delegate gains from the educational experience and the amusement from the entertainment experience, however delegates tend to participate more in the event. When delegates and speakers participate in the discussion at the AIDS conference, it can be regarded a relevant example.

These tourism experiences can motivate the consumption of tourism services (Sørensen & Jensen, 2015). The level of satisfaction the business tourists experience during any of the identified four experience categories will contribute to their post-consumption behavior and whether they will attend the AIDS Conference again.

INTENTION

Hutchinson et al. (2009), Jang and Namkung (2009), and Udo, Bagchi, and Kirs (2010) support research related to a tourist's intention to return to a destination, while Swart (2013) provides evidence applying it to the business tourism industry. Intentions aim to explain how business tourists' attitudes result in satisfaction and behavior. It is therefore necessary to investigate this concept as an experience value and satisfaction variable in the proposed business tourist experience value model.

ENGAGEMENT

In an experience-intensive industry, such as tourism, the paradox is providing efficient and standardized services. Engagement is one of the fundamental elements of experiences (Pine & Gilmore, 1999, 2013), but is often ignored (Sørensen & Jensen, 2015). As the outcomes of tourist experiences are experimental, intangible, and unpredictable (Osti, Turner, & King, 2009), the emotional, intellectual, and physical engagement support the shaping of the overall experience (Lauring, 2013). Two-way interaction between the emotional involvement of the customer (i.e., the business tourist) and business (i.e., the professional conference organizer – PCO) is used to co-create, co-perform, or co-design experiences (Sørensen & Jensen, 2015). The PCO can create a robust and integrated service environment in which the delegate can take the initiative to customize unique experiences in an attempt to meet each individual's needs. Through engagement two-way communication is supported, as it is less concerned with facts and more focused on creativity in an attempt to develop new knowledge about the tourism business. Engagement and job satisfaction increase the employees' involvement in the business (Sørensen & Jensen, 2015). However, the roles of frontline (business) tourism employees in the experience economy are not well known (Baerenholdt, Haldrup, & Larsen, 2008), but this literature discussion can provide insights on how engagement can influence experience value and satisfaction in the proposed business tourist experience value model.

Relationships between Value Experience and Satisfaction

The relationship between quality and service quality is known (Dabholkar et al., 2000; Haelsig et al., 2007; Iyengar et al., 2007), as well as the relationship between service quality and experiential value (Sørensen & Jensen, 2015). Sørensen and Jensen (2015) highlight the role of service encounters and its relationship to customer satisfaction in the evaluation value. In tourism, a poor service experience can affect the satisfaction of a business tourist for the duration of the business tourism trip (WTO, 1999). Yet, it is important to generate new knowledge given the value derived from business tourists' satisfaction needs and unique experiences.

However, after the author had a closer look at the known characteristics of tourism service encounters, it was observed that separate measurements of expectations can affect the reliability, discriminant validity, and variance restriction of constructs (or variables) negatively if scores are computed differently. Therefore, it is argued to include the same societal discourses advocating experiential value and satisfaction, namely *engagement* (Pine & Gilmore, 1999, 2013), *experience* (Sørensen & Jensen, 2015), and *intension* (Fishbein & Ajzen, 1975; Swart, 2013) as additional factors on how business tourists make their evaluations, and to enhance the value for business tourists. These dimensions may play an important role in acquiring information and knowledge creation on how business tourism organizations apply experiential value and satisfaction to become more successful. This combination of dimensions also aims to overcome any measurement problems (Dabholkar et al., 2000), to enhance the overall assessment of the model (Kuo, Chou, & Sun, 2011), and to provide literature support for the development of the business tourist experience value model.

Thus, based on the above discussion we suggest the following research proposition:

RP1. Experience, intention and engagement are variables of experiential value for the development of a business tourist experience value model.

RP2. Experience, intention and engagement are variables of satisfaction for the development of a business tourist experience value model.

Next, the outcome variable, namely post-consumption behavior, is discussed.

Post-Consumption Behavior

Two complementary motivating forces, namely intrinsic and extrinsic motivation, explain why a customer engages in an activity for their own benefit. Business managers use both types of motivation to align the post-consumption behavior of employees with business strategy. According to Han, Back, and Barrett (2009) tourists may engage in repurchase behavior without any psychological affiliation. Ajzen and Fishbein (1980) as well as Fishbein and Ajzen (1975) postulate that the best prediction of a person's behavior is through his or her future intention to perform the behavior. Behavior is defined as "... a person's observable response when studied in its own right" (Fishbein & Ajzen, 1975, p. 53). Therefore, Ajzen and Fishbein (1980) suggest strategies to change that behavior, which can be explored in a business tourism context further. For example, on return from the business trip, the business tourist can relax in knowing that they are partly responsible for the value of their experience (Lauring, 2013), which emphasizes their co-creative role (Peric & Wise, 2015) and results in a specific post-consumption behavior, such as loyalty or recommendations to name a few. In this discussion the literature support the inclusion of post-consumption behavior as a variable for the development of the business tourist experience value model.

Thus, based on the above discussion, we suggest the following research proposition:

RP3. Post-consumption behavior is an outcome variable in the development of a business tourist experience value model.

Relationship between Experience Value, Satisfaction, and Post-Consumption Behavior

Quality is a perception in the mind of a customer (Swarbrooke & Horner, 1999). Quality is therefore an essential force for customer satisfaction and behavior in the marketplace (Townsend & Gebhardt, 2005), as it improves a business's efficiency and competitiveness strategically (Hafeez, Malak, & Abdelmeguid, 2006). Scholars also support the direct relationship of satisfaction with behavioral intention (Hutchinson et al., 2009). According to Bonfield (1974) the correlation between intention and behavior is high, especially if the time between these two measures is very short. It is argued that behavioral intention can be operationalized as a surrogate indicator of authentic behavior (Fishbein & Ajzen, 1975). A positive perception of the tourism experience can result in tourist satisfaction and the intention to return to the destination (Gountas, Ewing, & Gountas, 2007), which is also evident in business tourism (Swart, 2013). Therefore, behavioral intention is defined as "... the conscious decision by a business tourist to engage in future activity with a business tourism service provider and/or to repurchase a tourism service" (Swart, 2013, p. 127). From these discussions the relationships between experience value, satisfaction, and post-consumption behavior is supported, to inform the development of the business tourist experience value model.

The Business Tourist Experience Value Model

Business models are considered as conceptual and practical outlines, which are designed to guide managers on how to design activities to offer identical and valuable experiences to tourists, and to create a sustainable business. Although business models facilitate theoretical development, there are different interpretations of how these business models are understood (Peric & Wise, 2015). According to Johnson, Christensen, and Kagermann (2008), the customer value perspective is one of the most important aspects in the business model, as this is the crux of how a business creates value and experiences for the customer (Peric & Wise, 2015), which will be applied in the development of the business tourist experience value model.

As mentioned in the introduction, different service quality models have been developed, however, only a few scholars (Booms & Bitner, 1981; Siu et al., 2012; Swart, 2013) acknowledge the impact on customers' or tourists' cognitive, affective, and behavior intention, from the Fishbein and Ajzen (1975) Behavior Intentions Model. Most of these models were criticized by scholars (i) due to the operational and conceptual issues in the definitions,

(ii) failure to draw on existing economic, psychological and statistical theories, (iii) negligence to adhere to the impact of physical surroundings on the post-consumption behavior of both employees and tourists, (iv) the inability of the models to include the effect of the relevant variables, and (v) the failure of the models to capture customers' complete evaluations of the service experience (Dabholkar et al., 2000; George, 2011; Kuo et al., 2011). In tourism, Barber, Goodman, and Goh (2011) are of the opinion that the achievement of guest satisfaction can be realized when exceptional value services are delivered at a hospitality establishment. While in air transport, Surovitskikh and Lubbe (2008) argue that passengers have different experiences of different airlines. From these studies, it is evident that the measurement of experience in the different tourism sectors is important. However, experience is perceived differently by different tourists and there is no clear indication of which variables are more and least important (Pakdil & Aydin, 2007). Swart (2013) argues that although more tourists travel for work-related activities, the value of the service quality they experience and its impact on the business tourism industry have been neglected. Based on these arguments it is proposed to develop a multi-item Business Tourist Experience Value Model, as a service quality modifications model (Dabholkar et al., 2000), where experience value addresses the cognitive, satisfaction the affective, and post-consumption behavior the cognitive intention of business tourists.

Thus, based on the above discussion, we suggest the following research proposition:

RP4. Experiential value, satisfaction, and post-consumption behavior are variables in the development of a business tourist experience value model.

Conclusion

Hume (2008) argues customers' service quality assessments can be used as guidance for managers to develop service quality strategies. Therefore, the suggested Business Tourism Experience Value model can support the existing business tourism strategies by focusing on the experience, intention, and engagement of business tourist, and to create a better understanding of their post-consumption behavior. When business managers subscribe to experience value and satisfaction practices it gives them the best chance to regain their vitality during favorable business environment, and to sustain the business practices during challenging economic times. This model aims to capture the conceptual, methodological, and practical aspects of experiential value research in a business tourism context. From a conceptual viewpoint, this research complements the existing literature by trying to integrate the theory of business models and experience economy in the context of business tourism. This model can contribute to assess the performance of suppliers of business tourism services, to suggest strategies to market business tourism experiences. However, the interpretation of this model must be done with caution as one cannot assume that this model considers the unique business tourism service offering and diverse cultural perspectives of the country in which the research is conducted. Future research is needed to empirically investigate, test, and validate the suggested Business Tourism Experience Value model.

References

Ajzen, I., & Fishbein, M. (1980). *Understanding attitudes and predicting social behaviour*. Englewood Cliffs, NY: Prentice Hall.

Baerenholdt, J. O., Haldrup, M., & Larsen, J. (2008). Performing cultural attractions. In J. Sundbo & P. Darmer (Eds.), *Creating experiences in the experience economy* (pp. 176–202). Cheltenham: Edward Elgar.

Barber, N., Goodman, R. J., & Goh, B. K. (2011). Restaurant consumers repeat patronage: A service quality concern. *International Journal of Hospitality Management, 30*(2), 329–336.

Baum, T. (2007). Human resources in tourism: Still waiting for change. *Tourism Management, 28*(6), 1383–1399.

Bigné, E., Andreu, L., & Gnoth, J. (2005). The theme park experience: An analysis of pleasure, arousal and satisfaction. *Tourism Management, 26*, 833–844.

Bigné, J. E., Sánchez, M. I., & Sánchez, J. (2001). Tourism image, evaluation variables and after purchase behaviour: Inter-relationship. *Tourism Management, 22*(6), 607–616.

Bonfield, E. H. (1974). Attitude, social influence, personal norm, and intention interaction as related to brand purchase behaviour. *Journal of Marketing Research, 11*, 379–389.

Booms, B. H., & Bitner, M. J. (1981). Marketing strategies and organization structures for service firms. In J. H. Donnelly & W. R. George (Eds.), *Marketing of services* (pp. 47–51). Chicago, IL: American Marketing Association.

British Tourist Authority. (2005). *Business tourism, including cruise tourism: International marketing opportunities 2005–2006*. London. Retrieved from http://www.visitBritain.com/ukindustry. Accessed in 2005.

Brunner-Sperdin, A., Peters, M., & Strobl, A. (2012). It is all about the emotional state: Managing tourists' experiences. *International Journal of Hospitality Management*, *31*(1), 23–30.

Campbell, J. (2009). *Oxford research study proves value of business travel.* Retrieved from www.thetransnational.travel.com/

Chou, C. C., Liu, L. J., Huang, S. F., Yih, J. M., & Han, T. C. (2011). An evaluation of airline service quality using the fuzzy weighted SERVQUAL method. *Applied Soft Computing*, *11*(2), 2117–2128.

Cronin, J., Brady, M. K., & Hult, Y. (2000). Assessing the effects of quality, value, and customer satisfaction on consumer behavioural intentions in service environments. *Journal of Retailing*, *76*(2), 193–218.

Cronin, J. J., & Taylor, S. A. (1992). Measuring service quality: A re-examination and extension. *Journal of Marketing*, *56*, 55–68.

Dabholkar, P. A., Shepherd, C. D., & Thorpe, D. L. (2000). A comprehensive framework for service quality: An investigation of critical conceptual and management issues through a longitudinal study. *Journal of Retailing*, *76*(2), 139–173.

Davidson, R. (1994). *Business travel.* London: Pitman.

Del Bosque, I. R., & Martín, H. S. (2008). Tourist satisfaction a cognitive-affective model. *Annals of Tourism Research*, *35*(2), 551–573.

Fishbein, M., & Ajzen, I. (1975). *Belief, attitude, intention and behaviour: An introduction to theory and research.* California: Addison-Wesley Publishing Company.

George, R. (2011). *Managing tourism in South Africa* (4th ed.). Cape Town: Oxford University Press.

Getz, D. (1997). *Event management and event tourism.* New York, NY: Cognizant Communications Corporation.

Gountas, S., Ewing, M. T., & Gountas, J. I. (2007). Testing airline passengers' responses to flight attendants' expressive displays: The effects of positive affect. *Journal of Business Research*, *60*, 81–83.

Grönroos, C. (1984). A service quality model and its marketing implications. *European Journal of Marketing*, *18*(40), 36–44.

Haelsig, F., Swoboda, B., Morschett, D., & Schramm-Klein, H. (2007). An inter-sector analysis of the relevance of service in building a strong retail brand. *Managing Service Quality*, *17*(4), 428.

Hafeez, K., Malak, N., & Abdelmeguid, H. A. (2006). Framework for TQM to achieve business excellence. *Total Quality Management*, *17*(9), 1213–1299.

Han, H., Back, K. J., & Barrett, B. (2009). Influencing factors on restaurant customer's revisit intention: The roles of emotions and switching barriers. *International Journal of Hospitality Management*, *28*, 563–572.

Hume, M. (2008). Understanding core and peripheral service quality in customer repurchase of the performing arts. *Managing Service Quality*, *18*(4), 349–369.

Hutchinson, J., Lai, F., & Wang, Y. (2009). Understanding the relationships of quality, value, equity, satisfaction and behavioural intentions amongst golf travellers. *Tourism Management*, *30*, 298–308.

IMEX. (2005). A meeting of hearts and minds. *Travel Inside. IMEX Daily Official*, 3: p.16.

Ismail, I., Haron, H., Ibrahim, D. N., & Isa, S. M. (2006). Service quality, client satisfaction and loyalty towards audit firms. *Managerial Auditing Journal*, 21(7), 738–756.

ITB Berlin Convention. (2008). ITB world travel trends report 2008/2009. Paper presented at the ITB Berlin Convention, Messe Berlin.

Iyengar, R., Ansari, A., & Gupta, S. (2007). A model of consumer learning for service quality and usage. *Journal of Marketing Research*, 44(4), 529–544.

Jang, S. C., & Namkung, Y. (2009). Perceived quality, emotions, and behavioural intentions: Application of an extended Mehrabian-Russell model to restaurants. *Journal of Business Research*, 62, 451–460.

Johnson, M. W., Christensen, C. M., & Kagermann, H. (2008). Reinventing your business model. *Harvard Business Review*, 86(12), 50–59.

Kong, M., & Jogaratnam, G. (2007). The influence of culture on perceptions of service employee behaviour. *Managing Service Quality*, 17(3), 275–297.

Kuo, Y. C., Chou, J. S., & Sun, K. S. (2011). Elucidating how service quality constructs influence resident satisfaction with condominium management. *Expert Systems with Applications*, 38(5), 5755–5763.

Kuo, M. S., & Liang, G. S. (2011). Combining VIKOR with GRA techniques to evaluate service quality of airports under fuzzy environment. *Expert Systems with Applications*, 38(3), 1304–1312.

Lauring, J. (2013). Creating the tourist product in the opposition between self-actualization and collective consumption: The case of charter tourism. *Journal of Hospitality and Tourism Research*, 37(2), 217–236.

Lehtinen, J., & Lehtinen, J. (1982). *Service quality: A study of quality dimensions*. Helsinki: Service Management Institute.

Lopez, J., Hart, L. K., & Rampersad, A. (2007). Ethnicity and customer satisfaction in the financial services sector. *Managing Service Quality*, 17(3), 259.

Medlik, S. (2003). *Dictionary of travel, tourism and hospitality* (3rd ed.). New York, NY: Butterworth and Heinemann.

Osti, L., Turner, L. W., & King, B. (2009). Cultural differences in travel guidebooks information search. *Journal of Vacation Marketing*, 15(1), 63–78.

Pakdil, F., & Aydin, O. (2007). Expectations and perceptions in airline service: An analysis using weighted SERVQUAL scores. *Journal of Air Transport Management*, 13, 229–237.

Parasuraman, A., Zeithaml, V. A., & Berry, L. L. (1988). SERVQUAL: A multiple-item scale for measuring consumer perceptions of service quality. *Journal of Retailing*, 64(1), 12–40.

Peric, M., & Wise, N. (2015). Understanding the delivery of experience: Conceptualising business models and sports tourism, assessing two case studies in Istria, Croatia. *Local Economy*, 30, 1000–1016. doi:10.1177/0269094215604131

Pine, B. J., & Gilmore, J. H. (1998). Welcome to the experience economy. *Harvard Business Review*, 76(4), 97–105.

Pine, B. J., & Gilmore, J. H. (1999). *The experience economy – Work is theatre and every business a stage*. Boston, MA: Harvard Business School Press.

Pine, B. J., & Gilmore, J. H. (2013). The experience economy: Past, present and future. In J. Sundbo & F. Sørensen (Eds.), *Handbook on the experience economy* (pp. 21−44). Cheltenham: Edward Elgar.

Ramsborg, G. C. (2006). *Professional meeting management: Comprehensive strategies for meetings, conventions and events.* Iowa: Kendull/Hunt Publishing Company.

Rogers, T. (2003). *Conferences and conventions: A global industry.* New York, NY: Butterworth and Heinemann.

Scottish Executive News. (2004). *International association of congress centres.* Retrieved from http://scotland.gov.uk/News/Release/2004/08/03140955

Shone, A. (1998). *The business of conferences, a hospitality sector overview for the UK and Ireland.* London: Butterworth and Heinemann.

Siu, N. Y. M., Wan, P. Y. K., & Dong, P. (2012). The impact of the servicescape on the desire to stay in convention and exhibition centres: The case of Macao. *International Journal of Hospitality Management, 31*(1), 236−246.

Sørensen, F., & Jensen, J. F. (2015). Value creation and knowledge development in tourism experience encounters. *Tourism Management, 46,* 335−346.

South African Tourism. (2004). *2003 annual tourism report,* April 2004. Johannesburg, South African Tourism.

South African Tourism. (2008). *Glossary of terms and acronyms.* Retrieved from http://www.southafrica.net/

Surovitskikh, S., & Lubbe, B. (2008). Positioning of selected Middle Eastern airlines in the South African business and leisure environment. *Journal of Air Transport Management, 14,* 75−81.

Swarbrooke, J., & Horner, S. (1999). *Consumer behaviour in tourism.* New York, NY: Butterworth and Heinemann.

Swarbrooke, J., & Horner, S. (2001). *Business travel and tourism.* New York, NY: Butterworth and Heinemann.

Swart, M. P. (2013). *A business tourist service quality scorecard for predicting business tourist retention.* DCom thesis, University of Johannesburg, Johannesburg.

Swart, M. P. (2007). *Service quality: A survey amongst convention consumers at the CSIR ICC.* MCom dissertation, University of Pretoria, Pretoria.

Tormala, Z. L., & Rucker, D. D. (2015). How certainty transformed persuasion. *Harvard Business Review, 93*(9), 98−103.

Tourism Australia. (2005). *Tourism info.* Retrieved from http://australia.com

Townsend, P., & Gebhardt, J. (2005). A bare bones look at the bottom line. *Quality Progress, 38*(5), 29−35.

Udo, G. J., Bagchi, K. K., & Kirs, P. J. (2010). An assessment of customers' e-service quality perception, satisfaction and intention. *International Journal of Information Management, 30*(6), 481−492.

Wagner, U. (1977). Out of time and place: Mass tourism and charter trips. *Ethnos, 42,* 38−52.

WTO. (1999). *International tourism: A global perspective* (2nd ed.). Madrid: WTO.

24

Consumer Travel Online Reviews and Recommendations: Suggesting Strategies to Address Challenges Faced within the Digital Context

Marios Sotiriadis and Ciná van Zyl

ABSTRACT

Purpose – The aim of this chapter is twofold: (i) to perform a synthesis of the academic research regarding the changes of tourist consumer behavior brought about by social media; and (ii) to suggest a set of strategies for tourism businesses to address resulting challenges.

Methodology/approach – Extensive literature reviews have been executed on the motivating factors and the effects of online reviews.

Findings – This analysis of the related research identified three main topics, namely: (1) the antecedents, the factors motivating tourists to write online reviews; (2) the impact of eWOM on providers of tourism services (business perspective); and (3) the influence of online reviews on consumers' behavior (demand perspective). This chapter focuses on the impact of online reviews on tourism businesses and suggests suitable strategies.

Research limitations/implications – This study is based on a literature review and implications indicated by previous studies; hence the suggestions are indicative rather than conclusive. A need exists for empirical studies to fully validate the chapter's suggestions.

Practical implications – This chapter outlines a series of adequate strategies formulated for business practitioners divided into two fields, namely managerial and marketing activities.

Originality/value – This study provides practical recommendations/suggestions for tourism businesses in addressing the challenges and opportunities raised within the online context.

Keywords: Social media; eWOM; online reviews; tourism businesses; management and marketing strategies

Introduction

The ongoing outputs of the digital revolution for the tourism industry are well documented in the literature (Benckendorff, Sheldon, & Fesenmaier, 2014; Law, Buhalis, & Cobanoglu, 2014). The major impacts have come through websites, Social Media (SM) and mobile telephony. The explosion in consumer use of SM has been highlighted by scholars (Leung, Law, van Hoof, & Buhalis, 2013; Sigala, Christou, & Gretzel, 2012). SM sharing and adoption is growing globally. According to a report by eMarketer, the number of SM users across the globe have exceeded the 2 billion users and more than 28% of people worldwide used SM regularly in 2015 (eMarketer, 2015). SM have become powerful social platforms for online communications, allowing tourists to interact and share their views, to collaborate and contribute to developing, extending, rating and commenting on tourism experiences (Ayeh, Au, & Law, 2013; Gretzel & Yoo, 2013; Leung et al., 2013; Sigala et al., 2012). Thus, tourists became co-marketers, co-designers, co-producers, and co-consumers of tourism experiences. These developments have important implications for digital marketing.

These Web 2.0 tools are presenting challenges and opportunities for tourism businesses. SM offer huge opportunities for customer feedback and open new channels of communication between the latter and their customers. One of the main functions of SM is to establish an interactive channel of communication, which is mutually beneficial to both parties involved: it offers a medium for tourists to express their desires and requirements, and provides tourism businesses a tool to acquire customer feedback (Leung et al., 2013; Oz, 2015). Furthermore, they have been recognized as innovative knowledge sharing networks by enabling customers to connect, share, and interact with others (Oz, 2015). For this reason SM, as knowledge sharing platforms, are gaining attention for the tourism industry (Benckendorff et al., 2014; Gretzel & Yoo, 2013; Law et al., 2014).

One of the main issues and challenges related to the stage of post-experience is the online reviews and evaluations. Within this context, this chapter attempts to review academic research on electronic Word-of-Mouth (eWOM) and online reviews (electronic evaluations and recommendations), with the aim to perform a synthesis of the main issues relating to changes in consumer behavior and the effects thereof on managerial and marketing functions of tourism businesses. The ultimate aim is to suggest a series of suitable business strategies.

Social Media Online Reviews

Advances in information technology and the introduction of new methods of communication have significantly altered consumer behavior. The Internet has become the consumer's first-choice place to search for information on tourism destinations and businesses (Benckendorff et al., 2014; Gretzel & Yoo, 2013; Law et al., 2014). These developments have caused a shift in focus in businesses' management and marketing strategies, especially in the tourism industry (Cantallops & Salvi, 2014). The challenges and opportunities for tourism-related industries that arise from the digital environment are obvious in everyday business practice (Leung et al., 2013; Sigala et al., 2012). During the last two decades scholars have shown an increasing interest in the growing role of SM in the tourism field, and this issue constitutes an interesting research topic (Law et al., 2014; Leung et al., 2013; Zeng & Gerritsen, 2014). According to literature SM play a significant role in many aspects of tourism, especially in consumer behavior (information search and decision-making), tourism marketing and communication/interaction with consumers (Bilgihan, Barreda, Okumus, & Nusair, 2016; Gretzel & Yoo, 2013; Law et al., 2014; Zeng & Gerritsen, 2014).

It is worth emphasizing that there is no universally adopted definition of SM. Based on the suggestions of Kaplan and Haenlein (2010) and Xiang and Gretzel (2010), Chan and Guillet (2011) define SM as "a group of Internet-based applications that exists on the Web 2.0 platform and enables the Internet users from all over the world to interact, communicate, and share ideas, content, thoughts, experiences, perspectives, information, and relationships." The main types include the following: blogs and micro-blogs, social networking sites, collaborative projects, content community sites and sites dedicated for feedback.

Litvin, Goldsmith, and Pan (2008, p. 461) suggest that eWOM can be defined as "all informal communications directed at consumers through Internet-based technology related to the usage or characteristics of particular goods and services, or their sellers." This definition includes communication between businesses and consumers, as well as that between consumers themselves — both integral parts of the eWOM flow. It is estimated that online reviews provide a trusted source of product information. The study by Trusov, Bucklin, and Pauwels (2009) has proven the relative effectiveness of eWOM compared to traditional marketing. The findings from this study also provide a strong motivation to better utilize the eWOM channel of communication.

Post-experience behavior in tourism refers to the customer's level of satisfaction with the undertaken vacation trip, image and attitudes formation, and recommending intentions. In the SM context post-experience behavior takes the form of the level of tourists' engagement in eWOM, contributing to the generation of consumer travel online reviews and recommendations (Kim & Fesenmaier, 2015; Morrison, 2013). Online reviews have a strong influence on consumers' decision-making process (Liu, Karahanna, & Watson, 2011; Sparks & Browning, 2011).

Within the context of increasing influence of SM in interpersonal communications and the importance of eWOM and online reviews in tourism, this chapter argues that the topic of reviews in SM needs a deeper understanding from two perspectives: (i) consumer perspective, in other words factors motivating and influencing tourists to post online reviews and (ii) provider perspective, in other words the effects of these reviews on managerial and marketing functions. The purpose of this chapter is, therefore, to synthesize the academic research with the ultimate aim to suggest a set of strategies for tourism businesses within the digital context.

Methodology

To achieve the above-mentioned aim, the present study reviewed related articles published in academic journals between 2009 and 2016. The role and use of SM in tourists' behavior and in tourism businesses management have been widely discussed in tourism research, since it constitutes one of the "mega trends" that has significantly impacted the tourism system. The present study reviewed journal articles published in the last seven years (2009–2016) regarding consumer online reviews related to the tourism industry, mainly the hotel industry. ScienceDirect was researched with the terms/keywords: online travel reviews, eWOM, user-generated content, consumer/customer reviews, social media, tourism experience. The implied methodology was similar to that implemented by the studies of Leung et al. (2013), Cantallops and Salvi (2014), and Zeng and Gerritsen (2014).

The articles were selected from scientific journals, based on their relevance to the topic investigated. Table 1 depicts the selected articles by journal in alphabetical order. In total 73 articles were analyzed for their findings, implications, and recommendations.

The review of literature indicated that the issues and aspects investigated by scholars could, from the perspective of the present chapter, be grouped into two main topics, namely: (i) the factors motivating and influencing tourists to generate online comments; and (ii) the effects of these online reviews on tourism businesses practices. The synthesis of this literature review is presented in the next section, followed by suggestions.

Table 1.   Related Academic Research (Years 2009–2016).

Journal	Number of Articles
Business Horizons	3
Computers in Human Behavior	6
Cornell Hotel and Restaurant Administration Quarterly	4
Current Issues in Tourism	1
Discourse, Context and Media	2
Electronic Commerce Research	2
Journal of Business Research	1
Journal of Hospitality and Tourism Management	1
Journal of Travel Research	6
Journal of Travel & Tourism Marketing	8
Journal of Vacation Marketing	1
Information Technology & Tourism	1
International Journal of Contemporary Hospitality Management	5
International Journal of Hospitality Management	16
Tourism Management	12
Tourism Management Perspectives	3
Other journals	3
Total	76

Consumer Travel Online Reviews: A Synthesis of Academic Research

As has already been pointed out, SM change the way in which tourists approach, see and experience their trip (Kim & Fesenmaier, 2015). eWOM communication increasingly attracts the attention of managers in the tourism industry, primarily because consumers make considerable use of online social platforms and often do not book without seeking online advice on tourism destinations and businesses (Kyoo Kim, Mattila, & Baloglu, 2011; Xiang & Gretzel, 2010). The literature review was based on a content analysis of the considered articles from both the consumers' and the providers' perspectives. The main findings are presented below.

CONSUMER PERSPECTIVE: SM AND TOURISTS' BEHAVIOR

This topic includes journal articles which examined the factors that motivate tourists to share their experiences online and the factors that influence them to generate online reviews and evaluations. All these studies contribute to improve our understanding of the behavioral consequences of eWOM (Cantallops & Salvi, 2014). The main issue is the impact of online travel reviews on consumer behavior. Oz (2015) suggests that the information gathered is used across all stages of the tourism experience, in other words before the trip (choice process), during the trip, and after the experience (post trip). We focus on the implications of online reviews on tourists' behavior.

Motivating factors: The motives of tourists to share their opinions and recommendations in SM have been examined by various studies. The majority of tourists consider helping other tourists or enabling them to make a good decision as an important reason (Bilgihan et al., 2016; Bronner & de Hoog, 2011; Liu et al., 2011; Wilson, Murphy, & Cambra Fierro, 2012; Yoo & Gretzel, 2009, 2011). Additionally, tourists tend to share knowledge online because they want to prevent other people from selecting incorrect products and services (Munar & Jacobsen, 2014). Let us observe the main motivating factors: (i) Service quality and customer satisfaction/dissatisfaction: studied by Boley, Magnini, and Tuten (2013), Browning, Fung, and Sparks (2013), Zhou, Ye, Pearce, and Wu (2014), and Kim and Fesenmaier (2015). (ii) Pre-purchase service expectations: an issue examined by Mauri and Minazzi (2013), Casaló, Flavián, Guinalíu, and Ekinci (2015), and Schuckert, Liu, and Law (2015). (iii) Sense of community belonging: highlighted by Casaló, Flavián, and Guinalíu (2010), Casaló, Flavián, and Guinalíu (2011), and Lee, Law, and Murphy (2011). (iv) Social identity/social support: this issue was examined by Kim and Tussyadiah (2013) and Kang and Schuett (2013). (v) Personality: investigated by Yoo and Gretzel (2011), who indicated that tourists' personality traits significantly influence perceived barriers to content creation, motivations to engage in online reviews, and specific creation behaviors.

The study by Kyoo Kim et al. (2011) noted three main motivating factors for tourists to seek eWOM, namely, convenience and quality, risk reduction, and social reassurance. These elements are essential to a consumer decision journey (Hudson & Thal, 2013).

Influence of eWOM on tourists' behavior: Various studies examined the factors influencing tourists' behavior, for example Boley et al. (2013), Wilson et al. (2012), Xiang and Gretzel (2010), and Ye, Law, Gu, and Chen (2011), Parra-López, Bulchand-Gidumal, Gutiérrez-Taño, and Díaz-Armas (2011) and Sotiriadis and Van Zyl (2013). Tourists are influenced by the following factors to adopt information from online reviews in their travel planning process and decision-making: (i) Perceptions of trust in the source, providing the advice and perceived usefulness, were explored by Casaló et al. (2011), Sparks and Browning (2011), Sparks, Perkins, and Buckley (2013), and Ladhari and Michaud (2015). (ii) Source credibility perception influencing consumers' attitudes and intentions toward online reviews (Ayeh et al., 2013; Casaló et al., 2015; Lee et al., 2011; Sotiriadis & Van Zyl, 2013). (iii) Evaluation of reviews dimensions was examined by Vermeulen and Seegers (2009), Viglia, Furlan, and Ladrón-de-Guevara (2014), and Tsao, Hsieh, Shih, and Lin (2015). (iv) Nationality: consumers from different countries have different posting behaviors (Schuckert et al., 2015; Wilson et al., 2012). (v) Information quality dimensions were explored by Filieri and McLeay (2014). (vi) Gender and expertise influence consumers' motivations to read online reviews, as indicated by Kyoo Kim et al. (2011). (vii) Perceived benefits of the use of SM were pointed out by Parra-López et al. (2011). Culture doesn't seem to have any influence on tourists' engagement patterns in their online hotel reviews (Tian, 2013).

Ring, Tkaczynski, and Dolnicar (2016) suggest that distinct segments of WOM behavior exist. Segments differ with regard to content shared (visual/verbal) and channel used (offline/online). Jacobsen and Munar (2012) found a complementary nature of Web 1.0 and Web 2.0 information sources. The role and uses of smartphones have been highlighted by Wang, Park, and Fesenmaier (2012).

The changes in consumer behavior have an impact on the approaches and strategies that tourism businesses have to adopt and implement in managing and marketing their services in the digital environment (Leung et al., 2013; Sigala, 2012; Sigala et al., 2012).

BUSINESS PERSPECTIVE: EFFECTS OF ONLINE REVIEWS ON TOURISM BUSINESSES

The second category of studies is the studies that examined the influence of online reviews on managerial and marketing practices of tourism businesses. Following are the main issues explored by business-related studies.

Business performance/sales management: Various studies analyzed the influence of customer online reviews and ratings on tourism business performance (Blal & Sturman, 2014; Kim, Lim, & Brymer, 2015; Phillips, Zigan, Santos Silva, & Schegg, 2015; Torres, Singh, & Robertson-Ring, 2015). Results indicated a significant relationship between online consumer reviews and business performance (Ye, Law, & Gu, 2009) and that tourists' reviews have a significant impact on online sales (Ye et al., 2011). A related issue, the booking and purchasing intentions, was investigated by Sparks and Browning (2011), Mauri and Minazzi (2013), Casaló et al. (2015), Ladhari and Michaud (2015), Tsao et al. (2015), and Zhao, Wang, Guo, and Law (2015).

Customer feedback: Customer feedback is "the transmission of negative information (complaints) or positive information (compliments) to providers about the services used" (Saha & Theingi, 2009, p. 354). Torres, Adler, and Behnke (2014) and Torres et al. (2015) suggested that online consumer-generated feedback is very useful for managerial purposes. This customer feedback might be used in the following managerial functions: (i) customer experience/service quality indicted by Mauri and Minazzi (2013) and Zhou et al. (2014); (ii) innovation management, suggested by Sotiriadis and Van Zyl (2015); (iii) service improvement, indicated by Torres et al. (2014).

Customer management: customer interactions and service recovery: This issue and related aspects (managing consumer dissatisfaction online/online negative reviews) were explored by Liu et al. (2011), Callarisa, Sánchez García, Cardiff, and Roshchina (2012), Leung and Bai (2013), Melián-González, Bulchand-Gidumal, and López-Valcárcel (2013), Wei, Miao, and Huang (2013), and Zhang and Vásquez (2014). Bradley, Sparks, and Weber (2015) demonstrated how negative online reviews can have adverse and diverse effects on restaurant industry employees and businesses and suggest four types of countermeasures (i.e., preventative, protective, positive, and palliative).

Marketing activities and practices: Tourism businesses develop specific marketing strategies: (i) strategic integration of SM into a company's marketing communications strategy (Hanna, Rohm, & Crittenden, 2011); (ii) improving brand-consumer relationships through SM (Su, Mariadoss, & Reynolds, 2015); (iii) online/SM marketing: the promotional mix must be the suitable by using wisely SM content posted (Hvass & Munar, 2012); (iv) strategies of multi-channel communications (Chan & Guillet, 2011; Sotiriadis & Van Zyl, 2013); (v) customer loyalty generated by online reviews in SM (Kim et al., 2015).

Reputation management: Corporate reputation is a valuable intangible asset for companies determining the business success, yet is increasingly difficult to manage in an era with hard-to-control online conversations (Dijkmans, Kerkhof, & Beukeboom, 2015; Gossling, Hall, & Andersson, 2016). This issue was investigated by Zhang, Ye, Law, and Li (2010) and Xie, Zhang, and Zhang (2014). Dijkmans et al. (2015) suggest that consumers' online company engagement is positively related to corporate reputation. Sparks, Fung So, and Bradley (2016) found that the provision of a response (versus no response) enhanced inferences of trust and concern. Finally, Gossling et al. (2016) examined the issue of online review manipulation strategies (i.e., tourism managers may be tempted to manipulate online content).

Other management functions/activities: Online reviews can be used by tourism businesses to support knowledge management activities (Schmunk et al., 2013; Sigala, 2011; Sigala & Chalkiti, 2014). Furthermore, the tremendous growth of SM and consumer online reviews on the Internet inspired the development of the so-called big data analytics to understand and solve real-life problems (Xiang, Schwartz, Gerdes, & Uysal, 2015). Capriello, Mason, Davis, and Crotts (2013) demonstrated three alternative approaches (manual content coding, corpus-based semantic analysis, and stance-shift analysis) for mining consumer sentiment from large amounts of qualitative data found in online travel reviews. Furthermore, tourism businesses adopted and make use of SM and online reviews for other purposes, such as (i) engagement and commitment: networking and social/customer intelligence of Web 2.0 by engaging customers (Sigala, 2011); (ii) relationship building/brand-consumer relationships: Calefato, Lanubile, and Novielli (2015) pointed out the importance of combining SM and traditional websites for effectively building a trustworthy online company image.

Table 2.   Suggested Managerial and Marketing Strategies.

Strategy	Content
Embrace SM, listening carefully to and learning from customers.	– Online reviews should be viewed as an opportunity to understand and respond to customers' needs.
Develop a clear and measurable strategy, integrating SM into business processes.	– Develop a methodically organized approach to tap ideas and inspiration from customers. – Provide training to employees regarding SM account management to ensure good performance.
Develop performance measurement to evaluate effectiveness of SM.	Monitor and evaluate effectiveness of SM activities.
Customer management.	– Transform website/SM pages dedicated to feedback. – Monitor and interact with customer opinions and evaluations of services.
Complaint management.	React positively (take advantage of positive postings and address negative comments) to online reviews.
Continuous improvement of experience service quality.	– Service recovery: acting promptly in addressing customer service problems. – Monitoring of customer satisfaction as a measure of system performance.
Innovation management	Exploit ideas that could be used to develop new concepts and to enhance improvements in services and processes.
Knowledge management/ data mining.	Exploit online data to better understand customer sentiment and behavior online.
Develop a multi-channel approach to communications with customers.	Do not treat SM strategy as stand-alone element, but part of an integrated system.
Use SM as additional tools in the marketing toolbox.	– Including both traditional media and channels and online channels. – Adopt a data-driven approach to optimization of marketing efficiency (customized marketing).
SM as a channel for interactive communication.	– Create content and design that are of customers' interest. – Proactive marketing action aimed at instigating eWOM behavior. – Enhance and exploit content generated by customers.
Market research.	Research is needed to (i) understand behavior choices, concerns and determinants of customers, and (ii) assess the effectiveness of SM strategies.
Performance monitoring and evaluation.	– Choose performance indicators and how they should be measured (performance metrics). – Monitor: put in place a control system as a tool to monitor performance.
Image/reputation management.	Nurturing good relationships with existing customers (online relationship marketing).

The above-mentioned literature review suggests that the field of the eWOM (online reviews and recommendations) constitutes a challenging topic for academic research. It also indicates that there is a need for suggestions for practitioners in performing their managerial tasks within a digital context. The next section outlines a set of suitable business strategies.

Suggestions: Business Strategies within the Context of SM Engagement

As already emphasized, SM have opened up a new world of dialogue among people, including conversations about tourism services, trips and destinations, since they facilitate direct interactions between businesses and tourists (Buhalis & Jun, 2011; Morrison, 2013; Sotiriadis & Van Zyl, 2013, 2015). The findings of the reviews thoroughly demonstrate the strategic importance of SM for all tourism business practices, as well as their performance and competitiveness. Online reviews and recommendations are considered one of the most significant innovations in tourism over the past decade (Xiang & Gretzel, 2010). These evaluations influence consumer perceptions and choices, and also affect price setting in businesses, inter-business and inter-destination competition, service innovation and host motivation (Gossling et al., 2016; Zhang et al., 2010). Therefore they are of great interest to management and marketing functions.

The ultimate aim of this chapter is to provide tourism businesses with a set of suggestions. In other words, the chapter's focus is not on identifying knowledge gaps and suggesting an agenda for future research. Therefore this section outlines a series of management and marketing strategies for practitioners. The strategies suggested by this study have as main underlying principle that the reviews in SM constitute customer knowledge and input that should be exploited to a greater extent by tourism businesses.

Tourism businesses have to adopt and implement suitable strategies. Two preliminary actions/strategies are necessary as a prerequisite: (i) understanding SM: it is essential for tourism businesses to understand what SM are and how social media should be used; and (ii) the need to truly understand how to execute digital marketing effectively.

The interaction of main challenges in the tourism market with the digital environment and the impressive adoption and use of SM clearly indicates that tourism businesses need to adopt new approaches and implement new strategies in performing their managerial and marketing activities (Table 2). Tourism businesses need to incorporate use of SM in their managerial and digital marketing activities. In doing so, they will have the input and knowledge needed to invest in creating innovative customer experiences.

Concluding Remarks

SM are expanding at a rapid pace, generating eWOM, online reviews and recommendations. It is therefore imperative for tourism businesses to understand what they are and how they can be effectively used in the digital environment for managerial and marketing purposes. This chapter performed a synthesis of the related academic research carried out during the past seven years. It outlined the main issues which arise by the adoption and increased use of SM and impacts of these changes on tourists' consumer behavior and the resulting influence on tourism businesses functions.

It is worth emphasizing that this chapter provides no more than a review of the literature and useful guidance, with a series of management and marketing strategies that could be adopted and implemented by tourism businesses. It attempts to outline existing knowledge in this challenging field and to provide tourism businesses with practical suggestions. Thus, it contributes to a better understanding of SM and the effects thereof on consumer behavior. This knowledge could contribute to a better understanding of customers' needs and desires, enabling the service provider to render a better service to the customer and making the experience more valuable.

It is believed that the SM and consumers' online reviews here to stay (Sotiriadis & Van Zyl, 2015). However, SM are not just only marketing and sales tools; they must be approached and used as a tool and a resource to harvest valuable ideas and inspiration from customers. By using SM effectively, tourism businesses are communicating directly and efficiently with their current and potential customers. Within a digital environment, the approach to digital marketing must be interactive. Tourism businesses which manage to create a virtual environment that builds a virtual community by engaging tourists to share their knowledge and insights will be more successful.

References

Ayeh, J. K., Au, N., & Law, R. (2013). Do we believe in TripAdvisor? Examining credibility perceptions and online travelers' attitude toward using user-generated content. *Journal of Travel Research*, 52(4), 437–452.

Benckendorff, P., Sheldon, P. J., & Fesenmaier, D. R. (2014). *Tourism information technology* (2nd ed.). London: CABI.

Bilgihan, A., Barreda, A., Okumus, F., & Nusair, K. (2016). Consumer perception of knowledge-sharing in travel-related online social networks. *Tourism Management*, 52(2), 287–296.

Blal, I., & Sturman, M. C. (2014). The differential effects of the quality and quantity of online reviews on hotel room sales. *Cornell Hotel and Restaurant Administration Quarterly*, 55(4), 365–375.

Boley, B. B., Magnini, V. P., & Tuten, T. L. (2013). Social media picture posting and souvenir purchasing behavior: Some initial findings. *Tourism Management*, 37(1), 27–30.

Bradley, G. L., Sparks, B. A., & Weber, K. (2015). The stress of anonymous online reviews: A conceptual model and research agenda. *International Journal of Contemporary Hospitality Management*, 27(5), 739–755.

Bronner, F., & de Hoog, R. (2011). Vacationers and eWOM: Who posts, and why, where, and what? *Journal of Travel Research*, 50(1), 15–26.

Browning, V., Fung So, K. K., & Sparks, B. (2013). The influence of online reviews on consumers' attributions of service quality and control for service standards in hotels. *Journal of Travel & Tourism Marketing*, 30(1–2), 23–40.

Buhalis, D., & Jun, S. H. (2011). *E-tourism*. Oxford: Goodfellow Publishers.

Calefato, F., Lanubile, F., & Novielli, N. (2015). The role of social media in affective trust building in customer-supplier relationships. *Electronic Commerce Research*, 15(4), 453–482.

Callarisa, L., Sánchez García, J., Cardiff, J., & Roshchina, A. (2012). Harnessing social media platforms to measure customer-based hotel brand equity. *Tourism Management Perspectives*, 4, 73–79.

Cantallops, A. S., & Salvi, F. (2014). New consumer behavior: A review of research on eWOM and hotels. *International Journal of Hospitality Management*, 36(1), 41–51.

Capriello, A., Mason, R. P., Davis, B., & Crotts, C. J. (2013). Farm tourism experiences in travel reviews: A cross-comparison of three alternative methods for data analysis. *Journal of Business Research*, 66, 778–785.

Casaló, L., Flavián, C., & Guinalíu, M. (2010). Determinants of the intention to participate in firm-hosted online travel communities and effects on consumer behavioural intentions. *Tourism Management*, 31, 898–911.

Casaló, L. V., Flavián, C., & Guinalíu, M. (2011). Understanding the intention to follow the advice obtained in an online travel community. *Computers in Human Behavior*, 27, 622–633.

Casaló, L. V., Flavián, C., Guinalíu, M., & Ekinci, Y. (2015). Do online hotel rating schemes influence booking behaviors? *International Journal of Hospitality Management*, 49(1), 28–36.

Chan, N. L., & Guillet, B. D. (2011). Investigation of social media marketing: How does the hotel industry in Hong Kong perform in marketing on social media websites? *Journal of Travel & Tourism Marketing, 28*(4), 345−368.

Dijkmans, C., Kerkhof, P., & Beukeboom, C. J. (2015). A stage to engage: Social media use and corporate reputation. *Tourism Management, 47*(1), 58−67.

eMarketer. (2015). Worldwide social network users: eMarketer's updated estimates for 2015. Report preview. Retrieved from http://www.emarketer.com/corporate/coverage#/results/1298?look. Accessed on November 5, 2015.

Filieri, R., & McLeay, F. (2014). E-WOM and accommodation: An analysis of the factors that influence travelers' adoption of information from online reviews. *Journal of Travel Research, 53*(1), 44−57.

Gossling, S., Hall, C. M., & Andersson, A.-C. (2016). The manager's dilemma: A conceptualization of online review manipulation strategies. *Current Issues in Tourism,* Accepted. Published online. doi:10.1080/13683500.2015.1127337

Gretzel, U., & Yoo, K.-H. (2013). Premises and promises of social media marketing in tourism. In S. McCabe (Ed.), *The Routledge handbook of tourism marketing* (pp. 491−504). New York, NY: Routledge.

Hanna, R., Rohm, A., & Crittenden, V. L. (2011). We're all connected: The power of the social media ecosystem. *Business Horizons, 54*(3), 265−273.

Hudson, S., & Thal, K. (2013). The impact of social media on the consumer decision process: Implications for tourism marketing. *Journal of Travel & Tourism Marketing, 30*(1−2), 156−160.

Hvass, K. A., & Munar, A. M. (2012). The take-off of social media in tourism. *Journal of Vacation Marketing, 18*(2), 93−103.

Jacobsen, J. K. S., & Munar, A. M. (2012). Tourism information search and destination choice in a digital age. *Tourism Management Perspectives, 1,* 39−47.

Kang, M., & Schuett, M. A. (2013). Determinants of sharing travel experiences in social media. *Journal of Travel & Tourism Marketing, 30*(1−2), 93−107.

Kaplan, A. M., & Haenlein, M. (2010). Users of the world, unite! The challenges and opportunities of social media. *Business Horizons, 53*(1), 59−68.

Kim, J., & Fesenmaier, D. R. (2015). Sharing tourism experiences: The post-trip experience. *Journal of Travel Research.* Published online on December 22, 2015. doi:10.1177/0047287515620491

Kim, J., & Tussyadiah, I. P. (2013). Social networking and social support in tourism experience: The moderating role of online self-presentation strategies. *Journal of Travel & Tourism Marketing, 30*(1−2), 78−92.

Kim, W. G., Lim, H., & Brymer, R. A. (2015). The effectiveness of managing social media on hotel performance. *International Journal of Hospitality Management, 44*(1), 165−171.

Kyoo Kim, E. E., Mattila, S. A., & Baloglu, S. (2011). Effects of gender and expertise on consumers' motivation to read online hotel reviews. *Cornell Hotel and Restaurant Administration Quarterly, 52*(4), 399−406.

Ladhari, R., & Michaud, M. (2015). eWOM effects on hotel booking intentions, attitudes, trust, and website perceptions. *International Journal of Hospitality Management, 46*(1), 36−45.

Law, R., Buhalis, D., & Cobanoglu, C. (2014). Progress on information and communication technologies in hospitality and tourism. *International Journal of Contemporary Hospitality Management*, 26(5), 727−750.

Lee, H. A., Law, R., & Murphy, J. (2011). Helpful reviewers in TripAdvisor, an online travel community. *Journal of Travel & Tourism Marketing*, 28(7), 675−688.

Leung, D., Law, R., van Hoof, H., & Buhalis, D. (2013). Social media in tourism and hospitality: A literature review. *Journal of Travel & Tourism Marketing*, 30(1−2), 3−22.

Leung, X. Y., & Bai, B. (2013). How motivation, opportunity, and ability impact travelers' social media involvement and revisit intention. *Journal of Travel & Tourism Marketing*, 30(1−2), 58−77.

Litvin, W. S., Goldsmith, E. R., & Pan, B. (2008). Electronic word-of-mouth in hospitality and tourism management. *Tourism Management*, 29(3), 458−468.

Liu, B. Q., Karahanna, E., & Watson, T. R. (2011). Unveiling user-generated content: Designing websites to best present customer reviews. *Business Horizons*, 54(3), 231−240.

Mauri, A. G., & Minazzi, R. (2013). Web reviews influence on expectations and purchasing intentions of hotel potential customers. *International Journal of Hospitality Management*, 34, 99−107.

Melián-González, S., Bulchand-Gidumal, J., & López-Valcárcel, B. G. (2013). Online customer reviews of hotels: As participation increases, better evaluation is obtained. *Cornell Hotel and Restaurant Administration Quarterly*, 54, 274−283.

Morrison, A. M. (2013). *Marketing and managing tourism destinations*. New York, NY: Routledge.

Munar, A. M., & Jacobsen, J. K. S. (2014). Motivations for sharing tourism experiences through social media. *Tourism Management*, 43(1), 46−54.

Oz, M. (2015). Social media utilization of tourists for travel-related purposes. *International Journal of Contemporary Hospitality Management*, 27(5), 1003−1023.

Parra-López, E., Bulchand-Gidumal, J., Gutiérrez-Taño, D., & Díaz-Armas, R. (2011). Intentions to use social media in organizing and taking vacation trips. *Computers in Human Behavior*, 27, 640−654.

Phillips, P., Zigan, K., Santos Silva, M. M., & Schegg, R. (2015). The interactive effects of online reviews on the determinants of Swiss hotel performance: A neural network analysis. *Tourism Management*, 50, 130−141.

Ring, A., Tkaczynski, A., & Dolnicar, S. (2016). Word-of-Mouth segments: Online, offline, visual or verbal? *Journal of Travel Research*, 55(4), 481−492.

Saha, G. C., & Theingi, A. (2009). Service quality, satisfaction, and behavioural intentions: A study of low-cost airline carriers in Thailand. *Managing Service Quality*, 19, 350−372.

Schuckert, M., Liu, X., & Law, R. (2015). A segmentation of online reviews by language groups: How English and non-English speakers rate hotels differently. *International Journal of Hospitality Management*, 48, 143−149.

Sigala, M. (2011). eCRM 2.0 applications and trends: The use and perceptions of Greek tourism firms of social networks and intelligence. *Computers in Human Behavior*, 27, 655–661.

Sigala, M. (2012). Social networks and customer involvement in New Service Development (NSD) the case of www.mystarbucksidea.com/. *International Journal of Contemporary Hospitality Management*, 24(7), 966–990.

Sigala, M., & Chalkiti, K. (2014). Investigating the exploitation of Web 2.0 for knowledge management in the Greek tourism industry: An utilisation–importance analysis. *Computers in Human Behavior*, 30, 800–812.

Sigala, M., Christou, E., & Gretzel, U. (Eds.). (2012). *Social media in travel, tourism and hospitality: Theory, practice and cases*. London: Ashgate.

Sotiriadis, M., & Van Zyl, C. (2013). Electronic world-of-mouth and online reviews in tourism services: The use of twitter by tourists. *Electronic Commerce Research*, 13(1), 103–124.

Sotiriadis, M., & Van Zyl, C. (2015). Tourism services, micro-blogging and customer feedback: A tourism provider perspective. In J. N. Burkhalter & N. T. Wood (Eds.), *Maximizing commerce and marketing strategies through micro-blogging* (pp. 157–176). Hershey, PA: IGI Global.

Sparks, A. B., & Browning, V. (2011). The impact of online reviews on hotel booking intentions and perception of trust. *Tourism Management*, 32(6), 1310–1323.

Sparks, A. B., Fung So, K. K., & Bradley, L. G. (2016). Responding to negative online reviews: The effects of hotel responses on customer inferences of trust and concern. *Tourism Management*, 53(1), 74–85.

Sparks, B. A., Perkins, H. E., & Buckley, R. (2013). Online travel reviews as persuasive communication: The effects of content type, source, and certification logos on consumer behavior. *Tourism Management*, 39(1), 1–9.

Su, N., Mariadoss, B. J., & Reynolds, D. (2015). Friendship on social networking sites: Improving relationship between hotel brands and consumers. *International Journal of Hospitality Management*, 51(1), 76–86.

Tian, Y. (2013). Engagement in online hotel reviews: A comparative study. *Discourse, Context and Media*, 2, 184–191.

Torres, E. N., Adler, H., & Behnke, C. (2014). Stars, diamonds, and other shiny things: The use of expert and consumer feedback in the hotel industry. *Journal of Hospitality and Tourism Management*, 21, 34–43.

Torres, E. N., Singh, D., & Robertson-Ring, A. (2015). Consumer reviews and the creation of booking transaction value: Lessons from the hotel industry. *International Journal of Hospitality Management*, 50(1), 77–83.

Trusov, M., Bucklin, E. R., & Pauwels, K. (2009). Effects of word-of-mouth versus traditional marketing: Findings from an Internet social networking site. *Journal of Marketing*, 73(5), 90–102.

Tsao, W.-C., Hsieh, M.-T., Shih, L.-W., & Lin, T. M. Y. (2015). Compliance with eWOM: The influence of hotel reviews on booking intention from the perspective of consumer conformity. *International Journal of Hospitality Management*, 46(1), 99–111.

Vermeulen, E. I., & Seegers, D. (2009). Tried and tested: The impact of online hotel reviews on consumer consideration. *Tourism Management*, *30*(1), 123–127.

Viglia, G., Furlan, R., & Ladrón-de-Guevara, A. (2014). Please, talk about it! When hotel popularity boosts preferences. *International Journal of Hospitality Management*, *42*, 155–164.

Wang, D., Park, S., & Fesenmaier, D. R. (2012). The role of smartphones in mediating the touristic experience. *Journal of Travel Research*, *51*(3), 371–387.

Wei, W., Miao, L., & Huang, Z. J. (2013). Customer engagement behaviors and hotel responses. *International Journal of Hospitality Management*, *33*, 316–330.

Wilson, A., Murphy, H., & Cambra Fierro, J. (2012). Hospitality and travel: The nature and implications of user-generated content. *Cornell Hotel and Restaurant Administration Quarterly*, *53*(3), 220–228.

Xiang, Z., & Gretzel, U. (2010). Role of social media in online travel information search. *Tourism Management*, *31*(2), 179–188.

Xiang, Z., Schwartz, Z., Gerdes, J. H., Jr., & Uysal, M. (2015). What can big data and text analytics tell us about hotel guest experience and satisfaction? *International Journal of Hospitality Management*, *44*(1), 120–130.

Xie, L. K., Zhang, Z., & Zhang, Z. (2014). The business value of online consumer reviews and management response to hotel performance. *International Journal of Hospitality Management*, *43*(1), 1–12.

Ye, Q., Law, R., & Gu, B. (2009). The impact of online user reviews on hotel room sales. *International Journal of Hospitality Management*, *28*, 180–182.

Ye, Q., Law, R., Gu, B., & Chen, W. (2011). The influence of user-generated content on traveler behavior: An empirical investigation on the effects of e-word-of-mouth to hotel online bookings. *Computers in Human Behavior*, *27*(2), 634–639.

Yoo, K. H., & Gretzel, U. (2009). What motivates consumers to write online travel reviews? *Information Technology & Tourism*, *10*, 283–296.

Yoo, K. H., & Gretzel, U. (2011). Influence of personality on travel-related consumer-generated media creation. *Computers in Human Behavior*, *27*, 609–621.

Zeng, B., & Gerritsen, R. (2014). What do we know about social media in tourism? A review. *Tourism Management Perspectives*, *10*, 27–36.

Zhang, Y., & Vásquez, C. (2014). Hotels' responses to online reviews: Managing consumer dissatisfaction. *Discourse, Context and Media*, *6*, 54–64.

Zhang, Z., Ye, Q., Law, R., & Li, Y. (2010). The impact of e-word-of-mouth on the online popularity of restaurants: A comparison of consumer reviews and editor reviews. *International Journal of Hospitality Management*, *29*(4), 694–700.

Zhao, X., Wang, L., Guo, X., & Law, R. (2015). The influence of online reviews to online hotel booking intentions. *International Journal of Contemporary Hospitality Management*, *27*(6), 1343–1364.

Zhou, L., Ye, S., Pearce, L. P., & Wu, M.-Y. (2014). Refreshing hotel satisfaction studies by reconfiguring customer review data. *International Journal of Hospitality Management*, *38*(1), 1–10.

25 Assessing Tourism Experiences: The Case of Heritage Attractions

Gaunette Sinclair-Maragh

ABSTRACT

Purpose – This chapter presents a research paper with empirical investigation on tourism experiences specific to heritage attractions. It analyses the five principles of experience economy within the context of heritage attractions. The study aims to find out if heritage attractions are using the principles of experience economy to provide a fulfilling experience for visitors. The principles of the experience economy are having consistent theme, using positive cues, eliminating negative cues, offering memorabilia, and engaging the five senses.

Methodology/approach – The survey method was used to collect data from three separate heritage attractions in Jamaica. Frequency distribution was used to determine the observations in the sample.

Findings – Results of the study reveal that majority of visitors either agree or strongly agree that many of the elements comprising the principles of experience economy are in place. One similar drawback among the attractions is that they all use visual and aural messages which can distract or contradict the theme and consequently visitors' experience.

Research limitations/implications – A limitation of the study is that it did not take into consideration the relationship between visitors' experience and their expectations as well as visitor satisfaction.

Originality/value – This study will inform management of heritage attractions of the importance of having implementing the principles of experience economy so as to provide a fulfilling experience for visitors.

Keywords: Tourism experiences; experience economy; heritage attraction; fulfilling experience; visitors

Introduction

The new generation of traveler is seeking more from their vacation experience. These "new tourists" are experienced, more flexible, independent, quality conscious, and harder to please (Poon, 1993). They do have respect for the host's culture and are participators rather than spectators (Raj, 2007). McKercher and du Cross (2002) state that the phenomenon of tourism involves the consumption of experiences. As persons accumulate more traveling experience and become more affluent they start looking for new tourist experiences in special interest tourism such as culture and heritage tourism and according to Wan and Man Cheng (2011) they are, likewise, demanding service quality. Hill (1986) believes that it is important for service providers to develop and provide offerings that will satisfy the needs of consumers.

Priori literature alluded to different types of experiences as they relate to travelers and visitors. Urry (2002) describes one experience as the tourist gaze which he suggested to be the landscape features that will separate the visitor from their everyday experience. Klerks and Kop (2008) refer to the concept of dematerialization as another type of experience. They believe that individuals in the post-modern society are more concerned about environmental issues and the less materialistically oriented lifestyle; focusing on immaterial features such as relaxation, experiences, stories, and perception, as well as nature, environment, and animal welfare. Additionally, Underhill (2005) identifies an emerging set of travelers who is demanding a private space during their short span vacation. They are considered to be among the wealthy and want to be segregated from the crowd. The new generation of travelers, therefore, is in quest of a fulfilling experience. Pine II and Gilmore (1999) postulate that people are moving away from only wanting to have a satisfactory service to wanting a memorable experience so that they can be engaged physically, emotionally, spiritually, and intellectually. They propose five principles of the concept of experience economy which they believe will provide a fulfilling experience for customers. The principles suggest that entities should create a consistent theme that will resonate throughout the customers' entire experience; use positive cues that are appropriate and easy to follow; eliminate negative cues that can either distract or contradict the theme, offer memorabilia to commemorate the experience of the customer; and engage all five senses through sight, sound, aroma, tasting, and feeling. These will heighten the experience and make it more memorable, thereby creating economic value through value perception.

Once these criteria are met, it is believed that the entity's performance will meet visitors' expectations, thus, confirming their satisfaction (Hill, 1986). Keeping customers satisfied is important in the hospitality and tourism industry (Wan & Man Cheng, 2011). Visitors have transitioned from the traditional sun-sea-sand concept and are demanding service quality considered as value for money (Sharpley & Forster, 2003). Additionally, Laws (1998) postulates that appropriate visitor management practices that underpin successful service delivery should minimize dysfunction and maximize satisfying experiences for visitors, hence, contributing to the organization's business objectives.

For the purpose of this study, the term customer is operationalized as visitor. The study, therefore, aims to find out if heritage attractions are using the principles of experience economy to provide a fulfilling experience for visitors. This is acceptable as Fodness (1990) used a customer interchange analysis to analyze Florida attraction visitors' perceptions.

Literature Review

EXPERIENCE ECONOMY

The concept of experience economy pose by Pine II and Gilmore (1999) is used to analyze the competitiveness of companies in the manufacturing and service industries. These companies can actually stage their performances to generate value through the creation of experiences for their customers. The experience created for customers is perceived to be a distinct economic offering that provides the basis for future economic growth, thus, the concept of experience economy. This is postulated as a move away from service economy since its focus is mainly on experiential offerings with the perspective that goods and services are no longer adding value to business economies. Additionally, the service economy is believed to be at its peak, leading way to the emerging experience economy, as mere goods and services are no longer sufficient to provide customer satisfaction.

In comparison to tangible goods and intangible services, experiences are memorable; people are looking for different experiences apart from those that are educational, escapist, and esthetic so as to enjoy themselves. When a customer buys a service, they receive the intangible aspect of the service, conversely, when they buy an experience, they actually pay for the memorable events in which they are personally engaged and the associated enjoyment (Pine II & Gilmore, 1999).

Experience economy is the foundation for a new competitive landscape and can be used to guide the transformation for customers, now and in the future. It is, however, important to refresh the experiences and so modification to this experience landscape is important. Pine II and Gilmore (1999) point out that although Walt Disney Company is faced with competition from new theme parks and technological innovations which include motion-based attractions, three-dimensional movies, and virtual reality experiences, they remain competitive. Throughout the years they have been modifying the offerings through "imagineering", using their experiential expertise to develop new concepts. The Disney experience, though lacking tangibility is highly valued by visitors as the experience resonates with them for a long time.

Similarly, Schmitt (2003) in explaining the importance of experiential branding proposes the concept of customer experience management (CEM) which is delineated as "the process of strategically managing a customer's entire experience ...." The experiences identified are sense, feel, think and act. He argues that managers should be paying attention to these in their marketing process. Pine II and Gilmore (1999) believe that more companies are incorporating the concept of experience economy into their existing offerings by improving their environment and engaging customers so as to achieve differentiation. The five principles of experience economy are explained as follows:

Having a Consistent Theme

Pine II and Gilmore (1999) suggest that creating a consistent theme that resonates throughout the entire experience will provide a fulfilling experience for the customers. They relate this perspective to the establishment of Disney World which is conceptualized as a theme park. Previously named Disneyland, this attraction depicts characters such as Peter Pan's Fight, Mark Twain Paddle Boat, and King Arthur Carousel, and theme areas such as Fantasyland and Frontier Land. This themed expression captivates the visitors by simultaneously entertaining and involving them in what is believed to be an unfolding story, and therefore, has become a place where persons find happiness and knowledge. The use of theme goes beyond entertainment as it involves engaging customers and connecting them in a personal and memorable way. For example, a theme restaurant such as Hard Rock Café not only entertains but also provides an *eatertainment* experience. The use of costumes can also commensurate the theme and add to the experience (Pine II & Gilmore, 1999).

Using Positive Cues

According to Pine II and Gilmore (1999), organizations that use positive cues that are appropriate and easy to follow as well as readable signs and symbols will provide customers with a fulfilling experience. Laws (1998) claims that design and resource decisions are important service management decisions. They clarify the parameters of the service encounter between customer and the customer-contact employee. This interaction occurs within the physical setting. Laws (1998) consequently designs a service blueprint to illustrate the techniques involved in a service system which can assist in improving the service delivery in a heritage setting. These include appropriate signage, parking facility, quality of catering, and even the cleanliness of the toilet facility. Likewise, Black (2001) examines the role of design and the physical environment on meeting visitors' needs, expectations and behavior and finds that this adds to their tourism experience.

Devesa, Laguna, and Palacios (2010) indicate that the existence of specific satisfactory elements is directly linked to visitors' reasons for making the visit. They also impact their satisfaction level. The authors point to some positive cues that are specific to cultural visitors; some of these are accessible roadways, signposting and parking facilities, and other general elements such as gastronomy quality, availability of restaurants, and access to information. Similarly, Boon, Sacha, Hayes, and Cave (2007) assess the effect of environmental elements on visitors to attractions in Tampa, Florida (museums, aquariums, and zoos) and discover that features such as signage, spaciousness and traffic flow are important in determining visitors' attitude toward repeat visit and recommendation of their experiences to family and friends. Huh and Uysol (2003) in Devesa et al. (2010) find that accessibility was among three important sources of visitor satisfaction.

In conducting a study on guests' satisfaction with health resorts in Slovenia, Ogorlec and Snoj (1998) indicate that 90 percent of the respondents perceive the hospitality nature of the facility to be the most positive element. Safety and security; and quality of the catering facilities are among the highest rating but the quality of the roads is given the worst rating.

Eliminating Negative Cues

Both visual and aural messages that can distract or contradict the theme will impact the customers' experience (Pine II & Gilmore, 1999). Negative cues are likewise extended beyond the visual and aural messages to include those attributes of an attraction that will not meet the expected level of satisfaction for the visitor. This takes into consideration the physical surrounding that does not have important features such as lighting, décor, and layout as indicated by the servicescape (Ryu & Jang, 2007) as well as lengthy wait time during the service delivery process (Wakefield & Blodgett, 1994).

Laws (1998) emphasizes that heritage sites should engage in "visitor ethic" practices which become necessary in catering to and caring for visitors. He posits that every step of the way of the visit should be dealt with strategically within the visitor management plan to ensure a fulfilling visitor's experience. The attitude of staff and their abilities to deliver quality service also have an impact on visitor enjoyment (Deary & Jago, 2001).

In examining visitors' perception of Maco's World Heritage Site, Frochot and Hughes (2000) find that although responsiveness got the highest rating in terms of convenient opening hours, empathy is scored the lowest due to inaccessibility by the less abled persons and children. This is due to the winding and narrow staircases that are typical of historical buildings. Leeds Castle has a similar issue (Laws, 1998). Furthermore, Frochot and Hughes (2000) state that communication is also rated low at Maco, as the visitors believe that more on-site information on the attraction is needed to enhance their experience.

Offering Memorabilia

Pine II and Gilmore (1999) posit that the offering of memorabilia will commemorate the experience of the customer and positively influence their experience. They add that the experience economy is staged; services are used as the stage and products as the "props" for engaging the customers. They also suggest the availability of items such as mugs, hats, T-shirts, key chains, stuffed animals, novelties, and souvenirs to extend the memory of the visitors' experience.

Engaging All Five Senses

Engaging all five senses through sight, sound, aroma, taste and feel to heighten the experience of customers and make it more memorable will provide a more fulfilling experience for them according to Pine II and Gilmore (1999). Additionally, the use of textured material, lights, audio-equipment, flavored ingredients, and fragrances can appeal to the senses. Boon et al. (2007) also allude to lighting and color as elements that impact attraction visitors. The Rainforest Café uses props and audio-animatronic animals and the All Star Café uses base-ball gloves to entice its customers.

Sensualizing the goods actually enhances customers' sensory interaction with them and by extension engages them. Pine II and Gilmore (1999) believe that items such as cotton candy, cigars, toys, photographs, colors, and wine are effective in creating sensory experiences. They add that employees are not just workers but should be perceived as cast members who stage the production using sights, sounds, tastes, aromas and textures to create an experience deem unique for the visitors.

This perspective is shared by Schmitt (2003), who poses the concept of sense experiences which involve sensory perception and feel experiences. The latter denotes affect/emotions as two of the five proposed CEM strategies to be considered for experiential marketing. Ryu and Jang (2007) likewise emphasize that music, aroma, and temperature are important operational tools to enhance customer perceptions. Hightower, Brady, and Baker (1999) indicate from their study on store atmosphere that servicescape has a significant and positive relationship with positive affect, service quality and service value.

In 1997, the Oyden Corporation invested in eight attractions which they named the American Wilderness Experiences. Visitors are fully engaged in motion-based nature scenes involving foliage, animals, events, and different cultural scenes in addition to a food service area. The first one opened in the Ontario Mills Mall in San Bernardino, California, depicts a staged experience in a shopping mall and appeals to the senses of visitors. Pine II and Gilmore (1999) emphasize that the focus of staging a rich, compelling experience is for engaging the visitors rather than entertaining them. Likewise, if visitors are allowed to create their own experiences, they will be able to contribute to the visual and aural experiences of others.

VISITOR EXPERIENCE AND VISITOR SATISFACTION

The literature points out that visitors who have a fulfilling experience will be satisfied and this is due to their perceived value as well as the quality of service received (Ogorlec & Snoj, 1998). These factors are believed to be antecedents of customer satisfaction (Fornell, Johnson, Anderson, Cha, & Bryant, 1996; Cronin, Brady, & Hult, 2000).

Ogorlec and Snoj (1998) believe that visitor's perceived value is one of the foremost underlying reasons for selecting a tourist destination. According to Woodruff (1997), value is the *"customer's perceived preference for an evaluation of those product attributes, attribute performances, and consequences arising from use that facilitate (or block) achieving the customer's goals and purposes in use situations"*. Ogorlec and Snoj (1998) also note that there is an increase importance on value and correspondingly on quality. It is believed that the quality of visitors' experience will determine the visitors' satisfaction level and will influence their decision to return (Laws, 1998) or using word of mouth communication to inform others of their experience (Laws, 1998; Ramseran-Fowader, 2007; Swanson & Kelly, 2001; Szymanski & Henard, 2011).

Methodology

This exploratory study examines the five principles of experience economy to determine if heritage attractions are using these principles to provide a fulfilling experience for visitors. These principles of the experience economy are having consistent theme, using positive cues, eliminating negative cues, offering memorabilia, and engaging the five senses.

MEASUREMENTS

Thirty-six items were used to measure heritage visitors' perception regarding the dimensions of the experience economy. These items were gleaned from the various literature reviewed, pertaining to the elements/features of the experience economy. Prior to this, both the SERQUAL (Parasuranman, Zeithaml, & Berry, 1988) and HISTOQUAL (Frochot & Hughes, 2000) scales were appraised to provide guidance for the measurements of this study. Their dimensions, however, could not be used as not all five measurements of experience economy (theme, positive cue, negative cue, memorabilia, and the five senses) had a fit with the measurements of those scales. A 5-point Likert scale was used for each item on the survey instrument. There is a rating from 1 to 5 with 1 representing strongly disagree to 5 being strongly agree.

The theme construct was measured using eight items and positive cues with nine items. Seven items were used to obtain responses pertaining to negative cues as pointed out in the literature review and four items for memorabilia. The five senses construct was measured using eight items. A total of eight items related to the five senses, three of which pertain in a general way to sensual, visual, and aural experiences. Refer to Table 1 for the measures.

DATA COLLECTION PROCEDURE

Three groups of tertiary students from an attraction management class conducted the survey while visiting three separate heritage attractions in Jamaica, a popular tourism destination in the Caribbean region (Sinclair-Maragh, 2014). The students were asked to observe the sites for the components of experience economy as indicated on the survey instrument. These attractions are heritage oriented because of their historical background and legacy. They are also different in nature as explained below.

Group one comprised 24 students who visited the Black River Safari in the south coast resort area in Jamaica. This ecological heritage attraction is located in Black River, capital of the parish of St. Elizabeth. Black River is one of the oldest European towns in Jamaica. Between the 18th and 19th centuries, it was a very busy seaport where logwood, cattle, rum, and pimento were exported to Europe. The safari played an important role as the logwood tree trunks were floated down the river to the port to be loaded on ships (Wikipedia Encyclopedia, 2016). The Black

Table 1.   Dimensions of Experience Economy.

Constructs	Measures	Cronbach Alpha
Theme	The theme is consistent throughout the tour	0.911
	Characters are used to depict the theme	0.908
	Costumes are used to match the theme	0.909
	There are specific themed areas	0.912
	Visitors are entertained throughout the experience	0.909
	Visitors are involved in the unfolding story	0.910
	Visitors are engaged throughout the tour	0.911
	The tour connects visitors in a personal and memorable way	0.908
Positive Cues	The heritage site is accessible by good roads	0.909
	There are adequate signposting/signage that are clear and helpful	0.912
	The parking facility is adequate	0.910
	Food and beverage facilities are available	0.907
	Food quality is good in terms of taste, appearance, and texture	0.911
	Information about the facilities and attraction is readily available	0.909
	The physical space is spacious and so there was no overcrowding	0.912
	The toilet facility is clean	0.910
	The visitors are safe and secure	0.912
Negative Cues	Visual messages can be seen and aural messages heard	0.912
	The facility has adequate and proper lighting	0.913
	The decor is attractive and interesting	0.909
	Visitors are able to move around the facility in an orderly way	0.911
	Visitors waited for a lengthy time before they were taken on the tour	0.914
	The facility is inaccessible by the less abled visitors	0.919
	It is very easy to communicate with the staff	0.912
Memorabilia	There is a wide assortment of memorabilia available	0.909
	Memorabilia are appropriate to the theme of the heritage site	0.910
	Adequate amount of memorabilia are available	0.911
	Souvenirs are available for purchase	0.915

Table 1.   (*Continued*)

Constructs	Measures	Cronbach Alpha
Five Senses	Textured materials are used to arouse visitors' sense of feeling	0.911
	Elements such as lights and props are appealing	0.911
	Visitors are able to sample the food/beverage items	0.910
	The facility has a fresh odor	0.914
	Audio-visual equipment are used to communicate the offerings	0.908
	Visitors are engaged in a rich and compelling atmosphere	0.910
	Cotton candy, cigars, toys, photographs, and colors appealed to the senses	0.913
	Visitors are able to create their own visual and aural experiences	0.911

River Safari is a wetland area with mangroves, palms, American crocodiles, and several species of birds (Jamaica South Coast, 2016).

There were 15 students in group two who visited the Rose Hall Great House located in the resort area of Montego Bay, capital of the parish of St. James. This legendary heritage attraction is a plantation on which the owner and slaves lived. The mansion is located on 650 acres of land. It was built in 1770 of Jamaican Georgian architecture. The attraction is based on a legendary story surrounding Annie Palmer, previous mistress of the plantation who is characterized as the White Witch of Rose Hall (Wikipedia Encyclopedia, 2016).

Group three comprised 16 students who visited the Coyaba River Garden and Museum which is located in the resort area of Ocho Rios. This resort is found in the parish of St. Ann and its offerings constitute a botanical garden with many of Jamaica's endemic and indigenous flora and fauna. The museum showcases the history of Jamaica before Columbus came to its shores with remnants of the Amerindians, the first inhabitants. There is also show of the Spanish architecture (Rainforest Adventures, 2016).

Methods

Frequency distribution was used to determine the number and percentage of observations in the sample. This data analysis was used as it is a simple technique that can determine the number of times the observations occurs in the data. Prior to the analysis, the measures were tested for their reliability. Table 1 shows that all 36 measures had high internal consistency as shown by the Cronbach Alpha coefficients exceeding 0.8 (Ryu, Ho, & Han, 2003). This indicates that the data is reliable and will produce stable and consistent results.

Findings

As presented in Table 2, majority of respondents in group one strongly agrees that all the components of a themed attraction were

Table 2. Frequency Distribution.

Measures	Black River Safari (%)	Rose Hall Great House (%)	Coyaba (%)
Theme			
Consistent theme	70.8 SA	73.3 SA	56.3 SA
Characters depict the theme	50.0 SA	40.0 A	31.3 NS
Costumes match the theme	41.7 SA	33.3 D	31.3 NS &D
Specific themed areas	58.3 SA	46.7 A	43.8 A
Visitors are entertained	62.5 SA	40.0 A	37.5 SA
Visitors are involved	45.8 SA	33.3 D &A	43.8 A
Visitors are engaged	70.8 SA	46.7 A	43.8 A
Tour connects visitors	6.7 SA	40.00	43.8 A
Positive Cues			
Site is accessible by good roads	50.00 SA	40.0 A	75.0 D
Adequate, clear, and helpful signs	58.3 SA	53.3 SA	75.0 A
Parking facility is adequate	54.2 A	53.3 SA	65.0 D
Food and beverage facilities available	62.5 SA	40.0 A	43.8 NS
Food quality is good	29.2 A	86.7 NS	75.0 NS
Information is readily available	66.7 SA	66.7 A	37.5 A
Physical space is spacious	66.7 SA	46.7 SA	56.3 A
Toilet facility is clean	58.3 SA	73.3 NS	37.5 A

Table 2. (*Continued*)

Measures	Black River Safari (%)	Rose Hall Great House (%)	Coyaba (%)
Visitors are safe and secure	54.2 SA	66.7A	56.3A
Negative Cues			
Visual messages seen and aural messages heard	50.0 SA	53.3 A	43.8 A
Adequate and proper lighting	41.7 SA	53.3 A	62.5 A
Decor is attractive and interesting	66.7 SA	60.0 A	50.0 SA
Visitors are able to move around	54.2 SA	53.3 A	50.0 A & SA
Visitors waited for a lengthy time	54.2 SD	53.3 A	56.3 DA
Facility is inaccessible by the less abled visitors	33.3 D	33.3 NS & D	31.3 D & NS
It is very easy to communicate with the staff	50.0 SA	53.3 SA	43.8 A
Memorabilia			
Wide assortment of memorabilia available	50.0 SA	60.0 A	37.5 A
Memorabilia are appropriate to the theme	45.8 A	53.3 A	50.0 D
Adequate amount of memorabilia are available	41.7 A	46.7 A	37.5 NS
Souvenirs are available for purchase	37.5 A	53.3 SA	50.0 A
Five Senses			
Textured materials are used	45.8 A	40.0 SA	31.3 SA
Elements such as lights and props are appealing	37.5 NS	33.3 A	31.3 A
Visitors sample food/beverage items	25.0 D &SA	40.0 SD	56.3 SD
Facility has a fresh odor	45.8 A	73.3 A	56.3 SA
Audio-visual equipment are used	50.0 A	53.3 D	37.5 D
Engaged in a rich and compelling atmosphere	58.3 SA	60.0 A	43.8 SA
Items for sensory interaction	25.0 SD & A	26.7 A	37.5 SD
Visitors create visual and aural experiences	66.7 SA	60.0 A	56.3 A

Strongly Disagree: SD; Disagree: D; Not Sure: NS; Agree: A; Strongly Agree SA.

present at the Black River Safari. This category includes having a consistent theme, characters, costumes and specific themed areas, as well as that the visitors were involved, entertained, engaged, and connected in a personal and memorable way. In terms of having positive cues, majority of group one strongly agree that all the measures were in place excepting adequate parking facility and quality of the food. With respect to negative cues, majority of respondents strongly agree that there were visual and aural messages, adequate lighting, decor, mobility, and communication. Majority of respondents agree that the memorabilia were appropriate and adequate, and that souvenirs were available for sale to the visitors. Majority of respondents agree that the five senses were used as there were textured material, fresh odor, and audio-visuals.

Group two response to their observation of the Rose Hall Great House shows that the majority agree that this heritage attraction uses characters and specific themed areas, and that visitors were entertained, engaged, and connected in a personal and memorable way. With respect to having positive cues, majority of respondents strongly agree that the attraction is accessible by road and has adequate signage parking facility and space. In terms of negative cues, majority of respondents agree that the attraction uses visual and aural messages, and has adequate lighting, décor, mobility, and communication. Majority of respondents also agree that there were memorabilia which were appropriate and adequate. Within this group, majority of respondents strongly agree that souvenirs were available for sale to visitors.

For group three, majority of respondents agree that there were specific themed areas and that visitors were involved in the story, engaged and had a memorable connection. The majority also agree that there were positive cues in terms of the heritage attraction having appropriate signage, information, space, clean toilet facility, and a safe and secure environment. Regarding the negative cues, majority of respondents agree that there were visual and aural messages, and proper lighting and communication. The respondents also agree that there were memorabilia and souvenirs for sale. They likewise agree that textured materials, fresh odor, audio-visuals, and sensory elements were in place.

Discussion

The study analyses the five principles of experience economy within the context of heritage attractions to find out if these attractions are using them to provide a fulfilling experience for visitors. Three groups of students visited each heritage attraction which is located in separate resort areas in Jamaica. The findings are discussed as follows:

BLACK RIVER SAFARI

Visitors strongly agree that this heritage attraction created a consistent theme as it had all elements in place. The areas were themed according to the nature of the attraction being a safari which the Europeans used to transport logwood to the seaport. Visitors were also involved, entertained, engaged and connected in a personal and memorable way. As indicated by Pine II and Gilmore (1999), these elements/principles will provide a fulfilling experience for visitors.

In terms of having positive cues, majority of visitors to this heritage attraction strongly agree that all the measures are in place excepting adequate parking facility and good catering quality. These areas to be improved as they are important components of a service delivery system and can negatively impact the visitor's experience. In fact, these two elements are identified by Devesa et al. (2010) as imperative in cultural visitors' decision making process to the visit the attraction. Sections of the roadway to this section of Jamaica tend to be in bad condition. According to Huh and Uysol (2003), accessibility can impact visitor satisfaction. However, there are plans in place to extend the current Highway 2000 to the southern parts of the island. When done, this will make the Black River Safari more accessible and traveling time.

Visitors strongly agree that there are visual and aural messages. The attraction management needs to assess these elements to ensure that they do not distract or contradict the theme. If this occurs it can prevent visitors from having a fulfilling experience. On the other hand, the attraction constitutes important features within its physical environment that can eliminate negative cues. For instance, there are adequate and proper lighting, and attractive and interesting décor. Additionally visitors can move around freely, hence, their mobility is not restricted. Another important element is that the visitors find it easy to communicate with staff.

There is also no issue with the waiting time during the delivery process and access for the disabled. The Black River Safari according to Laws (1998) is engaged in "visitor ethic" practices as it caters to and cares for its visitors in eliminating the majority of negative cues alluded to in the literature.

Visitors agree that the memorabilia were appropriate and adequate. As pointed out by Pine II and Gilmore (1999) this commemorates the visitor's experience and positively influences their experience. Souvenirs were also available for sale. Wherever the visitors go, these souvenirs will help them to recall their visit to the attraction. In terms of the use of the five senses, majority of respondents agree that there were textured material, fresh odor and audio-visuals. Some visitors strongly agree that there was food sampling and the atmosphere was rich. These are among several elements that are known to engage the five senses. In doing so, these sensory interactions make the visit more memorable and provide a fulfilling experience for visitors. The management of Black River Safari nonetheless needs to give consideration to the use of lights and props and other sensory elements that can appeal to visitors' senses and improve their experience.

ROSE HALL GREAT HOUSE

The visitors agree that this heritage attraction uses characters and specific themed areas. They were also entertained, engaged and connected in a personal and memorable way. There was strong agreement that the theme of the attraction was consistent throughout the tour. Agreeably, the Rose Hall Great House is agreed to be themed excepting that costumes were not worn. This is a mansion where former slave owners lived and visitors are taken on a tour of the premises to see the layout and furnishings that existed then. Based on the theme and nature of the site, tour guides could wear clothing from that era as costumes to show what the fashion design was at that time. This according to Pine II and Gilmore (1999) would commensurate the theme and add to the experience of visitors.

With respect to having positive cues, visitors strongly agree that the attraction is accessible by road. This is because it is located on the Rose Hall main road and this thoroughfare adjoins the second city, Montego Bay, to the northern parts of the island. The heritage attraction also has adequate, clear and helpful signs as well as adequate parking facility and space. These are important physical features which according to Black (2001) will meet the needs and expectations of visitors, determine their behavior and add to their tourism experience.

The attraction uses visual and aural messages and as expressed earlier, these can contradict the theme of the heritage attraction and negatively impact visitors' experience. On the contrary, having adequate lighting, décor, mobility, and communication can actually eliminate any existing negative cues and enhance visitors' experience. There were appropriate and adequate memorabilia as well as souvenirs for sale to visitors. Having these items serves as reminders of the visits which can remain in the memory of visitors for a long time.

COYABA RIVER GARDEN AND MUSEUM

This combined natural and physical attraction is of historical significance because of its collection of indigenous flora and fauna as well as artifacts and architecture. Visitors agree that there were specific themed areas and that they were involved, engaged, entertained, and had a memorable connection. This relates to the expectations of the new type of tourist alluded to by Raj (2007) who are participators rather than spectators.

Some visitors, however, were either not sure or disagreed about the use of costumes. This element of the experience economy can be considered since the site is of historical significance, showing remnants of previous habitants such as the Amerindians and Spanish. This is likely to improve visitors' experience (Pine II & Gilmore, 1999) and encourage more appreciation of the heritage and culture.

The important elements for providing positive cues were identified. Ogorlec and Snoj (1998) indicate that a safe and secure environment is highly rated by visitors of attraction. Regarding the negative cues, there were also visual and aural messages as observed at the other heritage attractions and these can cause some level of distortion from the theme. On the other hand, the proper lighting and communication identified are important in eliminating negative cues as previously pointed out. Memorabilia are also available for sale.

Visitors agree that textured materials, fresh odor, audio-visuals, and sensory elements were in place. This is in keeping with the literature which posits that these are necessary in creating a memorable experience for visitors.

In summary, all three heritage attractions despite their distinctiveness in offerings have the majority of elements in place that will create a fulfilling experience for visitors. However, noticeable similarities exist with the use of visual and aural messages which as suggested can be negative cues. Since these are being used, most likely for the purpose of communication, the management of the attractions needs to ensure that they are in sync with the themes to prevent distortions.

Conclusion and Implications

The purpose of the study is to analyze the five principles of experience economy to determine their influence in providing visitors to heritage attractions with a fulfilling experience. Three groups of students each visited a heritage attraction in a separate resort area in Jamaica. Overall, the study shows that the three groups of visitors either agree or strongly agree that many of the principles of experience economy were in place at the three heritage attractions, despite their distinctiveness in terms of offerings.

The major contribution of this study is that it will inform management of heritage attractions of the importance of having a theme that is consistent, elements of positive cues, elements that will eliminate negative cues, and memorabilia and sensory elements to provide a fulfilling experience for visitors. The study was done at three heritage attractions and this presents the platform for a comparative analysis from the findings. One limitation of the study is that there were no measures for visitor satisfaction to analyze the relationship between visitors' fulfilling experience and their satisfaction. Future studies can, however, take this into consideration and use a plausible theory such as confirmation-disconfirmation paradigm to explain the findings. Scholars can also examine the impact visitors' fulfilling experience has on the attraction's performance.

References

Black, G. (2001). Whats, whys and whos of concept design. In M. Devesa, M. Laguna and A. Palacios. (2010). The role of motivation in visitor satisfaction: Empirical evidence in rural tourism. *Tourism Management*, *31*(2010), 547–552.

Boon, M. A., Sacha, M. M. D., Hayes, S., & Cave, J. (2007). Heritage/cultural attraction atmospherics: Creating the right environment for the heritage/cultural visitor. *Journal of Travel Research*, *45*(February), 345–354.

Cronin, J. J., Brady, M. K., & Hult, G. T. (2000). Assessing the effects of quality, value, and customer satisfaction on consumer behavioral intentions in service environments. *Journal of Marketing*, *76*(2), 193–218.

Deary, M. A., & Jago, L. K. (2001). Managing human resources. In M. Devesa, M, Laguna and A. Palacios. (2010). The role of motivation in visitor satisfaction: Empirical evidence in rural tourism. *Tourism Management, 31*(2010), 547–552.

Devesa, M., Laguna, M., & Palacios, A. (2010). The role of motivation in visitor satisfaction: Empirical evidence in rural tourism. *Tourism Management, 31*(2010), 547–552.

Fodness, D. (1990). Consumer perceptions of tourist attractions. *Journal of Travel Research, 28*(4), 3–9.

Fornell, C., Johnson, M. D., Anderson, E. W., Cha, J., & Bryant, B. E. (1996). The American Customer Satisfaction Index: Nature, purpose and findings. *Journal of Marketing, 60*(October), 7–18.

Frochot, I., & Hughes, H. (2000). HISTOQUAL: The development of a historic house assessment scale. *Tourism Management, 21*, 157–167.

Hightower, R., Brady, M. K., & Baker, T. L. (1999). Investigating the role of the physical environment in hedonic service consumption: An exploratory study of sporting events. *Journal of Business Research, 55*(9), 697–707.

Hill, D. J. (1986). Satisfaction and consumer services. *NA-Advances in Consumer Research, 13*, 311–313.

Huh, J., & Uysol, M. (2003). Satisfaction with cultural/heritage sites: Virginia Historic Triangle. In M. Devesa, M. Laguna and A. Palacios. (2010). The role of motivation in visitor satisfaction: Empirical evidence in rural tourism. *Tourism Management, 31*(2010), 547–552.

Jamaica's South Coast. (2016, January 17). *The hidden side of Jamaica.* Retrieved from Jamaica-southcoast.com/blackriver/. Accessed on January 17, 2016.

Klerks, P., & Kop, N. (2008). Societal trends and crime-relevant factors … An overview of the Dutch national threat assessment on organised crime (2008–2012). Police Academy of the Netherlands, Politieacademie Apeldoorn.

Laws, E. (1998). Conceptualizing visitor satisfaction management in heritage settings: An exploratory blueprinting analysis of Leeds castle, Kent. *Tourism Management, 19*(6), 545–554.

McKercher, B., & du Cross, H. (2002). *Cultural tourism – The partnership between tourism and cultural heritage management.* New York, NY: Haworth Hospitality Press.

Ogorlec, A., & Snoj, B. (1998). Guests' satisfaction with tourism services: A case of health resorts in Slovenia. *The Tourist Review, 53*(2), 38–47.

Parasuranman, A., Zeithaml, V. A., & Berry, L. (1988). SERVQUAL: A multiple item scale for measuring consumer perceptions of service quality. *Journal of Retailing, 64*(1), 12–37.

Pine II, B. J., & Gilmore, J. (1999). *The experience economy: Work is theatre & every business a stage* (1st ed.). Boston, MA: Harvard Business School Press.

Poon, A. (1993). *Tourism, technology and competition strategies.* Wallingford: CAB International.

Rainforest Adventures. (2016, January 13). *Coyaba river gardens and museum.* Retrieved from www.rainforestadventure.com. Accessed on January 13, 2016.

Raj, A. (2007). *The new age of tourism — And the new tourist.* Jhansi: Institute of Tourism and Hotel Management, Bundelkhand University. Retrieved from www.indianmba.com/Faculty_Column/FC565.html

Ramseran-Fowader, R. R. (2007). Developing a service quality questionnaire for the hotel industry in Mauritius. *Journal of Vacation Marketing, 13*(1), 19—27.

Ryu, K., & Jang, S. S. (2007). The effect of environmental perceptions on behavioral intentions through emotions: The case of upscale restaurants. *Journal of Hospitality & Tourism Research, 31*(1), 56—72.

Ryu, S., Ho, S. H., & Han, I. (2003). Knowledge sharing behavior of physicians in hospitals. *Expert Systems with Applications, 25*(1), 113—122.

Schmitt, B. H. (2003). *Experience management: A revolutionary approach to connecting with your customers.* Hoboken, NJ: Wiley.

Sharpely, R., & Forster, G. (2003). The implications of hotel employees' attitudes for the development of quality tourism: The case of Cyprus. *Tourism Management, 24*(6), 687–697.

Sinclair-Maragh, G. M. (2014). Resort-based or resource-based tourism? A case study of Jamaica. *Emerald Emerging Markets Case Studies, 4*(2), 1—19.

Swanson, S. R., & Kelly, S. W. (2001). Service recovery attributions and word-of-mouth intentions. *Journal of Marketing, Hospitality & Tourism Research, 35*(1/2), 194—211.

Szymanski, D. M., & Henard, D. H. (2011). Customer satisfaction: A meta-analysis of the empirical evidence. *Journal of the Academy of Marketing Science, 29*(1), 16—35.

Underhill, W. (2005). In search of privacy. *Newsweek Magazine.* Retrieved from www.newsweek.com/id/51974/output/print. Accessed on March 18, 2012.

Urry, J. (2002). *The tourist gaze* (2nd ed.). London, England: SAGE Publishers.

Wakefield, K. L., & Blodgett, J. G. (1994). The importance of servicescapes in leisure service settings. *Journal of Services Marketing, 8*(3), 66—76.

Wan, K., & Man Cheng, E. I. (2011). Service quality of Maco's heritage site. *International Journal of Culture Tourism and Hospitality Research, 5*(1), 57—68.

Wikipedia Encyclopedia. (2016, January 17). *Black River Jamaica.* Retrieved from https://wikipedia.org/wiki/Black_River_Jamaica. Accessed on January 17, 2016.

Wikipedia Encyclopedia. (2016, January 17) *Rose Hall, Montego Bay.* Retrieved from https://en.wikipedia.org/wiki/Rose_Hall,Montego_Bay. Accessed on January 17, 2016.

Woodruff, R. B. (1997). Customer value: The next source for competitive advantage. *Journal of the Academy of Marketing Science, 25*(2), 139—153.

Conclusions: Issues and Challenges for Managing and Marketing Tourism Experiences

The final chapter of the *Handbook of Managing and Marketing Tourism Experiences* summarizes the issues and aspects highlighted, as well as conclusions formulated by authors in previous chapters, and provides suggestions and recommendations for local planners, destination and business managers to successfully design, manage, and market tourism experiences. As discussed earlier, a tourism experience refers to a chain of events. A tourism experience creation begins with an event where an individual experiences (activity) an attraction or business (resources) within a particular context or situation. This event generates a reaction and that reaction results in a memory upon which the individual reflects and creates a new meaning. Ultimately the individual, through this meaning-making process, both increases his or her understanding of the world and of the self as well. Studies suggest that the experience formation takes place in consumers' mind, and the outcome of experience consumption depends on how consumers, based on a specific situation or state of mind, react to the series of encounters that forms an experience.

There is no question that successfully designed, managed, and marketed tourism experiences are critical determinants of a destination/business' success in a highly competitive tourism marketplace. However, creation and delivery of highly successful tourism experiences heavily depends on how well the destination/business managers understand customers' experiential needs, wants and expectations, and how well hospitality and tourism businesses work together to create a memorable experience for their customers by addressing those experiential needs, wants, and expectations. Considering the fact that hospitality and tourism products are multidimensional, and usually consists of a "series of experiences" achieved through a combination of a diverse array of products and services, it is vital for destination and business managers to understand the importance of the interplay among various suppliers of those experiences. The quality of each experience delivered by a variety of providers is of vital importance to the overall tourism experience quality. From consumers' perspective, the product they purchase is the total experience, covering the entire amalgam of all aspects and components of the experience, including attitudes and expectations. Accordingly, the overall tourism experience is a "series of experiences" achieved through a combination of a diverse array of products and services; an amalgam of multiple components supplied by a range of businesses. The tourist experience is the result of a process where facilities, services, and attitudes from multiple businesses are configured to produce an experience of value to customers. In other words, tourism experience is a "multifaceted" and a "hybrid" experience, taking place in phases and tourists use services from more than one organization.

Tourism experiences are "deconstructed" products because they bring together a number of services from a number of individual businesses. In other words, a tourist's experience consists of a series of services and products, which are offered by businesses that operate separately. Ideally, each of those services a tourist receives from different companies is a value-adding service or a value-adding experience. The value chain of a tourist experience includes a number of players that are involved in offering and delivering all tourism-related services. Furthermore, a series of businesses, interactions, resources, and knowledge streams are involved in the creation and delivery of a memorable tourism experience to the end-consumer. This creates the need for integration of the whole range of supply chain activities because service delivery failures of any businesses involved in the delivery of a tourism experience can have significant negative consequences for the whole system. Any dissatisfactory experience with any service aspect decreases tourists' satisfaction with their overall tourism experiences. Furthermore, those dissatisfactory experiences may deter the total value of the hybrid tourism experiences offered. As a result, this may decrease the total value of the tourism experience and may decrease the overall satisfaction with tourism experience and may have significant negative influences on loyalty, which may have a significant impact on financial performance of companies involved in the delivery of tourism experiences. Therefore, it is crucial for companies to make sure that other companies involved in the process provide satisfactory experiences.

From the above discussion, it is clear that planning, design, management, and marketing of experiences for tourism markets constitute a focal challenge for tourism destinations and providers in a highly competitive marketplace. All businesses and organizations involved in have to address challenges and issues of providing high-quality experiences to tourists. This handbook was designed to bridge the gap in contemporary literature by carefully examining management and marketing issues of tourism experiences. Large number of scholars who contributed to this handbook have explored and analyzed the main issues and challenges in the field of tourism experiences from a strategic management and marketing perspective. Furthermore, those scholars have provided critical insights and discussed a number of approaches for planning, managing, and marketing experiences for tourists. Overall, contributions from distinguished scholars in the area have (i) provided a detailed analysis of the main issues and challenges related to tourism experience management and marketing; (ii) presented and discussed analytical frameworks and tools; (iii) explored theoretical and practical approaches for managing and marketing experiences in various tourism contexts and industries; and (vi) discussed and analyzed case studies illustrating approaches adopted, methods implemented, and best practices in addressing related issues.

This handbook examined design, management, marketing, and customers' evaluation of tourism experiences under four main parts. The first part titled "Planning: Design and Creating Tourism Experiences" examined theoretical and practical issues and concerns related to design and creation of tourism experiences. The second part titled "Managing: Organizing and Delivering Tourism Experiences" explored theoretical and practical issues and concerns related to managing tourism experiences within various contexts, industries, and settings. The third part titled "Marketing: Communicating and Promoting Tourism Experiences" focused on theoretical and practical issues and concerns related to marketing of hospitality and tourism experiences within various contexts, industries, and settings. The last part of the handbook titled "Monitoring and Evaluating Tourism Experiences" examined theoretical and practical issues and approaches related to monitoring the quality of tourism experiences and those experiences impact on travelers post experience behaviors including satisfaction, loyalty, and word of mouth behaviors.

Part I: Planning: Design and Creating Tourism Experiences

The first part titled "Planning: Design and Creating Tourism Experiences" consisted of six chapters focusing on experience-based service design, design of experiences, experience-centric approach and innovation, crucial role and contribution of human resources in the context of tourism experiences, social media and the co-creation of tourism experiences, and creation and marketing of tourism attraction experiences.

A service design path built around various elements such as sensations, emotions, human relations, innovations, and values was presented in Chapter 1. In this chapter, the author provided an extensive review of literature on the topic and utilized the Singapore Airlines web page as a case to investigate the appropriateness of the instructional path discussed in the chapter. The author argued that experience-based service design contains several components, and that this service design should be established within three-steps, namely explore, design, and positioning. Based on the extensive review of the literature, the author highlighted the instructional path for experience-based service design and implementation process. The author suggested that the instructional path can be used to guide business managers/ experience engineers. Author further argued that since the experiences are formed based on a set of emotions, by focusing on creating meanings and relating to the moment aspects of the experience-based service design, destinations and businesses can develop and deliver experiences that meets/exceeds customers' expectations. With this foresight, the author suggested that an instructional path for experience-based design implementation process should start with trying to understand customers' expectations and continue with building up the experience scene and focusing on the configuration of the customer interface.

The experience-centric strategy from the perspective of innovation management, its contribution to designing and managing valuable tourism experiences, especially in context of guided tours were discussed in Chapter 2. The chapter provided an extensive review of the literature on experience-centric approaches and innovation. The author also provided a conceptual discussion on the concepts of experience-centric innovation and experience innovation, particularly the role of experience design and market intelligence in experience-centric service processes. The conceptual discussion was further enhanced by analyzing empirical data from interviews with 11 tour providers. The author concluded that creation of novel experiences through product innovation is the most common type of innovation on frames of guided tours. While the group size is found to be an influential feature of the experience design, imitation is found to be a major threat. The author also explored the role of knowledge management and dynamics of knowledge on experience creation. Tour guides were identified as experiential knowledge collectors and/or creators, thus their role in knowledge management is crucial alongside the market intelligence. In contrast, costumer-driven innovation was not seen by tour providers as a crucial issue in creating memorable experiences.

The importance of human resources in creation and delivery of tourism experiences was discussed in Chapter 3. Authors provided an extensive literature review on issues and aspects of human resources management and its role in tourism experience creation and delivery. Authors also provided micro-cases and examples to illustrate utilization of various human resources management tools and practices. Their findings suggested that human resources play a critical role in overcoming the challenges faced during the creation, management, and delivery of experiences that meet customer expectations. Furthermore, authors argued that managing human resources strategically and enabling employees to develop new skill sets to deliver satisfactory experiences is critical because consumption experience has shifted from the servicescape to the experiencescape environment. Therefore, strategic human resources management is a must for tourism businesses that aim to provide valuable tourism experiences. There is an urgent need for development of tools that can be utilized for experiential intelligence and development of skill sets that can be used to deliver customized tourism experiences to contemporary tourists.

A conceptual model of tourist experiences in a destination was proposed in Chapter 4. The model was developed after reviewing the literature on tourist experiences and exploring a brief case. Authors argue that although there is an increasing interest in literature on customer experiences, the definition, conceptualization, components, and measurement of tourist experiences are still ambiguous. Measuring the overall experience in destinations is more complex than measuring it for individual service experiences because it extends a period of time and involves a synergistic interaction and consumption of integrated products and services simultaneously. The holistic destination experience model proposed in this chapter emphasized the important roles DMOs, host community, and industry play in the creation of the overall experiencescape. Authors argued that participation of local community in tourism experience delivery is critical for the delivery of a proper destination experience. DMOs also play an important role in the creation of an environment that facilities the creation and delivery of a satisfactory service experiences. DMOs can play an important role through coordination of various public and private actors, promotion of the destination, investing on infrastructure and lobbying with decision makers. Secondly, DMOs can also encourage and promote cultural events, festivals, arts, and other cultural activities that can improve tourist experience. Furthermore, the level of service provided by the industry acts as a supporting experiential factor for travelers. Authors further argued that both DMOs and individual service suppliers must understand the holistic experiential attributes the destination offers. Destinations should focus on developing new programs that people can experience and learn new things unique to the destination. Activities that involve both locals and tourists and motivate them to explore their talents, skills, and capabilities, increase the level of social interaction both with the locals working in tourism services (e.g., hotels) as well as with locals who are not involved in the tourism industry (e.g., in public transportation) would enhance experiences. Individuals who experience local culture are more likely to have a positive experience. Promotion of local food, local architecture, farmers markets, and other activities that increase interaction with locals would also improve tourist experiences. These can also be used in destination marketing. For example, local food is rarely utilized as a part of destination promotion. Using local clues is much more effective than using the images of beaches or international facilities that can be found pretty much in every destination in the World.

The role and the impact of social media in influencing and shaping tourism experiences was examined in Chapter 5 utilizing a Service Dominant Logic and co-creation approach and concepts for examining how the social media can influence interactions and participation that represent two major sources of tourism experiences. The author has argued that the social media do not only alter the nature of current experiences but also facilitate the transformation and continuous formation of experiences as well as the formation and creation of new types of tourism experiences. The author further argued that social media assists and facilitates tourism experiences (when tourists share travel resources for assisting others' travel planning processes); enriches and augments tourism experiences (when online travel resources enable tourists to make experiences more personalized, meaningful, imaginative, and emotional); forms tourism experiences (when social media interactions amongst various actors at micro, meso, and macro level enable an iterative co-construction process of experience meaning, understanding, and evaluation); mediates tourism experiences (the virtual experience of a destination); becomes the tourism experience itself (the use of the social media while traveling is the core and major purpose of having a tourism experience, that is, the social media become a tourism experience); empowers tourism experiences (when customers are empowered to participate and engage in the value co-creation processes of the firm, that is, the customer is embedded within the firm's value system); and enables tourism experiences (i.e., the use of social media for creating new types of tourism experiences, e.g., when the customer uses the social media for becoming a tourism entrepreneur providing tourism experiences, e.g., sharing economy, the customer uses the firm's infrastructure and value system for providing – marketing tourism experiences). The author concluded that social media co-created tourism experiences are enabled and supported through interactions and participation that change the major dimensions of the co-creation generating processes.

The current trends toward both creative and experiential tourism in cities in terms of development and marketing of local attractions were explored in Chapter 6. Authors provided a profile of creative tourism in cities through a literature review and further investigated by utilizing of a case study at a local attraction in Toronto, Canada. The choice of a site was one of a creative city and the repurposing of a formerly industrial site for visitation. The study of Evergreens Brickworks has demonstrated the use of market segmentation and product-market match techniques to identify markets and match visitors with experiences. These techniques are of particular importance for attractions with a local audience that also wish to attract tourists. Authors argued that the visitor segmentation method can help managers to identify the fit between the profile of their attraction to local visitors and tourists, thus identifying the motivations and interests of tourists that might differ and may lead to product innovation. For example, in the case of the Evergreen Brickworks pre-scheduled and bookable activities offered to locals would need to be offered on a different basis in order to be of interest to tourists, who may be one time visitors to the site. Likewise, the product-market match process can identify the suitability of current product offerings for both existing local audiences and visitors, suggesting areas in which products could be modified or indeed created. An example from the Evergreen Brickworks is the identification of the diversity of product elements including a restaurant, sustainability efforts (e.g., innovative energy uses, utilization of heritage and nature within interpretive tours), heritage building, and nature-based activities that can be matched with different visitor segments. The study of the Evergreen Brickworks also demonstrates how a site can employ experiential and creative tourism in an urban setting to differentiate themselves from other local visitor attraction offerings. This is a lesson that could be employed by other local attractions desiring to expand their visitor reach, by attracting tourists visiting their areas. The study of the Evergreen Brickworks also demonstrated the importance of increasing awareness of their sites to potential audiences. Authors argued that the product-market match process can help sites such as the Evergreen Brickworks to profile their unique selling points (USP's) that can be optimized to engage, educate, and advocate, thereby increase visitation and improve the visitor experience.

Part II: Managing: Organizing and Delivering Tourism Experiences

Delivery process and the issues faced in the management of the tourism experience delivery process within various contexts, industries, and settings were addressed in Part II of this handbook. The second part of the handbook features nine chapters that focus on a wide variety of management issues ranging from impact of culture on delivery of experiential tourism, collaboration between tourism operations, authenticity of experiences, creativity, sustainability, innovation, managing rural and event tourism experiences.

Cultural sensitivity in event design and its impact on ongoing management and tourism experiences was examined in Chapter 7. The author argued the importance of local arts ecologies in creating a unique tourism experience. As long as there is a refreshing diversity of sculptors/artists prepared to present their work at local art festivals, there will be new and different art for participants to enjoy. The author utilized a case study approach and used a new assessment tool, sustainable creative advantage (SCA) to assess SCA for the Sculpture by Sea, Bondi, Sydney 2015. This study was the first to utilize the new SCA assessment tool outside of Hong Kong. Author concluded that the SCA evaluation approach and the results of this application are of interest to academics studying glocality and events, the relationship of curatorial power to content/experience or how such events add to the leisurescapes in tourism.

The growth of Dragon Boat racing from humble beginnings in 1976 as part of a local tourism strategy by the Hong Kong Tourist Association (HKTA) to position Hong Kong as more distinctive than a destination for shopping or with British colonial history appeal was examined in Chapter 8 as an event that offers unique experiences to visitors. Authors indicated that the initial steps of the HKTA to incorporate Dragon Boat racing as a local strategy for tourism experience distinctiveness has rapidly evolved into a global strategy for developing a world sport. In this case, a special cultural event, élite, and community sport are combined to create a new tourism niche market, and one that tourism managers can capitalize on by ensuring that the distinctive intangible cultural heritage elements of waking the dragon, and putting it to sleep at the end, the decorative dragon heads on the boats and the drumming style remain quintessential ingredients of the total experience. The author, Fleur Fallon, identified three trends emerging from a review of the literature, namely: concern with balancing authenticity and profit-chasing; the phenomenal fast growth of the sport and the challenge to develop and maintain international control and governance; and seeking evidence of health and wellbeing benefits of Dragon Boat racing for breast cancer survivors. The author argued that the cultural legitimacy and authenticity debate may have some merit, but its focus is narrow and detracts from what has been happening in the last four decades in the growth of Dragon Boat racing as an international competitive and community sport. According to the author, the Dragon Boat racing is alive and well, and honors the original purpose of the Festival for promoting and supporting community, with a focus on health and wellbeing benefits. Since each race begins with some rituals, adapted from the original awakening the Dragon spirit, and with Dragon heads on the bow, plus the rhythmic beating of the drum, intrinsic linkages with the Chinese origin are clearly on display during the event.

Consumer experience within the context of the hotel industry and the impact of collaboration between businesses on providing valuable hospitality experiences in hotel settings was examined in Chapter 9. Authors argued that hotel operators and a destination's visitor attractions often share common strategic aims. Literature suggested that to be successful in the industry, hotel operations must provide a superior customer experience, and this must be done continuously and efficiently. In addition, hotels need to put more emphasis on improving the quality of their experience offerings and ensure that the needs and expectations of their guests are being met. From a managerial perspective, the customer experience has to be planned for, resources deployed, and personnel put in place to implement the plan. Value is a lived experience for the customer and there is generally a trade-off between benefits and costs. In the hospitality industry, customer experience is delivered through a number of vehicles including partnerships, which provide more attractive guest experience opportunities. By entering into a business venture, hotels can also provide extra customer value and may gain a competitive advantage. Authors argued that analyzing and understanding the guest experience as an emotionally and symbolically rich phenomenon, and anchoring it in a common, appealing, significant and distinctive route or theme (for instance, "Grand Tour"), may be a powerful way to combine the various elements and dimensions of the experience. Authors further argued that investment in business ventures and alliances is a good investment in the sense that it constitutes a potential source of sustainable competitive advantage. The main aim of a business network is, in authors' view, to generate business and market diversification. A collaborative platform wisely designed can offer a way of extending, enriching, and deepening the hotel guests' experience, based on endogenous resources. The later and other distinctive elements might be used as a means of diversifying the experience and making it appealing to different individuals within the same market segment. The ultimate aim is to make the experience attractive, pleasant, interactive, diverse, and meaningful.

How the methodology of service blueprinting may contribute to managing and offering high-quality experiences to sport tourists was discussed in Chapter 10. Authors utilized a combination of theoretical tools to develop a finalized services blueprint map for sport events. They argued that observation, diaries, service blueprints, comment management, and FMEA (Failure Mode and Effects Analysis) are a range of corporate research approaches and management tools that can offer new insights into the theory and praxis of service management applications and can improve the sport tourism experiences. Authors suggested that sporting event managers can utilize blueprints to make sure that the sporting events have all of the internal support systems and technological aspects of an event in place, as well as the employee-customer interactions that are required to create a distinctive customer experience. They further suggested observation, diaries, service blueprints, comment management, and FMEA (Failure Mode and Effects Analysis) can act as a range of corporate research elements and management tools that can provide new insight into the theory and the praxis of small-scale sporting event customer and experience focused management applications. The case study presented indicated that synthesis of different tools can offer an alternative approach for services blueprinting improvement-planning procedures that arise from a diary-based selection of comments. These comments can reflect the problematic areas (failures) in different contact points of a service blueprint system. The management of the contact points in this blueprint system can be coordinated more easily, if the management can identify those problematic areas that negatively affect the whole tourist experience. Given that these problem areas play a critical role in planning and organizing the customer quality improvement strategy of the event, the management can build a long-term data pool about the failures and effects with the aim of avoiding similar circumstances and situations that may occur in the future and can affect satisfaction, word of mouth, the tourist experience and tourist loyalty, and hence the sustainability of the small-scale sport event. Authors further argue that the analysis of Services Blueprinting can be combined with other useful managerial tools, like the Failure Mode and Effects Analysis to better manage the contact points, the "moments of truth" of tourist experiences in the sport event service system.

The authenticity of tourism experiences and the commodification of tourism offering were discussed in Chapter 11 by utilizing a case study approach. The author argued that destinations rely not only on authenticity of their attractiveness but also strive to attract tourists by tailoring experiences that can meet high-order needs of tourists. However, these destinations are under threat by commodification and McDonaldization due to excessive use of resources as a result of mass tourism. As suggested by theories on authenticity, commodification and McDonaldization are critical in understanding dimensions of tourist experiences. Hosting individuals traveling to specific destinations who are trying to satisfy their high-order needs such as authenticity seeking, prestige, and learning requires managers and planners to endeavor to maintain the authenticity of their destination, culture, and events. Indeed, the case study has demonstrated that destinations rely on not only the object authenticity of their attractiveness but also strive to create experiences that would differentiate themselves from their competitors. Authors argued that a competitive edge will be gained by providers who are able to satisfy a consumer's search for personal achievement and transformation. Therefore, it is crucial for the political and developmental agendas to preserve their authenticity rather than develop places, cultures, and communities. Although the authenticity of the tourist experience is of importance, it is more important to ensure that local communities feel comfortable with their role as performers and entertainers. This includes the degree to which they are prepared to allow the commodification of their culture for touristic purposes. In this chapter, the author has argued for greater attention to be paid to the role of authentic experiences in attracting and satisfying individuals. However, the author also suggested that contemporary tourism may appear to be moving into the "post-authentic" age, but authenticity may be lurking beneath the surfaces of post-modern attractions, though in an inverted, and in the eyes of some, perverted guise. Therefore, the ultimate goal for destination managers and planners is to focus on the experiences without compromising on authenticity, uniqueness, and genuineness of the attraction while refraining over-commercialization and McDonaldization of the destination.

Best practices and guidelines for managing experiences within the field of creative tourism were presented in Chapter 12. After examining the best practices in managing experiences, the author proposed some basic guidelines for DMOs and DMCs interested in designing activities that cater to travelers who are seeking for creative tourism experiences. Most of the analyses, examples, and observations presented in this chapter were based on management of the *Creative Tourism Network®* and the approaches adopted by its members in managing their creative tourism offerings all over the world. The author argued that the emergence of the creative and experiential tourism in general is only the visible part of the paradigm shift that is affecting the tourism industry, involving new challenges and opportunities. The author suggested that the emergence of the creative tourism implies a completely new form of management for both cultural and tourist fields, that can lead to the creation of specific skills and general guidelines to be adapted to different contexts.

A brief overview of green principles associated with developing ecotourism destinations was presented in Chapter 13. Furthermore, green ecotourism destination planning was discussed within the context of the tourists' experience to highlight critical factors necessary for sustainable ecotourism destination development. Authors suggested that even though the green market is still in its infancy, tourists are increasingly demanding green accommodations. Tourists across the globe are much more conscious of their impact on the natural environment and are continuously finding ways to be more environmentally friendly. They are willing to pay higher prices if it means that local labor conditions are fair, products and services provided are organic, the negative impact on the environment is minimized, environmental sustainability is guaranteed, and more funds are used to increase the conservation of natural areas and decrease the footprint of tourists in significant natural tourism attractions. Authors further argued that a green, sustainable ecotourism destination can only be developed if green principles are incorporated from the input phase. The input phase (e.g., building materials and infrastructure systems for water and energy) determines the output phase (e.g., operational materials, activities, suppliers, activities, and marketing) and, subsequently, the level of sustainability. It is therefore crucial to plan for these aspects and the level to which the destination aims to adhere to these aspects, as they are costly. Authors also suggested that ecotourism destinations have to ensure that they are continuously identifying factors that influence the experience of tourists at the destination and manage these factors accordingly to maintain optimum visitor experience which could lead to a competitive advantage. This supports the notion that tourists' experience is based on the perception, expectations, and level of satisfaction whilst visiting the ecotourism destination. Ecotourism destinations have to be proactive in ensuring tourists a memorable experience before, during, and after their visits to an ecotourism destination. This could lead to a more conscious tourist and support of global sustainability.

Rural tourists' experiences in relation to travel motives and activities performed in rural areas in Cyprus were examined in Chapter 14. Authors also explored tourists' overall satisfaction with rural tourism experience with regard to several physical, social, and symbolic attributes derived from the literature and elicited recommendations that can improve tourists' experiences in rural areas. The author argued that the rural tourism experience is fragmented and largely influenced by tourist motives, expectations, prior experience, and regional characteristics. The rural tourist space can be adjusted, with elements combined, in order to appeal to different market segments. The author suggested that rural tourists differ from other tourists and the need to categorize them into distinctive segments with relation to their motives, degree of interest with specific aspects of rurality, and level of involvement in activities is imminent. The study also reported varying opinions with regard to the rural tourism experience in Cyprus. Specifically, the lack of activities and attractions seems to be a focal point which the tourism authorities need to address if the experience of rural tourists is to be improved. Authors argued that prolonging the length of stay of visitors in the rural regions and enriching the tourist experience depend on the variety of activities and attractions appealing to different groups of tourists. In addition, a better organization and coordination of development and marketing efforts is required among key stakeholders in providing an enjoyable experience to rural tourists. The availability of attractions and facilities is not adequate as the effectiveness of service delivery is pivotal in the tourist experience. Lack of business knowledge and expertise are the key obstacles in the development of rural tourism in Cyprus. Thus, training rural tourism entrepreneurs and providing marketing support are essential tactics that regional tourism boards need to take into consideration.

The relationship between service innovation and experience creation within the context of spas, wellness, and medical tourism was discussed in Chapter 15. Authors examined the relationship between service innovation and experience creation in the context of spas, wellness, and medical tourism with the aim of providing an overview of service innovation theory and models and applying them to the spa, wellness, and medical tourism sectors. Authors argued that the inseparable nature of the spa, wellness, and medical tourism sectors suggests that it is critical to consider service innovation in the creation of guest experiences. Treatments and therapies depend on close interaction with healthcare practitioners and therapists, and they are essential to the quality of the service delivery. Authors suggested that the models of delivery should include strong elements of co-creation with tailor-made packages and treatments because customers are more and more involved in their own experience creation. Although the research data presented in this chapter suggested that technology might not be as important as operators imagined, "flexible solutions" (e.g., wearables) are becoming more and more sophisticated and can easily be used on holiday as well as at home. Authors argued that tourists are never far from specific medical advice, even when away from home. There are also significant efforts being made to make the medical experience more comfortable and less anxiety-inducing. The servicescape can be of considerable importance for spas, wellness, and medical facilities, and even though the research data presented suggested that design may not be as important as operators thought, the atmosphere of spas and wellness facilities depends very much on highly subjective and intangible elements such as design, light, color, scent, and music. While service innovation factors may not be as important as market orientation, service orientation, or organizational factors, service innovation nevertheless play an extremely significant role in the (co)creation of spas, wellness, and medical tourist experiences.

Part III: Marketing: Communicating and Promoting Tourism Experiences

Conceptual and practical issues related to marketing tourism experiences were discussed in Part III of this handbook. In this part, approaches and communication strategies utilized to market tourism experiences were examined from both theoretical and practical perspectives. This part included a total of six chapters. These chapters specifically focused on marketing and communication strategies designed for marketing tourism experiences, role of social media in experience sharing and communication, the role of internet in marketing tourism experiences, marketing niche tourism experiences such as culinary tourism and sport tourism, and the role of marketing in managing risk perceptions.

Utilizing a case study approach, the role of social media in experience sharing and communication of a gay film festival in one of the most popular world tourist destinations was examined in Chapter 16. The study presented in this chapter was focused on a single gay cultural event of a relatively small scale (2,000–3,000 attendees) organized by a militant association. Authors reported that the event's utilization of online promotions was relatively poor; maybe due to the size of the event, organizers underestimated the importance of OSMs for the event's promotion and development. Authors also reported that most of the attendees were not very happy about the lack of online advertising and communication about the festival. Authors suggested that providing communication opportunities about the festival via OSMs could have enabled organizers to attract more people, build up a loyal audiences and thus ensure that more external audiences will attend the next events. Authors discussed a number of benefits of OSMs in marketing such as cost, speed, anonymity, and the size of storage of information. However, authors argued that communicating information through OSMs may not be enough because it has to be passed on to the right relays and transmitters. Authors suggested that the best strategy may be to communicate through individuals who are planning on attending the event; this can help form a large OSM community for the festival with a dedicated Facebook page and ensure a greater success of the festival by fostering a real online experience. For the post-event communication, authors suggested that the organizers can build a "collective intelligence" hub on socio-digital media to gather feedback and comments from the attendees. A well-structured online communication tool through the social media may play a critical role in loyalty formation for the festival.

Importance of theming in creating an experience was discussed in Chapter 17 by examining the similarities between the experience economy and Disneyization, with a specific focus on theming as a means of enhancing tourism experience. The authors presented several issues and guidelines related to theming to highlight important factors that visitor attraction managers need to consider when seeking to use theming to enhance or create a visitor experience. The author compared several models, with specific emphasis on finding similarities between the experience economy and Disneyization. Even though authors reported several similarities, theming was found to be the overarching aspect that combines all other similarities (such as the physical environment, staff, tourists, and souvenirs). The author strongly suggested that for successful delivery of a tourism experience, the theme should be planned meticulously as the theme is the most critical factor not only in the experience itself but also in the experience cycle.

Marketing and communication strategies and approaches for promoting culinary tourism experiences were discussed in Chapter 18. In this chapter, the author specifically focused on identifying issues and approaches utilized in the development and marketing of culinary tourism experiences with the goal of determining the value of collaborative forms of product development and marketing. The author argued that collaborative approaches in developing and marketing of culinary tourism experiences through networks, partnerships, and alliances are critical for the success and beneficial to all stakeholders. The chapter highlighted the importance of collaborative forms of product development and innovation in marketing in terms of both networking and collaboration for both academics and practitioners in the growing area of experiential culinary tourism. Furthermore, the author indicated that this chapter contributes to our understanding of how strategic approaches to developing culinary tourism experiences can benefit destination branding and marketing, a lesson that might be applicable to other cities wishing to identify themselves with regional cuisines.

A comprehensive review of the risk perception literature in the tourism field and conceptual and operational definitions of risk perceptions was discussed in Chapter 19. Furthermore, based on the extensive literature review, a conceptual model of risk perceptions and operationalization of risk perception variables were provided in this chapter. Authors first provided an overview of major criticisms of the travel risk literature. In an effort to address these criticisms, authors proposed a conceptual model to understand the risk-related constructs of perceived risk (perceived vulnerability, perceived severity, affective risk perceptions), perceived efficacy (self-efficacy, response efficacy), and engagement in a recommended risk reduction behavior. Authors argued that adopting a theory-based, interdisciplinary approach to the conceptualization and operationalization of risk-related constructs can provide a more holistic understanding of the role of risk in travel decision-making. Authors further argued that a majority of risk-related variables (i.e., perceived severity, affective risk perceptions, self-efficacy, response efficacy, and engagement in a recommended risk reduction behavior) have not been studied in the context of international travel. Therefore, testing of the proposed conceptual model can provide a better understanding of the dynamic processes between the risk-related constructs, as well as their role in the destination choice process. The authors considered this study to be a one of the first steps in the process of moving the travel risk literature forward. An obvious next step in the process is to test the proposed conceptual model. As previously noted, going from theory to operationalization has been a challenge for travel risk scholars. Current measures have mainly failed to capture the multidimensional nature of perceived risk. A possible solution to this challenge is to look outside and turn to other fields that have extensively studied these constructs. For example, tourism scholars can adopt the measures used in health behavior and psychology. However, it should be noted that the measures will need to be adapted to reflect the dynamic nature of tourism because in the health behavior literature, for example, studies have focused on risk associated with topics such as AIDS prevention and breast cancer screenings. Another next step in the process is to test the proposed conceptual model in a variety of settings (e.g., different destinations, different types of risk, different tourist origin markets). Such research is necessary to refine the proposed conceptual model.

Marketing strategies and promotional tools used in marketing of sport tourism experiences in a mature tourism destination were discussed in Chapter 20. In this chapter, authors first investigated the success of specific marketing tools used to promote sport tourism and sport tourism experiences in Barbados by examining the responses of various sporting and tourism bodies. Afterwards, authors examined how marketing/promotional tools can contribute to better market sport tourism experiences. Authors reported that many of the promotional tools implemented in Barbados during their marketing process correspond with those used internationally. However problems of poor and insufficient sporting facilities as well as little collaboration between tourism and sporting entities hamper the success of Barbados as a sport tourism destination. This further minimized Barbados' ability to market favorable tourism experiences. Based on the findings, authors concluded that while promotional tools are essential in attracting tourists, other elements must also be taken into consideration to ensure sport tourists have positive experiences which can lead to a successful sport tourism destination.

The role of information and communication technologies in marketing tourism experiences was investigated in Chapter 21 by analyzing and examining the role of ICTs and the emerging trends and issues in marketing tourism experiences. Authors first reviewed the previous conceptual frameworks and then identified the key issues and trends that are considered to be for ICT-based tourism marketing. This chapter illustrated the many types of ICTs (web-based, social media, location-based, virtual and augmented reality, mobile and smart technologies) and their varied impacts on tourism experiences, tourist expectations, and visitor needs. It painted a picture of a highly technology-based tourism experience that offers new interplays between marketers and tourists and lots of avenues for experience as well as marketing content co-creation. The chapter offered a conceptual framework to show how ICTs have disrupted the exclusive rights of tourism marketers to tourism experience creation and promotion by facilitating new connections among tourists themselves, with marketers, with residents, and with employees. The chapter discussed not only emerging opportunities for marketers to take advantage of new ICTs but also urged tourism marketers to realize its increasing dependence on technology and its need to adjust strategies and tactics aimed at developing and selling compelling tourism experiences. A number of trends were listed in the chapter that illustrate how tourism marketing is changing and presented examples of how tourism marketers have tried to use emerging ICTs for the marketing of tourism experiences. The chapter further emphasized the changing role of marketing and the need of marketers to redefine themselves as trusted experts, curators, experience facilitators, reputation custodians, and storytellers. The trends identified in the chapter raised important questions about the type of knowledge and skills these new tourism marketers need and to what extent tourism marketers have shifted their assumptions and implemented new practices. Authors strongly suggested that more research is needed to answer the questions raised in this chapter. Authors also argued that there is a growing need or research that looks at marketing effectiveness in these new technological contexts.

Part IV: Monitoring and Evaluating Tourism Experiences

Issues and approaches related to the stage of post experience encounter was discussed in Part IV of this handbook. In this part, specific approaches and tools used to monitor and evaluate the performance of tourism destinations and businesses in developing and delivering memorable tourism experiences were discussed. This part features four chapters that examine conceptual foundations and managerial implications for program design, delivery and performance measurement, an experiential value model within the context of business tourism experiences, peer-to-peer review sites and social media strategies, and evaluations of tourism experiences.

A conceptual framework for guiding destination managers who seek to design and deliver memorable experiences appropriate to their particular destination was proposed in Chapter 22 in order to overcome the current theoretical lack of understanding of the memorable tourism experiences (MTEs) phenomena. The review of the tourism and memory literature related to experiences and the subsequent content analysis and overall synthesis of the author's findings revealed that MTEs are composed of seven underlying conceptual components. Thus, the author argued that tourism visitation experiences should be carefully designed to ensure they include the six positive components of a potential MTE – and, to the extent possible, avoid negative, or adverse, components, which can easily undo many months and years of careful planning. Author suggested enhancing visitor involvement as co-producers of their experiences, remedying negative experiences and enhancing positive ones (e.g., dealing with stressful events and surprising visitors in positive ways), and diversifying memorabilia as ways to enhance the probability of delivering MTEs. The framework developed in this chapter provides recommendations for designing and delivering tourism programs and "experiencescapes" that can provide visitors with the underlying components of MTEs a destination can deliver. The author also argued that destination managers can use the study results to develop rating or evaluation criteria. They may learn how their businesses rank against others across memorable experiential factors and management practices by asking visitors' questions about competitors. Since consumers have become more information oriented when deciding on destination areas, this competitive information could be transferred to advertising efforts and program development.

A theoretical framework for the development of a multi-item Business Tourist Experience Value Model was proposed in Chapter 23. The proposed model consisted of an integration and re-assessment of different elements from a range of empirical studies. The author argued that customers' service quality assessments can be used as guide by managers to develop service quality strategies. The author argued that the proposed Business Tourism Experience Value model can support the exiting business tourism strategies by focusing on the experience, intention, and engagement of business tourist to create a better understanding of their post consumption behavior. When business managers subscribe to experience value and satisfaction practices it gives them the best chance to regain their vitality during favorable business environment, and to sustain their business practices during challenging economic times. According to the author, the proposed model captures the conceptual, methodological, and practical aspects of experiential value research in a business tourism context. From a conceptual viewpoint, this research complements the existing literature by integrating the theory of business models and experience economy in the context of business tourism. This model can be used to assess the performance of suppliers of business tourism services. However, the author suggest that the interpretation of this model must be done with caution as one cannot assume that this model considers the unique business tourism service offering and diverse cultural perspectives of the country in which the research is conducted.

Changes in tourist consumer behavior brought about by social media and the possible strategies for tourism businesses to address resulting challenges were discussed in Chapter 24. Authors identified three main topics through extensive literature reviews, namely: (1) the antecedents (the factors motivating tourists to write online reviews); (2) the impact of eWOM on providers of tourism services (business perspective); and (3) the influence of online reviews on consumers' behavior (demand perspective). Authors also examined the impact of online reviews on tourism businesses and outlined a series of adequate strategies formulated for business practitioners. Authors argued that tourism businesses have to adopt and implement suitable strategies. Two preliminary actions/strategies that can be utilized are: (i) understanding SM: it is essential for tourism businesses to understand what SM are and how social media should be used; and (ii) the need to truly understand how to execute digital marketing effectively. Authors concluded that the interaction of main challenges in the tourism market with the digital environment and the adoption and use of SM clearly indicates that tourism businesses need to adopt new approaches and implement new strategies in performing their managerial and marketing activities. Tourism businesses need to incorporate use of SM in their managerial and digital marketing activities. In doing so, they will have the input and knowledge needed to invest in creating innovative customer experiences.

An evaluation of heritage tourism experiences was presented in Chapter 25 in a research study with empirical investigation on tourism experiences specific to heritage attractions. The study analyzed five principles of experience economy within the context of heritage attractions with the goal of finding out if heritage attractions are using the principles of experience economy to provide a fulfilling experience to visitors. The principles of the experience economy are having consistent theme, using positive cues, eliminating negative cues, offering memorabilia, and engaging the five senses. Results revealed that majority of visitors either agree or strongly agree that many of the elements comprising the principles of experience economy are in place. One similar drawback reported in the study among the attractions is that they all use visual and aural messages which can distract or contradict the theme and consequently visitors' experience. Author suggested that the major contribution of this study is that it informs management of heritage attractions of the importance of having a theme that is consistent, elements of positive cues, elements that will eliminate negative cues, and memorabilia and sensory elements to provide a fulfilling experience for visitors.

Overall, the *Handbook of Managing and Marketing Tourism Experiences* provided conceptual and practical evidence for the critical importance of adopting and implementing appropriate management and marketing approaches and strategies to address the challenges and opportunities in the emerging field of tourism experiences. It is worth noting that there is no magic recipe to guarantee the successful planning and efficient management of tourism experiences. All involved actors, stakeholders, planners, managers, and marketers must be aware of the challenges, obstacles, and difficulties in this field as discussed in previous chapters. They have to devote energy and resources to surmount them and achieve a sustainable and successful partnership in order to develop and deliver tourism experiences that exceeds customers' expectations. It is quite clear that the challenges, problems, and opportunities will continue to evolve as all tourism destinations and businesses strive to offer better tourism experiences in an increasingly competitive business environment.

Dogan Gursoy
Marios Sotiriadis
Editors

About the Authors

Elricke Botha is a Senior Lecturer in the Department of Entrepreneurship, Supply Chain, Transport, Tourism and Logistics Management at the University of South Africa (Unisa). She has been a faculty member here since 2012. In her short working career at Unisa, Elricke participated in curriculum development, taught several undergraduate and post-graduate modules, and served on academic committees (academic and research-related committees). Elricke completed her Ph.D. in Tourism Management as well as her undergraduate and post-graduate qualifications at the North West University, Potchefstroom, South Africa. Her research interests are related to ecotourism management and aspects associated with the field. Her thesis in particular focused on an interpretation framework for the Kruger National Park, South Africa and would like to pursue several topic-related aspects in the years to come.

Gurel Cetin is Assistant Professor at Istanbul University, Faculty of Economics. He holds an MS in Tourism Management and Ph.D. in Business Administration. He is currently a visiting researcher at European Tourism Research Institute (ETOUR). His research focuses primarily on tourism marketing, sustainable tourism, destination planning, ICT in tourism and tourist experience. Dr. Cetin also serves at the editorial board of Journal of Tourismology.

S. Christofle is Associate Professor at the Department of Geography, University Nice Sophia Antipolis. Sylvie holds a Ph.D. from the University of Montpellier, France and a Certificate of Tourism Planning and Architecture from the School of Architecture of Languedoc-Roussillon, France. She is a specialist in event and cultural tourism. Sylvie's research interests include event tourism, convention tourism, urban tourism, and culture tourism. Sylvie is also the Head of the MA in Tourism and Hospitality, University of Nice Sophia Antipolis, France.

Caroline Couret is expert in creative tourism; she co-founded and manages the *Creative Tourism Network*® and the *Barcelona Creative Tourism* program. She was born in France where she graduated in Management of Culture and Postgraduate in Cultural Policies. She is regularly invited to speak in conferences as well as to teach in universities around the world. She publishes articles about creative tourism in different languages. She is an external expert for the European Union, the *International Institute of Gastronomy, Culture, Arts and Tourism* (IGCAT), and the *International Creative Tourism Associate* (US). Since 2001 she has been in charge of the international area of the Foundation Society and Culture from which she has been managing a wide range of projects, including the coordination of European funds projects and the organization of festivals for the Barcelona City Council. She lived and worked in different countries: La Casa de Velázquez (Madrid), Festival de Cannes (France), as well as various projects in Louisiana, Mexico and Morocco. She speaks French, English, Spanish, Catalan, and Italian.

Rachel Dodds is Professor at the Ted Rogers School of Hospitality and Tourism Management at Ryerson University and is a specialist in sustainable tourism. She is also an Adjunct Professor at the University of Waterloo and an Honorary Reader at University College London. Rachel's research interests include sustainable tourism development, certification, corporate social responsibility, business marketing/development, and island issues. Rachel is also the Director of Sustaining Tourism, a boutique consultancy. With over 20 years of experience in the industry, Rachel has lived and worked on four continents and has travelled to over 80 countries.

Hilary du Cros is currently Honorary Research Fellow of the University of New Brunswick, Canada. She has taught and worked in the Asia Pacific region over the last 30 years (including projects for the United Nations World Tourism Organization or UNESCO). She has an interdisciplinary perspective on heritage and arts management, marketing, and sustainable tourism development.

Willy Hannes Engelbrecht is a Senior Head of Programme at the Independent Institute of Education (IIE) within the Faculty of Commerce where he manages various diploma, degree, and postgraduate programmes within the field of Business Management.

Willy has been seconded to the position Acting Head of Faculty for the Faculty of Commerce to oversee the overall academic development and timely delivery of modules and programmes within Faculty. He obtained his Ph.D. with the North-West University (NWU) focusing on developing a competitiveness model for South African National Parks. His research interest is within the field of ecotourism, national parks, strategic tourism, and visitor experience. He is also collaborating with a research expert in conducting research within the South African exhibition sector. Willy taught on various online programmes at both undergraduate and postgraduate level at the University of South Africa (Unisa) for two years and is actively involved in online tutoring. Furthermore, Willy is a co-researcher at the NWU in which emphasis is placed on teaching and learning in a digital environment.

Fleur Fallon is Independent Researcher, formerly with School of Tourism Management, Sun Yat-sen University, Zhuhai campus, Zhuhai 519082, Guangdong province, PR China. Fleur Fallon has a corporate background in human resource management in Australia. After completing her doctoral thesis on sustainable tourism development for the island of Lombok, Indonesia, she has led teaching in business, tourism, and events-related subjects in Australia, China, and Germany. She has published several articles and chapters based on her doctoral case study, Chinese leisure tourism to Indonesia, events management and learning and teaching themes.

Anna Farmaki is Lecturer in Tourism Management in the Department of Hotel and Tourism Management at the Cyprus University of Technology. She has a Ph.D. from Nottingham Trent University, a MA in Marketing from Kingston University and a BA (Hons) in Business from the University of Westminster. Prior to joining the Cyprus University of Technology, she worked for several years in private institutions of tertiary education in Cyprus and was course leader of the undergraduate hospitality and tourism management programme at the University of Central Lancashire (Cyprus). Her research interests lie in the areas of tourism planning and development, with emphasis on sustainable tourism, and tourist behavior. She has published in several reputable peer-reviewed academic journals and has presented her work in various international conferences, seminars, and workshops.

Sonia Ferrari is associate professor of Tourism Marketing and Place Marketing at the University of Calabria, Italy. She has been a researcher in the same University since 1993. She has also taught Management, Service Management, Event Marketing, Marketing of Museums, and Tourism Management at the University of Calabria. She is President of the Tourism Science Degree Course. Her main fields of study and research are: services management, tourism marketing, place marketing, event marketing, wellness tourism.

M. Ferry is Associate Professor at Institut Paul Bocuse in Lyon. Martine holds a Ph.D. from the University of La Sorbonne, France. She is a specialist in event, tourism, and hospitality. Martine's research interests include event tourism, experience, sustainability, tourism trends. Martine is also the Head of the Master in International Hospitality Management and the Master in Culinary Leadership & Innovation, Institut Paul Bocuse, Lyon, France.

Anestis Fotiadis (e-mail: anesfottiadis@isu.edu.tw; skype: anestis. fotiadis) is member of the academic teaching and research staff of the Department of Entertainment Management of I-Shou University in Kaohsiung, Taiwan. He researches and lectures in the field of Human Resource Management, Project Management, Events, and Venue Management. He has published more than 70 research papers in international academic journals and conferences along with two books.

Ulrike Gretzel is Professor of Tourism in the Business School at the University of Queensland. She held previous appointments at the University of Wollongong and Texas A&M University. She received her Ph.D. in Communications from the University of Illinois at Urbana-Champaign. Her research focuses on persuasion in human-technology interaction, information search and processing, big data, adoption and use of social media, interorganizational information systems, and other issues related to the development and use of intelligent systems in tourism. Her research has been funded by the Australian Research Council, the Hong Kong Research Council, the National Research Foundation of Korea, the US National Science Foundation, the US National Endowment for the Humanities, the US National Park Service, Parks Canada, TripAdvisor, the Bush Presidential Library and Museum, and a number of national, regional and local tourism organizations in North America, Europe, Australia, and Asia.

Özlem Güzel is Assistant Professor in the Tourism Faculty at the Akdeniz University in Turkey. After her bachelor's degree in tourism, she worked as a tour guide in travel agencies and tour operators in cultural and nature tours, as being a travel and history lover. She received the Master of Tourism and Hotel Business Management in 2007. After her professional experience in tourism and master degree, she gave courses at the Travel Management department as a lecturer. She completed her Ph.D. in Business Management at the Süleyman Demirel University in Turkey with the Ph.D. thesis on Experience Marketing in 2012. Her research interests are in tourism marketing, cultural tourism, and sustainable tourism.

Lee Jolliffe is Professor, Hospitality and Tourism at the University of New Brunswick, Canada. She combines an academic background in sociology and museum studies and practical experience in hospitality studying the intersection between culture and heritage related to tourism. Publications include the edited books with Channel View Publications: Spices and Tourism, Destinations, Attractions and Cuisines (2014) and Sugar Heritage and Tourism in Transition (2013), and the co-authored book with Hilary du Cros, The Arts and Events (2014) (Routledge). She sits on the editorial boards of a number of international hospitality and tourism journals and is the Resource Editor (Museums) for Annals of Tourism Research.

Cristina H. Jönsson is Lecturer in Tourism and Hospitality Management at the University of the West Indies (UWI), Cave Hill Campus, Barbados. Prior to joining UWI Cristina worked as a regional tourism development manager in Sweden where she worked in various projects ranging from sustainable tourism development to regional branding and marketing. Cristina is well travelled and has worked and served as a consultant in both private and public sector organizations in different countries. As a polyglot mastering seven languages Cristina has added richly to international projects and research as well as translation and interpretation. Cristina's research interests include Foreign Direct Investment (FDI) in Tourism, Sport Tourism, Medical Tourism, Sustainable Planning & Development, and Tourism Motivation.

Eyup Karayilan is Research Assistant at Istanbul University, Faculty of Economics, Tourism Management Department. He holds an MS Degree in Tourism Management and currently working on his Ph.D. thesis on tourist experiences. His research areas include tourist experience, tourism policy and planning, and tourism sociology.

Jong-Hyeong Kim, is Professor in the School of Tourism Management at Sun Yat-sen University. He received his Ph.D. in Leisure Behavior from Indiana University-Bloomington. His research focuses on consumer behavior in tourism and hospitality. Over the years, he has extensively published in the areas of memorable experiences and consumer behavior in top-tier journals, such as *Journal of Travel Research, Tourism Management, International Journal of Hospitality Management,* and *International Journal of Contemporary Hospitality Management.*

Maximiliano Korstanje is editor in chief of *International Journal of Safety and Security in Tourism* (UP Argentina) and *International Journal of Cyber Warfare and Terrorism* (IGI-GlobalUS). Besides being Senior Researcher in the Department of Economics at University of Palermo, Argentina, he is a global affiliate of Tourism Crisis Management Institute (University of Florida, USA), Centre for Ethnicity and Racism Studies (University of Leeds), The Forge (University of Lancaster and University of Leeds, UK). With more than 700 published papers and 25 books, Korstanje was awarded as Outstanding Reviewer 2012. *International Journal of Disaster Resilience in the Built Environment.* University of Salford, UK, Outstanding Reviewer 2013 *Journal of Place Management and Development,* and Reviewer Certificate of Acknowledgement 2014. *International Journal of Contemporary Hospitality Management (IJCHM).* He had nominated to five honorary doctorates for his contribution in the study of the effects of terrorism in tourism. In 2015, he was awarded as Visiting Research Fellow at School of Sociology and Social Policy, University of Leeds, UK.

Crystal C. Lewis has had numerous years within the health and fitness industry in Barbados and Venezuela which has led to her position as manager of a fitness facility in Barbados. However, with a need to expand her knowledge she pursued studies in tourism, later attaining a master's degree in tourism and sport management. Her tourism journey has allowed her to co-author in a previously published journal article and this opportunity has increased her enthusiasm to add to the enhancements of the tourism industry through continuous research and documentation of findings.

C. Papetti is Associate Professor at the University of Nice Sophia Antipolis and is a specialist in marketing, online social media, and tourism. After graduating from the Ecole Supérieure de Commerce de Paris (ESCP), she received her Ph.D. in Marketing, at the University of Nice. Her research interests include online social networks and media, their influence on consumer decisions and experiences, particularly in the tourism industry. She is the author of several articles edited in journals and presented at conferences and published business cases on aspects of tourism and hotel sector. Catherine is also the Director of the Master in Marketing, at the IAE, Business School of the University of Nice Sophia Antipolis.

Lori Pennington-Gray is the former Director of the Eric Friedheim Tourism Institute and the current Director of the Tourism Crisis Management Initiative at the University of Florida. Dr. Pennington-Gray received her Ph.D. from Michigan State University (1999), her MS from The Pennsylvania State University (1994), and her BS from Waterloo University in Canada (1993). She has expertise in tourism marketing, planning and development, policy and crisis management. In the area of planning and development, she has consulted on several strategic tourism development plans, including consultations for Belize Foundation for Research & Environmental Education (BFREE) and Fort Walton Beach, Florida. She has been involved with a number of tourism studies globally and has worked with a number of countries on tourism policy initiatives. Dr. Pennington-Gray has published more than 75 refereed articles, has brought in more than $3M in external research dollars and made over 120 presentations. Dr. Pennington-Gray teaches both undergraduate and graduate students the concepts of tourism marketing.

László Puczkó is Director of the Tourism and Leisure Knowledge Centre at the Budapest Metropolitan University of Applied Sciences. He has been working as travel and tourism expert for over 20 years. He was manager at KPMG between 2001 and 2004. He founded The Tourism Observatory for Health, Wellness and Spa (2012). He participated in more than a hundred projects in research, planning, product development, experience mapping and design, impact assessment, and marketing. He is the (co-)author of numerous books and articles.

Christos Sarmaniotis is Professor at the Department of Business Administration (Marketing Course) of the Alexander Technological Educational Institute of Thessaloniki, Greece and Dean of the School of Business and Economics. He is also Tutor at the Hellenic Open University. He received his MBA degree from Concordia University, Canada and his Ph.D. in Marketing from Aristotle University of Thessaloniki, Greece. He is co-chair of ICCMI (International Conference of Contemporary Marketing Issues) 2012, 2014, 2015, and 2016. He is author of a textbook in Management, author/co-author of many papers published in international journals and/or presented in international conferences. Moreover, he is a Marketing and Management consultant for many private and public organizations in Greece and has undertaken many projects. His research interests include Marketing, and Tourism and Hospitality Marketing.

Ashley Schroeder is an Assistant Professor at the University of Hawaii Manoa and the Managing Director of the Tourism Crisis Management Initiative at the University of Florida. Dr. Schroeder received her Ph.D. (2015), MS (2012), and BA (2007) from the University of Florida. She has expertise in destination management, with an emphasis on how destinations prepare for, respond to, and bounce back from crisis situations that affect consumer confidence or normal business operations in a destination. Within the area of tourism crisis management, she is particularly focused on understanding the underlying nature and subsequent influences of tourists' destination risk perceptions. She has worked with several destination management organizations on tourism research and tourism crisis management initiatives. She published 14 refereed articles during her graduate studies, has presented her research internationally, and has managed a number of external research grants. Dr. Schroeder teaches undergraduate courses in the areas of tourism management, tourism marketing, tourism planning and development, and research methods.

Marianna Sigala is Professor at the University of South Australia. Prior to her current position she has been an academic staff at the Universities of Strathclyde and Westminster in the United Kingdom, and the University of the Aegean (Greece). She also has professional hospitality industry experience. Her interests include service management, Information and Communication Technologies (ICT) in tourism and hospitality, and e-learning. She has published four books and her work has also been published in several academic journals, books, and international conferences. She is currently editor of the Journal of Service Theory & Practice and the Journal of Hospitality & Tourism Cases. She is a past President of EuroCHRIE and has served on the Board of Directors of I-CHRIE, IFITT, and HeAIS.

Gaunette Sinclair-Maragh, Ph.D., is Associate Professor at the School of Hospitality and Tourism Management in the College of Business and Management, University of Technology, Jamaica. She is a Fulbright Scholar and pursued doctoral studies in Business Administration with a specialization in Hospitality and Tourism Management at the Washington State University, USA. Her research interests focus on tourism planning and policy, residents' perceptions and support for tourism development, culture and heritage tourism and sports tourism. She currently serves as the Head of the School of Hospitality and Tourism Management at the University of Technology, Jamaica.

Geoffrey Skoll is Associate Professor emeritus in the Criminal Justice Department, Buffalo State College, Buffalo, New York. He was previously at the University of Wisconsin-Milwaukee. Work on fear and terrorism includes the monograph *Social Theory of Fear* (Palgrave Macmillan, 2010). New monograph titled *Dialectics in Social Thought: The Present Crisis* published June 2014 by Palgrave. He is currently working on a book length study of the conjuncture of a fear culture and globalization. His areas of specialization range from terrorism, jurisprudence, human right violations, and so forth.

Melanie Kay Smith is Associate Professor in the Department of Tourism, Leisure, and Hospitality at the Budapest Metropolitan University of Applied Sciences in Hungary where she specializes in cultural tourism and health tourism. She has worked for over 15 years as a Tourism academic in both London and Budapest. She has been the Director of BA and MA programmes, has undertaken extensive curriculum development, organized, hosted or chaired several conferences and events, and has more than 60 academic publications.

Marios Sotiriadis is Visiting Professor at Department of Entrepreneurship, Supply Chain, Transport, Tourism and Logistics Management, University of South Africa (Unisa). Formerly, he was Professor of Tourism Business Management Department, TEI of Crete, and Tutor of the Hellenic Open University, Greece. He received his Ph.D. in Tourism

Management from the University of Nice Sophia-Antipolis, Nice, France. He is the author of eight books and monographs, three distance learning manuals, and three e-learning materials on aspects of tourism marketing and management. He has undertaken a variety of research and consultancy projects (e.g., feasibility studies, business plans, marketing researches and plans, human resources projects) for both public and private organizations of the tourism and travel industry. His research and writing interests include tourism destination and businesses marketing and management. His articles have been published by international journals and presented at conferences.

Magdalena Petronella (Nellie) Swart is Senior Lecturer in the field of Tourism at the University of South Africa, a Certified Meetings Professional, an event organizer and part of the City of Tshwane's Ambassador Programme. She holds a DCom in Leadership Performance and Change (University of Johannesburg) in which she developed a Service Quality Scorecard to predict business tourist retention on grounds of variation in business tourist satisfaction. Forthcoming from her thesis, Nellie co-authored accredited journal articles and a number of accredited conference proceeding articles and also received the Outstanding Paper Award at the international Pan Pacific Business Conference in 2012. Her Community Engagement Project includes the offering of various guest lectures as part of the National Department of Tourism's Capacity Building Programme. Nellie is an EXCO member of the Tourism Educators South Africa committee and the Southern African Association for the Conference Industry Tshwane branch committee.

Ciná van Zyl is Professor in Tourism Management and Chair of the Department of Entrepreneurship, Supply Chain, Transport, Logistics and Tourism Management, College for Economic and Management Sciences, University of South Africa (UNISA), South Africa where she has been employed since 1988. She obtained HonsBEcon in Transport Economics at the University of Stellenbosch, MPhil (cum laude) in Tourism Management at the University of Pretoria, and DCom in Tourism Management at UNISA. Her special research interest is the leisure and business tourism market, more specifically, the festival and events sector of the tourism industry. She is author or co-author of specialist publications in national and international professional journals and has also read papers at national and international conferences.

Stelios Varvaressos is Professor at Department of Business Management (Degree/Course: Tourism Business Management), at the Technological Educational Institute (T.E.I) of Athens and Tutor of the Hellenic Open University, Greece, on the post-graduate program (MSc) Tourism Business Management. He received his Ph.D. in Tourism Economy from the University of Paris VIII, Paris, France. He is the author of seven books, on aspects of tourism economy, tourism development and tourism policy. He has undertaken a variety of research and consultancy projects of the tourism industry (public and private sectors). His articles have been published by international journals and presented at international conferences. He is a member of the editorial board of four scientific journals in tourism. His research and writing interest includes tourism economy, tourism development, and tourism policy.

Chris A. Vassiliadis is Associate Professor of Marketing at the University Macedonia, Department of Business Administration, Thessaloniki, Greece, where he teaches marketing courses in postgraduate and graduate level. Also, he is collaborating member of the Greek Open University. His research interests focus in the marketing of services and the management of tourist destinations and his work has been published in various international journals, and conferences. In addition, he is the author of two books (e-mail: chris@uom.edu.gr). The author is the director of the Master of Tourism Management – University of Macedonia, Thessaloniki program and instructor in other MBA and International Master Programs.

Medet Yolal is Associate Professor in the Department of Tour Guiding in the Faculty of Tourism at Anadolu University, Turkey. He received his Ph.D. in Tourism and Hotel Management at Anadolu University. His research interests mainly focus on tourism marketing, consumer behavior, event management, regional studies and tourism development.

Kyung-Hyan Yoo is Associate Professor of Communication at William Paterson University of New Jersey in the United States. She received her Ph.D. in Tourism from Texas A&M University focusing on Information Technology & Tourism. Her research focuses on electronic word-of-mouth, online trust, social media communication, persuasive technology, online information search and decision-making and other issues related to the role of information communication technology in tourism. She has worked on research projects on online travel reviews and social media use by travelers funded by TripAdvisor, Travel Industry Association of America, and several local destination marketing organizations. Yoo has authored journal articles and book chapters on social media marketing, consumer-generated media, and online trust. Her manuscripts have published in top peer-review journals including Public Relations Review, Computers in Human Behavior, and Journal of Information Technology & Tourism.

Anita Zátori, Ph.D., is Assistant Professor at Tourism Center, Institute of Marketing and Media, Corvinus University of Budapest, Hungary, and currently a Visiting Scholar at Department of Hospitality and Tourism Management, Pamplin College of Business, Virginia Tech, USA. Her actual research interest is in cultural tourism and urban tourism with a special focus on tourist experience.

Index

Aaran Taste Trail, 367
ADBF. *See* Asian Dragon Boat
Federation (ADBF)
Addo Elephant National Park,
354–359
AIMS. *See* Alliance of
Independent recognized
Members of Sports
(AIMS)
Alliance of Independent recog-
nized Members of Sports
(AIMS), 167
Alternative tours, 34–35
Arts events, 134–136, 139,
140, 143, 147
Asian Dragon Boat Federation
(ADBF), 163
Authentic culture, 222
Authenticity
in creative tourism, 250–253
in cultural tourism, 219–224

Barbados, 399, 402, 403
Barcelona Creative Tourism,
244
Big-group tours, 33, 34
Black River Safari, 501–502
Brand experience, 12
Buhr & Dugas's Intolerance of
Uncertainty.
Loewenstein's personal
safety scale, 388
Building glocality, 136
Business origami technique, 9

Business performance, 477
Business' self-sufficiency,
exploring, 5–6
Business tourism, 454–456
context, 453
engagement, 460
experience value model,
463–464
experiential value, 456–457
extraordinary experiences,
458–460
intention, 460
knowledge development, 454
post-consumption behavior,
463
satisfaction, 457–458,
460–462
value creation, 454
value experience, 460–462

Caribbean, 399
CED. *See* Customer experience
design (CED)
CEM. *See* Customer experience
management (CEM)
China's Dragon Boat festival
authenticity and profit-
chasers, 160–162
symbolic authenticity and
new alliances, 169–170
theoretical and cultural
context, 158–160
threats and opportunities,
162–168

Chinese cultural heritage
festival, 159, 171
Chop Chop, 370–371, 373
Collective intelligence, 338
Communities' empowerment,
239–240
Community center, 119
Community cultural
development, 138
Conceptual uniqueness,
137–138
Consumer-driven innovation,
39–40
Controllable convenience, 305,
306
Co-value creation, 200
Coyaba River Garden and
Museum, 503–504
Creative cities, 116, 117
Creative economy, 115
Creative industries, 115
Creative tourism, 114, 116,
122
active participation, 246
analysis and best practices,
246–255
assets and opportunities for,
239–240
authentic experiences, 246
authenticity, 250–253
challenges, 243–246
creative potential
development, 246
creativity, 248–250
essential awareness of
changes, 243
experience economy,
237–239
experience's eco-system,
243–245
guidelines, 255–258
opportunities and challenges,
237–246
sharing economy, 245–246
skills development, 246

tourist organizations,
240–243
Creative Tourism Network®
(CTN), 237, 240, 242,
248, 518
CTN. See Creative Tourism
Network® (CTN)
CTO. See Cyprus Tourism
Organisation (CTO)
Culinary Tourism (Long), 365
Culinary tourism experiences
developing and marketing,
368
experiential tourism products
found in, 366
market for, 364
Cultural heritage
design and strategic manage-
ment of, 157
Cultural tourism, 134
authenticity, 219–224
commodification of,
224–226
Customer-contact employees/
staff, 46, 49, 56
Customer experience
perceived value and
outcomes, 184
Customer experience design
(CED), 4
Customer experience
management (CEM), 4,
490
Customer experiences
as entertainment, 68
Customer feedback, 477
Customer interface, 12–13
Customer management,
477–478
Customers expectations, 6–7
Customers mind and
memorability, 13–14
Cyprus, 284, 286, 287
Cyprus Tourism Organisation
(CTO), 287

Data collection procedure, 495–497
Destination experience, 67–70
  process of designing, 70
Destination management, 283
DINESERV, 452
Disney Corporation, 345
Disneyization, 345–347
Disney World, 227
DMOs, 73–74
Double Fifth (Duan Wu) Festival, 156–158
Dragon Boat racing, 156–164
  history of, 164–166

Eatertainment experience, 491
Eco Atlas, 275
Ecolabeling, 270
Economic and tourism development, 135
Ecotourism, 263–266
EDBF. *See* European Dragon Boat Federation (EDBF)
Electronic Word-of-Mouth (eWOM), 471–475, 527
Emergent authenticity, 227
Emergent strategy, 159
Emotional intelligence (EI), 54, 55
Environmental economics, 271–272
Ephemeral tourist experience, 255
European Dragon Boat Federation (EDBF), 163
Event experience, 138
Event implementation and management, 139
eWOM. *See* Electronic Word-of-Mouth (eWOM)
Existential authenticity, 221
Experience atmosphere, 10–12

Experience-based design first phase of, 5
Experience-based tourism, 412
Experience-centric approach and concepts, 23–25
  and experience innovation, 25–26
Experience-centric innovation, 26–27
  for competitive advantage, 41
Experience-centric strategy, 510
Experience-centric value creation, 27–30
Experience co-creation opportunities, 100
Experience design
  experience-centric value creation, 27–30
  explore, 5–7
  innovation and creativity, 9
  and market intelligence, 27–30
  process, 5
  Singapore airlines, 13–16
  tour, 31
Experience economy, xii–xiii, 135, 236, 237–239, 345–347
Experience economy concept, 236
Experience innovation, 27
Experience market, 12, 16, 27
Experiential tourism, 125
  tourism services, providers of, 178–180
  tourists' aspirations and requirements, 178
Experiential value promise (EVP), 7–8
Explore, design and positioning (EDP), 5

Failure mode and effects analysis (FMEA), 201, 203, 517

Fairy chimneys, 228
Firm's value chain system
    operations, 103–108
Free-guided tours, 35
Frequency distribution,
    498–499
Fulfilling experience, 489–491

Gay cultural events, 326–327
Gay experience, 333–334
Gay film festivals, 326–329
Genuine culture, 222
GLES. *See* Green Leaf
    Environmental Standard
    (GLES)
Green development, 267–270
Green ecotourism destinations,
    263–266
Greening, 268, 270
Green Leaf Environmental
    Standard (GLES), 268
Green operations, 269–270,
    272–274
Guests' experiences
    boutique hotels and activities,
        190–191
    business alliances, 185–187
    characteristics and
        influencing dimensions,
        182–185
    management and marketing
        benefits, 187–188
    network's marketing concept,
        189
    service experience, 180–182
    venture's profile, 189
Guided tours, 23, 30–31

Haenerstburg, 271–275
Heritage attraction, 493–495
HISTOQUAL, 495
HKTA. *See* Hong Kong Tourist
    Association (HKTA)
Holistic approach, 241–242,
    254–255

Hong Kong Tourist Association
    (HKTA), 154, 158, 162,
    171, 515
Host community, 71–73
Hotel industry and guests'
    experiences
    characteristics and influencing
        dimensions, 182–185
    service experience, 180–182
Humanic clues, 8
Human resources (HR)
    crucial role, 46
    developing experiential skills,
        58–60
    in tourism field, 48–51
Human resources management
    (HRM)
    critical role of, 47
    importance of, 48–51
    strategic approach to, 52–54
Hybrid experience, 508

Imitation, 37–38
Information Communication
    Technologies (ICTs),
    xxiv, 525
    advances in, 410, 412
    experience hierarchy, 414
    impacts of, 410, 411
    and tourism experience,
        412–414
    in tourism marketing,
        414–417
Intangible cultural heritage,
    156, 157, 158, 161
Intellectual capital, 8
International Canoeing
    Federation (ICF), 163
International Dragon Boat
    Federation (IDBF), 163
International Olympic
    Committee (IOC), 167
International sporting event, 162
International Sports Federation
    (ISF), 167

Internet, 86, 471

Knowledge management, 29,
    38–39

Leisure, 201
Leisurescape, 135, 145
Lesbians, gays, bi, and trans
    (LGBT), 324, 329
Life cycle assessment (LCA),
    268
Life-enhancing products, 177
Loewenstein's personal safety
    scale, 388

Macro-environment., 10
Magoebaskloof Tourism, 275
Marketable tourist experience,
    244
Marketers, changing role of,
    417–418
Marketing tourism experience,
    417–420
Market segmentation, 117, 120,
    122
McDonaldization, 226–228,
    346, 433
Meetings, Incentives,
    Conventions and
    Exhibitions/Events
    (MICE), 455
Memorabilia, 493
Memorable tourism experiences
    (MTEs), 526
  adverse feelings, 439
  component of, 432, 441
  conceptual and theoretical
    components of, 436–439
  design and delivery of,
    439–442
  essence of, 434–439
  fundamental factors of, 432
  hedonism, 436–437
  knowledge, 438
  meaningfulness, 438–439

novelty, 437–438
  refreshment, 437
  social interaction and local
    culture, 438
Meso-environment, 10
Micro-environment, 10
Mobile marketing, 418–419
Multifaceted experience, 508

National Dragon Boat
    Associations, 163
Natural resources, 267
Negative cues, 492
Netnographic analysis,
    330–331, 334–335
Non-professional sport-tourists,
    197

Office du Tourisme et des
    Congrès (OTC), 332
Online communication, 325,
    329, 334, 335
Online reviews, 471–473,
    476–479
Online social media (OSM),
    325, 326, 522
Otium, 188–191

Pacific Asia Travel Association
    (PATA), 380, 381
Pärnu Hospital, Estonia,
    309–310
Penn State Worry
    Questionnaire, 388
Philadelphia, 420
Positive cues, 491–492
Post-modernism, emblem of, 222
Post tourists, 222
Product-market match, 114,
    122–125, 128, 135
Professional conference
    organizer (PCO), 460
Professional sport-tourists, 197
Promotional tools, 398, 400,
    401

Protection motivation theory (PMT), 384–385
Public-spirited orientation, 137

Refined service and exquisite hospitality, 53–54
RENTQUAL, 452
Reputation management, 478
Risk-as-feelings hypothesis, 385–386
Ritz-Carlton "gold standards", 50–51
Ritz-Carlton Hotel Company, 50–51
Rose Hall Great House, 502–503
Royal Ontario Museum, 422–423
Rural tourism experience, 284–286
    activities, 285
    conceptualization of, 285
    in Cyprus, 287
    evaluation of, 286
    management of, 286, 295

Saint-Jean-Port-Joli (Québec), 241–242
Sales management, 477
Sculpture trails, 142, 143–144
Sea, sculpture by
    assessing event experience, 147–148
    brand/conceptual uniqueness, 143–144
    event experience, 144–146
    global orientation, 141–143
    planning, management, and operation, 146–147
    SCA, assessment of, 149–150
    unique concept, 140–141
SERQUAL, 495
Service dominant logic (SDL), 47
    tourism experiences, 88–91
Service innovation

market-creating, 305, 306
    in medical tourism, 303–316
    in spas, 303–316
    in wellness, 303–316
Service Quality Scorecard (SQSC), 452
Services blueprinting, 201, 203
Servicescape, 452
SERVPERF, 452
SERVQUAL, 452
Sfendami Mountain Festival (SMF)
    area map of, 204
    small-scale sport event., 204–205
    sport event, 202
Singapore airlines (SIA), 13–16
Small and medium tourism enterprises (SMTEs), 185, 186
Small-group tour providers, 32
Small-scale sport service system, 206
Social context, contextualization, 91
Social context mobile marketing, 422
Socially constructed experiences, 90
Social media (SM)
    co-creation opportunities and processes, 100
    individualized and socially constructed experiences, 97–98
    interactions and tourism experiences, 93–100
    marketing strategies, 480
    motivating factors, 475
    multimedia content, 92
    online reviews, 471–473
    participation and tourism experiences, 100–102
    and tourism experiences, 91–93

Socio-cultural environment, 7
Socio-digital media, 338
Special interest tourism (SIT), 453
Sport tourism, 196
  data analysis procedures and validity, 404
  data collection procedures, 403
  diary design, 206–209
  implementation of, 402
  research approach and sampling, 402–403
  research instrument, 403–404
  service encounters and servicescapes, 199–200
  service quality, 197–199
  SMF, 2013, 201–202
  tourist experience and satisfaction, 200–201
Stakeholders, 70–71
Statistics Canada Motivations Survey (TAMS), 118
Strategic human resources management (SHRM), 52, 53, 62
Strengthen the customer, 7
Suburbanization, 115
Sustainability, 263
Sustainable creative advantage (SCA), 135, 515
Sydney Organizing Committee for the Olympic Games (SOCOG), 141, 142
Symbolic authenticity, 159

Tactile tours, 146
Technological product innovations, 36
Technology-empowered experience, 411
Theming, 347, 351
Toronto, 117–119

Total quality management (TQM), 60–61
Tour experience design, 31
Tourism attraction, 118, 119, 127
Tourism businesses manage service, 49
Tourism context and settings, xv–xxvii
Tourism Crisis Management Initiative (TCMI), 380
Tourism destinations, 264
Tourism experiences, xiii–xiv, 156, 157, 160, 161, 508
  creation, 507
  definition, xi
  developing experiential skills, HR, 58–60
  emotional labor and intelligence, 55–56
  experience encounter, 56
  experiential intelligence and skills, 57–58
  hotel, tourism experience encounters, 57
  managing and marketing, xiv–xv
  social media, 91–93
  total quality management (TQM), 60–61
Tourism Grading Council of South Africa (TGCSA), 268
Tourism industry, 74–76
Tourism marketing, 403, 405
  and management, 134
Tourism pursuits, 201
Tourist experiences, 67–71, 283, 286, 288
  factors influencing the, 349
  McDonaldization of, 226–228
Tourist moments, 221
Tourist paradigm shift, 236
Traditional mass tourism, 66

Traditional tourist
  behavior concepts, 66
Travel motives, 286, 288
Travel risk
  conceptualization and
    measurement of, 381
  criticism of, 381
  operationalization of, 382,
    388–392
  theory-based conceptual
    model, 387–388
Trip Advisor, 274
Turkey, 228–230
Tzaneen, 271–275

UNESCO, 158, 160
United Nations World Tourism
    Organization (UNWTO),
    380, 381

UNWTO report, 366
User-driven innovation, 30, 40

Value co-creation, 89, 109
Value co-destruction, 94
Visiting friends and relatives
    (VFR), 120
Visitor attractions, 345, 348
Visitor experience, 494
Visitor satisfaction, 494
Visitphilly photo spots, 420–422

Waterloo-Wellington Ale Trail,
  367
Waterwheel, 271–275
World Tourism Organisation
    (WTO), 454
World Travel Market, 400